Y0-DJN-078

THE
MODERN ITALIAN LYRIC

The Modern Italian Lyric

F.J. JONES

CARDIFF
UNIVERSITY OF WALES PRESS
1986

British Library Cataloguing in Publication Data

Jones, F.J.
The modern Italian lyric.
1. Italian poetry – 20th century – History and criticism
I. Title II. La Paesia italiana contemporanea. *English*
851'.914'09 PQ4113

ISBN 0-7083-0902-X

Typeset in Wales by Keystrokes, Cardiff
Printed by The Bath Press, Bath.

FOR
MAIR

ACKNOWLEDGEMENTS

Acknowledgement is due to Casa éditrice d'Anna for permission to publish an enlarged and revised English version of this book, which first appeared under the title, *La poesia italiana contemporanea* (Florence, 1975). Grateful thanks is also expressed to Cav. Dino Cipriani and the Italian Institute, London for supplying photographs of Eugenio Montale and Salvatore Quasimodo; to the BBC Hulton Picture Library for permission to reproduce the photograph of the Futurists and to the Moro Roma for permission to reproduce the photographs of Dino Campana and Giuseppe Ungaretti.

CONTENTS

ILLUSTRATIONS

PREFACE

This book first appeared in an abridged Italian translation under the title of *La poesia italiana contemporanea (da Gozzano a Quasimodo)* published by D'Anna, Messina-Florence, in 1975. It has since been revised and updated, and a half-chapter on Rebora included in the original manuscript but omitted from the Italian edition has been restored. The intention behind the work is to analyse the lyrical trends in Italian poetry between 1900 and 1945. It in no way claims to be all-inclusive but aims simply at examining the verse of the significant poets whose formative collections were published between the dates indicated, even though in some cases a considerable proportion of their lyrical output – as opposed to the elaboration of their aesthetic manners – may well have appeared after 1945. Whenever this occurs, the poets concerned have been assessed from the standpoint of their entire literary development and the terminal date of 1945 ignored.

The book is divided into two parts: the first part deals with the aesthetic innovations of the period and the various literary movements which have evolved in modern Italy within the wider framework of the European, and especially the French, tradition; the second with certain selected poets who have either marked a point of crisis or represented the highest lyrical achievement of the movements within which they have developed. The inclusion of poets like Ungaretti or Montale requires no special pleading, since their work has received a wide response within Europe and beyond; but, in order not to distort the cultural background from which the major poets have emerged, it is necessary to examine not only the writers who have most fully reflected the lyrical tensions of the first half of the century but also those who, while being perhaps less prominent from the point of view of poetic achievement, have nevertheless succeeded in widening the canvas of modern lyricism through the introduction of certain new aesthetic modes and procedures. Among these Govoni is a case in point: for, although he often shows an incapacity to synthesize on the lyrical plane, he was undoubtedly the initiator of a fresh baroque perspective which deeply influenced his contemporaries and successors. The relative disorder of his poetic output (though perhaps exaggerated) thus marks a point of change in modern taste which, while being first detectable in his work, was eventually given more adequate expression by others.

A further aim throughout the book has been to minimize theoretical issues and to concentrate the reader's attention on the unfolding of the sensibilities of the various poets treated. Even so, it has been necessary in the first part to refer to the 'orphic' patterns of imagery and the 'associative' rather than 'logical' manner of writing employed by the majority of contemporary poets to achieve their lyrical effects. An 'orphic' trend is already discernible in the works of Mallarmé in France and of Pascoli in Italy in the late nineteenth century, but it finds its highest existential and transfigurative – as opposed to its earlier theoretical and idealist – expression in the poetry of Campana and the Italian hermetic movement. Its modern form does not, however, amount to a coherent or logically developed doctrine, it is simply a bifocal way of looking at the world through the intellect and the senses. It is, in short, nothing more than the assertion of a dual state of consciousness which aims at distinguishing the eternal rhythm which subsists behind human existence from the chaotic flow of each individual poet's sense impressions; and, stylistically, it tends to find its highest lyrical expression in emblematic writing rather than in a modern transformation of the allegory. Its modalities are nevertheless peculiar to the present age and they have permitted the contemporary poet to record his inner vision in a manner which is less rationalized, less idealistic or transcendental in implication than was the case with the classical or romantic writers. Consequently new methods of representation and fresh lyrical perspectives have been discovered which were largely unsuspected by the poets of the past.

For the assistance of the general reader prose translations have been provided for all significant quotations from foreign languages (except for titles) on their first appearance in the text; but, since the notes deal largely with supportive evidence of specific interest to experts, translations in this area have been considered unnecessary. One further problem concerning the translations from modern Italian poetry – especially hermetic poetry – should also be mentioned: namely, that it rarely proves possible to reproduce in English all the ambiguities and polyvalencies of the original texts. However, it is to be hoped that sufficiently accurate translations have been provided to allow the reader to follow the main trends in the thought and imagery of the poets examined.

My thanks are due to Professor S. Gamberini for checking my translations from Italian poetry, and to Mrs M.M. Slowikowska and Dr G.L.C. Bedani for the many hours spent in proof-reading, although I hasten to add that any residual errors are entirely my own.

F.J.J.

University College,
Cardiff,
August, 1984.

PART ONE

CHAPTER I

Modern Italian poetry : origin and aesthetics

In contrast with the novel, it would probably be true to say that poetry is nowadays regarded by most readers of literature as an activity somewhat remote from their normal lives. This view has gained considerable ground over the last hundred years because poets themselves have seemed determined to write almost exclusively for an intellectual élite and to have cared little whether they communicated with – let alone reflected – the feelings of the average man. What lies behind so clear a breakdown in communication? Is it the inevitable result of a pretentious snobbery or has some more fundamental and genuine difficulty arisen concerning the expressivity of language? The answer one gives to such a question will depend on what one considers poetry to be. Does it aim at providing a *conceptual* message summing up life's problems in a particular time and place or is its primary intention to evoke new and surprising modes of feeling and to interpret the poet's specifically *emotional* responses to his circumstances? On the whole, traditional verse has succeeded in achieving both these goals simultaneously, even if perhaps with varying degrees of emphasis. This is because its conceptual element has consistently tended to be the dominant force, and so the poet has been able to convey his message in readily understandable terms. But ever since the time of Bergson and Croce modern poetry has stressed intuitive and emotional associations largely at the expense of a clear conceptual symbolism and this sudden change of direction has perplexed, if not alienated, wide sections of the public.

Although the situation has long since drifted into crisis, at least from the layman's point of view the possibility of a compromise has always seemed to be available. Given sufficient goodwill, it has been argued, the contemporary poet could attempt to smooth the way for his reader by partly conceptualizing or simplifying his message instead of setting up virtually impossible imaginative barriers to be cleared before the reader can come to grips with its implications. Yet to do any such thing would frequently mean the sacrifice of the poetic vision itself, because the tremendous complexities of modern life, as Eliot has emphasized, require equally complex modes of expression.

To a certain extent, admittedly, the problem of communication existed in more leisurely times than our own, though in the past the gap separating the poet and his reader never proved to be so wide as seriously to endanger meaning. Yet today it appears to grow more and more unbridgeable with every passing generation, with the result that the complexity of the pressures exerted on his sensibility has left the average man floundering. The reason for this is that the poet's views on the sacred and the profane have virtually been inverted. Until modern times, as Nietzsche once observed, art always acted as a psychological antidote to the stark absurdity of the human condition, providing it with a range of values transcending the blind forces of chance. Its sacred elements have thus always been composed of all those impulses and ideas, both social and religious, through which mankind has considered itself capable of controlling its fate. The profane, on the other hand, has tended to be identified with the inexplicable, the absurd, or the mysterious – with all those forces, in a word, which have threatened to overwhelm individuals or indeed whole societies when least expected. Even as late as the end of the nineteenth century this attitude remained virtually unchallenged and accounts for Mallarmé's admission that a cast of dice can never abolish 'le hasard' ('chance'). Yet in the case of the modern poet it is no longer true, since he adopts a very different attitude to the sacred and the profane. Although he does not revel in a show of irrationality, he clearly recognizes a form of 'déraisonnement' or 'unreason' as an important element in his work. So – largely, perhaps, thanks to science – he has come to accept that this whole vast area of experience has been waiting to be explored by the artist since time immemorial and he has wasted no time in his attempts to probe its outer defences.

In other words, as soon as science itself began to limit the area of the irrational and to make it a less frightening prospect for exploration, the poets also lost their fear of the unknown. Baudelaire was perhaps the first poet to take a significant step in this direction by placing himself on the very periphery of life, until the mystery of death almost became a hallucination of his imagination and senses:

> O mort, vieux capitaine, il est temps! Levons l'ancre!
> Ce pays nous ennuie, ô mort! Appareillons!
> Si le ciel et la mer sont noirs comme de l'encre,
> Nos cœurs que tu connais sont remplis de rayons!
>
> Verse-nous ton poison pour qu'il nous réconforte!
> Nous voulons, tant ce feu nous brûle le cerveau,
> Plonger au fond du gouffre, Enfer ou Ciel, qui'importe?
> Au fond de l'Inconnu pour trouver du *nouveau*![1]

O death, old captain, it is time! Let us lift anchor! This land bores us, o Death!

> Let us set sail! If the sky and the sea are as black as ink, our hearts which you know are filled with rays! Pour your poison for us so that we may be comforted! We wish, since this fire burns our brains so deeply, to plunge into the depths of the abyss, who cares if it be Heaven or Hell? Into the depths of the Unknown, to find the *new*!

Here death is depicted as an old sea-captain setting sail for a mysterious new world; and perhaps in the eyes of the decadent poets the mystery of death was likewise a natural starting-point for the exploration of the irrational, since it is by far the most absurd event to befall the individual. During their meditations upon its inner significance, they stumbled upon certain constants in the human condition which enabled their modern successors to revolutionize the ethical and aesthetic perspectives of art by closing the gap between social and metaphysical perceptions. As a consequence, poets have gradually abandoned those time-hallowed restraints formerly imposed on the investigation of the unknown and have created for their lyricism a fresh kind of transfigurative dimension – one which is concerned with seemingly irrational associations of moods and sensations but which implies a deeper, if somewhat less articulate, rationality lying not behind but within the elusiveness of their language and imagery.

At first sight the changes may not seem startling, but they imply that contemporary poets have invented a way of generalizing experience which no longer relies for its effects on a rational idealism with a Neoplatonic teleology. Instead their commitment is wholly aesthetic and their lyrical substance is largely sensory and contingent, not conceptual. Nevertheless, the poet's moral responsibility is by no means lost on that account: it emerges as a series of implications conditioned by the lyrical 'transfiguration' rather than the 'intellectualization' of feelings and symbolic aggregates. In short, its truths tend to operate on a higher level of awareness, where their meanings appear less as imaginatively expressed, moral assertions and more as figurative changes in tastes and perspectives within the social fabric. Probably the subtlety of such an approach explains why the content of modern verse rarely seems to impinge immediately on the everyday experiences of the reader, who is himself involved in *direct*, rather than *imaginative* or lyrically *involuted*, judgements on events and situations. And yet, it is the lyrical judgement which still appears to have the greater impact in the long run, and this fact alone shows that the apparent remoteness of modern poetry is illusory. In fact, many of the difficulties of the earlier hermetic writers have nowadays wholly evaporated and much of the obscurity of the later ones is in the process of clarification, revealing a much deeper range of perception in hermetic verse than was at first suspected.

To obtain some historical perspective on the revolution which has taken place, let us for a moment reconsider, partly through the views of the poet Mario Luzi, the essential evolution of the poetic sensibility over the centuries. The problem of how to adapt the traditional sensibility to modern trends has existed everywhere in the last hundred years, but nowhere in more demanding a form than in Italy. This is because the romantic period which represents so vital a stage in European tastes left Italian poetry virtually untouched. True, by Italian standards at least, there is a muted romantic strain in the apparent classicism of writers like Manzoni, Leopardi, Carducci and D'Annunzio; yet none of these writers can be considered romantic in the European sense, since they rarely fall into the trap of the pathetic fallacy and few of their works are underscored by a deep vein of sentimentality. So eventually the post-romantic influx of new aesthetic modes from beyond the Alps struck the still classical world of Italian culture like a whirlwind and had its most immediate effect on its poetry.[2]

Evidently, however, such radical lyrical transformations did not occur overnight. The aesthetic gap between the Italian and European sensibilities was first noted by the generation of the 'Scapigliati' ('dishevelled ones') and in their particular case it soon led to a great deal of confusion. The bewildered literary experimentation it prompted nevertheless seems typical of what normally takes place whenever a dynamic culture comes into contact with a static one. Hence one of the school's principal claims to fame is its uninhibited emotionalism and its plagiarizing of French themes and lyrical techniques. Unfortunately, the self-indulgence shown by Italian writers at that time seems to have weighed heavily ever since with European critics, giving the impression that modern Italian lyricism is a backwater chiefly indebted to French models for its achievements. But, although it would be absurd to deny the considerable influence of French aesthetics, it would be equally absurd not to try and assess its limits, and yet this is what few critics outside Italy itself have attempted in the past. Even as late as the mid-fifties, for instance, Georges Mounin reaffirmed that 'toute la poésie italienne du vingtième siècle est nourrie – même quand elle se coule en formes très originalement italiennes – de problèmes et d'expériences et de débats poétiques surtout français ... Ce qui explique pourquoi les trois quarts de ce qu'ils nous renvoient, ce sont nos propres reflets; enrichis d'irisations propres, mais reflets où nous nous reconnaissons trop, reflets qui ne nous apprennent plus rien que, peut-être, le vieillissement de nos propres modes.'[3] ('all the Italian poetry of the twentieth century is nourished – even when it flows in highly original Italian forms – with problems and experiences and poetic debates which are above all French ... This explains why three-quarters of what they send back to us are our own reflections; enriched with their own iridescent effects, but reflections in which we recognize ourselves all too much, reflections which no longer teach us anything, perhaps, except the ageing of our own modes.') This attitude on the part of the French was, needless to say, largely echoed by other European critics, until the growing reputations of Montale and Ungaretti somewhat disturbed them in their complacency. Consequently in the last two decades it has become apparent to all concerned that Italy has produced some twentieth-century poets of European stature and that the time has arrived for a reassessment of the position.

Probably it will be best to start our reappraisal, as Luzi does, with a contrast between modern symbolism and the allegory of the Middle Ages, and on this point he asserts that in the medieval poet's view the allegory counted for more than the quality of the poetic texture clothing it. The latter, in other words, was more concerned in projecting the spiritual joys of the afterlife than with the nature of life in this world, and so his figurative procedure must be regarded as 'un'operazione intellettuale esterna ai mezzi propri della poesia che in un certo modo le sono subordinati o concorrenti.'[4] ('an intellectual process external to the proper modes of poetry which in a certain sense is subordinate to or competitive with it'). Its implications are, therefore, extra-lyrical, in that they aim at adumbrating a type of reality composed of speculative attitudes, and these in turn are expressed largely at the expense of feeling and lyrical perception.

Not surprisingly, the Renaissance poets tended to reverse this type of outlook, since they were more concerned with the city of Man than with the city of God; and they tried to depict a state of serene wisdom in which aesthetic elements replaced metaphysical ones and in which ethics also played a vital part. Their type of perfection was limited rather by the horizons of the *Zeitgeist* of the period, which was itself modelled upon the perspectives of classical antiquity. So the best way of assessing the art of that time is perhaps to consider the way in which the poet tries to create for himself a second self or *persona*[5] to mediate between the pre-ordained pattern of classical tastes which he employs as a frame of reference and his own personal responses to his situations. Whenever this *persona* achieves an authentic form of mediation, we at once sense the radiance and sobriety of the classical canon of art; and, when it does not, merely the conventions of what Ungaretti once called a lifeless neo-classicism.

Modern art has, by contrast, progressed beyond the aesthetics of the Renaissance by bringing about a widening of the artist's social and metaphysical perspectives. In this regard it has tended to hold purely rational attitudes, as we have already seen, at something of a discount and to replace them with analogical or associative ones. However, the lyrical changes which have emerged have been developed in two stages. The first of these – the romantic stage – is possibly by modern standards an aberration from the true path of lyrical evolution, at least in the eyes of the hermetic poets, because it is based on a cult of Neoplatonic idealism revived during the Renaissance by Ficino and his followers. Ficino provided the humanist age with a metaphysical superstructure to justify it, conceiving the universe as the orphic poem of God. Such a view led to the revival of the ancient belief that the poet's inspiration was a divine frenzy, with the result that art gradually ceased to be a calm ethical and aesthetic activity and came to resemble a speculative fury in which the poet tried increasingly to identify himself with God. As this tendency became more and more uncontrolled, the process gave rise to the romantic idea of the Artist-God, whose overweening ego suppressed the humanist *persona* altogether and captured the centre of the stage for itself.

Such a posture eventually tended towards solipsism as the poet lost contact with the social realities around him; and so a nagging awareness of the basic insincerity of his position might well be at the bottom of the romantic poet's *mal du siècle*. This solipsist pose in turn caused the poet to feel a sense of disillusionment and dissatisfaction as he became more and more aware of his isolation and of living in a detached sentimental world of complete unreality. As his disillusionment intensified, he gradually abandoned all the myths, both sacred and profane, which had hitherto given human experiences their validity; and then, instead of filtering his feelings through the matrix of tradition like his Renaissance predecessors, he found that he had to justify them directly in his art. Eventually he transformed the whole nature of art, which afterwards no longer dealt with the problem of *how* one should live but *why* one should continue to live at all. So, when the initial timid introspection of the pre-romantics yielded to a complete form of egocentricity, the romantic hero was born.

Typical romantic heroes like Hernani or, in real life, Byron are pure revolutionaries with no function or purpose outside the revolution itself. At length they suffer a metaphysical *échec*[6] because they fail to direct their iconoclastic aspirations towards positive ends. Their evident sentimentality eventually forced the next generation of poets to try to re-establish some kind of equilibrium between the sensibility and reality, and the main problem confronting them was how to interpret the absurd towards which the romantic mind was increasingly attracted as it became more and more solipsist. When dealing with this problem, the poets of the late nineteenth century in France created new techniques in the hope of forging stronger links with the concrete, the results of which were the verbal alchemies of the symbolist poets with whom the figurative use of language underwent a truly decisive mutation.

This change may be summed up as a method of treating the Mallarmean 'hasard' by means of an associative rather than a deductive logic. Thereafter the symbolic implications which had traditionally been based on an image's conceptual element were radically displaced, so that it gradually acquired its principal effects from the tonal impressions surrounding its deployment in varying contexts. Poetic tension, in short, ceased to inhabit the overall discourse and relied far more on unexpected verbal juxtapositions and insights to impound its lyrical charge. Eventually syntactical links were either wholly severed or deliberately blurred because the new sensations demanding expression lay beyond the bounds of rational explanation, and the articulation of the image-chain then followed an *analogical* rather than a *logical* pattern. The hallucinatory type of impressionism so produced permitted the poet to convey his moods in a manner not requiring recourse to a deeply conceptual language; and, although the exploitation of the new technique was at first far more extensive in French than in Italian poetry, the following description of a summer storm in Pascoli's lyric 'Temporale' shows that the new linguistic alchemies were also thriving in Italy at the time:

Un bubbolío lontano . . .

Rosseggia l'orizzonte,
come affocato, a mare;
nero di pece, a monte,
stracci di nubi chiare:
tra il nero un casolare:
un'ala di gabbiano.

A distant rumbling . . . The horizon reddens, as if fiery, seaward; black as pitch, towards the hills, wisps of clear clouds: amid the blackness a cottage: a seagull's wing.

Here the principal expressive modes are the *analogia* and the *poesia delle cose* ('poetry of things'), both of which soon became autonomous techniques in Italian verse.[7] The former is related to the French device of the *correspondance* and aims at depicting eruptions of emotion similar in intensity to solar flares in a poet's lyrical texture; while the latter attempts to reflect the poet's mood through the deployment of complex arrangements of object-symbols. As a result of their pent-up emotional charge, both procedures lead to an involution of the symbols and ideas implicit in the image, and they give the impression that the classical poet's rational discourse has been replaced by a series of dissociated poetic flashes or interacting aggregates of objects. Their startling compression, moreover, is frequently responsible for the difficulties of comprehension arising in modern poetry.

If, therefore, we examine closely the last hundred years of lyrical output we note a growing complexity of experience necessitating the creation of ever more complex modes of expression. At first lyrical technique tended to lag behind the poet's extended range of feelings, a fact which may account for the virtual obsessive preoccupation of the symbolist poets with the enunciation of their lyrical principles in their poetry to the exclusion of most other types of lyrical content; yet, since they were still ensnared by a Neoplatonic and absolute vision of beauty, they too gradually adopted solipsist solutions when confronted with the problem of lyrical catharsis. So, as Luzi rightly emphasizes, in Mallarmé's verse 'la sostanza reale della poesia ... è l'illusione continua per analogia e simboli della creazione poetica impossibile'[8] ('the real substance of poetry ... is the continual illusion through analogies and symbols of the impossibility of poetic creation'). And, despite the fact that this leads directly to the metaphysical cult of 'la page blanche' ('the blank page') as the ideal poem because it is as yet unformed, the French poet's attitude to art may nevertheless be regarded as mediatory between romantic and modern aesthetics, inasmuch as he underlines the impossibility – through his own *échec* – of setting metaphysical or teleological goals for human aspirations. In theory his ideal of absence is wholly Platonic, defined by the much quoted formula: 'Je dis une fleur! et, hors de l'oubli où ma voix relègue aucun contour, en tant que quelque chose d'autre que les calices sus, musicalement se lève, idée même et suave, l'absente de tous bouquets'[9] ('I say a flower! and, out of oblivion where my voice relegates all shapes, as something different from known calyces, musically there arises, the soothing idea itself, the absent of all bouquets'). In practice, however, it gave rise to something quite different, to a recall of intense states of emotion which replaced the platonic ideas with a series of musically based ideations. In this sense an ideation amounts to a mutation of the philosophical concept of 'essence', so that, in fact, even for the symbolist and decadent poets the absoluteness of Ideas and Essences had already begun to dissolve. They were no longer seen as eternal Forms or Substances but rather as temporarily crystallized images drawn from the flux of life and producing a momentary lyrical synthesis of the emotions.[10] The introduction of these transiently felt emotional 'absolutes' or 'suspended' images ultimately provoked a tremendous upheaval in aesthetic attitudes; so that not even Mallarmé himself foresaw all the repercussions which the exploitation of his approach to art was to have on successive generations of poets.

The principal change which was to emerge from his writings was the new mode of creativity open to poets once the possibility of 'ideative' poetry had finally been demonstrated. For, whereas the logicality of traditional poetic discourse allowed only a gradual ascent towards distant forms of intellectual generalization, the associative processes pervading the 'ideative' manner ruled out the gradual intellectual approach altogether and demanded the development of more powerful, instantaneous techniques like the *analogia* or the *poesia delle cose*. Thus in symbolist verse one either finds oneself in the presence of an *absolute* state of emotional beatitude, the perfect reflection of a mood in its objective correlative, or else in a degraded sphere of *gratuitous* material flux. Moreover, since in symbolist aesthetics the property of wholeness belongs to the 'musical' unfolding of the emotions alone, it follows that the poet cannot hope to unify his feelings and perspectives unless he can ensure that everything he expresses immediately touches an absolute scale of Being.

The ambiguity running through the entire symbolist aesthetic seems to lie in the fact that its exponents did not thoroughly understand the nature of the imaginative poetry which they were attempting to produce and ultimately felt compelled to identify it with Platonic generalizations of events and images. Admittedly, they often sensed in some obscure fashion that the *logical* transcendence of existence could never be the goal of artistic transfiguration; and they were equally aware that without an infusion of the poet's galvanizing emotion into his verse his objects and situations would tend to slip back into their original chaotic states of mere 'subsisting'; yet in most cases they failed to conceive of any other solution to the problem of art than a process of intellectual rationalization. So, since they also considered traditional rationalizations as false forms of catharsis, they tended to sink into an ironic state of alienation in which (as Baudelaire illustrates in his poem significantly entitled 'Spleen') man's positive joy in transfiguring life is replaced by a soul-destroying ennui:

Rien n'égale en longueur les boiteuses journées,
Quand sous les lourds flocons des neigeuses années
L'ennui, fruit de la morne incuriosité,
Prend les proportions de l'immortalité.
– Désormais tu n'es plus, ô matière vivante!
Qu'un granit entouré d'une vague épouvante,
Assoupi dans le fond d'un Saharah brumeux;
Un vieux sphinx ignoré du monde insoucieux,
Oublié sur la carte, et dont l'humeur farouche
Ne chante qu'aux rayons du soleil qui se couche.

> Nothing equals in length the limping days, when under the heavy flakes of the snowy years, ennui, fruit of a dismal lack of curiosity, takes on the dimensions of immortality. – Henceforth you will no longer be, o living matter! but a granite rock surrounded by a vague fear, drowsing in the depths of a misty Sahara; an ancient sphinx ignored by the careless world, forgotten on maps, and whose fierce temper sings only to the rays of the setting sun.

This type of *ennui* was the natural condition of the romantic poets once they had stripped away the ethical and mythological accretions of humanism and replaced them with a sentimental dreamworld. Yet what neither Baudelaire nor the symbolist poets fully acknowledged was that the only valid way open to them of rehabilitating their own shattered inner reality was by means of a reformulation of the beliefs of the humanists upon a fresh plane of transfigured emotion. Thus, when confronted with the urgency of the problem, all they succeeded in doing was to turn aesthetics into a speculative science, so as to open up, as Poggioli once described it, 'una specie di scalinata mistica che serve a colmare l'intervallo tra una realtà inferiore e una piú elevata'[11] ('a kind of mystical staircase serving to bridge the gap between an inferior and a higher reality'). They continued, in short, to generalize in a Platonic manner because the 'ideation' had not yet become an inner conviction with them. Similarly a sense of lyrical empathy or 'feeling-within' objects and landscapes was not yet a firm principle of their aesthetics, but at most only an experimental line of investigation.

In Italy Pascoli is the clearest example of this type of poetic reflection and he proves to be the most important lyrical mediator between the symbolists and the hermetic poets. At times he is even more sensitive to the lower grades of existence, to the material reality and metaphysical unreality of things abandoned to themselves, than the French were. Let us take, for instance, the terrifying isolation of an abandoned plough in 'Lavandare':

> Nel campo mezzo grigio e mezzo nero
> resta un aratro senza buoi, che pare
> dimenticato, tra il vapor leggero.

> In the half-grey and half-black field stands a plough without oxen, which seems forgotten, amid the light mistiness.

This kind of 'suspended' perspective foreshadows modern orphic procedures. One of its prominent features is the transformation of objects into symbols of completely 'suspended' emotion. It is indeed from such perspectives that multiple insights arise and reflect the whole lyric tradition together with the poet's personal experiences through subtle poetic resonances. Here, for example, the physical existence of the plough dissolves into an atmosphere of 'absolute' emotion which aims at representing in a wholly 'detached' manner the feelings associated with modern man's sense of solitude and alienation.

What, one might ask, is the property inherent in poetic emotion which permits an object or an image to shed its existentiality or contingency and move away from an absurd state of meaninglessness to a higher plane of meaningful emotive Being? The symbolist poets who were the first to be faced with the problem insisted that it was a musical quality, and it was accordingly through the cult of an inner musicality that they hoped to transform the material world.[12] Although they did not all agree about the nature of this musicality, only two dominant views on the problem eventually prevailed, the one held by Mallarmé himself, the other by René Ghil. According to Mallarmé, the word-music of modern poetry is a form of spiritual cement binding together the various impulses of the conscience. By adhering to the thread of a poet's imagery as it unfolds, it raises his lyrical vision instantaneously to an absolute, unified state. To illustrate the point, he added: 'toute âme est une mélodie qu'il s'agit de renouer; et pour cela sont la flûte et la viole de chacun,'[13] ('every soul is a melody which it is necessary to retie; and for that purpose everyone has his own flute and viol'). He meant by this somewhat involuted statement that an authentic musical rhythm in a poem is capable of establishing the metaphysical unity of a poet's sensibility and of expressing that unity in an intensely emotional form. René Ghil, by contrast, while acknowledgedly paying lip-service in his doctrine of 'instrumentation verbale' to the thesis that all word-music is a spiritual harmony imposed by the poet on his sense-impressions, nevertheless in practice frequently tends to identify musicality with purely phonic combinations.[14] In so doing, he is perhaps guilty of confounding technique with lyrical principles and his partial substitution of the one for the other at times had disastrous effects on poetry, leading to a cult of otiose jingles.

Fortunately a number of poets have been able to combine Ghil's largely phonic doctrines with an underlying imaginative tension of the kind advocated by Mallarmé. In their work a display of musical virtuosity thus proves to be an integral part of their lyrical charm. The supreme example in Italy is D'Annunzio, especially the D'Annunzio of 'La pioggia nel pineto', where a remarkably delicate balance is struck between sound and sense:

Odi ? La pioggia cade
su la solitaria
verdura
con un crepitío che dura
e varia nell'aria

secondo le fronde
piú rade, men rade.
Ascolta. Risponde
al pianto il canto
delle cicale
che il pianto australe
non impaura,
né il ciel cinerino.
E il pino
ha un suono, e il mirto
altro suono, e il ginepro
altro ancora, stromenti
diversi
sotto innumerevoli dita.

Do you hear ? The rain falls on the solitary greenery with a pattering which endures and varies in the air according to whether the foliage is dense or less dense. Listen. To its weeping there replies the song of the cicadas, which the south wind's moaning does not frighten nor the ashen sky. And the pine has one sound, and the myrtle another sound, and the juniper another, different instruments under innumerable fingers.

Here the poet shows such mastery over the lyrical effects of assonance, alliteration, internal rhyme and enjambement that this highly contrived poetic orchestration is never in danger of degenerating into a jingle. Even so, its success depends not only on the artful choice of phonic combinations but is also closely linked with an underlying imaginative activity which fuses together a number of finely woven conceits into a delicate pattern of rarefied sensations.

Such verbal orchestrations nevertheless have obvious limitations when they are used alone as a process for unifying the sensibility. Thus the principal method adopted by the symbolists and decadents for the purpose of bringing about their lyrical ascensions was one in which an intimate relationship was established between the symbol and the perceiving mind. Its first stage consists of an absorption of external objects into the poet's inner space where they become elements of a new qualitative dimension defined by Bachelard as an 'espace intime'.[15] In this condition each image acquires the property of occupying simultaneously the centre of the poet's attention, and by virtue of this 'co-naissance' of powerful emotional foci (the term is Claudel's) the artist manages to identify external objects with the arcana of the psyche. The poet makes the reader pass, in short, from a world of spatial *extension* to one of emotional *intension*, and the degree of 'intension' itself depends upon an incandescent, inwardly-looking emotivity which has the effect of anthropomorphizing the universe and making it flesh of the poet's flesh. By virtue of the magical emotive spell he casts over his sense-impressions, the poet becomes capable of liberating himself from his dependence on material forms, and as long as his state of 'intension' endures, he possesses the independence of a creator predicating his own universe of lyrical structures.

Clearly the initial step in this mysterious process is the most difficult. According to Baudelaire it can only be attained by means of a 'magie évocatoire' ('evocative magic'). It often involves the creation of a verbal alchemy which establishes powerful emotional links between two widely differing objects in such a way that their lyrical attraction seems to possess all the compulsion of a revelation. This is the essence of the original Baudelairian *correspondance*, such as the one in 'Le voyage' admired by Eliot:

> Notre âme est un trois-mâts cherchant son Icarie.

Our soul is a three-master seeking its Icaria.

Normally Baudelaire's use of the device is simple and linear, but later poets began to extend it to include whole series of analogies cleverly blended together to produce complex lyrical textures. Not infrequently the first terms of these analogies were suppressed, leaving the secondary ones to produce a sheaf of startling and intuitively understood metaphors, such as the one found in Pascoli's 'Gelsomino notturno':

> La Chioccetta per l'aia azzurra
> va col suo pigolío di stelle.

The Chicken goes through the blue farmyard with its chirping of stars.

Here the hen is implicitly identified (by use of the capital) with the constellation of the Pleiades, the farmyard with the heavens, and her chicks with a scattering of stars. Not content with this interfusion of earthly and heavenly objects, the poet also uses a synesthesic device in the word 'pigolío' to convey the impression of a galactic scattering in auditory rather than visual terms. By such artifices all the segments of the comparison fall together and the imaginative co-presence of its spatially separated elements demonstrates the vast possibilities of the new qualitative dimension of 'intension'.

At the turn of the century a metaphorical language of tremendous suggestiveness had consequently already been elaborated for the modern poet's use, and the complexity of its field of reference was bound to increase dramatically as soon as poets became more skilled in handling it effectively. Almost at once it led to an involution of forms which caused the communicatory gap to widen still further between the poet and his reader. No doubt this, above all, explains why it is that the subtle allusiveness of hermetic imagery cannot be immediately understood by sensibilities unattuned to the modalities of symbolist and post-symbolist aesthetics.

Even so, the symbolists differ from their modern counterparts in their desire to cling to a tradition of mystical idealism instead of transfiguring reality by ringing the changes on a range of emotional intensities. It seems as if they were prepared to follow the will-o'-the-wisp of transcendence wherever it led them, even though they were half-aware of its aesthetic irrelevance. They tended, therefore, to behave like Neoplatonic magicians and confused the task of extending the resources of language with the theological aim of opening up 'uno spiraglio verso Dio'[16] ('a spy-hole towards God'). Such aspirations were bound to fail as similar romantic ones had failed before them. And, as a result, the decadent poets, although by no means as intellectual in outlook, can often be said to hold a more advanced lyrical perspective.

Until recently, however, the decadent movement has been somewhat neglected, since its very ethos has been regarded as the negation of art.[17] The word itself has been taken as being synonymous with an extreme spiritual exhaustion, inasmuch as some of the movement's prominent writers advocate a philosophy of sensuous nihilism. The dominant characteristics of the school have accordingly been defined as consisting of a vacillating moral indifference, an effete linguistic preciousness, and a self-confessed creative impotence. So perhaps, as a first step in any attempt to rehabilitate it, we need to distinguish its modes of expression from those of the virtually contemporary symbolist movement. Its much greater awareness of the importance of realism in art seems crucial in this respect, because a valid sense of human emotivity and of 'convivenza' (sociability) forms the bedrock of its inspiration. Therefore, after the speculative flights of Mallarmé and the symbolists, we are immediately struck by the decadent writers' interest in concrete situations and in their determination to assert their solidarity with their fellow-men.

On the other hand, the relations they envisage with the rest of humanity are by no means normal or balanced. They tend instead to consider all social intercourse to be invalid unless it operates on a level of attenuated and suspended emotions or, alternatively, unless it displays a sensual frenzy. The first of these attitudes emerges in a sentimental memorialism typified by Francis Jammes in the opening of a poem addressed to a childhood friend:

> J'aime dans le temps Clara d'Ellébeuse,
> l'écolière des anciens pensionnats,
> qui allait, les soirs chauds, sous les tilleuls
> lire les *magazines* d'autrefois.[18]

I loved in the past Clara D'Ellébeuse, the school-girl of the old boarding-houses, who walked, on warm evenings, under the lime-trees, reading the *magazines* of the past.

Later in the same poem, however, the sentimental note becomes highly sensual, erupting among the faded delights of yester-year in the form of a senile licentiousness:

Viens, viens, ma chère Clara d'Ellébeuse:
aimons-nous encore si tu existes.
Le vieux jardin a de vieilles tulipes.
Viens toute nue, ô Clara d'Ellébeuse.

Come, come my dear Clara d'Ellébeuse: let us love once more if you still exist. The ancient garden has faded tulips. Come quite naked, o Clara d'Ellébeuse.

Binni has described the particular literary perspective which this procedure creates as a cult of the *jenseits der Dinge*[19] ('the hindside of things'). Its divinatory element is also associated with Rimbaud's doctrine of the 'poète voyant' whose insight into the nature of things is defined in his well-known *Lettre d'un voyant*: 'Je dis qu'il faut être *voyant*, se faire voyant. Le poète se fait *voyant* par un long, immense dérèglement de tous les sens. Toutes les formes d'amour, de souffrance, de folie; il cherche lui-même, il épuise en lui tous les poisons, pour n'en garder que les quintessences. Ineffable torture où il a besoin de toute sa foi, de toute la force surhumaine, où il devient entre tous le grand malade, le grand criminel, le grand maudit, – et le suprême Savant! – Car il arrive à l'inconnu.'[20] ('I say that one must be a *seer*, make oneself a seer. A poet makes himself a *seer* by a long, immense disordering of all his senses. All forms of love, suffering, madness; he searches out himself, he exhausts within himself every kind of poison, to keep only quintessences. An unspeakable torture in which he needs all his faith, all his super-human powers, in which he becomes for everyone the great invalid, the great criminal, the great accursed one, – and the supreme Sage – Because he reaches the unknown.') Such ideas clearly aim at 'explaining' the irrational through a rationalization of chance or unreason, and they express the belief that it is by letting the sensibility wander into irrational by-ways that the poet will acquire his more important lyrical perceptions and greatest insights into his condition. Nevertheless, most of the decadent poets interpret this doctrine in an emotional and ethical, rather than in a metaphysical sense, and the perspectives they create consist of moods and sensations seen in a distant twilight world of hypersensitivity far from the realms of logic or even of unsentimentalized reality. Their lyricism thus displays as its most characteristic feature a strange penumbral sensitivity towards delicate and fleeting emotions, and in their efforts to express them adequately they tend to bring about, as Scrivano explains, 'una rivoluzione di mezzi espressivi, di contenuti e di gusto'[21] ('a revolution in modes of expression, in content and in taste').

The cult of 'le vague' invented by Verlaine also tends to make decadent imagery less intellectualized from an evocative standpoint than the poetry of the symbolists, and yet it is no less perceptive on that account. The decadent poets exist on a different – more modern – plane of lyrical responsiveness altogether and are less interested in using this world as a stepping-stone to soar into the next than in the multiple emotional disturbances which they experience by living in a given social climate. They thus try to detach themselves to see these disturbances in a fresh light, but their detachment normally alienates them from their times. They are nevertheless only partially, not completely alienated, and the art of the following poem by Verlaine addressed to his disaffected wife reveals the typical tone to which the decadent poet aspires. It amounts to a statement of melancholy serenity set in the minor key, which we can consider a variant on the sentimentality of the romantics. This is followed (or rather rounded off) by an objective correlative to the mood, expressed in delicate and yet intensely concrete imagery in the last line:

Écoutez la chanson bien douce
Qui ne pleure que pour vous plaire,
Elle est discrète, elle est légère:
Un frisson d'eau sur de la mousse![22]

Listen to the gentle song which weeps to please you alone, it is discreet and airy: a quiver of water on moss!

So plaintive an appeal for sympathy not only reveals the quivering of a hypersensitive mind but also indicates the presence of another shadowy figure in the background in whose emotional hinterland the poet wishes to immerse himself. In this case the person is Verlaine's estranged wife, and he hints that he would be prepared to submerge his personality wholly in her emotional aura if only such alienation could offer him an unalloyed form of decadent beatitude.

Such an attitude is typically *fin de siècle* and accounts for the decadent writer's normal religious outlook. Petrocchi has defined it as follows: 'La religione di un poeta decadente non è piú l'energico slancio dell'anima romantica verso Dio. È invece il subire la presenza di Dio, un sentirsene dominati in tutti gli atti e le visioni, non una corsa ma un'agitazione interiore, triste e chiusa nei propri pensieri.'[23] ('The religion of a decadent poet is no longer the energetic thrusting of the romantic soul towards God. It is instead a submission to the presence of God, a feeling of being dominated by Him in all acts and perceptions, not a racing forward but an inner agitation, sad and enclosed in its own meditations.') The poet's dominant and all-controlling Deity need not be God himself but more frequently a substitute on earth, and yet the principle remains the same. True, the decadent poet no longer feels himself imprisoned in a web of egocentric falsehoods like his romantic counterpart and so avoids all the latter's grandiloquent and unauthentic gestures; but, far from considering his regained personality as an inner sanctum, he is prepared to alienate himself by leasing it to a spirit other than his own. So from a psychological standpoint he is one of nature's eternal children, who wishes for nothing better than to be absorbed in the emotional field of a father or mother figure, because only when he finds himself, as it were, aestivating in that childlike condition does he feel sufficiently free to give full play to his over-refined senses. Later, on the other hand, when he discovers that personal alienation is an inadequate poetic attitude to adopt, he tries to expand his emotional experiences virtually to cosmic proportions, although he never takes refuge in a Neoplatonic, but rather in a social, absolute. Normally he attains to this infinite purview by fetishizing the tastes and perspectives of the past and reliving his own experiences within their temporally remote and musty atmospheres. But to satisfy his desires for a touch of modernity, the decadent poet requires a social ambience for his dreams which is not too far removed from the present. So, as is particularly the case with Gozzano, we find that he opts for the romantic and pre-romantic eras as his favoured periods and tends to idealize them both, just as if they represented lost paradises on earth.

How then do we account for the implicit changeover by the decadents from a metaphysical to a social ideal? Probably because their line of affiliation runs from Flaubert to Jammes rather than from Baudelaire to Mallarmé and onwards to Valéry. They consequently prefer to linger over insignificant events and exploit their innumerable ramifications rather than soar towards metaphysical goals by evolving a sense of transcendence. Briefly, their only lyrical aim is to endow the banal and homely images associated with the daily round with a heady emotional charge, and in so doing their sense of artistic propriety requires them to compose their attenuated lyrical harmonies in the minor key. Because of their inability to make purposeful choices, they hardly ever attain to the poetic resilience of the symbolists. Yet in their more vigilant moments their verse is far more than a languid impressionism.

We can, perhaps, accept Marcazzan's view that both the French and the Italian decadents are essentially disillusioned romantics.[24] Yet, while they are deprived of the tremendous enthusiasms of the romantic era through their opting for the microcosm of the senses rather than the macrocosm of the spirit, their anguish is in compensation a good deal milder, because they are able to take refuge in the tepid warmth of the immediate past and inflate it into an idealized way of life. Just as was the case with their romantic predecessors, their awareness of the inadequacy of experiences drawn from an insulated sphere of sentimentality eventually proved traumatic, and by reaction they clung more desperately than ever to their fetishes – the faded crinolines, the languorous word-music and musty perfumes of the past. Frequently they tried to fetishize the present as well in their work, as we can see from the following vignette written by Betteloni for the purpose of consoling himself with a vicarious breath of romantic fortitude:

> Passo dalla tua casa a notte nera,
> né di tue stanze ancor la luce è spenta;
> che delizia vegliar con te la sera
> che in dolce loco siedi all'ago intenta!
>
> Qua sulla strada, l'invernal bufera
> me stringe invece, e i baci suoi m'avventa;
> pur io mi perdo in mia gentil chimera,
> mentre il sigaro langue e si lamenta.[25]

I pass by your house in the black night, and the light is not yet extinguished in your room; how charming to keep vigil with you in the evening, when you sit in a sweet spot intent on your sewing! Here in the street the wintry gust enclasps me, however, and it rains its kisses on me; still I drift into my gentle fantasy, while my cigar languishes and sputters.

Here the same self-willed alienation is apparent as we saw earlier in Verlaine, and it eventually results in a poetic 'échec' since the writer remains a supine, outside observer caught up in the icy blast of contingency and cannot participate in the absolute emotive ambience enjoyed by his lady. In fact, Betteloni removes the object of his contemplation into a sphere of memorial still-life and then seeks to bask momentarily in his mistress's contrived emotional serenity. Through such self-imposed absorption into her state of domestic bliss he finally hopes to transform the lyric into an eternal repository of his mood. By adopting all the ruses of oleography, similar series of lyrical word-pictures are created by many of the decadent writers, and in the end it becomes clear that they wish to replace – not to complement – the present with the past. The musty aesthetic perfumes of the dead then engulf the sensibilities of the living and draw them into a closed and frigid circle of burnt-out experiences.

This kind of substitute living gives rise to its own spiritual attitudes of soul-death. Artistically its main characteristic is an idolatry for pure aesthetic values so typical of the period at the turn of the century. Usually such aestheticism is accompanied by complete moral indifference, yet it is also spiced with a residual desire on the part of the poet to live at a high level of sensuous enjoyment. The combination of these contradictory longings and tensions creates a most peculiar atmosphere composed of a complacent irony, a refined sensuality, and a ferocious, yet muted, anguish. Variations on this type of atmosphere were prevalent in Italy in the decadent period, especially in the work of D'Annunzio, and they proved to be the dominant feature inherited by the crepuscular and futurist schools from their predecessors. Yet neither the irony nor the almost hysterical sensuality of the decadent poets offered any lasting satisfaction. Instead, they left the basic problem of modern art largely unsolved: namely, how the poet was to strike the necessary lyrical chords to evoke harmonious responses from the sounding-board of his age in accordance with the symbolist doctrine of musicality.

The spiritual exhaustion and emotional disarray of many of the decadent writers also gave rise to heterogeneous stylistic effects. Their language proves to be transitional in character and relies partly on associative and partly on discursive techniques for its effects. Their principal problem was consequently how to produce a unity of tone, for their imaginative procedures (and this is particularly the case with the 'Scapigliati') tend to be centrifugal ones in which the separate parts of their lyrics appear to possess greater unity than the whole. All too often there is an excess of descriptiveness for its own sake, which is sometimes even present in a poet of Pascoli's stature; so that, despite the startling visual acuity of a poem like 'Il lampo', we are left with an uncomfortable feeling of its underlying purposelessness:

> E cielo e terra si mostrò era:
>
> la terra ansante, livida, in sussulto;
> il cielo ingombro, tragico, disfatto:
> bianca bianca nel tacito tumulto
> una casa apparí sparí d'un tratto;
> come un occhio, che, largo, esterrefatto,
> s'aprí si chiuse, nella notte nera.

And heaven and earth showed what they were: the earth panting, leaden, writhing; the heavens overcast, tragic, shattered: starkly white in the silent tumult, a house appeared disappeared in a flash; like an eye which, large, terror-stricken, opened closed, in the black night.

Here we can hardly complain of any lack of visual perception, for Pascoli's representation of the fleeting and fragmentary effects of the lightning flash could scarcely be more detailed. This is particularly noticeable in the two brilliantly contrived examples of asyndeton towards the end which echo syntactically the rapidity of the lightning flash itself. But the poem nevertheless gravitates towards a level of writing which we can only describe as oleographic, and its seeming lack of an interpretative element is characteristic of the decadent manner. In fact, far more than Pascoli, many other Italian decadent writers fail to liberate themselves from their preoccupations with the minutiae of their sense-impressions and thus prove incapable of seeing events and situations in a valid spiritual perspective.

On the other hand, despite its intense descriptiveness this present poem does nevertheless evoke a certain mystical atmosphere for which we shall offer a partial explanation later. In the meantime, we can perhaps put the symbolist and decadent schools into final perspective by considering them to represent two sides of one and the same coin. During the evolution of culture towards a modern form of lyricism the symbolists first created the necessary metaphysical outlook by changing the analogy into a *correspondance* with its speculative overtones and implications; while the decadents later infused a deep sensuous realism into the idealistic structures of the former movement. Neither school, however, felt entirely at home in the contingent world which provides the substance of modern art; yet both were painfully aware of the concessions and compromises which it required from the poet. They therefore tried to distil immortal visions from their experiences – Rimbaldian quintessences whose implications they were convinced were wholly detached from the fleeting impressions and momentary insights on which they were founded. In a word, they failed to grasp that the underlying basis of modern art is process, not conclusion, and that it amounts to a statement of moods and human experiences, not to a speculative investigation into human destiny. Hence, even if it is less evident in the decadents than in the symbolists, it is precisely the dominance of a speculative intellectualism over a transfiguring emotion that most distinguishes late nineteenth-century poetry from its modern counterpart.

★ ★ ★ ★ ★ ★

So far we have mainly discussed French aesthetic influence on the forms and structures of modern Italian verse, but it would be false to imagine that indigenous Italian art had been wholly eliminated in favour of the French tradition. In processes of cross-fertilization such occurrences rarely take place, since the overriding aim is not to replace one culture by another but to assimilate a new tradition to a pre-existing one. So, although a vast amount of lyrical assimilation was already achieved by the turn of the century, we still find that the previously established Italian standards of lyrical clarity and classicism advocated by Leopardi and Carducci continued to act as subconscious guiding lights. No doubt this explains why there is a healthy sensuousness in the modern Italian lyric which is often absent from its French counterpart. Even Mounin acknowledges its effectiveness despite his other strictures and he stresses that 'la grande vertu d'une anthologie de la poésie du vingtième siècle italien, ce serait celle de ses thèmes.' ('the great virtue of an anthology of twentieth-century Italian poetry is associated with its themes'). On the other hand he denounces the cult of 'la poésie pure' in France, where he sees abstract and speculative attitudes predominating; and he finally reaches the following striking conclusion: 'Par un paradoxe parlant, c'est la critique italienne crocienne qui s'est épuisée dans ses analyses sur l'art et le non-art, la poésie et la non-poésie; mais c'est la poésie française, – où le débat pauvrement technique et formel ouvert par l'Abbé Brémond, Valéry, Jaloux fut vite oublié, – qui s'est appauvrie par une sélection toujours plus épurée de ses thèmes, au point que la *matière* de notre poésie contemporaine est trop souvent impalpable.'[26] ('By a startling paradox, it is Italian Crocean criticism which has become exhausted in its analyses of art and non-art, poetry and non-poetry; but it is French poetry, – where the threadbare technical and formal debate opened up by Abbé Brémond, Valéry and Jaloux was quickly forgotten – which has been weakened by a more and more purified selection of its themes, to the point where the *content* of our contemporary poetry is often intangible.') We can perhaps account for this by noting that the development of the lyric away from a common decadent and symbolist base followed very different directions in the two countries.

If we consider the mainstream of French poetry between the two wars, we immediately see that under the aegis of Valéry it continued to evolve along highly intellectual lines. Indeed, before the Second World War the majority of French poets – despite their sincere attempts to come to grips with pre-logical material – were still largely tied to rational rather than associative lyrical structures. By reaction, they developed Dadaism and Surrealism, and yet not even these movements achieved authentic associative syntheses. They tended instead to evolve as highly refined intellectual theories and had little more than a marginal effect on modern poetic symbolism. As such, their relative impotence was soon noted by the major Italian poets, a fact which no doubt explains why they were so little imitated; and, therefore, apart from the early experiments of the futurists and neo-futurists, Italian writers have tended on the whole to cling to their own cultural traditions whose classical restraints have provided an effective barrier against the more dispersive trends in surrealist verse. It would, in fact, hardly be an exaggeration to say that the Italian cultural inheritance has held so firm a grip that Petrarchan modes are still the stock-in-trade of many major poets. Their present-day prestige is no doubt due to Leopardi's revival of them, for like Petrarch before him he was basically an ethical rather than a metaphysical poet. His view of the world is mirrored in poems like 'La sera del dí di festa' where simple everyday activities acquire universal implications by revealing the stark realities of the human condition:

Ahi, per la via
Odo non lunge il solitario canto
Dell'artigian, che riede a tarda notte,
Dopo i sollazzi, al suo povero ostello;
E fieramente mi si stringe il core,
A pensar come tutto al mondo passa,
E quasi orma non lascia.

Ah, along the street I hear not far away the lonely song of the artisan, who returns late at night, after his amusement, to his poor lodgings: and my heart is fiercely racked when I think how everything in the world passes away, and hardly leaves a trace behind.

This adherence to a meditative realism is very different from the attitude of Valéry in 'Le cimetière marin'. The French poet upturns reality from the outset as the heat of high noon and the liquid motion of the sea plunge him into a speculative dreamworld. Afterwards, it is only with the greatest reluctance that he returns to more earthly levels, and even then his reconciliation with life is a mere *pis-aller*:

Le vent se lève . . . Il faut tenter de vivre!

The wind rises . . . One must try to live.

Such Neoplatonic soarings, however, are difficult to locate in modern Italian verse, especially in the concreteness of poets like Montale. Instead, Leopardi's reflective miniatures are raised to a level of a corruscating emblematic symbolism in which an aspect of life is so transfigured that universal implications are liberated. The following poem describing a Jewish refugee, Liuba, is a case in point:

Non il grillo ma il gatto
del focolare
or ti consiglia, splendido
lare della dispersa tua famiglia.
La casa che tu rechi
con te ravvolta, gabbia o cappelliera?
sovrasta i ciechi tempi come il flutto
arca leggera – e basta al tuo riscatto.

> Not the cricket but the cat on the hearth now counsels you, a splendid laric symbol of your scattered family. The house you carry with you, well-wrapped, a cage or a hat-box? overcomes these baleful times like a bobbing ark the flood – and is sufficient for your redemption.

If this poem is speculative at all, its speculation remains on an intensely human level. Its emotional associations and realist elements are in no way subjugated to the transcendental processes which even the humblest of Valéry's symbols undergo. From this we can deduce that the source of most contemporary Italian poetry was the decadent school, though in the course of its development its socially-orientated decadent substratum suffers a sea-change and is ultimately restructured and transformed into an emblematic realism. Montale's realism is indeed already present in Leopardi, but his emblematic quality (emerging here from an aggregate of objects) is wholly modern and opens up *symbolically* rather than *discursively* the many-sided character of Liuba, who is both an individual and a representative of the Jewish race at a time of oppression.[27] The hermetic emblem is accordingly a symbolic figure, landscape or disparate aggregate of objects, summing up an entire aspect of life and providing simultaneously the lyrical grace and wider reverberations of a complete poetic mood. Moreover, whereas such moods maintain a single unified appearance despite their often asyntactical mode of expression, the seeming unilaterality of their message tends to dissolve on closer inspection into a series of multilateral implications, reflecting a much wider pattern of feelings and experiences. It is probably in this sense that the hermetic school of poets in Italy enlarges the range of Mallarmé's original notion of musicality. For with them its function is to suggest a series of interlocking perspectives by transfiguring, rather than transcending, the real. Its only hint of transcendence lies in its reforging of the techniques of the decadent and symbolist poets into a higher form of emblematic representation in which the 'orphic' constants or 'eternal' rhythm of human nature can be seen emerging from within the contingent elements of personal experience.

The less speculative nature of modern Italian poetry – its transfigurative rather than transcendental tendencies – is thus the mark of its originality. Why should this have occurred? Partly, it seems, because of the attraction of the mainstream of Italian lyricism from Petrarch onwards, in which the setting has been social rather than metaphysical. This also accounts no doubt for its predominantly decadent rather than symbolist flavour, at least at the beginning of the century, in spite of the fact that Petrarch's own grasp on the real was at best indirect. For, as Ungaretti has often stressed[28], between him and the senses we find a constant play of memory and meditation. His inspiration is very largely confined to the inner man and rarely attempts to depict an external world-order like Dante's. Yet his peculiar type of inwardness offers a fertile area for development, so that it would not perhaps be an exaggeration to suggest that the contemporary poet's sense of an inner 'orphic' space and even his principal psychic processes are already implicit in Petrarch's lyrical method.

It is nowadays axiomatic to claim that Petrarch's lyricism of consolation is a transfigured morality springing from the recollection of his bitter-sweet experiences in relative tranquillity. Not only is he the inventor of a memorially-based emblematic pose, as Montanari has demonstrated, in lines such as

> Erano i capei d'oro a l'aura sparsi,[29]

> Her golden hair was scattered to the breeze

where a classical attitude to beauty is subsumed in Laura's nonchalant grace, but he is also the creator of a form of objective correlative in which certain timeless object-symbols are set in a memorial hinterland for the purpose of evoking a state of sensuous, contemplative serenity:

> Chiare, fresche e dolci acque,
> Ove le belle membra
> Pose colei che sola a me par donna;
> Gentil ramo, ove piacque
> (Con sospir mi rimembra)
> A lei di far al bel fianco colonna;
> Erba e fior, che la gonna
> Leggiadra ricoverse
> Co l'angelico seno;
> Aere sacro sereno,
> Ove Amor co' begli occhi il core m'aperse;
> Date udienzia insieme
> A le dolenti mie parole estreme.[30]

> Clear, fresh and gentle waters, where she who alone to me seems a woman rested her lovely limbs; gentle branch, where it pleased her (I recall with a sigh) to make a support for her lovely side; grass and flowers, which her beautiful dress covered, together with her angelic bosom; sacred, serene air, where love opened my heart through her lovely eyes; together pay heed to these final grieving words of mine.

Here the sensuous fluidity of the first line helps to link a series of metonymic object-symbols (*ramo, erba, fior*) with a few generic adjectives, creating the after-imaging of a memorial perspective which characterizes the poet's style. For Petrarch memory is, in fact, a springboard for the projection of his sensibility towards richer states of feeling, and one suspects that it is an intricate combination of memorial perspectives, far more than a feeling of unrequitedness, which binds all the major Petrarchists together. This is certainly the case with modern Petrarchan practice where the love-theme is frequently transformed into an aesthetic contemplation of ethical and aesthetic perfection. Such contemplation incidentally carries along with it a further effect, a tendency to invert the world of the spirit and the senses, or at least to interfuse the one with the other. An inversion of relationships within the real is a favourite Petrarchan device of traditional origin which the French call 'le monde mis à l'envers' ('the world turned upside down'). In Italy its main – though by no means its only – modern exponent is Ungaretti who inverts life and death so as to make the memorial kingdom of death a state of living sensitivity and the crude immediacy of life a realm of mere sensuous oblivion:

> È nei vivi la strada dei defunti,
>
> Siamo noi la fiumana d'ombre,
>
> Sono esse il grano che ci scoppia in sogno . . .[31]

In the living runs the path of the dead, we are the torrent of shadows, they are the seed which bursts on us in dreams . . .

For poets like Ungaretti death amounts metaphorically to rebirth, to a recapturing of any given situation in its pristine wholeness from the past, through the whispering of tradition. By contrast, life's experiences lack all insight and are simply envisaged as elements of an anguish-stricken sub-state. But, as one moves through life like a somnambulist, death's immortal image-suspensions leave deeply-felt sandy deposits in the blood, and Ungaretti believes that they provide him with his most valuable atavistic perspectives:

> Morte, muta parola,
> Sabbia deposta come un letto
> Dal sangue,
> Ti odo cantare come una cicala
> Nella rosa abbrunata dei riflessi.[32]

Death, silent word, sand deposited like a bed by the blood. I hear you singing like a cicada in the darkened rose of reflections.

Just how the modern poet uses the modalities of memory to extend and exploit these lyrical insights will be a subject dealt with in more detail later. For the moment it will suffice to note that the cult of death's inner perspectives is again orphic in character. It is, in fact, a vital factor in the orphic doctrine of art, one of whose principal features is, as Flora once put it, 'il perenne accrescimento che la poeticità umana fa delle poesie passate rivivendole'[33] ('the perennial enhancement which human lyricism gives to the poetry of the past by re-living it').

The ethical tension resulting from the interplay of life and death is also an important feature in modern poetry. It creates a more intense form of 'dolore' than Petrarch's bitter-sweet melancholy and imbues the poet with a dual sense of awareness. This bifocality amounts to a dialectic between the perennial and the contingent which allows him to reorganize his steadily maturing experiences against the back-cloth of a timeless tradition, viewed over a period of many generations. The symbolic elements required for such a type of representation prove to be curiously adaptable to emblematic and analogical structures, although they demand at the same time an unswerving fidelity by the poet to the temporal unfolding of his inner feelings or personality: the kind of adherence which accounts for the autobiographical nature of the work of much modern Italian lyricism, an anti-idealist posture which would have shocked Mallarmé and the symbolists. Ungaretti draws particular attention to this psychological realism inherent in modern poetry when claiming for his own verse that 'l'autore non ha altra ambizione, e crede che anche i grandi poeti non ne avessero altre, se non quella di lasciare una sua bella biografia.'[34] ('the author has no other ambition, and believes that the great poets had no other, than to leave behind a fine biography.') The point leads us straight back to Mounin's contention that the greatest achievement of present-day Italian verse is the deep-seated realism of its themes. So, whereas over the last hundred years French poetry has provided us with ever more rarefied sensations[35], its Italian counterpart has normally drawn its substance from immediate and tangible forms of experience.

However, despite the great prestige of the Petrarchan tradition, its influence has not so much derived from Petrarch himself as from the major Petrarchists like Tasso and Leopardi. It has subsequently been further refined by Croce's ideas on the identity of intuition and lyrical expression. Pure poetry has in consequence been directed into a psychological mould (as even the poetry of so Gallic a poet as Fiumi will show), and Ungaretti hints that the 'pure' psychological lyricism of Tasso's *Aminta* is a source for the general trend. In this pastoral drama emphasis tends to fall on the emotional response rather than on conceptualization, although in some other areas Tasso is himself suspect in the eyes of modern poets because his artistic approach tends to be idealistically inclined. We can no doubt account for this suspicion by the fact that contemporary poets practise their creativeness at the point of intersection between reality and the imagination, whereas Tasso tended to displace his inspiration towards a cult of baroque fantasy while including only a leavening of realism for the sake of verisimilitude.[36]

Leopardi's firmer grasp on the concrete has, on the other hand, proved much more satisfying to modern tastes. Not only was he a realist at heart, but he also possessed a tremendous insight into the evolution of art forms and into the so-called 'racial' memory.[37] Hence it has been claimed that his sensibility was virtually attuned to modern aesthetic tastes even before the basis on which the modern sensibility was intended to operate was remotely understood. In his *Zibaldone* he gives a definition of art which has fascinated contemporary writers, for he describes poetic texture as consisting of 'una folla d'idee simultanee, o cosí rapidamente succedentisi che paiono simultanee' ('a crowd of simultaneous ideas, or so rapidly succeeding each other that they seem simultaneous') and that these ideas 'fanno ondeggiar l'anima in una tale abbondanza di pensieri, o d'immagini e sensazioni spirituali, ch'ella o non è capace di abbracciarle tutte...o non ha tempo di restare in ozio, e priva di sensazioni'[38] ('make the soul linger in such an abundance of thoughts, or images and spiritual sensations, that it is either not capable of embracing them all ... or has no time to remain unoccupied and deprived of sensations'). Here a cult of sensuous intensities is foreshadowed which is not just the obverse of purely rational trends but even of Petrarch's religiously based conviction that material things lead man to perdition and need to be transcended in verse. His views on the sensuous aspects of life are laid down by St. Augustine in the *Secretum*, where the Saint tries to wean him off the delights of this world: 'Conglobantur siquidem species innumere et imagines rerum visibilium, que corporeis introgresse sensibus, postquam singulariter admisse sunt, catervatim in anime penetralibus densantur; eamque, nec ad id genitam nec tam multorum difformiumque capacem, pregravant atque confundunt. Hinc pestis illa fantasmatum vestros discerpens laceransque cogitatus, meditationibusque clarificis, quibus ad unum solum summumque lumen ascenditur, iter obstruens varietate mortifera.'[39] ('Indeed, the innumerable types and images of material things accumulate and, by penetrating through our bodily senses, coagulate in hosts within the inner reaches of the soul, once they have been received there individually; and, since it was not created for that purpose nor is capable of receiving such discordant forms, they confound and encumber it. Hence that plague of phantasmata rending and tearing your thoughts, which with a pernicious inconstancy blocks the way to sublime meditations whereby it ascends alone to the single almighty light of God'). However, as a poet Petrarch was at the same time keenly aware that these deplorable material things were the very stuff of the lyrical imagination, so what Leopardi succeeded in doing was to laicize Petrarch's paradoxical attitude towards material forms and produce a modern view of poetry as a combination of interlocking and mutually illuminating images.

The main residual ideological element in Leopardi's verse was on the other hand a virtual religion of cosmic futility, a foreknowledge of the limits of the human condition, which led him to a type of universal pessimism. Yet this attitude too is capable of being turned into its obverse, just as Petrarch's was before him. Its positive aspect is Ungaretti's existential 'dolore', which is subtly mediated through the works of Pascoli and D'Annunzio. These two poets stand, in fact, halfway between Leopardi's and Ungaretti's outlooks and they reveal their residual idealism in curious ways. With Pascoli it appears as a fruitless cosmic yearning for a higher state of insight, while with D'Annunzio it operates even more surprisingly through the senses, prompting their intense but nonetheless futile exasperation.

Although both attitudes are fundamentally decadent, Lugli assures us that Pascoli, at least, stood aloof from contemporary French trends and may have developed parallel modes of expression like the *analogia* or *poesia delle cose* for himself.[40] Whenever he is truly inspired, his lyrics are highly integrated and coherent, although his overall ratio of success to failure is perhaps not as marked as we would expect it to be. His lyrical structures in consequence often prove to be very fragile, especially his more impressionistic poems, revealing a certain inability to conclude. By contrast, D'Annunzio tends to turn Leopardi's universal pessimism into an emotional nihilism, so that while Pascoli is a Leopardian poet writ exceedingly small, D'Annunzio is one writ impossibly large, in which an inflationary emotionalism is accompanied by a feverish sensuality and counterbalanced stylistically by a self-conscious cult of classical perfection.[41] Whenever he writes a valid poem, it is largely composed of delicate imaginative conceits and a good deal of phonic ingenuity, as previously illustrated in 'La pioggia nel pineto'. Thus, in the last resort it is through their success in introducing novel forms and fresh ways of perceiving the world that these two poets exert an influence on modern poetry.

It was through a combination of D'Annunzio's rarefied sensationalism and musicality and Pascoli's fetishized landscapes and symbolic aggregates that the next vital step forward was accomplished. We have already seen a mild form of fetishization of a scene of domestic bliss in the vignette quoted earlier from Betteloni. Soon after the turn of the century this type of art was brought to a high state of perfection by Gozzano who tried to transmute imagery into a series of 'vecchie stampe' ('old engravings') or daguerrotypes. He attempted to write, in other words, poems possessing all the detachment of still-lifes by employing a curious form of decadent image-suspension; and, although in themselves such word-pictures seem frigid and negative, they are nevertheless the forerunners of Montale's use of the objective correlative as a 'laric' form of symbolism to plumb new depths of experience. Whereas we may feel in Montale's case that the wheel has come full circle and that his extreme agnosticism is more closely linked with Leopardi's pessimism than with Ungaretti's more positive sense of 'dolore', the fact remains that both these lyrical attitudes are already implicit in Leopardi's verse.

Two further features also implicit in his verse are a sense of human *durata* and of personal *disponibilità*. These are both important aspects of any existential outlook since *durata* may be regarded as involving an awareness of the finitude and uniqueness of individual experience, while *disponibilità* is an attitude of continuous receptivity which combats the recurring desire of the poet's sensibility for a condition of emotive stasis. To illustrate them, let us take an example by Bartolini which is reminiscent of Rimbaud's 'Sonnet des voyelles' and which represents the 'soubresauts de la conscience' ('quiverings of conscience') depicted in modern art, and another from Adriano Grande, the first lyric of *La strada al mare* (1943), where a reflective lyrical perspective emerges from a thorough-going existential setting. Bartolini's poem 'Colori' is a veritable alchemistic riot of colours and temporally extended sensations:

> Nero: sei Nero, Inferno, le oscure sue porte,
> l'arco di Stige sei, l'ombra di sera, il fiato di notte,
> la coltre triste, che in ultimo ci ricopre;
> nero, odore dispensier di Morte.
>
> Rosso, oh tu, fra i colori, il piú giovane,
> per te si dilegua, in fuga si pone malinconia;
> colore delle corolle fragranti, di labbra accese,
> tu l'anima sei dei sensi, oh colore terrestre!

Black: you are Black, Hell, its dark gates, the meandering of the Styx, the shadow of evening, the gasp of night, the sad sheet which finally covers us; black, a smell dispensing Death. Red, oh you, among the colours, the youngest, through you melancholy takes to flight, melts away; colour of fragrant corollas, of burning lips, you are the soul of the senses, oh terrestrial colour!

On the other hand, Grande's lyric 'Destino' tries to provide a perspective or sense of *durata* by evoking the psycho-sensuous enchantment of transient experiences within an overall pattern or framework:

> Amo le cose passate
> e quelle che saranno.
> M'afferro, uccello, al ramo
> dell'esistenza e sbatto come vuole
> il vento della storia. Me ne resta
> dentro, talvolta, il lieve
> sapore che la gente oblia.

> I love things past and those to come. I cling like a bird to the branch of existence and shake as the wind of history desires. Within me there sometimes remains the slight flavour which people forget.

Hence we can claim that between them they illustrate the entire range of lyrical effects available to modern poets in their attempts to plumb the existential depths of contemporary life and feeling.

★ ★ ★ ★ ★ ★

The peculiar intermingling of sensory and ethical material in the transfigurative processes of modern Italian verse has permitted aestheticians to add to their theories on the nature of art a further element deriving from mass-psychology. It is one which purports to demonstrate that art is not intended to function within an intellectual sphere of eternal ideas; its aim is rather to reflect that powerful nexus of moral and emotive forces which make up the social fabric of a society at a given time and place. The modern poet, among others, has consequently regarded it as his duty to reassess the values of his own age in the light of the cultural tradition and not to propound any specific or dogmatic theology, because he has finally become aware that 'la verità non è né in Dio né nella terra, ma nell'atto unitario dello spirito'[42] ('truth, is neither in God nor the earth, but in the unifying act of the spirit').

The philosophical background which has most attracted Italian theorists in this area is that of the phenomenologists, especially Husserl's doctrine of the *Lebenswelt*, from whom the hermetic school also obtains its concept of *epoché*. Both these terms require some explanation. The *Lebenswelt* may be defined as the traditions and cultural tensions persisting in a society at a given time, while *epoché* – sometimes called hypostasis in Mallarmean criticism[43] – amounts to the momentary suspension of the image as an 'ideation' in the poet's sensibility so that it may be interpreted in isolation (by putting the world in parentheses) and made vibrant with the reflections of an 'absolute' lyrical charge. Its emotion is impressed on the reader's mind through a form of empathy, and it is by means of this 'revelationary' emphatic charge that it is claimed that a new form of communication is achieved. Precisely speaking, the process is a 'transfigurative' one, although the phenomenologists tend to use transcendentalist terms to describe it, a point which explains why even so realist a poet as Montale argues that lyrical communication is attained through the 'io trascendentale'.[44] Nevertheless for him the process involved does not consist of a stepping-beyond but of a breathing-within the real.

A parallel point expressed in similar transcendental terms is made by Battaglini who stresses that the real aim of poetry is to 'trascendere la fisicità delle cose che ci attorniano, a procedere all'*epoché*, a cogliere la *Lebenswelt*'[45] ('transcend the physicality of the things which surround us, to proceed to *epoché*, to accept the *Lebenswelt*'). Moreover, in the post-war world the process has produced a modern humanist outlook which, as Leonetti has explained, aims at creating a poetry which is 'una rappresentazione storico-attuale misurata col proprio cuore'[46] ('a historico-synchronic form of representation measured out with one's own heart'). However, during the period between the two wars which is our main centre of interest, this particular outlook gave rise to a modern religion of art, a modern orphism, which we can consider to be the aesthetic counterpart of the psycho-ethical doctrine implicit in Husserl's *Lebenswelt*.

Somewhat surprisingly, the modern concept of orphism has definite connections – though mostly analogical ones – with ancient orphism. In Greece, ancient orphism was a religion of salvation through metempsychosis, and its aims were achieved by means of a progressive purification of the spirit which involved religious ceremonies and the carrying out of a number of rituals or *teletae*. Most of these rituals appear to have involved the practice of abstinence and the singing of songs, so that even in ancient times the cult had an aesthetic as well as a religious aspect. But, presumably before such refinements were evolved, the cult's founder, Orpheus – a singer of Thrace – was confused with Dionysus and Demeter, the Gods of vegetation. From them orphism acquired a ritual which re-enacted the rending of Orpheus's body by the Bacchants under the influence of wine. This eventually led to the symbolism of the 'One in the Many'[47], which is considered the central feature of the cult.

Probably the most important element of ancient orphism from a modern lyrical standpoint is the underlying myth of purification leading to salvation. Most of the information we possess about it is given in the form of a series of travelogues which were intended to help the orphic adept in his fateful journey through the underworld after death, and one of the most illuminating is the Tablet of Petelia now in the British Museum:

> 'You will find a spring to the left of the Halls of Hades and beside it a white cypress growing. Do not go near this spring. And you will find another from the Lake of Memory flowing forth with cold water. In front of it are guards. You must say "I am a child of Gê and starry Ouranos"; this you yourselves know. "I am dry with thirst and am perishing. Come, give me cold water running from the Lake of Memory." And they themselves will give you to drink from the divine spring and thereafter you will reign with the other heroes.'

The so-called realm of the 'white cypress' depicted here finds its modern counterpart in Campana's 'panorama scheletrico del mondo' ('skeletal panorama of the world'), as we shall see later. However, if we follow the myth a little further, we discover that the road to Hades was forked and, while the purified took the right-hand fork, the impure took the left. The impure proceeded, that is, to the Spring of Lethe because they were condemned by their sins to a process of reincarnation in this world, to further purification within the 'Great Wheel of Being'. Hence their aim was not to drink too deeply of the spring of forgetfulness in case they lost the memory of their past errors. The pure, on the other hand, drank immediately of the Fountain of Mnemosyne, the spring of memorial omniscience and creative intelligence, and thereby attained to a godlike level of perception and insight, even though at the time this state was envisaged largely as the passive or static contemplation of the Platonic Ideas.

In the modern theory of orphism the ancient realm of memorial omniscience is replaced by the *Lebenswelt*, which is never static but constantly changing, and this accounts for the fact that modern orphism is existential rather than absolutist in nature. The aim of the modern orphic poet, in short, is to recapture the multiple elements of life in their totality, but at the particular time and in the particular place in which he lives. He does this by saturating his verse with echoes and cultural reminiscences drawn from tradition and by modifying tastes through the introduction into the *Lebenswelt* of those subtle shifts of emphasis and perception characteristic of all temporal processes.[48] In other words, the modern poet is alienated at the outset of his career from the set patterns of the society in which he develops, but he is gradually modified by, as he himself modifies, its dominant tastes and feelings. In so far as he tries to resolve the problem of his reintegration into society by combining traditional ethico-aesthetic values with his own individual outlook he therefore becomes an 'experimental traditionalist' whose aim, unlike that of the futurists, is not to disrupt the culture of the past but to encourage its gradual evolution.

A secret cult of orphism with a concomitant infolding of the poetic image has had a long history in European art.[49] Already in the Renaissance period, for instance, Chastel points out that Ficino 'aime montrer Dieu comme un pasteur orphique veillant sur le monde'[50] ('loves to show God as an orphic shepherd watching over the world'), while Wind has also noted that at times the infolding of the image was then a deliberate expressive technique.[51] The cult has more recently been taken up once again in Mallarmé's poetry, although the symbolists tend to remain pure Platonists at heart and their view of orphism is not essentially different from that of the Ancients. They even reintroduce some of ancient orphism's rich pastoral imagery, as the opening of Mallarmé's 'L'après-midi d'un Faune' will show:

Ces nymphes, je les veux perpétuer.
Si clair,
Leur incarnat léger, qu'il voltige dans l'air
Assoupi de sommeils touffus.

Aimai-je un rêve?
Mon doute, amas de nuit ancienne, s'achève
En maint rameau subtil, qui, demeuré les vrais
Bois mêmes, prouve, hélas! que bien seul je m'offrais
Pour troimphe la faute idéale de roses.

These nymphs, I would wish to eternalize them. So clear their light complexion that it flutters in the air made drowsy by tufted slumbers. Did I love a dream? My doubt, a gathering of ancient darkness, ends in many a subtle branch, which, remaining the real woods themselves, proves, alas! that all alone I offered myself as a triumph the ideal error of roses.

The Faun's dream in this poem, although it is based on sexual yearning, is nevertheless eidetically orientated, aiming at a static tableau of purity and eternity, even though it may well be unattainable. But in modern Italian poetry the orphic goal of revealing the One through the Multiple changes subtly into a revelation of the perennial through the multiple, which amounts to the creation of a myth of 'absoluteness within change'. Hence, when Ungaretti offers a perspective of human sexuality in 'Canto' written in 1932, the yearning is sublimated not into a form of intellection but into an echoing, existential myth whose perenniality evokes a dialectic of love and separation symbolically repeated down the ages:

Rivedo la tua bocca lenta
(Il mare le va incontro delle notti)
E la cavalla delle reni
In agonia caderti
Nelle mie braccia che cantavano,
E riportarti un sonno
Al colorito e a nuove morti.

E la crudele solitudine
Che in sé ciascuno scopre, se ama,
Ora tomba infinita,
Da te mi divide per sempre.

Cara, lontana come in uno specchio . . .

Once more I see your slow mouth (the ocean of night flows towards it) and the mare of your loins casting you in trepidation into my singing arms, and sleep bearing you back to a coloured world and new deaths. And the cruel solitude which each of us discovers within himself, if he loves, now an infinite tomb, divides me from you for ever. Dear one, distant as if in a mirror . . .

Here, of course, the perspective slowly emerges from the imagery and is made allusively explicit in the last line, because the mirror-image suggests the phantomatic fading of immediate reality and its replacement by the perennial recurrence of the archetypal orphic agony of love. The poet's aim has thus been to transfigure human relationships instead of trying to transcend them through forms of conceptual statement, because, as Battaglini explains in phenomenological terms, the artist is now no longer as he was in romantic times 'un Dio creatore, ma come uno sperimentatore instancabile di nuove e complesse situazioni umane'[52] ('a creative God, but as it were an indefatigable experimenter with new and complex human situations'). The difficulty with which we shall be confronted in what follows will be that the hermetic poets believed that these complex situations could only be made to emerge from certain preconceived metaphysical perspectives expressed in an intense involution of language and imagery.

CHAPTER II

Modern Italian poetry : movements and polemics

The literary realities on which the modern lyric is based can be traced back to the sixties of the last century when the dominant mood among avant-garde writers was one of revolt against the *status quo*. A group particularly noted for its opposition to authority and tradition was the *Scapigliatura* whose name was borrowed from the seventeenth century and was first employed by Carlo Righetti in one of his novels, with a meaning approximating to the French word 'bohème'.[1] In all essentials the 'Scapigliati' adopted the same iconoclastic attitudes and expressed the same revolutionary ideas as the 'bas romantiques' in France. Indeed like the latter, violence, sadism and a gruesome form of realism all play a part in their work and were frequently used as a mask to conceal a lack of positive aesthetic values.

We can ascribe the birth of this peculiar form of frenzied romanticism to two main causes: first, to the prevailing hegemony of French cultural fashions and, second, to the pressing social changes occurring in Italy itself. As Romanò has explained, it was precisely at that period that Northern Italy was beginning to feel the full impact of its belated industrial revolution and a sense of industrial alienation and rootlessness was already undermining the previously close-knit pattern of Italian life.[2] In such conditions it was only to be expected that writers would turn to French sources for their raw materials, because the same kind of revolution had already taken place in France much earlier, manifesting itself in the movement known as *Les Jeunes-France*.[3] Yet, while French writings were responsible for setting the trend, it was later maintained by the ever-increasing rate of cultural change in Italy itself, especially after its Unification. This explains why the steadily growing momentum of Italian social transformation had a significant influence on literary developments in the nineties and why the time actually arrived in the first decade of the twentieth century when Italian avant-garde groups even seemed marginally ahead of their French counterparts in the violence of their revolutionary fervour. At that time Marinetti and his followers succeeded in imposing the doctrines of futurism on the rest of Europe, with articles on the subject appearing even in right-wing newspapers like the *Daily Telegraph*. Nevertheless, the futurists still resembled the 'Scapigliati' in a sense, since they were far more conscious of the rate of change in social and cultural conditions than they were of the need to reduce their responses to these changes to a valid representational pattern. Thus, from 1860 to 1914, we can regard the underlying cultural ethos as highly unsettled, despite the presence of a trilogy of major poets such as Carducci, Pascoli and D'Annunzio.

At the one end of the time-scale we find the 'Scapigliati' who soon turned their attention to social as well as aesthetic agitation. They hoped, in so doing, to bring about a regeneration of society by continually challenging the established order and shaking it out of its mental and physical inertia. However from an aesthetic standpoint, despite the efforts of Giuseppe Rovani[4] to work out the movement's aesthetic principles (which he believed should be centred around the fusion of the three arts of music, painting and poetry), all sense of artistic cohesion gradually faded away and the dominant trends became sociological ones, amounting virtually to the setting up of an anti-establishment. The outcome of such a programme on the cultural level can readily be predicted: the great majority of the 'Scapigliati' abandoned all thought of originality and degenerated into a set of ineffectual revolutionaries tending to mimic the most advanced and fashionable French tastes, themes and stylistic mannerisms. Since their artistic experience was almost completely vicarious, they rarely formulated aesthetic or moral values of their own, and therefore failed to re-synthesize a major Italian tradition out of their borrowed plumes.

Although the *Scapigliatura* was by no means a compact or self-conscious group and the range of its lyrical content proved vast, most of its members nevertheless possessed – as Rovani insisted – at least one tendency in common: a feature which Flora has described as 'la tendenza (o la velleità o l'illusione) di trasporre un'arte nell'altra: ad esempio il canto verbale in colore, la parola in nota musicale'[5] ('the tendency (or the whim or illusion) of transposing one art into another: for example, the verbal song into colour, the word into a musical note'). If we confine our examination of their work to this area, we discover that the two principal poets of the school, Emilio Praga and Arrigo Boito, gravitate respectively towards the visual and musical ends of the literary spectrum.

The early Praga of *Tavolozza* (1862) proves to be a colourful, if sometimes an idyllic, landscape painter. But there is always an undercurrent of ironic shading in his work to counteract any trace of sentimentality, and it finds its highest expression in a sustained – yet colour-punctuated –

realism. This is typified by his description of the features of a rapacious old monk in 'Un frate':

Tra una pelle liscia, gialla,
scintillavan come faci
occhi ceruli e rapaci,
segno questo che non falla;

e il naso uscía schiacciato,
monco, nero, raggrinzato,
come il naso di un chinese,
strano pur nel suo paese.

In a smooth, yellow skin there glistened like torches blue, rapacious eyes, an unfailing sign this; and the nose was shattered, snub, black, wrinkled, like the nose of a Chinese, though strange even in his country.

Here one can almost say that a human character has been transformed into a coloured landscape in keeping with the poet's dominant pictorial manner. Praga often underlines this kind of artifice by introducing into his literary textures the sordid realism and the extravagant gestures of the 'bas romantiques' in France. So much so that eventually, in *Penombre* (1864), we are presented with discordant chiaroscuro colourings and a perspective of cynical detachment, and such an attitude soon becomes identified with the fragmented poetic principles of all the writers of the *Scapigliatura*.

Again, a single example will suffice to illustrate the point. In the 'Preludio' to this volume the poet adopts a Baudelairian stance (similar to the one appearing in the poem 'Au lecteur' at the beginning of the *Fleurs du mal*) and depicts with little modification of tone or meaning the type of moral degeneracy to which the French poet had already felt himself a prey:

O nemico lettor, canto la Noia,
L'eredità del dubbio e dell'ignoto,
Il tuo re, il tuo pontefice, il tuo boia,
Il tuo cielo e il tuo loto!

O hostile reader, I sing of Ennui, the inheritance of doubt and the unknown, your king, your Pope, your executioner, your heaven and your mire!

Wholesale plagiarizing of this type is not uncommon with the 'Scapigliati' and it is sometimes practised with so little discrimination that entire collections of verse appear to be rag-bags of second-hand emotion. *Penombre* itself, admittedly, is not without its merits, but its tonal fragmentation and lack of symbolic unity reveal that Praga's visual acuity was not matched by a sensibility capable of rising to a heightened imaginative and affective sphere. Hence what he and his contemporaries saw as a profound cultural revolution turned out to be largely a damp squib, a moody regurgitation of romantic banalities; and, even if the group did genuinely attempt to create an unsophisticated, realist style to rescue the Italian lyric from neo-classical rhetoric, their lack of an authentic perspective virtually obscured its originality. Thus only infrequent sparks of a modern authentic lyricism appear in Praga's work and these are mostly verbal felicities rather than the result of poetic insight.

Similarly we find at times prefigurations of a modern lyrical vein in Boito, although this well-known librettist had, if anything, an even more fragmented sensibility than Praga. He was certainly more melodramatic in his gestures, and his poetry is marked by the dualism which runs right through the movement: a paradoxical cult of angelism and satanism. In Boito the two moods are not juxtaposed by means of colour-contrasts but by an interplay of light and shade within the musical fluidity of his verse. A typical example is the following passage from the poem 'Dualismo' itself, where the decadent posture is somewhat redeemed by a persuasive word-music:

> Son luce e ombra; angelica
> farfalla o verme immondo,
> sono un caduto chèrubo
> dannato a errar sul mondo,
> un demone che sale,
> affaticando l'ale,
> verso un lontano ciel...

I am light and shadow; an angelic butterfly or foul worm, I am a fallen cherub condemned to wander upon the earth, or a demon rising by wearily flapping his wings towards a distant heaven...

Sometimes the word-music is further heightened by a symbolic style which borders on a *poesia delle cose*, as the following lines reveal:

> L'illusïon – libellula
> che bacia i fiorellini,
> – l'illusïon – scoiattolo
> che danza in cima i pini,
> – l'illusïon – fanciulla
> che trama e si trastulla
> colle fibre del cor,
> viene ancora a sorridermi...

Illusion – dragonfly which kisses the flowerets, – illusion – squirrel which dances on the pine-tops, – illusion – girl who plots and trifles with the heart's strings, returns once more to smile upon me...

Lines like these, indeed, suggest that there exists in the aesthetics of the decadent poets a secret development away from conventional romanticism towards a more resilient poetry involving a symbolic realism; and, as we shall see later, this kind of figurative language slowly progresses through Gozzano's fetishized lyricism towards the emblematic style of the hermetic writers. Accordingly, even if Boito does not possess the necessary insight fully to exploit it, he certainly helped to clear the ground for a subsequent step forward in poetic representation. Sporadically he even went further and, by adopting Praga's colour technique, achieved a full measure of verbal alchemy. The effect again derives from a fusion of his word-music with a perceptive range of object-symbols, which together produce veritable firework displays of auditory and visual contrasts. One of his brilliantly contrived examples of alchemistic counterpoint involving colour, echo-rhyming and assonance reads:

Il cielo è di cenere – il suol di carbone
e par che ogni platano – annidi un dimone.
Le stelle s'estinguono – la luna s'asconde,
i tumuli, i culmini – le rupi, le fronde,
le curve fantastiche – dell'erto sentiero
son torvi profili – che spiccano in nero.
Chi ulula? Un'upupa – del lito montano.
Chi vola? una nuvola – che va all'uragano.
Chi passa? una foglia – dell'irta mandragola,
Un grillo che cigola – il vento che miagola.
Lassú tra le nebbie – la stella diana
par l'occhio verdognolo – di qualche befana.[6]

The sky is ashen – the earth like coal, and it seems that every plane-tree – houses a demon. The stars are extinguished – the moon hides, the graves, the summits – the cliffs, the foliage, the fantastic curves – of the steep path, are wild silhouettes – which stand out darkly. What howls? A hoopoe – from the mountainous strand. What flies? a cloud – which moves towards a hurricane. What passes? a leaf – of the shaggy mandragola, a cricket which chirps – the wind which caterwauls. Up there among the mists – the morning star seems like the greenish eye – of some apparition.

By virtue of their lyrical intensity, we can expect verbal alchemies of this kind to provide Boito with some standing among the modern poets, and the above-quoted lyric does, in fact, remind us of Montale's manner, though on a purely descriptive rather than on a reflective plane. His alliterative technique is also reproduced in a sense by Rebora, Campana and others; and yet, at the same time, it has to be acknowledged that his twentieth-century successors are normally much more parsimonious in their use of these artifices than he is. Needless to say, such a tendency is wholly explicable in terms of the differing levels of critical awareness prevailing in the two periods under discussion.

In effect, what is notably lacking in the poets of the *Scapigliatura* is a self-conscious understanding of the function of art. They often tend to use it for propaganda purposes and fail to realize that in the modern era its true function is to express complex states and feelings. So, although we find hints at later lyrical developments in nearly all of this movement's representative writers, they are more accidental than premeditated lyrical responses. In the majority of cases, as Romanò points out, 'la sintesi espressiva, la intuizione di una verità storica in movimento, la visione rappresentativa di una situazione cui concorrono componenti eterogenei, non viene neppure sfiorata'[7] ('an expressive synthesis, the grasping of a progressive historical truth, the representational vision of a situation which focuses heterogeneous elements, is not even touched upon'). This suggests that the entire movement is largely an imitative one and that its adherents tend to treat contemporary French literature as a kind of Pandora's box from which to draw eye-catching turns of phrase and exotic moods, with nothing more than an intermittent show of critical selection or lyrical appropriateness. Yet, even though it soon became evident that such attempts at wholesale transplantation of a foreign culture into Italy were doomed to failure, the final outcome of the experimentation of the 'Scapigliati' nevertheless proved positive. For the welter of partly digested romantic and post-romantic themes which the latter left suspended in the Italian literary firmament tended to spur subsequent generations of poets to meditate more seriously on the deeper aesthetic problems involved in the process of assimilating the broader European culture of the last century to the exigencies of Italian taste.

★ ★ ★ ★ ★ ★

It would be largely inaccurate to speak of the existence of any definite school of poetry engaged in the task of assimilation towards the turn of the century, although a number of modern trends became more and more perceptible, some of them pioneered by major poets like Pascoli or D'Annunzio. Of the two Pascoli is probably the more significant from the standpoint of hermetic culture, because D'Annunzio's supercharged decadent sensibility tended to have only a piece-meal effect upon the art of his successors. He may therefore be more readily considered in his relationship with single poets such as Gozzano or Montale than in a wider perspective. This being the case, we shall take as the main example of cultural mediation between the nineteenth and twentieth centuries the poetry of Pascoli, especially since the first recorded hints at modern notions like pure poetry or reflective insight are first found in the Italian language in his well-known lyrical manifesto, *Il Fanciullino.*[8]

What Pascoli understood by insight was the visionary power of the child, a theme which becomes important in modern lyricism since it provides a fundamental distinction between the unreflective modes of feeling at work in infancy and the self-conscious ones operating in the adult. This is largely because the intellect in adulthood tends to become dominant over the intuition. As Bàrberi Squarotti notes[9], the intuitive insight of the child is normally the mainspring of Pascoli's lyrical procedures. The point may be illustrated by his typically decadent concept of the 'casa-nido' ('house-nest') with its closed and inward-looking emotional security, as opposed to the open and menacing indifference of the cosmos, where the laws of chance hold sway. Such an attitude is probably the hidden implication behind the sudden revelation of the house caught in the lightning flash in 'Il lampo' quoted earlier, for the most satisfying aesthetic interpretation of the poem is that it is not mere description but represents the resistance of the *foyer* to the senseless onslaughts of cosmic power symbolized by the storm. In other words, Pascoli's aesthetics and lyrical themes are directed towards the strengthening of man's inner reality while acknowledging the absurdity of cosmic indifference or even cosmic hostility. At first sight such a posture suggests that he may be upholding reason and attempting to use it as a shield against the vagaries of chance, but the opposite proves in fact to be the case. For Pascoli's world consists of the mysterious emotional bonds uniting the family over the generations and is itself highly irrational, depending more on the instincts and their associative powers than on the reason for its lyrical cohesion.

The largely instinctive base on which he builds his imaginative structures nevertheless guarantees a certain infusion of concrete, realist elements into his themes. These are, of course, closely linked with the intricate, almost hallucinatory forms of transfiguration – the *jenseits der Dinge* – cultivated by the decadent poets. Frequently Pascoli's hallucinatory effects lead to oniric, or even onanistic, interpretations of moods and feelings, to which he sometimes adds a touch of racial mysticism and perspective. Like contemporary French poets, he appears to have regarded the racial ethos as a touchstone for lyrical consolidation, especially when it helps to counter the individual's sense of isolation. Therefore in this sense he, too, tends to regress into an atavistic dreamworld (as did Mallarmé in 'Igitur') in the hope of finding a personal absolute.

His attitude to the dead is perhaps the supreme illustration of this feature in his work, because he seems to consider the present, living family and its ancestors as a single, self-contained unit. The obsessive presence of the dead is accordingly a constant, if perplexing, reality for him:

Io vedo, vedo, vedo un camposanto,
oscura cosa nella notte oscura;
odo quel pianto della tomba, pianto

d'occhi lasciati dalla morte attenti,
pianto di cuori cui la sepoltura
lasciò, ma solo di dolor, viventi.[10]

I see, I see, I see a graveyard, a dark object in a dark night; I hear the mourning of the tomb, the weeping of eyes left alert by death, the weeping of hearts which the tomb has left alive, but only through grief.

Here the poet's dead not only continue to rub shoulders with the living, they also tend to control the customs and habits of the living through their silent reproaches and endless vigil. However primitive and superstitious such an attitude may seem, it nevertheless already foreshadows the preoccupation of the hermetic poets with the intelligence of the dead as mirrored in the inflections of the lyric tradition. Indeed, in hermetic art the very presence of the poets of the past appears to determine the bounds of expressiveness in the present which living poets dare not overstep except at their peril; and, likewise, the recurrent imagery of night, of shadows and a spectral whiteness typified by Pascoli's 'pallidi morti' ('pallid dead') reveals an orphic background and an atavistic framework for the entire modern lyrical ethos.

This secret world of the dead has its counterpart in the equally secret sphere of childhood perceptions. Pascoli's poetry is not merely a re-penetration of the kingdom of death but also a head-spinning regression into the arcana of childhood feelings and fears; so that all the intricacies of the pre-rational sensibility are deployed to complement the poet's visions from beyond the grave. The effects produced by these explorations often deal with the closed, sensuous delights of hearth and home, as typified by the following description of the drowsing household in 'Gelsomino notturno':

Da un pezzo si tacquero i gridi:
là sola una casa bisbiglia.
        Sotto l'ali dormono i nidi,
        come gli occhi sotto le ciglia.

For a while all cries have been silenced: there alone a house whispers. Nests slumber, under wings, like eyes under lids.

It should be noted how personification and metonymy are the chief artifices operative in this passage. For together with the analogy and the objective correlative they prove to be the most prominent lyrical devices of hermetic poetry.

Broadly speaking, therefore, these two areas of insight characterize Pascoli's originality and form the two poles of his imagination. Yet, although his desire to put the deeper feelings of life and childhood perceptions into lyrical perspective was orphic in intention, his failure to fuse together the contradictions latent in the decadent school's aesthetics frequently resulted in an inability to transfigure. So the main feeling which we experience when reading his poetry is a tremendous sense of instinctive insight and spatial depth in which the links between the microcosm and the macrocosm are explored with all the hallucinatory *visività* that the poet is capable of mustering; yet at the same time this mode of expressiveness frequently fails to create an 'espace intime' of the type mentioned by Bachelard and consequently does not convey to the reader a coherent state of *veggenza*. It tends instead to linger on the periphery of insight in spite of the ingenuity of single images and analogies, since it lacks an overall transfigurative potential. Again the point may be illustrated by a specific text, 'L'imbrunire':

> Case sparse: Sirio, Algol, Arturo!
> Una stella od un gruppo di stelle
> per ogni uomo o per ogni tribú.
>
> Quelle case sono ognuna un mondo
> con la fiamma dentro, che traspare;
> e c'è dentro un tumulto giocondo
> che non s'ode a due passi di là.
>
> E tra i mondi, come un grigio velo,
> erra il fumo d'ogni focolare.
> La Via Lattea s'esala nel cielo
> per la tremola serenità.

Scattered houses: Sirius, Algol, Arcturus! A star or a group of stars for every man and every tribe. Those houses are each a world with a flame inside it, which shines out; and within there is a a joyful commotion which is unheard a few paces away. And amid the worlds, like a grey veil, the smoke of the hearth wanders. The Milky Way breathes in the sky through the tremulous serenity.

Here the analogies are cleverly arranged to give the maximum lyrical effect, especially those concerned with the linking of the houses of the living with the celestial abodes of Sirius, Algol and Arcturus or the smoke from their chimneys with the Milky Way. But in the last resort the passage from the microcosm to the macrocosm hardly provides any significant interpretation of those deeper mysteries of life at which the poet is constantly hinting. Indeed, the constant weakness of Pascoli's art is that he often stretches our desire to understand the inwardness of his lyrical vision to breaking-point, then leaves us stranded on a spatial image which – for all its transfigurative promise – does not stand up to reflective analysis.

D'Annunzio's contribution to the modern lyrical ethos, by contrast, is perhaps more narcissistic than orphic in intention, even though he also shows almost an unbounded faith in the powers of song. As previously suggested, the labyrinthine complexity of his sensations and rhetoric has had a somewhat fragmentary impact on the sensibilities of his successors, despite the fact that his techniques certainly helped to foster the attitudes which later become the basis of modern artistic representation. In this respect his *Poema paradisiaco* is a key text since it contains a suggestive decadent background while at the same time providing early examples of image-suspension. Its results are, however, to be interpreted mainly in an ancient, not a modern, orphic sense, especially in the crucial sections of *Hortus conclusus* and *Hortus larvarum*, where the dominant figures are certain god-like, statuesque creatures emergent from some distant decadent paradise:

. . . e piú bianche nel silenzio intente
le statue guardavan la profonda
pace e sognavano indicibilmente.

. . . and whiter in the silence the statues gazed intently over the deep peace and dreamed ineffably.

Significantly, too, these figures are static, not dynamic emblems, and so they are far from being the active symbols used by modern poets as stepping-stones to higher states of perception. Nevertheless they still depict powerful orphic images of half-light, fountains, shadows, flowers and stars, all of which are bathed in an obsessive whiteness reminding us of the skeletal evocations characteristic of the lyrical inscapes of the majority of contemporary poets.

On the other hand, when D'Annunzio's inspiration moves towards the doctrine of 'superuomismo', we find that the process of assimilation of decadent culture to modern tastes passed to more sensitive hands. For, quite apart from the major poets practising at the time, a number of minor ones also contributed to the grafting of European modes on to the Italian sensibility, and among these were Gnoli, Graf, and above all Thovez.[11] Their contribution was, perhaps, twofold: the creation of a subtle irony which ultimately undermined the romantic order, and the final stabilization of those tentative crepuscular atmospheres which began to emerge in the tonalities of the *Scapigliatura*. Their relative success was no doubt attributable to their greater authenticity as artists than their rather iconoclastic predecessors. They therefore produce a more unified tone and manage to temper their imagery in the quicksilver of sincere experience instead of in mere literary recollections. Together their efforts gave something of a new impetus to the tradition, and this fresh approach has subsequently been endowed with a wider range of implication by successive generations of twentieth-century poets.[12]

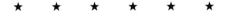

The first coherent attempt to synthesize a radically new form of lyricism in Italy from romantic and post-romantic sources was made by the crepuscular poets. The school was Roman in origin and only acquired its name somewhat belatedly from what was intended to be a derogatory article by G.A. Borgese in *La Stampa* in 1910.[13] In contrast with the flamboyance of the 'Scapigliati', the crepuscular poets were noted for their mildness and resignation, and the group counted among its chief exponents such timid and retiring figures as Corazzini, Moretti, Martini, Novaro and Chiaves. Two other more significant poets – Govoni and Gozzano – also gravitate around it, although neither of them can be regarded as specifically crepuscular in their inspiration.

Because of their lack of assertiveness, the crepuscular movement was as loosely-knit a school as the 'Scapigliati' had been before them. They only appear to have galvanized themselves into a self-conscious artistic group for a brief period around 1905-6 when they published the short-lived review *Le cronache latine.*[14] At the beginning their themes and imagery were decadent in origin, so that their aesthetics was clouded by a sense of world-weariness typical of a society which no longer had any faith in itself and was desperately seeking some way out of its moral torpor. At first the crepuscular poets' awareness of the prevailing nihilism of their age tended to paralyse their minds and drive them towards aesthetic escapism. They then refined their experiences and sensations to such a degree that they reduced life almost to a deliquescent dreamworld. Only when they discovered that the romantic dream was untenable as an authentic lyrical position in the twentieth century did the more courageous among them attempt a compromise between its sentimental blandishments and the realities of their more modern environment. Even so, their participation in human affairs amounted at most to a graceful resignation to their fate and tended to operate within the limits of an extremely narrow range of themes and experiences.

The main difficulty for them was that at the same time as they were gingerly grasping the nettle of concrete reality they still wished to linger on the very confines of sensation, just as if they were terrified to confront the wide variety of experiences in the real world. So they tried to attain some degree of sensuous repose by deliberately decreasing the number and scale of their daily contacts with life. But the process did not lead them back to a decadent attitude of complete alienation because they possessed a greater sense of artistic responsibility. It induced them instead to cast aside their original tenuous sentimentality in favour of a modern existential 'dolore' which stressed man's constant sense of dying by reflecting his contingency in the fragility and ailments of the body. From this feeling of inevitable disintegration there gradually arose an acute understanding of the limits of the human condition, a feature which is indeed present in all modern lyricism. Even so, the deep existential perceptiveness to be found in the major crepuscular poets is not shared by the minor ones. On the contrary, the latter's lack of self-awareness soon gave rise to a long critical controversy about the very relevance of crepuscular attitudes to the development of contemporary aesthetics which perhaps, even now, has not been wholly resolved.

The first point which strikes us when we read the verse of the crepuscular school is that the very few genuine poets are swamped by the mere versifiers who may for convenience be described as purveyors of its group-consciousness. This no doubt explains why the dispute among the critics about the value of the school appears to be based on the use of two different sets of criteria – the one providing a historical and the other a largely aesthetic perspective. Whenever aesthetic considerations are uppermost, critics normally class the crepusculars as *prima facie* modern poets; but, when historical and thematic considerations are predominant, they tend to emphasize their many decadent traits. The truth lies naturally between these two extremes, although it is perhaps more profitable from our present standpoint to consider the movement as consisting of 'attenuated' modern poets rather than of so many literary throwbacks to the nineteenth century.

The polemics about the school's actual status gradually crystallized in the fifties around the respective attitudes of Spagnoletti and Anceschi, the former holding the historical and the latter the aesthetic point of view.[15] In themselves, neither of these attitudes can provide a definitive solution to the problem, although the weight of evidence since they were formulated does appear to favour the view asserting the aesthetic modernity of the school. This is especially the case when we bear in mind Montale's definition of modern lyricism as 'la nuova arte del tormento critico'[16] ('the new art of critical torment'), since our standard of comparison must always remain the verse of the *Scapigliatura* with its relative lack of critical acumen and its large-scale plagiarizing of French sources. In contrast with that particular movement there can be little room for doubt that crepuscular aesthetics is a mild attempt at assimilating more modern forms of art to the Italian sensibility.

However, the actual degree of critical self-awareness shown by the crepuscular writers provides a further field for dispute, since an autocritical faculty is hardly apparent in a good deal of their poetry. We can easily detect, for instance, Gozzano's critical acumen as he selects, transforms and refines decadent materials for his own specific purposes, and the same can be said to a somewhat lesser degree of Corazzini. But this particular feature is largely lacking in the bulk of the verse written by poets like Moretti or Martini, although no one has so far denied them a place in the crepuscular movement. Probably, because he had foreseen such an objection, Anceschi defined the verse of the minor crepusculars as being that of a 'nitida e povera esemplarità'[17] ('a clear and impoverished exemplarity'). He denied, that is, any moral validity to their lyrical perspectives but offered them as paradigms of the group's dominant tonalities and lyrical tastes.

Of the two, Moretti is the writer who most clearly illustrates the point. A crucial collection in this respect is *Poesie scritte col lapis* (1910) whose compositions, as Flora once wryly observed, are 'da leggere con la gomma'[18] ('to be read with the rubber (in hand)'). In this collection we find paradigmatic themes and tonalities ranging right across the crepuscular spectrum. One technique, for instance, which the poet particularly prized is a process of scenic dissolution, and it appears to a greater or lesser degree in all crepuscular art:

> . . . nel mattino che par sera
> fra la nebbia fine fine
> vanno insieme le beghine,
> le beghine alla preghiera.[19]

> . . . in the morning which seems evening amid the fine, fine mist the beguines walk together, the beguines to their prayers.

Another is a pose of tremulous sensitivity, amounting to an evident exasperation of the senses and deriving from decadent sources:

> Il tintinno d'una folla
> di campane fa tremare
> lievemente la corolla
> d'uno smorto nenufare.[20]

> The tinkling of a host of bells makes the corolla of a pale water-lily quiver slightly.

Likewise, a further decadent procedure in the school's make-up is a certain preciousness of tone and imagery accompanied by a sad satiety of the senses:

> Oh dolcezza del mio cuore,
> de' miei sensi un poco stanchi!
> Vanno i cigni, i cigni bianchi,
> van sul pio Lago d'Amore . . . [21]

Oh, the sweetness of my heart, of my somewhat weary senses! The swans, the white swans, move on the pious Lake of Love . . .

And, needless to say, this type of lyrical perception ultimately results in a touch of crepuscular mystery, arising from a gentle, hallucinatory merging of its various tonalities:

> Tacque il sanato, ché sentí un bisogno
> strano di buio; e, al suo volere, scese
> la notte, immensa palpebra, sul mondo! [22]

The convalescent was silent, for he felt a strange need for darkness; and, at his wish, night descended, as a huge eyelid, on the world!

Yet, however characteristic of crepuscularism these elements may be, it can hardly be maintained that they strike an original note in the decadent sensibility. Their outcome, as Petronio has stressed, is one which produces 'versi scolasticamente crepuscolari in cui i temi e motivi di moda si ripetono senza una particolare accentuazione' [23] ('Schoolboyish crepuscular verses in which themes and motifs drawn from fashion are repeated without any particular emphasis'). So, if we are still to assert that a genuine form of crepuscular poetry actually exists, we must seek it elsewhere than in those lyrics reflecting the group-consciousness.

The deeper implications of Anceschi's criteria were first made explicit in Tedesco's studies on Quasimodo and the crepuscular ethos. [24] Tedesco draws the obvious conclusion that there exist two different forms of crepuscular art, a major and a minor trend, and he distinguishes them as follows: 'Nel maggiore crepuscolarismo la dolente luce crepuscolare che, a volte, fascia e ovatta come nube i sentimenti del poeta, soltanto apparentemente sembrerà non essere originata dalle cose . . . Nel minore crepuscolarismo, al contrario, la dolente luce crepuscolare è la morfina che addormenta e di cui non si può fare a meno, tanto da violentare sul serio il senso delle cose'. [25] ('In the major form of crepuscularism the anguished crepuscular light, which at times swathes and encompasses the feelings of the poet like a cloud, seems only in appearance not to originate from reality . . . In the minor form of crepuscularism, on the contrary, the anguished crepuscular light is the morphine which tranquillizes and which one cannot do without, so much so that it seriously violates one's understanding of reality.') We can broadly accept this distinction as a valid one, while adding the further gloss that the crepuscularism of the minor poets is nothing more than a reflection of the all-pervasive mood of the age. What, on the other hand, gives the major crepuscular poets their greater lyrical resilience is the coherence of their symbolism and the appropriateness of their emotional overtones to the unfolding of that symbolism.

In addition to Guido Gozzano and Corrado Govoni who, as previously stated, are not really classifiable as crepuscular writers at all, the most significant poets of the school are Corazzini and Novaro. Since the former will later be studied in an attempt to trace out the development of the greater coherence of the movement's symbolism, let us for the moment take a poem by Novaro as an illustration of the positive side of the crepuscular muse. Given, however, the predominant lyrical ethos at the time, we should bear in mind that the most that can be expected of the adherents to the school is a series of variations upon the muted lyricism of the decadent writers combined with the conceptual involution of the symbolists. Whereas the minor poets opt wholly for the first trend, the major ones attempt a synthesis of the two and introduce a touch of symbolist toughness into a basically decadent lyrical texture. This is precisely what we see in Novaro's finer poetry, for it contains a sinuous thread of lyrical grace underscored by appropriate symbolic aggregates, and these two elements separate it markedly from the stereotyped forms found in the work of a Moretti:

> Questi pini
> questi cipressi
> e le rose come sangue rosse,
> quante volte ancora,
> quando io piú non sia,
> stupita guarderà la luna,
> mute cennando guarderan le stelle,
> sul colle che solo
> restava con me
> nel silenzio notturno,
> a meditare![26]

These pines, these cypresses, and the roses as red as blood, how many times again, when I am no more, will the astonished moon gaze on them, and the silent stars, winking, watch over them, on the hill which alone remained with me to meditate in the nocturnal silence!

Here we can clearly detect the presence of an objective correlative to the poet's mood. His poetry thereby acts as a mirror to his overall purview on life as he withdraws momentarily from the crude realities of the senses to meditate detachedly on the limits of the human condition. The underlying anguish in the poem may be regarded as an awareness of human transiency, and this sense of being conscious of one's continual state of dying is one of the hallmarks of the crepuscular outlook. But what distinguishes the poem above all is the clarity and precision of its symbolism, so that the melancholy of the theme can no longer be considered decadent but rather a muted existential 'dolore' not unlike that which we find in Ungaretti.

Even so, we have to acknowledge that the crepuscular sensibility is much less robust, much less resilient, than that of the later hermetic poets. The reason for this is probably the crepuscular poets' tendency to retreat before the impact of immediate experience, which often provokes peculiar responses in their art. In particular, there is an inclination to immerse the whole of reality in a monochrome colour-scheme, or at least in a colour-scheme where the range of contrasts is exceedingly narrow, lying almost wholly between the impalpable nuances of half-light and shade. Normally such over-delicateness of tone would rank as a definite drawback, but despite the self-imposed evanescence of their landscapes, the cutting-edge of crepuscular symbolism is still far sharper than that of their decadent predecessors. So poets like Novaro, even while participating selectively in the real world, reveal a clear understanding of its diverse tensions, especially its metaphysical and emotional issues. This implies that the crepuscular movement is a further step forward in the process of assimilating European aesthetics to Italian tastes, because the poetry produced not only meditates in a fresh way on life's problems, but its melodic line is one which is unified and touched with a self-conscious sorrow which defines a wholly new region of the human heart.

When we consider Spagnoletti's and Anceschi's hypotheses in the light of the above facts, we find that the former's thesis based on historical criteria fails in the case of a poet like Novaro but not in the case of a poet like Moretti, while the converse holds for Anceschi. So we are eventually compelled to seek some overriding criteria to account for the originality of the crepuscular ethos itself. Some inkling of what such criteria could be may be obtained by comparing a genuine crepuscular tone with its earlier adumbration in one of the 'Scapigliati', and here once again Praga proves to be a useful poet for the purposes of comparison.

Superficially his poetry sometimes seems to possess pure crepuscular tonalities, as may be illustrated in the poem 'Teco errando':

> E teco errando, pallida Sofia,
> Come una chiesa, era piena di squilli
> L'anima mia;
> Come una selva era piena di trilli

L'anima sacra alla malinconia!
Errando teco, pallida Sofia.

And wandering with you, pale Sophia, like a church my soul was full of tinklings, like a wood it was full of twitterings, my soul dedicated to melancholy! Wandering with you, pale Sophia.

Nevertheless, although these lines seem at first sight to be little removed from those characteristic of a Moretti, Praga hardly ever attains the tonal compactness of even the minor crepuscular poets. Here the impropriety of words like 'squilli' and 'trilli' clearly indicates the heterogeneity of his inspiration, since they introduce a jarring sensual excitement out of keeping with the passive melancholy of the theme. Yet this type of tonal aberration is rarely encountered in the crepuscular poets proper, because their melancholy was authentic, not a pose. Moreover, in their art the firmly based aesthetic principle of detachment, of keeping reality at arm's length, also proves to be a further tonal regulator by holding their senses in check. As a result, one of the advantages the crepuscular poets gain by stepping back from their immediately sense-impressions is an ability to create harmonious tonal perspectives, and these eventually become the touchstone of their art by guaranteeing its authenticity. The fundamental advances which they make over the 'Scapigliati' are perhaps twofold: first, the reintroduction of emotional sincerity, of living within the genuine configuration of one's moods; and, second, the reassertion of a tonal unity in their lyricism, although the latter is no doubt a corollary of the former. By such means they ensured from the outset that twentieth-century poetry would regain a sense of moral responsibility as well as a more satisfying aesthetic appropriateness.

After disporting ourselves with the crepuscular lambs, a first encounter with the futurist wolf-pack in full cry and howling

Uccidiamo il chiaro di luna[27]

Let's kill the moonlight

proves to be a somewhat chastening experience. Still, such an encounter had to be faced by all the poets of the first decade of this century, since the futurists were all-embracing in their artistic relations and one feels that the only qualification needed for enforced enrolment into their ranks was any vaguely enunciated assertion that all was not well with the cultural activities of the past. Even so, we should by no means be overhasty in condemning the movement, since it is surprising how great a hold stereotyped neo-classical art still had on Italian culture at the time. In a few short years the futurists brought these time-hallowed modes of expression into complete disrepute and created the necessary literary climate and stylistic experimentation for a new culture to develop. Their principal shortcoming was that they worshipped experimentation for its own sake, so that their general aesthetic approach was largely, though not wholly, negative, whereas that of other writers outside the movement was generally positive. The significant difference between the futurists and their non-futurist counterparts at the time was thus not a question of greater revolutionary zeal but one of greater perception. For, while the latter sought to re-create the poetic tradition from within, the futurists themselves believed that it first had to be destroyed from without.

On the surface the futurist movement – like its fascist counterpart in the political field at a later date – possessed a monolithic unity, although its artistic principles were wholly heterogeneous and its inner contradictions frequently led to incoherent works of art. Moreover, it claimed to be not simply a literary movement but to encompass the whole spectrum of cultural activities, and in this respect it had clear affinities with the *Scapigliatura*. So, just as the writers of the earlier movement were largely distinguished by the radicality and yet the incoherence of their revolt against society, similarly the futurists can be singled out for the relative incoherence of their artistic revolt, although they could hardly have failed to introduce at least some of the literary innovations which were to prove invaluable later. One of their main features was the way in which they inveighed apocalyptically against traditional rhetoric, prompting one leading futurist poet, Auro d'Alba, to express the following revolutionary desire:

In una notte in un'ora in un attimo
liberarsi di tutto il passato . . . [28]

In a night, in an hour, in a moment to free oneself from the entire past . . .

Yet in the futurist manifestos intending to condemn traditional rhetoric an incredible amount of rhetorical oratory is deployed for the purpose of denouncing the rhetorical manner.

The earliest – and fundamental – futurist manifesto was published by F.T. Marinetti in 1909 and it first appeared in the French newspaper *Le Figaro* (February 20). Later the French text was reproduced in Italian in *Poesia,*[29] a periodical edited by Marinetti and two of his friends, Sem Benelli and Vitaliano Ponti. The manifesto is a politico-socio-psychologico-lyrical document written in a typically polysyllabic futurist manner. It lists in all eleven points on which futurist attitudes should differ from conventional ones, but we shall consider only the eleventh at present since it deals with the content of futurist verse. Its rolling, bombastic tone reveals its author's straining after effect:

> 'Noi canteremo le grandi folle agitate dal lavoro, dal piacere o dalla sommossa: canteremo le maree multicolori e polifoniche delle rivoluzioni nelle capitali moderne; canteremo il vibrante fervore notturno degli arsenali e dei cantieri incendiati da violente lune elettriche; le stagioni ingorde, divoratrici di serpi che fumano, le officine appese alle nuvole pei contorti fili dei loro fumi; i ponti simili a ginnasti giganti che scavalcano i fiumi balenanti al sole con un luccichío di coltelli; i piroscafi avventurosi che fiutano l'orizzonte, le locomotive dall'ampio petto, che scalpitano sulle rotaie, come enormi cavalli d'acciaio imbrigliati di tubi, e il volo scivolante degli aeroplani, la cui elica garrisce al vento come una bandiera e sembra applaudire come una folla entusiasta.' [30]
>
> ('We shall sing of the great masses racked by toil, by pleasure and revolt: we shall sing of the multi-coloured and polyphonic tides of revolution in modern capitals; we shall sing of the quivering nocturnal fever of arsenals and shipyards lit up by violent electric moons; of the greedy seasons, devourers of smoking snakes, of the workshops hanging from the clouds by the twisted threads of their smoke; of bridges like gigantic gymnasts which cross rivers gleaming in the sunlight with the glint of knives; of adventurous steam-ships which sniff the horizon, of locomotives with broad chests, which go clattering on the rails, like enormous iron steeds bridled with tubes, and the slithering flight of planes whose propellers whirr in the wind like banners and seem to applaud like an enthusiastic crowd!')

If we discount for the moment the somewhat naïve personifications which clearly lessen the impact of this passage for the serious reader, then the principal aim of futurist art – that of introducing the various aspects of industrial life into poetry – might well be considered a meritorious one. Indeed, had the activities of the members of the movement continued strictly along these lines, they could have brought into existence a new form of lyricism, as Flora was the first to acknowledge.[31] Even the grandiloquent Marinetti in his more sober moments proposed some sensible ideas, and he was particularly perceptive in noting the need for an art which 'si fonda sul completo rinnovamento della sensibilità umana avvenuto per effetto delle grandi scoperte scientifiche'[32] ('is founded on the complete renewal of the human sensibility brought about by the effects of the great scientific discoveries'). However, his own attempts at creating such an art through a torrential, though dislocated, eloquence were much too crudely made to be successful. Hence, despite his and the other futurists' full-scale assault on the bastions of romantic thought, they eventually fell into the trap of producing neo-romantic industrial atmospheres themselves, thereby depriving their revolt of all its bite and penetration.

Ironically, too, one of their main preoccupations seems to have been to revive in a more modern key the romantic technique of 'local colour', since they introduced into their verse elements of a facile industrial topography, consisting of festoons of electric cables, contorted ganglions of gas and sewer-pipes, gaunt steel factory frames, belching smoke-stacks and the roar of mammoth machines. They identify these machines with man's straining muscles and the limbs of the body, while simultaneously providing a background glare of arc-lamps or the fierce glow of furnaces. Yet in this welter of industrialization both Man and Nature are largely reduced to insignificance and the only things still retaining some semblance of the natural order are the poet's brutal personifications of machines. Indeed, the inhuman scale of modern neo-futurist architecture already appears to have been foreshadowed in designs associated with this immediate post-decadent trend; and so, just as many modern buildings prove to be the very negation of human perspectives, likewise futurist atmospheres and lyrical landscapes often seem to be the very negation of any human type of art.

Admittedly, not all the changes wrought by the futurists were lyrically negative ones. One evident gain was the rapid introduction of industrial scenery into the conservative fabric of Italian lyricism. Although the more sophisticated writers evoke it by allusion rather than by a crude and direct descriptiveness, the fact remains that between the two extremes of futurism – its raw sensationalism and cult of materialistic description – many interesting forms of mediation were attempted. The intention was normally to try and strike a balance between artifice and realism, though most of the experimentation was weighted towards realism, and this accounts for the innumerable poem-documents produced by the movement. Soffici's poetry will perhaps serve as a useful illustration both of the range and of the partial success of twentieth-century forms of experimentation. In an early poem 'Sul Kobilek' published in 1918 we still find many crude futurist images, yet the style is nevertheless somewhat enhanced by the introduction of elements emanating from the poet's intensely baroque imagination:

Sul fianco biondo del Kobilek
Vicino a Bavterca,
Scoppian gli schrapnel a mazzi
Sulla nostra testa.

Le lor nuvolette di fumo
Bianche, color di rosa, nere
ondeggiano nel nuovo cielo d'Italia
Come deliziose bandiere.

On the fair flank of the Kobilek, near Bavterca, the shrapnel bursts in showers over our heads. Their clouds of white and rose-coloured smoke stir darkly in Italy's new sky like delightful banners.

The short poem 'Estate' taken from *Marsia e Apollo* (1938) is, on the other hand, much more successful, since it combines a residual futurism with an infolded hermetic structure. As a consequence, the kaleidoscopic violence of the earlier poem is now constrained within a rich allusive form of descriptiveness:

Estate, disco bianco, bianca
Vampa,
Liquefazione d'oro,
Cembalo di silenzio sonoro
Sulla terra stanca.

Respiro infiammato, bollore
Di tetti, di giardini e d'orti,
Stupore di campi smorti
Abbandonati nell'immensità.

Summer, white disc, a white blaze, the liquefaction of gold, a cymbal of resounding silence on the weary earth. Flaming breath, boiling of rooftops, of gardens and orchards, the astonishment of pallid fields abandoned to its immensity.

In the above-quoted poems, in other words, we are in the presence of two stages of a self-conscious and meditative type of futurism whose results are far more impressive than the conventional rhetoric of Marinetti and his closest collaborators. It was, in fact, recognized from the very outset that the leader of the school sailed rather too near the wind of sheer materialism for comfort and he was frequently baited by the satirists. One of the epigrams levelled against him was the following, which subtly emphasizes the monolithic as well as the 'absurd' aspects of the school:

Futurismo è quella cosa
che fa capo a Marinetti,
mentre poi, se ben rifletti,
non ha capo e non ha piè.[33]

Futurism is that thing which has Marinetti at its head, and yet, if you think carefully, it has neither head nor tail.

Such criticisms give us an insight into the attitude of the man in the street to the futurist movement: it was either dismissed as a manifestation of an extravagant iconoclasm or as an attempt by charlatans to hoodwink the public.

However, before we proceed to an examination of the poetry of the futurists proper, the verse of one other writer calls for brief comment since he stands as a transitional figure between the crepuscular and futurist schools. This poet is Aldo Palazzeschi. As Getto has stressed[34], in his work the crepuscular 'bambino innocente' ('innocent child') becomes a 'bambino corrotto' ('corrupt child'), a child who attaches all sorts of ambiguous or vacuous interpretations to the earlier school's plaintive lyrical insights. Furthermore this implicit 'corruption' is accompanied by a deep-seated sense of renunciation concealed behind an intricate form of sophistry involving both the intellect and the imagination. Like the crepuscular pose before it, Palazzeschi's renunciatory attitude is based on a delicate sense of irony, which is fundamentally destructive despite the fact that it is frequently created by means of witty conceits and sudden transformations of situations. Probably it is most cleverly deployed in half-serious poems like 'Habel Nasshab', in which an otherwise meditative discourse on the mysteries of the East is first initiated and then rounded off by the following playfully deflating refrain:

> Habel Nasshab, sei bello tu,
> con quegli enormi calzoncioni blu![35]

Habel Nasshab, how bonny you are, in those enormous, baggy-blue trousers!

Unfortunately this ironic undermining of serious thought can easily degenerate into a gratuitous mannerism, although the specifically futurist trend in his work is perhaps mainly highlighted by his predilection for onomatopoeia. But at the same time his verse rarely lapses into complete linguistic incoherence, because Palazzeschi possessed a remarkable sense of artistic restraint. Even he himself, however, was all too aware of his over-reliance on ingeniously contrived technical devices, and in summing up his own character he once wrote:

> Chi sono?
> Il saltimbanco dell'anima mia.[36]

Who am I? The clown of my own soul.

His most effective lyrical antidote to his technical demon was his whimsical imaginative power, although not even he was capable of supplying his verse with a continuous lyrical resilience. When it faltered, he was compelled to rely on the pegs of narration for support, which has led some critics to regard his poetry as a half-serious and half-gratuitous prelude to his career as a novelist.[37] What his poems usually evoke in the reader's mind is a gaily-coloured void, a sparkling wasteland, whose underlying aridity in the area of feeling inclines it towards the negative side of the futurist spectrum. Oddly, such spiritual 'aridity' stands in opposition to Sbarbaro's more 'positive' tone, despite the fact that the latter appears on the surface to be the complete pessimist. This is because Sbarbaro's curious 'nominalism', as we shall see later, has a peculiar quality about it which eventually points towards a mature hermetic style. So the most satisfactory definition we can provide for Palazzeschi's early verse is that it is futurist in implication, if not in form and craftsmanship. Although he rarely sinks to the level of incoherence found in the minor futurist rhymers, in the last resort he tends to share their ethos and sows the seeds of a cult of gratuitousness which erupts openly in the futurist technique of the *parola in libertà* ('word in liberty').

If we now return to the futurist poets proper, we find that Falqui distinguishes two distinct moments in futurist literary output, both of them initiated by Marinetti himself or receiving his wholehearted support.[38] The first period runs from around 1905 to 1914 and can be described as the age of the *verso libero* ('free verse'), while the second extends from 1914 onwards and may be regarded as that of the *parola in libertà*. The free-verse period still retains some pretensions to artistic discipline, but the latter renounces all claims to lyrical patterning or logicality and in its practice of free associations releases a flood of imagery which flows endlessly on in disjointed and apparently gratuitous sequences.

A cult of free verse was an early love of the futurists for two reasons: first, because the technique was a fashionable import from France and, second, because it lent itself to that unrestrained futurist 'will-to-power' which Marinetti defines as a 'perpetuo dinamismo del pensiero, corrente ininterotta d'immagini e di suoni, e il solo mezzo per esprimere l'effimero, instabile e sinfonico universo che si fucina in noi'[39] ('perpetual dynamism of thought, an uninterrupted current of images and sounds, and the only means of expressing the ephemeral, unstable and symphonic universe which glows within us'). Frequently his own dynamic but largely uncritical imagination tends to thresh like a flail in a spiritual void and the results of his cult of the *verso libero* are disordered and unimpressive. Nevertheless, they are far more comprehensible than his attempts to demonstrate the technique of the *parola in libertà*, and convenient examples of his achievements in the *verso libero* can be drawn from *Destruction* (1904) and *La ville charnelle* (1908), both written originally in French but later translated into Italian either by Marinetti himself or by others. The style of a passage drawn from the first volume reminds us of a hysterical D'Annunzio,[40] for Marinetti's attitude to the sea is one of a baroque sexual frenzy:

> Mi tuffo a mani giunte
> e affondo, agitando le braccia
> nella mollezza diafana del tuo seno che ondeggia,
> per cercare il tuo sangue piú fresco
> nelle verdi tue viscere profonde . . .[41]

> I plunge with hands clasped and sink, waving my arms, into the diaphanous softness of your shimmering bosom, to seek out your freshest blood in the depths of your green viscera . . .

On the other hand, when he is not a prey to sexual paroxysms, the poet often tends to indulge in paeans of praise to the power of the machine, as for instance in 'Automobile da corsa', which includes the following grotesque eulogy of a racing-car:

> Veemente dio d'una razza d'acciaio,
> automobile ebrrrro di spazio,
> che scalpiti e fremi d'angoscia
> rodendo il morso con striduli denti,
> formidabile mostro giapponese,
> dagli occhi di fucina . . .

> Vehement god of a steely race, motorcar drrrunk with space, which quivers and clatters with anguish, gnawing at the bit with grinding teeth, formidable Japanese monster, with furnace-like eyes . . .

Briefly, therefore, these two passages sum up Marinetti's entire early manner. In them he exults in a cosmic sexuality and an idolatrous cult of mechanical objects, and he places them both on an equal footing as the tutelary gods of the twentieth century. Often a certain sexual inebriation is even imparted to the machine itself, either through its constant personification or its sensuous fondling. As a result, the machine gradually replaces man; but the metamorphosis from the one to the other is so mechanically contrived that this type of poetry hardly offers any form of original experience despite its many artifices. What is attained is perhaps a glorification of a new poetic absolute of speed, in which it could be argued that hallucinatory forms of simultaneous, synesthesic effects are produced by the merging of the five senses in the very rapidity of the futurists' *estetica della velocità* ('aesthetic of speed').

Marinetti's later collection *Zang tumb tumb* (1914) is likewise the model and exemplar of the art of the *paroliberista*. In this collection the poet decides to have no further dealings with cautious innovators and attempts to abolish the normal syntactic structures of language altogether. Hence neither the title of the work nor its contents offer much scope for intellectual edification and play almost wholly upon the senses. We are, in fact, presented with free associations of syllables, words and images which seem to flash like shooting stars through a gratuitous poetic firmament. Admittedly, associative writing in itself, as for instance Pound's *Cantos* demonstrate,[42] is not without its proper function in modern art. Indeed, it could be argued that the changeover from a discursive to a self-controlled associative manner is a dominant feature of modern lyrical practice distinguishing it from its romantic counterpart. But the kind of art produced by the futurists is not normally the self-conscious form of syntactic dislocation to be found in Rimbaud's *Illuminations* where disruptiveness is ultimately redeemed by a vigilant lyrical intelligence; it is instead an impressionistic (often haphazard) loosening of all intellectual and artistic restraints and the abandonment of the sensibility to the vagaries of chance. So, although the following description of a battlefield is perhaps vaguely recognizable in one of the long prose-poems appearing in *Zang tumb tumb*, a lyrical quality is hardly detectable at all in its totally asyntactic texture:

> Mezzogiorno 3/4 flauti gemiti solleone *tumbtumb* allarme Gargaresch schiantarsi crepitazione marcia Tintinnío zaini fucili zoccoli chiodi cannoni criniere ruote cassoni ebrei frittelle pani-all'olio cantilene bottegucce zaffate lustreggío . . . ecc. ecc.[43]

> Midday 3/4 flutes groans dog-days *tumbtumb* alarm Gargaresch shattering crackling march tinkling knapsacks rifles hooves nails cannon manes wheels caissons Jews fritters oil-bread sing-songs tiny shops stenches flashes . . . etc. etc.

The various stages of development in Marinetti's aesthetic of chance associations may be discovered by reading his increasingly rhetorical manifestos. His first step was to abolish the past by establishing his aesthetic of speed in the present. This new 'absolute' – possibly inspired by a nebulous understanding of Einstein's theory of relativity – was intended to fuse together all the multitudinous clashes of emotion in the modern world, and its technical results were his doctrine of a *simultaneità* of sensations and an accompanying telegraphic, asyntactic style, both of which aimed at providing a new imaginative harmony.[44] It was hoped that a multidimensional perspective on life would emerge from the new aesthetic of speed and, in the manifesto *Distruzione della sintassi* (1913), it was defined as the creation of 'coscienze molteplici e simultanee in uno stesso individuo' ('multiple and simultaneous consciences in single individuals'). Yet, in reality, the lyrical effects of such uncontrolled intersubjectivity appear to amount to little more than linguistic sleight-of-hand. To bring his illusionist tricks to fruition the poet thought it sufficient to range along the whole scale of human emotions from the extremes of eroticism to an unbridled sense of chauvinistic patriotism. By such means he hoped to create a new ethos, but what was actually produced was simply a tumultuous emotionalism, as Marinetti and his followers paraded before their astonished public every startling image or juxtaposition of images that they could conceive. What they tried to attain was an absolute psycho-sensuous ecstasy justifying modern life, the intensity of which would be so great that none of the intermediate grades of lesser emotivity would be apparent at all. Yet later, when their lyrical vision did not live up to expectations, they asserted that the conventions of language were too crude to reflect the deeper insights of the futurist sensibility and its 'simultaneità degli stati d'animo' ('simultaneity of states of mind'). They accordingly abandoned normal syntax for a process of catachresis similar to the type of linguistic dislocation first appearing in the symbolist and decadent movements. But they did not understand the scope and limitations of the technique and all it offered to them was a means of clearing the mind of its intellectual superstructures so that they could indulge in hallucinatory effects for the purpose of mesmerizing their readers. Their images thus tended to develop as a whirlwind of fleeting impressions whose sole object, as Marinetti himself admitted, was to create a form of 'immaginazione senza fili' ('imagination without links').

By so proceeding the futurist poets transported themselves into a state of verbal inebriation, which proved to be their substitute for inspiration. As long as they were immersed in the flux of matter, they felt themselves to be in an 'immanent' lyrical mood capable of producing mind-shattering displays of pyrotechnics. Yet even they eventually noticed their lack of control and tried to remedy it by offering pseudo-mathematical formulas for artistic creation:

Scomposizione		Onomatopee
	Forma + espansione	
Trasformazione		Suoni Rumori [45]
Decomposition		Onomatopoeia
	Form + expansion	
Transformation		Sounds Noises

Marinetti himself was an advocate of the above formula and released in his *poesia paroliberista* trains of kaleidoscopic images and strange analogies to justify it. These were all fused together in a frenzied tableau of absolute speed and simultaneity of impact, so that the poet moved on to vaster and vaster planes of being until finally he attained a transcendent anthropomorphic universe in which a polychromatic symphony of relationless and centrifugal images bedazzled his sensibility.

Since one cannot avoid a certain amount of rhetoric even when describing the futurist approach to art, this very fact again reinforces suspicions of its lyrical shallowness. One thing is abundantly clear: despite their cult of the 'aggettivo atmosfera' ('atmosphere adjective') or the 'aggettivo semaforico' ('semaphoric adjective') the futurists were unable to control their

The Futurist High Command (1912)
From left to right: Russolo, Carrà, Marinetti, Boccioni, Severini

imaginative fervour and extreme sensuality. Most of the other volumes of poetry produced under the aegis of the *parola in libertà* consequently tended towards the pattern established in Marinetti's *Zang tumb tumb*; while later poem-pictures such as Govoni's compositions in *Rarefazioni* (1915) were also developed to give the process greater visual impact. The gratuitousness of the whole trend nevertheless soon became apparent, so that it was not surprising that Marinetti's less revolutionary supporters finally turned away from his extreme form of imaginative dissociation. Indeed, as early as 1914 Papini was already hinting in the futurist periodical *Lacerba* that the school's latest lucubrations were a somewhat inane attempt 'di sostituire alla trasformazione lirica e razionale delle cose le cose medesime'[46] ('to substitute things themselves for the lyrical and rational transformation of things').

Notably Soffici's doctrine of an inner rhythm in art represents a withdrawal from the extremes of futurist dissociative imagery since he always stressed the ultimate supremacy of the artist's intelligence. In his view the artist's task was to 'sottrarre la realtà alle sue proprie leggi contingenti, per sottoporla a una legge nuova, che è un ritmo, un nesso armonico e non altro'[47] ('remove reality from its own contingent laws and impose on it a new law, which is a rhythm, a harmonic link and nothing else'). For this purpose he created 'chimismi lirici' ('lyrical alchemies') which produced a 'compenetrazione dei piani plastici'[48] ('interpenetration of plastic planes'); and, when speaking of Apollinaire's *Calligrammes*, he claimed that verbal alchemies tend to 'stimolare nello spirito come un'interferenza, una rete vibrante di sensazioni multiple e simultanee'[49] ('stimulate, as it were, in the spirit an interference-pattern, a vibrant network of multiple and simultaneous sensations'). Like all authentic artists, in other words, he advocated a restrained, associative use of words and images, because he considered that only by yoking the intellect and the intuition together in double harness could the poet penetrate into those areas of inarticulate truth where conceptual language alone is incapable of reaching.

Insights of this kind prove to be the positive side of futurist experimentation. Through them some of the more meditative writers of the school, but more particularly their immediate successors, succeeded in surpassing in lyrical achievement the Dadaists in France and a fair section of the Surrealist writers as well. But, even so, all three schools were essentially attempts at evolving a pre-rational vision of life based on those deep emotional forces which according to Freud lay close at hand in the subconscious mind. Hence, if we accept Mathieu's thesis that 'à toutes les époques la décadence des civilisations s'est traduite en trois phases: la sclérose, la boursouflure et finalement la dissolution des formes'[50] ('in all eras the decline of civilizations has been enacted in three phases: sclerosis, bombast, and finally the dissolution of forms'), then it seems likely that the futurists telescoped the last two phases. On the other hand, they exerted a tremendous pressure on Italian literary conventions through their sweeping away of the neo-classical sensibility, and as a result of their iconoclasm a dramatic change took place in cultural circles. The reaction they provoked soon led to the production of a highly original type of poetry which controlled and at the same time profited from futurist exuberance.

From a purely Italian standpoint we can trace the literary affiliations of the futurists back to the 'Scapigliati', and in the last analysis the two movements are complementary to each other. Just as the first sparked off the revolt against the neo-classical world-order which had persisted in Italy during the romantic period, so the second tried to complete the revolution on the technical and aesthetic levels. Yet what is disturbing about Marinetti and his group who form the mainstream of futurism is their relative incompetence in the literary, as opposed to the propagandist, field. Despite their mountainous output, only a few positive doctrines emerge from their work, and the most important of these is perhaps the concept of *simultaneità*, mentioned earlier. It even stirred Apollinaire's imagination,[51] but unfortunately the artistic methods the futurists adopted to express it were far too crude to permit its satisfactory exploitation in their own works, except in the field of painting. The result was that the task of producing further lyrical developments was left to poets either marginal or positively opposed to the movement.

A significant writer in this respect was Giuseppe Ungaretti. The essentialized syntax of his early collection, *Allegria di Naufragi* (1919), seems at first sight to have some affinity with futurist experimentation – perhaps even with *la parola in libertà* – although we should hasten to add that his schematic syntax was more a call to order than a further stylistic indulgence. In this volume he used analogies and dislocated language so skilfully that he often achieved that very simultaneity of sensations which the futurists themselves totally failed to attain. The point may be illustrated by quoting the final stanza of 'I Fiumi', a poem written in 1916. In the stanzas preceding it he had referred to the waters of certain rivers along whose banks he had grown up and with whose atavistic emotions he had been involved. Then at the end he informs us that he had combined them all in his imagination into a whorl of memories:

Questa è la mia nostalgia
che in ognuno
mi traspare

ora ch'e notte
che la mia vita mi pare
una corolla
di tenebre.

This is my nostalgia which in each one emerges for me, now that it is night, that my life seems to me to be a corolla of shadows.

No doubt the reason why the futurists failed to produce poetry of a similar suggestivity was because they became so involved in the material aspects of their sense-impressions that they lost their ability to stand at a distance from their subject-matter, despite the object-lesson in detachment offered by their contemporaries in the crepuscular movement. Normally their art possesses few cathartic qualities, a defect which they share with certain modern baroque poets like Govoni within whose lyrical orbit they can often be said to fall. In fact, both movements appear to hold the view that in order to transcend one's immediate sensations it is first necessary to immerse one's sensibility completely in the material world in all its Protean forms. Yet, while the baroque poets feed on the past, the futurists try to sweep the past away, because they consider it irrelevant to the modern condition. In its place they put forward a set of new, if undigested, ideas which despite their strangeness helped to clear the ground for a more fruitful era to begin. Their revolutionary tactics must accordingly be regarded as a healthy, if chaotic, reaction, in so far as they had the ultimate effect of breaking down the deepseated conservativism in diction and imagery which had bedevilled Italian poetry ever since the eighteenth century.

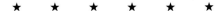

The futurist movement was followed by the development of the hermetic school of poetry, but before we can properly examine the movement's principal features we shall need to make some preliminary reference to the literary controversies surrounding it. Post-war Italian critics have divided the school into two separate parts: an early period they describe as an age of 'pure poetry'[52] and a later one which they alone regard as truly 'hermetic' and date from the thirties. The division is by its very nature disputable but, in order to put the issues squarely before the reader, we need to digress briefly and turn our attention away from the various literary groups themselves and concentrate more on the periodicals disseminating their doctrines. Indeed, it is often difficult to separate modern trends from the reviews which gave them expression, and this is particularly the case between 1900 and 1940 when literary circles were highly conscious of the changes taking place in aesthetics and were hotly debating the impact these changes were likely to have on the future of culture. Although some of the debates were sterile and highly speculative, others were intelligently concerned with the continuous process of assimilating the Italian tradition to the European one, a process, we recall, which had begun to emerge with the work of the *Scapigliatura*. The reviews to which we refer were both far-ranging and perceptive in their approach, but despite their literary interests and the importance they attached to aesthetic matters, the initial stimulus behind them was largely philosophical in origin.

The earliest periodical to examine the new trends was the *Leonardo* (1900-7). Its main function was the dissemination of pragmatist philosophy in Italy but at the same time it held an advanced literary outlook. The credit for this must be given to the two editors, Giuseppe Prezzolini and Giovanni Papini, both of whom were later to become eminent men of letters. Nevertheless, in spite of its perceptiveness the *Leonardo* was rather short-lived, and after it ceased publication in 1907 the same two editors founded a second periodical, *La Voce*. Again it was intended to be broadly cultural rather than specifically literary in scope, yet it soon began to play a significant part in the development of fresh literary theories and ideas.

Although much of its space was necessarily given over to politics and other social problems, the chief function of *La Voce* was to provide a national forum for the dissemination of advanced literary attitudes. On the whole its approach was a rational one, though at times this broad rationalism was tinged with a touch of intuitive mysticism already perceptive in the pragmatist philosophy of the *Leonardo* and in Prezzolini's personal outlook. In any case the concept of rationalism had to be regarded as a relative one at that time, given the almost demonic irrationality of the futurist movement. So, in contrast with the latter's chaotic and self-contradictory trends, the Vocians may be considered the very epitome of common sense. Their aim, as Anceschi has insisted, was to erect a barrier 'di fronte alle minacce del *vuoto* e del *non autentico*'[53] ('before threats of *emptiness* and a *lack of authenticity*').

There were two clear periods of Vocian activity, the first extending from the review's inception in 1908 until the resignation of Prezzolini as general editor in 1914, and the second running from 1914 to the discontinuance of the review in 1916. The earlier period was regarded as that of *La Voce* proper, the latter as that of *La Voce letteraria*. Likewise, from the very beginning the trends apparent in the periodical were twofold, because a muted futurist tendency perceptible in the work of Papini and Soffici coexisted with a more traditional one involving writers like Cecchi, Serra and Boine, whom we suspect were implicitly supported by Prezzolini himself. The most important function of the general editor, however, was to mediate critically between them and to fuse them together into a coherent editorial pattern.[54] The approach which he and his collaborators favoured was one which sought to break down the problems of the day into their constituent parts so that they could be tackled as a series of 'esami di coscienza'[55] ('examinations of conscience'). Each contributor was given a free hand with the subject he had chosen to treat, even though Prezzolini's own critical outlook inclined towards the idealism advocated in various ways by Croce, Bergson and others.

One of the solid advantages of *La Voce*'s breadth of culture was its success in reinserting men of letters into the life of their times. By way of its many analyses of contemporary cultural institutions, closer links were established between literary and socio-political circles;[56] and from such cross-fertilization there arose new solutions both to aesthetic and to social problems. Naturally, what was considered a relative lack of direction in the new periodical's policy was at times sharply criticized, and Gaetano Salvemini once noted that 'i gruppi della *Voce* non sono due, sono dieci, sono venti: *siamo tutte persone in margine dei gruppi*'[57] ('The groups of the *Voce* are not two, they are ten, they are twenty: *we are all people on the periphery of groups*'). Yet, as he himself suggests, this lack of direction was probably more of an asset than a disadvantage because, if the periodical had had more rigidly literary aims, it might well have lost its importance as the first great cultural landmark of twentieth-century Italy.

The breadth of vision of the first *Voce* nevertheless became more restricted with the passage of time and after Prezzolini's resignation in 1914 the balance of contributions was weighted towards purely literary matters, when the *Voce letteraria* emerged as a powerful formative force. Under the editorship of De Robertis it finally changed from a cultural review in the widest sense to one of literary ferment and achievement. The new editor's approach became more programmatic with the passage of time, and this was especially the case after he had elaborated his doctrine of *saper leggere* ('learn how to read'), a form of close textual criticism 'a piè di pagina' ('at the foot of the page') somewhat reminiscent of Serra's 'poetica del lettore'[58] ('poetics of the reader'). But, although De Robertis quickly acquired a firm grip on the direction of the periodical, it took some little time before the art-life connection which had been its mainstay under Prezzolini was completely cast aside. As Scalia has explained, its outlook was then slowly transformed from an 'activist extraversion' to a 'dogged introspection'[59] as emphasis was placed more and more on the 'dato letterario' ('literary datum'). Such an attitude was consonant with the editor's own critical approach which he defined himself in the following words: 'La critica è tutta da creare. Critica frammentaria di momenti poetici. Riduzione dell'esame a pochi tratti isolati, e quel che si dice essenzialità.'[60] ('Criticism is still wholly to be created. A fragmentary criticism of poetic flashes. Reduction of the analysis to a few isolated points, and what we call essentialities.')

The intuitive approach to literature which this implied had considerable influence outside the field of criticism itself, particularly in determining the nature of poetic structures. Indeed, some time before De Robertis had formulated the doctrine, it had already been responsible for the lively interest shown by the Vocians in the lyrical fragment or *frammento*. This type of composition derives from the French cult of the poem in prose, but the Italian version differs from the French since equal weight was placed on both prose and verse forms. On balance, however, the verse form predominates in Italy, despite the popularity accorded to Rimbaud's *Illuminations* after they had been translated by Soffici in 1911.[61] In fact, the doctrine underlying the *frammento* goes back much further, to Poe's theory that the only valid poem is a short one. Moreover, his belief that structural material was fundamentally unartistic was at that time being repropounded by Croce in his doctrine identifying poetic expression with the intuitive flash of insight. Thus the *frammento* soon found a ready acceptance in Italian culture and, with the help of Rimbaud, fostered a new type of impressionism.

Whereas the verse fragment was a notable success, the prose one, with a few honourable exceptions, was a distinct failure, probably because it did not possess sufficient lyrical compression to bring about catharsis. No doubt it provided Croce with material to develop his distinction between 'poesia' and 'non-poesia', while indirectly it also introduced the parallel distinction between *veggenza* and *visività*, again of French, and more particularly, Rimbaldian origin. In Italian criticism the first of these terms measures lyrical insight and profundity, while the second merely indicates a tendency to reflect visual superficialities, albeit sometimes in a hallucinatory manner. An apt illustration of the distinction can perhaps be drawn from French literature, from the sterile descriptive alchemies of Aloysius Bertrand and the *alchimie en profondeur* ('alchemy in depth') of Rimbaud himself.[62]

Although many Vocian poets tried their hands at writing *frammenti*, perhaps one of the most successful was Arturo Onofri. He produced them both in prose and verse, and the following is one of his finest verse fragments whose opening stanza clearly reaches a state of lyrical *veggenza*:

Melodie di fontane alzano in fresche
gole d'azzurrità sorsi d'argento,
aprendo in mattutine ali i germogli

della diafana terra; e alle voraci
brame, che sfanno il bozzolo di fuoco
da petti antichi in verginità d'oro,
son guarigioni e bianco brio di voli.[63]

Melodies of fountains raise in fresh throats of blueness draughts of silver, opening in morning wings the buds of the diaphanous earth; and for those voracious desires, which unwind the cocoon of fire from ancient breasts in a virginity of gold, they are healing balms and the white glee of flights.

The importance of the above passage is that, despite the fact that it still seems grounded in a Dannunzian style, it nevertheless manages to introduce a fresh alchemy of analogical elements. Vigolo attributes this feature to Onofri's ability to 'ridurre l'immagine a un puro aggregato associazionistico di nuova formazione' ('reduce the image to a pure associative aggregate of new formation'),[64] and it certainly emphasizes the scope and range of the new lyricism. On the other hand, a less intense practice of *visività* is apparent in his prose-poems collected in the volume *Orchestrine* (1917):

'I palazzi al menomar del sole, metallizzato laggiú dalle nubi gelate, si làminano di rame; e i cornicioni obliqui, lucendo di taglio, splendono a lancia sospesa, nella chiara freddezza dell'aria.'[65]

('The buildings in the waning of the sunlight, metallized down there by frozen clouds, are streaked with copper; and the slanting cornices, glistening in silhouette, shine like suspended lances, in the cold clarity of the air.')

Even so, these lines have a certain metallic tone about them whose hidden effects will reappear later in Montale; while their atmosphere also describes the idea of dying as a crystallization into total inanimacy which is an equally important theme in modern poetry.

However, since the prose fragment fails to concentrate the flash of lyrical insight with the same potency as its verse counterpart, it tended over the period to broaden down into the more discursive *capitolo*. The type of *prosa d'arte* which was then produced was brought to perfection by the collaborators of another important periodical, *La Ronda*, especially by one of its editors, Cardarelli. But this subsequent development is scarcely germane to the present discussion and so our conclusion must be that, although the associative techniques of the verse *frammento* were widely adopted, its prose version gradually withered away, to such an extent that it might not be too uncharitable to describe it as a literary fossil.

With the demise of the early *Voce*, on the other hand, the torch of cultural innovation, as opposed to that of literary consolidation, was passed to *Lacerba* (1913-15), a periodical founded by two ubiquitous but by now dissident Vocians, Papini and Soffici.[66] Under the title of 'Introibo' they proclaimed as their aim a state of futurist libertarianism, and, whether by accident or design, the review soon became the mouthpiece of Marinetti and his circle. This implies, of course, that its programme was revolutionary and highly extravagant; so much so that the recently converted Papini was forced, as soon as he realized the monster he had begotten, to denounce its many absurdities. But he left it too late to engineer any radical change of direction in its editorial policy and a whole range of futurist manifestos dealing with fine art, architecture, music and literature was published in its pages.

Nevertheless, despite its extravagance *Lacerba* clearly provided a national outlet for the wilder mentalities of the time and also acted as a convenient vehicle of expression for the many divergent views on aesthetics fermenting in the minds of the younger generation. Yet, paradoxically, its very irrationality soon prompted a call to order, though this was in the political rather than the literary field. One of the most significant attitudes adopted by the editors was that of making the review the champion of Italian intervention in the First World War on the side of the allies, although when we recall that Mussolini was one of its adherents and that he was even then envisaging futurism as a kind of literary wing for his burgeoning vision of fascism, such a posture may seem somewhat incongruous.[67] The inner tensions of *Lacerba* were, however, never allowed to resolve themselves because, when Italy did eventually enter the war in 1915, the periodical closed down, its editors having decided that art could with advantage be dispensed with for the duration of hostilities. Its last number contained a cry of triumph by Papini under the title of 'Abbiamo vinto' and an anti-German propagandist poem called 'Wir müssen' by Jahier. It is therefore fitting to contrast this avant-garde enthusiasm for war with the temperate attitudes of the writers contributing to *La Voce letteraria*. De Robertis, its editor, still believed that art was important enough to continue during wartime, while Serra, even more uncompromisingly, went further and asserted that war changed nothing in the literary field.

After the disappearance of *Lacerba* in 1915 (and *La Voce letteraria* itself for different reasons in 1916) a good deal of cultural reassessment still continued underground. A number of milder polemical battles did erupt, it has to be admitted, from time to time, notably in anti-futurist journals like *La Raccolta* edited by Giuseppe Raimondi; but, fundamentally, if we discount the noisy but largely irrelevant neo-futurist polemic between the movements of *Strapaese* (the traditionalists) and *Stracittà* (the innovators) in the twenties, the most important literary review to emerge at the time was *La Ronda*. It was edited by Riccardo Bacchelli and Vincenzo Cardarelli, both of whom advocated a return to modern forms of classicism.[68]

In some ways we can consider *La Ronda* and *La Voce letteraria* as complementary to each other; for, as a consequence of the doctrine of *saper leggere* put forward by the earlier review, there appeared in the later one the idea of *saper scrivere* ('know how to write'), which can aptly be described as its artistic counterpart. In its first number *La Ronda* announced its intention to return to the pure Italian literary tradition of classical restraint, although this was not intended to imply a return to neo-classical conventions. Such an attitude might seem at first sight to be a direct reaction against futurism, but the 'Rondisti' clearly understood the earlier movement's merits as well as its defects. So, in spite of the fact that he chose other modes of representation, even Bacchelli could be drawn at one stage to admit that the futurist revolt against the decadent ethos possessed 'qualcosa di autentico e di eroico'[69] ('something authentic and heroic').

On the other hand, the outlook of the 'Rondisti' was very different from that of their predecessors. Their main contention was that the modern writer needed to express his originality within the tradition: 'Eviteremo . . . di proposito di fare fracasso con delle formule che mandano odore di muffa e di giovinezza. Il nostro classicismo è metaforico a doppio sfondo. Seguitare a servirci di uno stile defunto non vorrà dire altro per noi che realizzare delle nuove eleganze, perpetuare insomma, insensibilmente, la tradizione della nostra arte. E questo stimeremo essere moderni alla maniera italiana, senza spatriarci.'[70] ('We shall purposely . . . avoid making a commotion with formulas which breathe forth the odours of fustiness and youth. Our classicism is metaphorical with a dual perspective. To continue to write in a defunct style means nothing more to us than to bring about new forms of elegance, to perpetuate, in a word, imperceptibly, the tradition of our art. And this we consider being modern in the Italian manner, without exiling ourselves.') So, precisely because of their return to traditional forms, the 'Rondisti' can be regarded as the first self-conscious assimilators of the European tradition with specifically Italian cultural aims in view. They were certainly not afraid of any possible dilution of their sensibilities by reasonable importation of themes and aesthetic principles from abroad, but they took exception to the practice of flagrant plagiarism which had, in fact, been going on in various degrees ever since the time of the 'Scapigliati'. As a result of their mature approach to art they found they could range much further than their immediate predecessors had done over other modern literatures, and we accordingly find in their works a return of Shakespeare and Goethe into the Italian literary sphere.

What marked their attitudes above all was their fascination for Leopardi. He was effectively their tutelary god and his *Zibaldone* their Bible.[71] Their admiration for him actually led them to blame Pascoli for much of the degeneration of Italian art at the turn of the century, and their attitude was summed up by Angelini who, in reply to an inquiry conducted by the editors, stated that he was 'una natura fortemente lirica, in una insufficienza artistica'[72] ('a strong lyrical nature, within an artistic insufficiency'). Lyrical synthesis was in other words more important for them than either a cult of empathy or surprise: they did not aim to startle, that is, as the futurists had done before them, but preferred to satisfy the reader by their maturity of tone. To achieve such maturity they slowly evolved a transcendent form of realism which does not so much imitate as re-create in a modern key the artistic modes and lyrical substance of the past. Moreover, since they were convinced humanists they believed it to be an irrefutable truth that stylistic perfection sprang – as Cardarelli put it – from 'una felice infrazione all'uso'[73] ('a happy break with usage'). They accordingly refused to accept any artistic doctrine which implied that the abolition of the past or any number of revolutions in technique could of themselves bring about a rejuvenation of art.

The importance of the collaborators to *La Ronda* was that they paved the way for a return to a sensible artistic climate after the extravagances of the immediate past. Yet, great as its influence was on literary affairs as a whole, its specific impact upon poetry was at best only indirect. Its fortunes were principally connected with the cult of the *capitolo*[74] which developed out of the prose *frammento*; but, since the evolution of the prose style of the period lies outside our present purview, its principal significance for us will be its cultivation of a resilient classicism: one which persists throughout contemporary poetry right up till the Second World War, despite the archness and involution of the hermetic school. To take an analogy from the past, we can regard the classicism of *La Ronda* as a sophisticated modern *trobar clar* as opposed to the *trobar clus* of the hermetic movement. Modelled as it was on traditional melodic patterns and a direct interpretation of experience, it illustrates a curious dualistic tendency of the modern style in Italy towards discursive and infolded manners of expression.

The open or discursive style first emerges with Gozzano and the crepuscular poets, later reappears with Saba and Cardarelli, and then extends to Pavese and in some senses to Penna and others. In their early work there is a touch of it also in a few hermetic writers, even though its main aim seems to be to counteract the so-called hermetic obfuscation of imagery by relying for its effects on subtle variations of traditional imagery and cadences. For instance, one poet whom we would later classify as hermetic but who introduces a leavening of discursive classicism into his style is Sereni. His first collection *Frontiera* (1941) could be regarded as an attempt to blend together the two manners, a fact which goes far to explain why his prewar verse retains a certain smoothness and fluidity reminiscent of Leopardi.

Poems like 'Terrazza' illustrate the point because they are enriched by the poet's attempt to represent mysterious and rarefied feelings by means of a narrative, and yet suspended, hermetic discourse:

Improvvisa ci coglie la sera.
                                        Piú non sai
dove il lago finisca;
un murmure soltanto
sfiora la nostra vita
sotto una pensile terrazza.

Siamo tutti sospesi
a un tacito evento questa sera
entro quel raggio di torpediniera
che ci scruta poi gira se ne va.[75]

Unexpectedly evening seizes on us. You no longer know where the lake may end; a murmur alone disturbs our lives beneath this hanging balcony. We are all suspended on a silent event tonight, in the ray of a torpedo-boat which peers at us, then turns, goes away.

On the other hand, the following lines from Pavese's 'I mari del sud' still retain orphic or hermetic overtones despite their open mode of presentation:

Camminiamo una sera sul fianco di un colle,
in silenzio. Nell'ombra del tardo crepuscolo
mio cugino è un gigante vestito di bianco,
che si muove pacato, abbronzato nel volto,
taciturno. Tacere è la nostra virtú.
Qualche nostro antenato dev'essere stato ben solo
– un grand'uomo tra idioti o un povero folle –
per insegnare ai suoi tanto silenzio.[76]

We walked one evening on the side of a hill, in silence. In the shadows of the advanced twilight my cousin was a giant dressed in white, who moved peacefully, his face sunburnt, unspeaking. To be silent was our virtue. Some ancestor of ours must have been very lonely – a great man among idiots or a poor madman – to instil into his family so much silence.

Here the orphic, ancestral perspective seeks to merge with the present to form a fresh substantial myth. So where Sereni's and Pavese's tendencies intersect we note a bell-like clarity of tone which still bears the distinct traces of the perceptual modes of the 'Rondisti'.

It thereby follows that the influence of *La Ronda* on later poetry lies specifically within the area of lyrical tone, largely because it permits delicate compromises between traditional forms and attempts at lyrical innovation. Its aesthetic sureness of touch on the one hand prevents the open discourse from degenerating into a flat *procès-verbal* type of style, while on the other it keeps the involutive trend in hermetic art within the bounds of a communicative art. Hence in both senses it can be regarded as setting the stage for the full flowering of the lyricism of the twentieth century and itself represents its first point of artistic maturity.

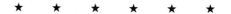

Although periodicals like *Solaria, Frontespizio* and *Primato* continue the polemics well into the thirties and forties, their work is largely one of consolidation rather than innovation, since by the time *La Ronda* ceased publication the principal art forms of the inter-war years had been fixed. So at this point we shall return to our main literary topic and discuss the development of the hermetic school. As previously indicated, the main bone of contention which has arisen about it is whether it was one or two interrelated movements. The weight of critical opinion in Italy inclines towards division, with the first generation of hermetic poets being considered an offshoot of the cult of pure poetry and the second alone regarded as representing the hermetic movement proper. Coupled with the word hermeticism in this sense, however, there is a slight suggestion of opprobrium, an implication of mannerism, which relegates the output of the thirties – when the movement is said to begin – to a lower literary level. This distinction between pure poets and hermeticists seems to imply that critics have aligned themselves either according to historical or purely literary criteria, and just as similar criteria produced a dualistic approach to the crepuscular poets, so too with the present school we find opposing groups of historically and aesthetically minded critics. Before we can ourselves reach any definitive conclusions, therefore, we shall need to examine the approaches of both sides.

The historical group tends to see the development of hermeticism in a social context, although in a rather attenuated one which we might define as a silent reaction to the flamboyance and theatricality of the fascists. They argue that in contrast with the bombast of the politicians of the period the authentic poets deliberately chose to lower their voices to a mere whisper.[77] Moreover, since they found it impossible to comment openly on the degenerate life of their times, they were forced to make an aesthetic out of necessity and deal allusively with their experiences through a form of symbolic involution. This they could do in relative safety because their intimate thoughts were concealed in a private jargon of esoteric images, for which the reader – especially, perhaps, the fascist reader – did not possess the key. Accordingly, their verse was bound to appear inherently difficult and socially irrelevant to their times and the term 'hermetic' was coined to describe it.

Even if we grant, however, that a stringent symbolic involution was practised by these poets for self-protection and not to extend the expressivity of language, a narrow historical account of the origin of the hermetic school will still continue to appear one-sided, if not grossly overstated. The most unacceptable point about the thesis is the premiss that literary movements – even under dictatorships – act as counterweights to political frustrations, especially when, as is the case here, the preoccupations of society only figure marginally in the hermetic poets' themes. If then we are to justify, even partially, this particular line of argument, we need to take a wider perspective and consider for a moment the ideological constants operating within the social scene in Italy at that period.

The polarization of local Italian politics was the result of the adoption of one of two broad choices available to European society as a whole at the turn of the century. The one was the advocacy of a liberal approach symbolized in politics by Giolitti and in the literary field by *La Voce*; the other the authoritarian solution already foreshadowed by the ambiguous socialism of Mussolini in the political arena and by *Lacerba* and Marinetti's futurist movement in the literary one. While Italian politicians gradually moved towards the latter, the men of letters tended towards the former; and, as things turned out, the former approach proved in the long run to be the more fruitful course. Indeed political dictatorship in Italy eventually showed itself to be a form of empty assertiveness concealing a deep-seated disorder: one whose explosive elements could be suppressed internally by the imposition of a high degree of regimentation, but which externally, between the major European nations, could hardly be controlled at all. On the level of language, this resulted in Italy in the creation of a bombastic fascist rhetoric which was as devoid of content as it was rich in verbiage. The horror in which it was held by the poets of the time might well have increased their introspection, but its influence was perhaps more noticeable on the younger than the older generation of hermetic poets. Internal prohibitions and fascist propaganda may then have limited the horizons of the younger writers and could explain why they tended to gravitate towards a lyrical formalism, in contrast with their elders who already possessed enough experience of wider European literary trends to protect themselves far more effectively against the encroachment of a similar type of artistic sclerosis. If so, we are oddly confronted with the curious spectacle that the initiators of the hermetic movement are normally more broadly based and successful in their poetry than its chief practitioners.

Such a paradoxical state of affairs appears to lie at the heart of the controversy which has raged since the fifties over the chronological limits of the school. Critics have at times been so disturbed by the qualitative gap separating the poetry of the two generations of hermetic poets that they have looked upon them as representing entirely separate lyrical trends. Such a dichotomy, however, within the same overall ethos gives rise to all sorts of gratuitous distinctions and even seems to imply that all second-generation hermetic poets are *ipso facto* inferior ones. This is untrue, as the case of Quasimodo will demonstrate. He was even considered to be the *caposcuola* of the movement in the thirties, yet his evident literary merits – though perhaps somewhat contended nowadays – originally threw the critics into disarray. The result was that the upholders of the distinction between the two generations were compelled to deny that he was a hermetic poet at all. They naturally sought to make their point while granting all sorts of concessions and qualifications, but if their argument is taken to its logical conclusion it simply spirits away one of the better hermetic poets and leaves behind a greater amount of detritus to prove the original contention. Now distinctions of this type are not made in conscious bad faith, but only in the interests of a spurious form of literary precision, and yet the outcome is exactly the same: the content of the word 'hermetic' thereafter becomes so whittled away that it hardly possesses any literary significance at all.

The main advocate of the dual classification of hermetic poetry in the fifties was Petrucciani, supported partially by the early Tedesco and more explicitly by Ramat.[78] By contrast, earlier critics like Giannessi and Romano tended to date the movement back to the publication of Campana's *Canti orfici* in 1914.[79] We consequently have a clear choice before us: either to accept Petrucciani's distinction between pure poetry and hermetic verse, thereby ignoring Soffici's oft-stated belief that the literary climate at the time was inimical to the cult of 'pure poetry', or alternatively we can regard the whole corpus of poetry written from Campana onwards till the outbreak of the Second World War as a single and continuous movement. Since we consider Petrucciani's outlook too narrowly based, we shall ultimately opt for the wider purview, in support of which we can paradoxically quote Flora's diatribe against hermetic poetry published in 1936. In this work Flora hardly mentioned the second generation of hermetic poets for the very good reason that at that time they had hardly begun to write; yet he levelled the same kind of criticism against the first generation – notably Ungaretti – as more recent critics have levelled against his successors. What then could be more suggestive of an identity of views and procedures? Again, Montale's attitude carries with it the same implication, for he too concluded that subtle distinctions between poets of largely the same lyrical ethos are otiose and that the wider the critical terms are to describe them the better.[80] Nevertheless, it would be unfair to let Petrucciani's case go by default, so let us examine briefly its main contentions.

His basic view is that hermetic poetry essentially proves to be 'la deformazione intellettualistica della nostra migliore poesia pura'.[81] ('the intellectualist distortion of our finest pure poetry'). To support this contention he adduces a wealth of evidence from second-generation hermetic sources. Yet, while everyone concurs that a certain corrosion of imagery reveals the hardening of the lyrical arteries of a small number of later hermetic poets, surely a corrosion of common elements implies in itself continuity of a single lyrical manner, not the existence of two? Besides, if a degeneration of poetic intensities is indeed an overall characteristic of the second wave of hermetic poets, how does one account for the clearly valid poetry of a writer like Luzi who – in sharp contrast with Quasimodo – lies completely within the movement's revised chronological limits? Here begin those endless series of concessions and tergiversations which finally deprive hermeticism of any useful meaning.

Although Quasimodo is marginal to the second generation from a chronological standpoint, he is still the key figure in the entire argument, because some of his earlier poems undoubtedly conform to Petrucciani's definition of a corrosion of forms. These poems were in fact recognized as such by De Robertis as soon as they appeared and he referred to them as 'una finzione di profondi sensi, che diventano nonsensi'[82] ('a pretence at deep meaning, which becomes nonsense'). Yet they differ only in degree – not in kind – from his successful lyrics with their deeper implications. Tedesco fully acknowledged this, although he remained a supporter of the narrower definition of hermeticism.[83] Neither he nor Petrucciani, it seems, could accept that the two generations of poets simply alternated between writing good and bad poetry. However, we could apply to the hermetic poets the same distinction which Tedesco had made himself between the authentic poets and the mere purveyors of conventions in the crepuscular movement. In which case the only point of difference between the two schools of lyricism would be that in the later hermetic movement the poets and poetasters tended to be largely successive rather than contemporaneous, unlike the position in the crepuscular movement.

Doubtless, Petrucciani would contend this conclusion of identity through continuity by pressing his point that there exists a 'discendenza involutiva poesia pura – ermetismo'[84] ('involuted descent (from) pure poetry (to) hermeticism'). But here there are really two separate issues: the suggestion that the reduction of an original manner to a technique changes the nature of the original manner, and a belief in the essential 'purity' of the first-generation hermetic poets. The first point seems to indicate an unacceptable identification of technique and inspiration, while the second prompts the question whether the frequent atavism of an Ungaretti or the Nestorianism of a Montale can in any meaningful sense be termed 'pure'. Certainly not in the sense attached to the term by the Abbé Brémond in France,[85] who advocated the reduction of poetic content to pure form and musicality. Moreover, we run into a further difficulty if we simply translate into Italian the French expression 'poésie pure', since that term itself has become derogatory in subsequent French criticism and implies the same kind of formalism as Petrucciani attaches to the Italian word 'ermetismo'. If therefore the hermetic movement is to retain any value and meaning at all in literary criticism, it will be preferable to find some less confusing terminology, and a reversion to the original meaning of the word would be the easiest solution. We shall accordingly use the term to cover the whole trajectory of development from Campana onwards, since it seems to be the only appropriate term to describe the involution of the poetry both of the twenties and the thirties.

Somewhat similar to Petrucciani's approach is the doctrine of 'la poetica della parola' ('the poetics of the word') expounded by Macrí as the aesthetic ideology of the second wave of hermetic poets, especially Quasimodo. His view is that in hermetic composition 'piú si esaspera la tensione verso una parola assoluta, una parola-essere, piú la parola sembra svuotarsi di ogni sostanziale verità umana e poetica'[86] ('the more one exacerbates tension towards the absolute word, towards the word-as-being, the more the word seems to divest itself of all poetic and human truth'). This theory seems to be Crocean in origin and to repeat in modified form Croce's doctrine that non-poetry is a technical sclerosis of positive inspiration, since all inspiration is *ipso facto* positive. Admittedly, Macrí produces many insights into Quasimodo's early poetry by using this theory as a background, but it nevertheless remains simply a means of distinguishing between poetry and non-poetry, and conventional critical methods have always yielded similar results without the necessity for their being underpinned by so elaborate a metaphysical theory. It is hardly surprising, then, that many of Petrucciani's and Macrí's insights into the art of the hermetic poets are the result of critical perceptions about the nature of first- and second-generation hermeticism.

One of Petrucciani's more important observations is the key rôle played by memory in modern verse, particularly in the writings of Ungaretti. On this point he notes: ' "Ciò che è stato è stato per sempre" annota Ungaretti . . . E perché ciò si realizzi, tutta la spiritualità e la fenomenicità dell'uomo si concentrano – dopo la morte – nella memoria, sopravvivono in lei nonostante il perire delle forme; ed è la memoria che nel suo slancio d'inarrestabile creatività, fissa in eterno le immagini della vita, dà loro una fermezza immutabile che le riscatta dal provvisorio'[87] (' "What has been has been for ever" Ungaretti observes ... And in order for that to be achieved, all the spirituality and phenomenality of man are concentrated – after death – in the memory, survive in it despite the dying of forms; and it is the memory which in its drive towards unstoppable creativity fixes for evermore images of life and gives them an unchanging stability which rescues them from the contingent'). Here we must take the expression 'dopo la morte' to mean after the passing of experience as well as after the death of the poet, and both factors enter into the hermetic poet's calculations when he is composing. The cumulative, memorial approach is as a result vital to the hermetic writer, for it helps him to build up complex imaginative patterns and resonances in a 'telescopic' fashion until eventually they seem saturated with the feelings of the past as well as the present. Imagery is, in short, to be viewed in hermetic poetry as becoming constantly enriched by its temporal dilation, through repetition in a number of contexts; and according to Montale the 'telescopic' process of gazing backwards through time for the purpose of acquiring perspective is normally to be likened to peering through a 'cannocchiale rovesciato' ('upturned telescope') in which objects and situations gain in intensity what they lose in size, precision and clarity.

Through such a process the past uses of a poet's imagery illuminate his present uses of it and vice versa, and indeed in Ungaretti we can actually detect two levels of memorial persisting, one active and therefore readily recalled and the other passive and thus only distantly perceived. The active memory or recollection deals with aesthetic processing, with the refraction of experience through the sensibility and its transfiguration; while the passive or mechanical memory is merely repetitive and not transfigurative: it lies in the realms of raw sense-data and forms part of that area of the absurd which the poet aims at transforming lyrically.

Other important modern poets like Montale or Quasimodo also use memory as a means of refining and providing a perspective for their experiences, although on the other hand some of the less original hermetic poets tend to obscure the issue of perspective by indulging in an extreme allusiveness of the type which Macrí called a 'parola-essere' and which at times seems to conceal a certain shallowness. Therefore, on balance, it seems as if the first generation of hermetic poets is less interested in involution for its own sake than the second generation and that some of the latter accept uncritically the ready-made techniques handed down to them by their predecessors and infold their imagery merely as a stylistic exercise. Nevertheless it would be unjust to accuse them of being corporately inferior because of the activities of the mannerists, even though the presence of significant numbers of mannerists does give the impression that there is an overall diminution of genuine inspiration in the second wave of writers.

One further issue needs to be examined before we pass on to a brief review of hermetic poetry in its texts. It is the problem of exegesis of individual hermetic lyrics. According to the critics of the thirties hermetic texts are multilateral in their meanings and it is a mistake to attribute to them any specific message, as opposed to an infinite range of meanings expressed in musical form. Carlo Bo, the principal hermetic critic of the time, put the point in an article entitled 'Nozione di poesia' in the periodical *Corrente* (15 June 1939), where he stated: 'La poesia non è se non realtà moltiplicata' ('poetry is simply a multiplied reality'). What he is asserting is, in fact, the twofold principle of Italian hermeticism: first, that poetry is a transfiguration, not a transcendence, of reality, which distinguishes the school from that of the French symbolists; second, that there is no specific truth in a hermetic poem, only a series of truths, each the harmonic of all the others. This view, therefore, seems to preclude a unilateral approach to interpretation altogether.

Montale, on the other hand, later makes a slightly different claim for hermeticism when he discusses his own creativeness, saying 'Io parto sempre dal vero, non so inventare nulla; ma quando mi metto a scrivere (rapidamente e con poche correzioni) il nucleo poetico ha avuto in me una lunga incubazione: lunga e oscura. *Après coup*, a cose fatte, conosco le mie intenzioni. Il dato realistico, però, è sempre presente, sempre vero.'[88] ('I always move from the truth, I do not know how to invent anything; but when I begin to write (rapidly and with few corrections) the poetic nucleus has had within me a long incubation: long and obscure. *Après coup*, when things are complete, I know my intentions. The realist datum, however, is always present, always true.') Here the implication is that there is in the first place a literal meaning of which the poet is alone conscious during the act of composition, and that later a symbolic intention emerges at a second stage. For Montale, at least, there is consequently a bilateral meaning – both literal and symbolic – in the hermetic poem; and, although this does not preclude further harmonics as overtones to the principal symbolic meaning, one dominant meaning in both senses exists in any authentic lyric. So, granted the difficulty of providing an infinite range of meanings, the exegeses given in what follows will be of the Montalian type, not of the type advocated by Bo. For, if an approximation to a key interpretation can be made, then its harmonics should also 'emerge' for the reader as overtones of that interpretation. It would, of course, be presumptuous to claim that the intentions of a poet are ever wholly uncovered in any interpretation; but one can perhaps hope to offer sufficient critical illumination for at least some of the harmonics to be awakened in the reader's mind. Certainly one risks accusations of unilaterality in such a process, but this type of unilaterality – like the individual text itself – is intended to convey through its ambiguities a broadly based, multidimensional perspective.

Since it is the intention to examine the major hermetics later, we shall for the present concentrate our attention on the minor poets of the first generation and the major and minor ones of the second. Indeed, the unoriginality of the second generation has been grossly overstated, even though there is evidently stiffness of tone and phraseology at times in poets like Solmi, De Libero, Pavolini and others whom Pozzi has labelled the hermetic Petrarchists.[89] What is perhaps a tendency towards a five-fingered exercise on the hermetic keyboard is De Libero's 'Testa' whose involution seems somewhat extreme:

Narrata e bruna all'aria che la cela
tutta negli occhi, quella testa, e un fuoco
stretto di labbra il suo segreto brucia
per la guancia che rapida matura
entro la notte bella dei capelli:
sulla fronte una luna si ricorda.

That head, wholly described and dark in the air which conceals it in the eyes, and a thin fire of lips burns its secret across the cheek which rapidly matures in the lovely night of the hair: on its brow one is reminded of a moon.

Yet, despite the fact that this poem might be regarded as tending towards what Anceschi would call a paradigmatic form, it is still far from being trite and unoriginal in expression. Accordingly, in the last analysis its only defect appears to be that it does not 'stretch' the expressivity of language quite to the same extent as lyrics of the major hermetic poets.

With the first generation of minor hermetic poets, on the other hand, the problem is not so much technical as spiritual, since their sense of alienation often leads to a persistent aridity of outlook. One of the more incisive of these minor poets is Camillo Sbarbaro who, with Gozzano, may be considered the initiator of that particular type of *poesia delle cose* in which aggregates of objects suffer a kind of *reductio ad essentiam* so as to create situations of purely mental dimensions. One of his early lyrics is a case in point, in which a hinterland of intentional aridity emerges from a flash-back technique of erstwhile participation and joyfulness:

> Talora nell'arsura della via
> un canto di cicale mi sorprende.
> E subito ecco m'empie la visione
> di campagne prostrate nella luce . . .
> E stupisco che ancora al mondo sian
> gli alberi e l'acque,
> tutte le cose buone della terra
> che bastavano un giorno a smemorarmi . . . [90]

> Sometimes in the heat of the roadway the song of the cicadas surprises me. And immediately I am filled with the vision of a countryside prostrated in sunlight . . . And I am astonished that there are still trees and water in the world, all the good things of the earth which were once sufficient to unburden my memory . . .

Here the poet's vision of a stupefying orphic reality is largely negative; and so, instead of producing a moral figuration of his attitudes to life, it casts him out of a meaningful somewhere into a meaningless nowhere. Yet in spite of this his acute state of self-awareness is highly important. It functions, as we have indicated, as a meditative hinterland behind the poet's immediate sense-impressions and provides them with a startling metaphysical perspective. Sbarbaro can therefore be regarded as the virtual creator of that speculative halo around the image which is normally responsible for keeping the hermetic lyric sharply in focus.

Not only does he achieve a heightening of lyrical perception in this way, he also provides the dominant wasteland atmosphere to be exploited later by poets like Eliot and Montale. This is no doubt why we are always aware of mixed sensations of awe and despair when we read hermetic verse as it endeavours to come to grips with raw sensory experience. These curious sensations probably derive from the recoil of the mind when faced with the starkness of its own contingency, and once again Sbarbaro catches this mood to perfection:

> Perduto ha la voce
> la sirena del mondo, e il mondo è un grande
> deserto.
> Nel deserto
> io guardo con asciutti occhi me stesso. [91]

> The siren of the world has lost her voice, and the world is a vast desert. In the desert I gaze with dry eyes at myself.

Such profound existential anguish marks a significant withdrawal from Pascoli's almost obsessive involvement in the sensuous qualities of things and events and stresses the present poet's attempt to reinterpret reality upon a detached and evaluative, rather than a sensuous and participatory, plane. Hence his type of *poesia delle cose* is the opposite of Pascoli's representational approach to art because, instead of allowing himself to become absorbed by his sense-impressions, Sbarbaro withdraws distrustfully from them and thereby provides a stark objectivity and lyrical toughness which in many ways are characteristic of the hermetic school's transcendental realism.

Similarly many other elements of hermetic aesthetics are forged in the works of the minor poets of both the first and second generations. These elements prove to be either fertile or corrosive in quality not so much as a result of the chronology of their appearance as by virtue of the degree of transfiguration which they provide for the poet. Not surprisingly, therefore, the better poets of the second generation often seem to be attempting to strike a balance between the two polarities of fertility and aridity in both a spiritual and technical sense, especially Gatto and Sinisgalli in their early work. Whereas the former is the master of almost a surrealist, stream-of-consciousness mode of writing, the latter inclines towards an aggregative and metaphysical form of hermetic symbolism.

Gatto's art creates its peculiar atmospheres by combining an impressionistic manner somewhat reminiscent of a restrained cult of the *parola in libertà* with a precise configuration of objects which he believes will mirror his mood. The point may be illustrated by the poem 'Mamma in carrozza con la luna del sud', appearing in *Nuove poesie* (1950):

Il palazzo che fugge ad altro rosa
alza la luna piena e le risate
delle carrozze splendide di buio.
E le mani pescose nei capelli,
nel sereno riverso delle donne
ora canta la notte, fresca guancia.
Una mano si posa sul mio nome
dolce a sentire ed a morir compiuto.

O consolato amore che nel soffio
del volto perdi la sembianza, uguale
al bianco seno dove parla il cuore,
gota su gota a ritrovarti, il sonno
della notte serena m'ha portato
di qua e di là, come il tuo capo inchina.
E la carrozza che allontana il mondo
ci avvicina ridenti, ed il silenzio
che tace l'aria ci rovescia vivi

nella pesca degli occhi, o mamma piena
come la notte, affaticata negra.
Il palazzo che fugge ad altro rosa
t'alza la luna nelle braccia, il frutto
della gioia terrena, è tua la vita
di tutti e la bontà che non perdona.
Il silenzio ci resta, l'incantato
trotto che da lontano veglia un lume.

The building which flees to another pink one raises the full moon and the laughter of the splendid carriages of darkness. And with its peach-like hands in its hair, on the serene backs of women, night, a fresh cheek, now sings. On my name rests a hand, sweet to hear and made replete by dying. O love consoled, which in the breath of a face loses the look, similar to a white breast, where the heart speaks; to find you again, cheek upon cheek, the sleep of a calm night has borne me here and there, inclined like your head. And the carriage which distances the world approaches us as we smile and the silence which fills the air upturns us, alive, in the peach of your eyes, o mother, replete with night, weary negress. The building which flees to another pink one raises the moon in your arms, the fruit of terrestrial joy; yours is the life embracing us all and the goodness which will not forgive. The silence remains for us, the enchanted trotting over which from afar a light keeps vigil.

At first sight the imagery in this composition may seem dispersive, resembling so much flotsam floating on a sea of emotion. Yet on a second reading we discover that its dreamlike fairy-tale effects mask a subtle interrelevance of images through which the poet's views on death and *post mortem* survival are communicated in a rich and allusive, though conceptually inarticulate, manner. Indeed, the poet's sensibility and his mother's feathery dream from beyond death gradually become so intertwined that the surrealist technique he employs seems ultimately the only appropriate one for its communication.

Whereas Gatto is like Ungaretti a master of analogical processes, Sinisgalli tends to resemble Montale since he attempts to avoid the pitfalls of incommunicability through the use of a *poesia delle cose*:

La luce ha la tua statura
E regge il gesto
Precisa, anche la pietra
Dà il petto al sole.
La tua voce questa mattina
Ci cresce nelle ossa,
In questo sangue
Che si ordina come le foglie.
E il giorno prende in terra
Misura dal tuo passo.[92]

Light has your stature and governs your gestures precisely, even the stone offers its bosom to the sun. Your voice this morning grows in our bones, in this blood which is ordered like the leaves. And day on earth takes its measure from your step.

Here, perhaps, the poet's engineering training appears to have had an effect, because the poem has precise contours but a somewhat allusive content. This allusiveness, however, is rather different from Gatto's, since it does not arise from imaginative and syntactic fragmentation; it springs instead from the very contrast between the clarity of the physical outline of the person described and the indeterminateness of the underlying symbolism. We suspect that the person concerned is a statuesque orphic deity controlling the poet's inner life; but, precisely because of the indefiniteness of her priestlike gestures, the poet's mood, far from being hindered in its communication, acquires a mysterious cloak of emotional shading which offsets the almost geometrical starkness of the deity's presentation as a mere silhouette.

Sinisgalli's emotional and aesthetic discretion accordingly teaches us a further point about hermetic techniques: it indicates that the imagery of its successful poets provides a vision which is sharp and lyrically unblurred despite the fact that it expresses inarticulate and often paradoxical feelings. It functions in other words as a focus for highlighting ineffable impressions and sensations which could hardly be rendered in conceptual language at all. So, once again, we see the infolded manners of both these poets attempting to 'stretch' the capabilities of language in true hermetic style, although we are also, at times, aware of the danger of a less successful form of mannerism lurking just around the corner and threatening to undermine their art. Indeed, even with Sinisgalli we sometimes find that his desire to set into relief just the 'disegno delle cose'[93] ('outline of things') produces a skein of meaningless 'geometrical' relations devoid of any significant emotional charge. Hence, just as Gatto's main literary danger is perhaps one of over-subjectivity, his is one of over-objectivity. At such moments each poet shows himself relatively incapable of rising above a passive, memorial attitude to art and so fails to bring about that form of recollective 'liberation' which Eliot associates with authentic re-evocations of scenes and events.[94]

Both Gatto and Sinisgalli are lay poets of the second generation, whereas Luzi tends towards a religious form of inspiration. In his verse the orphic resonances of the hermetic movement are normally overlaid with a rapt religious awe, and this quality – though certainly by no means dogmatically Christian – is detectable even in his Petrarchan-type lyrics such as *Donna in Pisa*, where the lady seems to be idealized to indicate her mediatory function:

Non sempre fosti sola con me, spesso guardavi
lunghe feste appassite nei canali

scorrere sotto i ponti inseguite dal tempo,
tra i pampini, tra i prati languidi e il lume
della sera discendere i fondali
e le spire del fiume.

E talvolta era incerto tra noi chi fosse assente:
spesso vedevi i limpidi tornei
snodarsi nelle vie sotto i soli d'inverno,
tra logge, tra fiori fumidi e il gelo
delle mura sospingere i trofei
nella luce d'averno.

Donna altrimenti – e niente piú simile alla vita –
calda d'impercettibili passioni
velata da un vapore di lagrime ideali
nel vento, sui ponti ultimi al fuoco
delle stelle apparivi dai portali,
dietro i vetri di croco.[95]

You were not always alone with me, often you gazed at long, faded processions in the canals flowing under bridges pursued by time, amid vines, languid meadows and the light of evening plumbing the depths and meanderings of the river. And sometimes it was uncertain between us who was absent: often you saw limpid tournaments unfolding in the streets beneath winter suns, amid loggias, amid smoky flowers and the ice on the walls thrusting trophies into the avernal light. A woman otherwise – and nothing more resembling life – warm with imperceptible passions, veiled by a mist of ideal tears in the wind, on the distant bridges in the fire of the stars you appeared from the doorways, behind crocus-like window-panes.

From this type of verse we can immediately deduce that Luzi is a highly literary poet and that his poetic textures contain all the elements of the century, ranging from a touch of crepuscular melancholy to a muted form of baroque hermeticism, in perfect equilibrium. Slowly, however, this somewhat self-centred form of hermetic involution moves forward to a broader pattern of human commitment with less narrowly religious overtones in the post-war period, after the manner advocated by Quasimodo and others.

Luzi's desire to broaden his spectrum while retaining his earlier orphic, atavistic and historical elements, is evident in the poetry of *Onore del vero* (1957). The approach now adopted is one which partly dissociates itself from the hermetic 'metaphysic' and replaces speculative with ethical considerations. Hence a poem like 'Come deve' reveals that the poet is in the process of reducing the 'absoluteness' of his emblematic landscapes to the level of a contingent human scene:

La vita come deve si perpetua
dirama in mille rivoli. La madre

spezza il pane tra i piccoli, alimenta
il fuoco; la giornata scorre piena
o uggiosa, arriva il forestiero, parte,
cade neve, rischiara o un acquerugiola
di fine inverno soffoca le tinte,
impregna scarpe ed abiti, fa notte.

> Life as it must perpetuates itself, branches into a thousand rivulets. The mother breaks her bread among her little ones, stokes up the fire; the day unfolds, full and gloomy, a stranger arrives, departs, snow falls, it clears up or a drizzle of late winter stifles every hue, soaks into shoes and clothes, night descends.

This is clearly a less speculative, more humane type of tableau than the one evoked in the earlier poem, although it possibly does not possess the high lyrical charge of the former composition. There thus appears to be a certain amount of narrative dilution of poetic effects in Luzi's more recent collections like *Nel magma* (1963) and *Su fondamenti invisibili* (1971), while in an intervening collection *Dal fondo delle campagne* (1965)[96] we sense once again the striking of a balance between hermetic and post-hermetic styles such as we saw in *Onore del vero*. Whenever such a balance is attained, entire scenes become concentrated transfigurations of dramatic human actions with perennial overtones, indicative of a circumspect attempt at a 'detached' participation in present-day events.

No doubt Luzi's and many other poets' post-war tendency towards the incorporation of a richer human content in their verse is a reaction against the more arid practices evolving in the later hermetic school; and this explains why only those poets who were wedded to the narrower, highly involuted, hermetic manner of the pre-war world failed to revitalize their poetry in the aftermath of the war. So even if it is true that a certain mannerism was rooted in the work of the second-generation hermetic poets, such mannerism as does exist is clearly of the same type as that which first emerged for a more functional purpose in the works of the first generation. It suggests, moreover, that we might find a general law which covers the output of both. It is that those hermetic poets who tend to be concrete and discursive in their art suffer at moments of lesser inspiration from a complete obfuscation of their imagery and this opacity appears to conceal a void of thought and feeling; while those who are syntactically more daring and lyrically dissociative in their approach border at similar moments on a neo-futurist display of *immagini in libertà* ('images-in-liberty'). Yet such a conclusion clearly supports the thesis of the unity of the two generations in a single school, and if any valid distinctions are to be made at all within the hermetic ethos, these should be distinctions of aesthetic intensities and not chronological ones. For the hallmark of the genuine artist in both generations is an ability to extend the expressivity of language and to convey new modes of feeling which in the course of time will actually provoke their conceptual clarification; while that of the poetaster is a constant repetition of the artifices and tonal paradigms of pre-existing hermetic conventions.

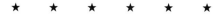

Since the hermetic trend remained the dominant lyrical movement until the end of the Second World War, at this point we shall conclude the main part of the present survey. But because some of the major poets with whom we shall later be concerned have also been influenced by post-war trends, it will be necessary to touch briefly on a number of later developments. What was perfectly clear in the immediate aftermath of the war was the fact that poetry was about to undergo yet another of its periodic transitional phases, despite the apparent continuity provided by the still active hermetic writers. For a time the hermetic poets even continued to acquire disciples and one of the most significant was Accrocca who soon proved himself capable of blending together an Ungarettian type of lyrical substance with a Montalian taste for melodic complexity. Atavism and a cult of internal rhymes are thus highlighted in poems like 'Anniversario' in *Ritorno a Portonaccio* (1959):

Allora una parola
m'avanza e mi consola
e mi rallegra, amica,
se dell'antica voce si ridesta
la solitaria festa che non nuoce
all'armonia che mesta
circonfuse la lesta
fanciullezza che ha mutato via.

Then a word helps me on, and consoles and cheers me, friend, if the lonely triumph of the antique voice is reawakened, one which does not harm the sad harmony that surrounded my alert childhood which has changed course.

Another of the more sensitive of these neo-hermetics was Cattafi who once wrote that poetry is not a formal but an intimately human affair: 'Quella del poeta è secondo me una pura e semplice condizione umana, la poesia appartiene alla nostra piú intima biologia, condiziona e sviluppa il nostro destino, è un modo come un altro di essere uomini.'[97] ('Being a poet is for me a pure and simple human condition, for poetry belongs to our intimate biology, it conditions and develops our destinies, it is one way among others of being a man.') This outlook no doubt accounts for his subtle combination of hermetic delicacy and more robust, outward-looking feelings in early poems like 'L'Agave' in *Nel centro della mano*

(1951). Equally worthy of notice is the post-war generation of poetesses who seem to have followed in the footsteps of their predecessors in the earlier part of the century. Ada Merini, for instance, reminds us of the spontaneity and emotionalism of a Sibilla Aleramo, while Margherita Guidacci suggests the kind of inspiration associated with the more meditative and hermetically inclined Antonia Pozzi. The strength of Merini lies in her psychological approach to the secrets and the ambivalence of the female heart, whereas Guidacci tends in *La sabbia e l'angelo* (1946) to offer us a wasteland, where a tenuous hope offsets the wilderness of the emotions:

> Ora il nostro amore si spanderà nella vigna e nel grano,
> Il nostro veleno nei cactus e negli spini crudeli.

Now our love will spread among the vineyards and the grain, our poison in the cacti and cruel thorns.

Probably, however, the most significant of these neo-hermeticist, post-war poets is Andrea Zanzotto. He appears to take the idea of involution to extremes, reducing the object to the word and the idea of eidetic essence to opacity. The result is that with him non-structure becomes the only structure worth pursuing, the random the only pattern or norm. His work is immensely complicated and combines a form of exasperated traditionalism (in which the intertext is turned into something approaching an extra-text) with a type of centrifugal experimentation reminding us of the futurists. A further tension is also apparent in his use of classical language and classical forms of expression for a destructive purpose, and this whole funambulatory exercise aims, as he tells us himself in 'Fuisse' from *Vocativo* (1957), at teaching him as a 'non-uomo' ('non-man')

> la vicenda non umana
> del mio fuisse umano.

the inhuman vicissitudes of my human "to-have-been".

At first sight the whole of his post-war work may seem gratuitous, but it is based on the serious idea of transcending hermeticism from within the very tenets of the school itself. From a literary point of view his logic of continuity is therefore absolute, but it involves a penetration into a sphere of the absurd which the layman finds puzzling, if not unacceptable.

For a long time it seemed – and indeed still seems to many – that the most valid post-war developments do not lie with these transitional or ultra-hermetic poets but with the many schools of experimentalists and neo-experimentalists who, unlike the latter, have really attempted a typical avant-garde disruption of lyrical forms. The original stimulus was provided by a few disillusioned and far-sighted hermetic poets led at first by Quasimodo. He and other poets of a similar cast of mind gradually directed their verse away from pre-war hermetic involution towards a more humane assessment of life and to the reconstruction of the moral values of humanity after the wartime upheavals. The break was not initially a complete one and Quasimodo himself evolved a hermetico-humanist compromise which we shall examine in greater detail later. At present it will suffice to illustrate with a single example the unfolding of the previous infolded hermetic imagery of one of the most involuted of the pre-war hermeticists, Sinisgalli. The poem is entitled 'Pianto antico' appearing in *Cineraccio* (1961); and, while it provides no startling innovations in technique, its temper is clearly open and non-hermetic, in complete contrast with the poem quoted earlier from the same author:

I vecchi hanno il pianto facile.
In pieno meriggio
in un nascondiglio della casa vuota
scoppiano in lagrime seduti.
Li coglie di sorpresa
una disperazione infinita.
Portano alle labbra uno spicchio
secco di pera, la polpa
di un fico cotto sulle tegole.
Anche un sorso d'acqua
può spegnere una crisi
e la visita di una lumachina.

The old are easily moved to tears. At high noon in a hiding-place in the empty house they break into tears as they sit down. An infinite despair seizes them. They put to their lips a dry segment of pear, the pulp of a fig cooked on tiles. Even a sip of water can extinguish a crisis and the visit of a snail.

Despite a lingering touch of mystery and hermetic perspective, these lines reveal a deeper and far more open commitment to life. Yet at the same time the changeover from the pre-war to the post-war Sinisgalli was never a slack, sentimental process. For, in effect, the poet's feelings still spring from the inner exigencies of his art and his desire to widen his emotional purview is counterbalanced by his intention to retain the self-conscious stylistic control of his hermetic period.

Whereas the post-war development of the hermetic poets evolved from within the previous tradition, the same thing, on the other hand, can hardly be said of most of the post-war groups proper. Consequently we find many instances of erstwhile hermetic poets reacting sharply to the charlatanism they believe they detect in their successors. Montale – although he was subtly influenced by certain post-war stylistic effects – voiced somewhat ironically his disapproval of the creeping cosmopolitanism of post-war poetic diction by giving a recipe for it. For him the final result is a 'cocktail multilinguistico delle parole messe nello "shaker" e poi rimescolate "prima dell'uso" '[98] ('multilingual cocktail of words put in a "shaker" and then mixed "before use" '). In justification of such remarks, perhaps, we have only to read the following passage from Sanguineti's *Laborintus* (1951-4) which appears to essentialize all the defects attributed to the then avant-garde:

tu Ruben
che sei il garantito visionario Filius Hermaphroditus in
  putrefazione
ma in questa véxeux senza risorse
  acqua senza coscienza dico
(vivo quando dormo) lasciati vivere
lascia che la vita scorra sopra di te (vivo quando dormo)
con l'epidermide intiera tocchiamo terra
che sarò nella pioggia e nel vento che la luna non entra
nell'acquario ma asciutta
occidit et vivere facit
  noi les objects à réaction poétique
riportiamo un linguaggio a un senso morale
che sarò nella lettura discreta del barometro nel dubbio
della metalessi tenace ma in questa morte impropria
dove l'amore non est aurum vulgi. . . .[99]

You Rubens who are a well vouched-for visionary, a Hermaphroditic Son in decay, but in this Hades without resources, consciousless water, I say (I live while I sleep) let yourself live, let life flow over you (I live while I sleep), with our whole epidermis we touch the earth, for I shall be in the rain and the wind which the moon does not bring in the aquarium but – dry – kills and re-animates us, we objects of jet-propelled poetry, restore a moral sense to language, for I shall be in the discreet reading of the barometer, in the doubt of the tenacious metalepsis, yet in this inappropriate death where love is not the gold of the vulgar . . .

When read carefully this poem is no doubt not so neo-futurist as it might at first appear, but it is nevertheless typical of the trend; and so with evidently similar mosaics in mind Luzi has deplored the spiritual laxity of the post-war artist, pointing out that a 'preoccupazione di nuovi contenuti e nuovi modi di comunicazione ha dato luogo a operazioni alquanto esteriori'[100] ('a preoccupation with new content and new modes of communication has given way to somewhat superficial practices').

One of the first groups to practise the new techniques of the post-war world were the 'neosperimentalisti'. Its leader was Piero Paolo Pasolini, who was at first a writer of dialect poetry but later assumed the roles of a novelist, film director and poet in Italian as well. He directed his crusade against hermetic involution and, while not rejecting its message outright, attempted to introduce into verse a greater 'impegno sociale' ('social commitment'). Admittedly, a number of his poems are poem-documents in various disguises, but despite their superficial affinities with the futurists, the 'neosperimentalisti' can hardly be equated with the 'paroliberisti' surrounding Marinetti. Not only did they have a far clearer view of the scope and limitations of their art, but their aesthetics was based on the belief that originality springs from 'un'identificazione dello sperimentare con l'inventare'[101] ('an identification of experimentation with invention').

In other words, since the neo-experimentalists had learned the lesson of history, they were much more conscious than the futurists that style is essentially a spiritual rather than a mere technical achievement. Even their revolt against the hermetic school is thus hardly denunciatory, it attempts rather to base itself on a positive effort to graft present humanistic tendencies on to pre-existing hermetic modes; and, as Pasolini himself pointed out, the entire movement 'tende semmai a essere epigono, non sovversivo, rispetto alla tradizione novecentesca'[102] ('tends, if anything, to be imitative, not subversive, of the twentieth-century tradition'). This is perhaps less true of more radical movements like 'Il Gruppo 63' or 'Il Gruppo 70' whose works appeared respectively in *Il Menabò* and *Marcatre*,[103] for a good deal of plurilingual and scientific jargon tends to come to the surface in their work. Indeed, some of the *Novissimi* as they were then called strike such crude neo-realist attitudes that at times their poetry was accused of showing complete aesthetic irresponsibility.

One reason for the relative lack of success of the poets of the late fifties, the sixties and the seventies was perhaps the nature of their subject-matter, for they ranged far afield in their search for originality, venturing into linguistics, sociology, medicine and economics. At first sight such a tactic might be regarded as a praiseworthy one, but what it normally produces is yet another series of poem-documents. Pagliarani's 'Vicende dell'oro' taken from the economic field in the late fifties is an apt example, since emotional participation on the part of the reader is hardly possible:

> Il valore della moneta non dipende tanto
> dalla misura delle riserve accumulate quanto
> dall'energia con cui questo valore è difeso
> in periodi di tensione.[104]

> The value of money does not depend so much on the quantity of reserves accumulated as on the energy with which this value is defended in periods of tension.

In this case as in other similar ones we can do no better than echo Petrucciani's comment on the difficulties inherent in contemporary cultural trends, for he observed that since the war 'le istanze etico-esistenziali tendono a prevalere – e di fatto prevalgono – su quelle letterarie'[105] ('ethico-existential postulates tend to prevail – and indeed do prevail – over literary ones').

As the post-war sensibility developed, the danger of over-cerebration and excessive theorizing at the expense of the sensuous and emotional elements of the lyric became more and more acute. As Cherchi has stressed,[106] an incredible number of new aesthetic attitudes were then struck and there was a constant preoccupation with the problem of how to write rather than with lyrical achievement itself. Not unexpectedly, poems written with some doctrinaire approach in mind normally tended to be inferior, and even now after more than thirty years of experimentation the position is still rather fluid.

Probably the most promising feature of post-war poetry has been its desire to reintegrate the individual poet into society after his clear alienation from it during the fascist era. Quasimodo once called this desire an attempt to 'rifare l'uomo'[107] ('remake man'), though his aim to create ethical transfigurations of life by transforming social tensions was partly misinterpreted by the younger generation, who seemed at times to consider that he was advocating the complete abandonment of the critical faculty and seeking to establish a new futurist era. In Cherchi's view the aim in the immediate post-war years was to create 'una poesia civile' ('a secular poetry') in which 'si deve eliminare tutto ciò che sa di decadentismo, di misticismo, di inconsapevole. Deve subentrare, come affirma De Martino, una riduzione al razionale, con cui si eliminino le tenebre e i miti, per costruire una cultura che risolva problemi terreni e civili, in luogo delle utopie che, pur sempre, sono espedienti di uomini caduti nelle superstizioni e nella magia'.[108] ('one must eliminate all that smacks of decadentism, of mysticism, of a lack of awareness. As De Martino states, a reduction to the rational level must be allowed to take place, through which shadows and myths may be eliminated, and a culture built up which will resolve civil and worldly problems, in place of the utopias which have always been the expedients of men who have yielded to superstition and magic.') In the light of experience since that time it is perhaps true to say that the best post-war verse has consistently resulted from a compromise with tradition and that the more heady of the experimentalists have produced only limited lyrical successes. Even so, the aim of art in the post-war world does not seem to have deviated much from Quasimodo's view in the immediate aftermath of the war. This was that the poetry of the new era should seek to reveal those deeper human and aesthetic truths which lie fallow in any given society until eventually they are made explicit through the insights of its mature poets.

PART TWO

CHAPTER III

Guido Gozzano and the modern tradition

Since Gozzano was basically a transitional poet his position in the evolution of the modern Italian lyric has proved to be a controversial one, and while some critics still regard him as the father of modern poetry, others deny him even a modest role in its development.[1] One particular factor which has always worked against him has been the widespread belief in literary circles that his poetry is pre-crepuscular in tone. At first sight this belief will seem surprising, because his subject-matter and somewhat decadent outlook bear a close resemblance to those of the crepuscular poets proper; but what distinguishes him from them is the quality of his anguish. The anguish of the crepuscular poets was basically positive, expressed as it was in reticent – though fully committed – imagery; while Gozzano's proves by contrast to be negatively directed, turning away from life and its immediate tensions towards a kind of soul-death. As a result, he tried to fossilize his sense-impressions by surrounding them intentionally with lyrical incrustations drawn in taste and decor wholly from the past.

His aim in cultivating these 'daguerrotypes' or 'vecchie stampe' ('old engravings') as he called them was to substitute mediate for immediate experience – to take refuge from the vagaries of the present in a cult of decadent fashion by resuscitating a closed world of historical sensations. The process gradually became his cultural profession of faith, so that in poems like 'Prologo' we see none of the contemporary crepuscular poets' understanding of man's continual state of dying nor their tragic awareness of the insubstantiality of individual experience. Instead there only subsists a desire to relive the encapsulated and largely fossilized feelings of the romantic and pre-romantic periods and to use their blandishments as a spiritual balm to distract attention from the uncertainties of the poet's own life:

> Dice il Sofista amaro . . . Il Passato è passato;
> è come un'ombra, è come se non fosse mai stato.
> Impossibile è trarlo dal sempiterno oblio;
> impossibile all'uomo, impossibile a Dio!

Il Passato è passato. Il buon Sofista mente:
basta un accordo lieve e il Passato è presente.
Basta una bianca mano sulla tastiera amica
ed ecco si ridesta tutta la grazia antica![2]

The bitter Sophist says . . . The Past is past; it is, as it were, a shadow, it is as if it had never been. It is impossible to draw it out of its everlasting oblivion; impossible for man, impossible for God! The Past is past. The good Sophist lies: a subtle chord suffices and the Past becomes present. A white hand on the friendly keyboard is enough and the entire grace of the past is reawakened!

Nevertheless, although his main intention was to absolutize the past and resurrect its closed traditions and ideology, Gozzano eventually acknowledged that such a goal was unachievable; and he then tried to reinsert himself into the present by fetishizing the past within the very texture of twentieth-century life. This practice was similar to that of the decadents and frequently he cultivated their social aims to the point of complete self-renunciation. Indeed, because he allowed his own emotions to be absorbed almost completely in the process of reproducing old-world engravings, his poetry risked becoming deprived of any vestige of personal feeling. On the other hand he did, paradoxically, pave the way in two respects for the development of a modern symbolism: negatively, by taking decadent prescriptions to their extreme consequences and blocking any further experimentation in that direction; and positively, by 'suspending' his imagery in such a way that it would later require little more than a reversal of his spiritual and artistic procedures to create a modern form of emblematic writing. In this sense he can be said to play an important part in the assimilation – as opposed to the mere imitation – of European tastes into Italian culture.

Precisely because his style is dependent upon the intense literariness of his manner, we shall need to put Gozzano's relationships with other writers into proper perspective. Like most of his contemporaries he was at first ensnared by the dominant lyrical atmospheres of Carducci, Pascoli and D'Annunzio and his youthful work shows varying degrees of their respective influences. However, the early maturation of his critical faculty quickly prompted him to detach himself from each and everyone of them by teaching him the importance of discriminating between invention within the tradition and a parrot-like reproduction of its conventions. Later this critical acuity proved a quality so adherent to his work that some critics have ventured to suggest that it was his only mark of originality. But it is difficult to see how a poet can be critically original in a lyrical vacuum no matter how refined his perceptions may be. So like all genuine poets Gozzano must be regarded in the last resort as exercising his critical acumen on his lyrical content, and the nub of the problem posed by his art lies at the point at which he selects and then transfigures his materials.

At first he carefully examined the lyrical procedures of his predecessors and drew certain significant conclusions from the results. We can therefore relive the various stages of his aesthetic development by analysing his relationships with the poets who interested him most. Of the above mentioned trilogy of major poets the one to have the greatest impact technically and the least ideologically was Carducci. At a superficial level we can immediately detect his presence in lines like the following ones taken from 'Il castello d'Agliè':

Poi che il romano Uccello lo stendardo
latino impose su l'itale terre
surgesti minaccioso baluardo.

Since the Roman Eagle planted the Latin standard on Italian ground you have stood as a threatening bulwark.

But estimating the influence of one poet on another simply by tracing back textual reminiscences is an unrewarding way of assessing their intimate relationships, and so we must attempt to discover some deeper spiritual or aesthetic affinities between them.

One connection which immediately springs to mind is the technique of image-suspension practised by both poets. Yet in spite of a superficial parallelism in their artistic procedures it soon becomes clear that Gozzano and Carducci mirror the world in widely different ways. Whereas Carducci, as Bàrberi-Squarotti rightly observes[3], has basically a historical sensibility which automatically transfers real situations on to mythological and ethical planes, Gozzano's is by contrast incipiently orphic in its approach: he does not indulge, that is, in moral idealizations of the past but prefers to recapture its moods and essential emotions in their tremulous existentiality, and he does this by immersing his imagery in the fragrance of historically defined tastes and atmospheres. Such a complete difference in outlook blocks from the outset any deep ideological communion between the two poets. Hence, precisely because their intentions remain poles apart, one is inclined to accept Antonielli's conclusion that any influence Carducci exerted over Gozzano must be confined to matters of artistic discipline and modes of representation.[4]

Pascoli's influence seems at first sight to go much deeper, since his spiritual climate is closer to Gozzano's than Carducci's, and there is also a clear connection between their imagery and lyrical topography. This similarity is sometimes very striking, because Gozzano's verse, like Pascoli's, abounds in decaying manor houses, deserted parks, overgrown gardens, guelder roses, wistaria, butterflies, moths, children at play, romping animals, and so on.[5] Critics likewise claim to have detected a certain cosmic mysticism of Pascolian origin in his early work, as for example in 'Ignorabimus':

> Certo un mistero altissimo e piú forte
> dei nostri umani sogni gemebondi
> governa il ritmo d'infiniti mondi,
> gli enimmi delle Vita e della Morte.

> Certainly, a very deep mystery and a more powerful one than our lamenting human dreams governs the rhythm of infinite worlds, the enigmas of Life and Death.

But here again the similarity can be deceptive, because the speculative note dies away completely in Gozzano's mature poetry as he directs his muse more and more towards an aesthetico-social form of mythology.

Their crucial divergence, however, lies in their differing lyrical techniques, for Pascoli's rudimentary *poesia delle cose* moves in the opposite direction from Gozzano's. From the outset Pascoli allows himself, as we have seen, to be hallucinated and then finally absorbed by the magical emotional overtones inherent in his object-symbols and images; but Gozzano never yields to this form of indulgence. Instead he becomes alienated from his lyrical substance at a later stage, through a failure to identify himself with his overall lyrical patterns once he has raised them to the level of a myth. Admittedly, in one sense the result is very much the same, for both procedures lead to an inability to conclude: a shortcoming which in turn produces a form of frustration emphasizing the inadequacy of the two poets' powers of catharsis. But, as Bonfiglioli points out, Pascoli courts defeat by continually searching for a unifying power in the expanding void of his sense-impressions[6] while Gozzano suffers his *échec* only when he tries to eternalize his immediate experiences by associating them with the fossilized myths of a half-forgotten social and literary past.

D'Annunzio's influence is perhaps the most difficult of the three to assess, because throughout the modern period his impact has been more technical and sensory than spiritual. Like all the younger generation, moreover, Gozzano's attraction to him was at first almost visceral. Yet his interest is mostly linked with D'Annunzio's lyrically negative cult of the Nietzschean superman and his hysterically refined sensuality, and such an uncritical relationship was sooner or later bound to provoke a violent reaction. So, when his own powers of discrimination had fully developed, Gozzano resisted the latter's influence ferociously, almost to the point of regarding his detachment from him as a matter of literary probity. But in spite of his conscious renunciation of his imaginative habits he still tended to use D'Annunzio's dominant attitudes as a foil to cast his own aesthetic innovations into relief. This tendency led Calcaterra to observe that during his whole lifetime he always remained 'quell'innesto singolarissimo di antidannunzianesimo sul dannunzianesimo'[7] ('that peculiar graft of anti-Dannunzian upon Dannunzian features').

The crisis in his relations with D'Annunzio appears to have been reached in 1905. Two years later, in 1907, he wrote a draft of an uncompleted poem entitled 'L'altro' in which he revealed his contempt for his erstwhile master, by saying in a prayer to God:

> . . . avresti anche potuto
>
> invece che farmi gozzano
> un po' scimunito, ma greggio,
> farmi grabieldannunziano:
> sarebbe stato ben peggio![8]

. . . you could have made me instead of gozzano, somewhat silly but genuine, grabieldannunzian: that would have been much worse!

Here even the metathesis deforming D'Annunzio's name and the omission of capitals from his own are significant. They reveal that Gozzano had at this point decided to 'sing small' and avoid all histrionic, yet gratuitous, Dannunzian gestures. But oddly the very influence he was constantly striving to eliminate from his art soon reappeared in his deeper psychological attitudes, especially in his relations with women. So much so that even Croce was finally led to observe that 'nel suo Canzoniere non sono poesie d'amore, ma solo ricordi di avventure con donne'[9] ('in his verse collections there are no poems of love, but only memories of affairs with women'). Equally strange is the fact that, while in his life his adventures were those associated with the Dannunzian superman, in art the position was reversed, so that women are usually the elect souls of his poetry and he himself becomes the exemplar of the childlike decadent or damned soul. Since, however, such a reversal of D'Annunzio's artistic modes is commonplace with the crepuscular poets, his approach is clearly an important pointer to the future.

Pancrazi presses the Dannunzian comparison even further by quoting letters written by him to the poetess Amalia Guglielminetti who had apparently become infatuated with Gozzano as early as 1907.[10] In his view the poet's normal reaction to her protestations of love and affection was the following dandified pose of Dannunzian indifference: 'Scrivetemi, Amalia, ma cose frivole, e non parlatemi, se potete, della vostra anima triste: non saprei consolarvi, non vi capirei, forse, nemmeno, in questa mia grande serenità.'[11] ('Write to me, Amalia, but about frivolous things, and do not speak to me, if you can help it, about your sad soul: I would not know how to console you, I would not even understand you, perhaps, in this great state of serenity of mine.') But perhaps this asexual serenity is already a sympton of his diseased, even pathological, sensibility; and, if so, it is the very opposite of D'Annunzio's lust for life, approximating instead to that passive, tubercular condition of exhaustion and insensitivity which reappears in his later work. As time passes, this attitude seems to become less and less of a pose and more and more of a reality, although again, by an identification of opposites, it still retains elements reminding us of D'Annunzio's somewhat supercilious attitudes to his cast-off mistresses. To illustrate the point we need only quote the following remarks, again addressed to Amalia: 'L'ambizione da qualche tempo mi artiglia in modo atroce. Non sento non vedo non godo non soffro d'altro ... Perdonami. Ragiono perché non amo; questa è la grande verità ... nessuna donna mai mi fece soffrire; non ho amato mai; con tutte non ho avuto che l'aridità del desiderio.'[12] ('Ambition for some time has racked me in an atrocious manner. I do not hear, see, enjoy, or suffer from anything else ... Forgive me. I reason because I do not love; this is the real truth ... no woman has ever made me suffer; I have never loved; with all of them I have only experienced the aridity of desire.') From such statements Pancrazi concludes that those Dannunzian features Gozzano managed to banish from his art re-emerge in his life and make it a 'controscena negativa' ('negative counterpart') of his poetry. There is indeed much to be said for his view, provided it does not imply that a similarity of psychological make-up leads to a similarity of poetic textures. For, in effect, the aesthetic differences between the two poets are no less startling than their psychological affinities, as an analysis of their respective manners will reveal.

Momigliano defines D'Annunzio's art as 'l'approfondimento magico della sensazione'[13] ('the magical deepening of sensation'). Through an extreme refinement of imagery his frenzied pursuit of sensation often becomes totally transfigured, and then his crude sensuality is miraculously replaced by a form of sensuous participation creating that diaphanous type of beauty seen in 'La pioggia nel pineto'. In such tone-poems the poet shows himself to be the very quintessence of the decadent aesthete, for whom, as Walter Pater claimed, art always approaches the condition of music. Not only does he use musical effects in such instances to divest his sense-impressions of their grosser, tactile qualities, but he also endows them with an extremely delicate and rarefied emotivity expressive of the inner rhythm of his sensibility. Gozzano ironically observes that the process amounts at times to a form of 'liquefaction';[14] and more often than not it appears to be accompanied by a touch of rhetoric and a lingering thread of unresolved sensation. On the other hand, in Gozzano's own verse, far from detecting a cult of sensation we feel that all sense-impressions are already dead or dying before the poet sets pen to paper; and this effect is accentuated by his tendency to absorb emotion into a distant myth rather than to transfigure it at an intimate or personal level. His objective dreamlands indeed frequently reach Lewis Caroll proportions, especially when he limits his art to creating 'una sua bella favola' ('a beautiful fable of his own') drawn from the past, which he subsequently tries to identify with his moods in the hope of escaping from the senseless flux of living.

The gap between D'Annunzio's full acceptance of life and Gozzano's ultimate rejection of it for suspended dreams could, therefore, hardly be wider. It leads the former to produce sheaves of exotic sensations and the latter to content himself with the construction of ironic myths from the shattered elements of the past tradition. Yet in the long run it was D'Annunzio's verse which proved the more artificial, justifying Serra's biting remark that it was 'una perfezione che suona falso'[15] ('a perfection which sounds false'). Gozzano's poetry, on the other hand, despite its narrow literary range, gradually acquired the unmistakable stamp of sincerity, reflecting in its very emotional dislocation and ambivalence the authenticity of a truly modern lyricism.

Probably, it was because of his initial difficulties in liberating himself from D'Annunzio's shallow decadentism that Gozzano first turned to contemporary French sources for inspiration. This prompted Papini's somewhat exaggerated description of him as 'il madrigalista prendingiro delle Clara d'Ellébeuse e delle Almaidi d'Estremont piemontesi'[16] ('the deflating madrigalist of the Clara d'Ellébeuses and the Almaide d'Estremonts of Piedmont'). In his introduction to his works Calcaterra lists among the French decadents read by Gozzano – probably at the suggestion of his friend Léon Coutras – such names as Verlaine, Jammes, Samain, Rodenbach, Henri de Régnier Gregh, Kahn and Mauclair. Moreover, it is equally interesting to note his attraction to certain Parnassian poets like Sully Prudhomme, Leconte de Lisle and Heredia, whose contribution to his technique of image-suspension has perhaps been underestimated. Of some significance, too, is the influence of a few French romantics such as Musset, from whom his delicate sense of irony may well have originated.[17]

Among his French sources those to whom he felt the greatest affinity were the *intimistes*, especially Jammes, who had a considerable influence on his sensibility. Martin tells us that the notebook designated as 'L'albo dell'officina' ('work-book') by Calcaterra[18] is full of transcriptions from contemporary French writers, although she adds that these often prove to be 'fragmentaires et infidèles' ('fragmentary and inaccurate'), a fact which was destined to have at least one curious consequence. At first sight it seems to make Gozzano a more derivative poet than ever, because Porcelli has conclusively shown[19] that many passages from *Le farfalle* are pure translations from Maeterlinck's *L'intelligence des fleurs, La vie des abeilles* and *Le double jardin*. But the surprising thing is that Gozzano nonchalantly applies to moths and butterflies what the French writer had previously applied to flowers and bees and he shows a complete disdain for scientific accuracy in his attempts to produce startling turns of phrase. This is indeed typical of his approach: he absorbs all the imagery of the French poets that he comes into contact with and redeploys it in his own specific manner. But the result is that all his dominant myths, even the blatantly borrowed one of Paul and Virginia, have more than a touch of originality about them. Any transcription of passages that he makes from other people's work does not, in short, amount to simple plagiarism, since their function is so changed that they are suffused with his own unmistakable lyrical outlook. We should not therefore be disturbed or dismayed at the range and extent of his French sources; for, at bottom, it is not his images or phraseology but his symbolic intentions which create his lyrical tone and these are as far removed from French lyricism as the symbolism of a Montale or a Quasimodo.

On the other hand, Gozzano may have acquired his orphic sensibility from Heredia because the French sonneteer similarly tends to use a 'detached' or 'suspended' lyrical content in order to emphasize the bouquet or flavour of an age at the expense of its temporal or factual detail. Admittedly, his historical purview is not nearly as broad as the French poet's in that he confines himself to the dramas of the romantic and pre-romantic ages and reduces them telescopically to a single composite period;[20] and yet his re-creation of historical *moeurs* is equally intense. Moreover, he does not attempt like the symbolists to crystallize abstract eternities out of his sense-data, and in this respect the absence of Mallarmé from Calcaterra's list of influences is significant. Unlike the latter, he never regarded the retention of content in verse as taboo, even though in a curious way he partially adopts in his narrative style a similar 'involution' of dramatic action, largely for the purpose of presenting us with an idealized, highly intuitive, vision of reality.

If, however, he was attracted to an infolding of imagery at all, it was in the sense of extracting mythical or orphically recurrent tableaus from historically based situations. Otherwise he was an upholder of the narrative manner of the previous Italian tradition which seemed to him to offer the only basis for the construction of his artfully planned lyrical illusions. Hence, while not foreseeing the later stylistic manifestations of the hermetic school, he was already beginning to create *ex nihilo* a mysterious inner world of the spirit, not unlike that defined by Bachelard as an 'espace intime'. What begins with him as a narration of events gradually transforms itself into an extended metaphor; so that poems like 'La signorina Felicita' or 'Paolo e Virginia' do not, despite appearances, tell a straightforward story, they tend rather to create the mood or lyrical atmosphere of an age.

This same manner of 'infolded', yet psychologically based narrative was later adopted by some, if not all, of Gozzano's successors. It could therefore account for the emotive realism of modern Italian verse, since few contemporary Italian poets have been willing to sacrifice the realistic basis of their personal responses to situations in favour of refined metaphysical dreams. Notably, the way in which the practice starts is through Gozzano's fetishization of a past age – a method which differs in degree but not in kind from the hermetic practice of evoking moods through the juxtaposing of a number of powerful analogies or objective correlatives. Nevertheless, while modern poets are able to handle their symbols with such deftness that they merge dynamically with their overall situations, Gozzano often sacrifices organic unity for an obsession with detail and a static form of neo-romantic bric-à-brac. As Montale has explained,[21] his imagery is often migratory and draws its effects not from the unfolding of a set pattern (since narrative elements can be transposed at will) but from distant emotional associations inherent in the object-symbols deployed. In order to complete his poetic effects he has to rely heavily on the sentimental overtones of the many keepsakes and mementos he has gathered so laboriously together, and at times these are the main, or even the sole, supports of his inspiration. Such a procedure is, of course, bound to lack the tremendous 'interiority' of the hermetic or symbolist schools; and so, whereas their work brings about a transfiguration of situations by dissolving them into shadowy and sensuous tonalities, his verse remains touched with a neo-romanticism in which a self-conscious irony conceals a simultaneous attraction for, and a suspicion of, the romantic world with its heady sentimentalized mythology.

The clash of temperament and intellect which this mode of writing produces is further stressed by Gozzano's awareness of the distinction to be drawn between 'altri tempi' ('other times') and 'i tempi nostri' ('our times'), normally to the detriment of the latter. He attributes the undermining of the social myths of the past by contemporary generations of poets to the destructive analytical clarity of modern society which encourages the poet to 'see through' rather than to reconstruct the sentimental and imaginative patterns of the romantics. But since these myths remained the only ones available in his own age, he found himself in the position of an unwilling agnostic in their regard, and he was forced to adapt them to his personal circumstances for lack of any more modern or substantial ones to replace them. This explains his dialectic of love-hate with the romantic ethos, and from it there springs a critical irony which prevents him from being totally absorbed by its idealistic forms of consolation.

Still, even if his residual romanticism is touched with irony, this faculty never descends with Gozzano to the level of the satire and sarcasm of a Laforgue; it is simply a self-conscious pose possessing sufficient critical penetration to undermine the vapid romantic attitudes within which it operates. It is, broadly speaking, a type of irony which momentarily lifts the veil of illusion and shows us that the poet is not the dupe of his senses or imagination, despite his almost perverse desire to anaesthetize his critical powers and abandon himself to the charms of previously established ideological patterns. Its ambivalence soon produces a dichotomy in his sensibility through which the poet, during the very act of participation in his carefully contrived romantic dreamworlds, is for ever looking over his shoulder at the aching void behind modern mythology and contrasting its aridity with the splendidly faith-provoking, if nowadays unconvincing, visions of bygone days. The process amounts to a kind of *pietas* (the word is Antonielli's) which simultaneously accepts and condemns his own ambiguous attitudes to life. It may well be that the residual, troubled sense of reality embedded in the heart of his romantic fantasies is derived from the influence of the school of *Verismo* ('Realism') dominated by Verga which was a very popular movement at the time. But whatever its origins it was destined to have a salutary effect on the Italian lyrical developments of the next sixty years, since it encouraged that subtle type of transfiguration of the real which is the hallmark of contemporary Italian poetry.

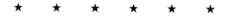

So far we have attempted to show in this examination of Gozzano's poetry the limits beyond which the main trends in modern European literature cannot be pressed into service to explain the nature of modern Italian culture. In spite of the very real pressures from beyond the Alps for social and cultural changes and the fact that the European attitudes had an important bearing on his and subsequent poets' works, nevertheless they did not exert a crucial impact on the intimate texture of his lyricism. At most they only helped to create a general mood and provide the necessary perspectives for the development of his critical awareness. The crucial lyrical influence on Gozzano, it seems, did not derive from non-Italian sources at all, but from certain minor Italian romantics like Prati and Grossi, together with a few post-*Scapigliatura* lyricists of the generation of Gnoli and Graf.

Already in Prati's complacent romanticism we find marginal tones and lyrical inflections with a definite Gozzanian flavour about them, as may be seen in the following lines:

La culla a ribaciar torna e sospira
Chi per suoi dolorosi esperimenti
Apprese l'arti, *onde si volve e gira*
Questa torbida razza de' viventi.[22]

He returned to kiss the cradle again and sighed, he who through his grievous experiences had learned the arts *whereby this turbid race of the living twists and turns.*

Yet, before these tones and inflections managed to permeate the entire fabric of Italian verse, they had to be filtered through an intricately evolving tradition, as Mariani's investigations have shown.[23] Gozzano was the ultimate inheritor of this tradition and, since the impetus behind his melodic line is largely a literary one, we find that he is an artist even before he is a poet, although certainly not the crude artist who plagiarizes instead of transforming the past like many of the adherents to the *Scapigliatura*. Accordingly, the most effective way of illustrating the process of refinement which ultimately leads to Gozzano's hypercritical approach to aesthetic and lyrical forms will be to compare an intimate domestic scene drawn from his poetry with similar ones found in the works of Prati, Gnoli and Graf.

Since he is chronologically the first among these poets, Prati imbues his verse, as we should expect, with a romantic tonality: one which in 'I conti di Viú' combines emotional and visual elements to create, through the deft use of local colour, a subdued, sentimental atmosphere:

Là di Viú nella tacita valle
Tra le frasche d'un ampio noceto,
Da un dirupo ombreggiata alle spalle,
Una casa antichissima appar.
   Or ne penzola l'embrice vieto,
Lungo i muri va l'edera attorta,
E sul rotto fronton della porta
Il ramarro si vede passar.

There in the silent valley of Viú among the boughs of a large walnut-grove, shaded at the back by a cliff, stands a very old house. Now an antiquated tile hangs from it, along the walls the twisted ivy climbs, and on the broken pediment of the door one sees the green lizards slip by.

Later his subdued romanticism is successfully transformed into a decadent tone by Gnoli and Graf, so that the stages of transformation up to Gozzano almost seem as if they possess the inevitability of a geometrical progression. In Gnoli, for instance, the incipient decadent atmosphere already perceptible in Prati is 'interiorized', stylized by way of a conscious artistic effort, and then touched with a dilated, spatial atmosphere which makes it a suitable transposition of the state of the poet's soul:

L'anima mia è una deserta
basilica: è umida e odora
di vecchio. Lo spazio colora
la luce del vespero incerta
che scende dai vetri appannati.[24]

My soul is a deserted basilica: it is damp and smells of age. Space colours the uncertain light of evening which falls from the misted-up window-panes.

With Graf, on the other hand, the same type of situation acquires a post-romantic analytical clarity which transforms a particular situation into a generic ethical state of spiritual inertia:

Nella mia cameretta ove l'amica
luna dal ciel traguarda e il sol morente,
sovra il camin pende uno specchio, antica
d'arte veneziana opra lucente . . .
Talor mi pongo a riguardar furtivo
entro il suo lume, quando il giorno muore,
e nel vedermi, e nel sentirmi vivo,
d'orror mi riempio, mi s'agghiaccia il core.
E l'empia Gorgo mi saetta addosso
l'atroce sguardo e mi trapassa drento;
vorrei fuggire e il piè mover non posso,
immobil guardo ed impietrar mi sento.[25]

In my little room where the friendly moon and the dying sun peep from the sky, there hangs over the fireplace a mirror, a gleaming work of ancient Venetian art . . . Sometimes I set out to look furtively into its light as day fades, and on seeing myself and feeling myself alive, I am filled with horror, and my heart grows icy. And the impious Gorgon casts on me her horrible glance and pierces me; I would like to flee and I cannot move a foot, motionless I gaze and feel myself turning to stone.

Finally, by a patient study of these previous poets' resources Gozzano succeeds in inventing a peculiar narrative technique, which we might well describe as a lyricism of supreme ironic intelligence:[26]

> Col suo giardino incolto, le sale vaste, i bei
> balconi secentisti guarniti di verzura,
> la villa sembra tolta da certi versi miei,
> sembra la villa-tipo, del Libro di Lettura . . .
>
> Pensa migliori giorni la villa triste, pensa
> gaie brigate sotto gli alberi centenari,
> banchetti illustri nella sala da pranzo immensa
> e danze nel salone spoglio da gli antiquari.
>
> Ma dove in altri tempi giungeva Casa Ansaldo,
> Casa Rattazzi, Casa D'Azeglio, Casa Oddone,
> s'arresta un automobile fremendo e sobbalzando,
> villosi forestieri picchiano la gorgòne.
>
> S'ode un latrato e un passo, si schiude cautamente
> la porta . . . In quel silenzio di chiostro e di caserma
> vive Totò Merúmeni con la madre inferma,
> una prozia canuta ed uno zio demente.[27]

> With its uncultivated garden, vast rooms, and fine seventeenth-century balconies garnished with greenery, the villa seems taken out of certain verses of mine, seems to be the villa-type, from the Story Book . . . The sad villa dreams of better days, thinks of joyful groups beneath the century-old trees, of illustrious banquets in the vast dining-room and of dances in the drawing-room despoiled by antique-dealers. But where in other times came the House of Ansaldo, Rattazzi, D'Azeglio, and Oddone, halts, quivering and shuddering, a motor car, shaggy foreigners knock at the Gorgon door-knocker. A bark and a footstep are heard, a door opens cautiously . . . In that silence of cloister and barrack-room lives Totò Merúmeni with his sickly mother, his grey-haired great-aunt and crazy uncle.

Such terrifying psychological lucidity and an equally terrifying ability to extend narrative and metaphorical situations to the dimension of entire moods constantly underline the ambivalence of Gozzano's poetic atmospheres. He brings about in his imagery what can only be described as a form of 'detached participation' in events, which Mariani suggests may be traced back to Betteloni's oleographic style.[28] The process is also akin to the doctrine of 'dépersonalisation' in art to be found in Mallarmé and the symbolists. But whatever its ultimate origin it is a factor of crucial importance for modern aesthetics because it allows poets to synthesize objectively instead of diffusing their emotion gratuitously and subjectively into their lyrical materials like the decadent writers.

With Gozzano the process often leads to over-concreteness and this is perhaps the greatest danger to which his poetry is subject. Whenever it occurs, his object-symbols become impermeable, massive, unresponsive phenomena, so intractable and opaque in quality that, if they are also fetishized by means of an anachronistic emotional charge, they tend to live an independent life of their own. Similarly they create the peculiar, detached lyrical continuum we have seen previously, a kind of Limbo 'tra il Tutto e il Niente'[29] ('between Everything and Nothing') in which there is neither a sensuous enjoyment of concrete forms nor a willing emotional acceptance by the poet of his own contrived situations. At such times the poet seems to abandon his verse to the faintly narrative mould in which it is cast, although even this is not always a disadvantage since his narrative technique aims at quintessentializing his feelings rather than presenting events in any logical sequence. In this way he slowly evolves a mode of representation which becomes integrated with his detached manner of perceiving and which proves to be frequently discontinuous in its unfolding. As a result acts, situations and even objects all tend to change into mere categories or classes of things in his mind. They function, that is, as abstract, cerebral elements playing a part in equally stereotyped and static events. A case in point is the following description from 'Torino', where an extremely delicate balance is struck between an abstract, categorizing tendency and a certain residual desire for historical realism:

Come una stampa antica bavarese
vedo al tramonto il cielo subalpino . . .
Da palazzo Madama al Valentino
ardono L'Alpi tra le nubi accese . . .
È questa l'ora *antica* torinese
è questa l'ora *vera* di Torino . . .

L'ora ch'io dissi del Risorgimento,
l'ora in cui penso a Massimo d'Azeglio
adolescente, a *I miei ricordi*, e sento
d'essere nato troppo tardi . . . Meglio
vivere al tempo sacro del risveglio,
che al tempo nostro mite e sonnolento!

Like an old Bavarian engraving I see the sub-alpine sky at sunset . . . From the Madama palace to the Valentino castle the Alps glow among the burning clouds . . . This is the *time-hallowed* Turinese moment, this is the real moment of Turin . . . The moment which I mentioned of the Risorgimento, the moment in which I think of Massimo d'Azeglio as a youth, of *My Memoirs*, and I feel I was born too late . . . Better to live in the hallowed time of the reawakening, than in our mild and somnolent times!

At present we need only examine the technical trend of this passage. In the first stanza it moves towards a static perspective of life, somewhat detached from that underlying historical reality which a Carducci, for instance, would eagerly have stressed. Yet simultaneously the whole poem is surrounded by a complacent irony undermining the illusion created and giving the impression that it is based upon a game of studied make-believe. The same artificial atmosphere is prolonged in the second stanza by reference to cultural reminiscences romanticizing the *Risorgimento*, the aim no doubt being to recapture the past in its totality and to reject the present – ostensibly because of its decadence but actually because of its cultural incompleteness and agonizing contingency.

The problem facing the critic is thus to establish whether a Parnassian cult of almost complete objectivity is a valid form of art. For those who regard poetry as solely the lyrical representation of feelings it evidently is not. For such critics the above-quoted tableau borders on descriptive absurdity by depriving art of its active emotional and moral commitment and by taking the Parnassian ideal to wholly unacceptable extremes. Yet what it does tend to represent authentically is the climax of Gozzano's anguish – the apotheosis of his revolt against his precarious existentiality which derives from his complete lack of any consoling mythical base. In his attempts to compensate for the imaginative poverty of his age by refurbishing the myths of the past he evolves a technique of schemátizing to the fullest extent the dimensions of his lyrical world; and this makes his efforts at rehabilitation easier, because the process of identifying himself with a restricted number of frequently repeated images is itself consolatory.[30] Furthermore, such repetitions – clearly a form of decalcomania – prove to be powerful instruments in the reduction of situations to situation-types; and, unless they are crudely deployed, they normally prefigure more modern techniques of telescoping imagery for the purpose of increasing its depth and resonance. However, once Gozzano reaches his *tabula rasa* state of complete objectivity, he changes direction and tries to find some valid escape from the condition of spiritual apathy he has so studiously fostered. Eventually the glimmering of a solution presents itself, and in poems like 'Acherontia atropos' the descriptive back-cloth begins to lose its preplanned cerebral structure, as all the protagonists and the situation itself become united in the unfolding of brief, but highly dramatic, emblematic scenes.

We can detect three main – though closely interrelated – stages in Gozzano's emblematic development of situation-types or 'daguerrotypes' as he himself sometimes calls them. They are the static drama, the extended metaphor, and the open conflict of emotions. The trend towards the static drama begins early and is already apparent in the probing, psychological episodes of *La via del rifugio* (1907). A typical example is the poem 'Le due strade'. At that time the influence of the 'veristi' on the poet was probably at its strongest, so that he seizes in his verse the elements of a decisive moment of life and presents it to us in a delicately narrative, yet orphically suspended, form. Equally, D'Annunzio's influence is still perceptible, and in his usual manner of acting as a foil to the latter's highly dramatic modes of writing Gozzano creates a 'superdonna' ('super-woman') while he himself appears as an ineffectual post-romantic dreamer.

The episode forming the substance of 'Le due strade' is a minor incident in the poet's everyday existence. When out walking with his now somewhat ageing but highly sophisticated mistress he meets a young girl, Graziella, along the road at the foot of a hill, and the latter, being a 'superdonna' of the period, is daringly riding a bicycle. She turns out to be a friend of the older woman's and they stop to talk. At once the poet lapses into a day-dream in which he sees Graziella as a figure of hope in his life, and she proves to be the first of a number of powerful, life-seeking feminine symbols appearing in his verse. He is gradually led to contrast her dynamic modernity with the decadent inertia of his companion, and his thought continues to move in this direction despite the fact that she impudently hands him her bicycle to push up the hill. As he muses upon the encounter he moves further and further away from reality into a world of sheer make-believe and fondly imagines the existence of an emotional attachment between himself and the young girl, a relationship which offers him 'la via della salute' ('the way to salvation'):

O Bimba, nelle palme tu chiudi la mia sorte;
discendere alla Morte come per calme rive,

discendere al Niente pel mio sentiere umano,
ma avere te per mano, o dolce sorridente!

O Child, in your palms you enclose my fate; oh to sink to Death as though along calm shores, to sink into Nothingness along my human path, but to have you by the hand, o sweet smiling girl!

Unfortunately, there remains the all too solid presence of his mistress at his side to remind him of his real fate; so that, after contemplating regretfully the ravages that time has wreaked upon her face, he proceeds to consider in parallel lines his far less attractive future with her:

Discenderai al Niente pel tuo sentiere umano
e non avrai per mano la dolce sorridente!

ma l'altro beveraggio avrai fino alla morte:
il tempo è già piú forte di tutto il tuo coraggio.

> You will descend to Nothingness along your human path and you shall not hold that sweet smiling girl by the hand! But the other brew you will have right up to your death: time is already stronger than all your courage.

At this point the young Amazon takes her leave and careers off down the hill without so much as a word of thanks to the poet for his services. As she disappears in the distance, the same *taedium vitae* comes flooding back as he experienced earlier before his chance encounter with her, and it is stressed at the end of the poem by the repetition of an earlier heavy, neo-classical rhythmical sequence:

> E seguitai l'amica, recando nell'ascesa
> la triste che già pesa nostra catena antica.

> And I followed my mistress, bearing up the slope that sad and already weighty ancient chain of ours.

Now the transparent symbolism of this poem hardly requires labouring, but its diffuse narrative manner is typical of Gozzano and it tends to allegorize man's frightening contingency. In this way it indicates an incipiently modern sensibility, a fact which is surprising when we consider that the lyric was written in a deliberately archaic style and possesses an equally archaic rhythm. But the cult of archaism has two highly functional purposes with him: in the first place it helps to create his orphically 'suspended' lyrical atmospheres and in the second it underlines the old-world charm – though evident falsity – of his pseudo-romantic situations. Hence, although it may seem at first that the poet is lulled into a beguiling sense of security as he allows himself to be caught up in a sentimental dream, in the last analysis he never becomes the victim of his own illusions. At moments of acute self-awareness he immediately casts doubt on his own spiritual procedures and sums up his preferred attitude to life in the eponymous lyric:

> Non agogno
> che la virtú del sogno:
> l'inconsapevolezza.

> I only desire the power of dreams: non-awareness.

Indeed, he hopes that his cult of 'non-awareness' will finally thrust him out of art into a less self-conscious way of life.

A similar desire for spiritual abnegation is evident throughout his poetry, although his critical self-consciousness rarely allows him to forget his involvement in the present. This probably explains why poems like 'Le due strade' are dramatic in structure despite their dreamlike atmospheres.

Frequently they even contain long passages of dialogue to increase the psychological tension, but here again we have to treat Gozzano's dramatic effects with caution, since in his verse there exist two very different types of dialogue. The one consists of realistic, cut-and-thrust speech emphasizing a clash of personalities, as illustrated in 'Invernale', 'Ketty', or even 'Cocotte'; while the other is simply a disguised monologue which masquerades as dialogue by being put into the mouths of two similar-minded characters. Most of these 'monologues for two voices' are, as we shall see later, sentimental in quality and propound – by cumulative means – a sheer escapist attitude to life. As such, they may be considered 'melodramatic' in direction and tend to turn the unresolved tensions of living into a weary desire for death. As the poet himself explains,

Verrà da sé la cosa
vera chiamata Morte:
che giova ansimar forte
per l'erta faticosa? [31]

The true thing called Death will come of its own accord: what use is it to go panting strongly up the tiring slope?

Often the starkness of this kind of world-weariness results in complete spiritual inertia, in a desire to take refuge in death's dream kingdom through self-conscious acts of renunciation. The suppression of dialogue in disguised monologues is thus one of the poet's subtler devices for achieving his decadent aims, and fundamentally it amounts to an extreme application to art of the decadent school's predisposition to a form of self-willed alienation.

In a sense the representational techniques which the poet adopts when he is immersed in this type of mood are pre-expressionist in nature, especially if we accept Mittner's definition of expressionism as a subversion of the decadent school's ontology, so that 'le cose ora esistono in sé, ma non esistono piú per l'uomo' [32] ('things now exist in themselves, but no longer exist for men'). By removing Pascoli's emotional aura from objects and using them as inert building-blocks, Gozzano turns the latter's highly emotive landscapes into his 'vecchie stampe'. Hence in his still-life tableaus, instead of experiencing an emotional 'dilation' of reality, we sense a deliberate contraction of it, a flight into a distant sunken dream, a typical example of which is a distilled memorial document like the opening of 'L'amica di nonna Speranza'. [33] In this poem objects are reduced to an absurd state of mere persisting, with just that touch of fossilized or fetishized emotion pervading them to justify their lyrical presence as keepsakes. Such then is the virtually neutralized base from which the positive emblems of modern verse were destined to spring:

Loreto impagliato ed il busto d'Alfieri, di Napoleone,
i fiori in cornice (le buone cose di pessimo gusto),

il caminetto un po' tetro, le scatole senza confetti,
i frutti di marmo protetti dalle campane di vetro,

un qualche raro balocco, gli scrigni fatti di valve,
gli oggetti col monito *salve, ricordo*, le noci di cocco.

Venezia ritratta a musaici, gli acquerelli un po' scialbi,
le stampe, i cofaní, gli albi dipinti d'anemoni arcaici,

. . . .

il cúcu dell'ore che canta, le sedie parate a damasco
chèrmisi . . . rinasco, rinasco del mille ottocento cinquanta!

A stuffed parrot and the busts of Alfieri, of Napoleon, flowers in a picture-frame (the good things of execrable taste), the somewhat gloomy fireplace, the boxes without sugared almonds, the marble fruit protected by domes of glass, an occasional toy, cases made of shells, objects with the warning *hail, remember*, coconuts. Venice depicted in mosaics, water-colours somewhat faded, prints, caskets, albums painted with archaic anemones . . . the singing cuckoo of the clock, the chairs adorned with crimson damask . . . I am reborn, I am reborn to eighteen hundred and fifty!

Here a process of accretion is clearly operating, but we are not merely presented with a gratuitous list of minutiae: the intention is to idealize the past in its own right, or at least to roll back the present until it coincides with it. In fact, the main difference between Gozzano and his successors lies precisely in this procedure; for, whereas the latter build up perspectives which connect their imagery with their immediate lives and emotions, he still sees his emotional perspectives as detached and precious essences, in which the aching heart may seek refuge by self-absorption but through which he soon discovers the sensibility cannot achieve any genuine form of transfiguration. All his 'buone brutte cose borghesi' ('good ugly bourgeois objects') accordingly resist the pressure of changing circumstances, and coagulate in groups swathed in an inert emotion and infused with just a touch of historical realism. In the last resort they become reduced to keepsakes whose only genuine function is to satisfy the poet's mania for reproducing historical tastes and settings as daguerrotypes or inert tableaus redolent with the fixed emotions, the musty perfumes, and the settled conventions of yesteryear.

Fortunately, this fossilization of situations is just one of the stages in Gozzano's lyrical development and later he evolves a more satisfactory manner.[34] It will, however, be interesting before we proceed to the next stage to see how fossilized situations of this type are treated. In the poem under discussion, 'L'amica di nonna Speranza', the poet continues to cut himself off from the present by insinuating into his imagery the values of a dead society, one whose immutable laws and customs offer a security which can in no way be challenged by the unpredictable passions of contemporary life. So, after the above-mentioned enumeration of objects intended to create an appropriate atmosphere, the lyric unfolds as a quintessentialized narrative, and the tableau which is paraded before our eyes is given a tenuous historical localization by the linking of individual characters to particularized events of the time:

> Giungeva lo Zio, signore virtuoso di molto riguardo,
> ligio al Passato, al Lombardo-Veneto, all'Imperatore . . .'

> Then my Uncle came in, a virtuous gentleman of high regard, bound to the Past, to Venice-Lombardy, to the Emperor . . .

In a similar manner melodramatic effects are obtained by the frequent introduction of historical detail in the form of desultory conversation:

> '. . . Radetzky? Ma che! L'armistizio . . . la pace, la pace che regna . . .'
> '. . . Quel giovine Re di Sardegna è uomo di molto giudizio!'
>
> 'È certo uno spirito insonne . . . è forte e vigile e scaltro . . .'
> 'È bello?' – 'Non è bello: tutt'altro.' – 'Gli piacciono le donne . . .'
>
> 'Speranza!' (chinavansi piano, con tono un po' sibillino)
> 'Carlotta! Scendete in giardino: andate a giocare al volano!'

> '. . . Radetzky? What nonsense! The armistice . . . the peace, the peace now holding . . .' '. . . That young King of Sardinia is a man of great judgement!' 'He is certainly a tireless spirit . . . and he's strong and vigilant and cunning . . .' 'Is he good-looking?' 'He is not good-looking: far from it.' 'He has a taste for women . . .' 'Speranza!' (they bowed down silently, in rather a sybilline mood) 'Carlotta! Go down into the garden: go and play battledore and shuttlecock!'

While the poet also lets drop at times a few allusions to contemporary fashion, as in the following lines:

> Il cerchio ampissimo increspa la gonna a rose turchine.
> Piú snella da la crinoline emerge la vita a vespa.

> The wide hoop ruffled the skirt with blue roses. More slender from the crinoline emerged the wasp-like waist-line.

Nevertheless the dialogue which takes place between Speranza and her friend Carlotta is perhaps more important than the local historical colouring in which it is framed. We soon discover that, although they are sent out into the garden to play battledore and shuttlecock when the conversation turns on the young king's taste for women, their heads had already been filled at school with that facile sentimentality typified by Gozzano in his allusion to 'i casi di Iacopo mesti nel tenero libro di Foscolo' ('the sad vicissitudes of Jacopo in Foscolo's tender book'). Hence the main result of their banishment from the drawing-room is a 'monologue for two voices' in true romantic style:

> 'Il lago s'è fatto piú denso
> di stelle' – ... che pensi?' – 'Non penso.' – '... Ti piacerebbe morire?'
>
> 'Sí!' – 'Pare che il cielo riveli piú stelle nell'acqua e piú lustri.
> – E l'ami? ...' – 'Che versi divini!' – 'Fu lui a donarmi quel libro,
>
> ricordi? che narra siccome amando senza fortuna,
> un tale si uccida per una: per una che aveva il mio nome.'
>
> 'The lake has become thicker with stars' – '... what are you thinking of?' – 'I'm not thinking.' – '... Would you like to die?' 'Yes!' – 'It seems that the sky is casting more stars in the water and more reflections. – And do you love him? ...' – 'What divine verses!' – 'It was he who gave me that book, do you remember? which tells how loving, though unrequited, a certain man killed himself for a girl: for one who bore my name.'

The protagonists have been fossilized here into such immutable poses that the interaction of their personalities has been effectively abolished, and they are both absorbed into a sphere of complete romantic egocentricity. For each of them the figure of 'l'altra' ('the other'), always a disturbing concept for Gozzano, has been completely suppressed by the reduction of their dialogue to the level of a monologue. As a consequence, the tastes and events of the time in which they live are closely woven together into a shared monolithic dream and the poetry becomes one of totally suspended animation.

Paradoxically, however, the dramatic dialogue suppressed within the actual texture of the verse reappears in another form, as a state of anxiety and conflict arising within the sensibility of the poet, involving a clash between his emotions and his carefully constructed myth of the past. For, in fact, as soon as Gozzano produces his escapist dreamland and seals it off hermetically from reality, he finds that he is unable to participate in it himself. His ideal of a completely harmonious and objective lyricism is thereby shattered and, instead of his art proving to be a mirror of a lyrically reconstructed life, it simply becomes an illustration of the impossibility of burying the present in the past and of resolving today's tensions by merging them with the dust of historical perfection. Even the poet himself realizes at the end of the present lyric that he has failed in his task and laments in elegiac tones over the unalterable fact that worlds of time and space lie between him and his perspective of inanimate serenity:

> Stai come rapita in un cantico: lo sguardo al cielo profondo,
> e l'indice al labbro, secondo l'atteggiamento romantico.
>
> Quel giorno – malinconia! – vestivi un abito rosa
> per farti – novissima cosa! – ritrarre in *fotografia* . . .
>
> Ma te non rivedo nel fiore, o amica di Nonna! Ove sei
> o sola che – forse – potrei amare, amare d'amore!

You are, as it were, borne off in a poem: your glance towards the depths of heaven, your finger on your lips, in accordance with the romantic pose. That day – oh, melancholy! – you were wearing a pink dress to have yourself – a wonderful new thing! – taken in a *photograph* . . . But I do not see you again in your flowering youth, o friend of my grandmother's! Where are you, o you alone who – perhaps – I could love, love with true love?

Needless to say, the sense of alienation implicit in these lines gathers momentum as time goes on, and the ultimate effect on Gozzano himself is that he revolts against his own artistic method – against the constant suppression of human values clearly demonstrable in the lifeless statuesque figures that people his dreams. Hence 'L'amica di nonna Speranza' can be regarded as the first conscious échec he suffers in his attempt to attain to that much desired state of 'inconsapevolezza' ('unawareness') characteristic of inanimate objects.

Despite the apparent rebuff he experiences at the close of this poem, his use of the daguerrotype technique does not peter out after the composition of 'L'amica di nonna Speranza': it continues – at times even in an exacerbated form – in other poems that appear in *I Colloqui* (1911). In his second stage Gozzano acts as a fabulous myth-maker and adopts attitudes lending support to Pancrazi's contention that his life gradually becomes 'una controscena negativa' of his art. But by now he has fully developed his potentialities as a portrayer of old-world tonalities and through them he still hopes to perfect his personality by absorbing it into a wholly suspended, a-historical sphere. The poem which most clearly illustrates the point is 'La signorina Felicita' where he again 'sings small' and writes his name without capitals as he momentarily considers a complete retirement from civilized life. The idea is symbolized in an extended metaphor in which he apparently yields to the temptation of abandoning the artificialities of the town in favour of a placid, even boorish, state of domesticity in the country with his lady-love Felicity. Similarly in 'Paolo e Virginia' he refurbishes the myth created by Bernardin de Saint-Pierre and tries to replace his tortured intellectual life with one based on the primitive innocence and joys of the senses.

The atmosphere of 'La signorina Felicita' is a skilful telescoping of the various stages of the romantic movement and is based on the sheer escapist belief that by ignoring the complex demands of civilization one can create for oneself a haven of complete emotional peace. Once more we encounter an accretion of old-world knick-knacks in the shape of trinkets, grandfather clocks, battered baroque furniture and romantic pictures. However, they are not now regarded with the same diffident sympathy as they were earlier and tend to underline the moral and social decline of the villa in which the action of the poem takes place. Depicted as it is in its utter isolation and solitude, it seems quite unreal, as if lifted wholesale – like the castle of the Sleeping Beauty – out of a children's story-book:

Vill'Amarena! Dolce la tua casa
in quella grande pace settembrina!
La tua casa che veste una cortina
di granturco fino alla cimasa:
come una dama secentista, invasa
dal Tempo, che vestí da contadina.

Villa Amarena! How soothing your house is in this tremendous peace of September! Your house which wears a curtain of Indian corn right up to the eaves: like a seventeenth-century lady, ravaged by time, and dressed as a peasant.

Similarly the lady Felicity herself – an ill-educated descendant of an impoverished landed gentry – is immobilized in an eternal pose, while the repeated subtle emphasis on her peasant-like awkwardness removes the last vestige of the fine sentimental bearing of the ladies formerly inhabiting her home:

Sei quasi brutta, priva di lusinga
nelle tue vesti quasi campagnole,
ma la tua faccia buona e casalinga,
ma i bei capelli di color di sole,
attorti in minutissime trecciuole,
ti fanno un tipo di beltà fiamminga . . .

E rivedo la tua bocca vermiglia
cosí larga nel ridere e nel bere,
e il volto quadro, senza sopracciglia,
tutto sparso d'efelidi leggiere
e gli occhi fermi, l'iridi sincere
azzurre d'un azzurro di stoviglia . . .

You are almost ugly, shorn of grace in your almost country clothes, but your good and homely face, your fair hair the colour of sunlight, tied up in tiny tresses, make you a Flemish type of beauty . . . And I see again your crimson mouth, so large when smiling and drinking, your square face, without eyebrows, completely covered with light freckles, and your steady eyes, their artless irises, as blue as the blueness of crockery . . .

This parody reminds us of a similar anti-Petrarchistic parody by Berni,[35] especially since like its predecessor it uses in an ironical fashion the props of the style it wishes to undermine. However, it does not perhaps go quite as far in that direction as Berni's poem, since Felicity tends to possess certain positive charms which clearly attract the poet. Her emotions, for instance, are straightforward, uncomplicated and sincere, and she shows an unspoilt enthusiasm for life similar to that found in Flemish paintings. Even so, the very terms of Gozzano's artistic comparison reveal that a cultural reflex subsists in his judgement and is about to detach him from his complaisant naturalism. We are thus left to wonder at this point whether so refined a soul as his could retain any attraction at all for a sensibility as untutored as hers. This last point is not lost on the poet himself and it enters directly into his calculations when he struggles desperately to make up his mind whether or not to marry Felicity and settle down with her to a life of rustic bliss:

Ecco – pensavo – questa è l'Amarena,
ma laggiú, oltre i colli dilettosi,
c'è il Mondo: quella cosa tutta piena
di lotte e di commerci turbinosi,
la cosa tutta piena di quei 'cosi
con due gambe' che fanno tanta pena . . .

Behold – I thought – this is Amarena, but down there, beyond those delightful hills, there lies the World: that thing full of struggles and tumultuous activities, the thing completely full of those 'thingummybobs with two legs' which cause so much trouble . . .

Here again, of course, reality is being contrasted with the dream, and in the process other destinies, other modes of living, continue to haunt Gozzano as he moves in his artificially created sphere of romantic beatitude. The result is that he tries to vanquish his doubts through yet another of his disguised monologues, one which borders on the ridiculous in its consciously intended naïveté but which again reveals his longing for the lifeless tranquillity of the 'vecchia stampa'. The scene is set in the attic of Felicity's villa, where the following conversation takes place:

'Sarebbe dolce restar qui, con Lei! . . .'
'Qui, nel solaio? . . .' – 'per l'eternità' –
'Per sempre? Accetterebbe? . . .' – 'Accetterei!'

'It would be nice to stay here, with you! . . .' 'Here, in the attic? . . .' – 'for ever' – 'For ever? Would you accept?' . . . 'I would!'

As we might expect, the fossilizing of the dramatic tension in this way produces an inner conflict similar to the one we saw earlier in 'L'amica di nonna Speranza', and the clash between the poet's feelings and his intellect derives at this juncture from the fact that he is again unable to associate his sensibility in any authentic way with the romanticized narrative he has constructed. Eventually he abandons his rustic maiden to her vegetables, while at the same time regretting that he lacks the spontaneity of the typical headstrong romantic who would undoubtedly have made a supreme sacrifice of himself at the moment the impulse seized him, without indulging at all in Gozzano's own decadent attitude of anguished reflection:

Giunse il distacco, amaro senza fine,
e fu il distacco d'altri tempi, quando
le amate in bande lisce e in crinoline,
protese da un giardino venerando,
singhiozzavano forte, salutando
diligenze che andavano al confine . . .

M'apparisti cosí come in un cantico
del Prati, lacrimante l'abbandono
per l'isole perdute nell'atlantico;
ed io fui l'uomo d'altri tempi, un buono
sentimentale giovine romantico . . .

Quello che fingo d'essere e non sono!

The parting came, an infinitely bitter one, and it was an old-world parting, when lovers in crinolines and smooth head-bands, hanging over some venerable garden, sobbed loudly, waving to stage-coaches which were heading for the frontier . . . You appeared to me, as if in a poem by Prati, bewailing your abandonment for islands lost in the Atlantic; and I was a man of yesteryear, a good, sentimental, youthful romantic . . . What I pretend to be and am not!

What clearly distinguishes 'La signorina Felicita' from the normal romantic poem is thus Gozzano's ability to see both sides of the question; and so here, as elsewhere, his autocritical faculty comes between his desires and their satisfaction. The continual crisis in his work no doubt has its source in the spiritual aftermath of the romantic and decadent movements, because it sums up both the sentimental escapism of the former school and the voluntary alienation implicit in the latter. The real tragedy in Gozzano's poetry was, in fact, his realization that however much he tried he could not entirely escape from his historical conditioning. Indeed Petrarch's experience, in which he took a great interest, had already taught him in his youth that a consolatory art could never overcome completely the existential anguish of the poet. Yet unlike Petrarch's serene humanist outlook his own self-defeating intellectual lucidity prevented him from enjoying even that lesser type of consolation which derives from consummate craftsmanship. Hence, as long as his mind remained involved in the ritual of producing extended metaphors, he found his own sensibility out of sympathy with the lyrical modes through which he was obliged to express his feelings. And, although he tried to conceal the fact by depicting his emotions vicariously in melodramatic poses, he was always driven back in the end to the conclusion that his entire artistic manner was a gigantic make-believe.

'Paolo e Virginia' constitutes yet another example of his creation of subtle forms of self-deception through imagery and is probably Gozzano's finest example of an attempted literary escape from a despairing state of existential perplexity. By wholly identifying himself with Bernardin de Saint-Pierre's hero, Paolo, the poet fervently hoped to free himself from his arid intellectualism, and so here once more he presents us with a fresh approach to his lyrical dreamland, with the prospect of yet another meditated avatar. But from the outset we can detect in the lyrical texture of this tropical idyll a gentle – though persistent – vein of irony, which breaks down the poet's attempt to identify himself with Paolo and eventually leads to a complete emotional échec. The despair which results is not simply that of the artist, it is also the despair of a human being who can neither participate in everyday life nor communicate his innermost feelings to others.

We can follow Gozzano's emotional trajectory by making an examination of the poem's development. For instance, the opening lines make the identification of the poet with Paolo an absolute condition for its understanding:

Io fui Paolo già. Troppo mi scuote
il nome di Virginia . . .;

I was once Paul. Too much Virginia's name upsets me . . .;

and once we accept this initial proposition we find that the French writer's isle of innocence and sweet sensuous pleasure is taken over in its entirety by Gozzano as an objective correlative of his mood. As the original story tells us, the young lovers spend a happy and unselfconscious youth almost entirely in one another's company. But the modern poet's description of the island's luxuriant vegetation contains an element of ironic detachment and suggests the imminent break-up of his identification with Paolo. From the outset he is by no means satisfied with the reproduction of the lush natural scenery of his French model, but aims instead at making it mediate and remote, with an overt literary flavour:

Rivedo gli orizzonti immaginari
e favolosi come gli scenari . . .

I see again the imaginary and fabulous horizons just like scenarios . . .

Even the actual vegetation shows a widening of the gap, because its orderliness suggests that it is tended by the hand of an expert gardener. In other words the riotous world of the senses and the ordered world of the intellect are never unified in this lyric, and the over-cerebral Gozzano is continually making mental reservations within the very fabric of his so-called neo-romantic dream. So, since sensation and concept are juxtaposed rather than blended, they produce a mutual repulsion and appear as two distinct and irreconcilable aspects of his creative power.

Needless to say, the poet's sense of aloofness and detachment from his myth is not wholly unintentional. He consciously accentuates it by various kinds of artifice. Not only does the tropical luxuriance of the island ring slightly false, but even certain symbolic events like the telling of time from the height of the shadows under the trees again imply a false and studied primitivism. On the other hand, it must be admitted that the imaginative discontinuities evident in some earlier poems have now been largely avoided, with the result that this poem does not consist of inert and disjointed accumulations of objects but is constructed from carefully interlocking images and associations. The outcome is an allusive narration of events which continues uninterruptedly until it is finally broken by Virginia's trip abroad. Symbolically this incident represents the intrusion of reality into the lovers' idyllic dreamworld, but the poet describes it once more as a melodrama. Its tone is highly melodramatic just as if Virginia, instead of setting out for France to complete her education, were being carried off by some old-time villain of vaudeville. By the same token her eventual return to the island is depicted as a flight from the degradation of modern society, and it is at this highly symbolic point, when the lovers are about to be reunited, that disaster overwhelms them. As Virginia's ship approaches the island a fierce storm arises and she is drowned. Drowned not in a real storm but once again in

una tempesta bella ed artificiosa
come il Diluvio delle vecchie tele . . .;

a fine and artificial tempest like the Flood on old canvases . . .;

so that nowhere is the detachment of art from reality more clearly emphasized than in the contriving of this traumatic event.

Nevertheless, in spite of the fact that the intrusion of artifice into the very heart of the drama tends to deprive it of its verisimilitude, it does not deprive it of its sincerity as a true record of Gozzano's state of mind. The real significance of the poem is that it faithfully represents an antinomy in the poet's sensibility – his inability to accept his deeply felt sentimental inclinations because of his overriding critical perceptiveness. Since then melodrama stands to drama as sentimentality to real sentiment in Gozzano's work, we are left in no doubt of the physical 'unreality' and the spiritual 'reality' of Virginia's flight, and the same thing can be said of her death in the artistically contrived disaster. In other words the poem seems to transport us intentionally on to an artificial plane of feeling in order to accentuate the true nature of the poet's spiritual dilemma.

The deeper implications to be read into Gozzano's technique of total figurative detachment are accordingly moral as well as aesthetic. On the moral plane he is condemning the pointlessness of a civilization which provides man with material wealth and yet deprives him of the mythologies – both lay and religious – which make the possession of that wealth significant. What he himself seeks above all from society is a spiritual purpose permitting him symbolically to write his name once more as Guido Gozzano in authentic capitals; and in this poem, because he despairs of finding a valid myth in his own age, he looks for a substitute in the Rousseauesque ideal of the noble savage.

In his view the man with spontaneous emotions is far superior to the man with a paralysing gift for self-analysis. This accounts for the implications in the conclusion of the lyric, where Gozzano again complains of the aridity of his decadent way of life and puts his finger on the evil which modern civilization has visited upon his sensibility:

Ah! Se potessi amare! Ah! Se potessi
amare, canterei sí novamente!
Ma l'anima corrosa
sogghigna nelle sue gelide sere . . .
Amanti! Miserere,
miserere di questa mia giocosa
aridità larvata di chimere!

Ah! If only I could love! Ah! If only I could love, I would sing so freshly again! But my corroded soul sniggers in its icy evenings, . . . Lovers! Have pity, have pity on this my playful aridity haunted by chimeras!

'Paolo e Virginia' might then be considered the elegy of modern man's dissociated sensibility. For, although the poet is now fully aware of the nature of his lyrical impotence and can even represent it adequately in a myth, he is still unable to provide a cure for the disease that has affected his whole generation. All he can do is to revolt against the outmoded shibboleths of the society in which he lives and hope to demolish its web of illusions by offering a destructive analysis of the type of moral climate it produces.

In his third stage of development he does precisely this and the poem 'Totò Merúmeni' (the self-destroyer) takes the process beyond the point of abnegation to a spurious form of consolation. Just how far the nihilism of the lyric is the result of Gozzano's pathological state – he was already by 1911 in an advanced state of consumption – it is difficult to assess. But his qualities of self-analysis and destructive clear-sightedness now dissolve the last vestiges of his belief in the validity of his experiences and lead to an art which Mariani describes as 'la realtà decomposta nell'artificio'[36] ('reality decomposed in artifice'). Henceforth a desire to bury himself in a pseudo-scientific cloister of entomological studies is symptomatic of his complete renunciation of life, although in the present poem he does once again assert, if somewhat desperately, the possibility of living on two planes of feeling.

On the surface it seems as if Totò's dual personality can produce two parallel states of serenity, yet his self-willed renunciations soon create their own disturbing atmosphere, one which is akin to madness or at least to a muted form of hysteria and neurosis:

> ... In quel silenzio di chiostro e di caserma
> vive Totò Merúmeni con una madre inferma,
> una prozia canuta e uno zio demente.

... In that silence of cloister and barrack-room lives Totò Merúmeni with his sickly mother, his grey-haired great aunt and crazy uncle.

Such a mood is the direct result of the suppression of all spontaneity in favour of a coldly calculated ritual of twofacedness. We are in other words confronted with the conditioned reflex of the intellect, with a *consciously* self-imposed regime of 'inconsapevolezza', which dichotomizes Totò's character into a barren analytical faculty and an amoral, sensual appetite, described in the following self-portrait:

> Totò ha venticinque anni, tempra sdegnosa,
> molta cultura e gusto in opere d'inchiostro,
> scarso cervello, scarsa morale, spaventosa
> chiaroveggenza: è il vero figlio del tempo nostro.

Totò is twenty-five, a disdainful nature, with great culture and taste in works of ink, little commonsense, little morality, a frightening clear-sightedness: he is the true son of our age.

Totò is largely a prefiguration of Eliot's 'hollow men' and he lives solely by enforcing a pointless self-regimentation and a ritualistic acceptance of his lot. Even his devitalized pleasures are mechanical ones and each is carefully ordered and regular. They range from a romp in the garden with his pets to a romp in bed with the cook. What does he acquire as a result of these self-imposed humiliations? The peace and contentment of a studiously cultivated insensitivity mingled with a bitter-sweet literary consolation:

> Totò non può sentire. Un lento male indomo
> inaridí le fonti prime del sentimento;
> l'analisi e il sofisma fecero di quest'uomo
> ciò che le fiamme fanno d'un edificio al vento.
>
> Ma come le ruine che già seppero il fuoco
> esprimono i giaggioli dai bei vividi fiori,
> quell'anima riarsa esprime poco a poco
> una fiorita d'esili versi consolatori . . .

Totò cannot feel. A slow untameable illness has dried up the inner founts of feeling; analysis and sophistry have made of this man what flames do to a building in the wind. But just as ruins which have already tasted fire bloom with fine gladioli flowers, so this burnt-out soul blooms little by little in a wealth of slender consolatory verses . . .

The sting in these lines is clearly in the tail. For we need hardly stress that the type of consolatory verse appealing most to Totò is to be identified with Gozzano's own: a verse which is sentimental, yet alienated and self-destructive in intention.

The real rebellion in this lyric can be seen simmering in the mood of suppressed madness lying beneath its surface, a madness fed by Totò's explosive sensuality and arid intellectualism. A similar mood reappears momentarily in 'Una risorta', where the dissociation of the poet's sensibility has regressed into the memory, so that a flaring of the senses, although immediate, is viewed as if in retrospect. Hence the pleasures of past love-making tend to become more keenly experienced than present ones, which are treated with clinical detachment like the following kisses:

> Vidi le nari fini,
> riseppi le sagaci
> labbra e commista ai baci
> l'asprezza dei canini.

I saw the fine nostrils, I tasted again the experienced lips, and mingled with the kisses the sharpness of her teeth.

Accordingly, it was because of Gozzano's inability to reintegrate these two clashing states of emotional and intellectual experience that he turned momentarily to the comforts of religion. But, although he wrote a film script on the life of Saint Francis in 1915, his attitude can hardly be called a conversion. It was at most an attempt to halt, without any real hope of curing, his continual process of emotional desiccation.

Even so, beneath the arid melodramas of his emotional crisis there gradually arises a strikingly new mode of lyrical representation, one which we have previously defined as a form of emblematic realism. By a subtle transformation of his earlier, inert fetishes into dynamic figures of life the poet occasionally manages to produce verse in which emotional tensions and lyrical settings are intimately united, through the agency of poignant human dramas. The first steps towards this kind of inspiration are the worldly-wise attitudes struck in poems like 'Ketty', even though this particular lyric was not finally completed until 1916; but more important from our present standpoint are a few evocative passages in *Le farfalle*, in which the static absurdity of the daguerrotype is transformed into a heightened existential drama. An incident drawn from the life-cycle of the death's-head moth in 'Acherontia atropos', for instance, reveals a sudden psycho-sensuous dilation of Gozzano's insight and is probably one of the most powerful examples of dramatic writing in his entire work:

L'Acherontia frequenta le campagne,
i giardini degli uomini, le ville;
di giorno giace contro i muri e i tronchi,
nei corridoi piú cupi, nei solai
piú desolati, sotto le grondaie,
dorme con l'ali ripiegate a tetto.
E n'esce a sera. Nelle sere illuni
fredde stellate di settembre, quando
il crepuscolo già cede alla notte,
e le farfalle della luce sono
scomparse, l'Acherontia lamentosa
si libra solitaria nelle tenebre
tra i camperops, le tuje, sulle ajole
dove dianzi scherzavano i fanciulli,
le Vanesse, le Arginnidi, i Papilî.
L'Acherontia s'aggira: il pipistrello
l'evita con un guizzo repentino.
L'Acherontia s'aggira. Alto è il silenzio
comentato, non rotto, dalle strigi,
dallo stridio monotono dei grilli.
La villa è immersa nella notte. Solo
spiccano le finestre della sala
da pranzo dove la famiglia cena.
L'Acherontia s'appressa esita spia
numera i commensali ad uno ad uno,
sibila un nome, cozza contro i vetri
tre quattro volte come nocca ossuta.
La giovinetta piú pallida s'alza
con un sussulto, come ad un richiamo.

'Chi c'è?' Socchiude la finestra, esplora
il giardino invisibile, protende
il capo d'oro nella notte illune . . .

. . . .

Ma già s'ode il garrito dei fanciulli
giubilanti per l'ospite improvvisa,
per l'ospite guizzata non veduta.
Intorno al lume turbina ronzando
la cupa messaggiera funeraria.

> The death's-head moth frequents the countryside, the gardens of men, their villas; by day it hangs against walls and tree-trunks, in darkest corridors, in the most deserted attics; under the guttering, it sleeps with its wings folded like a roof. And it emerges in the evening. In the moonless, cold and starry evenings of September, when twilight is already yielding to night and the butterflies of day have disappeared, the wailing death's-head moth hovers alone in the darkness among the brush-palms, the thuyas, on the flowerbeds, where earlier the children played, and the vanessas, the arginides and the papilas. The death's-head moth wanders around: the bat avoids it with a sudden dart. The death's-head moth wanders around. Deep is the silence, commented upon, but not broken, by the screech-owls, by the monotonous chirping of the crickets. The villa is immersed in darkness. Only the windows of the dining-room stand out, where the family is eating. The death's-head moth approaches, hesitates, reconnoitres, counts the diners one by one, hisses a name, strikes against the window-panes three or four times like a bony knuckle. The palest young girl gets up with a start, as if at a recollection. 'Who is there?' She half-closes the window, gazes over the invisible garden, stretches her golden head into the moonless night . . . But already the squabbling of the children can be heard, joyful because of the unexpected guest, the guest which darts about but is not seen. The dark, funereal messenger drones and whirls around the lamp.

Here one certainly senses a 'frisson nouveau' ('a fresh shudder'). The interaction of the nocturnal landscape, the death's-head moth and the family upon which it makes, as it were, a visitation opens up a new dimension in Gozzano's lyrical manner. At this stage the emphasis is no longer laid upon the static qualities of the scene, but on the existential drama which momentarily links together a number of anguished and existentially conditioned creatures within their mysterious and vaguely terrifying background. Hence, as the moth with its horrifying sphinx-like form circles the lamp and reacts against the narrow confines of its sphere of activity, we are at once led to think that the same kind of limit restricts the human consciousness in its state of sheer contingency. In other words the poet has at last passed beyond the dissociated worlds of intellect and sensation and by means of a spiritual mutation he has acquired an insight into the manifold perspectives of a deeper orphic world. This world turns out to be the principal focus of modern lyrical attention and its modalities are tremulously associative rather than discursive or rational in nature. Admittedly, such a high level of emblematic intelligence only appears occasionally in Gozzano's lyricism and even then almost as a troublesome by-product of quite a different standard of values. Yet even its sporadic manifestations show us that the poet was already hovering on the verge of a representational revolution, one which would eventually involve the upturning of his inert symbolic aggregates and their transformation into dynamic emblems of life.

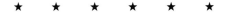

Perhaps Gozzano's greatest misfortune was that he did not fully realize the immense possibilities of the spiritual and technical processes he had fortuitously created. So, instead of moving towards an ideative realism like many subsequent poets, he reverted to a Neoplatonic idealism in which he sought salvation by turns in a feckless cult of mysticism, a dilatory stoicism and a dubious adhesion to eastern religions and Christianity. We can clearly account for these multiple responses by bearing in mind his complete moral bewilderment when confronted with the dynamic complexity of the contemporary world surrounding him. Blinded as he was by bankrupt decadent attitudes, he failed to grasp that the way towards a solution of his spiritual antinomies was a radical change of direction. His positive poetry, from a twentieth-century standpoint, is thus almost an accidental consequence of his symbolic modes, arising from the fact that he was attracted by the 'esterna fenomenicità del mondo'[37] ('external phenomenality of the world') and yet could not justify its attractions in the depths of his conscience. In this case Montale probably came nearest to a definition of his lyrical method when he described him as 'una coscienza tragica e teorica della sospensione'[38] ('a conscience, both tragic and theoretical, of a state of suspension').

Briefly, the love-hate relationship which Gozzano lived with romanticism and decadentism represents the spiritual trauma which finally awakens the modern sensibility. It derives from his feeling of having been thrust willy-nilly out of the cosy world of fixed customs and traditions inherited from the past into a relativistic society with multifarious – though largely meaningless – activities. In his bewilderment he failed to discern the true sphere in which the modern lyricist was to operate, a sphere which tends to lie at the point of intersection between the senses, the imagination and the evaluative faculty. By reaction, he strove to regress into the apparently more substantial sphere of sentimentality cultivated by the romantics, although such an anachronistic process was doomed to failure from the outset. The tragic destiny he represents is perfectly illustrated later by Ungaretti in his contrast between the figures of Aeneas and Palinurus in *La terra promessa*, where the former stands for the hermetic ideal of the creative and thrusting spirit and the latter for the tendency of ancient orphic aesthetics to produce figures representative of a statuesque passivity. Like Gozzano, Palinurus can be described as the 'controscena negativa' of the hermetic ethos, for in the words of Paci 'non sa vivere l'idea, irraggiungibile, come "senso" della vita presente: la feticizza già nel sogno e nella scienza, la fa diventare cosa, cosa alienata, e alla fine egli diventa cosa, si trasforma "nell'immortalità ironica di un sasso" '[39] ('he does not know how to live the unattainable idea as a "feeling-for" presentday life: he already fetishizes it in his dreams and in his science, he makes it become a thing, and in the end he becomes a thing, and is transformed into "the ironic immortality of a rock" '). Similarly the present poet's failure to reach a positive solution to his anguish explains why at every turn his lyricism reveals a dissociation between his imagination and his intellect. The critical acuity which this dissociation produces leads him both to a sense of disillusionment with the present because of its contingency and with the past because of its inaccessibility. Hence to resolve his dilemma he tries to fossilize his emotions in a series of extended, memorially based metaphors; yet powerful tensions continue to subsist beneath the surface of his artfully constructed myths and finally detach his sensibility from their lyrical structures.

Oddly enough, the negativeness of his overall ethos does not detract from the quality of his poetry and a close examination of his lyrical patterns is always rewarding, especially in such intricately literary productions as 'La signorina Felicita'. Indeed, by accepting the richness of his textures and meditating deeply on the nature of his échec, later poets like Montale have succeeded in inverting his symbolic techniques and endowing his inert and sunken imagery with a dynamic emblematic significance. So, precisely because Gozzano is the literary figure providing the initial stimulus while not actively participating in the development of twentieth-century lyricism, we can at best only describe him as the *deus ex machina* of contemporary poetry. He normally stands aloof with a mild and dandified disdain from the trends he was instrumental in promoting; and yet, although he may have regarded himself as the last of nineteenth-century poets, he was in fact a wholly subversive epilogue to its tastes and ideological beliefs.

CHAPTER IV

The originality of Sergio Corazzini

The crepuscular poets are such a retiring and loosely organized group that it is virtually impossible to speak either of a leader or of disciples in the movement. But if we have to single out the name of its most representative poet then the palm must undoubtedly go to Sergio Corazzini. The brevity and unassuming modesty of his life together with the delicacy and resilience of his artistic temperament mark him out as the very incarnation of the crepuscular ethos.[1] So much so that Fontana has attributed his ever-increasing skill at avoiding the commonplaces of the minor crepuscular poets to what he calls his 'air de verginité désenchantée'[2] ('aır of disillusioned virginity'). Beneath a veneer of unaffected charm and naïveté he constantly shows an ability to suffuse with a touch of irony the neo-romantic attitudes adopted by his companions. Moreover, in his work the ironic vein is not wholly complacent as it was the Gozzano, but aims instead at discriminating between those elements specific to the decadent movement and those which might in the future serve as a basis for more modern lyrical developments. Hence at the moment of his premature death at the age of twenty in 1907 he had already transformed his art into a very subtle instrument for reflecting his moods and lyrical outlook.

Corazzini's most important contribution to modern verse was the singular way in which he used first the allegory and then the symbol to blaze a trail towards the emblem. Although the process started from very modest beginnings, its constant driving force was the poet's determination to abandon the crude literary eclecticism of the 'Scapigliati' and represent in a significant, authentic manner the realities of the world he perceived around him. Where he showed himself superior to his contemporaries was in his ability to maintain a coherent tonal structure. His imagery – unlike Praga's, for instance – does not appear to be detached from his inner experiences but stands as a genuine imaginative transliteration of the subtle relationships linking the poet's intimate feelings with the world outside himself. Intuitively at least, if not always consciously, he seems to have recognized that the main field of experience open to modern poets should be an emotional and ethical one and that present-day lyrical responses ought rightly to consist of a series of meditative reactions to the immediate realities of human existence.

That part of Corazzini's inspiration which lies beyond rational comprehension is, by contrast, broadly orphic in character. His outlook is not only determined by his acute sense of life's transiency but also by a continual sense of dying: an unabating 'sentirsi morire di tristezza' ('feeling oneself dying of sadness'), which he emphasizes in 'Il fanale' and which at times seems like a shadowy premonition of his own impending death from consumption. Essentially, death and despair form the basis of the stereotyped naturalistic world he hopes to transcend in his poetry; and in one of his later compositions, 'La sera della domenica', he describes the poet's condition – and, by extension, that of all mankind – as a continuous struggle for survival against impossible odds:

Il Poeta, ebro di morte,
viene a patti
con la Disperazione
che gli offre il domani con tutte
le sue piccole ire sorde,
le sue facili rassegnazioni,
mentre gli ride in faccia
perché non seppe ancora
morire di fame!

The poet, drunk with death, comes to terms with Despair which offers him tomorrow with all its dull little angers, its facile resignations, while it laughs in his face because he has not yet managed to die of hunger!

His normal manner of transcending his anguished, existential state is by means of a meditation on death's inner meaning, by an analysis of its secret potentialities and their subsequent elevation to the level of myth. In order to exploit fully death's hidden resources he postulates an afterlife which matures in the confined space of the coffin and whose infinite vistas are revealed by certain analogical techniques. This entire theme, of course, will only receive its complete lyrical treatment later in Ungaretti's atavistic outlook on life and culture; but what needs to be stressed at present is that it requires for its expression positive – if still resigned – lyrical responses from the poet. Corazzini's verse is in this sense by no means a nihilistic descent to the quietude of death as Gozzano's daguerrotypes tended to be. His poetry deals realistically with the deeper issues of existence, seen from the standpoint of the individual's inner 'durata'; and his incipient sense of personal maturation with the passage of time awakens feelings of artistic self-awareness destined to pervade the whole of twentieth-century verse.

Lyrical awareness with Corazzini, admittedly, falls short of a full participation in life. Despite his basic positiveness, his grasp on reality is often as highly attenuated as that of the other crepuscular poets. Nevertheless, he appears to have understood from the outset that a tremulous realism was at the root of his originality and tried to protect it from two distinct literary temptations: from a Gozzanian corrosion of the senses on the one hand and the self-defeating alienation of the decadent poets on the other. Gradually his efforts sharpened his already vigilant critical faculty and prompted him to steer a course halfway between the nihilism of the former and the desperate, though false, 'giocondità' of the latter. In fact, the texture of his lyricism is normally strengthened by a quality of tender hope, a word he often writes with a capital, although once again this is not a note he strikes openly in a form of full-throated lyricism: it is simply a resilient undertone which suffuses his melodic line as a by-product of his deeper view of the poet's function.

Because of their acknowledgement of the need for authenticity in their poetic expression all the crepuscular poets tended to stand aloof from futurist trends, with perhaps the single exception of Govoni. Normally they felt so great a revulsion for its chaotic sensationalism that they suppressed all forms of brash assertiveness in their imagery, especially violent clashes of colour or vivid tonal contrasts. Likewise, they were even suspicious of visual, tactile or olfactory flashes of sensuousness in case they too provoked meretricious effects.[3] Such extreme reserve before the impact of the senses imparted to Corazzini's poetry, in particular, a touch of dandified asceticism; for, as a general rule, he saw no reason for widening his narrow but subtle and sophisticated poetic spectrum unless the inner exigencies of his art made it imperative for him to do so. Whereas this type of excessive restraint sometimes diminished the influence of his poetry on his successors, it had on the other hand the advantage of saving it from the uncontrolled enthusiasms of his futurist contemporaries, a fact which probably explains why he was a relatively successful poet in a cultural climate largely preoccupied with second-hand aesthetic views imported from France. It also explains why with the wisdom of hindsight wc can now see that his extreme selectivity and anguished awareness of the precariousness of existence amounted to an early attempt to apply modern criteria to poetic composition. To some extent, indeed, this element was already latent in the ethos of his entire age; and so, according to Fontana, not only Corazzini but all the crepusculars 'possèdent un peu ce don de se faire pardonner leur incertitude et leur inconstance ... Cette incertitude et cette inconstance deviennent dans leurs œuvres, plutôt qu'un défaut, une grâce'[4] ('possess something of a gift for having their uncertainty and inconstancy forgiven ... This uncertainty and this inconstancy become in their works a grace rather than a defect.').

Yet, however subtle and persuasive they may have been within their narrow range of experience, it has to be conceded that most members of the movement remained transitional poets, possessing neither a wholly modern outlook nor a wholly modern sensibility. So particularly valuable in assessing their relative merits and demerits is a distinction made by Tedesco who claims that there are broadly two separate groups of crepuscular writers: the genuine poets whose main characteristic is their self-sincerity and the versifiers who do no more than reflect uncritically the group-consciousness. Precisely because Corazzini rose above the commonplaces to which the minor poets were addicted he became its most significant figure; although at the same time it has to be acknowledged that much of his early work also tends to merge thematically – and at times even technically – with the broad stream of their more conventional practices.

A typical example of a banal thematic element which continually dogs his steps and obtrudes on occasion, even when he has acquired an original poetic tone, is his obsession with churches; and, in fact, a similar obsession by all the other crepusculars caused Moretti to remark later that 'il nascente crepuscolarismo estetizzava i confessionali'[5] ('crepuscularism at its birth aestheticized the confessional'). According to some critics such detritus – together with certain tonal aberrations they claim to detect throughout his verse – is sufficient to condemn both Corazzini and the entire movement to which he belongs by providing conclusive proof of its neo-decadent character. In their view crepuscularism is nothing more than a cult of decadent extremes, involving a pallid sensuality, a moral fecklessness, a deepseated sense of disease, and an incipient neurosis.[6] Although it is difficult to accept such judgements as adequate descriptions of Corazzini's mature poetry,[7] it would be quite futile to deny that part of his early lyricism falls into this category. Normally two diametrically opposing tendencies can be detected in his work: the one a critical acuteness manifesting itself as a delicate and probing form of irony, and the other a clear vein of romantic sentimentality. At first the quality of his individual poems depends on which of these two elements is dominant in his acts of poetic creation. When the sentimental note is uppermost it can sometimes vitiate even his better poems by producing too melodramatic or too plaintive a lyrical inflection. This is especially the case when the poet poses as a naïve, decadent 'bimbo'[8] ('child'); and so, despite its otherwise tonal maturity, even the successful lyric 'Desolazione del povero poeta sentimentale' underlines the point. In this poem Corazzini's conception of his poetic function amounts to a form of inverted romantic egocentricity, and he diminishes the poet's rôle as much as the romantic writers overstated it:

Perché tu mi dici poeta?
Io non sono un poeta.
Io non sono che un piccolo fanciullo che piange.

Why do you call me poet? I am not a poet. I am only a little child who weeps.

On the other hand, when the ironic vein predominates, he often succeeds in suppressing his latent sentimentality altogether, although sometimes at the cost of sensuous warmth.

This type of bipolarity is not eliminated even in his finest work, but its elements are then combined in just the right proportions to provide his melodic line with subtle lyrical qualities. As a result, his gentle – though corrosive – bitterness and his sentimental slackness often fuse together to produce delicate and perceptive images which express the exact configuration of his moods. This is especially the case when he traces out his lonely and premature journey to the grave. Admittedly, he only managed to write a limited number of poems of this type, despite the fact that they represent the highest expressions of his genius; but it is clearly against the background of their formal and spiritual maturity that we have to measure all the other stages of his lyrical development.

Although Corazzini's poetic evolution extends only over five or six years, he made some incredible advances during that period. Consequently, despite its brief span the most satisfactory way of approaching his art will prove to be a chronological one. Here a difficulty has been overcome by Jacomuzzi's publication of his complete poetic works[9], because all previous editions had simply contained his later compositions and excluded his juvenilia altogether. Fortunately the latter were saved from oblivion by Donini's study of his life and work published in 1949, and it is on his research that we shall rely, just as Jacomuzzi did, for our illustrations of his early texts.[10]

An important element we detect in Corazzini's early manner is surprisingly his poetic irony. At first it is rather complacent and playful, but later it may be equated with that remarkable 'consapevolezza di sé' ('self-consciousness') which Anceschi lays down as one of the basic ingredients of contemporary poetry. Strange as it may seem for so serious an artist, his ironic vein first appeared in satirical poems written in the Roman dialect for humorous magazines like the *Marforio*, the *Rugantino* and *Il Capitan Fracassa*. But precisely because it manifested itself at so early a stage it seems to have saved his lyricism from falling a prey to the morose sentimentality which was soon to prove the distinguishing feature of the minor crepusculars. In contrast with their effeteness Corazzini's own poetry gradually becomes interiorized and highly authentic in utterance, and the first step he took in this direction was to develop a certain laconic incisiveness of expression, as may be seen in the following fragment concerning the experiences of a shipwrecked sailor:

La mattina appresso
tutto meravijato
ariscoprí 'na palla de fucile,
e dopo un'ora
vide 'na forca co' un impiccato.
– Alla bon'ora! –
disse subito contento, – so' arrivato
a un paese civile' – [11].

> The morning after, completely astonished, he discovered a rifle bullet, and an hour later he saw a gallows with a hanged man. 'All well and good!' he said immediately content, 'I have arrived in a civilized country'.

Although the Voltairian reminiscence is barely concealed, the clipped tone of the passage already shows the psychological tautness of the poet's mature writings. Normally his irony is most effective when it is most subdued and merely casts a delicate shadow of ambiguity over his moods. It then provides an underlying intellectual resilience which is hardly ever perceptible when the sentimental attitudes inherent in the normal range of crepuscular conventions dominate his inspiration.

A clear example of such sentimental slackness is the following passage which amounts to little more than decadent simpering:

Io porto tanto amore
a una crocetta d'oro
che s'apre, sul mio cuore.

È un tenue lavoro,
non è un ricordo, no,
come l'ebbi, l'ignoro.

Io l'amo perché so
che croce fu dolore,
e assai ne spasimò

un mio dolce Signore! [12]

> I bear so much love for a little cross of gold which opens on my heart. It is a delicate work, not a keepsake, no, how I acquired it, I know not. I love it because I know the cross spelled anguish, and my sweet Lord suffered deeply on it!

In contrast with such jaded artificiality we find lines of a much more resilient lyrical level in 'A Carlo Simoneschi' published in *L'amaro calice*

(1905). Here too the poet's melancholy and nostalgia tend to be religiously orientated and romantic, thereby appearing to acquire almost a note of a cosmic wretchedness. Yet the underlying ironic touch clearly saves the poem from crepuscular banality:

Carlo, malinconia
m'ha preso forte, sono
perduto; cosí sia.

Charles, melancholy has gripped me firmly, I am lost; so be it.

A similar type of ironic resilience before the blows of fate will become predominant towards the end of Corazzini's life, especially in poems like 'A Gino Calza'. At that stage a feeling of bitterness cuts across the thread of his sentimentality and sometimes reduces his verse to a frigid state of ironic realism. An apt example is to be found in 'Dialogo di marionette'[13] where the puppet queen shows an extreme awareness of her inanimate condition and repeatedly interrupts the poet's professions of love by making such ironically objective remarks as:

Poeta! non vedete
che i miei capelli sono
di stoppa?

Poet, don't you see that my hair is made of tow?

or:

Oh, come
vorrei piangere! Ma che posso farci
se il mio piccolo cuore
è di legno?

Oh, how I would like to weep! But what can I do if my little heart is made of wood?

From these illustrations we can deduce that, as Corazzini's irony develops, it moves away from a gentle, participatory humour of the type we find in his early verse towards a much more allusive, detached and perceptive form of expression, before finally ending on a note of gentle sarcasm in 'Bando'. Consequently his finest poetry was composed between these two extremes, during a period when a sense of critical self-consciousness tended to offset his highly charged sentimental themes. Through his muted irony and growing understanding of the human condition he gradually learned, in short, to found his sense of values on inner fulfilment and the authentic representation of his moods rather than on the vapid romanticism and residual, metaphysically based idealism of his age.

This immediately places him from an ethico-aesthetic standpoint on the same footing as the majority of hermetic poets.

But, although his ironical vein and crepuscular sentimentality provide us with insights into the various stages of Corazzini's spiritual development, at first the sentimental note clearly dominated his inspiration. Fundamentally his early crepuscularism proves to be a decadent melodic experience which is slowly refined and uplifted by the consolidation of his steadily maturing critical intelligence. At the outset of his career he draws on powerful romantic sources for his themes and these – when set in a minor key – cause his nostalgic melancholy to deliquesce into the facile musicality of the opera-song:

Mio dolcissimo mare,
sotto la luna bionda
io vedo da la sponda
la nave lontanare.

Sento la morbid'onda
che mi viene a baciare,
come per consolare
la mia pena profonda.

Ella parte, e il mio pianto
va a morire sul mare
come l'anima mia . . .

Ahi, non si può pensare
che il mare, ch'io ho amato tanto,
il mar la porta via! . . . [14]

My gentle sea, under the fair moon I see from the shore the ship moving away. I feel the soft waves coming to kiss me, as if to console my deep grief. She is leaving, and my weeping dies away over the sea like my soul . . . Ah, one could not have thought that the sea, which I have loved so much, that the sea would bear her off! . . .

At first sight one can hardly detect a touch of self-consciousness – let alone irony – in these lines; but what distinguishes even this lyric from typically decadent compositions is its melodic flow. Its melodiousness gives rise in turn to a unity of tone and Corazzini's tonal compactness is a quality which we rarely come across either in the poetry of the Italian decadents or in that of the 'Scapigliati'. Accordingly, his main achievement at this juncture is his ability to establish a tonal equilibrium in his verse by an appropriate selection of image-patterns and lyrical cadences. What he still lacks, on the other hand, is a sufficiently developed critical awareness to allow him to avoid the blandishments of the romantic dream.

However, not only does he later attenuate his sentimental strain by the introduction of a graduated form of irony, he also succeeds in fashioning a perceptive symbolism to give his verse more of a cutting-edge. In his juvenilia this symbolic element is hardly noticeable since it is overlaid by the decadent materials he finds lying at hand in the folklore of his age. But even in his early period he began to develop certain technical procedures which were destined to stand him in good stead when his symbolism had eventually matured. These techniques are closely associated with the crepuscular conventions of the minor poets and the devices on which they are based could no doubt be described as a form of 'basso crepuscolarismo' ('base crepuscularism'). Take, for instance, the following lines:

A te, piccola visione bianca.
Oh, un bacio, un bacio lieve
su la tua bocca rossa,
un bacio breve, breve,
piccolo, senza scossa;[15]

To you, tiny white vision. Oh, a kiss, a light kiss on your red mouth, a brief, brief kiss, a tiny one, without impact!

Although the lyricism they contain is of extremely doubtful quality, the way in which it is expressed is nevertheless highly significant. From the outset the poem's residual sensuality is clearly due to the prevailing cult of Dannunzian aesthetics; but it is already evident even in this lyric that Corazzini's sensibility is moving steadily towards a 'poesia delle piccole cose' ('poetry of tiny things') of the kind he will later practise in his maturity. Such a cult of symbolic aggregates likewise determines a number of his poetic modalities, especially the reduction of his object-symbols to a few essentialities like 'bocca', 'visione bianca' and 'bacio'. These elements are then offset by a momentary flaring of colour-contrasts, as may be seen in the phrase 'bocca rossa' which acts as a foil to the earlier evocation of 'visione bianca'. In fact, these two colours – associated with the redness of blood and the pallor of disease – will henceforth become rooted in Corazzini's sensibility and form for him the two poles of crepuscular experience. On the other hand, equally important at present is yet another artifice, the spatial restrictiveness of sensations produced by such phrases as 'bacio lieve', 'bacio breve, breve' and 'piccolo, senza scossa'. As we have stressed earlier, a conscious restriction of feelings by a retraction of the poet's senses is a normal feature of crepuscular art; and, although it is crudely effected in these lines, it will later become a vital feature in the self-conscious lyrical attenuation of feeling which Corazzini aims at producing in his imagery.

What these devices in combination tend to create is that gentle irritation of the senses which so often overlays the purity of lyrical intention characteristic of the crepuscular muse. So we already find Corazzini practising here in schematic fashion a calculated withdrawal from reality for the sake of providing a perspective for his mood; and this is achieved despite the fact that the situation he evokes is a singularly naïve one. Such a growing sense of perspective emerging from his otherwise muted sensations may perhaps be attributed to his pathological state of mind, especially to his obsession with death; but the air of 'participatory detachment' that the process suggests has considerable lyrical implications for the future. Admittedly, we are still far removed from the type of lyrical suspension perfected by the hermetic poets, but at least a small – though significant – step towards it has been taken.

We can no doubt also detect in this poem that 'traccia di sensibilità dannunziana'[16] ('touch of Dannunzian sensibility') which Baldacci claims is at the base of all crepuscular experience; and yet the point is to be interpreted in a positive rather than a negative sense. Crepuscular attenuation of the cult of sensation is fundamentally more than a refinement of Dannunzian aesthetics, it is an attempt to see the world in a fresh lyrical light. This explains why the crepuscular view of death is not as macabre as D'Annunzio's normally was, and why the very idea of dying is normally associated with a sense of fulfilment. Likewise many other artifices in the crepuscular armoury, while appearing to be derived from D'Annunzio, may well have been drawn from other sources. Even the technique of colour-contrasts, for instance, illustrated above could have had its origin with the French decadents, where it also served as a sensory stimulus within otherwise gently muted imagery; and in this respect the poet enjoying the highest prestige with the crepusculars was undoubtedly Francis Jammes.

Even so, the crepuscular poets are clearly to be distinguished from the French decadents because of their greater attenuation of sensations. This is particularly the case with Corazzini who avoids both the garish imagery of a Verhaeren and the insidious lubricity of Jammes himself. The latter, indeed, often produces a sexual undertone in the intimate texture of his lyricism, one which is based on a delicate chiaroscuro technique, as may be seen in the following polychromatic line describing Clara d'Ellébeuse:

La lumière bleue de sa gorge blanche.[17]

The blue light of her white throat.

But with Corazzini any similar touch of sensuality is linked with death rather than with sexually-based desire, with the result that a form of dark funereal beauty is highlighted in lyrics like 'Amore e morte' through the almost tactile imagery of certain pallid, yet flesh-textured, flowers. Symbols of this kind seem to represent in his mind the freshness of young life cut off in its prime, together perhaps with a possible promise of rebirth beyond the tomb. The following suicide scene with its aura of hopeful despair is a case in point:

Venne la morte; piansero le rose,
Petali tristi sopra i corpi belli;
Egli, confusi aveva i suoi capelli
con le chiome di lei, fresche e odorose.[18]

Death came; the roses wept, sad petals on lovely bodies; he had intertwined his hair with her fresh and perfumed tresses.

A further step has also been taken here in Corazzini's technique of sensory attenuation, because in the three sonnets dealing with this dual suicide the palpable qualities of the flesh are nuanced by a cult of generic adjectives such as 'fronte pallida' ('pale brow'), 'labbra divine' ('divine lips'), 'corpi belli' ('lovely bodies'), 'grandi occhi' ('large eyes') and 'manina bianca' ('tiny white hand'). Moreover, there is a touch of drama in the description as well as a note of sensuality because the emphasis now clearly inclines towards tragedy. Thus, what this sombre mood actually delineates for the first time is the poet's evolving metaphysic of dying, in which at the moment he takes only a vicarious pleasure but which later, during his own protracted illness, will afford him the opportunity of experiencing all the stages of a personal decline and of describing them with complete artistic fidelity.

A variant upon the image of death is the previously mentioned image of blood which now tends to become an obsession with the consumptive Corazzini.[19] At times blood, flowers and death all combine to form one of his earliest perceptive aggregates of object-symbols. Normally they are associated with his elemental colour transitions which emphasize the two polarities of his moral world, the full flush of life on the one hand and the pallor of mortal disease on the other:

Oh un bacio di morente
sulla bocca, permetti!

Su quella bocca ardente
che pare un fior di sangue
trionfante fra i mughetti![20]

Oh, permit the kiss of a dying man on your mouth! On that burning mouth which seems like a blood-red flower triumphant among the lilies!

One other function of his colour-contrasts at this stage is to convey a residual feeling of sensual excitement which at certain points the poet still continues to filter through his sensibility. But simultaneously he tends to exorcise most of his other sensuous reactions by using muted images and nuances. Only occasionally is even a mildly provocative image produced, and then the allusion is normally Petrarchan, amounting to no more than a metonymic reference to a 'bocca vermiglia' ('crimson mouth') or a 'manina bianca' ('tiny white hand'). In themselves, such images would hardly cause a stir, but so neutral is the background against which they are set into relief that they seem to highlight the very nature of his tenuous desires. If, on the other hand, he does tend to indulge at all in any open sensuality, it is generally for the purpose of indicating his deep sense of mystery and the anguished timidity he experiences while he attempts to explore the arcana of his emotions, as illustrated in such lines as

La voluttà dei vostri occhi grevi
di ombre . . . [21]

The voluptuousness of your eyes heavy with shadows . . .

or:

La fiamma azzurra dei vostri occhi azzurri . . . [22]

The blue flame of your blue eyes ...

The hallucinatory quality of these lines leads us to suspect that they are modelled on Pascoli's equally hallucinatory eye-images, although the sensuality of their *chiaroscuro* evocativeness also links them with Jammes' sexually-stimulated evocations of feminine beauty. But whatever their origin, they mark the utmost limit of Corazzini's incursion into the field of the senses in his early verse, and later he will consciously refine away all residual concrete elements, replacing them with a series of 'sonate in bianco' ('sonatas in white') which do no more than linger on the very periphery of emotion and sensory experience.

Although the crepuscular device of undermining the concreteness of imagery is perhaps not overemphasized in *Dolcezze* (1904), the very title already suggests that the emotions expressed will hardly be passionate or violent in quality. The stress falls instead on a kind of childlike humility, while the rhythms of the collection remind us of those which predominate in D'Annunzio's *Poema paradisiaco*. The general atmosphere of the work is one of physical and mental exhaustion, which gives rise to a false sense of intimacy: one in which a complacent sense of grief is artificially cultivated to conform with the conventional crepuscular pattern. Most of the compositions it contains thus tend to lack the robustness and the inner perceptions we encounter later, and the following example is no exception:

Voglio dirti in segreto
de la dolce follia
che mi fa triste e quieto

tanto; vedi, la mia
anima è nel mio cuore,
il cuore è nella mia

anima e se dolore
l'anima un poco sente,
soffre un poco anche il cuore,

bimbo, quietamente.[23]

I want to tell you in secret of the gentle madness which makes me so sad and resigned; you see, my soul is in my heart, my heart is in my soul and if my soul feels a little anguish, my heart too suffers a little, quietly, like a child.

This effete lucubration reminds us of the naïve chop-logic sometimes produced by poets of the Middle Ages, especially by the Tuscan school and the minor *stilnovisti*; and a hint at such an origin is given in the poem's epigraph drawn from Cino da Pistoia. Needless to say, its complacency and lack of moral tension sound almost completely false, while the simplistic quality of the argument is inappropriately combined with a form of naïve ratiocination which almost appears to be syllogistic in its unfolding.

Similar types of lyrical insincerity are to be found in other poems, and indeed Corazzini seems at his most jejune when he attempts to fuse together atmospheres of childlike innocence and religious piety. His obsession with ecclesiastical images, for example, reasserts itself in 'Follie', but its completely conventional framework and imitative rhythmical structure tend to deprive the poem of all persuasiveness and conviction.[24] Few of Corazzini's images of nuns, priests, altars, crosses and so on ever adhere in any satisfactory way to his moods at this stage, although we do come across an occasional exception. One of these is his early bell-symbol which unexpectedly borders on the type of emblematic image he develops in his mature verse.

Probably we can describe the bell-symbol as the first coherent emblem in his work, and, although he does not subsequently develop it to the full, it already has generic sensuo-religious implications in his early poetry:

Campana dondolante
In un cielo di rose,
Dolci note armoniose,
note di bocca amante . . .[25]

Swinging bell, in a sky of roses, sweet harmonious notes, notes from a lover's mouth . . .

No doubt this stanza is also a little too decadent for the modern ear, but by way of compensation it is one of Corazzini's first attempts at analogical writing, and its general emotional fabric is already suffused with the melancholy timbre we shall later find predominant. Most of its subsequent appearances will be variations on a single key mood, which combines the poet's reverence for the act of worship with his feeling of sensuous awe before the mysterious resonances of Christianity or – more often – 'la tetra rovina delle cose' ('the dark ruin of things'), which are again powerfully expressed by a similar tolling of a bell in 'Chiesa abbandonata'. It is consequently a symbol galvanizing his spiritual life and filling him with a sense of stoic fortitude as he contemplates the ever-lengthening shadow which death was beginning to cast over his personal destiny.

Other symbols rise more slowly to an emblematic state, but some are eventually even more fully exploited than the bell-symbol; and in the process of their elevation we find them passing through a virtual allegorical phase. One of the most significant is the sun-symbol, already appearing in schematic allegorical form in 'La tipografia abbandonata' (1903):

Oh, ma tu fuggi, o sole!
Ritornerai domani?
O ci abbandoni come già gli umani
ci abbandonarono?

Oh, but you flee, o sun! Will you return tomorrow? Or will you abandon us as humanity already abandoned us?

At first it represents a life-giving force and its appearance contrasts with the decay implicit in the poet's dominant atmospheres: but later it tends to act as a kind of symbolic stimulus, for the purpose of evoking moments of attenuated joy. Already in a poem like 'Gabbia' in *Dolcezze* (1904) it has this function, emphasizing the liberation felt by birds after their escape from a cage, although the cage itself – an allegorical rendering of the poet's soul – is then left desolate by their absence:

. . . di fuori
benigno sole offriva a' bei canori
pennuti la dolcezza di suoi raggi . . .

. . . outside a benign sun offered to the beautiful feathered songsters the gentleness of its rays . . .

A similar function of the symbol is to be noted in association with Corazzini's evocation of distant religious paradises. In lyrics like 'Follie' the two object-symbols act in combination to encourage the poet to continue his 'spiritual viaggio' ('spiritual journey'), even if in a somewhat vague and still neo-romantic sense. Finally, the Virgin Mary is likened to the sun, and then the poet is unceasingly attracted like a madman to her light:

Voi siete il Sole, io sono
un pazzo che lo segue
e non concede tregue
allo spirto mai prono.

You are the Sun, I am a madman who follows it, and it offers no truce to my undaunted spirit.

In his mature work, on the other hand, religious allegories of this type play a subsidiary rôle to the immediate sensuous warmth of the sun-symbol, which becomes transformed into a complete tonal element and offers an insight into that orphic state of serenity to which the poet or his characters aspire. At this stage Corazzini's faith appears to have more of a humanist than a narrow Catholic meaning and his religious images consequently appear in a subservient – even a decorative – light.

In a similar way the season of the year changes with this maturing of his sensibility, so that in the highly aestheticized atmosphere of a lyric like 'Sonata in bianco minore' the sun-symbol emerges against a background of tepid autumnal warmth:

– Sorelle, venite a vedere!
– C'è il sole nell'orto, c'è il sole!
– È un povero sole che ha freddo, non senti?
– Che piange le sue primavere . . .

. . . .

– Come è gelido il convento.
– È piú gelido il mio cuore.
– Oh, Sorelle, invece, io sento
tutto il sole nel mio cuore.
– Stelle in cielo e vele in mare,
tante vele e tante stelle . . .
– Accendiamo le candele sull'altare . . .
– Che faremo, se non torna?
– Se non torna piú, morremo.

Sisters, come and see! – There is the sun in the garden, there is the sun! – It is a weak sun which feels cold, don't you think? – Which grieves over its springs . . . – How cold the convent is. – My heart is colder still. – Oh, Sisters, on the contrary, I feel the whole sun in my heart. – Stars in heaven and sails on the sea, so many sails and so many stars . . . – Let us light the candles on the altar . . . – What shall we do, if it does not return? – If it no longer returns, we shall die.

The very pathos of these lines shows conclusively that the previously overt religious images contained in Corazzini's lyrical repertoire must now be considered as mere background elements intensifying the gentle spiritual warmth and sensuous bliss denoted by the return of the sun. Very often it is within these wider atmospheres of almost metaphysical proportions that his other symbols and sub-symbols develop to produce an emblematic transcription of his states of mind. Some of them, it has to be admitted, continue throughout his work to retain allegorical overtones, but most are now transformed into symbolic, tonal pointers, interpreting concretely the significance of the poet's thought by turning it into tremulous existential imagery.

Another significant example of this symbolic intersection of idea and sensation is the leaf-image. It is even to be found in poems as early as 'Follie' where falling leaves are used allegorically to represent spiritual decay and the continually dashed hopes of the poet:

O morta ch'eri in cielo
e nel mio cuore anelo
di te, di te, creatura,

per cui arsero tutte
le mie fiammee voglie
e cadder come foglie
le speranze distrutte.

O dead girl who were in heaven and in my heart, I long for you, for you, sweet creature, for whom all my flaming desires burned and all my shattered hopes fell like leaves.

Still, the fact that this poem is an early text is quite clear from the archaic, almost stilnovistic, quality of the language. Later, however, the idea of fading hope continues to be associated with the falling of leaves; and once the poet has changed his dominant season from the spring to the fall of the year, as in the 'Sonetto d'autunno', we immediately note that his associative network has been vastly extended to bring in the implication of autumnal ripeness and decay:

Foglie e speranze senza tregua, foglie
e speranze; non hanno rami e cuori
cadute eguali allor che i primi ori
Autunno triste su la terra accoglie?

L'anima poi che nell'audaci voglie
si disfece con gli ultimi rossori
della sua giovinezza, in foglie e fiori
malinconicamente si discioglie.

> Leaves and hopes without cease, leaves and hopes; do not branches and hearts have equal falls when autumn sadly gathers on the earth its first golds? The soul, when it melted with bold desires in the last flush of its youth, unburdened itself sadly in leaves and flowers.

Lines like these clearly establish an allegorico-symbolic meaning for the falling of leaves in Corazzini's imagery, and pave the way towards a more mature emblematic style. So, ultimately, when we come across the leaf-symbol again in 'Dopo', it is transformed into an emblematic statement, carrying along with it a train of inarticulate associations and multi-dimensional resonances adding depth and feeling to the lyrical texture:

> Il passo degli umani
> è simile a un cadere
> di foglie . . . Oh! primavere
> di giardini lontani!

> The human footstep is like a falling of leaves . . . Oh! the springs of distant gardens!

Consequently his poetry can be said to be one of the first in modern Italy to provide over the entire temporal span of the poet's life an ever-deepening and interlocking imaginative consistency.

Another symbol which develops into a full-blown emblem is the image of distant, peaceful garden-paradises. As is already evident in the above-quoted lines from 'Dopo', gardens gradually tend to become drowsy havens of peace for the poet and prove to be his psycho-sensuous substitute for a state of religious beatitude. Again these images spring from more generalized origins and we can detect their concealed presence in early landscapes, especially in hallucinatory ones associated with eye-images such as the stagnant pools punctuating the green plains of Lombardy:

> Acque serene ch'io corsi sognando
> ne la dolcezza de le notti estive,
> acque che vi allargate fra le rive
> come un occhio stupito . . . [26]

> Serene waters which I sped across in dreams in the balminess of summer nights, waters which widen out between banks like an astonished eye . . .

Gradually, however, such broad hallucinatory expanses give way to restricted visions of tiny gardens dozing in the tepid sunlight of Corazzini's everlasting and ideal spring:

> O piccoli giardini addormentati
> in un sonno di pace e di dolcezze,
> o piccoli custodi rassegnati
> di sussurri, di baci e di carezze . . . [27]

O little gardens sleeping a peaceful slumber of sweetness, O tiny resigned custodians of whispers, kisses and caresses . . .

This is as far as the garden-image is taken in *Dolcezze*, but in the next collection *L'amaro calice* (1905) the poet continues to associate its inner tranquillity with an appropriate crepuscular tone. The opening poem 'Invito' illustrates the process to perfection, because its formal clarity depends on the elaboration of a virtually monochrome spiritual equilibrium, emphasizing the purity of the poet's resignation as he bows before the inevitability of death:

Anima pura come un'alba pura,
anima triste per i suoi destini,
anima prigioniera nei confini
come una bara nella sepoltura,

anima dolce buona creatura,
rassegnata nei tristi occhi divini,
non piú rifioriranno i tuoi giardini
in questa vana primavera oscura . . .

Soul as pure as a pure dawn, soul saddened by its fate, soul imprisoned within its confines like a coffin in the sepulchre, soul, sweet and good creature, resigned within sad, divine eyes, your gardens will reflower no more in this dark and vain spring . . .

From this point on a mutation takes place in Corazzini's art. He abandons the cruder decadent effects and the red-white contrasts of his youth and replaces them with a chiaroscuro form of lyrical synthesis, together with a tonal consistency more in keeping with genuine crepuscular inspiration. This fusion of aggregates of object-symbols – the soul, dawn, the coffin, leaves, eyes and gardens – with an overall lyrical tone, is achieved by a mingling of visual and auditory effects. Thereafter both the poet's word-music and his image-chains are modulated upon a chromatic scale which at most ranges through pure whiteness to various degrees of transparency and liquidity. In the process the garden-symbol becomes an important feature in the landscapes correlative to Corazzini's moods and their further integration with purely phonic or melodic effects provides a musical solution to his anguish.

The symbolic aggregate which now makes its appearance – though hardly noticeable at first because of Corazzini's high tonal compactness – marks the beginning of a new form of *poesia delle cose*. Its diverse elements will appear as so many variants on his basic lyrical configurations as they attempt to mirror his moods as authentically as possible. In 'Invito' the tendency is to regress to a delicate orphic afterworld dominated by the pale serenity of death; yet death, as we have already hinted, is not a wholly negative feature with him: it promises instead a mysterious form of regeneration in a sensuous sphere beyond the tomb. In this respect the poet's attempts to nuance his visual and emotional perceptions by the progressive dematerialization of imagery has more than a technical impact on his work: it also tends to represent a self-conscious metaphysic of dying in which a gradual loss of sensuous acuity will form an essential part of the process of refining experience and fitting it for ultimate lyrical transfiguration. The embodiment of the technique into Corazzini's art consequently ensures that mood and imagery will cohere, that his emotional responses and visual impressions will become broadly reciprocating, and that both will be associated with a set of object-symbols whose lyrical patterning will represent a 'precise' imaginative rendering of his mood.

The use of virtual objective correlatives in poems like 'Invito' clearly marks a major step forward, because the device represents the confluence of the two main stylistic aspects of the twentieth century – the analogy and the symbolic aggregate. The subtle implications which they are capable of evoking may be further examined by considering the development of Corazzini's coffin-symbol. Naturally this symbol is closely associated with the grave and is part of his analogical representation of death. At first death seems in his view to be a frightening concept, the ghost at the feast in all his moments of 'giocondità'; but slowly he adopts, as we have stressed, a more positive view of dying and he then tries to explore the inner meaning of the phenomenon by ringing the changes on its dominant imagery. His investigation soon convinces him of death's infinite resourcefulness and leads him to postulate an orphically purified afterlife, the essential qualities of which are enunciated in 'Elegia':

> la bella
> Vita imagineremo in una chiara
> morte . . .

a fine Life we shall imagine in a clear death . . .

The 'chiara morte' of which he speaks amounts here to a sense of self-fulfilment after the suffering experienced in this world; and, despite the ecclesiastical imagery in which it is clothed, a similar meaning can also be detected in the ending of the prose-poem 'Esortazione al fratello', where the essence of an authentic personality is retained beyond the tomb as 'una mortale felicità':

> 'Oh, che tu debba inginocchiarti e orare e sudar sangue, novizio, in fin che la sua cantilena, incomprensibile e monotona come le parole di un folle, ti lacrimi la Morte, dolce sorella, e tu a lei ti doni a simiglianza dell'esule che

ritorni e all'anima delle vecchie cose tutto se stesso affidi, colmo il cuore di una mortale felicità.'

('Oh, you should kneel and pray and sweat blood, novice, until Death, our sweet sister, weeps on you its singsong, as incomprehensible and monotonous as the words of a madman, and you should give yourself to it like an exile who is returning and entrusting his entire self to the soul of time-hallowed things, his heart brimming with a mortal happiness.')

Here the key expression is 'anima delle vecchie cose' because the road towards authenticity and self-fulfilment is a lyrico-memorial one for Corazzini and it consists in consolidating things poetically as part of oneself. This is why he indulges in a cult of what he himself calls 'le povere piccole cose' ('poor tiny things') and tries to make them correlatives of his moods.

The difficulties involved in attaining this consubstantiation of mood and object-symbol are examined in the *Poemetti in prosa* (1906). In 'Esortazione al fratello' quoted above the emphasis is still placed on the human being's self-sincerity and on an acceptance of one's contingent human condition. By contrast, in the 'Soliloquio delle cose' we are confronted with the other side of the coin, with the anguish of things which, after they have long become merged in a cohesive form of empathy with a human sensibility, find that they are slowly slipping back into that void of gratuitous subsisting which we have described earlier as the ground-state of cosmic absurdity. No doubt the basic procedures involved in such a *poesia delle cose* were derived by Corazzini from the French decadents and Pascoli; but we have nevertheless to make a clear distinction between his and Pascoli's form of empathy. For, whereas objects gradually tend with Pascoli to 'possess' their perceiver and absorb him into the mysterious atmospheres which their hallucinatory presence creates, with the crepuscular poet the flow of emotion is reversed: it no longer passes from objects to poet and seeks to implicate him in the situation of which they form part, but flows instead from the poet to certain objects which he himself selects as the necessary symbols for the configuration of his mood. In other words the crepuscular poet imposes his own emotive order on the external world, while the decadent one is often completely absorbed by its flux.

What then, we might ask, do the 'povere piccole cose' of Corazzini's prose-poems complain about? What powers do they feel that they are in danger of losing? They are afraid most of all of shedding their emotional relations with a single human soul and sinking back into the shadows of inanimacy or death. Their drama actually takes place in the room of a man who has departed forever. And with his absence his emotional aura also becomes diminished, to such an extent that the objects involved feel that they are no longer alive and part of him, but are regressing into a void of almost complete inanimacy:

> 'Qualche cosa in noi si schianta, qualche cosa che il nostro amico direbbe: cuore. Siamo delle vecchi vergini, chiuse nell'ombra come nella bara. E abbiamo i fiori. Egli avanti di andarsene, per sempre, lasciò sul piccolo letto nero delle violette agonizzanti. Disperatamente ci penetrò quel sottile alito e ci pensammo in una esile tomba di giovinetta, morta di amoroso segreto. Oh! come fu triste la perdita cotidiana inesorabile del povero profumo! E se ne andò come lui, con lui, per sempre. Noi non siamo che cose in una cosa: imagine terribilmente perfetta del Nulla.'

> ('Something within us has shattered, something which our friend would call: heart. We are aged virgins, enclosed in shadow as if in a bier. And we have flowers. Before going away for ever, he left on his little black bed some fading violets. Despairingly that subtle perfume entered into us and we thought we were in the narrow grave of a young girl who had died of secret love. Oh! how sad was the daily inexorable loss of that poor perfume. And it disappeared for ever like him, with him. We are only things within a thing: a perfect image of the Void.')

The bearing which this passage has on Corazzini's lyrical method is that it shows that he sees art as a struggle between the poet and his materials as he attempts to shape and define his moods. If he fails, his object-symbols simply lapse back into their original state of fragmented sense-impressions; while, if he succeeds, his poetry becomes interpretative simultaneously of external reality and of the inner qualities of his own sensibility. Such an attitude clearly makes Corazzini's type of empathy very different from that of the decadent poet's because, instead of being wholly absorbed by his sense-data, he succeeds in infusing the objects of his perceptions into his own elemental grief. As Montale's experience will later prove, this was a peculiar and necessary form of detachment which the modern poet's symbolism had to undergo before it could hope to rise to the level of emblematic representation. Broadly speaking, the essential feature of the technique lies in the fact that it injects into the imaginative substance of a lyrical composition an emotivity which is so complex and suggestive that it becomes expressive of a mood or state of mind in its organic totality. Yet precisely because Corazzini was aware of the difficulty of bringing such a transfiguration about, he quotes as one of the epigraphs he associates with this poem Hugo's telling phrase that 'les choses ont leur terrible "non possumus" ' ('things have their terrible "no further" '), and this was an artistic problem he was determined to overcome.

Needless to say, the kind of transfiguration of which we are speaking can only take place when the poet manages to complete the change-over from an 'allegorical' to a 'symbolic' manner of writing. During Corazzini's allegorical period objects still tended to remain as detached, sentimental elements in the texture of his verse, and this probably explains why the coffin-symbol has no analogical value in 'Follie', although it is already associated with a possible resurrection:

Io vi vidi tranquilla
in una bara morta,
e vi sognai risorta
e il sogno ancor m'assilla.

I saw you lying still in a coffin, dead, and I dreamt you were resurrected and the dream still dazzles me.

But in the course of time it loses its lesser decorative function as a part of a sentimental allegory of death and acquires a new and more intense form of suggestivity whose greater depth of insight indicates a parallel deepening of the poet's entire aesthetic manner.

The greater allusiveness of the symbol in Corazzini's work is first apparent in 'Invito', where the soul is depicted as being imprisoned in the body in the same way as the body is eventually imprisoned in the coffin. Likewise in 'Il cuore e la pioggia' the original image of the poet's childhood home is given a universal – almost an atavistic – dimension as it is gradually metamorphosed into a repository of fossilized memories. The house is envisaged, moreover, as a kind of tomb set in the degraded paradise of a 'muto giardino' ('silent garden'); and in this way it becomes a spatially restricted reliquary of faded hopes in the true crepuscular manner. Such restrictiveness is again evoked though a cult of lilliputian terms and attenuated sensations; but, unlike the early poem 'Un bacio', the somewhat simpering tone is now redeemed by a genuinely felt sense of dismay and foreboding:

O mia piccola dolce casa, vergine rossa
c'hai vergogna e ti celi in un manto di foglie
qua e là strappato, ancora nell'occhio si raccoglie
un pianto triste e il cuore prova una fredda scossa
s'avvenga che ripensi le tue diserte soglie,
il tuo giardino, la terra non rimossa
da tempo grande, come la terra d'una fossa,
la fossa ch'ogni mia dolce speranza accoglie.

O my tiny sweet home, a blushing virgin who is ashamed and hides herself in a mantle of leaves torn here and there, still in my eye there gathers a sad tear and my heart feels a cold shock should I happen to think again of your deserted threshold, your garden, the earth for long undug, like the earth on a grave, the grave where all my sweet hopes are gathered.

The coffin-symbol in the form of the 'fossa' is perhaps emotively negative here, but this was no doubt a necessary transformation after its earlier usage. More significantly, it is still surrounded in this context by that cloying use of diminutives and endearments which all the crepuscular poets employ to avoid the main issue before them: the problem of evolving a deeper association between their moods and the figurative language in which it is expressed. Although effective in its lyrical structure, 'Il cuore e la pioggia' thus continues to be a product of crepuscular conventionalism; and, if we need further proof that this is so, we have only to note the use of the colour red in the poem which, as a purely visual contrast, highlights by its opposition the pallor of the poet's languid mood of resignation.

Later a further deepening of Corazzini's understanding of the technique of spatial and emotional restriction gives his poetry much subtler resonances. And, as his *poesia delle piccole cose* becomes a category of his spirit, the coffin-symbol with its highly restrictive spatial dimensions is transformed into a symbol of hope and acts as a crucible in which his mind is fired by an atavistic insight into the nature of things. What at first appears to the poet, therefore, as a cosy and complacent dream of death soon takes on a deeper significance, because by ringing the changes on the coffin-symbol Corazzini endeavours to explore the emotions associated with death almost to a point beyond the limits of human perception. This is precisely what Ungaretti also attempts later; although he, as we shall see, went further and managed to convey through a heightened sense of death's resources a fully orphic perspective of the human predicament.

The coffin-symbol ultimately acquires its symbolic implication of hope in lyrics in the collection *Le aureole* (1905); and, although a poem like 'Sonetto della neve' conveys its sense of mystery and orphic regeneration through other symbols as well, this symbol nevertheless acts as a stimulus to an effective emotional repenetration of the kingdom of death. At first the poet combines a number of personal elements to form a chiaroscuro pattern in order to devise an emblematic landscape offering the promise of a sensuous salvation. Then, as the process culminates in an analogical image-chain, it creates a state of insight, of 'chiara morte' ('clear death'), through the refinement and gradual desubstantialization of concrete forms into symbolic aggregates.

In the first quatrain the colour-pattern no longer oscillates between white and red as it did in his early verse, but between 'bianco' ('white') and 'tetro' ('dark'), so that the interplay of light and shadow produces an atmosphere of intimate mystery. Simultaneously, too, the sharp contours of the real world are abolished by a deep and emotionally charged snowfall which envelopes the entire scene. A type of orphic empathy is thereby established between the poet and his landscape and he uses it to objectivize his mood. Indeed, it almost seems as if the snow is falling from the sky for the specific purpose of enduing the earth with a secret power of regeneration:

Nulla piú triste di quell'orto era,
nulla piú tetro di quel cielo morto
che disfaceva per il nudo orto
l'anima sua bianchissima e leggera.

Nothing was sadder than that garden, nothing darker than that dead sky which shed over the bare garden its light and pure white soul.

The promised transformation will naturally take place within one of Corazzini's by now typical garden-paradises; but first a few further remarks on the pictorial technique involved will perhaps be appropriate. The whole process of lyrical empathy, as we have hinted, evolves within the traditional orphic colour polarities of whiteness and darkness, and between these two rather impalpable limits the adjectival charge is always carefully graduated, both in a visual and ethical sense. The combination 'triste-tetro-morto' ('sad-dark-dead') represents the downward path of the senses and 'nudo-bianchissimo-leggera' ('bare-white-light') the upward path of the spirit. Moreover, through their interaction the real world slowly loses its concreteness and acquires overtones which connect it with that skeletal scenery which orphic poetry normally associates with the metaphysical problems of human destiny, as we shall see later in Campana's poetry.

In the second quatrain, on the other hand, a touch of allegory is still detectable in the mention of spring and regeneration, because the poet is probably drawing a connection between human existence and the cycle of dormancy and regeneration of seed in the ground. At least the emphasis laid on the purity of the offering of the snow, its maternal acceptance by the garden, and the latter's momentarily muted heart all seem to indicate a state of dormancy which proves a prelude to vigorous rebirth:

Maternamente coronò la sera
l'offerta pura e il muto cuore assorto
in ricevere il tenero conforto
quasi nova fiorisse primavera.

Maternally the evening crowned the pure offering and the sad heart absorbed in receiving the tender comfort as if a new spring were flowering.

However, the allegory is now so concealed that it acts simply as an attenuated background to the underlying implications of the verse, whose lyrical texture is already approaching the quality of an associative emblemism.

Afterwards the featureless wilderness made by the snow and its accompanying atmosphere of wintry silence – both of which appear to denote a state of suspended animation – tend to fade as the distant brightness of a new dawn drives away the orphic darkness of mere dormancy. In one of the poet's mature lyrics, 'Dopo', this kind of dawn is later referred to as an 'alba originale' ('dawn original') and has religious connotations suggesting a new awakening. Here, by contrast, it represents no more than a realistic psycho-sensuous revivification, brought about by a secret gestative process within the confined space of the bier:

> Ma poi che l'alba insidiò co' 'l lieve
> gesto la notte e, per l'usata via,
> sorrisa venne di sua luce chiara,
> parve celato come in una bara
> l'orto sopito di melanconia
> nella tetra dolcezza della neve.

But when the dawn undermined with its slight gesture the night and, along its accustomed path, came smiling with its clear light, the garden drowsy with melancholy seemed as if it were concealed in a bier, in the dark sweetness of the snow.

In these lines, in short, the coffin-symbol acquires a cultural quality arising from an extreme refinement of the Petrarchan tradition, with its quality of 'dolcezza'; and it is also well on its way to prompting those subtle resonances of an orphic nature it later possesses in the poetry of Ungaretti. But, although Ungaretti's name rises naturally to the lips at this point, we can also see the makings of the symbolic aggregate in the poem, especially in its imaginative transformation of a landscape. As we have indicated earlier, this is the technique for which Montale has since become renowned, yet it is already implied in Corazzini's cult of his 'povere piccole cose'. So, just like Montale's, we can also claim that his manner conforms to Anceschi's definition of a *poesia delle cose* ('poetry of things'), which the latter once described as 'un modo di fermare gli oggetti, di caricarli intensamente di emozioni, un modo di trasformare gli oggetti in equivalenti di determinate emozioni'[28] ('a way of crystallizing objects, of charging them intensely with emotion, a way of transforming objects into the equivalents of pre-determined emotions'). In point of fact the major symbols in the 'Sonetto della neve' support this definition because they are all so skilfully arranged that they represent by cross-reference and implication the entire teleological perspective of Corazzini's myth of a 'chiara morte'. From here on, therefore, he will test his symbols against an inner analogical keyboard before use, in order to see whether they mediate adequately between his lyrical situations and the overall mythology of death to which he now feels himself ever more closely bound.

The poet's finest symbolic productions – though few in number – appear in his last collections, in the *Piccolo libro inutile* and *Libro per la sera della domenica*, both published in 1906.[29] Although we can attribute their lyrical quality mostly to the gradual maturation of his symbols, the fact that the waning of his irony has now been definitely arrested is also not wholly without significance. In the more sensitive of his mature poems his irony is no doubt more subtly controlled than it was earlier and, in particular, it is never allowed to disrupt his underlying lyrical tone. With the result that he now shows himself capable of synchronizing his musical, rhythmical and imaginative elements so effectively that he raises the original fluidity of his style to a far more intense – though still perhaps slightly plaintive – level.

Before we proceed to examine the final integration of Corazzini's word-music with his symbolic structures, a few points about his rhythmical patterns need to be emphasized, for one of the principal ways in which he weaves the various strands of his lyricism together is through a sustained attempt to produce satisfying metrical equivalences. His importance in this field is that he was one of the first to attempt to use rhythmical effects to echo the temporal duration and lyrical transfiguration of his moods;[30] and, as he achieved greater and greater success in this direction, his poetry moved away from the conventions of the minor crepusculars (whose work was founded rhythmically on the languid repetitions of the *Poema paradisiaco*) towards a much more modern form of prosody.

Before we can discuss the problem meaningfully we need to define more closely the type of free verse about which we are speaking. There is a great difference between the *vers libre* practised in France and supposedly invented by Gustave Kahn and the Italian notion of the *verso libero*. The French form is something of a mystification and Marcel Raymond has indicated that 'le vers libre n'est (pas) parvenu . . . à se distinguer de la prose rythmée'[31] ('free verse has not succeeded . . . in distinguishing itself from rhythmical prose'). Moreover, if we accept Pius Servien's definition of the difference between prose and verse, to the effect that 'la prose représente un mouvement sonore libre, les vers un mouvement sonore contraint,'[32] ('prose represents a free movement of sounds, verse a constrained movement of sounds'), it immediately becomes clear that there are so few constraints in the *vers libre* that it inclines to the prosaic end of the rhythmical spectrum. This, by contrast, is far from being the case with free verse in the Italian sense, at least until the prose-poems of the Vocian period appeared. Instead, the Italian conception of the *verso libero* (even with the futurists) remains much closer to traditional prosody. Such is also the case with the crepuscular poets, because their adaption of the idea of free verse was rarely anything more startling than a series of perfectly acceptable poetic lines whose innovations lay in their distribution within the stanza or in their varying inflections and length; and both procedures were intended to articulate the pangs of conscience experienced by the poet as he wrote. In Corazzini's case the rhythmical quality of his early verse perhaps conforms to this ideal only in externals, despite Donini's strong advocacy of the prosody of poems like 'La tipografia abbandonata'; but by the time we reach mature poems such as the eponymous lyric in 'Sera della domenica' we cannot fail to notice the deployment of a much more flexible form of *verso libero*. Here the novelty does not lie so much in the rhythmical beat, although the *sdrucciolo* (sliding or antepenultimate) stress is clearly important, as in the varied articulation of the sense-groups within the stanza. Their fluctuation in length and frequent lack of correspondence with external, typographical arrangements are the essential features which combine to produce a novel form of prosody. So in this lyric particularly we find a fully developed twentieth-century rhythmical structure which attempts to echo in its varying cadences the trepidation of the poet's forsaken heart:

Ora che li organi
di Barberia singhiozzano al crepuscolo
li ultimi balli e le ultime canzoni
ancora una volta, quasi una paura
folle di rimanere
soli nell'imminente ombra li tenga . . .

Now that the barrel-organs sigh at twilight the last dance-tunes and the last songs once again, almost a wild fear of remaining alone in the growing darkness grips them . . .

Even this brief passage taken from a much longer sequence shows how the antepenultimate stresses, the dying falls of the melody, and the frequent enjambements combine to create a metrical configuration which reproduces on an auditory level the melancholy nonchalance of Corazzini's dominant mood. Accordingly, one need hardly add that once he had perfected such a subtle prosodic manner he rarely looked back to the faded conventions he had used in his earlier poetry. So here, once again, our standpoint coincides with that of Donini who acutely emphasizes the underlying similarity between the present poet's lyrical procedures and those of his hermetic successors.[33]

At this point we can revert to our main thesis that Corazzini's handling of the *verso libero* was part and parcel of his wider design to fuse together all the various elements which make up his lyrical tone. As we have stressed repeatedly, his finest poems are those that relate word-music to symbolic content, and in this regard Donini notes that whenever he abandons conventional crepuscular rhetoric for an authentic symbolic realism 'gli si affluano le immagini, prendono una maggiore evidenza le sue figure, e i suoi pallidi personaggi, e nascono dei simboli suggestivi, poeticissimi'[34] ('images flow towards him, his figures acquire a greater definition, as do his pale characters, and suggestive, intensely poetic symbols are created').

The poem which best illustrates this kind of synthesis is 'Per organo di Barberia'. It raises the hurdy-gurdy to the level of a symbol of the merry-go-round of life:

Elemosina triste
di vecchie arie sperdute,
vanità di un'offerta
che nessuno raccoglie!
Primavera di foglie
in una via deserta!
Poveri ritornelli
che passano e ripassano
e sono come uccelli
di un cielo musicale!
Ariette d'ospedale
che sembra domandino
un'eco in elemosina!

Vedi: nessuno ascolta.
Sfogli la tua tristezza
monotona davanti
alla piccola casa
provinciale che dorme;
singhiozzi quel tuo brindisi
folle di agonizzanti
una seconda volta,
ritorni su' tuoi pianti
ostinati di povero
fanciullo incontentato,
e nessuno ti ascolta.

Sad alms of scattered, old-fashioned ditties, the vanity of an offering which no one accepts! A springful of leaves in a deserted street! Poor refrains which pass and pass again, and seem like birds in a musical sky! Hospital ditties which seem to ask for an echo in alms! You see: no one is listening. You leaf through your tiresome sadness in front of the drowsing little provincial house; you sob out that wild toast of dying men for a second time, return to your obstinate laments of a poor discontented child, and no one listens to you.

Although the meaning of this poem may seem straightforward, behind its apparent simplicity it deals with two fundamental issues in human existence: its terrifying ephemerality and the even greater transiency of the cultural patterns and fashions which condition the sensibility of individual artists. Its tension, in fact, results from Corazzini's observation that these two dominant processes can fall out of step. Whenever they do so, the individual tends to become a living fossil in the cultural sense even before his death makes the implications of his alienation irrelevant.

Around the poem's archetypal images there also gravitates a whole galaxy of subsidiary objects or 'povere piccole cose' intended to reveal the deeper implications of the poet's mood. Moreover, all the lyrical effects are enhanced by means of a telescopic method of image-creation, through which symbols acquire a train of undertones by flashbacks to similar combinations evoked in the past. This may be illustrated in the image of a springful of leaves, because its cumulative associations (as seen in earlier poems) provide it with additional symbolic depth and significance. The same thing may be said about all the other archetypes employed, so that by examining these symbols closely we can gain some understanding of how Corazzini – and indeed most other modern poets – fuse together their themes, symbols and allusive musical qualities.

The first point to be noted is that the barrel-organist's repertoire is composed of a number of old-fashioned tunes; yet these melodies, while being evocative of a sentimental past to be associated with Gozzano's 'buone cose di pessimo gusto' ('good things of execrable taste'), are nevertheless irrelevant to the new cultural ethos emerging in the poem. Even the image of the deserted street and its old-world gaiety symbolizes a plaintive appeal for sympathy and alms. Similarly, the poet himself shows that he has an understanding of the barrel-organist's alienated state of mind, for in part he too feels himself conditioned by the illusory security of outmoded aesthetic standards. Hence the fading hopes expressed by many of the ditties stir memories in both their hearts and these memories are cruelly juxtaposed with the image of an unresponsive wilderness, the deserted street itself. Within this sonorous void the songs of both protagonists seem like flowers wasting their sweetness on the desert air. All they achieve is the evocation of an artificial world encapsulated in the image of birds soaring toward some fossilized musical heaven; and the result is a gradual corrosion of any appetite for life which makes even the tunes themselves seem sickly and feckless. Finally, the stanza ends on a note of sombre melancholy and despair, again depicting a mood of deepseated alienation.

In the second stanza the cold light of reality enters and it immediately shatters the iridescent sphere of the barrel-organist's self-nurtured illusions. The outside world's indifference to his fate is mirrored in the image of the sleepy provincial house, recalling once more the fossilizing of the poet's memories in the symbol of his birthplace in 'Il cuore e la pioggia'. Its sheer unresponsiveness has an immediate effect on the nature of his song: it makes his word-music sound petulant, melodramatic and splenetic as he doggedly persists in repeating these anguished 'toasts' of yesteryear before the unheeding ears of a public with whom they have lost their powers of communication. The last stage in the drama is consequently all too predictable: the childlike music-maker, not unlike the poet, is completely abandoned to his fate; and, as his music fades away into oblivion like the unsatisfied desires of infancy, we are led to imagine that he too descends to the grave, unwept and unsung, scarcely noticed by the changing world about him.

Again the metrical invention of the composition can by no means be ignored. As we have already suggested, the lyric achieves virtually for the first time in crepuscular verse the Mallarmean ideal of an inner word-music which follows the articulation of the poet's conscience and unifies the various elements of his sensibility. In this respect we have only to refer to the fact that the false gaiety of the barrel-organist's tunes is reinforced on the prosodic level by the many 'parole sdrucciole' in the two stanzas, which almost create the lively effect of a modern *cursus velox*. As a result, Fontana was prompted to observe that eventually 'la métrique de Corazzini perdra ce qu'elle possédait jusqu'alors de mélodique, et la mélodie nouvelle suivra toutes les évolutions de l'âme'[35] ('the metrics of Corazzini will lose what it once possessed of melodiousness, and his new melody will follow all the convolutions of his soul'). No doubt what the French critic is really at pains to stress in these words is the distinction which exists between personal and conventional melodic notations within the crepuscular ethos, a feature which first forces itself upon our attention in Corazzini's relatively small number of mature poems. In one of them, at least, it seems as if that orphic vision of life to which he had aspired from the outset of his career had at last come within his grasp. But unfortunately this poem, 'La morte di Tantalo', was only completed shortly before his death and so he had no opportunity of consolidating the new type of symbolism which it so clearly displays.[36]

What is the message contained in the lyric? It is the tantalizing one of an orphic subsisting beyond death, attained through the purification of earthly love. All the separate elements of the poet's orphic insight seem to have fused together in its composition, but its weakness lies in the relative lack of any references back to previous imagery and the subsequent difficulties of interpretation which result from such a dramatic change of direction. Even so, the central archetype of the garden-paradise is again prominently featured and at times we seem to be reverting to the paradise lost of biblical memory. Likewise the paradise eventually regained has the humanist clarity of a Leopardian moonlight scene about it, and it is existential and perennial in quality containing none of the idealizing tendencies still implicit in the Gozzanian daguerrotype:

Assaporammo tutta la notte
i meravigliosi grappoli.
Bevemmo l'acqua d'oro,
e l'alba ci trovo seduti
sull'orlo della fontana
nella vigna non piú d'oro.

O dolce mio amore,
confessa al viandante
che non abbiamo saputo morire
negandoci il frutto saporoso
e l'acqua d'oro, come la luna.

E aggiungi che non morremo piú
e che andremo per la vita
errando per sempre.

We tasted all night long the wonderful grape-clusters. We drank the golden water, and dawn caught us sitting on the edge of the fountain in a vineyard no longer of gold. O my sweet love, confess to the passer-by that we did not know how to die by denying ourselves the tasty fruit and the golden water, like the moon. And add that we shall no longer die and shall go through life wandering for ever.

These lines are only capable of interpretation in the light of later lyrical developments in twentieth-century poetry. But they are already expressive of a modern orphism in embryo and their meaning can perhaps be paraphrased as follows: 'We tasted during our whole existence (*notte*) the rich fruits of experience (*grappoli*). We drank life to the lees (*l'acqua d'oro*) and the dawn of a higher state of consciousness (*alba*) found us meditating near the fountain (of Mnemosyne?) in the skeletal world of Hades (*nella vigna non piú d'oro*). O my sweet love, confess to the passer-by that we could not contemplate any kind of 'ideal' death by denying ourselves the fruits of existence and the golden water of life. And add that we shall now never die but linger memorially in the human consciousness for ever.' This is clearly the consummation of the marriage of the ancient orphic myth of absolute memorial insight with a modernized existential myth of Tantalus and his infinite thirst for experience. It is to be noted, however, that whereas in the myth of Tantalus the waters always receded at his feet and the grapes hung just out of reach above his head, in the Corazzinian version the fruit and the waters are both enjoyed. They are made 'absolute' emotionally, that is, by becoming part of the protagonists' personalities and are expressive of a perennial sphere of 'contingent eternity' to which poets like Campana and the hermetic writers later aspire. Likewise the whole atmosphere is expressed emblematically in a modern orphic idiom in which word-music and symbolism are subtly interfused. In consequence, the lyrical flow no longer requires the conceptual statements of a worn-out allegorical method of transfiguration to convey its meaning.

In the light of these tremendous aesthetic advances it is clearly impossible to uphold Spagnoletti's contention that the innovations of the crepuscular writers are wholly illusory, despite the large amount of decadent detritus which appears in their work. We have to admit, of course, that the process of liberation from the earlier school's conventions was a tortuous one, as our excursion into Corazzini's poetic workshop has shown; but it is only the minor crepusculars like Chiaves, Moretti or Martini who fail to free themselves eventually from mimetic writing: major ones like Novaro or Corazzini himself foreshadow in their lyricism genuine qualitative changes in the modern sensibility. Since these changes tend to be orphic and symbolic in nature, they probably account for the residual crepuscularism which we find even in the inspiration of the majority of the hermetic writers.

CHAPTER V

The Vocian Poets: Clemente Rebora and Dino Campana

Through its very complexity and the breadth of its cultural range the Vocian period offers us an embarrassingly wide choice in our attempt to characterize its main trends. This is largely because all the well-known poets of the time – Palazzeschi, Jahier, Onofri, Soffici and others – contributed in their own particular ways to the literary revolution which it initiated. But, on reflection, and especially if we bear in mind the distinguishing feature of Vocian practice defined by G. Titta Rosa as the creation of a 'realtà morale vissuta'[1] ('lived moral reality'), the field becomes somewhat narrower and two specific writers, Clemente Rebora and Dino Campana, stand out among all the rest as symbols of its inner aspirations. Oddly enough, these poets were among the least committed of the group. Nevertheless Rebora's tortured religious outlook now appears in retrospect to be the very incarnation of the moral and spiritual principles which the movement postulated as the motive force behind its development of fresh aesthetic values, while Campana's attitudes – although he was perhaps even more of a marginal figure than Rebora[2] – similarly tend to essentialize the *Voce letteraria*'s glorification of the 'fatto letterario' ('literary factor') above all extra-literary considerations. In order to reduce our inquiry into Vocian aesthetics to manageable proportions, therefore, we shall confine ourselves at present to an examination of its impact upon the minds and sensibilities of these two poets.

As a preliminary, we should perhaps remind ourselves briefly of the cultural situation prevailing at the time. Although the intense literary and philosophical agitation stirred up by the *Leonardo* at the turn of the century had already begun to bear fruit, the early numbers of *La Voce* nevertheless opened up several completely new fields of aesthetic and sociological inquiry. This renewed ferment – by substituting a far more insistent and compelling cultural atmosphere for the highly attenuated and barely understood existential anguish of the crepuscular writers – gradually disrupted the entire fabric of Italian literary life and forced the artist to leave the comforts of his ivory tower and consider afresh the problems arising from his relationship with a dynamic and rapidly evolving society.

Needless to say, the problems of social adjustment alone were more than sufficient to preoccupy the minds of most of the writers contributing to the review; but Rebora's social adjustment was further complicated by another problem which largely overshadowed it – the problem of the poet's relations with his God. Likewise, an apparently extraneous problem – the link between his outlook and the orphism of the pre-Socratic philosophers – tended to fill the canvas of Campana's poetic vision. So in the last resort it seems as if these two poets were really casting about in the quicksands of existence for some theological, ethical and aesthetic solutions which would allow them to relate the contingent experience of the present moment to the eternal values of the European cultural tradition. Just how far they succeeded in achieving this aim it will now be our intention to assess.

Clemente Rebora

From the outset of his career ethical and theological problems form a considerable part of Rebora's field of investigation, although even in his early poetry he was fully aware of the fact that art amounted to something more than philosophical speculation. In a sense the difficulties he encountered in his musical studies in his youth may be regarded as analogous to those he was later to encounter in his lyricism. Of his musical ability he wrote at the time: 'Sono nella condizione di dover *sillabare* . . . mentre è nell'anima un prodigio di suoni che non posso e non potrò mai *esteriorizzare*. S'io riescirò a vincere la noia invincibile dei principi, a guadagnare il mio strumento col quale operare, non mi potrò piú assolutamente lagnar di me stesso. E forse, presto mi inoltrerò nel cuore stesso della musica, nell'armonia. Avrò le doti e le intuizioni necessarie? O il mio mare non darà una goccia alla mia sete?'[3] ('I am in the position of having to *play my scales* . . . while there is in my soul a profusion of sounds that I cannot and shall never be able to *exteriorize*. If I can ever manage to overcome the overwhelming boredom of first principles, to master the instrument through which I work, I shall no longer be able to complain about myself in any absolute sense. And perhaps I shall soon enter into the very heart of music, into harmony. Shall I have sufficient talent and intuition? Or will my sea not yield a single drop to slake my thirst?'). Already then his artistic problem was one of control, of instrumentation, rather than a lack of enthusiasm or inspiration. What he realized he had been unable to achieve initially was the transformation of his free-flowing concrete imagery and passionate emotional vitality into the ordered spirituality of art, and he acknowledged the fact in the following words: 'Se io ne posseggo una, è mia dottrina la "scienza dell'amore" alla maniera che l'intende Socrate o Platone: cioè l'intuito spirituale delle cose; ma nel concreto, ahimè!'[4] ('If I possess a doctrine at all, mine is the "science of love" after the fashion that Plato and Socrates understood it: that is, a spiritual intuition of things; but in the concrete, alas!'). We need hardly add that the combination of his titanic feelings and high religious seriousness soon created tremendous tensions within his sensibility, the result of which was a soul-searing anguish of the kind characterized by his first collection of verse, the *Frammenti lirici* (1913). In this work Rebora's self-torment is clearly generated by the clash between the imperious demands of his senses and the aspirations of his spirit, and it unfolds as a drama of conflicting desires whose paradoxes he spends the whole of his lifetime trying to resolve. Indeed, as his brother Piero once noted, the very intensity of his theological doubts together with the force of his pent-up moralizing fervour gave rise to a 'moderno religioso esistenzialismo jacoponico'[5] ('modern religious Jacoponian existentialism'); and its purpose was virtually to compel the underlying light of the divine spirit to illuminate the world by shining through the very opaqueness of its material forms.

What then was the real nature of Rebora's faith? One thing at least remains abundantly clear: it was no abstract view of reality as an inert mass of lifeless matter overtopped by a skein of metaphysical relations which the poet sought mysteriously to fuse together to form a pattern of idealistic images. On the contrary, his work was so adherent to the tactile qualities of the living world about him that Montale once defined his religion as a vision 'tutta nutrita di succhi terrestri, di una fede attivistica che fu detta mazziniana e piú tardi persino tolstoiana'[6] ('nurtured entirely on terrestrial humours, an activist faith which was called Mazzinian and later even Tolstoyan'). His lyrical manner in other words possessed not only a hard core of thought, but also a heavy emotional charge: one which at times amounted to a virtual passion for the real. This explains why his religious feelings are more adaptable to poetic treatment than any abstract, doctrinal approach would have been, although it has also to be conceded that theological and ratiocinatory modes later tend to gain the upper hand in his work and cause a gradual diminution of its sensory impact.

In fact, salvation only seemed possible to the young Rebora as a result of a constant participation in the sufferings of mankind, and he rushed headlong into a life of imaginative sensuousness, confident that nothing less than a comprehensive understanding of all the vicissitudes of human experience would provide him with the means for an authentic transcendence of original sin. In the course of time the validity of this approach became a veritable article of faith and he once described his spiritual evolution as consisting of 'una certezza di bontà operosa, verso un'azione di fede nel mondo' [7] ('a certainty of committed goodness, towards an act of faith in the world'). In his early verse, however, the true quality of his work-a-day goodness is somewhat obscured by the very depth of his passion for things and sensations. On some occasions a heavy emotional charge not only informs but even tends to blunt in Dannunzian fashion his responses to his lyrical situations; and this is especially the case when he aims at mirroring in his imagery the dark seething of instinctive forces. Moreover, because he always applied theological standards in the end to his interpretations of experience, his general attitude towards existence proves to be one of love-hate. Normally, he envisages life as an attractive but labyrinthine state of depravity, in which the very fabric of human experience pulsates with a diabolical rhythm; and this rhythm is normally held together by the double thread of sin and ignorance. His poetic approach thus acts as a foil to the opposite elements highlighted in D'Annunzio's *Laus vitae* and contains an equally powerful lyrical fervour:

L'egual vita diversa urge intorno;
Cerco e non trovo e m'avvio
Nell'incessante suo moto:
A secondarlo par uso o ventura,
Ma dentro fa paura.
Perde, chi scruta,
L'irrevocabil presente;
Né i melliflui abbandoni
Né l'oblioso incanto
Dell'ora il ferreo bàttito concede. [8]

A life both similar and diverse stirs all about me; I seek and do not find and I labour on in its incessant motion: it seems that custom or chance favours it, but deep within it causes fear. Whoever scrutinizes it loses the irrevocable present; and the iron-beat of time concedes neither mellifluous languors nor oblivion-laden enchantments.

From so paradoxical an attitude the dynamics of Rebora's faith rises plainly for all to see: it is a faith in a poetic vision which fills him with a desire for regeneration and at the same time for a special, sensuous communion with God's divine aims:

Se a me fusto è l'eterno,
Fronda la storia e patria il fiore,
Pur vorrei mutar da radice
La mia linfa nel vivido tutto
E con alterno vigor felice
Suggere il sole e prodigar il frutto . . .[9]

Though for me the eternal be a stalk, history foliage, and my fatherland a flower, I would still wish to change from the very root my sap in this vivid universe and with a happy alternating vigour suck in the sun and teem with fruit . . .

In place of the bewilderment and pessimism of the decadents he consequently displays a positive attitude towards the senses, and his sensory perceptions play a significant part in elaborating his transcendent view of beatitude. Indeed, it is only through their mediation that he can hope to hypostasize and so reconcile the flux of the external world with the hidden designs of God. By pinning his hopes from the outset on a wholly metaphorical transcendence of his situations – a process which looks beyond the Platonism dominant in Italian letters from Ficino's time onwards – he soon learned to exult in the changing world about him and glory even in its dialectic of creation and destruction, both attitudes which to poets less religiously inclined than himself have always been a source of despair:

Nel vortice m'esalto della lotta
Che lusinga e s'indraca
E concrea e distrugge.[10]

I exult in the vortex of the struggle which soothes and breathes fire, concreates and destroys.

Such utterances with their harsh interplay of plosives, of gutturals and sibilants can perhaps be considered a belief in the sanctity and finality of cosmic processes; and it is eventually around his profound faith in Christian salvation that all Rebora's imagery tends to gravitate. Likewise he draws from this belief not only the entire range of his aesthetic effects, but also his powers of suggestion and of lyrical cohesion.

His sense of exultation in God's creation naturally could not be expressed in anything less than a torrent of colourful images; and, granted the neo-futurist tastes of the day, most of his metaphors are inclined to be richly baroque in quality. Their distinctive feature is a white-hot emotional intensity springing from the poet's tactile delight in the solidity, simplicity and even at times the incongruity, of his object-symbols. By using his image-chains as stepping-stones in an arduous ascent towards a vision of God's glory, he manages to endue his poems with a form of concrete insight directly proportional to his efforts at obtaining a clearer understanding of divine processes. Their implications range far beyond the material objects serving as their points of departure; and, since the procedures he adopts are cumulative in their effects, whenever he finally reaches a peak of religious fervour he writes like a man possessed by divine inspiration.

The anguished doubt to which he sometimes fell victim is also existential in quality. It is largely to be identified with that restless Christian anguish which has gripped the minds of most religious poets in Europe ever since the Fathers of the Church cast aside the unified mythology advocated by Plotinus and replaced it with the separate, but interrelated, worlds of the creature and the Creator. Precisely because its source is logical and metaphysical, its underlying presence endures throughout the whole span of Rebora's life; and, while its effects are diminished in intensity by occasional miracles of faith, its antinomies are in all essentials so deeply rooted in his being that they can only finally be overcome by death.

The way in which he justifies his moments of doubt serve to confirm us in our assumption of their logical and theological origin. On this point he is completely traditional and attributes the waywardness of his feelings to the all-pervasiveness of original sin. As a result, the violence and insidiousness of his senses are reflected in scenes of tortured beauty, like the storm described in 'Bufera' which is virtually a cacophonous hymn to Satan:

Viene un vento di bufera
Velocissimo, e scoppia
In un fragore di grandine.
Anche tu, immortal natura,
Perdesti oggi l'ineffabile
Saggezza: lode a Satana!
Ma dopo? Uguale a te,
Non a me, tornerà il tempo.

A swift stormy wind comes and bursts in a shattering shower of hail. Even you, immortal nature, have lost today your ineffable wisdom: praise be to Satan! But after? Similar to you, not to me, the weather will return.

He even suggests in 'Soffrire' that the secret of the truly Christian life is to adhere consciously to this pattern of universal flux, though without ever allowing oneself to be carried away by the current:

. . . O realtà, essere in te vorrei:
Ma in un concreto e alterno
Svarïar perdo il senso
Del tuo vortice eterno.

. . . O reality, I would like to be within you: but in a concrete and fluctuating diversity I lose my sense of your eternal spiral.

Basically such an attitude is anti-romantic in quality, and the view of time it implies is a complete subversion of the kind of dreamlike perfection advocated by the romantics in their ideal of an eternal, sentimentalized present. In contrast with their somewhat static and falsely optimistic outlook, Rebora considers the stagnation of the single moment as the habitat of sin; so that he upturns the ideal of the romantic poets and suggests that it was their attempt to stop the clock, not the continuous cycle of growth, change and decay, which accounts for the contemporary enfeeblement of humanity's will-to-salvation. Since then the romantic dream proves ineffective, the only recourse he sees remaining for the modern poet is to cultivate a sense of complete participation in events and to involve himself inseparably in God's cosmic processes and designs. In so doing, a sense of belonging, not of alienation, will become an intimate part of his nature and he will gradually come to consider man's temporal condition as a humanized counterpart to cosmic change. In this sense the poet notes in 'Il consolatore' (through an apparent adaptation of 'Unanimist' views to religious beliefs) that

Io vivo con voglia nel tempo;
E del sangue di tutti è il mio polso.

I live with desire in time: and my pulse shares the blood of all.

Identification with the Will of God through its reflection in the material universe is, therefore, Rebora's innermost desire at this stage in his career.

The importance of such an outlook is that it is fundamentally dynamic and positive in quality and provides a modern flavour for his poetry. Accordingly, he proves to be one of the founders of the dominant contemporary view that art should deal with the concrete elements of life in their continual transformation, and his lyricism always tends to mediate between his spirit and his momentary sense-impressions. This means that he utterly rejects an aesthetic like Gozzano's which aims at providing little more than a storehouse of congealed memories. His conception of the sublime in art is instead the very opposite of such decadent views, insofar as it is receptive – not impermeable – to the tensions arising from social change; and for that reason he is always careful to distinguish between a superficial sensationalism of the kind practised by D'Annunzio and a true unison of the senses and the spirit. In his opinion D'Annunzio's art is a sheer indulgence in the chaos of sensation, a wallowing in the humus which feeds original sin; whereas his own method – though by no means divorced from the tactile qualities of the real world – is a continual attempt to illuminate imagery by irradiating it with the light of God's grace. In fact, in his art there arises a novel manner of responding to the sense-impressions of the external universe. For he considers all images evoked in the sphere of time to be anguish-torn, abstract and inert, until eventually they are placed in historical and religious perspective. Then alone do they mysteriously spring to life by being touched with that quality of divine insight associated with the secret rhythm of human destiny.

One example of the 'accidia' ('slothfulness') from which the modern poet suffers when he is confronted with the prison of the present is to be seen in 'Tempo'. In this lyric Rebora immediately establishes a connection between the modern feeling of 'noia' and original sin:

Apro finestre e porte –
Ma nulla non esce,
Non entra nessuno:
Inerte dentro,
Fuori l'aria è la pioggia.
Gocciole da un filo teso
Cadono tutte, a una scossa.

I open windows and doors – but nothing goes out, no one comes in: inert within, outside the air is damp with rain. Drops from a taut wire all fall, at a single tremor.

What he is striving to define here is the lowest common denominator of sin in our material existence on which he can subsequently build his ethical and theological system. As his experience of life increases, he tends to conflate this early ontological quest to determine the basis and limits of human depravity with a teleological investigation into human destiny; and at a certain point in his development he establishes a balance between the two processes by producing a remarkable type of 'metaphysical' poetry in the English meaning of the word. Needless to say, this balance is a precarious one and is not maintained for long. Indeed, its loss is particularly noticeable whenever he openly expresses his increasing concern with dogma and other religious problems in his later life. Nevertheless, for a short period in the twenties a fine equipoise between conceptual and imaginative elements was finally achieved in his religious poetry, before the crushing of his senses by his intellect led at length to the stifling rationalizations of his liturgical verse.

In the *Frammenti lirici*, however, Rebora's art was still in its first flush, and his powers of lyrical synthesis were so strong that the type of artistic sclerosis which we shall encounter later was scarcely more than a distant possibility. The very effectiveness of his early poetry may be attributed to the fact that he uses his imagination to 're-create' archetypal human situations in concrete and particularized circumstances. His manner of proceeding is in many respects similar to that adopted by Montale, even though their spiritual outlooks are poles apart; and, curiously, it often leads to equally interesting results. Essentially Rebora considers the aridity of the present to be the cause of the bondage of the human mind and points out the dangers of materialism and over-mechanization by representing them as non-cathartic yet 'condensed' states of 'noia'. In practice, these despairing evocations take the form of dense, baroque series of images in which concept fuses with symbol and symbol with ethical tone. An apt example is the ending of the same poem, 'Tempo', where the entire import of the lyric is crystallized into a handful of object-symbols – a few water-drops, tears and the 'filo teso' of life – all constantly buffeted by the blows of time:

Quello che fu non è piú,
Ciò che verrà se n'andrà,
Ma non esce non entra
Sempre teso il presente –
Gocciole lagrime
A una scossa del tempo.

That which once was is no more, what will come will go away, but the ever-taut present neither enters nor departs – water-drops, tears, at a single tremor of time.

In Rebora's view poetic catharsis is actually brought about by the personal 'dolore' of the individual interacting with the spiritual suffering of humanity as a whole. Consequently, he always emphasizes the efficacy of the activity of the single human conscience whose suffering has the peculiar effect of universalizing the implications of our contingency and providing it with a unique validity. As he explains in 'Cantico famigliare',

. . . nulla è vano
Se per qualcuno è dolore,

. . . nothing is vain if for someone it means pain,

so that for him human anguish proves to be a positive quality whenever it helps the sensibility in its attempts to make subtle readjustments in its dynamic relations with God, humanity, and the external world. The assessing of the strength and quality of these shifts in his own conscience at significant moments in his career is, therefore, Rebora's true artistic aim. His poetry, when seen in this light, may be considered as a struggle to transpose into imagery the metaphysical tensions and ethical aspirations of the Christian way of life.

The stark, expectant anguish of 'Tempo' shows us that he had failed to arrive at any overall synthesis at that point, although it also indicates the immense spiritual efforts that he was prepared to make to achieve one. His relative failure to integrate the various tensions in life explains why moments of distress and anxiety so greatly outnumber at the outset of his career his moments of joy. Indeed, even when poetic liberation does occur in the *Frammenti lirici*, it is frequently due to 'alchemistic' rather than to purely 'spiritual' effects. Here again, however, while Rebora was not averse to using the instruments fashioned by the French symbolist poets to increase his poetic suggestiveness, as a general rule his desire for sincerity of utterance prevented him from indulging in analogical writing for its own sake. He was, as Costanzo has stressed, fundamentally a traditionalist at heart[11] and tended to keep all technical innovations strictly under control. Perhaps then the only modern device to which we can really say he was addicted was the 'frammento' form itself. This, we recall, was a mode of composition which became exceedingly popular with the Vocian writers after the appearance of Soffici's translations of Rimbaud's works in 1911.

The kind of perceptiveness we associate with the 'frammento' is the sudden, fulminatory poetic flash, which was already implicit in Rimbaud's use of the English word *Illuminations* as the title for his prose-poems.[12] Equally the French poet's dislocated syntax had a deep influence on the 'genre' and caused the emotional charge to fall impressionistically upon the single word or phrase rather than to be more widely distributed over the entire lyrical discourse as is the case in classical art. In the course of time this process led to the breakdown of logical patterns altogether, and afterwards the 'frammento' had to rely on subtle associations and careful interrelationships between its various images for its cohesion. However, at that point the traditionalist Rebora rebelled and refused absolutely to abandon the classical convention of developing his poetry from thesis to conclusion by way of imaginative illustrations of all the intervening phases of his moods. Not only did he find such an approach a perfectly adequate one for his needs, but he also retained too much respect for the doctrine of tonal appropriateness to indulge in anything more than the occasional practice of anacoluthon or the cult of striking, fulminatory analogies. This does not mean that his work is totally devoid of disjointed similes and metaphors, far from it; but he always tended in the end to subordinate metaphorical vividness to rational exposition in his attempts to illuminate the arcana of the Divine Intelligence; and, as a result, his imaginative procedures appear to be largely propelled, if not entirely dominated, by his spiritual preconceptions.

On the other hand, he recognized that spiritual regeneration could only be accomplished by giving full expression to the emotions spontaneously arising within the human heart. In his view its responses to certain situations could even supply unshakeable proof of the immanence of a personal God, precisely because the imagery which it created had the emotive power to orchestrate sensations and produce forms of perceptive ecstasy. Such a belief explains his highly concrete and emotional representations of his Faith, which is frequently intensified by being mirrored in the very solidity and intractability of the physical world:

Tutta è mia casa la montagna, e sponda
Al desiderio il cielo azzurro porge;
Ineffabile pàlpita gioconda
L'estasi delle cose, e in me si accorge.[13]

The mountain is wholly my home, and the blue sky offers a landfall for my desires; ineffable and joyful beats the ecstasy of things, and is perceived within me.

Clearly, by giving such a concrete texture to his imagery, Rebora – like many other contemporary poets – moves away from the attenuated realism of the crepusculars, despite the fact that a nucleus of crepuscular procedures is still to be detected in his early verse. So, whereas the former school tended to suffer existence in a wholly passive manner and to keep its more violent sensations at arm's length, the present poet positively seizes life in both hands, extracts from it its charge of immanent spirit, and then translates that charge into a resilient poetic tension. In a way, however, his procedures are not so much a break with crepuscularism as a transcendence of its dominant tonalities, a bursting of its artificially drawn perceptive limits through the very urgency of his faith. He thus replaces its fastidious detachment with a form of overall involvement in the vicissitudes of human experience, a point which is underlined in the following stanzas from 'Sera al lago' where we see a neo-crepuscular tone disrupted from within by an explosive faith in the unifying powers of God:

Ma quasi fiume che rigiri lento,
In una blanda opacità di perla
L'ombra procede con liscio fermento:
E il plenilunio in luce sembra berla.

Pulsa l'eterno anelito e s'invera
Il creato, proteso in su la bocca;
Per non destar chi dorme, piú leggera
Il vecchio campanile l'ora scocca.

Yet like a river which meanders slowly, in a bland, pearly opaqueness the shadows proceed with a smooth agitation: and the full-moon seems to drink them with its light. The eternal yearning pulsates and all creation redeems itself, extended towards the river's mouth; so as not to arouse those who sleep, the aged belfry more softly strikes the hour.

The lyrical synthesis produced in this poem may be described as an attempted theology of the emotions; and it manifests itself artistically in the contrast made between the tranquillity of the scenic elements and the tremendous spiritual energy of the poet. The languorous melancholy and shadowy limpidity of the decadent age have consequently now disappeared for ever. In their place we discern a metaphysical clarity of outline virtually of Leopardian dimensions, suffused at every turn with the irrepressible power of Rebora's sense of salvation. The authenticity of this new tone is assured by the fact that it emerges spontaneously from within the previous tradition and is not, like futurism, an arbitrary imposition upon it from without. It is almost as if a gust of fresh air has finally blown away the musty perfumes and dank luxuriance of the decadent ethos and offered us a more modern and dynamic outlook on life.

Because Rebora is basically a discursive rather than an associative lyricist, the balance in his work tends ultimately to be inclined towards a rational outlook on life rather than towards spontaneous lyrical flashes. And yet, precisely because his poetry is intended to alleviate the gloom of Man's apparent damnation, it often manages to achieve through the magic of the senses remarkable figurative ascensions towards the light of the spirit. In the process analogies and emblematic aggregates play an important part, although not principally – as we have suggested before – by creating verbal alchemies in the symbolist manner. If we detect any 'chimismi' ('alchemies') at all in Rebora's case, we soon realize that all such artifices are stiffened by a powerful thread of logic. Occasionally, perhaps, an associative image may gain the upper hand, as in the following lines from 'Giorni dispersi':

Sciorinati giorni dispersi,
Cenci all'aria insaziabile . . .;

Unfurled, scattered days, rags in the insatiable air . . .;

but even here the early associative style of the opening lines later gives way to a well-developed rational discourse and the poem closes on a theological note. On the other hand, despite the logical unfolding of the lyric as a whole, its imagery still remains remarkable for its analogical appropriateness, as may be illustrated in the following passage:

Oh per l'umano divenir possente
certezza ineluttabile del vero,

ordisci, ordisci de' tuoi fili il panno
che saldamente nel tessuto è storia
e nel disegno eternamente è Dio.

O for powerful, human becoming, ineluctable certainty of truth, weave, weave the cloth from your threads, which is solidly history in texture and in design is eternally God.

Rebora's peculiar manner of compelling the abstract to seep through his concrete evocations disturbed some of his early critics who tended to stress the conceptual danger threatening his lyricism. But as long as he was able to leaven his doctrinal discourse with carefully drawn analogies of this type, his poetic flair remained dominant over his tortured metaphysics. In the above-quoted composition, in particular, he proves to be so successful in integrating his images with the conceptual pattern of his discourse that his lyrical exposition clearly transcends any mere statement of doctrine.

Broadly speaking, this expertise in handling the analogy is repeated with the object-symbol. But it needs nevertheless to be emphasized once more that this form of representation is still in a state of transition in Rebora's early work. The mode had not yet fully evolved away from Pascoli's and the crepusculars' *poesia delle piccole cose* ('poetry of little things') and often fails to achieve the lyrical stature associated with Montale's sterner *poesia dell'oggetto* ('poetry of the object'). Its effectiveness is nevertheless far greater than the symbolism of the impressionists, since symbolic aggregates are closely connected in Rebora's work with metaphysical atmospheres. Already, therefore, we find that certain selected object-symbols give body and vividness to the process of lyrical ascension, as may again be illustrated in the previously quoted early lyric, 'Sera al lago':

Nella sommersa pace il guardar mio
Sembra che in fiammei pòllini s'incieli,
E va nel tenue senso un crepolio
D'aria che a galla su per l'acqua levi;

Cammino in nimbo, e rarefatto inclino
Sinuoso al fosforico sentiero:
Ciò che men dissi, tutto m'è vicino;
E per l'amante cuor nulla è mistero.

In the sunken peace my glance seems to become heavenly in a flaming of pollen, and in my attenuated senses passes a quiver of air which, floating, rises from the water; I walk in a cloud, and, having become rarefied, I incline sinuously to the phosphorescent path: what I have least expressed is now close to me; and for the loving heart nothing is mystery.

An attraction for the hills and lakes of the poet's native Lombardy indeed persists throughout his life, and everywhere it stirs up half-forgotten memories and insights in his mind. To intensify their impact he often inserts into their distant charms a number of intensely concrete images such as the 'fiammei pòllini', 'un crepolio d'aria' and 'fosforico sentiero' seen here, all of which provoke powerful reactions in the reader's imagination. They also serve, incidentally, to internalize or intimize the situation by suggesting a progressive deepening of the poet's responses to reality. This ultimately leads to the climax of the poem in which he senses that God's love pervades all things.

Such hallucinatory aggregates thus cast further light upon Rebora's art. From them we deduce that he is searching for what Bachelard once called 'une ontologie de la profondeur humaine'[14] ('an ontology of human profundity'). Yet primarily his intention was not to use this sense of lyrical depth as an aesthetic justification for his craft, as other modern poets have done; he wished instead to upturn the contingent and purely artistic message of poetry and to illustrate by means of its very concreteness Man's teleological goal. His object was to demonstrate in other words that mankind's intended destiny is to ascend by means of the stepping-stones of the real to a purposeful identity with God. A prerequisite for the attainment of such a goal is an absolute 'possession' of the material world and its inner spirituality, because it is only by direct experience of the range and limits of the human condition that Man can finally hope to transcend it and reach a state of beatitude. No doubt it was with this thought in mind that Betocchi once asserted that 'la fine di possesso, nella poesia di Rebora, significa conoscere ...'[15] ('the aim of possession in Rebora's poetry signifies knowledge'). At bottom it was only by an intellectual and emotional 're-possession' of the universe that Rebora could finally convince himself of its inner sanctity. His artistry, accordingly, turns out to be an instrument for detecting *sensorially* the Divine Intelligence through the tactile qualities of things; and, wherever he feels capable of enduing the material world with God's illuminating grace, he attains to fresh heights of participatory fervour and to new pinnacles of religious faith.

The crests and troughs of his inspiration lead, of course, to a dialectic between opposing feelings of damnation and salvation, and this explains why his verse is never smooth or dulcet in tone. His word-music – reflecting as it does at all times the immensity of his spiritual struggle – is often, as we have already suggested, purposefully cacophonous, and its sharps and flats clearly militate against the achievement of any facile lyrical cadences. To overcome the effects of his jarring melodies Rebora thus sometimes creates a semi-allusive form of imagery within which a strange one-to-one equivalence is suggested between the absent world of the spirit and the turmoil of the senses. Eventually the growing influence of this process provides an underlying intellectual resilience and prevents his poetry from straying into the lyrical preserves of the *paroliberisti*, despite his often vastly extended series of comparisons. The effect of the process on his word-music is such that, as the crushing weight of the claustrophobic world of sin is temporarily lightened by spiritual insights, entire lyrics are freed from its disruptive cacophonies; and the poet's anguished tone then drops to a neo-crepuscular – though still spiritually robust – whisper, as is the case in 'Soffrire' where the everyday experiences of life merge with the secret presence of God:

Terso vigor di zampillo,
Quiete di riso tranquillo,
Paga blandizie del senso,
Labile cosa del tempo
Tra labili cose, io sia:.
Ma nell'urto del piccolo piede
Il passo divino ascoltare,
Tacita guida a chi crede.

Smooth vigour of a flash, the calm of a tranquil smile, the contented blandness of the senses, a transient object of time among transient objects let me be; but in the tread of a tiny foot, listen to the divine footstep, a silent guide to those who believe.

Here once again theological postulates lie concealed behind the blandishments of the senses; but they are at present portrayed through analogical and emotional gradations rather than by rational demonstration. Thus in moments of unwariness we might almost be led to believe that Rebora's emotions and not his metaphysics are the main regenerative forces in his lyrical manner. At least his faith in the redemptive value of feeling is amply supported by the following passage from 'Cuore' in which he sums up in emotio-conceptual form his entire religious humanism:

Quando si nutre il cuore
Un nulla è riso pieno,
Quando s'accende il cuore
Un nulla è ciel sereno:
Quando s'eleva il cuore
All'amoroso dono,
Non piú s'inventan gli uomini, ma sono.

When the heart is well nourished, a mere trifle is a fulsome smile, when the heart burns, a trifle is blue sky: when the heart rises to the gift of love, men are no longer evolving, but are.

Yet, even now, this momentary identity between his senses and his spirit presupposes a prior – if not habitual – dichotomy which becomes particularly marked in the *Canti anonimi* (1920-22).

In fact, the world of emotional relationships as opposed to the rational world was never more than half-open to Rebora, and therefore he was unable to resolve his deeper spiritual problems either by moments of impassioned participation in existence or by the cultivation of aesthetic alchemies. What more readily satisfied his ratiocinative cast of mind was a theological system, although once he had perfected it, his muse immediately tended to wither away and die. Clearly, then, we are much less interested in his finalistic pronouncements on life than in his searching investigation into all aspects of living before their ultimate theological formulation; and we are less moved by his eventual assertion of dogmatic certainties than by the hesitations and doubts which assailed him before they became articles of faith. In this respect the philosophical enigmas which confounded him in his early manhood are of particular importance, since they demonstrate his typically Vocian habit of facing up to problems in the hope of bringing order out of chaos. Although these problems range through the whole of his life's activities, we intend to confine ourselves here to two aspects of them only, his attitudes to love and society. At first they may seem to be somewhat marginal to his literary production, but they are notable pointers to the various stages of his psychological development; and they also throw light on the reasons which led him to make an eventual renunciation of the world.

Women play a muted, though significant, part in the poet's life, and Guglielminetti regards his early affection for his mother and his friendships with Ada Negri and Sibilla Aleramo as conclusive proof of his desire to consider various members of the opposite sex as mediators – or at least as help-mates – in his journey towards salvation.[16] This attitude persists both during and immediately after the First World War, because during that period he lived for a time with a young Russian pianist called Lydia Natus, with whom he experienced the joys and sorrows of an intimate emotional relationship. He actually addressed ten short lyrics to Lydia, but all but one of them were excluded from his collected works, until they were eventually published in 1959 by Marchione.[17] They mark perhaps three stages in the development of his love. The first attitude he strikes is one of frank sensuality mingled with a naïve tenderness, already suggestive of a transcendent purity:

Quando al mattino
Negli àttimi belli
Sorridi a me beata
Se ti guardo e schiudi
La pupilla ch'è baciata,
Vorrei lavarti il musino,
Volger dai tuoi capelli
Una treccia alla cintura
Con un fiocco tra i nastri,
Vestirti una montura
Fresca da ragazzetta:
Poi, la cartelletta,
La colazione nel cestino,
E con carezze di parola
Accompagnarti a scuola,
Dove il mio amore
Fosse il tuo candore.

When in the morning in your finest moments you smile contentedly at me, as I look at you and you open your eye which I kiss, I would like to wash your tiny face, unroll from your hair a tress down to your waist tying a knot among the ribbons, dress you in a fresh uniform like a little girl: then, with your satchel and lunch in a basket, and with caressing words accompany you to school, where my love would be your innocence.

The second shows the poet abandoning his mystico-absolutist outlook and allowing himself for a moment to slip into the sensuous darkness of an un-intellectualized emotional union:

Scendo con l'ombra
Slittando nei fiori
Verso la valle
Che ninna i monti;
M'inghirlanda
La donna che accorre,
Alta quanto un'occhiata,
Giusto al mio cuore.

I go down with the shadows, sliding among the flowers, towards the valley which lulls the mountains: the woman who runs up, as tall as my glancing eye, garlands me right to the heart.

But Rebora was not the type of person to be satisfied with this type of relationship for long without attaching to it unjustifiable moral and theo-logical superstructures. So in the third stage we find the two lovers slowly drifting apart, until the point was reached in 1919 when Lydia finally left Italy to take up residence in Paris.

The immediate impact of the break on the poet's sensibility was to drive him into a period of frenzied intellectual activity, during which he read Mazzini, the Christian mystics, Hegel, and many books on the religions of the Orient. At the same time he was a much sought-after lecturer, especially by the fashionable, upper-class ladies of Milan; and his lecturing activities prompted in 1926 a correspondence with the Countess Bici Rusconi. In these letters he defines the virtually 'orphic' and spiritually creative rôle he envisaged for woman in the modern world and explains that 'è piú mamma, ma proprio organicamente e positivamente, una creatura che viva secondo la legge di maternità della vita, come e quanto può, *mettendo alla luce le tenebre* che ha in sé e ha intorno, che non la femmina fisiologicamente genitrice . . .'[18] ('she is more of a mother, but even organically and positively, the woman who lives according to the law of maternity in life, bringing to the light as far as she is able, the darkness she has within and around herself, than the creature who is physiologically a progenitor. . .'). Whether the Countess showed full understanding of this attitude we do not know, but evidently Lydia did not. Hence, if we are to read back into the poet's relationship with her a similar attitude of mind, it is obvious that in the long term she found it insufficiently perceptive and emotionally enriching. Later, in fact, Rebora actually came to conceive of love in a wholly religious sense and attributed to his women-friends virtues which seem to border on a cult of mariolatry. Thus, in 1930, he was already able to consider one of his students as a kind of stilnovistic intermediary in his quest for salvation, observing: 'Erano almeno trent'anni che io, non educato all Fede, andavo cercando la via del Paradiso su tutte le deviazioni dell'inferno. E io penso che Lei è stata certamente una delle creature mosse dal Signore per aiutarmi a salvezza in un momento grave della mia vita. . .'[19] ('For at least thirty years, not having been brought up in the Faith, I wandered in search of the road to Paradise along all the highways and byways of Hell. And I think that you have been certainly one of the creatures inspired by our Lord to help me towards salvation in a grave moment in my life . . .') Probably, therefore, his love-affair with Lydia should be regarded merely as a sensuous interlude in the poet's otherwise continual search for a platonic relationship offering nothing more than a vague spiritual guidance.

Even so, his perplexity before the implications of emotional love was hardly sufficient in itself to have caused him to make an ultimate renunciation of the world. Social pressures and above all moral tensions also played a significant part. As a convinced follower of Mazzini he tended to see the world through a veil of idealistic humanism – one in which physical and ethical forces acted as thesis and antithesis in a process of Hegelian synthesis of truly apocalyptic proportions. Needless to say, this religious vision grew progressively stronger with the passage of time, and already in a letter to his brother Piero in 1922 he expressed his current outlook in the form of philosophy of social action, whose ultimate sanction was mankind's re-unification with God through the acquisition of knowledge: '*L'Educatore* è Iddio e noi dobbiamo essere solo i realizzatori, e cominciare ad aiutare la realizzazione della Vita che attende tutti nel progresso del tempo . . .'[20] ('*The Educator* is God and we should only be his agents, and begin to help the flowering of Life that awaits us all in the fullness of time . . .')

The converse of this doctrine was also true in his opinion. Man should not overstep the bounds of Nature in his immediate aspirations, because it is only when he has shunned any attempt to transgress that the purposive design of God's Will can become illuminated through human toil. One of the gravest acts of transgression perpetrated by modern Man was, for Rebora, his cult of mechanization. At the time when he was writing, we recall, scientific literature was already hinting at the prospect of the wholesale mechanization of human affairs. Yet the poet himself was totally opposed to any such behaviourist philosophy and claimed that it led to a peculiarly insidious form of damnation – mechanistic determinism. Even by moving towards it, modern science was in his eyes becoming little less than blasphemous. Not only was it upsetting the divinely ordered harmony between man and his environment, it was also denying the exercise of free-will by blocking the path towards creative self-transcendence. So he denounced the whole process in a Guinizellian type of scientific analogy, while simultaneously upholding an ideal akin to Bergson's life-force, which, in 'Scienza vince natura', he regards as acting as a pious channel for progress throughout the ages:

Scienza vince natura:
Quasi in corrente acqua pura e immonda,
Dei secoli l'errore
E la virtú nell'atto si feconda;
. . . .

Affiorar sento l'ignota bontà
Che nei millenni trasse l'uom dal bruto,
E nell'urto civil, per la vicenda
D'ogni dí, scopro il fremito d'un Dio.

Science conquers nature: as in a current filthy and pure water, the sin of the ages and its virtues nurture each other in action . . . I feel the unacknowledged goodness rising, which in the millennia lifted man above the beast, and in the social struggle, through the affairs of everyday life, I discover the quivering of God.

Rebora is indeed at his most socially perceptive when describing the peculiar state of sin and transcendence which tends to rise from pitiless industrialization. At such moments the 'buon lavoro' ('good work') of the toiling masses appears to act as a counterweight to life's damnatory tendencies, and so in the same poem his description of workers setting out in the morning to work, although apocalyptic in tone and hinting at the kind of dragooning we find in the ant-hill or bee-hive, nevertheless ultimately suggests an eventual emergence of salvatory forces:

Oh per le vie all'alba
Fulmineo ridestarsi,
Quando – uccelli dei nidi cittadini –
Per l'aria dai camini
Vòlano le sirene
Negl'incensi del fumo
Chiamando al buon lavoro!

Oh the fulminatory stirring along the streets at dawn, when – like birds from city nests – the sirens pass through the air in the smoky incense, calling people from their hearths to wholesome work!

On the other hand, he contemplates society's frequent deviations from the true path of salvation on a broader front and suggests that social sins are particularly apt to proliferate in the modern world because they are aided and abetted by industrial techniques. In one sense, of course, he still acknowledges that all new skills and processes are a boon and that Man transcends his condition by eliminating the drudgery attached to the human lot in the ancient world[21]; but equally often modern technology puts a more soulless labour in its place, the repetitive drudgery of mass-production which destroys creativeness and initiative altogether. An appropriate symbol perhaps of this type of profanation is – to link his ideas back with his views on love – the debased, almost mechanical, sexual act. For, as the 'volgo in desiderio occhiuto' ('plebs in wide-eyed desire') becomes more and more bestialized, its sexual relationships are also cheapened and prove meaningless and mechanical. Finally the point is reached when the sexual act seems to dominate everything, yet at the same time it is reduced to the level of a futile conditioned reflex:

– Stanca si affretta l'età sverginata,
E tutto sa di coito! –[22]

– Wearily the deflowered age hastens on, and everything smacks of coitus! –

By universalizing this debasement the poet provides reasons for all the ills besetting modern society – from its symptomatic aridity to its complex neuroses and anxiety states. If then we consider the carnival in 'Fantasia di carnevale' to be a pageant symbolizing the various aspects of contemporary life, the following lines strike us as representing in all its horror the despair experienced by individuals who are forced to participate in a neurotic, materialistic society which does not possess any leavening of idealism:

Noi siam dell'inquieta brigata
E scontentezza ci guida:
Spietata alla gente è la sfida,
Ma dentro si accascia gemente.

We are the restless throng and discontent guides us: our challenge to people is pitiless, but inside ourselves we collapse, whining.

Broadly speaking, the present-day city is the place where Rebora sees the diabolical rhythm of sin reaching a crescendo. In its maw even the Idea, normally the fount of salvation, becomes corrupt and evil, and when he is in such moods he allows a strain of sarcasm to take possession of his mind. He then dismisses modern forms of morality in the following biting terms in 'Fantasia di Carnevale', XI:

Ai passanti innocenti
Scaglieremo le bombe
Colmeremo le tombe
Che la carie dell'ore ci aprí.
Del resto, il destino
Ha stomaco sano,
Per smaltire anche noi . . .

On innocent passers-by we shall hurl bombs, we shall fill the graves brimful, which the decay of the passing hours opened for us. Moreover, destiny has a strong enough maw to digest even us . . .

Yet despite his disillusionment, Rebora still remains basically Mazzinian at heart and sees the good eventually emerging from the social interaction of human passions and greed. Teleologically, in other words, mankind cannot seriously deviate from its Christian destiny, though evil and goodness will always subtly offset each other in the process of our regaining a state of innocence and beatitude.

During the twenties Rebora created novel technical procedures for forging his deeply felt emotional links with God. They largely consist of forms of metaphysical emblemism whose symbolic aggregates take his cult of a *poesia delle cose* a stage further than in his early verse. They operate in a vast existential universe of space and time, a sphere in which the young Rebora had earlier imagined all spiritual progress to evolve. Already in the *Frammenti lirici*, for instance, we note from time to time a macrocosmic dilation of imagery produced by various direct and indirect means. One such example is the opening of 'Salve' where we sense the immensity of midday emerging from a country scene:

Per le deserte strade alla campagna
Il sol schioccando si spámpana
Immane nel sovrano meriggio . . .

Along the deserted roads to the countryside the sun flaunts itself, cracking its whip, huge in the sovereignty of noon . . .

Equally, at the other end of the scale the microcosm is not ignored, and the intensity of anguish in poems like 'Grillo del focolare' indicates that there is a certain qualitative immensity even in the rasping song of the cricket:

Grillo del focolar
Rodi in fretta il tuo grigio dolore
Grillo del focolar
Ch'è vicin nuovo ardore.

Cricket on the hearth, you gnaw hastily at your grey sorrow, cricket on the hearth, for fresh ardour is close by.

The scaling of these elements is indeed carefully handled and a wide range of subtle perspectives is thereby gradually constructed.

Normally the background state against which the scaling of temporal and spatial elements is conducted is one of Christian anguish clearly illustrated in 'Dall'immagine tesa':

Dall'immagine tesa
Vigilo l'istante
Con imminenza di attesa –
E non aspetto nessuno.

From the taut image I survey the passing instant with the promise of expectancy – and I expect no one.

But at the end of the poem, despite the fact that the keyed-up expectancy of the poet is as intense as ever, his faith is so strong that he feels sure that he is living in a state of incipient redemption, as he anticipates apparently a Second Coming of Christ:

Ma deve venire,
Verrà se resisto
A sbocciare non visto,
Verrà d'improvviso
Quando meno l'avverto.
   Verrà quasi perdono.
Di quanto fa morire,
Verrà a farmi certo
Del suo e del mio tesoro,
Verrà come ristoro,
Delle mie e sue pene,
Verrà, forse già viene
   Il suo bisbiglio.

But he must come, he will come, if I persist in blossoming unseen, he will come unexpectedly, when I least anticipate it. Forgiveness, as it were, will come. Inasmuch as he causes death, he will come to assure me of his and my treasure, he will come as a reliever of my and his anguish, he will come, perhaps his whisper is already arriving.

Such faith is the outcome of a kind of spirito-spatial compression which we often encounter in his work and which can be said to reach complete fruition in poems like 'L'infinito riposa'. In that lyric Rebora transforms the landscape into a curious inner space composed of dynamic scenic features, in which a spatial restrictiveness, reminiscent of the crepuscular poets, at first provokes a compressive heaviness of the soul:

Non è piú su di un palmo
Oggi il ciel dalla terra:
Timido, opaco, calmo,
L'anima in ombra di poca aria serra.

Today the sky is no more than a palm's breadth above the earth: timid, opaque and calm, it compresses the soul in the shadow of a small airy space.

Yet, suddenly, this restrictive and oppressive weight is lifted by the poet's participation in life, and a Christian harmony is then attained in which a human rhythm gives meaningfulness to the cosmos:

In un volger lieve
L'infinito riposa:
La quotidiana e breve
Vicenda è il suon concorde d'ogni cosa.

Allor, sorto da ignote
Nicchie vapora piano
Un senso sopra note
Forme: e gioisce del suo ritmo umano.

The infinite rests in a gentle turning: the short, daily round is the harmonious sound of all things. Then, rising from unknown recesses, a sense slowly diffuses over well-known forms: and enjoys its human rhythm.

This particular kind of religious ecstasy is typical of the *Frammenti lirici*; but, later, in the *Canti anonimi* (1920-22) such ascensions through the senses are abandoned for a form of approach which is somewhat more meditative: one in which Rebora infuses into his lyrical procedures a resilient analogical element pointing the way towards a taut and highly intellectual, one might almost say an antithetical and aphoristic, style:

E giunge l'onda, ma non giunge il mare:
E ciascun flutto è nostro, che s'infrange,
E la distesa è sua, che permane.[23]

And the wave arrives, but the sea does not arrive: and each inflow is ours as it breaks, yet the expanse belongs to it, which remains.

The final outcome of this type of writing is a cult of ingenious baroque images whose disparate elements are forcibly yoked together to magnify and intensify the poet's feelings. A good illustration is the following description of psycho-sensuous harmony:

Facevan le fusa
I miei sensi, e zampilli i pensieri.[24]

My senses purred, and my thoughts were like water-spouts.

Such finely woven incongruities remind us more of the 'metaphysical' poets in England than of the Italian *Seicento*, although perhaps the immediate source of Rebora's wit was not so much Donne, Tesauro or Gracián[25] as the parallel tradition of the Lombard stylists at the turn of the century, especially the work of Carlo Dossi.[26] Whenever Dossi's style appears therefore to influence the poet, his analogies at once tend to become bold and arresting and his language takes on a distinctly northern flavour.

A case in point is 'Gira la trottola viva' where the normal geometrical pattern of relations associated with 'metaphysical' wit is combined with another device which Gamberini has described in Donne's case as a subtle blending of 'il sacro nel profano o del profano nel sacro'[27] ('the sacred in the profane or the profane in the sacred'). Donne's lyric 'The Flea' is the supreme illustration of the stratagem, but in the present poem the profane object chosen to bear the weight of the poet's symbolism is a child's top. Symbolically speaking, the top is made to stand for the Earth as it spins through space while the whip that drives it represents God. From this basic situation Rebora develops a number of ingenious images and analogical parallels which together underline the meaning of the poem. At first we are presented with an axiomatic description of the top's spinning which is so tautologically expressed that it reminds us again of the syllogistic chop-logic of a Guittone d'Arezzo:

Gira la trottola viva
Sotto la sferza, mercè la sferza;
Lasciata a sé giace priva,
Stretta alla terra, odiando la terra.

The living top spins beneath the whip, thanks to the whip; left to itself it lies helpless, flat upon the ground, hating the ground.

Then, after this deliberately laconic statement of the toy's motion, we see it in action. The impetus given to it by the whip is gradually deepened in significance by a clever conceit, one that could be described as the identification of the great multitude of forms and emotive tensions found in life with the colours on the top's surface; and all of them are unified into a single trascendent colour by the speed of its spinning:

Gira – e il mondo variopinto
Fonde in sua bianchezza
Tutti i contorni, tutti i colori;

Gira – e il mondo disunito
Fascia in sua purezza
Con tutti i cuori per tutti i giorni.

It spins – and the multi-coloured world melts into its whiteness all its configurations, all its colours; it spins – and it swathes the disunited world in its purity with all its hearts for every day.

In the last stanza this whole series of parallel images is finally fused together into a vision of God's cosmic design, so that the poet's Christian Faith is mirrored and subsumed in the top's incessant gyrations. Likewise, the various forces acting upon it are identified in the end with the all-embracing concept of Divine Love:

Vive la trottola e gira,
La sferza Iddio, la sferza è il tempo:
Cosí la trottola aspira
Dentro l'amore, verso l'eterno.

The top lives and spins, God whips it, the whip is time: thus the top aspires within love, towards the Eternal.

Naturally, poems of this kind represent the high-water mark of Rebora's inspiration, yet at the same time they hint at an impending crisis – one which later will lead to the poet's complete alienation from the world. As he plunges deeper and deeper into the study of a rigorously intellectualized theology, a form of emotional sclerosis seems to affect his sensibility and to exert a profound influence on the texture of his verse.

The *Poesie religiose* (1936-47) are accordingly marred by a cerebral type of inspiration and most of the collection has been classified by Bàrberi

Squarotti as 'le strutture date *ab aeterno* della preghiera'[28] ('the structures fixed *eternally* for prayer'). Much the same thing may be said of the *Canti dell'infermità* (1956) in which the following example of versified doctrine occurs:

Senza Confiteor non si sale Altare,
Magnificat conclude il Miserere
e il De profundis nel Te Deum ascende.[29]

Without the Confiteor no Altar can be mounted, the Magnificat rounds off the Miserere and the De profundis rises in the Te Deum.

Since verses of this type are fundamentally non-cathartic, we can assume that aesthetic problems had by now ceased to be the poet's central preoccupation and that the major activities in his life were prayer and other forms of religious devotion. Spasmodically, perhaps, he still succeeds in re-evoking in these collections the vibrant qualities of his genuine lyricism, although we only become conscious of them when we encounter isolated, concrete images leavening the anguish embedded in the very texture of his religious homilies.

One example of such concreteness, even though it is used for a clearly didactic purpose in the end, is the short poem 'La cima del frassino':

La cima del frassino
approva, disapprova
con lenta riprova
la vicenda del vento;
e in fine sempre afferma
il tendere massimo al cielo.

The top of the ash-tree approves, disapproves with a slow reproving the chance effects of the wind; and in the end always reasserts its fulsome striving towards heaven.

So, not surprisingly, because of his desire to impose an intellectual straitjacket upon his sense-impressions, new doubts now tend to emerge from beneath the surface of Rebora's verse. One of the most poignant is his feeling of having thrown away the substance of life for its shadow by limiting his participation in human affairs to a priestly and detached form of intellectualism. Indeed, basically the poet admits of no easy resignation, of no facile acceptance of the comforts of religion, even at the end of his life. Each spiritual gain he makes is always accompanied by further doubts and further anguish, and the point may be illustrated by the disillusionment expressed in the first of his *Epigrafi* where he revives an earlier image of putrefaction and deploys it with more despairing overtones than ever before:

Dopo aver agognato alle cime,
e perso vita per vivere sublime,
grazia m'è data di far da concime.

After having longed for the summit, and wasted life to live sublimely, the opportunity is granted me to act as manure.

Such stoic fortitude makes us wonder in the last resort whether Rebora, once he had fossilized his religious aspirations into dogma, ever managed to draw a more permanent comfort from his Christianity than he did from his aesthetics. Of his lyricism Carlo Bo notes that 'la poesia non poteva fornire a Rebora nessun elemento valido di sicurezza, di risoluzione. La poesia tutt'al piú lo aiutava a riconoscere la radice del dolore . . .'[30] ('poetry could not provide Rebora with any valid form of assurance, of solution. At most poetry helped him to recognize the root of anguish . . .'); and indeed at times, it seems, the same thing can be said of his religious beliefs. What is clear is that his renunciations and self-imposed asceticism ran directly counter to his temperament and tended to stifle not only his feeling for the sufferings of his fellow-men but also his sense of involvement in the real. Yet, in the same way as his humanity previously caused him to overstep the limits of aesthetic appropriateness in his early verse, so now it breaks through occasionally in his religious imagery in spite of all the doctrinal and liturgical barriers erected in its path. And it is these glimmers of his earlier fervour which provide the principal lyrical insights of his later collections.

★ ★ ★ ★ ★ ★

Rebora's language and lyrical technique also had a profound effect upon modern poetic diction, because he was one of the first poets to foresee the possibility of a new type of syntax – one which compromised between the iconoclasm of the futurists on the one hand and the jaded conventions of the neo-classicists on the other.[31] From the outset his language tends to be eclectic in quality and derives its stylistic effects from a wide range of sources, including the *trecento* lyricists, Foscolo, Leopardi and the late nineteenth-century Lombard stylists. The result is that his style proves to be highly literary and yet at the same time by no means lacking in vigour and spontaneity. Indeed, on occasion its power is such that even Montale once described his lyrical manner as a form of 'raptus espressivo'[32] ('expressive rapture').

Normally Rebora still strives to observe the rules of rational discourse despite his intense linguistic urgency; and so his occasional disregard for authority on the syntactic and idiomatic levels – while giving spice to his art – never becomes an all-absorbing preoccupation. Especially important is his ability to adapt and digest the various devices lying at hand in the literary ethos of his age, but without allowing them to disrupt his fiercely classical and traditional notions of lyrical structure. As an illustration of this point we have only to refer back to his uses of the analogy and emblem which, while undoubtedly effective, were only marginally indebted to the symbolists' alchemistic inventiveness for their impact. Indeed, he probably learned to deploy syntactic associations of this kind from indigenous sources, especially from the nineteenth-century Lombard stylists like Dossi and his group. This explains why their influence is more marked on his linguistic and imaginative procedures than that of the then dominant French sources. What Dossi's influence ensured above all was that his language would be predominantly Lombard in quality with just an appropriate smattering of Tuscan elements. Stylistically the effect of this type of procedure is that a Tuscan leavening tempers and nuances the brusque transitions and linguistic violence of his basic northern manner, thereby providing an aesthetic shading which would not otherwise have been present. Contini has made a useful distinction between the two styles under discussion which will help us to put Rebora's linguistic practice into perspective. He notes that 'lo stilismo lombardo si differenzia essenzialmente dallo stilismo o purismo toscana o centrale in quanto esso è "verbale", non "nominale"; spetta cioè alla rappresentazione dell'azione invece che alla descrizione, alla nomenclatura.'[33] ('Lombard style is essentially distinguishable from Tuscan or central style or purism in so far as it is "verbal", not "nominal"; that is, it touches on the representation of action instead of description, of nomenclature.')

In support of this thesis it can be stated that not even the most casual perusal of Rebora's work can fail to detect the profusion of his verbal forms. Frequently they take on the appearance of baroque firework displays and possess the peculiar property that one verbal explosion generates the next, upon the level of sound as well as sense:

> O poesia, nel livido verso
> Che *sguazza* fanghiglia d'autunno
> Che *spezza* ghiaccioli d'inverno
> Che *schizza* veleno nell'occhio del cielo
> Che *strizza* ferite sul cuor del cielo . . .[34]

O poetry, in the bruised verse which *spatters* mud in autumn, which *shatters* icicles in winter, which *squirts* poison in the eye of heaven, which *spurts* wounds on the heart of heaven . . .

These harsh alliterative effects are not intended to be merely eye-catching and gratuitous: they are a vital ingredient in the contorted type of poetry which the poet creates as a result of his efforts to grapple with the powerful, yet labyrinthine, emotions he experiences during the process of living.

Often Rebora's enthusiasm and the sheer lyrical pressure of his style are themselves sufficient to stimulate him to create neologisms or at least resuscitate archaisms, of which 'ondare' ('wave'), 'sbirbonare' ('to play the rogue'), 'risbaldire' ('to cheer up') and 'inspeloncare' ('to put in a cave') are typical examples. Not unexpectedly, many of these new coinages or restorations reflect Rebora's own cataclysmic outlook, as is the case with 'inalveare' ('enchannel'), 'ingoire' ('to swallow up'), 'mulinarsi' ('to whirl'), 'incielarsi' ('to raise oneself to heaven'), 'indracarsi' ('to breathe fire like a dragon'), and so on. Not only do such terms have a Dantesque ring about them, but they also combine the idea of violent movement with that harsh form of articulation Dante gave to his *rime petrose* ('stony rhymes'); and these effects produce calculated cacophonies both in Rebora's verbal forms and in his nouns and adjectives.

The consistency with which he chooses harshly articulated words and phrases indeed suggests that his phonic combinations have spiritual as well as technical implications; and here we have to remember that his main lyrical effort was not concentrated on the linguistic field but was orientated towards the re-establishment of moral and spiritual values. Hence the measure of his poetic success may be gauged by the degree of integration he achieves between his spiritual attitudes and his technical procedures. As soon as his alliterative combinations begin to sound off-key, we can in fact be sure of the presence of some unresolved or partially unresolved spiritual problem in his mind. So intense at times do the stridencies of his word-music prove to be that they deeply shocked contemporary critics who were perhaps pre-conditioned to what might be called the *feu sucré* ('sugary fire') of crepuscular inspiration. Yet, in spite of the artistic function which his anti-arcadic revolt sometimes acquired, there can be little doubt that Rebora's cult of cacophonies often tended to be over-provocative, especially when he produced virtually ear-splitting combinations of plosives, sibilants and gutturals of the type to be found in 'Sole':

Con àliti e gorghi
Con guizzi e clangori
Ebbra l'ora si stordiva.

With breezes and whirls, with flashes and clangs the drunken hour bemused itself.

How far these effects were intentional and how far they were due to a certain insensitivity on Rebora's part it is difficult to decide. But, while we acknowledge that at times his spiritual development consciously drove him to produce excruciatingly discordant sounds, the very fact that their harshness became a lyrical habit also suggests that he was basically a man with precious little music in his soul.

Such a conclusion, moreover, seems justified when we consider that his linguistic cacophonies are everywhere matched by strange, uneven rhymes, forced and unexpected enjambements, heavy rhyming assonances and frequent ellipsis. All these forms of syntactic dislocation are no doubt the inevitable outcome of his tortured thought processes and give rise to his many inversions, interpolations and lengthy parentheses. Eventually such complexities and distortions make his language appear to be symptomatic of his wider spiritual unease and they can perhaps in retrospect be defined as the very stylization of his anguish.

The main function of Rebora's style is thus to facilitate his process of spiritual clarification, and its basic aesthetic objective is the establishment of new representational norms. In this respect few critics would deny nowadays that the poet's attempt to create a fresh type of emblematic writing has borne important fruit. We have only to turn to Montale's art to see how often strident phonic combinations later serve as a basis for alchemizing a more satisfying modern musicality; while the same can be said of another by-product of Rebora's experimentation – his cult of ennui and spiritual ugliness, which he uses as a mood correlative to the social degradation he sees in his own age. A broadening of the range of what was previously acceptable in poetry was accordingly an important feature of his work; and in this sense his style can be considered to have had an impact even in the field of aesthetic philosophy. Art was no longer regarded by him as an autonomous activity, to be judged solely by criteria internal to its own structures: it had also to reflect the social, religious and moral commitments of the poet whose duty it was to range over the whole spectrum of human problems and provide, at least in the lyrical field, valid solutions for them.

It is precisely because he was one of the first poets to try and reintegrate art into life that Russi once described Rebora as a writer who had discovered for himself and for his entire generation the 'dolore che ha per limite l'azione'[35] ('anguish which has action as its limit'). Everywhere in his lyricism we sense an existential anguish and a participatory grief whose intensity marks a decisive retreat from post-symbolist Narcissism. His one major failing, perhaps, was his inability to understand to the full the modern use of metaphor as a means of heightening, and thereby interpreting, the real. This explains the revolt in his later verse against the concrete demands of his sensibility and his obsessive desire to express conceptually rather than figuratively his views on Man's relations with God.

On this subject a useful contrast may be drawn between Rebora and Petrarch to demonstrate the way in which each tries to combine and offset imaginative and religious tensions. From the very outset it is clear that both elements operated under much greater control with Petrarch than with Rebora because the modern poet never possessed the fourteenth-century poet's two basic aids to imaginative concentration – a capacity for resignation and a gift for dispassionate contemplation. As Marvardi has explained[36], it is in the nature of all religious poets to run two kinds of thought in double harness. The first of these – lyrically speaking the more important – may be described as the natural religion of Man. It is a religion which provides writers with a 'social' foundation for their inspiration and with a coherent emotional tradition within which to work. The second is, by contrast, a far more doctrinaire approach, one whose dogmas tend to corrode the poet's imagination by confining his thought within a narrow circle of intellectual speculation, and even at times by limiting it to a mere show of casuistry.

Clearly, in their youth both Petrarch and Rebora were largely governed by their humanist tendencies, by their passionate involvement in life; and then later, with the passage of time, each of them moved imperceptibly towards a more Catholic or theological view of existence. Yet of the two Rebora was the one who ventured much the further in this direction; so that, while Petrarch never attempted to make any specific identification of Laura with the Virgin Mary and always tended to keep his religious feelings somewhat in the background, Rebora slowly allowed his theology to gain the upper hand over his sensibility. Eventually a point was reached where his imaginative faculty became stunted and every image he produced then began to bear the stamp of an inflexible dogmatism. As a result of this intellectual fossilization of his feelings his style gradually grew crabbed, arid and disputatious, and likewise his tonal fabric lost much of its lyrical cohesion. So, broadly speaking, his increasing commitment to doctrine can in the last resort be regarded as the measure of his alienation from life.

Rebora's poetic experience may in this sense be considered to serve both as a stimulus and as a warning to his successors – as a stimulus by virtue of its provision of an imaginative and linguistic framework within which a new lyrical texture might be developed, and as a warning insofar as its regression from imaginative to doctrinal modes led to an increasing aridity. On the one hand we find that his anguish was similar to that experienced by contemporary poets in their attempts to transfigure the moral as well as the aesthetic aspects of modern society; but on the other his ultimate solutions which lay within the dogmas of an orthodox Catholicism had little real lyrical relevance to modern art at all. Hence, like Gozzano, he was fundamentally a transitional poet and his sensibility gradually atrophied because of the dichotomy he perceived but was unable to overcome between his senses and his ideological preoccupations. Nevertheless it has to be conceded that his early verse not only revealed to his fellow-men the importance and relevance of Christian suffering in the modern world, but also reintroduced a strong note of realism and emotional sincerity into Italian poetry as a whole. In so doing, it paved the way for Rebora's successors to transpose their 'dolore' on to more perceptive and figurative levels, and the process ultimately enabled them to garner a rich poetic harvest whose intense alchemistic imagery and poetic values unfortunately lay just beyond Rebora's own lyrical grasp.

Dino Campana

Campana is so different a poet from Rebora that at first sight it would seem impossible to associate them with the same literary trend. But we have to remember that the Vocian movement was itself composed of two distinct periods, the early *Voce* of Prezzolini and the *Voce letteraria* of De Robertis. While the former advocated a broad humanist outlook, the latter, as a result of De Robertis's doctrine of *saper leggere* ('know how to read'), was responsible for establishing the hermetic doctrine of the absolute autonomy of art. As a consequence, we find under the umbrella of the Vocian ethos the coexistence of two diverse – if not antithetical – literary movements, the one adopting a robust, discursive approach to the problems of poetic expression and the other a more inward-looking and kaleidoscopic style whose aim is to imply imaginatively rather than to state conceptually the lyrical truths inherent in modern society.

It was to the second and not to the first trend that Campana was attracted, and so the distinction to be drawn between his poetry and Rebora's is that it illustrates the other side of the Vocian coin – its introspective and intuitive side rather than its sociological and theological attitudes. But here again – because opposites inevitably meet – we still find certain affinities between the two writers, the most important of which is that they both strive to discover some lyrical process which will act as a life-line and raise them out of their anguished state of contingency.

One other point of contact which remains between them is their attitude to language or syntax because, in spite of a certain linguistic flamboyance, Campana still retained a belief in the effectiveness of discursive modes of expression. Fundamentally his linguistic manner developed along traditional lines, although it has also to be acknowledged that the proportion of imaginative to rational elements is much greater in his work than in that of most earlier Vocian poets. Probably the controlling influence in this regard was his desire to erect an effective barrier in his art against the *paroliberisti*. For later when discussing futurism he wholly deplored the gratuitousness and senselessness of its inspiration and at one point was drawn to remark: 'Ogni tanto scrivevo dei versi balzani ma non ero futurista. Il verso libero futurista è falso, non è armonico. È un'improvvisazione senza colore e senza armonia. Io facevo un poco di arte.'[37] ('Every now and again I wrote strange verses but I was not a futurist. Futurist free verse is false, it is not harmonious. It is an improvisation without colour and without harmony. I contrived a modicum of art.') From such an observation we deduce that he conceived his poetic duty to be that of steering a middle course between the classical style advocated by Carducci and the tumultuous outpourings of a Marinetti. Needless to say, he does not always strike the right balance between them and on such occasions he clearly introduces into his poetic line a note of neo-futurist rhetoric. But only in the view of a few critics do these features bulk so large in his work that they are considered as obscuring his authentic poetry altogether. With most other readers they tend rather to be dismissed as of relatively little importance. More dangerous, on the other hand, was his neo-romanticism, because even an admirer like Macrí concedes that his finer verse can sometimes unexpectedly dissolve into 'il vacuo melodismo illimite della musica romantica'[38] ('the vacuous and unbounded melodiousness of romantic word-music').

The link between him and the romantic period is, however, not a direct one: it is partly influenced by Carducci's idealistic suspension of the historical image and is partly filtered through Rimbaud's mysticism. In fact, Campana's irregular bohemian existence, like the French poet's before him, has always held a fatal fascination for the critics, and their untiring interest has caused a Rimbaldian type of myth to spring up around his name which it would take a second Étiemble fully to analyse and assess. Yet basically we can hardly claim for the Italian poet the same steadfastness of purpose as we detect in Rimbaud, so that despite the intermittent brilliance of his insights he always remains a very uneven writer. His overriding importance is more closely associated with modern aesthetics and cultural history than with his actual lyrical achievement, although in a few outstanding lyrics his impact is so decisive that we can regard him as one of the principal precursors of the hermetic movement. At first, perhaps, he was considered to have held this position simply because he introduced Rimbaud's 'alchemie du verbe' ('verbal alchemy') into Italian lyrical textures; but nowadays it is widely accepted that his originality goes much deeper than a mere technical or linguistic dexterity. Moreover, because he and Rimbaud initiated the same type of lyrical revolution into their respective languages, they both encountered at first the same kind of critical antagonism.

The main reaction of their early critics was one of shock and incomprehension, and in Campana's case he himself can hardly be said to have helped his cause since he ostentatiously tore out those pages which he thought the more conventional among his readers would not understand before selling them his *Canti orfici*. But to justify a link between him and Rimbaud on a mere similarity of critical repercussions would be a highly dubious procedure if there were not also some clear affinities in their metaphysical and aesthetic outlooks. At bottom, both were visionary poets who aimed at raising everyday experience to the level of an orphic plane of consciousness. To achieve this end they strove to create an 'absolute' world of aesthetic and emotive beauty behind the real world of the senses, in the hope that a regressive mental perspective would add depth and interpretative power to their lyrical perceptions. In Rimbaud's case the messianic atmospheres created often overstep the bounds of art and border on a mysticism of the senses and the intellect; but in Campana's verse the principal intention is not to transcend the real nor to express 'une rage de l'Absolu' ('rage for the Absolute'): it is instead to evoke an emotively tinged, though non-transcendent, vision of beauty in an aesthetico-historical perspective. Such a form of beauty is one which he hopes will satisfy his craving for perfection while at the same time allowing his responses to his situations to remain within the bounds of human experience. Essentially it amounts to nothing more idealistic than a concrete transfiguration of events and feelings. This explains why the Italian poet rejects the symbolist way of escape from the real through the device of the *correspondance*. Instead, he endeavours to heighten the impact of his sense-impressions by linking them with unexpected orphic associations. His outlook is in other words psycho-sensuous and it never runs the risk of crystallizing into a cult of theology of the type we frequently encounter in Rebora's Christianity. Its prescriptiveness stops short of erecting metaphysical superstructures for transcending reality and contents itself with representing in hieratically-orientated gestures each human being's historically determined yet personal myth. In short, therefore, his sense of orphic 'absoluteness' is of a second, indirect order: its aim is to provide human perspectives through depicting the *regressive perenniality of historico-aesthetic forms*, not to make a direct assault on the bastions of Being as Rimbaud appears to have attempted. No doubt this accounts for the intense plasticity of his descriptions which, as we shall see, reaches a climax in poems like 'Genova' despite their tendency towards fragmentation.

Such an attitude offers a humanist alternative to the Promethean ambition of the symbolists to escape from the narrow confines of the ancient orphic cycle by means of a carefully devised ritual of artistic 'liberation'. But unfortunately Campana did not quite possess the singleness of purpose nor the lyrical power to present this new, modern orphic vision of the world in a definitive and well-rounded form, and so his verse normally proves inferior to Rimbaud's in poetic quality. Probably the reason for the fragmentation of his sensibility was an incipient madness which was latent in his personality from boyhood and which prevented him from sustaining a coherent line of inspiration. Thus, although he felt himself drawn inexorably towards the highly intellectual Vocian programme of moral and aesthetic revaluation, his intermittent awareness of his own shortcomings drove him at times to outbursts of unruly romanticism.

These outbursts usually took the form of a facile and repetitive rhetoric, or even an inability to conclude; and the coarseness of their lyrical textures often clouded the poet's field of vision, causing him to thresh about aimlessly in an imaginative and spiritual void. Contini has described the whole process as 'un tentativo di captare l'ideale magari attraverso l'assurdo verbale'[39] ('an attempt to seize on the ideal, even through verbal absurdity'); and, although examples of it do not appear quite so often in his work as some critics would have us believe, one cannot help admitting that at times, just as we are expecting him to transfigure the initial data of a poem, the entire composition dissolves into a frenzy of visual impressions and auditory jingles.[40]

Nevertheless his finest work is definitely not of this kind: it is firmly based on subtle visionary perceptions which illuminate the very depths of the previous tradition and have no connection whatsoever with a sterile cult of rhetoric. These authentic insights spring from the poet's ability to establish a virtually intuitive communion between his imagination and the material world of the senses. In consequence, it is only occasionally, when an illuminating catharsis fails to emerge from his mood, that he attempts to take possession of a situation by direct neo-futurist assault. Then, however, too close a participation in the world-flux leads paradoxically, as indeed it did with the futurists themselves, to a loss of plasticity, and his words and images immediately tend to resemble those inert building-blocks deployed by Gozzano to create his neo-romantic dreams. Even so, Campana's apparent 'vecchie stampe' are always more concerned with dramatizing Man's inability to pass beyond certain perceptive limits than with fossilizing his tastes and experiences.

If Campana can be said to suffer from any spiritual stasis at all, it is of a second order deriving from a periodicity which, as previously explained, he sensed he had detected in the workings of nature. He describes the process in such a way that its implications are mythical and aesthetic rather than metaphysical in character, and he notes particularly on the aesthetic level that 'nel giro del ritorno eterno vertiginoso l'immagine muore immediatamente'[41] ('in the circle of the vertiginous eternal return the image dies immediately'). This emergence and successive dying away of the image is in one sense a parallel to the perennial and senseless periodicity of the cycle of Becoming in which the Impure are trapped in ancient Orphism; yet with him it is to be interpreted *aesthetically* in a positive sense as a purifying process, as an ascent towards a stable mythological reinterpretation of the world. His poetry is consequently an attempt to overcome the opaqueness and gratuitousness of the vortex of material existence by rendering the image interpretative, diaphanous, limpid and resonant; and so, whenever he manages through a ritualistic purification of imagery to perceive the orphic rhythm or pattern behind the flux of the senses, his poetry reaches its highest point of lyrical communication. On the other hand, the vicious circle of repetitive and 'reincarnated' imagery to which he often falls prey in his moments of lesser inspiration is no more than a materialistic descent into the world of sensations. Yet, attractive as such short-lived bacchanalia of the senses tend to be, they are clearly incompatible with that higher state of orphic awareness through which he highlights the recurrence of cathartic events and attitudes behind the transient flow of his sense-impressions.

As we might expect, whenever Campana's art does not spiral inwards towards distantly perceived orphic perspectives it tends to crystallize into Parnassian tableaus with only limited poetic implications. But, when it regresses towards an authentic orphic mood, its plastic rhythm is never lost or hypostasized into sterile oleographic forms, because for Campana true lyrical insight is always infinite process and response, not the achievement of a preconceived goal. Indeed, his art seems to imply that there should be an endless delay in the final consummation of the orphic process of attaining memorial omniscience, which normally results in the hypostasis of the image through its ultimate orphic purification. From such delaying tactics we can deduce his aesthetic doctrine. It is one which affirms that the aim of lyricism is to suggest, not to define or demonstrate, the unpremeditated delight the poet takes in the plastic and tangible forms of the passing moment. For him poetry cannot be a conceptual art at all, although it must at all times offer a definitive interpretation of life by enunciating lyrical truths symbolically, as a subtle rhythm within tradition. In his aesthetics, therefore, the Neoplatonism practised by the symbolists loses its idealistic component and is transmuted into a form of art based on a 'transfigured' realism. Equally, the identification of poetry with music is now taken a step further because Campana reveals how the plastic forms of the real world need to be lyrically orchestrated before they can be transfigured and reshaped into image-chains revealing the perennial pattern behind the poet's contingent states of feeling.

However, we are already in danger of anticipating our conclusions, because clearly not even Campana could have hoped to attain to such a mature conception of artistic composition from the outset of his career and, like all other artists, he needed time to explore the potentialities of his method. During this period of experimentation the touchstone of his art seems to have been a compelling desire to change the metaphysical aridity of ancient orphic doctrine into a series of dynamic imaginative figures representing a metaphorical transcription of his moods.

He was thus convinced that the poet could foreshadow solutions to human problems without ultimately changing those solutions into arid and intellectualized principles, as the ancient orphic priesthood had attempted to do. But, not surprisingly, once he had realized the full implications of his task he ran into all kinds of expressive difficulties, one of the most recurrent of which was that vicious circle of obsessive sensations to which we have already alluded. Nevertheless, even in such moments of lyrical opacity he frequently managed to compensate for his lack of interpretative insight by developing incantatory effects. Hence, in spite of the rhetorical devices apparent in the following fragment, a striking admixture of musical and visual qualities casts a spell over the reader's mind and causes him to forget that he is, in fact, being treated to nothing more than a series of fleeting, almost gratuitous, impressions:

Le vele le vele le vele
che schioccano e frustano al vento
che gonfia di vane sequele
le vele le vele le vele
che tesson e tesson: lamento
volubil che l'onda che ammorza
ne l'onda volubile smorza
ne l'ultimo schianto crudele
le vele le vele le vele.[42]

The sails the sails the sails, which crack and whip in the wind that swells in vain bursts, the sails the sails the sails, which weave and weave: the changing lament which the wave that dies away within the changing wave extinguishes in a final cruel wrench, the sails the sails the sails.

No doubt we can partly account for the fragmentary and hallucinatory nature of this composition by reference to Campana's recurring bouts of madness, since an early medical report had already diagnosed a 'pazzia dissociativa primaria'[43] ('a primary dissociative madness'). Likewise on a literary level we find Solmi, as early as 1928, stressing the 'aura di follia' ('atmosphere of madness') which often surrounds his work.[44] But a moment's reflection will show that a certain emotive unity nevertheless persists throughout, with the result that the kind of *visività* which the poet displays in the above description of flapping sails has considerable lyrical power. Similarly, on a purely technical level the poem is not without merit, despite its circularity: for by means of his sheer virtuosity Campana manages to lull our sensibilities to sleep and substitute the artful and insidious rhythm of plastic imagery for the lack of a deeper inner perspective. Clearly then, we must always be on our guard against sweeping condemnations of his poetry as a series of gratuitous evocations; and this is especially true of his mature verse written from 1912 onwards, for he invests it with such subtle orphic implications that despite its obscurity it transcends – both imaginatively and prosodically – his earlier somewhat vacuous romantic melodiousness.

On the other hand, this poem is an excellent example of the kind of mental block which frequently short-circuits his imagination and provokes a vicious circle of obsessive sensations. Whether it is wholly ascribable to his unbalanced state of mind is a moot point and one whose investigation is unlikely to throw much light on the nature of his art. What we do know, however, is that at a conscious level at least he held the random dissociative techniques of the futurists in utter contempt. So in his *Taccuinetto faentino* he insists on the necessity for an underlying spiritual unity in all authentic lyricism and notes that 'il valore dell'arte non sta nel motivo ma nel collegamento e, quindi, nel punto di fusione si ha la grande arte'[45] ('the value of art does not lie in the motif but in its relationships and, therefore, one has great art at a point of fusion'). The nature of this aesthetic fusion is for him an imaginative, rarely a mystical or intellectual act; and, even though he regards man as a 'pastore del gregge infinito/ Del mondo fenomenale'[46] ('shepherd of the infinite flock of the phenomenal world') whose duty it is to mirror in his verse the memory of 'una divina/ serenità perduta'[47] ('a lost divine serenity'), he never envisages the function of the artist as that of crystallizing the phenomenal world into any meditative absolutes. Instead he adds a rider to the above definition by emphasizing the necessity for the artist to effect an immanent transfiguration of experience by bridging gaps within the real, because 'la grande arte, come la grande vita, non è che un ponte di passaggio' ('great art like great life is only a mediatory bridge').

Dino Campana

The bridging process hinted at here is one which connects the poet's awareness of perennial change with the unifying powers of his lyrical perspectives, and the same idea is repeated at the end of the second section of 'La Notte'. It is, in fact, put in the form of a question by the hallucinated protagonists of the poem, who have actually bridged the orphic void and penetrated to the deeper rhythm behind reality, and who then ask: 'Non era dunque il mondo abitato da dolci spettri e nella notte non era il sogno ridesto nelle potenze sue tutte trionfali? Qual ponte, muti chiedemmo, qual ponte abbiamo noi gettato sull'infinito, che tutto ci appare ombra di eternità?'[48] ('Was not then the world inhabited by sweet spectres and in the night was not the dream stimulated once more in all its triumphant powers? What bridge, we silently asked, what bridge have we cast over the infinite, so that everything seems to us a shadow of eternity?') This enchanted world, be it noted, is not static but dynamic or, as the existentialists put it, intentional in nature. As such, it does not fossilize life but represents human situations and gestures ritualistically, producing a continuous and open-ended commentary on the richness and yet the inevitable sameness of mankind's inner existence.

If Campana aimed at such a startling new dimension of experience, why is it that he has not been acclaimed as one of the major poets of the century? The answer to this is twofold: first, as we have already mentioned, because his work seems to be so fragmented; and, second, because he lived in the shadow of Rimbaud whose inspiration was nevertheless moving in quite a contrary and idealistic direction. This explains why Mounin brushes aside the Italian poet's achievement and writes:

> 'Je me demande franchement si les *Chants orphiques* de Dino Campana, qui jouit dans l'histoire de la poésie italienne du double prestige d'un Rimbaud par ses voyages, et d'un Reverdy par ses dix-huit ans d'asile de fous, – un fois traduits, ne feraient pas penser à Gabriele D'Annunzio, ses paroxysmes verbaux, ses trépidations, plus qu'à Reverdy, plus qu'à Rimbaud: tandis que son orphisme, à nous lecteurs de Whitman et des nocturnes allemands, semblerait probablement vieillot. Campana, notable dans l'histoire lyrique italienne, hors d'Italie ne compte pas.'[49]

> ('I ask myself frankly if the *Orphic Songs* of Dino Campana, who enjoys in the history of Italian poetry the double prestige of a Rimbaud through his voyages and a Reverdy through his eighteen years in a mental institution, – once translated, would not cause one to think of a Gabriele D'Annunzio, his verbal paroxysms, his trepidation, rather than of Reverdy, rather than of Rimbaud; while his orphism, to us who are readers of Whitman and the German poets of night, would probably seem old-fashioned. Campana, notable in the history of the Italian lyric, outside Italy does not count.')

Now, although such perfunctoriness is to be deplored, it is also partly to be excused, precisely because of the incompleteness and obscurity of the *Canti orfici* themselves. Their fragmentary nature moreover has, if anything, been increased recently because successive editors of the text – no doubt in a wholly praiseworthy desire to add substance to its depressingly slender lyrical achievement – have included in it a large number of half-completed poems and much of the poet's juvenilia. The result is that his art now seems to contain all the faults of a *bas romantisme* without any of the romantic movement's major saving graces. And, when one adds to this process a whole series of investigations into his sources, which have had the effect of portraying his verse as a regurgitation of Baudelaire, Rimbaud and the decadents, one cannot blame the average reader for drawing the conclusion that Campana is largely to be identified with the 'Scapigliati' and the futurists, even though in all essentials he has little to do with either. As a corrective to this impression, let us examine briefly his cultural interests and, by elucidating his aims and lyrical range, try to bring into clearer focus the deeper implications of his poetic vision.

As a preliminary, we need to assess the breadth of his culture, which extended over three of four European literatures. Clearly the most spectacular of his masters were the French symbolists and decadents, especially Baudelaire and Rimbaud, yet an indigenous Italian influence is hardly less in evidence. Of particular note, perhaps, is the way in which he adapts Carducci's modes of landscaping and lyrical suspension while adding to them D'Annunzio's decadent cult of sensuous description.[52] Again, the influence of these poets is tempered by that of Novalis, Heine and Nietzsche[51], while the poet himself claims to have been influenced by Edgar Poe and Walt Whitman. In considering his American sources we are faced with the problem of his knowledge of English;[52] but even if we admit that the poet had sufficient knowledge of the language to read Whitman in the original, it is still difficult to see any conclusive link between their manners. Apart from a vague ritualistic primitivism, those connections which do exist probably amount to nothing more than Costanzo's observation, that 'la libertà delle forme e il ritmo musicale di Whitman siano stati per Campana un *incitamentum* a realizzare le sue aspirazioni piú segrete',[53] ('the freedom of forms and the musical rhythm of Whitman were for Campana an encouragement to actualize his own most secret aspirations'). Substantially the same thing may indeed be repeated about his other literary influences, since even his blatant plagiarisms form nothing more than a general cultural background upon which he consciously stamps his own metaphorical designs.

His new figurative method consists in the first instance of an intense *visività* which tends to attain to higher levels of perception by colouring 'la nostra voluttà di riflessi irreali'[54] ('our voluptuousness with irreal reflections'). Normally the poet manages to abstract an orphic pattern from the riot of sensations emerging from his sensibility; but, although his deeper insights are constantly bifocal, at the lower level of sensation he always adopts towards reality the attitudes of the primitive, instinct-driven voluptuary. Indeed, it seems that it is only by cultivating the Dionysian spirit of the Bacchants that he believed he could re-acquire the intense mythological creativity of the Ancients and present life as a ritualistic, orphic stylization of everyday acts and poses. So, while somewhat lacking in intellectual brilliance, we find that most of the people he evokes manifest a time-hallowed and pre-reflective grace with immense symbolic potentialities. Since these primitive archetypes, moreover, find themselves simultaneously in harmony with the forces of external nature and with the imaginative powers latent in the human mind, they act as creatures reborn and stand awe-stricken and breathless before the beauties of their orphico-naturalistic settings – indeed not unlike Rimbaud's hare before the magic of nature in the prose-poem 'Après le déluge'. What we witness in them is, in fact, a kind of rebirth, the re-creation of mankind within a sphere of pre-conscious wonder; so that normally Campana's living creatures are all figures of mature, 'regained' innocence, inebriated by space and cosmic yearning. Yet at the same time they remain earth-bound and authentic by being ritualistically immersed in the solemn drama of living.

The ritualistic behaviour of Campana's characters at all focal points of his narrative is, according to Solmi, responsible for the fact that the poet's sense of reality 'trabocca insensibilmente nel sogno'[55] ('overflows imperceptibly into the dream'). Even so, his dream is no mere escapism but rather an intensification of earthly existence, in which his stylized orphic priests and priestesses mediate between everyday events and his powerful yet orphically recessive imagination. Gradually these creatures appear to create their own historically saturated, visionary sphere, in which his feminine figures in particular seem to arise like so many freshly born Aphrodites from the foam of the sea.[56] The transfigured imaginative atmospheres which surround them tend to suggest that the entire ritual of their lives unfolds within a world of 'contingent eternity': a world which seems so fragile and intangible and yet is so firmly delineated that it never degenerates into an abstract ideal. Indeed, it appears to possess at times such an earthy flavour that we suspect that Campana was somewhat influenced by the painters of the *fauviste* school. Hence the realism of what he calls the 'aspro succo della verde vita'[57] ('the bitter humour of green life') which emanates from his descriptions (especially those evoking South

American scenes) makes us feel he is communing with nature at her most elemental level. The starkness of his *tabula rasa* effects may be gauged from the following passage:

> 'Gettato sull'erba vergine, in faccia alle strane costellazioni io mi andavo abbandonando tutto ai misteriosi giuochi dei loro arabeschi, cullato deliziosamente dai rumori attutiti del bivacco . . . La luce delle stelle ora impassibili era piú misteriosa sulla terra infinitamente deserta: una piú vasta patria il destino ci aveva dato: un piú dolce calor naturale era nel mistero della terra selvaggia e buona. Ora assopito io seguivo degli echi di un'emozione meravigliosa, echi di vibrazioni sempre piú lontane: fin che pure cogli echi l'emozione meravigliosa si spense. E allora fu che nel mio intorpidimento finale io sentii con delizia l'uomo nuovo nascere: l'uomo nascere riconciliato con la natura ineffabilmente dolce e terribile: deliziosamente e orgogliosamente succhi vitali nascere alle profondità dell'essere: fluire dalla profondità della terra: il cielo come la terra in alto, misterioso, puro, deserto dall'ombra, infinito. Mi ero alzato. Sotto le stelle impassibili, sulla terra infinitamente deserta e misteriosa, dalla sua tenda l'uomo libero tendeva le braccia al cielo infinito non deturpato dall'ombra di nessun Dio.'[58]

> ('Cast upon the virgin grass, confronted by strange constellations, I abandoned myself to all the mysterious patterns of their arabesques, delightfully lulled by the deadened noises of the bivouac, . . . The light of the now impassive stars was more mysterious on the infinitely deserted earth: destiny had given us a vaster fatherland: a gentler natural heat lay in the mystery of the wild and good earth. Now drowsy, I followed the echoes of a wonderful emotion, echoes of more and more distant vibrations: until with those echoes the wonderful emotion also died away. And then it was that in my final bewilderment I felt with delight a new man being born: a man being born who was reconciled with an ineffably gentle and terrible nature: I felt bursting from the depths of Being, proudly and delightfully, vitalistic humours: their flowing from the depths of the earth: the sky above like the earth was mysterious, pure, deprived of shadows, infinite. I had arisen. Under the impassive stars, on the infinitely deserted and mysterious earth, from his tent a free man extended his arms towards heaven, infinite and no longer blemished by the shadow of any God.')

It would perhaps be no exaggeration to assert that this evocation sets the dominant mood and provides the dominant tone for the whole range of Campana's mythological dreams. One senses that within it all the vitalistic elements of ancient and modern orphism subsist in suspended animation; and, in fact, the only lyrical element which it perhaps to some extent underplays is the poet's keen feeling for the age-old memorial culture of the human tradition. So what Campana is attempting to do here is to evoke a vision of the vastness of life's spiritual possibilities, and from this point on one realizes that his particular process of transhumanization can never be theological in quality:[59] it is simply an ethical and figurative converging of tensions which move towards a psycho-sensuous state of insight.

Essentially the poet gains from his art a sense of 'liberation' which permits him to release himself from his dependence on a rationally based religion and to make (or re-make) himself a primitive god in his own right.

At first we still detect in his work the presence of ancient theological dichotomies separating Being from Existence, the Saved from the Damned. But in his contemplation of a time-hallowed, man-made landscape in the following passage we encounter the previously missing historico-cultural dimension of life. The setting is the town of Faenza, seen as a kind of rose-red city half as old as time; and the stylization of the gestures of its inhabitants is so effectively achieved that their orphic perenniality saves the tableau from degenerating into a mere Gozzanian daguerrotype:

> 'Ricordo una vecchia città, rossa di mura e turrita, arsa su la pianura sterminata nell'agosto torrido, con il lontano refrigerio di colline verdi e molli sullo sfondo. Archi enormemente vuoti di ponti sul fiume impaludato in magre stagnazioni plumbee: sagome nere di zingari mobili e silenziosi sulla riva: tra il barbaglio lontano di un canneto lontane forme ignude di adolescenti e il profilo e la barba giudaica di un vecchio: e a un tratto dal mezzo dell'acqua morta le zingare e un canto, da la palude afona una nenia primordiale monotona e irritante: e del tempo fu sospeso il corso.'[60]

> ('I recall an ancient city, with red walls and turreted, burning on the endless plain in a torrid August, with the distant coolness of green and damp hills as a background. The arches, grandiosely empty, of bridges over the river stagnating in shallow leaden pools: the black silhouettes of silently moving gipsies on the bank: in the distant dazzle of a reed-bed distant naked forms of youths and the outline and Jewish beard of an old man: and suddenly from the depths of the stagnant water the gipsy-women and a song, from the speechless swamp a monotonous, irritating primeval lullaby: and time's course was stilled.')

This entire landscape mirrors a stagnant and reflective eternity, and subsumes an age-old culture whose mysteriously orphic flavours have saturated the very walls of the city. In Apollonio's words we can almost consider the scene as a 'paesaggio capovolto in una negativa fotografica'[61] ('a scene upturned in a photographic negative') and it may be contrasted with another, very different spectral description, an evocation of Campigno near Campana's home-town of Marradi, which has a haunting, almost a diabolical, rhythm about it:

> 'Campigno: paese barbarico, fuggente, paese notturno, mistico incubo del caos. Il tuo abitante porge la notte dell'antico animale umano nei suoi gesti. Nelle tue mosse montagne l'elemento grottesco profila: un gaglioffo, una grossa puttana fuggono sotto le nubi in corsa. E le tue rive bianche come le nubi, triangolari, curve come gonfie vele: paese barbarico, fuggente, paese notturno, mistico incubo del Caos.'[62]

('Campigno: barbaric, fleeing hamlet, nocturnal hamlet, mystical nightmare of chaos. Your inhabitants open up the night of the ancient human animal in their gestures. In your heaving mountains a grotesque element stands out: a lout, a fat prostitute flee under the passing clouds. And your banks as white as clouds, triangular, curved like swelling sails: barbaric hamlet, fleeing, nocturnal hamlet, mystical nightmare of Chaos.')

In contrast with the static, block-dream of Faenza, the dynamic flux of the poet's modern Hades is thrown into relief here in a turbulent and hallucinatory circularity of imagery, in a fantasmagoria which once more reminds us of the 'eternal return' and that damnatory reversion to the status quo always implicit in the orphic doctrine of reincarnation. Yet, while both these passages undoubtedly possess greater evocativeness and mythological resonance than the average 'daguerrotype', they still do not in themselves produce that inner perspective on life which Lalou once defined as 'la sensualité consciente de l'art'[63] ('the conscious sensuality of art').

How does Campana attain this level of insight? Largely in the same way as Rilke achieved it, by replacing ancient orphic religious absolutes with dynamic imaginative processes. So, although the poet feels himself as much caught up in the great wheel of Being as the ancient orphic adepts and also assumes that he is no less a child of Gê and starry Ouranos than they were, his main intention is to 'transcend' his earthly nature and purify himself wholly by aesthetic, not by religious, means. He is determined, in other words, to use the material world simply as a stepping-stone for the purpose of ascending *metaphorically* instead of *metaphysically* 'nello spazio, fuori del tempo'[64] ('into space, out of time'). What this evaluative, yet highly lyrical, process strives basically to achieve is to probe the inner depths of our human experiences through an intermingling of visual and musical effects: it certainly does not postulate any intellectual goal beyond a sense of self-fulfilment which is to be attained by the artist; and it stops well short of the desire of the ancient orphic adepts to rival in knowledge the Gods on Olympus. For Campana it is always better to travel hopefully than to arrive, and his mature art proves to be an endless regress towards the ever-receding goal of a perennial human myth. It is in this non-teleological sense, therefore, that his orphism must be regarded as 'modern' and to differ from that fostered earlier by the symbolist poets.[65]

His divergence from the traditional orphic pattern, by contrast, does not imply an unwillingness to transmit his lyrical message through traditional orphic imagery. On the contrary, his topography of springs, fountains, lakes, streams and woods, to say nothing of his constant rendering of the dismal Halls of Hades in desubstantialized earthly settings, all remind us of the realm of the 'white cypress' previously evoked in the ancient orphic tablet from Petelia now in the British Museum. It would indeed be no exaggeration to say that the time-hallowed custom of evoking the afterworld in terms of a spectral whiteness or transparency obsessed Campana, and he drew from this pattern of visual imagery his technique of conflating the past and the present in what he called his 'panorama scheletrico del mondo'[66] ('skeletal panorama of the world'). The process is the basis of an orphic 'colour regression' in his work which may be traced back to its hesitant beginnings in his early descriptions of the statuesque stillness and memorial omniscience of the ancient orphic heroes. A case in point appears in an immature poem in *Quaderno* (1908-14) significantly entitled 'Convito romano-egizio', where an appropriate orphico-mythical regression seems under way:

Le coscie bronzine s'imbiancano
E gli occhi son madreperla
I suoni lontani e monotoni
Carezzano il cuore fanciullo
E noi berremo alle fonti
Eterne della vita come il sole
Ci scalderemo al suo seno inesausto.

Our bronze thighs whiten and our eyes are mother-of-pearl. Distant and monotonous sounds caress our childlike hearts and we shall drink at the eternal founts of life, like the sun we shall warm ourselves in its inexhaustible bosom.

Now orphic tableaus of this kind stand halfway between the ancient and modern ideals of the cult, and the colour 'bronzino' marks the beginning of the poet's later developed, yet highly significant and orphically based range of colour-patterns. It depicts in this case a moment of transition from the demonic flux of life to the divine stillness associated with a statuesque form of godhood – a transition which suggests a silent orphic rhythm similar to the one Eliot detected surrounding a chinese jar in 'Burnt Norton':

At the still point, there the dance is,
But neither arrest nor movement. And do not call it fixity,
Where past and future are gathered.

The evoking of such skeletal musical and colour-patterns is gradually brought to a fine art by Campana who sums up his 'contingent eternity' in a voluptuous baroque manner. The stylization of his dynamic orphic stillness may be illustrated in the following passage from *Il viaggio e il ritorno* in 'La notte', where it reaches a point of maturity:

'A l'ombra dei lampioni verdi le bianche colossali prostitute sognavano sogni vaghi nella luce bizzarra al vento. Il mare nel vento mesceva il suo sale che il vento mesceva e levava nell'odor lussurioso dei vichi, e la bianca notte mediterranea scherzava colle enormi forme delle femmine tra i tentativi bizzarri della fiamma di svellersi dal cavo dei lampioni.'

('In the shadow of the green lamplight colossal white prostitutes dreamed vague dreams in the strange glow, in the wind. The sea in the wind poured out its salt which the wind poured forth and cast aside in the lustful smell of the alley-ways, and the white mediterranean night played with the enormous silhouettes of the women between the bizarre attempts of the flame to uproot itself from the inside of the street-lamps.')

Accordingly, if we compare this passage with the above-quoted verses describing a Roman-Egyptian banquet, we shall see that while the first regresses towards a form of deification, the second is by no means as Neoplatonic nor as intellectually fossilized in orientation. Instead it forms part of one of the poet's 'enormi miti solari' ('vast solar myths') in which his orphic creatures retain their fleshly substantiality despite the fact that the world around them has degenerated into a colourless and insubstantial Hades. In short, a new kind of 'depersonalization' is now beginning to evolve out of the ancient ritualistic process of orphic purification, and after it has developed Neoplatonism will never again be considered by Italian poets as a satisfactory mode of lyrical representation. Its modalities will be replaced by that contingent form of image-suspension or myth-making subsumed in the process of *epoché*, despite the fact that Campana himself did not attempt to theorize upon this subject but simply put it into practice in his verse.

Although, as Gerola has stressed,[67] feminine figures tend to predominate in his evocations of skeletal situations, Campana's women are normally 'depersonalized' in a peculiar way and rarely appear as the immediate objects of his affections. Instead of behaving as individuals in their own right they are stylized so as to become the performers of a series of ritual acts, so many 'portatrici di mistero' ('bearers of mystery') whose gestures tend to express 'racchiusi enigmi vitali' ('closed vitalistic enigmas'). Their enigmatic function is emphasized all the more by the poet's predilection for describing them in certain sphinx-like poses, which endue their personalities with a Baudelairian touch of baroque strangeness.[68] They all emit, moreover, a mysterious translucence deriving from their apparent ability to understand the deeper secrets of the universe, and each one of them holds in her eyes the key to some vital aspects of the arcana of the psyche. At the same time they are by no means to be considered vestal virgins in the ancient sense of that word. All of them are so fully versed in the arts of love that in 'La Notte' sexuality appears to form an integral part of their orphic natures. Likewise, there is no attempt by Campana to cultivate an upper class élite, either on a social or intellectual level; if anything, he shows a distinct preference for the lower classes whose way of life lies closer than the intelligentsia's to the realities of his primitive sense of vitalism.

Even the very range of Campana's characters is itself impressive. At the lower end of the scale we find the 'ancella ingenua e avida' ('naïve and greedy maid-servant'), the 'matrona ruffiana' ('matronly go-between') and the innumerable prostitutes haunting the highways and byways of the mediterranean ports. At the upper end, by contrast, there are a few ladies like the sophisticated and impenetrable baroque beauty of 'La chimera', who only seems to subsist within a distant sphere of aestheticism. Yet what all these creatures have in common are their hieratic poses, their attitudes of pensive and tranquil beauty, which are both derivative from, and transcendent of, the traditional orphic mode of transfiguration. Quite clearly then, this feature is consciously intended by Campana to remind us of the statuesque gestures and hieratic symbolism – though not perhaps of the purity of intention – of the priestesses of the ancient world.

Such serene and stylized acts should not consequently be taken on their face-value as an indication of incipient godhood. At most they only express the poet's belief in the absoluteness of human relationships within the overall orphic pattern evolving in society. Behind their individuating features his priestesses embody the Goethian and Nervalian concept of the Eternal Feminine, although their ritualistic and aesthetic prescriptions are also filtered, it seems, through a Rimbaldian ethos before attaining their final expression in his lyricism. It may also be from Goethe that he obtained his technique of enacting aesthetically orientated ritual dramas, and this explains why at one stage Faust becomes the orphic hero of 'La Notte'.[69] On the other hand, although Nerval's own dreamland defined as 'l'épanchement du songe dans la vie réelle'[70] ('the spreading of the dream into real life') appears at first sight somewhat removed from Campana's 'sogno della vita in blocco' ('block-dream of life'), no doubt inherited from Carducci, in practice the combination of the multiple elements of reality with a dreamlike orphic hinterland is a feature common to them both. As a result, the airy mystery of poems like Nerval's 'Delfica' is expressed with a rather more earthy opulence in Campana's archetype of the great mediterranean mother evoked in 'Genova':

> O Siciliana proterva opulente matrona
> A le finestre ventose del vico marinaro.

O impudent, opulent Sicilian matron at the gusty windows of the coastal alley-way.

The sexual luxuriance introduced here is again derived from Baudelaire, and at times it tends to reach a level of paroxysm, especially when Campana views the world through the eyes of a primitive voluptuary. His most overt linking of sex with orphic mystery is to be found in 'Furibondo', where the sexual act itself is seen as a process of orphic initiation:

> Ardendo disperatamente allora
> Raddoppiai le mie forze a quell'appello
> Fatidico e ansimando la dimora
> Varcai del nulla e dell'ebbrezza, fiero
> Penetrai, nel fervore alta la fronte
> Impugnando la gola della donna
> Vittorioso nel mistico maniero
> Nella mia patria antica nel gran nulla.

> Then burning desperately I redoubled my efforts at that fateful call and panting I crossed the threshold of the void and intoxication, proudly as a victor I entered, my brow held high in my fervour and seizing the throat of the woman, into the mystic mansion into my ancient motherland and into the great void.

In other words not even so vitalistic a pleasure as procreation is considered as an experience in its own right by him: it is regarded as a means of intensifying desire to such an extent that it leads directly to the annihilation of the self in the twin processes of mythification and dematerialization. In the ultimate analysis, therefore, woman is not even admired for her sensuous or sexual attractions by Campana, but solely for her powers of mediation. On occasion, he even refines away her aura of sensuality, after which we are left with a purely disembodied spirit endowed with mystical potentialities and typified by the wraith mediating over the scene in 'Piazza Sarzano': 'Una donna bianca appare a una finestra aperta. È la notte mediterranea' ('a white woman appears at the window. She is the mediterranean night').

Occasionally, on the other hand, between these two extremes of sensuality and disembodied spirituality we come across a woman of flesh and blood: a fulfilled personality whose only overt orphic traits are her stylized gestures and the radiance of the enigmatic smile lurking behind her benign appearance. A case in point is 'Donna genovese' where the lady so intimately combines her sphinx-like qualities with the poet's fleshly ideal of the *bête fauve* ('tawny beast') that she symbolizes his ideal earthly companion:

> Tu mi portasti un po' d'alga marina
> Nei tuoi capelli, ed un odor di vento,
> Che è corso di lontano e giunge grave
> D'ardore, era nel tuo corpo bronzino:
> – Oh la divina

Semplicità delle tue forme snelle –
Non amore non spasimo, un fantasma,
Un'ombra della necessità che vaga
Serena e ineluttabile per l'anima
E la discioglie in gioia, in incanto serena
Perché per l'infinito lo scirocco
Se la possa portare.
Come è piccolo il mondo e leggero nelle tue mani.

You brought me a piece of seaweed in your hair and a scent of wind, which has come from afar and reaches me heavy with passion, was on your bronzed body: – Oh, the divine simplicity of your nimble limbs – not love, not pangs, a phantom, a shadow of necessity which drifts serenely and ineluctably through the soul and liberates it in tranquil joy, in enchantment, so that through the infinite, the scirocco wind can carry it off. How small and light the world is in your hands.

Here her 'corpo bronzino' again reminds us distantly of the statuesque figures found in 'Convito romano-egizio', while her condition as a sea-creature and the wind as a metaphor of the life-force are both symbols laden with consequences for the hermetic poetry of the twenties and thirties. Such effects clearly deepen the otherwise pure existentiality of the woman depicted, so that behind all her actions we sense a ritualistic and hieratic purpose. It is as if her very grace and movements are insidiously touched with some arcane significance which makes her the bearer and communicator of a profound psycho-sensuous wisdom, possibly a sense of orphic fulfilment, through a complete adaptation to life at all levels of experience.

In contrast with the Genoese woman's assertion of almost a plebeian simplicity, the lady of 'La chimera' symbolizes the orphic priestess in the guise of a baroque 'femme fatale'.[71] Her beauty is the very essence of the Eternal Feminine which the poet envisages as being steeped in the cultural reminiscences of the past; and she seems to emerge from her surroundings like some intermediary between matter and spirit. She too is gradually disembodied by a dematerialization of the scene within which she is framed, although she also continues to retain a certain aura of sensuousness about her like her Genoese counterpart. Moreover, far from being distant and wraith-like at the outset, she reminds us of the sensual baroque temptress whose special function it is, according to Baudelaire,[72] to compound a sense of 'volupté' ('voluptuousness') with a touch of 'amertume' ('bitterness'). A similar point is made by the Pre-Raphaelite critic Walter Pater in his celebrated description of *La Gioconda*, although actually in this particular poem the woman is not modelled on the latter figure but on Leonardo's *Vergine delle rocce* described as her younger sister:

Non so se tra roccie il tuo pallido
Viso m'apparve, o sorriso
Di lontananze ignote
Fosti, la china eburnea
Fronte fulgente o giovine
Suora della Gioconda:
O delle primavere
Spente, per i tuoi mitici pallori
O Regina o Regina adolescente:
Ma per il tuo ignoto poema
Di voluttà e di dolore
Musica fanciulla esangue,
Segnato di linea di sangue
Nel cerchio delle labbra sinuose,
Regina di melodia:
Ma per il vergine capo
Reclino, io poeta notturno
Vegliai le stelle vivide nei pelaghi del cielo,
Io per il tuo dolce mistero
Io per il tuo divenir taciturno.

I do not know whether your pale face appeared to me among rocks, or whether you were a smile of unknown horizons, with your inclined ivory brow, o young Sister of the Mona Lisa: O Queen, o youthful Queen of past springs, by virtue of your mythical paleness: but for your unknown poem of voluptuousness and grief, o musical bloodless girl, marked with a line of blood on the circle of your sinuous lips, o Queen of melody: but for your virgin reclining head, I, a poet of night, surveyed the vivid stars in the oceans of heaven, I for your sweet mystery, I for your silent becoming.

The 'divenir taciturno' of this mysterious creature seems to represent for Campana the unfolding of the whole range of human passions, because – as Pater would put it – she has all the experience of the world, both past and present, etched upon her sphinx-like countenance. She is simultaneously ancient and modern in other words, both an example of the post-Baudelairian baroque canon of beauty and of ancient orphic myth. Her chief characteristic is her ability to transmute contingent effects into absolute gestures by associating the entire landscape and atmosphere about her with her distant imperious smile. This last effect is best illustrated at the end of the poem where at one and the same time she dematerializes and is symbolically dematerialized herself by the rocks on which she reposes. In her stylized attitude she becomes as impalpable and as inaccessible as that hushed orphic state of transition between life and death which is a favourite theme with Campana and which she is no doubt intended to represent:

Guardo le bianche rocce le mute fonti dei venti
E l'immobilità dei firmamenti
E i gonfii rivi che vanno piangenti

E l'ombre del lavoro umano curve là sui poggi algenti
E ancora per teneri cieli lontane chiare ombre correnti
E ancora ti chiamo ti chiamo Chimera.

I gaze at the white rocks, the silent founts of the wind and the impassivity of the firmament and the swollen streams which weepingly pass by and the shadows of human toil bent over the freezing hills, and still gazing through tender skies at flowing and distant clear shadows, still I call you, I call you Chimera.

Her dissolving silhouette, in fact, even reminds us somewhat of the ancient myth of Orpheus and Eurydice; for, just as Eurydice faded away and vanished when her husband looked back at her in the Underworld, so Campana's baroque archetype tends to melt away into a deliquescent musical rhythm as he tries to divine her inner significance. She leaves behind her a sense of uneasiness and frustration arising from the secret desire of the mind for absolute serenity and the poet's awareness that any such state is humanly and aesthetically unattainable, despite the perennial re-emergence of similar figures of grace.

From poems of this kind the link between Campana and Rilke becomes apparent, even though the Italian poet may not actually have read his German counterpart's early orphically orientated verse. Both poets nevertheless possessed in large measure that mysterious quality which Pellegrini defines as a power of 'illuminazione medianica'[73] ('medianic illumination'). On the other hand, whereas Rilke moves easily in a world of orphic revelation, Campana often seems to stand breathless before its portals. The reason for this is not so much the Italian poet's lack of insight (even though his relative lack of intellectual power clearly has some bearing on the problem) as his fundamental belief that movement is more orphically effective than stasis in the struggle for artistic representation. As previously indicated, he undertakes his orphic journeys in order to travel hopefully rather than to arrive. So what he requires from his art is simply that his bifocal view of experience should radiate outwards in all its vibrant contingency from the imagery in which it is transfigured. To ensure this he creates the illusion of an infinite regression, a sense of infinite descent, to express the issue in orphic terms; and such a process is not so easy to grasp as, say, the concrete hypostasis of Rilke's metaphysical yearnings depicted in the angel-symbols of the *Duino Elegies.*[74] For Campana, in other words, the moment of fulfilment lies in the chase, never in a final possession of the receding myth, and in this respect his work seems to run parallel to Nerval's ideology in the *Filles du feu*. For just as the latter are dramatic symbols of the contingent – yet mystic – love of the French writer for his ever-changing human condition, so the Italian poet's emblematic creatures fuse together in a similar way the apparently incompatible elements of a transient realism and an eternal orphic perspective. This dynamic mythification of reality is thus precisely what makes Campana's poetry a landmark in modern Italian aesthetic development.

But in order to bring into sharper focus the various levels of his shadowy orphic atmospheres we need to examine closely his colour alchemies, especially since he has long been accused of unburdening himself in a riot of gratuitous, if colourful, fantasies. Such an examination may indeed at first sight suggest a link between him and the futurists; consequently, if we are to justify his own assertions that his work has nothing in common with the chance-effects of the *parola in libertà*, we shall need to offer a convincing explanation for the use of colours in his image-patterns. Their effects should not in other words be merely the result of hallucinations induced by his madness but should follow an inner logic of their own. Campana's personal statement on the subject reported by Pariani during a discussion in the asylum of Castel Pulci is that he aimed at creating 'una poesia europea musicale colorita'[75] ('a coloured, musical European poetry'). But, unfortunately, few critics have ever read any specific meaning into this observation and at best have chosen to link his colour-symbolism with Rimbaud's *alchimie du verbe*, especially with those particular alchemies suggested in the 'Sonnet des voyelles'. In reality, however, the Italian poet profoundly modifies Rimbaud's approach to colour-sequences, and his own colour-patterns have little or nothing to do with medieval alchemistic practices.[76] Instead, they are intended to punctuate his regressions into an orphic dreamworld and their immediate origin may well have lain in his early scientific training.

One possible influence on his colour-system, for example, might have been the work done by Charles Henri, a one-time director of the laboratory of the physiology of sensations at the Sorbonne, on the properties of the chromatic circle. Like Campana, Henri considered red to be symbolic of dynamic change and essentially ascensional in direction; while green seemed to him to be an inhibitory or non-transcendent colour acting in a psychological depressant sense.[77] Soon this scientific investigation of colour-patterns was applied to artistic practice by Guaita in *La scienza dei colori e la pittura* (1893) and further aesthetic and psychological effects brought about by colour changes were worked out by various schools of painters after the turn of the century. Bigongiari has even suggested that the orphic aesthetic of colour expounded by Delaunay[78] may have influenced Campana, while Soffici equally stressed his wide knowledge of contemporary trends in fine art. Nevertheless, for our present purposes the origins of his development of a psychology of colour are not so important as the more or less regular colour-pattern which the poet gradually evolved. This proves ultimately to be a subtle mnemonic system whose functioning can best be illustrated by the examination of two texts, the verse-poem 'Giardino autunnale' and the prose-poem 'La Notte'.

The goal of Campana's colour-sequences is naturally to highlight the orphico-aesthetic process of dematerialization which results from his regressions away from the real, and in a small number of his finest compositions colour-gradations mark vital stages in this orphic ritual of purification as he moves towards a 'panorama scheletrico del mondo'. For instance, 'Giardino autunnale' has as its setting the Boboli gardens in Florence; but, as Campana's orphic regression from reality gets under way, the gardens lose their original concrete greenness and the scene becomes desubstantialized by stages, both from the visual and auditory standpoints. The process is perhaps the supreme example of the poet's many attempts at providing a twofold state of *veggenza* by creating a 'sogno della vita in blocco' ('block-dream of life'):

Al giardino spettrale al lauro muto
De le verdi ghirlande
A la terra autunnale
Un ultimo saluto!

To the ghostly garden, to the silent laurel with its green garlands, to the autumnal earth a final farewell!

Evidently the intention here is to transmute the garden into a kind of antichamber of Hades by gradually removing the limitations imposed by the greenery of the real garden and evoking an atmosphere of boundless memorial insight, not unlike that found in the ancient Tablet of Petelia. At first the process of continual metamorphosis is emphasized in the gradation of the adjectival effects, which suggests on a variety of levels (*spettrale – verde – autunnale – ultimo*) a form of dissolution. The trend becomes more pronounced in subsequent stanzas, all of which attempt to bring about an 'immanent' transfiguration of the real. At first such a state may be considered to be a motionless one such as we so often find in Neoplatonic stylizations of ancient orphism; but, as might be anticipated, Campana's colour-changes never congeal into a final hypostasis: they aim instead at creating a sense of infinite possibility, of limitless insight and liberation.

The initial atmosphere of incipient regression is thus immediately followed by an evocation of the setting of the sun where the colour red predominates. The sunset suffuses the entire scene with a ruddy glow and is presumably symbolic of the sunset of earthly life as the soul prepares to pass over into the world of shadows beyond death. Indeed, the momentary vision of the antechamber to Hades presented here has a distinct Dantesque flavour about it, probably an intentional one:

A l'aride pendici
Aspre arrossate nell'estremo sole
Confusa di rumori
Rauchi grida la lontana vita:
Grida al morente sole
Che insanguina le aiole.

To the arid slopes harsh and reddened by the dying sun, distant life cries out, confused with raucous sounds: it cries to the dying sun which stains the flowerbeds blood-red.

Once again we note that the regression to a faraway world is accompanied by a general muting of all kinds of harsh sensations, especially sounds, until finally this apocalyptic vision of dying suns and muffled cries is buried like the river of life (for water represents both the *élan vital* and a purificatory medium for the orphics) in the yellowing sands of eternity. Afterwards, there erupts over the entire scene, like the sound of the last Trump, the searing blast of a bugle:

S'intende una fanfara
Che straziante sale: il fiume spare
Ne le arene dorate: nel silenzio
Stanno le bianche statue a capo i ponti
Volte: e le cose già non sono piú.

A fanfare is heard which rises agonizingly: the river disappears into the golden sands: in the silence the white statues stand, turned at the head of the bridges: and already things are no more.

The stridency of the bugle's blast is intended in a symbolic sense to sever the soul's last connections with life on an auditory level, thereby reinforcing the visual attenuation of sensations in the preceding colour-pattern; and the only objects then surviving in the poet's parched desert of eternity which had been moments before a highly animated Florentine scene[79] are certain white marble statues rising, pale and immutable, over transitional bridges and representing, or so it seems, the deified heroes of the ancient orphic cult. They alone have escaped from the 'Wheel of Being' and become immobilized as part of the block-dream of an omniscient memorial eternity.

At this point, indeed, hardly a noun or adjective fails to increase our sense of orphic mystery, and the process of dematerialization has now wholly undermined the concrete imagery originally presented to the reader's gaze. In particular, the colour-gradations of the lyric – the ghostly garden, the blood-red sunset, the yellowing sands and white statues

– all stand as a mnemonic means of punctuating the progressive dissolution of the real world and its replacement by a picture of death's dream kingdom. But for Campana the picture is not yet complete: it still lacks the mythical element of 'contingent eternity' which is the hallmark of his modern orphism. So he now postulates a further transformation, almost an ectoplasmic liberation from the everlasting insentiency of godhood; and in the closing stanza the immobility of his godlike statues gives way to a perennial, transfigured symbol of the flesh re-emerging in the form of a *Chimera*. Since the restored fleshliness of this vision is compounded both from existence and eternity it tends to insinuate into the kingdom of death a subtle living presence; and in the present case it amounts to the 're-emergence' of the Campanian Eternal Feminine, whose reactivated sensuousness is highlighted by the decadent, olfactory atmosphere in which she is immersed:

E in aroma d'alloro,
In aroma d'alloro acre languente,
Tra le statue immortali nel tramonto
Ella m'appar, presente.

And in the scent of laurel, in the languid, acrid smell of laurel, among the immortal statues in the sunset She appears present to me.

In other words, Campana's 'chimera' is now no longer a wild romantic dream, as it has so frequently been considered to be: it depicts instead a new type of existential creature who moves in an artistic sphere of 'suspended' emotion, that is to say, in a sphere of 'epochized' or 'suspended' myth.

In this sense Campana is the creator of a new type of *stilnovismo* in which his ladies – instead of being angelic creatures mediating between the poet and his God – are sensuous intermediaries guiding the poet towards redemptive visions of orphic beauty. Hence, while Beatrice, for example, mediates between Dante and his goal of Christian redemption, Campana's 'chimere' mediate between his existence and his aesthetico-mythical values. They prove to be the creators of unique yet perennial inscapes crystallized out of the flux of human experience, the weavers of a pattern which can alone give meaning to life in the absence of any dogmatic religious sanction. By so acting they serve, oddly enough, as prototypes for other emblematic figures appearing later in the works of Ungaretti, Montale and Quasimodo, because it is precisely through similar entities that these poets also explore the arcana of experience and the inner reaches of their consciences.

On the other hand, in spite of Falqui's assertion of a 'combustione lirico-visiva del sostrato realistico e letterario'[80] ('a lyrico-visual combustion of the realist and literary substratum') in 'Giardino autunnale', it would perhaps be pertinent to ask if its rich lyrical texture is, in fact, the exception rather than the rule in Campana's literary output. In this regard, we can only assert that the poem is indeed representative of the general drift of his mature inspiration, although its orphic unity is not a feature typical of most of his juvenilia. On the other hand, nearly all his other mature poems adumbrate a similar visionary insight into the long mythical shadow cast by human experience and culture upon the screen of history. Consequently, even though Campana's colour-schemes cannot be said to be absolutely consistent, we can legitimately maintain that they do consistently punctuate the various stages of his orphic regressions.

In the light of this discovery we can dismiss the suggestion that his art depends on a gratuitous *visività* for its effects. Essentially his orphic patterns are a powerful means of probing into the secrets of human destiny and sometimes – as, for instance, at the end of 'La Notte' – the colour-scheme is so interwoven with the overall myth that it reveals an outlook of almost epic proportions. In this particular passage the order of the colours is virtually the same as in 'Giardino autunnale' and at the end they again synthesize its thought, even though they have in the past normally been taken as a mere visual leavening for the imagery:

> 'Nel tepore della luce *rossa*, dentro le chiuse aule dove la luce affonda uguale dentro gli specchi all'infinito fioriscono sfioriscono *bianchezze* di trine. La portiera nello sfarzo smesso di un giustacuore *verde*, le rughe del volto piú dolci, gli occhi che nel chiarore velano il *nero* guarda la porta d'*argento*. Dell'amore si sente il fascino indefinito. Governa una donna matura addolcita da una vita d'amore con un sorriso con un vago bagliore che è negli occhi il ricordo delle lacrime della voluttà! Passano nella veglia opime di messi d'amore, leggere spole tessenti fantasie *multicolori*, errano, polvere luminosa che posa nell'enigma degli specchi. La portiera guarda la porta *d'argento*. Fuori è la notte chiomata di muti canti, *pallido* amor degli erranti.'

> ('In the tepidness of the *red* light, inside the closed halls where the light sinks evenly to the infinite within the mirrors, a *whiteness* of lace emerges and fades. The lodge-keeper in the subdued magnificence of a close-fitting *green* jacket, the wrinkles on her face softer, and her eyes in the half-glow veiling their *blackness*, gazes at the *silvery* door. One feels the indistinct fascination of love. There rules a woman both mature and mellowed by a life of love, with a smile, with a vague glitter, which in her eyes, is the memory of the tears of voluptuousness! In her vigil there pass by, loaded with harvests of love, slender bobbins weaving *multi-coloured* fantasies; they wander, like a luminous dust, which comes to rest in the enigma of the mirrors. The lodge-keeper gazes at the *silvery* door. Outside is the night crowned with muted songs, the *pallid* love of wanderers.')

When we bear in mind the symbolic interpretation we attributed to similar colour-contrasts earlier, the significance of this myth takes on an entirely fresh complexion. But, before we attempt to analyse it, we have as a preliminary to emphasize that Campana tends to indicate colour-transitions by indirect as well as direct means. Thus a sense of whiteness not only appears directly in the phrase 'bianchezze di trine', but it is also evoked indirectly in phrases like 'la porta d'argento' (where perhaps it expresses a value-judgement), or even in adjectives like 'pallido'. Likewise the blackness of pure orphic existence is either evoked directly or is associated with 'la notte'; while again the whole mythological universe of Campana's kaleidoscopic imagination is clearly subsumed in the phrase 'fantasie multicolori'.

Once we have accepted this extension of the poet's colour-system, we immediately note how his various colours again possess precise symbolic functions. In 'Giardino autunnale', we recall, red represented a transitional stage in which all sensations were gradually muted, and white the skeletal contours of the ancient orphic realm of Hades. As such, these colours stood in complete opposition to the green of the Boboli gardens, and here once more green represents a concrete reality, the fleshly solidity of the 'portiera'. To the chromatic scale developed in the earlier poem, on the other hand, we now have to add black, because as a typical 'poeta notturno' ('nocturnal poet') Campana uses the symbol of Night as a backcloth against which to project his orphic dramas.

In the present case the orphic process is one of regression into a mirror-universe. The multiple reflections appearing in the mirrors around the room are mythicized and transformed into the colourless realm of the 'white cypress', while at the same time the 'portiera' acts as a symbol of an earth-mother guarding the portals of her mirror-eternity. The portals themselves are probably silvery images of the actual doors of the porter's lodge reflected in the mirror, while the abundant white lace curtaining the windows no doubt is intended to increase the suggestion of the imminent 'emergence' of the poet's 'mondo scheletrico'. Needless to say, the 'portiera' herself is yet another of those corpulent and over-mature symbols of baroque beauty so dear to the poet's heart and her carnal substantiality is visually emphasized in her 'giustacuore verde' ('green close-fitting jacket'). We are in fact told that she has been fully matured by life and the implication is that the broad sweep of her experiences reaches over into the nether world. This is because she is probably the guardian of a brothel and has herself tasted love in all its voluptuousness, bitterness and perceptive ecstasies. Hence her eyes shine darkly with the innermost secrets of existence, while at the same time her nimble fingers spin fantastic multi-coloured patterns in the enigmatic hinterland of the mirrors. Perhaps, then, like Rilke's blind man in the lyric 'Pont du Carrousel',[81] she stands at the very centre of her mysterious universe. Placed in so strategic a situation she appears to acquire a twofold function: her prime duty is no doubt to act as an orphic priestess or intermediary for the poet, but in her apparent activity as a spinner of life's thread she also goes far beyond this rôle and seems to be connected with one or other of the three Fates who spin, weave and eventually cut the thread of life. Like them, she becomes the fountain-head of recondite knowledge and seems to weave the very warp and woof of experience. As she spins and guards her mystic portals, there pass outside in the street the pale and insubstantial figures of the uninitiated, those half-conscious human creatures who are too mentally short-sighted to appreciate her true powers and significance.

Oddly enough, the spiritual movement evoked by the colour-pattern in this passage is not primarily one of regression but one of fluctuation between reality and the orphic dream, and the order of the colours evoked (*rosso – bianco – verde – nero – multicolore – argento*) is probably intended to indicate precisely this type of dialectic. From an artistic standpoint such a rhythm is more adherent to human realities than the more regressive procedures seen in 'Giardino autunnale'; although at the same time the latter poem is perhaps more traditional and reminds us of the orphic bifocality of Baudelaire's visionary experience in poems like 'Les sept vieillards' in the *Tableaux parisiens*:

> Fourmillante cité, cité pleine de rêves
> Où le spectre en plein jour raccroche le passant!

> Teeming city, city full of dreams, where the spectre in broad daylight buttonholes the passer-by!

From this we can perhaps conclude that it was in the area of a dual vision of the real that the French decadent poets influenced Campana most, because he was certainly not in sympathy with the Neoplatonic absolutism of a symbolist poet like Mallarmé, despite the latter's manifest orphic features.

Campana's colour-system also works in double harness with his melodic patterns to provide a deeper resonance for his imagery, and his lyrical cadences are consequently a major feature of his art. His aim was to fuse together his sense of pure plastic existence with the rhythm of his orphic conscience, and in the process a musical liquidity and a dynamic visual perceptiveness, as illustrated in 'Il canto della tenebra', are skilfully interwoven:

> La luce del crepuscolo si attenua:
> Inquieti spiriti sia dolce la tenebra
> Al cuore che non ama piú!
> Sorgenti sorgenti abbiam da ascoltare,

Sorgenti sorgenti che sanno
Sorgenti che sanno che spiriti stanno
Che spiriti stanno a ascoltare . . .

> The light of twilight fades: restless spirits, let the darkness be sweet to the heart that no longer loves! Springs, springs we must heed, springs, springs which know, springs which know that spirits linger, that spirits linger to listen. . .

We note in this passage how phonic, rhetorical (especially the device of anaphora) and muted visual elements are carefully blended together to produce an orphic half-light with mysterious, suggestive overtones emerging from its lyrical cadences. Elsewhere perhaps this type of lyrical equilibrium is short-circuited, as we saw earlier in fragments like 'Barche amarrate', where the poet becomes momentarily a prey to his hallucinations. Yet equally frequently a momentary hallucination can be uplifted by rhythmical inventiveness, and this is clearly the case in poems like 'Tre giovani Fiorentine cammino':

Ondulava sul passo verginale
Ondulava la chioma musicale
Nello splendore del tiepido sole
Eran tre vergini e una grazia sola
Ondulava sul passo verginale
Crespa e nera la chioma musicale
Eran tre vergini e una grazia sola
E sei piedini in marcia militare.

> With their virginal step undulated, undulated their musical hair, in the splendour of the tepid sunlight. They were three virgins and a single grace. There undulated with their virginal step, curly and black, their musical hair. They were three virgins and a single grace and six little feet in military step.

Here again visual elements support and deepen the musical inflections. Consequently the blackness of the girls' hair contrasts with the luminosity of the sunlight and its constant undulations cause imaginative and rhythmical elements to merge in an artfully contrived pattern of movement which transcends a mere repetitive lilt and provides a metrico-visual glimpse of the orphic rhythm itself.

By contrast, it seems as if the poet's musical dexterity is inevitably weakened whenever his imagery becomes loose and dissociative during his bouts of madness; although even then the result is rarely a complete lyrical failure but rather a series of disjointed fantasies whose individual parts are more coherently articulated than the whole structure. Perhaps the supreme example of this is the unfinished lyric 'Genova' which may well have been intended as a cubist vision depicting the city's life on a series of dramatically intersecting planes. Unfortunately the interrelevance of its various sections is not always apparent and this is because they have not been galvanized into a satisfactory unity by Campana's normally haunting melodic effects. Hence the poem dissolves into a number of isolated visionary fragments, although admittedly most of them still possess great hallucinatory power. Within these fragments, on the other hand, the free flow of repetitive rhythmical patterns adds considerably to the lyrical quality, especially in the process of dematerialization, as when, for instance, the city dissolves into an impalpable, shadowy dreamworld which emerges from behind realistic scenes:

> . . . sorgeva un torreggiare
> Bianco nell'aria: innumeri dal mare
> Parvero i bianchi sogni dei mattini
> Lontano dileguando incatenare
> Come un ignoto turbine di suono.

. . . a host of towers arose, white in the air: innumerable from the sea seemed the white dreams of the mornings, threading, as they melted into the distance, a virtually unknown whorl of sound.

Significantly, many of these half-integrated visions have their origin in a cult of statuary, especially in the figure of Michelangelo's statue of Night, which gradually becomes obsessive with Campana and which he adopted as the overall archetype of his regenerated humanity. Yet in the last resort statuesque poses prove so many false artistic trails in his work, and they produce imagery akin to ancient rather than modern orphic symbolism. Fortunately, the main feminine figure of 'Genova' has a more flexible purpose and she appears to be a true denizen of the poet's sphere of 'contingent eternity'. She is presented as a corpulent Sicilian matron who only just fails in her desire to actualize his dream. Therefore, while eventually casting him back into the chaos of existence at the end of the poem, this 'piovra de le notti mediterranee' ('octopus of mediterranean nights') tends to haunt and revitalize the entire scene, and seems even to be offering the distant promise of a lyrical beatitude after an apocalyptic period of cosmic disintegration:

> La finestra avevi spenta:
> Nuda mistica in alto cava
> Infinitamente occhiuta devastazione era la notte tirrena.

You had blotted out the window: naked, mystic, hollow, infinitely-eyed, high above there lay the devastation of the Tyrrhenian night.

The result is that despite its disjointed development the overall impression which the poem provides is not one which veers too dramatically towards a neo-romantic dream, but contains instead hints at a deeper state of colour-punctuated orphic transfiguration.

One other rhythmic technique which Campana synchronizes with a stylistic device equally deserves mention: a tendency to round a poem off on an image possessing an ascending or descending cadence. This again is perhaps a Rimbaldian device which, as Gustave Kahn has put it, aims at opening up 'une marge de rêverie sur l'infini' ('a margin of dreaminess on infinity'). Normally it relies for its effects on an accompanying stylistic feature, especially one involving the sudden resolution of a situation by an incisive analogy or an unexpected exclamation. An apt model is to be found in the ending of Rimbaud's 'Le châtiment de Tartufe':

> Peuh! Tartufe était nu du haut jusques en bas.

Pha! Tartufe was naked from head to toe.

A similar ending occurs in Campana's 'Il canto della tenebra' where a new protagonist is unexpectedly introduced to dominate the scene. As the gentle play of fountains dies away, a masculine figure – apparently a suicide[82] – looms up and takes on a function parallel to the female wraith in 'Piazza Sarzano'. Not only does he brood over the entire scene but he is also instrumental in evoking the orphic perspective within which the lyric is ultimately framed:

> Guardiamo: di già il paesaggio
> Degli alberi e l'acque è notturno.
> Il fiume va via taciturno . . .
> Pùm! mamma quell'omo lassú!

Let us look: already the landscape of trees and water is nocturnal. The river flows away silently . . . Bang! mother, that man up there!

From such examples it becomes clear that Campana's bifocal view of reality is amply supported and reinforced by rhythmical inflections closely integrated with his emblematic effects and that he attempts to produce cadences which are analogous to the deeper unfolding of his orphic insight. In consequence, although it has to be admitted that his *Canti orfici* contains a fair sprinkling of *bas romantisme*, his intentions and the imaginative sphere in which he operates are both in the last resort identical with those of the major hermetic poets. In many senses Campana already functions as a hermetic writer, and the type of involution which he practises may be defined as one which depends on a process of infinite, existential regression of imagery. By endlessly delaying its hypostasis he produces a poetry of action rather than of pure contemplation such as is characterized by the ancient orphic manner; and when his plastic techniques are combined with his deepseated realism – sometimes even with the earthy realism of primitive passions – he frequently discovers poetic harmonics permitting the integration of his personal tastes and outlook with the continuously evolving fabric of the Italian lyrical tradition.

CHAPTER VI

Govoni and the development of a modern baroque outlook

From the very beginning that keen sense of the contingency of human life appearing in the works of the Vocian poets is a constant feature with Govoni. Yet he soon shows himself to be so completely immersed in the trivia of everyday existence that his poetry is normally little more than a farrago of gratuitous – though highly intensified – sensations. He aims almost exclusively at depicting the mutable contours of reality in all their multiple nuances, but he does this without attempting to organize his sense-impressions into significant interpretative patterns or even to impart to them any symbolic meaning transcending their own startling immediacy. At first sight he strikes one as being a demonic image-maker, a virtuoso of the imagination; and yet he only manages to exert a quantitative, not a qualitative, influence upon his contemporaries and successors. Thus, although from the point of view of lyrical output he bestrides the modern Italian lyrical scene like a colossus, his fame depends more on the hallucinatory richness of his imagery than on its intellectual resilience. Likewise he becomes a prey to all sorts of literary temptations, the gravest of which are his relative lack of critical awareness and his fluctuating poetic aims.

His intellectual confusion, however, is to some extent counterbalanced by the incredible density of his lyrical textures which, although they frequently dissolve into a neo-futurist riot of colour-contrasts, are sometimes highly effective, precisely because of their extreme heightening of sensations. If then we compare his lyricism with that of the Vocian poets proper, we feel that he possesses the spiritual violence of a Rebora without the discipline of his religious idealism and the waywardness of a Campana without the saving grace of his orphic outlook. Of the two poets the latter perhaps comes nearer the mark, because Campana, we recall, was also at times caught up in that kaleidoscopic pageant of luxuriant sensations which Govoni paraded for nearly sixty years before his astonished audience. Yet normally his associative style is non-functional, running quite contrary to the self-conscious hermetic trend. So, before we attempt to come to grips with the fantasmagoria of his imagery, we should perhaps pause for a moment and consider the basic psychology of the modern man of letters.

We can discern in contemporary European writers two widely differing approaches to art. On the one side we find the highly self-conscious poet like Valéry who deliberately isolates himself from his fellow men and surrounds his aesthetic procedures with a thousand critical precautions in case they should become contaminated by extraneous, unauthentic material; and on the other a more broadly based type of poet who acts largely out of instinct and feels that it is his duty to trace out the trajectory of his age in all its multiple aspects and aspirations. The former naturally shows a high degree of lyrical control, while the latter is often willing to abandon any pretence at self-criticism in the hope of handing down to posterity a complete compendium of the tastes and attitudes of his age. It is to the second group rather than the first that Govoni belongs, though by making so difficult a choice he placed himself from the outset in an unenviable position. This is because few poets – apart from the notable exception of Hugo – have ever been able to adopt a thorough-going epic stance in the modern world with any significant degree of success, and in Govoni's case the assumption of such an attitude was particularly unwise because by temperament he possessed only the first of the two paradoxical qualities of mind that the epic manner requires: a boundless desire to participate in life and an equally keen sense of critical detachment.

Why then did he take up this stance? Probably the choice was not a self-conscious one: it was forced upon him by the fact that he was equally ill-equipped to practise any of the more resilient forms of artistic activity. What he lacked above all was a sense of self-awareness which is bred in the bone of most modern poets. Hence he was largely incapable of providing a perspective on life which would either transcend the banalities of everyday affairs or attain to that state of self-consciousness which makes one's art a logical consequence of one's inner lyrical vision. So, even if to a certain degree the most self-possessed modern poets also seem to be driven along pre-determined paths by the power of some irresistible inner demon, unlike him they never allow themselves to be deflected from their poetic purpose by the pressure of contingent events. They know that any such course would compromise their inner reality; and, because they realize that their spiritual integrity is the hallmark of their genius, they resist determinedly all literary and extra-literary temptations, especially the spurious attractions of the cultural fashions of the world in which they live.

It is, however, this kind of rigour of thought and expression which modern 'epic' poets like Govoni risk sacrificing in their constant attempts to paint gigantic, all-inclusive frescos of their age. They indeed become so involved in the multifarious activities of society that all its dominant cultural trends – its côteries, fashions and exclusive literary poses – exert a powerful influence on their minds. At length these irrelevancies – the flotsam of a lifetime – accumulate disastrously in the work of the unwary poet stifling his originality, and Govoni is a case in point. So, if we compare him with Valéry, we soon have to concede that, whereas the French poet impresses his personality and poetic ethos upon his work with a great economy of lyrical means, the Italian one tends to eliminate his personality from his work by subordinating his critical faculty to his sensory appetites. His art thus tends to resemble a process of lyrical fission rather than fusion, and the cosmic firework displays to which his imagination treats us are eventually left suspended in mid-air, to sputter and die away like shooting stars or damp squibs in his own particular pre-lyrical firmament.

Because of the similarity of their accretive approaches to art we should perhaps compare briefly the manners of Govoni and Gozzano. Where the present poet scores over his predecessor is in the freshness and modernity of his imagery. And yet, since he does not possess the incisive critical and interpretative powers of Gozzano, his lyricism is, as Francesco Flora noted, 'troppo leggeramente visiva; bolle di sapone sgargianti; se il poeta sapesse fissarle sarebbe immenso'[1] ('too frivolously visual; showy soap-bubbles; if the poet knew how to crystallize them he would be tremendous'). Whenever one approaches even his most cohesive lyrics, one consequently has the feeling that he has not succeeded in living up to his potentialities. Nevertheless, so boundless is his enthusiasm for life and so fascinating the baroque personality which shines intermittently through his shoals of gratuitous images that one can at times excuse – if not condone – his lack of critical perception.

From a very early stage in his career Govoni appears to have sensed that his love of sensation for its own sake was undermining his authenticity as a poet; but, instead of trying to remedy this pernicious tendency, he preferred to involve himself in a vexatious literary dispute which he pursued with various protagonists over a period of fifty years. His principal contention was that he should be acknowledged as the creator of crepuscular art. The first time he raised the issue was in a letter to Prezzolini, the editor of *La Voce*, in which he deplored the fact that the latter had omitted his name from his recently drawn-up crepuscular hagiography. Then, having once referred to the omission as being 'interamente gratuita' ('wholly gratuitous') he goes on to explain that 'è proprio impossibile essere preceduti e accompagnati quando si viene irrefutabilmente prima'[2] ('it is indeed impossible to be preceded and accompanied when one comes irrefutably first'). He also quotes the dates of publication of four of his volumes of verse, beginning with *Le Fiale* (1903) and ending with *Gli Aborti* (1907), to prove his point. But his plea for recognition fell on deaf ears and he received the following dusty reply from Prezzolini in the very next number of the periodical: 'Caro Govoni, le date – dovrei insegnarlo a un poeta? – non decidono nulla. Se le sue *Fiale* son del 1903 e le *Armonie in grigio e in silenzio* del 1904 (*sic*) non è però detto che vi si trova quella "nuova sensibilità" del quale io parlavo a proposito suo, di Corazzini, di Palazzeschi e di altri . . . In quel tempo lei non si sollevava gran che sulla turba comune: Le *Fiale* sono poesie dannunziane . . .'[3] ('Dear Govoni, dates – do I have to point it out to a poet? – decide nothing. If your *Fiale* are of 1903 and the *Armonie in grigio e in silenzio* of 1904 (*sic*), it does not mean that one can find in them the "new sensibility", of which I spoke appropriately in the case of Corazzini, Palazzeschi and others . . . At that time you had not emerged far above the common herd: the *Fiale* are Dannunzian poems . . .'). Despite the fact that this judgement has been echoed down the years by a large number of other Italian critics, it certainly did not prevent Govoni from returning to the charge from time to time and trying in a variety of ways to substantiate his claim.[4] As a result, it is difficult not to suppress a smile nowadays at the poet's repeated efforts to carve out for himself this particular niche in the historical development of the twentieth-century lyric, especially since we know perfectly well that his position – although a modest one – has been assured for other more obvious reasons. But such touchiness and sensitivity once again indicate Govoni's own understanding of the major weakness of his manner: his relative inability to distinguish the essential from the purely decorative in art. Accordingly, while he had a proven capacity to produce felicitous images in isolation, his fundamental drawback always tended to be his failure to give an overall structural unity to his poems.

It is precisely for this reason that he soon became the victim rather than the leader of fashion. Even so, his appetite always remained sufficiently voracious to enable him to participate in a large number of literary climates and reflect in a personal manner their dominant themes. Chief among these were the crepuscular and futurist movements in the early part of his career, although these were subsequently followed by a surrealist, neo-hermetic, and even a narrative period. It is not, however, possible to separate the various moments of his inspiration into watertight compartments strictly delimiting each phase. This is partly because he allows one trend to merge with its successor and partly because he is never willing totally to relinquish his earlier acquisitions, however inappropriate they might prove to be, when practising his later lyrical manners.

As a result of such literary covetousness, we shall not be surprised to find that the cumulative effect of his first manner – crepuscularism – has the greatest influence on his poetic tone. In its purest form it ranged, as Govoni himself affirmed, from the much maligned *Le Fiale* to *Gli Aborti* and perhaps reached its climax in *Armonia in grigio et in silenzio* (1903). After 1907, on the other hand, it progressively declined, as his crepuscular modes were submerged by his futurist ones. Nevertheless it continued to persist as an undercurrent throughout his entire work and may even be detected in the poetry of the fifties. Despite the presence of this and other tonalities, however, we must immediately draw a distinction between the many literary fashions he employed and his own distinctive tone. What is undoubtedly far more decisive an influence on his poetry than any indulgence in passing cultural enthusiasms is his peculiar cast of mind, which reacts against the literary pressures that tend to stifle his genius and produces an inner region of perception which can only be described as a genuinely modern baroque outlook. When we consider his poetry in this light, we are soon driven to the conclusion that the secret behind his lyrical development rarely lies in his degree of mastery over the various styles which he temporarily adopts, but in the degree of baroque complication and suggestiveness which he introduces into his imagery. In fact, this baroque insight is the only constant feature in his verse; so that even on those occasions when he appears to be striving after complication for its own sake, his imagination – in spite of its dispersive tendencies – struggles instinctively to create a central core of baroque analogies of surprising lyrical clarity.

On the other hand, although we have to acknowledge the limits of the influence of literary fashions on his more significant verse, we soon discover that they serve as useful referential backgrounds against which Govoni sketches the true outline of his lyrical development. It is indeed almost as literary backgrounds that he considers them himself, for he always appears to have felt the need for a cultural screen on which to throw the kaleidoscopic patterns of his baroque inspiration. In default of a ready-made modern baroque tradition he accepted any other cultural movement that came to hand, though he tended to work on the periphery of his borrowed literary backgrounds, never within them. Even his crepuscularism is hardly identifiable with the normal crepuscular texture, as Ravegnani rightly notes when he says '. . . in Govoni il "crepuscolarismo" non era né un'idea polemica della poesia, né una moda; e nemmeno era un'esperienza, o un'affinità di temperamento, o una ricerca di sé. Govoni in concreto fu un crepuscolare *sui generis*, un crepuscolare fuori del crepuscolarismo, come piú tardi fu un futurista fuori del futurismo.'[5] ('. . . in Govoni "crepuscularism" was neither a polemical conception of poetry nor a fashion; and not even an experience, or an affinity of temperament, or a search for himself. In substance, Govoni was a crepuscular *sui generis*, a crepuscular outside crepuscularism, as he was later a futurist outside futurism.') In this case it will probably be easier to explain what his crepuscularism does not consist of rather than attempt to indicate its more positive qualities, although from the beginning we sense that the texture of Govoni's crepuscular imagery is far more concrete than Corazzini's ever was. Likewise his manner of representation is more objectively Parnassian, less deliquescent, than a Moretti's or a Martini's; and its merely half-suppressed vivacity suggests that the pose of moral exhaustion typical of the genuine crepuscular poets is a very superficial attitude with him. At most he only employs crepuscularism as a convenient ethos within which momentarily to project his own baroque effects; and, even if crepuscular and later futurist themes bulk large in his verse, they never stifle his baroque personality altogether. At times, admittedly, he hardly seems able to utter a word or make a single gesture without tingeing them with the specific hues and colours of these two schools or without casting them in their peculiar syntactic and rhythmical moulds. They accordingly take on the appearance of aesthetic religions in his eyes, though without ever obtaining the sanction of being his own particular religions. And in this sense they tend to obtrude in a rather arbitrary manner in his poetic textures while leaving the deeper sphere of his baroque temperament relatively untouched.

The first manifestation of his baroque outlook is a strange orientalism deriving from his attraction for the 'art nouveau' style. This style, known as the 'Liberty style' in Italian, normally coincides with his early crepuscular inspiration and prevents it from freeing itself from the type of ornate Parnassianism in which it soon found itself imprisoned. The manner probably owes as much to D'Annunzio's baroque cult of refined sensations as it does to the 'art nouveau' movement in painting, but whatever its origin it at once reveals the kind of aesthetic weakness which was destined to dog Govoni's steps throughout his life: a tendency to juxtapose rather than integrate the diverse cultural undercurrents appearing in his work. A case in point is the following passage from *Le Fiale* (1903):

> Sul limitare siede una musmé
> trapuntando d'insetti un paravento
> e d'una qualche rara calcedonia:
>
> vicino, tra le lacche e i netzké,
> rosseggia sul polito pavimento,
> in un vaso giallastro una peonia.[6]

On the threshold there sits a mousmee, embroidering a screen with insects and a few scattered chalcedonies: nearby, among the lacquer-work and netzkés, there glows in a yellowish vase on the polished floor, a peony.

Here, quite clearly, the poet's attempt to fuse together his two dominant poetic tonalities has failed. What we note at once is that an oriental tone is preponderant in the first stanza and a crepuscular one in the second, especially in the decadent atmosphere evoked by the peony in the yellowish vase. Consequently the poem contains an inherent tonal clash which will be raised at times elsewhere to grotesque proportions: and, indeed, even in this lyric the cult of a precise eastern ornateness and a wilting crepuscular languor can hardly be regarded as a particularly good combination. As the collection unfolds, such tonal clashes tend to become the norm, and Govoni's crepuscular atmospheres are then frequently disrupted by inappropriate shows of lyrical violence, an element which becomes increasingly noticeable in his sensibility as time passes. It usually manifests itself in his choice of verbs, and direct evidence of the tendency is apparent even in such paradigmatic crepuscular lyrics as the sonnet 'Autunno'. In this poem we are no sooner plunged into a state of dreamy melancholy than we are jerked out of it again as twilight, instead of creeping insidiously upon us, almost menacingly flings open its red portals:

Ecco autunno con le piogge tetre,
e il funebre corteo di foglie morte;
ecco i crepuscoli che su le pietre
spalancano le loro rosse porte.[7]

Here is autumn with its gloomy rain, and its funereal procession of dead leaves; here are twilights which on the stones *fling open* their red portals.

This technique already borders on the baroque cult of surprise and it is no doubt to similar effects that Ravegnani referred when describing Govoni's crepuscularism as wholly *sui generis*. We suspect, however, that at first his tonal clashes were unconscious ones and that he really did strive during his early crepuscular period to deploy his images in ways which would minimize them. But because his emotions were so strong his poems gradually built up to a crescendo; and, as his zest for life broke through, the tonal unity of his lyrics became splintered by the introduction of brusque or violent gestures into largely meditative, crepuscular scenery. If then the date of the present collection was not the early one of 1903, we might be tempted to attribute such a phenomenon to futurist influence. Though precisely because it antedates futurist activism by more than five years, it can only be convincingly associated with the poet's inner baroque mentality. Probably this baroque mechanism predates all the overt cultural patterns in Govoni's style and provides that hidden unity lurking behind his otherwise fragmentary manner.

Even in *Armonia in grigio et in silenzio*, which may be considered his most typical crepuscular work, we again discover unexpected tonal dislocations. Some of them amount to rapid transitions from a sense of gravity to bathos and frequently they prove to be introduced by means of verbal forms. For instance, the poet's impatience with the placid melancholy of his crepuscular tonalities is clearly accentuated in the inappropriateness of the last line of the following passage from 'Il lampione':

La sua fiamma claustrale
sembra una fiamma provvisoria
e instabile. Si direbbe che *sternuta*.

Its claustral flame seems an unstable and provisional flame. One would say that *it sneezes*.

Here not only does the bathos of the final comparison disrupt the preceding melancholy effect, but it also cuts across the crepuscular poets' cult of high-seriousness and muted sensations. So, whereas the normal adherents to the school retreat before their sense-impressions, Govoni seeks instead to glory in them, until the point is reached where his whole crepuscular tone breaks down under the strain.

One particular facet of his growing inner violence and hypersensitivity is to be found in *Gli Aborti* which is noted for its heightened responses to olfactory stimuli. Poems like 'I profumi' offer powerful synesthesic effects and their interplay of olfactory, visual and tactile images is worthy of a Baudelaire at his most acute moments of perception:

Vi sono dei profumi d'un candore
di neve intatta, bianchi e affascinanti
come miraggi tremuli, abbaglianti
come pupille di gatte in amore.

There are perfumes as pure as unblemished snow, white and as fascinating as tremulous mirages, dazzling as the pupils of cats in heat.

The almost convulsive sensuality of these lines is again typically baroque in flavour, even though its actual presentation owes much to the Parnassian manner of image-suspension. Indeed once more in this collection we find an oriental Parnassianism obtruding in the form of a wealth of intense and finely chiselled details. It is a representational mode which by now has become so intimate a part of Govoni's oblique manner of perceiving that it often results in frigid mirror-images of tortured baroque plenitude, not unlike those found in poems of the *seicento* ('seventeenth-century') mannerists:

Odalische che ignude e voluttuose
prendono il bagno, tra gli specchi astanti
uguali a grandi eunuchi noncuranti,
nei vasi di majoliche preziose.[8]

> Naked voluptuous odalisks who bathe among surrounding mirrors, like large nonchalant eunuchs, on precious majolica vases.

Whereas we can describe such displays of oriental virtuosity as attempts to recapture the traditional forms of a sensuous baroque realism, elsewhere we find the poet trying to add a more detached dimension to his crepuscular inspiration by introducing a quixotic melancholy or else a somewhat complacent irony into his imagery. With him, however, irony is more a social than a personally based phenomenon, even though in all other tonal respects his poetry still retains the muted complacency typical of a Corazzini:

> Strane città anodine
> dove tutti i sentimenti
> s'affinano in gentili malattie,
> dove persino l'amore
> assume una mitezza clericale.[9]

> Strange anodyne cities where all feelings are refined into gentle maladies, where even love assumes a clerical mildness.

Again within this social matrix we can already detect at times the development of a cult of realism, and in *Fuochi d'artifizio* (1905) Govoni's realism has a peasant-like earthiness about it which passes beyond the bounds of crepuscularism altogether. The following lines are a case in point:

> Nell'orto in mezzo ai fiori di patate
> *Scarrucola* il selvatico paone.[10]

> In the garden among the flowers of the potatoes the wild peacock *wheels like a pulley*.

Here, in short, there reappears the same disruptive verbal element as we saw in *Le Fiale*, but it now brings into focus one of Govoni's finest baroque gifts, his talent for a powerful and felicitous choice of metaphor. The verb 'scarrucola' is indeed an evocative masterpiece in this context, and, although it might seem somewhat violent and futurist in tone, it is really indicative of a trend destined to become widespread in the mature Govoni – an ability to replace traditional similes with colourful chains of baroque analogies.

Not that we should underestimate the rôle of traditional similes in his early verse, however; they often introduce a psychological factor identical with that to be found later in the poetry of a Saba or a Cardarelli. A case in point is his description of a melancholy day by means of a comparison evoking the distressing image of a blind child playing a mouth-organ in a lonely alley:

> O pallida giornata malinconica,
> triste come il lamento d'un'armonica
> che in fondo ad una solitaria via
> suoni una scalza bimba cieca.[11]

O pale melancholy day, as sad as the lament of a mouth-organ which at the end of a lonely road a bare-foot blind little girl plays.

At first similes of this type proved to be highly effective, but in the long run they too tended to degenerate into obsessions. So later, whenever he felt that his poetry was beginning to lose its cutting-edge, he would try to revive its flagging tension by making his comparisons more elaborate, more sensational and far-fetched. Inevitably the process led to a loss of emotional balance in certain lyrics and to the fracturing of their tonal consistency; with the result that in contrast with Corazzini's crepuscularism Govoni's seems to be constantly adulterated by external elements.[12]

At most, therefore, he can only be regarded as the peasant of the crepuscular movement, because he was exclusively concerned with the marketing of his wares in the most flamboyant way he could devise, and he had little or no understanding of the qualitative restraints required by the tradition within which he had chosen to work. Admittedly, he was able to imitate its dominant tonal features with a certain degree of success, yet beneath his verbal felicities we sense a deep-seated spiritual disorder: one which is particularly stressed in the lack of gradation of his tonal transitions and their evident incongruity. As his career progressed these aberrations become more and more marked, and at their worst they ranged from clumsy combinations of baroque and crepuscular features to strange – though sometimes effective – types of metamorphosis. An example of the first is a description of autumn as wearing 'una tiara di nebbia grigia e di pioggia' ('a tiara of grey, mist and rain') in 'Ore di pioggia', and of the second the transformation of dew-filled flowers into 'specchi vegetali degli occhi' ('vegetative mirrors of the eyes'). In the lyric 'Le azalée' from *Gli aborti* (1907) Govoni even seems willing to sell his soul for such effects, a point which is, perhaps, already evident in *Fuochi d'artifizio* (1905). In these two collections the sheaves of gratuitous images with which he regales us may well then be considered to announce the arrival of his futurist demon.

A casual perusal of a volume like *Gli aborti* reveals the perplexing disjointedness which springs from an aimless parading of sensations for their own sake and verifies the fact that these works are both take-off points for the poet's futurist experimentation. Yet when adopting his new literary stance Govoni neither manages nor wholly intends to abandon his former manner; he hopes instead to create from both movements a new synthesis of active, but attenuated realism. As a result his futurist trend, far from eliminating or merging with his crepuscular one, merely grows up alongside it, and the way in which his mixture of these two trends is ultimately presented has been castigated by at least one critic as a crepuscular-futurist confusion.[13] At first their juxtaposition does not lead to any noticeable interaction, except for the previously indicated splintering of tones. But gradually the type of symbiosis which Govoni fosters between them becomes somewhat more ingenious than we might have anticipated. A few poems in his main futurist collections – *Poesie elettriche* (1911) and *L'inaugurazione della primavera* (1915) – consequently possess a crepuscular undertone controlling their otherwise exuberant futurist violence: a feature which at times allows the poet to turn his very defects into positive factors in his struggle to unify his sensibility. Moreover, the passive crepuscular back-cloth he provides for his futurist enthusiasms brings into clearer focus the baroque elements which up till that point had lain partially dormant in his mind; and the result is that from here on his poetry is characterized by an obsessional cult of metaphor.

Gradually the peculiar effects emanating from his baroque image-chains distinguish him from the futurists proper just as they had distinguished him previously from the crepuscular poets. So, while he too is capable of sloughing off interminable series of analogies with the apparent nonchalance of a Marinetti, he never actually descends to the practice of the *parola in libertà* ('word-in-liberty'). His verse always retains a certain sense of unity and relevance, either by virtue of his use of embryonic conceits or, more often, as a result of his colourful visual patterns; and in general these restraints also guarantee some form of syntactic cohesiveness. It would not then be too much of an exaggeration to say that in his hands the violent aspects of futurism are partly submitted to a retributive violence, because he consciously strives to reconcile its gratuitous procedures with the earlier and more coherent modes of his neo-crepuscular writing. In the end his futurist experimentation hardly proves to be futurist at all: it is basically a polychromatic outpouring of baroque images which sometimes approach surrealist levels in their development of powerful subconscious analogies.

Frattini has described the entire process as 'una sarabanda di figure e di analogie'[14] ('a wild dance of figures and analogies') and most of its effectiveness derives from emotively-based – if congruous – transfigurations of the world of the senses. When they are at their most perceptive these transfigurations acquire a curious hallucinatory power characteristic of all modern baroque writing. A clear instance of their strange evocative power appears in 'Venezia elettrica' as a result of the use of the traditional baroque device of personification:

> . . . la tua luna esaltante
> che la laguna ingoia
> come una pastiglia di chinino
> per guarire la sua febbre lancinante . . . [15]

. . . your exulting moon which the lagoon swallows like a quinine pill to cure its piercing fever . . .

Quite apart from his relative comprehensibility, a further element which also distinguishes Govoni from Marinetti is a distant aura of *veggenza*. It is produced by a touch of anthropomorphic mystery which he infuses into his evocations of everyday effects, and it goes far to tone down through its interplay of light and shade the grotesque associations of many of the images he deploys. Hence the most he shares with his futurist contemporaries is a certain atmosphere of stylistic and structural gratuitousness; and, even if his great trains of similes and metaphors often fail in the same way as theirs to crystallize into significant lyrical patterns, they nevertheless remain meaningful and self-sufficient in their separate parts. This implies that, although one often senses that they could be continued *ad infinitum* without reaching any intellectual or emotive conclusion, they do function as true Vocian 'frammenti' and offer a series of disconnected insights into the nature of modern life.

A small number of the shorter poems of the period quite clearly also succeed in overcoming the problem of the poet's inability to conclude. One of them, in particular, fuses together crepuscular, futurist, Parnassian and impressionist techniques to produce a new type of rustic realism, in which the poet's dynamic everyday activities are underscored by a sense of orphic mystery:

> Esplodon le simpatiche campane
> d'un bianco campanile sopra tetti
> grigi; donne con rossi fazzoletti
> cavano da un rotondo forno il pane.
>
> Ammazzano un maiale nella neve
> tra un gruppo di bambini affascinati
> dal sangue, che con gli occhi spalancati
> aspettan la crudele agonia breve.
>
> Gettan i galli vittoriosi squilli.
> I buoi escono dai fienili neri;
> si spargono su l'argine, tranquilli,

scendono a bere gravi acqua d'argento.
Nei campi, rosei, bianchi, i cimiteri
sperano in mezzo al verde del frumento.[16]

The pleasing bells explode from a white belfry over grey roofs; women with red handkerchiefs take bread out of a round oven. They are killing a pig in the snow among a group of children fascinated by the blood, who with eyes wide open await the brief and cruel death-throes. Cocks crow triumphantly. Bullocks emerge from dark barns; they spread along the bank, calmly, go down heavily to drink the silvery water. In the fields, pinkish, white, the cemeteries live in hope among the green of the corn.

This sonnet is almost a symphony in sounds, colours and violent actions and undoubtedly represents one of the highwater marks of Govoni's poetic inspiration. Its somewhat disparate images are artfully blended together to create a well-rounded tableau suggestive of the subdued mystery and drama of human life. Like Campana we note that Govoni uses colours to evoke a stylized eternity behind the contingency of his everyday existence, and his verse is usually most effective when it is being suggestive and dissociative yet at the same time restrained in its lyrical procedures. In fact, it is largely because of a lack of this kind of restraint that the longer, more discursive poems appearing in his other collections prove to be entirely fragmentary by comparison.

If then we grant that we have to search for Govoni's lyrical successes in his explosive bursts of imagery rather than in his overall poetic structures, we soon discover that some of his finest writing is detectable in his analogical creations, especially when the first term of an analogy is suppressed in favour of its second element. A typical illustration is the opening stanza of 'I mendicanti di campagna' where the bizarre, baroque image of the bodiless limbs of beggars is merged with the plaintiveness of a crepuscular tonality to express a feeling of obsessive vagrancy:

Non son che mani e piedi,
piedi per camminare
mani per mendicare.

They are only hands and feet, feet to walk with, hands to beg with.

In contrast with this phantomatic evocation we also find in the same poem the very opposite, a colourful tableau producing a hallucinatory disquiet; so much so that the beggars whom the poet depicts appear to inhabit a somnambulist world of carefully calculated lyrical intensities:

Con degli immensi ombrelli,
verdi come la tela cerata
che copre gli organi di Barberia, tristi
come quelli dei brumisti

che aspettano in una piazza deserta,
spauracchi ambulanti,
vanno sotto la pioggia
che li bersaglia
aizzando, coi loro brandelli
inquieti e aggressivi,
i cani e i monelli.

With immense umbrellas, green as the waxed cloth which cover barrel-organs, as melancholy as those of the coach-drivers who wait in the deserted square, like ambling scarecrows, they walk through the rain which beats upon them, prodding with their restless and aggressive sticks both dogs and urchins.

Such a technique is perhaps Baudelairian in origin and it seems as if Govoni is trying to give the same hallucinatory perspective to country scenes as the French poet gave to the town in his *Tableaux parisiens*. Not only does he evoke the spectral reality we associate with Baudelaire's lyricism, however, but he is also equally aware of the baroque grotesqueness of society's forgotten inhabitants, of which Baudelaire's poem 'Les petites vieilles' is the paradigm:

Dans les plis sinueux des vieilles capitales,
Où tout, même l'horreur, tourne aux enchantements,
Je guette, obéissant à mes humeurs fatales,
Des êtres singuliers, décrépits et charmants.

In the sinuous folds of ancient capitals, where everything, even horror, becomes enchantment, I spy, obedient to my baleful humour, on strange, decrepit and charming creatures.

Now, admittedly, the Italian poet's hallucinatory realism is not quite as effective as the French poet's, but in the field of baroque complication he can even outdo his master. So that, whereas Baudelaire's 'vieilles' are abject and monstrous, a similar kind of old woman in Govoni's poem 'La vecchia' is curiously baroque. Hence the contorted beauty of her smile is described with a degree of ingenuity bordering on a 'metaphysical' conceit:

Un organetto di rughe
che suona il mendicante
del suo sorriso.

A tiny organ of wrinkles played by the beggarliness of her smile.

Here again the suppression of the first term in the comparison has the effect of disembodying the person described and causes her to regress to the same dreamlike, somnambulist world as that seen earlier in the case of the beggars.

On the other hand Govoni normally uses more conventional imagery – a type of *bas romantisme* – in his longer descriptions. In a far-fetched image of the moon, for instance, in 'L'usignolo e gli ubbriachi', the object of comparison which is usually noted for its age-old chastity is unexpectedly identified with the hideous immodesty and vulgarity of a prostitute:

> . . . la luna
> come una grassa puttana bruna
> di pelo e di capelli
> si solleva con una mano
> cicatrizzata d'anelli
> sul ventre lucido la veste di zafferano.

... the moon like a fat prostitute with dark skin and hair lifts above her shining belly her saffron robe with a hand scarred by rings.

When taken together these last two passages accordingly appear to represent the extremes of the poet's lyrical range and we normally find that he is most perceptive when he is operating between them. His conceits then sometimes acquire an airy grace bordering on the *fantaisiste*, as the following lines from 'Roma' will indicate:

> Nell'agro, intorno alla via Appia,
> si scorgono i treni deragliati degli acquedotti.

In the plain, around the via Appia, one sees the derailed trains of the acqueducts.

Even so, such felicities are isolated ones and fail in themselves to guarantee the success of the bulk of his poems in the collections which precede *L'inaugurazione della primavera* (1915). Furthermore, while this volume is perhaps the best production of the poet's early career, even its lyricism is still too fragmentary in structure for it to be considered a completely satisfactory poetic monument.

Probably the best way of underlining Govoni's structural inadequacies in this period is to examine his symbolism, since its consistency proves to be more verbal than spiritual. As a general rule the poet tries to use symbols as focal points around which his imagery can gravitate, but in practice his images and their symbolic import rarely cohere. This is true even for his most persistent symbol, the nightingale. Only in the short lyric 'Poesia e realtà' does it really attain to any kind of psycho-sensuous unity, when the purity of its song is used to offset the ugliness of reality:

> L'anima mia è come l'usignuolo
> che canta canta sopra il biancospino
> fiorito inebbriandosi al suo canto
> come preso in una vortice di sogno
> come in preda ad un fascino maligno;

e non s'accorge che sotto la siepe
lo fissa e attira coi suoi occhi molli
l'immondo rospo a bocca spalancata
ove presto avran fine e canto e sogno.

My soul is like the nightingale which sings, sings on the flowering hawthorn, inebriating itself with its song as if caught up in a whorl of dreams, as if a prey to a malign fascination; and it does not notice that under the hedge the filthy toad fixes and attracts it with its damp eyes and gaping mouth, where soon both song and dream will end.

But even this kind of treatment is of an external or thematic type, more closely associated with allegory than with a truly inherent symbolism. Its extra-literary moralizing implications, moreover, are clearly stressed in 'l'usignuolo e gli ubbriachi' where the nightingale's song is first contrasted with that of drunkards and prostitutes and then linked grotesquely in a duet with the former to emphasize the inevitable decline of the poet's ideals:

E l'usignolo innocente
continua il duetto sguaiato e divino
con gli ubbriachi turpi
sotto il fanale nauseoso
contro il muro schifoso.

And the innocent nightingale continues its open-throated and divine duet with the disgusting drunks under the nauseating street-lamp against the befouled wall.

Essentially such a duet perpetuates the dichotomy of inspiration which runs right through Govoni's entire lyricism: his tendency to juxtapose thought and sensations instead of bringing about their lyrical synthesis. In the long run even the purity of the nightingale's song is bound to be undermined by such a technique; and in a play written during his neo-futurist period we see a first stage in its degeneration, for the bird is gradually turned into a phallic symbol.[17] At this point it becomes evident, however, that sexual sublimation is no more effective as a catalytic process than crepuscular detachment or futurist violence, and so most of Govoni's images continue ineffectually to illustrate certain ingenuous allegorical themes without offering any definite intellectual focus for his feelings. They become, in short, part and parcel of his directionless stream of *immagini senza fili* ('images without links') which, like the futurist *parola in libertà* they parallel at a slightly higher level of intellection, rush for ever onwards in the hope of arriving by mere accretive means at some distant and undefined poetic goal.

Not surprisingly, Govoni's pursuit of rarefied erotic imagery and other figurative will-o'-the wisps soon leads him to ransack the technical armoury of the symbolists and the decadents, and he himself gradually becomes obsessed with the riotous word-pictures he evokes. Not only is he enchanted by their shape and colour, but also by their taste and smell; and he takes a particular delight in the active physical presence of objects, in their intractable solidity and inexplicable permanence. Yet the more he participates in material realities the less he is able to put them into perspective, except perhaps as displays of mere visual intensities; and so, by being excluded in this sense from the absolutes of spiritual life, he finds himself condemned to juggle with the existential elements of the universe in their apparent endless flux without either understanding or interpreting them. The only valid solution to his spiritual dilemma would be the substitution of a form of lyrical synthesis for his art of almost pure descriptiveness, but this he is quite unable to achieve. Thus he seizes on the cult of the marvellous which had served his forerunners – the *seicentisti* ('seventeenth-century mannerists') – so well, and he uses it as a means of dazzling his readers by undermining their critical perceptions.

With the passage of time surprise or at least a form of childlike wonder becomes his chief artistic weapon and he employs it unashamedly in an attempt to conceal his lack of interpretative power. In order to spring his imaginative surprises more effectively he even tries at times to take over the futurist doctrine of simultaneity; although here once more, because his doctrine is like theirs an external one of *extension* and not an internal one of *intension*, the practice rarely leads to satisfying poetry. All that he manages to do is to produce a type of verse in which the thread of emotion is strained to breaking-point by shoals of perceptive, yet largely irrelevant, images; and these too are produced in the pious hope that sheer weight of numbers will provide a cathartic effect.

The technique may be described as a fluvial one and is perhaps typical of the modern epic style which we also encounter in poets like Saint-John Perse. With Govoni, however, its main feature is an aimless neo-narrative accompanied by an exasperation of the senses in an intensely baroque direction. Through a grotesque magnification of reality and its subsequent dematerialization within a sensuously attenuated dreamworld the Italian poet actually turns the normal baroque epic typified by Marino's *Adone* away from its concrete realist base towards a cult of highly artificial analogical relations; and, even though his lyrical texture on occasion is by no means less complicated nor less luxuriant than that of his seventeenth-century counterpart, the human gestures and sense of corporeal solidity which characterize Marino's imagery are removed by him on to a purely abstract plane. Let us take as typical examples two poems by Marino and Govoni respectively. For instance, in the former's 'Arianna (Sampogna)' a realist sense of drama is maintained by the very deliberation of the female figure, against her hypersensitive background of rich sensations:

> Le vezzose piante
> scalze e senza coturno
> toccando la vicina umida sponda
> si lavavan nell'onda,
> e nel margine erboso,
> a cui da l'onda istessa
> intessuto di lino
> verde, rosso, ceruleo, azzurro e giallo
> orlava il lembo un natural ricamo,
> sovente il mar con mormoranti baci
> a lambirle il bel piè stendea la lingua . . . [18]

Her delightful feet, quite naked and without buskins, were washed by the wave as they touched the nearby dank strand, and right up to the grassy shore, where a natural embroidery woven with green, red, blue, azure and yellow by the wave itself hemmed the verge, the sea often thrust out its tongue to lap at her fair foot with murmurous kisses . . .

But a similar figure in one of Govoni's most successful lyrics, 'Ballerina', is present only in a metaphysical sense – as a disembodied lyrical harmony. Having, in fact, little or no existence outside the ritual dance she performs, the modern poet's personified butterfly is no more than a baroque incarnation of his concept of pure movement, though expressed in intense sensory terms:

> L'elegantissima vanessa
> che s'allontana e s'avvicina
> a questo fresco fiore di peonia,
> è come una stupenda ballerina
> che turbina magicamente
> su un tappeto di fuoco e di profumo,
> sulla punta delle dita,
> e, tra i cuscini morbidi di rose
> cade sfinita.
> Eccola, s'avanza,
> tutta vestita di baci,
> sulla peonia rossa di garanza;
> agita i veli fantasiosi, e danza.

The elegant butterfly which approaches and moves away from this fresh flowering peony, is like a stupendous ballerina who whirls magically on a carpet of fire and perfume, on the tips of her toes, and, among the soft cushions of roses, falls in a swoon. Behold, she moves forward, dressed wholly in kisses, over the peony as red as madder; waves her fantastic wings, and dances.

Now no one will deny that certain associative elements in the poet's inspiration have fallen together here to create a remarkable, if ultimately disembodied and synesthesic, lyrical pattern; but the difference between Govoni's lyricism and Marino's is that the earlier poet's work is still intensely concrete, still conditioned by human tensions and a humanist sense of values, whereas the modern writer's is not merely more abstract in conception, its hierarchy of values has also changed. So here we are no longer confronted with a social grace illuminated by aesthetic effects, we find ourselves instead in the presence of a wholly aesthetic grace with metaphysical not social overtones: one in which there is at most only a slender thread of emotive authenticity to counterbalance the complete abstraction of the lyrical situation. In other words the humanism of the seventeenth century has been sacrificed on the altars of a contemporary orphic aestheticism which depicts and essentializes a decorative extreme, the ritual dance of a butterfly seen analogically as a ballerina.

Throughout the whole of his literary career Govoni was, in fact, all too aware of the need for a call to order and tried energetically at times to toughen his analogical manner by means of a cult of intellectual conceits. His successes in this direction are again to be counted more in fragments than in complete poems, although one partial success (which proves, however, to be simultaneously a structural failure) is the poem 'Ho mangiato una donna in un gelato'. As the very title suggests, the basic conceit is incredibly weak when compared with, for instance, the one appearing in Rebora's 'Gira la trottola viva'; but at the same time certain passages and analogies have a lyrical grace of their own. At first the lady's sensual, almost sexual, presence is symbolized by her gaily-coloured dress and parasol and these baroque effects captivate the poet. He subsequently indulges in a daydream at her expense as he orders a waiter to bring him an ice-cream. When it arrives he enjoys her analogically, by eating her symbolically as he devours the ice-cream's multi-coloured layers.

Now such a situation is perhaps full of baroque possibilities, but Govoni does not possess the razor-sharp elegance of mind to draw all its analogical threads together, and so his images again remain decorative rather than purposeful. His conclusion is illustrative of his ingrained lyrical slackness, even though the waiter appears to aid and abet his plan to take analogical possession of his victim:

> Ed il giovane mago sbarbato
> m'allunga sorridendo
> il cilindrico gelato
> che finalmente mi libererà
> dalla tua malia.
>
> Ho finito. E nessuno mai saprà
> che nel gelato rosa e viola

> ho mangiato la bella avventuriera
> con la gonna cannelloni color nocciuola
> e il cappello malva a giardiniera . . .

And the young smooth-shaven magician, smiling, offers me the cylindrical ice-cream which will finally free me from your bewitchment. I have finished it. And no one will ever know that in the pink and purple ice-cream I have eaten the fair adventuress with the striped, nut-coloured skirt and the mauve, flowered hat . . .

How do we account for the poet's lyrical inadequacy at a moment of apparent triumph? It simply results from his tendency to slip away from the overall logic of his conceits towards grotesquely distended descriptions of their constituent parts. Such a manner of proceeding is clearly characteristic of Italian baroque poets like Marino rather than of more cohesive baroque traditions headed by Góngora in Spain or Donne in England; and there seems little doubt that Govoni modelled his poems far too closely on the former. So, while the parallel between the woman's clothes and the layers of ice-cream offer ample scope for a show of ingenuity, the conceit is soon transformed into a parade of hallucinatory visual images.

Even so, it would be unfair to deny Govoni occasional successes in the practice of neo-baroque wit. These successes amount to sporadic moments of visual acuity or hallucinatory abstraction which are embedded in his otherwise relatively aimless narrative structures. One powerful example of his ability to penetrate and display the secret visual relationships between things appears in 'Ricordo alpino':

> . . . le rondini giú per le chine
> tosavano la prateria fiorita,
> tutta arazzi di sole e vellutate ombre fuggenti,

. . . the swallows down the slopes shaved the flowering meadowland, all tapestries of sunlight and fleeting velvet shadows,

where the baroque verbal imagery associated with the swallows as they interact with the sunlight is lyrically unifying as well as being hallucinatory. Again, on the quainter, more abstract plane which we encountered in his earlier descriptions of beggars or of an old woman's face, we find the following image in 'Paesaggio magnetico':

> Va e viene lungo la scorza
> l'aritmetica delle formiche . . .

There comes and goes on the bark the arithmetic of the ants . . .

However, not even the most enthusiastic of Govoni's admirers would claim that such images blend functionally with his overall patterns, although there is certainly a progressive accentuation of the baroque element in his poetry with the passage of time. On the whole, therefore, his cumulative approach to imagery tends to support Boine's view that he held as his central aesthetic belief that 'la bellezza sia fare un inventario del mondo'[19] ('beauty is to make an inventory of the world').

In the collections *Brindisi alle notte* (1924), *Il flauto magico* (1932) and *Canzoni a bocca chiusa* (1938) the poet's baroque perceptiveness gradually becomes dominant, and perhaps it can be said that in the last of these volumes his poetry reaches both a point of maturity and crisis: a point of maturity because he now attains to some level of awareness of the harrowing irrelevance of his image-streams, and of crisis because of the equally harrowing intellectual shortcomings that he senses within his creative faculty. At long last he seems to realize that his analogical demon is driving him towards a spiritual desert and that his poetry will have to be totally transformed if he wishes to preserve it. In his attempts to do so he aims at developing an inflexible will-power, for the purpose of controlling his deep draughts of sensation; and he hopes that his thirst for sensuous imagery will gradually give way to a desire for authentic experiences. In judging his own past at this point he writes:

Invano hai camminato e corso:
tutto è ancora da raggiungere:
la strada della vita è sempre da rifare:
sei ogni giorno al punto di partenza
con la gola bruciata
dal pepe della polvere
e davanti agli occhi ubbriachi
l'acqua fuggente del riverbero . . .[20]

Vainly you have walked and run: everything is still to be attained: life's journey is still to be redone: every day you are at the point of departure with a burning throat from the pepper of the dust and before your drunken eyes the fleeing water of reflection . . .

Clearly this constant willingness to grapple with life at new levels reaffirms Govoni's modernity of outlook, but it does not give him any firmer control over his style, except perhaps in a few short poems where a unity of tone results from a baroque reconstruction of simple visual scenes.One such poem is 'Cavallo' in which the poet's normal *visività* is raised to a higher plane of intensity:

Violenta primavera del cavallo!
Ad ogni suo elastico passo
intorno allo zoccolo viola
che stampa lune di rumore, fuma

un biancospino di polvere,
sboccia un cespuglio di fango.

Violent spring of the horse! At each one of its elastic steps, around its purple hoof which prints out half-moons of sound, there smokes a hawthorn of dust, there blossoms a shrub of mud.

Already these images are neo-hermetic in their implications and from the standpoint of imaginative cohesion few can rival them in his entire work. At this juncture, therefore, he has evolved an authentic *magie évocatoire*, both by virtue of the poem's lyrical unity and by way of its depth of sensory insight.

If short poems of the highest quality like 'Cavallo' are rarely found in *Canzoni a bocca chiusa*, longer poems of the same quality are rarer still. However, at least one, 'Ritratto di donna', is carefully structured as an extended baroque metaphor, and in this poem the human body is treated agronomically by being progressively metamorphosed into a vineyard or fruit-garden:

Sotto,
molli viti di braccia
e pampini di ascelle,
dolci pere cassane hanno una goccia
di sidro ghiotto
fragolato
da cui scacci i miei diti come vespe
con un grido
cieco annaspante
con artigli di falco di nido.

Underneath, soft vines of arms and vine-leaves of armpits, sweet cassant pears bear a drop of tasty strawberried cider, from which you drive away my wasp-like fingers with a blind delirious shout, with the claws of a nesting falcon.

Here again the texture of the poem is illustrative of both the strong and the weak features of Govoni's art, though fortunately the strong points momentarily overshadow the weaker ones. On the credit side we can obviously place his sensitive treatment of a contingent situation – the description of a naked woman engaged in washing her hair and spied upon by the poet through a half-open door. While on the debit side there is the over-complicated conceit identifying ablution with the harvest, although it too blends here so appropriately with the simple coquetry of the woman that the lyric's somewhat creaking structural mechanics is hardly noticed.

What, in fact, tends to unbalance the structure side of the majority of the poems in this volume is paradoxically the very strength of the poet's perceptions, since their power leads to such a determined show of ingenuity and visual acuity that certain lyrics become sensuously overloaded, even though their individual images remain incisive and provocative. We thus tend to linger over their constituent parts longer than we ought, and when this occurs we find our attention being so completely wrenched out of focus that we are unable to discern the overall significance of the lyrical patterns developed.

Cases in point are abundant at this stage of Govoni's career and they seem to be linked with his taste for synesthesia and abstract-concrete contrasts. We shall examine the abstract-concrete contrast first, although at times it is rather difficult to distinguish between this device and parallel synesthesic ones. A striking rendering of auditory effects involving, once again, a partial suppression of concrete elements (this time through metonymy) emerges from the following description of birds in 'Giardino d'uccelli':

> . . . è tutto il giorno
> una fiera di chiacchierine gole . . .;

> . . . all day long there is a festival of chattering throats . . .;

while equally powerful visual imagery is deployed in 'Autunno' to describe the effects of mist in a countryside scene:

> Freddi buoi di nebbia
> camminano sugli argini
> tra i calici violacei del colchico.

> Cold bullocks of mist walk on the banks among the violet calyces of the autumn crocuses.

This form of imaginative intensity clearly borders upon a visionary insight and there can be no doubt that the visual sense is the most acute of all the senses with Govoni. But since there is no lack of examples drawn from the other senses as well, it might perhaps be instructive to survey briefly the whole spectrum of his synesthesic effects. To achieve complete coverage we need to draw on images appearing in various volumes from *Il quaderno dei sogni e delle stelle* (1924) right up to *Govonigiotto* (1943).

On the visual plane the poet regularly seems to succumb to hallucinations when evoking certain objects. A good example is the cat-image, because in 'Le sere orfane e tristi . . .' he describes how

> I catenacci rugginosi
> sbarrano le porte, come gatti neri.

> The rusting chains bar the doors, like black cats.

Later, in 'Ho visto . . .' in the same collection, this image is reinforced by a similar one employing the opposite colour-scheme:

Sopra un lembo di muro il sole
era come un dolce gatto bianco.

On a fragment of wall the sun lay like a gentle white cat.

But perhaps more successful than such far-fetched comparisons are his delicate images of movement which are capable of evoking in a single line of verse an entire landscape, as in 'Bagattelle del mattino':

Tremola un falco dietro il campanile.

A falcon quivers behind the belfry.

Just where the line is to be drawn between this visual baroque style and the sort of 'metaphysical' abstraction mentioned earlier it is indeed difficult to say, but images like 'gli occhi birichini/ della pioggia d'aprile' ('the imp-like eyes of the April rain') in 'Patria morta' or 'un gracil nevicar di biancospini' ('a graceful snow of hawthorn') in 'Passeggiata' clearly play on our sensory and rational faculties at one and the same time. The same can be said of the following lines from 'La stella pulcinaia', although the imagery has abstract, possibly Pascolian, elements in its texture as well:

. . . il carro in un angolo non è piú
che un mazzo di ruote
in preda alla ruggine dell'immobilità . . .

. . . the cart in the corner is nothing more than a bunch of wheels preyed on by the rust of inactivity . . .

Olfactory images are perhaps rarer and often concern themselves with certain homely smells like that of the weekly washing. But again it is the interplay of the olfactory elements with the visual image which accounts for their surprising depth of synesthesic penetration:

Un fresco amaro odore di bucato
viene dal biancospino in fiore.[21]

A fresh bitter smell of laundry comes from the flowering hawthorn.

Likewise auditory and visual imagery are often very closely associated, sometimes in a virtually orphic sense, as in the following line from 'Sanguigna':

. . . passano calme l'ombre soffianti dei buoi . . .

. . . the panting shadows of the bullocks pass calmly by . . .

Again, auditory imagery and tactile impressions tend to become intermingled on occasion:

. . . si sentivano dei piccoli piedi nudi ancor caldi
come uova nel nido.[22]

. . . one could hear little bare feet still warm like eggs in the nest.

Hence, when Govoni is in his most perceptive moments he either manages to blend together the responses of the various senses into vast analogical perspectives like the following one from 'Paesello':

> Paesello
> fra smeraldi di monti,
> una penna nera dietro un muro sereno,

A hamlet between emeralds of mounts, a black feather behind a calm wall,

or else he uses them to increase the impact of one particular sensation or effect, such as the one to be found in the opening of 'Come il fuoco sornione':

> Mi entrasti nella carne viva
> come il fuoco sornione nella stoffa . . .

You entered my living flesh like a sly fire in cloth . . .

Yet, oddly enough, what the poet's firm grip on his senses now shows is his relative lack of control over the purely baroque complications of many of his comparisons. The quaintly surrealist effect of the following comparison from 'Plastico di Roma' is perhaps still acceptable:

> Le donne al posto del seno
> portavano un semplice neo.

The women in the place of their breasts had a simple mole.

But comparisons like the following one from 'È l'ora' border on the ludicrous and show an exaggerated cult of Marinesque surprise in Govoni's lyrical method:

> È l'ora in cui dolgono agli alberi
> le radici come denti.

It is the time when the roots of the trees ache like teeth.

Even so, we can perhaps conclude that this profusion of sensory images based on abstraction or on synesthesia indicate in their relative effectiveness that the poet is now largely the master of his individual perceptions, although their baroque orientation and overall looseness of structure are still largely dissociative.

Eventually Govoni was only liberated from the meshes of his own verbal magic by a personal tragedy, the death of his son Aladino, who was shot as a hostage at the 'Fosse ardeatine' by the Nazis in 1945. As soon as he heard of his son's death the poet's baroque idyllicism collapsed and his dominant mood changed from one of irrepressible delight in natural forms to a brooding melancholy and despair. With this radical change of mood his neo-hermetic technique of image-suspension was also largely discontinued, and in its place we see the emergence of a sombre narrative strain. What the tightening up of his inspiration for the purpose of expressing his despair really required from him at this juncture, however, was a new poetic outlook in the broader sense of the word, not just the adoption of new representational techniques. So, when we ask ourselves whether this traumatic experience of personal loss deepened the poet's insight in any way, we find that we have to introduce into our assessment all sorts of qualifications.

From the stylistic standpoint Govoni aimed at creating in *Aladino* an inner chronicle of events, and his story begins with a re-evocation of his son's childhood and ends with his tragic martyrdom. But the poet can hardly be considered to be at ease in his new manner and this prompts Spagnoletti to observe that he possessed 'un cuore di poeta non rassegnato ai suoi facili miti, ma non preparato però all'angoscia'[23] ('the heart of a poet not resigned to his facile myths, yet not prepared however for anguish'). Moreover, we soon discover that such a narrative discourse demands from him a greater artistic consistency than his previous dissociative impressionism and he is rarely able to achieve it. He therefore becomes a prey to two separate kinds of literary temptation: a shallow, though passionate, form of rhetoric and a desire to give vent to inarticulate cries of grief and despair. Yet his despairing, denunciatory style rarely acquires any deep lyrical resonance and his rhetorical one tends to inveigh more or less apocalyptically against society rather than attempt to represent the inner drama associated with his personal loss. This does not mean that *Aladino* is a complete failure as a work of art, although in its weaker moments the lyrical texture does underline the fact that rhetorical fulminations are no remedy for a lack of genuine poetic tension.

What emerges almost immediately is a suspicion that the poet has lived far too long within his egocentric shell of neo-hermetic experiences to act like anything other than a fish out of water when he is forced to return to an appraisal of the real world. One even senses at times that, despite himself, the death of his son has failed to make any profound impression upon his hide-bound sensibility. As a consequence, the whole emotional focus of the work appears out of joint; and, instead of conveying to us his intimate responses to the tragedy of his son's death, the poet simply gives voice to a form of social posturing in which he denounces human wickedness and deplores the paradoxes inherent in human life:

> Quando sento suonare un organetto
> mi si annebbia la vista anche di dentro
> e il cuore mi si spezza dallo strazio:
> il mio triste passato di dolore
> è chiamato a raccolta da quel suono.

Gli ideali traditi, la sinistra
lotta con l'uomo, le sconfitte amare
e la crudele beffa dell'amore,
mi prendono alla gola come un tossico
infiammato. E su tutto, il tuo martirio
con quel gran sangue . . . È niente, o benedetto,
il morire in confronto a quel che io provo
quando sento suonare un organetto.[24]

When I hear a barrel-organ playing, my eyes become misty even within, and my heart breaks from the agony: my sad past full of grief is gathered together by that sound. My betrayed ideals, my sinister struggle with men, my bitter defeats and the cruel mockery of love, seize me by the throat like a burning poison. And above all else, your martyrdom, with that great bloodletting . . . It is nothing, o blessed one, to die in comparison with what I feel when I hear a barrel-organ playing.

However, even the egocentric self-pity which appears at the end of this lyric is typical of his present mood, because it follows logically from the recriminations he now directs against humanity as a whole; and no doubt such recriminations are intended to reveal the contrast between the airy beauty of his former dreamworld and his present traumatic despair. Significantly, he also returns here to a neo-crepuscular type of inspiration, to the Corazzinian image of the hurdy-gurdy, to express his new-found anguish; and yet this fact again underlines the anachronistic rhetorical vein stifling his true emotive responses as a father.

The principal message behind *Aladino* is consequently the melancholy fact that Govoni is quite unable to break out of the convolutions of his own carefully constructed lyrical *persona*. His self-centredness is always uppermost throughout the tragedy and not even a religious motif can wholly undermine his egotism. A case in point is the following lyric in which the poet makes a half-hearted attempt to liken Aladino's death to that of Christ. Nevertheless at the end the real martyr again appears to be Govoni the father and not the son, because his son's martyrdom has burdened him with the whole weight of humanity's remorse and sorrow:

Quante croci ho portato in vita mia!
Croci d'amore, croci di poesia.
Tante ne vidi, e tante ne portai
che persino le braccia in fiore al mandorlo
vidi alzar disperatamente in croce.
Ma la croce piú perfida ed amara
è quella che ora porto nel mio sangue,
inchiodata con chiodi incandescenti:
la croce della tua povera bara.[25]

How many crosses have I borne in my life! Crosses of love, crosses of poetry. I have borne as many as I have seen, so that even the flowering arms of the

> almond-tree I have seen raised despairingly in a cross. But the most bitter and insidious cross is that which I now carry in my blood, nailed there with white-hot nails: the cross of your poor coffin.

Elsewhere we encounter a still more overweening form of egocentricity, in which Govoni's genuine grief as a father is set against his tetchiness as a great – though misunderstood – poet, in the eleventh lyric:

> Io scontai con la tragica tua fine
> la mia crudele povertà di padre;
> e scontai nell'Italia analfabeta
> la mia grandezza oscura di poeta.

> I redeemed through your tragic end my cruel ineptitude as a father; and I redeemed in an illiterate Italy my obscure greatness as a poet.

We can only conclude from this that a deeper and unavoidable form of artistic insincerity underlies his honestly felt anguish as a man, and its very existence shows the poet once again to be the victim of fashion. At this time, we recall, a reaction was setting in against the hermetic movement and Govoni was beginning to become aware of it. So, while paying his due to personal grief, he was trying simultaneously to evolve a new manner of narrative discourse in harmony with the trend then being established by Quasimodo and others. He thus continued to write with one eye on his personal feelings while the other was intent on keeping abreast of the cultural innovations emerging in the postwar world.

Nevertheless, this collection is perhaps not wholly a literary exercise. It strikes at least one genuine note insofar as it reveals a change of perspective in the poet's attitude to death. Death is now conceived by him as a waste-land, as a withering away of animal pleasures, and it tends to reduce his imagination to its lowest creative level by replacing his earlier luxuriant imagery with a somewhat unimaginative form of rhetoric. Here again, however, there is a subtle connection between Govoni's present and past manners, because both his baroque and rhetorical moments accentuate a certain inability to rise above gratuitous ornamental flourishes. Furthermore, his escapist proclivities are once more evident in *Aladino* and cause his inspiration to slip from a central area of personal grief towards extraneous social and religious considerations. To cover up so clear a failure to objectivize his emotions he thus continues to practise a quantitative approach to his art and still hopes, it seems, to equate lyrical insight with sheer weight of productivity.

Eventually he himself became conscious of the impotence of his new manner and in *Conchiglia sul quaderno* (1948) questioned the whole range of his inspiration.[26] But in contrast with his earlier self-indulgence he now claimed to see through the world of illusion he had previously created for himself and tried to depict life without nurturing false hopes of any kind:

Ora che la crudele realtà
ha fermato quel giuoco degli specchi
con cui tutto il creato inganna e illude
sé stesso con le creature ignude;
so troppo bene tutto l'universo
che bugia di fulgore in lontananza
di pestiferi fuochi e marci fiati
sia per gli ignari miseri viventi:
immenso spaventoso niente, fatto
di niente come me a ripetizione.[27]

Now that cruel reality has halted that play of mirrors through which the whole of creation deceives and deludes itself with its defenceless creatures; I know all too well what a lie of distant refulgences with pestiferous fires and stinking exhalations the whole universe is for the wretched, ignorant living: an immense, frightening void, made of nothingness, like myself, by repetition.

Not only his cult of sensations but also his irrepressible optimism seem to have abandoned the poet at this juncture leaving in his mouth only a taste of bitterness and a sense of lyrical aridity. The result is that in an attempt to counter their effects and to conceal his diminishing hunger for life he once more tries to indulge in a profusion of rustic images, and his old poetic stand-bys – nightingales, swallows, starlings, variegated flowers, animals and children – again appear in profusion in certain of his neo-narrative lyrics. The style he now practises, in short, is a regressive one harking back to his early baroque period; and, as was previously the case, his evocations tend to resemble inventories of the natural order of things.

To these somewhat inert tableaus he also attempts to add in his later collections a cult of scientific or pseudo-scientific jargon which he uses as a substitute for imaginative creation. In this respect the poetry of *Conchiglia sul quaderno* is by no means the worst example, though its astronomical perspectives remind us of Pascoli's non-cathartic, cosmic soaring:

Anche il tempo verrà che la Galassia
(men di un minuto per l'eternità
i milioni di secoli passati)
spegnerà la beffarda luminaria.
E i miliardi di soli giganteschi
che la gremiscono ora penderanno
calcinati nel greto dello spazio
come ciotoli calvi levigati
dalla corrente dell'eternità.
Oltre quel ghiaccio nero, inesorabile,
salirà il grido vano del mio strazio.[28]

> The time will also come when the Galaxy (less than a minute for eternity the millions of centuries that have passed) will extinguish its mocking light. And billions of gigantic suns which now teem in it will hang mineralized in the gravel-bed of space like bald pebbles polished by the current of eternity. Beyond that black ice will inexorably rise the vain cry of my anguish.

Here a sense of baroque disproportion is all too obvious and the feelings expressed are also despairingly egocentric and sentimental; but the dominant feature of the style is not yet a scientific verbalism in the true sense of the word. In fact, a far more important characteristic in this volume is the resuscitation of the poet's analogical demon. For, baulked as he now found himself in life as well as in art, he gradually slipped back into his earlier mode of writing in a baroque frenzy; and with the resuscitation of such a frenzy there reappears the irrepressible panache and the dank luxuriance of his erotic fantasy. This becomes evident in the anthropomorphic imagery of 'Nozze celesti':

> Com'è bella la terra, col suo mare
> che si solleva, grembo palpitante,
> e i monti che digradan come seni
> gonfi del latte delle bianche nuvole!
> Languida, d'erbe nuove e d'acqua bionda
> irresistibilmente si offre; e il cielo,
> lacerandole il verginale velo,
> dei suoi fulmini d'oro la feconda.
> Erra a lungo sui prati dell'Aprile
> l'odore elettrico del Dio virile.

> How fair is the earth, with its heaving sea, a palpitating bosom, and the mountains which slope down like breasts filled with the milk of the white clouds! Languid, with fresh grass and fair water, irresistibly it offers itself; and the sky, tearing away its virginal veil, impregnates it with its golden thunderbolts. There stalks for a long time over the fields in April the electric incense of a virile God.

In other words the Govonian leopard had been quite unable to change its spots as a result of the harrowing experiences of *Aladino*. So the fact remains that evocations of this kind rarely hold any interpretative power beyond their reassertion of the regenerative forces of nature; and they only achieve even these effects by baroque sexual personifications and the repetition of fertility-symbols. Perhaps, however, the one area where these lyrics appear to have made some sort of poetic advance is in their rhythmico-imaginative orchestration; although, oddly, even their rhythmical variations are partially offset by an impression that the searing experience of his son's death has temporarily removed the vitalistic element from the poet's sensibility. Accordingly, in place of the spontaneous, if contorted, imaginative grace we find in *Canzoni a bocca chiusa*, we are now presented with a flaccid reversion to the artificiality and commonplace anthropomorphism of the *seicento*. Over-indulgence in such practices soon causes Govoni's fantasies to fall flat, so that beneath the veneer of his tumultuous imagery we continue to detect a sense of emotional aridity.

Fortunately a revival of his spirits takes place in *Preghiera al trifoglio* published in 1953, where once again we sense a genuine return to his earlier sensory insights. What the poet attempts in this volume is a regression into a world of childhood innocence in order to bring about a reconciliation between his sensibility and his destiny as a man. Although he does not always succeed, it is evident that the discursive method he adopted in *Aladino* is now beginning to find an authentic place in his art. So, although his image-chains are less dense than previously, they certainly no longer suffer from any slackness in their narrative structure; they acquire instead a certain poetic luminosity which in his previous volumes had largely disappeared.

It is to be regretted, therefore, that in *Manoscritto nella bottiglia* (1954) the tender plant of Govoni's renewed sensory perception again tends to wilt. It is replaced by exercises in self-imitation, almost in self-parody, since all his former manners are now crudely regurgitated and starkly juxtaposed. For instance, we detect a crepuscular tone in a poem like 'Una volta mai piú', a baroque one in 'Brasso Cattleya', and an apocalyptic, mechanico-futurist one in 'La bomba H', to mention but a few. A typical example of the accumulation of such detritus is a poem like 'Madrigale alla luna' where the initial lunar motif is quickly forgotten and the lyric founders beneath the weight of hyperbolic and self-generating imagery:

Ninfomane regina delle notti,
febbre bianca di gufi e d'usignoli;
gazza ladra celeste
attirata da tutti i luccichíi:
acque stagnanti, vetri rotti, ghiacci;
chitarra
di neve morta assassinata
con corde
di sangue e di lagrime filate;
pura sacerdotessa uscita
a spargere sul gregge dei dormienti
foglie d'issopo e brine arborescenti . . .

Nymphomaniac queen of the night, white fever of owls and nightingales; thieving magpie of heaven attracted by all its glitterings: stagnant waters, broken glass, ice; guitar of dead murdered snow with strings of blood and threaded tears; pure priestess emerging to scatter over the herd of sleeping humanity leaves of hyssop and arborescent hoar-frost . . .

As previously indicated, Frattini calls this type of writing so common with Govoni an example of his 'famose catene analogiche' ('well-known analogical chains'); but he adds that all too frequently they tend to undermine his true inspiration because of their almost exclusive reliance on an 'automatica matrice psichica'[29] ('automatic psychical pattern').

That such a manner of composing should ultimately produce stereotyped and repetitive verse is hardly surprising, and the same type of self-imitation and self-parody is perceptible in *Stradario della primavera* (1958) and *I canti del puro folle* (1959). But, although these collections rarely strike a fresh lyrical chord in our sensibilities, they are nevertheless praiseworthy for their renewed vigour and autumnal serenity. So that, while in a subdued mood in 'Dopo il temporale' the poet feels keenly the approach of old-age and reflects it in images of serene wisdom:

> Bello e triste è ascoltare la pioggia
> e guardare il vento,
> senza pensare al sangue
> e sentirne l'oscuro tormento,

> Fine and sad it is to listen to the rain and gaze at the wind, without thinking of the blood and feeling its dark torment,

elsewhere in 'Furberia d'amore' he can still talk of love in his old manner and shows conclusively that the dark torment of the blood is still capable of erupting within his ageing flesh:

> In ogni senso le diramazioni
> della vita infinita godrò in te,
> carne di donna, neve, luce, fiori,
> come un'unica carne intelligente.
> . . . .
> A casa nei tuoi occhi berrò l'anima
> al fiume, ubbriacato di capelli;
> godrò con spasimi di voluttà
> nelle tue carni ancora piú divine
> le curve delle tenere colline.

> In you I shall enjoy in all senses the ramifications of infinite life, flesh of woman, snow, light, flowers, as a unique intelligent flesh . . . At home in your eyes, I shall drink your soul in a river, inebriated with hair; with quivers of voluptuousness I shall enjoy in your even diviner flesh the curves of tender hills.

What these poems achieve, therefore, is finally to set the seal on Govoni's stupendous lyrical output and provide once again – as if for good measure – a distillation of his favourite themes and images. Indeed, as he looks back over his life's work in poems like 'Povertà', he can now see his joys and sorrows in some kind of lyrical perspective and the prospect fills him with an impetuous feeling of memorial self-fulfilment and maturity:

Anche se vi nascondo
la mia pena segreta
sono il vecchio piú ricco del mondo;
ho un tesoro piú grande dell'amore:
ho il dolore.
Non mi chiamate piú povero;
se volete chiamatemi pazzo,
chiamatemi poeta . . .

Even if I conceal from you my secret sorrow, I am the richest old man in the world; I have a greater treasure than love: I have anguish. Do not call me poor any more; if you wish, call me a madman, call me a poet . . .

Accordingly, although one might still entertain doubts about the depth and the cathartic effects of Govoni's 'dolore', one has to acknowledge that his feelings of satisfaction and contentedness were not completely unjustifiable. Above all, he was well aware that he had assembled in his work the greatest repository of startling images to be found in modern Italian literature and in this respect he was truly the lyrical colossus of his age. Although we still cannot discount the fact that he never possessed a critical power comparable with his imaginative capacity, we sense on the other hand that, if he had been more of an intellectual and less of a 'visivo', contemporary Italian poetry might well have lost a whole dimension of its lyrical perceptiveness – to say nothing of that rich and luxuriant humus on which other modern poets have unconsciously drawn to enliven the imagery of their own verse.

CHAPTER VII

The development of Saba's lyricism

When we compare Saba's poetic work with that of Govoni we are immediately struck by its essential clarity and simplicity. Not only does it deal exclusively with the minor and apparently insignificant experiences of everyday life, but its very directness of approach and immediacy of impact imply that it will be relatively easy to understand. Such an impression is deceptive, although his poetry does at first sight seem to invite the reader to lay aside his critical faculty and abandon himself to the limpid unfolding of his imagery and the traditional magic of his cadences. Accordingly, we are soon convinced that the poet's inner feelings will tolerate no prevarication or deceit. Yet behind his artless style and touching innocence of expression one detects a highly responsive and subtle sensibility which unaccountably succeeds in endowing the time-hallowed forms of the Italian lyric with a surprising and quite unexpected contemporary relevance.

On the other hand, it immediately becomes clear that Saba is an isolated case in modern Italian culture. So unpretentiously 'open' is his lyrical discourse that we have to regard his entire literary presence as having been cast disturbingly into the modern nightmare world of baroque involution. The reason why we gain this impression is because his verse possesses none of the violent elliptical imagery associated with the French symbolists or Italian hermetic poets: it aims instead at the communication of emotive states in all their immediate purity. At all points of expression the poet shows himself to be quite unwilling to proceed beyond this limited purview of life in order to involve himself in the whys and wherefores of human destiny, or even in analogical transcriptions of his moods. Yet despite its apparent simplicity Saba's melodic line demonstrates that he is the master of a half-submerged world of resilient psychological tensions, of an unsophisticated area of authentic emotion, which the hermetic movement through the very intensity of its involution tends progressively to obscure.

But because his poetry is humbler, less intellectualized, than that of his contemporaries one should not assume that it reveals no constancy of purpose. On the contrary, by moving instinctively within his chosen sphere of evanescent feelings he acquires a tremendous insight into the elusive ebb and flow of the emotions and the senses. At one moment his imagery will reflect a hidden pang of conscience, at another the instantaneous recoil of crushed feelings, and at yet another those almost imperceptible shifts in sensitivity which can suddenly reverse or transform entire situations. Not even a blush, an involuntary sob or the half-concealed glow of love and enthusiasm are beneath his notice. He makes each a part of that delicate thread of sentiment which forms the matrix of his work and against which the most insignificant details or the humblest gestures are brought into proper relief. Since moreover, these elements are evoked in all their temporal fragility, his emotional responses tend to be transformed into images with a truly gossamer-like texture, just as if the poet were spinning a delicate fabric of dreams over the sheer void of existence. Such a manner of composing appears to link his approach with that of the 'poeti puri', but he never moves like them into involuted areas of inspiration. His lyrical texture is more in the nature of a wakeful dream than the product of a subconscious drift or stream of consciousness technique, and he always keeps the aesthetically refined but never dematerialized contours of reality sharply in focus, while at the same time refusing to sacrifice his integrity on the altars of dissociative lyrical alchemies.

No doubt it is his unique capacity to offset realist and imaginative elements and to combine them with penetrating psychological observations that accounts for the underlying resilience of his art. His basic manner not only prevents him from detaching himself from the psychological realities underlying human intercourse, it also permits him to invoke imagery with the necessary depth and authenticity to strike a chord in his readers' sensibilities. Admittedly, single poems are at times somewhat coarsened by touches of mawkish sentimentality; but, even when this quality seems uppermost, he still manages to redeem himself by means of a remarkable ability to reflect those fractional changes of mood and attitude which provide variety and meaning within the continual unfolding of life. Undoubtedly this deftness of touch, this skill at revealing organically the deeper responses of the sensibility to its historical and social settings, ensures for him a well-consolidated position in modern Italian literature. So, although his art seems intuitive rather than meditative at first sight, we soon realize that it possesses a lyrical toughness which reveals a lively intelligence operating at all critical points of expression.

By contrast, its intrinsic elusiveness makes it difficult to characterize adequately Saba's authentic line of inspiration. Let us therefore limit ourselves at present to noting that his art neither drives him to a form of intellectual isolation like Mallarmé's nor causes him to fall victim to literary fashions like Govoni's. Even so, he is always ready to venture into whatever fresh fields of experience his personal talent leads him, and no matter how disastrous he felt his complete rejection of verbal alchemies might prove to be for his immediate lyrical success, he still placed himself consciously outside the heady, but to him unauthentic, atmospheres of hermeticism and futurism. On the other hand, he did retain a connection with the type of 'classical' inspiration associated with the group surrounding *La Ronda*; and, although not contributing actively to the review himself, he gave it his silent support by pursuing steadfastly his chosen rôle as a poet of pure existence and subtly decanted human feelings.

Heroic as this stand was, Saba nevertheless soon discovered that without the analogical devices of modern art to support him he was faced with the problem of inventing some alternative means of orchestrating his emotions, and the technique he eventually elaborated permitted him to use his highly egocentric personality as a lyrical filter for his feelings. Such a fact might lead us to assume that a knowledge of the vicissitudes of his life will offer a series of clues for use in the interpretation of his poetry, but this is certainly not the case. On the contrary, as Borlenghi explains, 'l'autobiografia è sempre da scontare in lui, come la condizione stessa dell'esistenza'[1] ('autobiography is always to be discounted with him, as the very condition of existence'). In short, biographical material always appears as accident to substance in his *Canzoniere*, a point which is so self-evident that not even the most perverse of his critics has ventured to suggest that his verse amounts to rhymed autobiography. His work is instead a study in depth of his own complex, yet unsophisticated, personality: a subtle modulation of his spirit and his senses in which, in the words of Debenedetti[2], he succeeds in fusing a single artistic temperament so completely with the constant elements of human nature that he depicts through his own experiences the innumerable facets of the unchanging destiny of man.

However, it has to be admitted that Saba was also at times painfully liberal with his supply of external data. This defect leads Marcazzan to claim that whenever he fails to resolve a situation lyrically he shows 'un eccesso di fiducia nell'occasione'[3] ('an excess of faith in the occasion'). Such a tendency persists throughout his entire work, although it is gradually offset by a growing capacity to absorb his general situations, if not their particular incidents, into an integrated lyrical tone. Hence we find that in his finer compositions each detail, though heterogeneous in itself, tends ultimately to fall into place within an integrated chain of psychological images, and through them he manages to illuminate the fleeting aspects of his experience almost as soon as they impinge upon his consciousness in all their radiant ephemerality.

Nowhere is the process more clearly exemplified than in his carefully contrived confrontations between individuals in everyday circumstances. On occasion a clash of temperament, for instance, prompts him to express himself in a form of delicate irony, as when a girl with whom he is in love tells him a downright lie:

Perché arrossire ? Io credo
pure alle tue bugie.
Hanno piú religione delle mie
verità;[4]

Why blush? I even believe in your lies. They have more religion than my truths;

while elsewhere he shows a vein of good-natured humour, when he tries to cheer up a fellow-prisoner in his *Versi militari* (1908):

Ed io che volli un poco di sereno
dentro l'animo suo, gli dissi: 'Credi
qui non c'è tutto il male che tu vedi;

che quando stai nella prigione, almeno
non ti mettono in mano la ramazza,
e puoi pensare in pace alla ragazza.'[5]

And I who wished to fill his mind with a little serenity, said to him: 'Believe me, here there is not all the unpleasantness that you see; for, when you are in prison, they do not put a broom in your hands, and you can think in peace about your girl-friend'.

Such delicate examples of coquetry and humour clearly bring out the full flavour of his moods in a way that pure narration would fail to do, and they will suffice for the moment to emphasize the point that the *Canzoniere* is an autobiography of states of consciousness or moods and not even remotely a prosaic curriculum vitae. The same point may also be deduced from the fact that Saba's aesthetic evolution is far from being predictably chronological in its unfolding. Precisely because his lyricism is most mature when he fuses historical data with his deeper emotional life, we find a rare felicity of expression in some poems written in his early career and, by the same token, some moments of painful unevenness re-emerging towards the end of it. He is, in brief, a born poet, not a cultivated one, and it is for this reason that his verse only intermittently achieves its highest form of expression in the unexpected yet refined illumination of his feelings. However, at such moments his level of perceptiveness is raised to a point where he absorbs his raw materials completely into his lyrical tone without leaving any obscuring factual residue behind.

In the process of lyrical absorption and transfiguration Saba's powers of psychological observation and analysis play a considerable part. At times the psychological tension created between himself and his circumstances leads to the formation of a type of 'cronaca interna' ('inner chronicle') in which images are transmuted into intricate archetypal representations of human nature and shed almost completely their contingent associations. Similarly, whenever his lyrical responses are supported by an indulgence in *badinage* or subtle ironical effects, we find a radiant air of enchantment surrounding his poetic line. On the other hand, only rarely does his sense of detachment evoke nihilistic attitudes or feelings of despair, since the dominant characteristic of his verse is an unreserved, if partly disillusioned, acceptance of life. So, precisely because he sees reality in terms of his own emotional responses, the intimate relationship between his senses and his lyricism is never broken or blurred by metaphysical speculation. Instead, it normally tends to be a faithful record of the development of his personality as it unfolds against the bedrock of his immediate sense-impressions.

Since the poet's outlook is in the final analysis a humanist one, he naturally subscribes to the doctrine that the development of the personality is a self-validating process and the ultimate goal in life. Yet he holds this conviction in all its purity and never looks beyond it or tries to meditate on the limits of the human condition like the hermetics. This explains why his verse is not as anguish-stricken as theirs and why its dramatic tension, especially its melancholy note, only reveals itself when he pits his conscience against the shortcomings of his own character rather than against the human condition as such. At first it may seem as if he is constantly acknowledging his own faults and foibles and accepting them with a high degree of complacency; but on further examination we see that each acceptance is mingled with an undercurrent of irritation at his inability to dominate the complexities of life and participate in all its manifestations without reservation. Occasionally he is even aware of the vein of decadent renunciation which insinuates itself into his lyricism and becomes manifest as a form of melodrama whenever his inspiration momentarily flags. But once again he is saved from the excesses of decadentism by the positive manner in which he reacts to the world outside himself. Eventually it becomes clear that his cast of mind is not really renunciatory at all but typical of the modern active poet. This point is already prefigured in an early poem 'Glauco' in *Poesie dell'adolescenza e giovanili* (1900-7), where the poet is eventually disposed to pay heed to his friend Glauco's blandishments and to participate whole-heartedly in the adventure of living, despite his shyness and his initial adoption of certain anti-social postures:

> Umberto, ma perché senza un diletto
> tu consumi la vita, e par nasconda
> un dolore o un mistero ogni tuo detto?
> Perché non vieni con me sulla sponda
>
> del mare, che in sue azzurre onde c'invita?
> Qual'è il pensiero che non dici, ascoso,
> e che da noi, cosí a un tratto, t'invola?

Tu non sai come sia dolce la vita
agli amici che fuggi, e come vola
a me il mio tempo, allegro e immaginoso.

> Umberto, but why do you waste your life without delight, so that your every word seems to conceal a grief or mystery? Why do you not come with me on the beach by the sea, which invites us into its blue waves? What is the unspoken thought you hide and which suddenly carries you away from us? You do not know how sweet life is for the friends whom you flee, and how joyfully and imaginatively time flies for me.

But, while accepting the kind of *disponibilità* which his friend offers, he nevertheless feels the necessity to maintain a certain detachment, and so he offsets an attitude of joyful participation with an equal assertion of the need for artistic restraint in all situations and experiences.

One of his more obvious acts of restraint is his acceptance of traditional poetic structures. His ability to compromise with traditional forms is evident at all stages in his work and is nothing more than the acknowledgement of his Italian cultural inheritance, underlined in his early poetry by numerous reminiscences drawn from other poets' verse. His rigorously formal, lyrical apprenticeship also prepares him for his later practice of basing his poetry on subtle psychological analyses; and these, when fused with his allusive resonances from the lyric tradition, account for the almost intuitive cultural saturation of his poetic line.

Perhaps then it would not be too improbable to assert that the creation of Saba's psychologically orientated imagery was itself a highly literary affair; and indeed the only thing which counterbalances his early cult of literary imitation[6] is the temper of his mind which is as fresh and innocent, but at the same time as perceptive, as a child's. So unusual a temperament tends to give free rein to the poet's fancy and on occasion his inspiration could be said to border on the *fantaisiste*, very much like that of a Musset or a Palazzeschi. Even so, from a spiritual standpoint its old-world charm and frequent expressions of disarming wonder may more appropriately be likened to the writings of an Anatole France in his lighter moments.[7] If, as Lalou has suggested, the French writer 'incarnait ... la plus délicate culture de l'humanisme européen'[8] ('made incarnate ... the most delicate culture of European humanism') in the late nineteenth century, then Saba can undoubtedly be said to do the same in the twentieth. Superficially both writers take a naïve delight in their 'chance' involvement in human affairs, but we soon discover that this apparently innocent pleasure is compounded from a deep existential suffering and a remarkably wide range of human understanding. The human sympathy possessed by both men was, in fact, so intense that they had to conceal it behind an indulgent scepticism to prevent it from lapsing into a form of sentimentality.

Not only was their cast of mind so similar, but even their lives and interests also bear remarkable resemblances. Both were, for instance, antiquarians and connoisseurs of ancient pictures, engravings, manuscripts and incunabula. Anatole France cultivated his taste for such things when employed in the *Bibliothèque du Sénat*, while Saba's curiosity for *objets d'art* of all kinds was aroused after he had opened his 'bottega d'antiquario' ('antiquarian bookshop') in the Via San Nicolò in Trieste just after the First World War. One can accordingly imagine the Italian poet's self-portrait in the fifteenth sonnet of *Autobiografia* (1924) to be equally applicable to the French novelist's spiritual physiognomy, and both men might well have been caught by an artist in the selfsame pose as they worked in the musty atmosphere of some old bookshop and pored over gold-bound volumes of medieval lore:

> Una strana bottega d'antiquario
> s'apre, a Trieste, in una via secreta.
> D'antiche legature un oro vario
> l'occhio per gli scaffali errante allieta.
>
> Vive in quell'aria tranquillo un poeta.
> Dei morti in quel vivente lapidario
> la sua opera compie, onesta e lieta,
> D'Amor pensoso, ignoto e solitario.

A strange antiquarian bookshop is open, in Trieste, in a remote street. The eye is gladdened as it wanders along its shelves by the varying gilt of ancient bindings. A poet lives tranquilly in that atmosphere. In that living lapidary of the dead he carries out his honest, joyful work, mindful of Love, unknown and alone.

This thumbnail sketch virtually gives the impression that Saba regarded himself a poet resuscitated from a bygone age who had reluctantly seized the opportunity afforded by his incredible restoration to life to complete his work. His grace has something indefinable about it; so that, as he continues to mature his tastes, he evokes an old-world charm whenever he puts pen to paper. Hence for this reason too he provides us with the same sort of culturally saturated wisdom as that which we note so often in the works of Anatole France.

Nevertheless, the French writer's courteous scepticism has a sharper cutting-edge than the Italian poet's evanescent irony and France undoubtedly surpassed Saba in literary penetration, if not in charm of utterance. This is particularly the case in his early period when the Italian poet's uncritical approach so weakened his art that his reputation suffered from it for the rest of his life. The effect on his sensibility was such that, when he finally realized he was being neglected by his contemporaries, a touch of bitterness entered his soul and exacerbated his already deepseated egotism.

Self-confession then seemed the only way in which he could square his account with posterity and he wrote a curious critical work, *La storia e cronistoria del Canzoniere* (1948),[9] in which he pretended to act as an independent critic and examined his own poetry with the detachment of a third person.

In spite of the rather eclectic nature of his critical opinions and the praise he sometimes lavishes on his weaker compositions, the *Cronistoria* is a work of great importance for all students of Saba's lyricism. Quite apart from the fact that it offers valuable insights into his lyrical procedures, it has plainly exerted a profound influence on the direction taken by all independent criticism of his verse ever since. In a sense, perhaps, this may be considered to be a mixed blessing, especially after the real work of revaluation had finally begun; but at least it has prevented critics from labouring under their former misconceptions.

Let us, however, leave aside for the moment the poet's own judgements on his lyrical achievements and try to approach the *Canzoniere* with the minimum of preconceptions. The first thing that strikes us when we read it is that it is based almost entirely upon Saba himself and on the city of Trieste. Within the provincial framework of his native town he depicts his personal responses to life in a refined and unobtrusively humanistic manner, casting light by turns on all the possible facets of his subtle – and indeed at times almost precious – character. As we become more immersed in his lyrical atmospheres we begin to realize that he has no highly developed visual sense, no real desire to attract attention by garish displays of colour like a Marinetti or a Campana; he tries instead to offset his lack of grasp on concrete elements by steeping his sense-impressions, as Petrarch did before him, in a pre-established, inner musicality whose secret function is to fuse together all the various sensations stimulated by his experiences. The result is that the rhythm of his conscience is ultimately the force dominating his lyrical effects and this procedure has often been equated with a form of extreme egocentricity.

Yet, if it is egocentricity, it remains a product of his emotions rather than his intellect; and, what is more, it never degenerates into any form of moral solipsism. It is simply a means whereby Saba creates objective lyrical images which, when filtered through his personality, appear to stand as eternal human values. His symbols, as previously suggested, thereby acquire at times an emblematic stature and delineate the fragile contours of a unique and highly significant human existence. True, his entire manner may on occasion be regarded as romantic or even pre-romantic in nature, and then it gives rise to beguiling lyrical tableaus which seem to be combinations of sketches by Fragonard and arias by Monteverdi. But the poet nevertheless rejects one of romanticism's most important features – its careful selection of themes, sentiments and diction. Far from being idealistic and restrictive, he tends to be wholly eclectic in his approach and thoroughly realistic and modern in his imagery. His vocabulary may perhaps seem a little archaic at first, precisely because of his cult of literary reminiscences; but he gradually dominates his innate literariness through his determination to present the whole spectrum of his life as an aesthetic unity. At length we discover that all that remains of his literary reminiscences is a suggestive halo of overtones; yet these have the advantage of crystallizing his momentary perceptions into images evoking a whole range of subtle lyrical resonances drawn from past tradition.

Sometimes his aesthetic treatment of events is in this regard reminiscent of crepuscular art, especially in the first edition of the *Canzoniere* published in 1921. So deliberately nuanced is the imagery of this first version that it often seems as if Saba merely wishes his fingers to graze his experiential data so as to make his sense-impressions act as mere touchstones confirming the reality of an inner word-music. At the very moment of prehension, in other words, he tends to abandon things once more to their fate, to translate all his feelings into terms of pure form, outline and rhythm – without, as Cardarelli would put it, ever allowing them to suffer 'il sudore umiliante dei contatti' ('the humiliating sweat of contact'). Examples of this sensory diffidence are frequent and they show that Saba's realism is basically psychological, not factual, in orientation. But in all cases his aesthetic transcendence of his sense-data depends on the relative intensity of his inspiration, and an apt illustration of an early incomplete transcendence is the following passage taken from 'Dormiveglia':

> Trillava un cardellino
> nell'attonita stanza,
> e il sole s'oscurava.
> Un rullo, una campana,
> il gallo a quando a quando
> s'udivano; e il mattino
> piú s'andava velando.

A goldfinch trilled in the astonished room, and the sun grew dim. A rumble, a bell, a cock from time to time could be heard; and the morning became more and more cloudy.

Here we have no doubt a gallant attempt at complete lyrical transfiguration; but the elusive quality of lyrical fluidity is somewhat weakened by the poet's inability to fuse together certain disparate sensory elements, and the result is a muted jarring of sensations. It reminds us almost of Pascoli's dislocated impressionism and even borrows from him his favourite object-symbols. Yet by the time we reach the *Quinta fuga* in 1928-9 the latter's influence will long since have disappeared and an audio-visual reintegration of the poet's moods is then achieved, through the subordination of purely sensory patterns to an alert, forceful, and dominant word-music:

> Io un lume verde,
> in una barca alla ventura andante.
> Che importa a me degli scogli? Non amo
> chi pericoli accenna; altro non amo
> che me sulla mia barca, e quel richiamo
> che si rispecchia nell'onda, che l'onda
> allunga giú fino ai porti.

I a green light, in a boat aimlessly drifting. What do rocks matter to me? I do not love those who point out dangers; I love only myself in my boat and that echo which is mirrored again in the waves, which the waves prolong right down to the port.

Saba's mature poetic discourse is accordingly shot through with delicate half-lights of emotion whose unifying powers are far superior to those apparent in poems like 'Dormiveglia'. Admittedly, there still remains the danger that certain isolated elements in it will not rise fully above 'il fatto prosastico grezzo'[10] ('the raw prosaic fact') but this peril is now greatly diminished, since in the interval the poet had learned how to create his own tonal inflections and is wholly capable of disciplining his emotions by filtering them through his lyrical *persona*.

The main thing which still puzzled and dismayed him at this stage was the continued intermittency of his inspiration. So, in order to justify the inclusion of some of his weaker lyrics in the *Canzoniere*, he made the claim in the *Cronistoria* that a poet's lyrical existence must be considered as an organic whole. His troughs of inspiration should have, that is, as much symbolic value as his finest transfigurations, because it is only when both are examined together that a complete assessment of his lyrical presence can be made. Are we then to discount aesthetics altogether in favour of his underlying poetic substance? Fortunately not: for Saba had an ulterior motive for propounding this view – his determination to level a veiled blow at hermetic obscurity which he regarded as a more serious danger to modern art than his own prosaic style. There is, nevertheless, more than a grain of truth in the suggestion that his work should be read as a whole rather than in selections. For, whenever we do so, we not only gain a deeper insight into his tremendous poetic range, we also obtain a clearer idea of the various aesthetic temptations in which he so frequently indulged.

In particular, the rise and fall of his lyrical tension shows how even his finest work is balanced on a knife-edge between a prosaic form of narrative on the one hand and a maudlin type of sentimentality on the other. Of the two the sentimental strain is perhaps the more damaging, because it imitates the neo-Romantic pose of universal suffering. When applied to the love-theme it produces anguish of an almost completely different quality from the existential anguish of modern times and tends to re-echo in a minor key Shelley's melodramatic cry of 'I fall upon the thorns of life! I bleed!':

Sanguina il mio cuore
come un cuore qualunque.
La dura spina che m'inflisse amore
la porto ovunque.[11]

> My heart bleeds like any other heart. The harsh thorn Love inflicted on me I carry everywhere!

Precisely because these lines possess a heavy sentimental charge they show that Saba, too, often wore his heart on his sleeve. But at the same time this type of lyricism is partly saved by the very preciousness of the poet's imagery and the airy grace of his word-music. On occasion it almost seems as if the poet was himself half-aware of the theatricality of the attitude he was adopting and he then tried to stiffen his modes of expression by means of a delicate touch of irony. So, as time goes by, the incisiveness of his irony tends to gain the upper hand and it transforms his gratuitous romanticism into something approaching a modern feeling of 'dolore'.

One successful attempt at toughening his poetic line is already apparent in the early poem 'La capra'. Within its lyrical texture narrative, imaginative and rhythmical elements are all carefully integrated to produce an astonishingly mature result:

Ho parlato a una capra.
Era sola sul prato, era legata.
Sazia d'erba, bagnata
dalla pioggia, belava.

Quell' uguale belato era fraterno
al mio dolore. Ed io risposi, prima
per celia, poi perché il dolore è eterno,
ha una voce e non varia.
Questa voce sentiva
gemere in una capra solitaria.

In una capra dal viso semita
sentiva querelarsi ogni altro male,
ogni altra vita.

> I have spoken to a nanny-goat. She was alone in a meadow, and tethered. Sated with grass, drenched with rain, she bleated. That even bleating was allied to my grief. And I replied, first out of mockery, then because grief is eternal, has a single voice and never varies. This voice could be heard moaning in a

> lonely nanny-goat. In a goat with a Jewish face could be heard a-mumbling all other ills, all other lives.

Here the secret behind the lyrical transfiguration is the poet's ability to blend a slender thread of autobiographical material with a conversational tone, and then to transmute both into feelings mirroring the whole spectrum of human destiny. The point at which his inner sentiment and an external symbolism intersect is clearly in the emblematic figure of the goat, especially after the phrase 'una capra dal viso semita' identifies the animal with Saba himself and with the long shadow of his Jewish background. Once this metamorphosis is made, the goat's suffering no longer seems bestial and meaningless, but realistically human; and the irony dies away as the entire situation is transformed from a melodramatic into a poignantly dramatic scene. So in contrast with the poet's previous imitative manner this lyric, written as early as 1910, proves capable of awakening poetic resonances simultaneously in a typically modern fashion upon moral and aesthetic planes.

Despite its early composition only a few other poems in the *Canzoniere* equal – much less surpass – the standards set by 'La capra', because nearly all of Saba's lyrics tend to become vitiated at a pre-poetic stage by one or another of his aesthetic failings. Even in 1910-11 he already seems to have appreciated the nature of these weaknesses and, as a general principle, ascribed such unevenness to an inability to distinguish between artificial and authentic forms of lyrical utterance. He even wrote an essay on the subject entitled 'Quello che resta da fare ai poeti'[12] and submitted it to the *Voce* for publication. It was rejected by Scipio Slataper for the editorial board and did not finally appear in print until 1959, yet it nevertheless highlights Saba's basic attitudes to artistic creation and indicates that even at that time he considered self-sincerity to be the touchstone of art. The vital illustration he provides in support of his thesis is the evident sincerity of Manzoni on the one hand and the blatant insincerity of D'Annunzio on the other; and, after enunciating the general principle, he insists that 'l'onestà dell'uno e la nessuna onestà dell'altro, cosí verso loro stessi come verso il lettore ... sono i due termini cui può benissimo ridursi la differenza dei due valori.'[13] ('the honesty of the one and the lack of honesty of the other, both towards themselves and towards the reader ... are the two extremes to which the difference in their two values may be reduced.')

From this essay it is evident that authenticity of feeling and the relationship between art and life remain crucial problems for Saba. He solved them by acting as if the watchword in life for the sincere man should be a continual *disponibilità*, and that of the sincere artist a rigorous *selettività*.

The lyrical tension produced by the application of these two doctrines manifests itself in the subtle interaction of his *figure* and *canti*. The former stand as so many free agents and symbolize the waywardness of life, while the latter represent highly egocentric musical patterns determined by the articulation of the poet's conscience; and they control and limit the innate waywardness of his protagonists by imposing a lyrical order upon their passions. In his finer moments of insight the centrifugal tendencies of his objectively conceived *figure* are thus offset by the centripetal movement of his subjectively controlled lyrical cadences; yet, even so, a regrettable imbalance persists in moments of lesser inspiration, whenever he indulges a purely rhetorical or narrative form of lyricism. Such a lack of constraint he once described as a yielding to Dannunzian 'intenzioni bottegaie o ambiziose' ('commercial or ambitious aims').

What is so surprising about this whole outlook is that it was developed and crystallized into an artistic doctrine so early. Hence from 1911 onwards Saba's views on aesthetics remain constant and he moves steadily towards a position in which he asserts that a poem does not depend for its brilliance on its individual images but on the inner cohesion of its tonal structure. The point may be illustrated by his gradually changing attitude towards crepuscularism as he matures. At first its languorous qualities act powerfully upon his sensibility and many of its atmospheres are still dominant in the *Canzoniere* of 1921. But by the time we reach the definitive edition of 1945 they have almost completely disappeared. Take, for instance, the first version of the poem 'Notte di Natale':

Io scrivo nella mia dolce stanzetta,
d'una candela al tenue chiarore,
ed una forza indomita d'amore
muove la stanca mano che s'affretta.

I am writing in my sweet little room, in the dim glow of the candle, and an untamed force of love moves my weary yet hastening hand.

Here the crepuscular mood is apparent even in the gradation of the adjectives *dolce-tenue-stanca*, and the entire lyric borders on that paradigmatic form of crepuscular rhetoric already seen in the work of Moretti. As such, it tends to undermine Saba's artistic sincerity, which explains why at a later date he decided to eliminate it from his verse altogether.

The actual process of elimination can be followed in certain other lyrics, and two variants of the poem originally entitled 'Lina', in the *Canzonieri* of 1921 and 1945, are from this point of view highly significant. A comparison between them will show that the poet's incursion in the crepuscular field was no more than a vague flirtation with its moods, a stop-gap measure which Saba accepted temporarily while casting around for the vital elements of his own personal manner.[14] The first version appears in *Poesie fiorentine* in the 1921 edition:

> Lina, già volge l'anno che ti vidi.
> Seduta alla finestra eri e cucivi.
> Io ti sorrisi, ma non mi dissi amante,
> ti accarezzai quell'anima tremante,

> Lina, already a year has passed since I saw you. Seated you were at the window, sewing. I smiled at you, but did not confess my love. I caressed that trembling soul of yours,

and these lines are clearly still touched with crepuscular features. They in fact linger over the image of the lady in a sentimental fashion very much like similar verses quoted earlier from Betteloni. But in the final version ('Fanciulle', 5) the lady is brought more objectively into focus when the earlier decadent atmosphere surrounding her yields to more robust and dynamic gestures:

> Questa è la donna che un tempo cuciva
> seduta alla finestra.
> Nell'ago era maestra
> e l'occhio, l'occhio nella via fuggiva.

> This is the woman who once sewed, seated at the window. She was mistress of the needle and her eye, her eye wandered along the street.

As the rest of the poem will show, even the syntax of the second version is more concise and sinewy than the first; with the result that its inspiration can be seen to move both emotionally and rhythmically right out of the crepuscular orbit. Consequently in the poet's mature work its influence is at most only a residual one.

Probably what most distinguishes Saba's attitudes from those of the crepuscular poets is the fact that he is patently optimist and extravert in outlook while they were morbidly introspective and elegiac. Thus, as he says himself, those critics who have talked of 'il Saba delle "piccole cose" ' ('the Saba of "little things" ') ought really to have tried to explain how in his poetry 'quelle "piccole cose" erano elevate ai vertici di un'alta spiritualità, che le trasfigurava in alta poesia'[15] ('those "little things" were raised to the pinnacle of a high spirituality, which transformed them into lofty poetry'). Although the poet had his own particular axe to grind when making such an assertion, nevertheless an objective examination of his lyricism will completely bear his contention out. Admittedly, some critics have still not been satisfied and have even accused him of eliminating his crepuscular features *a posteriori* for the sake of proving his point; but this is hardly a telling criticism since, whether by accident or design, he did ultimately eliminate all crepuscular detritus, and significantly he managed to do so without disrupting the tonal quality of his work. Surely, then, such a feat must indicate that its original function was no more than a superficial colouring and that it never formed an integral part of his spiritual make-up? Indeed, most of his borrowings from the school (mainly adjectival effects) are concerned with the evoking of emotional atmospheres rather than with lyrical attitudes and substance, and their peripheral rôle later permits him to shed the crepuscular poets' complacent acceptance of man's alienation from society and the world at large in favour of a detached – though nonetheless whole-hearted – commitment to life.

Similarly the quality of his irony grows deeper and more resilient with the passage of time and this is further proof of his independence. With the crepusculars, we recall, irony took the form of a *Schadenfreude*, which became all the more poignant when it was based on their truly frightening sense of passive suffering. But with Saba irony is used solely as a means of highlighting his disillusionment and is neither renunciatory nor masochistic in nature. Its principal concern is with the delineation of those fundamental ambiguities implicit in the human condition, whose source is found in what the poet himself calls his 'ambivalenza affettiva' ('emotional ambivalence'), a complicated interplay of emotional opposites whose psycho-analytical origin he on the whole manages effectively to conceal in his lyricism. By synthesizing its opposing tensions in his verse he is indeed able to produce a psychologically founded form of objectivity and a personal set of ethical values. In turn these lead him to respect the uniqueness of the human personality as it works out its own particular form of compromise with society, and to acknowledge that all personal experiences need to be measured lyrically by reference to the uniqueness of that compromise alone.

The consequence of this approach to life is that Saba's irony coalesces with his desire for objectivity and provides his melodic line with its sense of realism and perspective. Normally he uses irony as an instrument to analyse his ambivalent feelings towards people, situations and things and to question any possible lack of sincerity in his responses to them. By so reducing his lyrical attitudes to the bedrock of authentic personal feelings he is ultimately able to cast overboard the intellectual nihilism implicit in the decadent world-outlook and makes his art a simple modulation of his tastes and experiences. Its ever-deepening validity is, in effect, the result of a growing self-knowledge and the constant sharpening of his powers of discrimination. So the positive side of his crepuscular experience in his view was that it helped him to explore the inner reaches of his conscience and to sustain a continuous process of mellowing in his sensibility. Where his art falls below this kind of subtle psychological analysis we can regard it as recessive, as moving backwards in the direction of neo-crepuscular forms of narrative. On the other hand, where it succeeds in exploiting the process to the full it leads to the attenuation of the melancholy and negative attitudes of his youth and produces a serene optimism, indicative of Saba's mature ability to live contentedly at all levels of experience.

With the passing of time we find that he tends to show an increasing interest in human relations and opts more and more for the pleasures of the senses, possibly with the aim of counterbalancing the over-cerebrality which he considered implicit in the hermetic age. But this could not have happened without an inborn sensuous disposition on his part, a characteristic we already detect in his early collections of poetry whenever he tries to recapture distant, though significant, sensations from the depths of memory. Take, for instance, the following reminiscence dealing with a momentary olfactory rapture recalled from childhood:

A Dio innalzavo l'anima serena,
e dalla casa un suon di care voci
mi giungeva, *e l'odore della cena.*[16]

I raised my soul serenely to God, and from the house a sound of dear voices reached me, *and the smell of supper.*

Gradually this nonchalant recall of intense sensations develops into a full-blown psychology of the memory, the chief effect of which is to stress how robust the spiritual and sensory impulses behind the *Canzoniere* really are. They function equally strongly in moments of anguish and moments of elation and authenticate both – a fact which is not surprising when we bear in mind that, given the ambivalence of Saba's emotional responses, laughter is always close to tears with him and that at times he is as adept at transforming states of pathos and despair as he is at evoking vibrant moments of joy and relief.

Often these rapid alternations of mood are facilitated by his use of language and rhythm, and his pangs of joy and sorrow are then transmitted to the reader through elusive falls in his lyrical cadences or in delicate shifts of his poetic intonation; and these, on occasion, may be introduced either through colloquial turns of phrase or enjambement.[17] By ringing the changes on such devices Saba succeeds in achieving a renewal of his poetic forms from their basic elements upwards; and, when all such elements are combined effectively, we note a withering away of the rigid classical symmetry of his early lyrical structures and their replacement by more flexible forms, mirroring in particular the wayward course of his own personal moods. A thorough-going empirical approach to life thus tends, as he matures, to replace generic moods and mimetic features in his work, and the process implies the assimilation of experience at first hand instead of through the medium of literary reminiscences.

On the other hand, despite the gradual 'illimpidimento' ('purification') of his imagery resulting from this process, it would be a mistake to assert that Saba's poetry is completely free from artificiality. Titta Rosa has even gone so far as to claim that the very fabric of his style is inordinately literary, while paradoxically adding that its tonal quality is, if anything, anti-literary.[18] In support of such a view we note the presence of a number of irritating 'tics' which are either crudely imitative or else seem deceptively artless in origin. One of the most prominent is a certain preciousness of diction evident when the poet deals with the nuances of his psychological impulses. Another is a specious cult of archaisms, rhetorical figures and, at times, even strange infantile spellings. A well-known poem combining several of these features (the infantile spelling 'quore' accompanied by the strange tmesis 'con' and 'quista') is 'Zaccaria':

io sono
un quore che con quista molti quori.

I am a heart which con quers many hearts.

In some contexts these unusual linguistic devices are no doubt justifiable and add an atmosphere of naïve charm to a lyric; but, on the whole, they tend to indicate a certain immaturity of taste which the poet himself later condemns in the *Cronistoria,* describing it as 'una stonatura' ('a dissonance'). Nevertheless, their persistence in a number of his collections emphasizes the lengthy duration of his lyrical apprenticeship and also the nature of the long pre-critical phase he underwent before learning how to assimilate in a genuine lyrical fashion the elements of his literary and linguistic inheritance.

Although his syntactic structures are consequently to be regarded as modern and contain little of the dead-wood bedevilling previous neoclassical forms of art, one period in his development must be excepted from this general rule: it is the early one in which he shows that he possesses a particular passion for Leopardi who was himself, we recall, a master of the elegant, refurbished archaism. Saba's misfortune at that stage was that in the changed circumstances of the twentieth century he was unable to handle traditional phraseology quite as effectively; so that, while the earlier poet's archaic turns of phrase harmonize with his poetic tone, Saba's often do not, and they even tend at times to disrupt his melodic flow. A brief comparison between the techniques of the two poets may accordingly prove worthwhile, since it will have the advantage of indicating how the modern poet sets about freeing himself from the yoke of literary imitation.

Probably the first – and essentially pre-poetic – stage in his liberation was his renunciation of Leopardi's cosmic pessimism. It resulted in a subtle displacement of Saba's perspectives, because it helped his essentially egocentric nature to invert the earlier poet's modes of perceiving. On the other hand, the modern poet did not dare at the time to meddle with the more fundamental temper of Leopardi's melodic line and normally reproduced its inflections and tonal colouring in their totality. Nowadays, with the wisdom of hindsight, we can see how judicious a decision this was, because without an intimate acquaintance with the nineteenth-century poet's richly modulated rhythms it is doubtful whether Saba could ever have saved himself from falling victim to the edulcorated word-music of the crepusculars, to say nothing of eliminating the various literary 'tics' which jar so much upon the sensibility of his readers in his early verse. But by reacting as he did he eventually managed to use Leopardi's lyrical grace as a stepping-stone towards – rather than as a substitute for – a personal mode of expression: a fact which largely explains the progressive 'illimpidimento' of his lyrical effects. Normally this continuing purification of tone and imagery ensures the cohesion of his literary *persona*, and so his debt to Leopardi in evolving a personal and definitive style is truly enormous.

As an illustration let us take the opening lines of Leopardi's poem 'La sera del dí di festa' and compare them with the admittedly inferior opening of Saba's own 'La sera', for which they probably served as a model. In the first lines of Leopardi's poem the shadowy mystery of the moonlight throws into relief the secret overtones of existence which are adumbrated in the poet's emblematic hinterland of gardens, rooftops and distant mountains:

Dolce e chiara è la notte e senza vento,
E queta sovra i tetti e in mezzo agli orti
Posa la luna, e di lontan rivela
Serena ogni montagna.

> Sweet and clear is the night and without wind, and calmly over the rooftops and amid the gardens hangs the moon, and from afar reveals serenely every mountain.

A similar, though by no means so clearly focussed, perspective is presented by Saba as follows:

Or che biancheggia in ciel sulla pianura
la solitaria falce della luna,
e abbandonano i monti ad una ad una
le mandre, ch'eran sparse alla pastura;

cosí buona la Terra, cosí pia
sembra in quest'ora devota dell'Ave,

che un inganno soave
tiene l'animo e i sensi in sua balia.

Now that there stands white in the sky above the plain the lonely sickle of the moon, and one by one the flocks leave the hills, where they were scattered in pasture; so good, so pious the Earth seems at this devout moment of evensong, that a sweet deception holds the mind and senses in thrall.

Here it is evident from the precision of Leopardi's and the diffuseness of Saba's evocation that the relative aesthetic values of the two texts are very different. It is not, however, this which most concerns us at present, but rather the fundamental divergence in the modes of perception of the two poets. In Leopardi's poem the eye of the poet moves outwards, away from the crisp outlines of nearby objects in order to follow a path which leads first to the distant horizon and then to a meditative sphere beyond it. As it opens up wider and wider vistas, Leopardi's mind gradually acquires a deeper understanding of existential suffering, until at last the point is reached where he experiences moments of emotional ecstasy and aesthetic insight. This is not the case with Saba. Cosmic longings are rarely a feature of his work and to immerse his mind in a universal state of consciousness is not his normal intention. If anything, it is the exact opposite: his principal poetic aim is to engulf the outside world in the folds and convolutions of his own personality. So, as we follow his particular line of sight, we find that it does not trace out a path away from nearby objects and move towards the horizon, but by contrast the line of the horizon itself first comes into view together with the distant moon. It is only later that he begins to illuminate things nearer at hand, at the moment when he is ready to absorb the entire external scene and transform it into an objective correlative of his state of mind. At that point his somewhat diffuse imagery becomes egocentrically concentrated and in the above lyric the process leads to a feeling of 'sovraumano amore' ('superhuman love') and an 'estatica calma' ('ecstatic calm'). These are moods similar in intensity but very different in meaning from Leopardi's own ecstatic 'dolore'.

Now this inversion of Leopardi's modes of perceiving fixes a precise limit beyond which Saba is unwilling to go in his imitations of his world. A reversed Leopardian 'naufragio' (a shipwreck of the universe in the mind of the poet rather than of the poet's mind in the universe) in fact soon becomes his regular poetic practice, and its manner of development throws an interesting light on the balance he strikes between centrifugal and centripetal elements in his imagery. Primarily the cohesive force of his egocentricity ensures a basic unity of tone in his poetry, but in his finest verse its procedures also imply that he has learned to relate the universal problems of existence to the microcosm of his own psychological evolution.

A feature which must always enter into our calculations when assessing the effectiveness of his lyricism is, therefore, whether his intimate and general visions of life are thoroughly interfused, or whether the result is fragmentary or merely ornamental. Doubtless it is the lower functionality of his imagery in this sense when compared with Leopardi's which accounts for the weakness of some of his early lyrics. For, indeed, in the ultimate analysis it is a poet's power of imaginative cohesion which determines his meditative position and lyrical effectiveness. So, whereas the Recanatese poet's images are always highly pertinent and cause his lyricism to cohere around a central nucleus of inspiration, Saba's are at first so loose as to be partly ornamental and dispersive, revealing only in a discontinuous fashion the deeper qualities of his lyrical insight. As a result, Leopardi seems like a musician with an ability to strike whole series of chords simultaneously in our sensibilities, while Saba's musical skill is limited to simple, if graceful, melodies which only awaken responses in our minds when composed of interrelevant sequences of single notes, as in *arpeggio* technique.

Nevertheless the poet's rapidly executed lyrical scales are eventually carefully integrated with the articulation of his intimate feelings; and, instead of moving in rational or meditative directions, they are then often guided by certain psycho-analytical procedures which he uses for exorcising his passions.[19] In his mature work the lyrical clarity he achieves is indeed almost exclusively due to meditative self-explorations followed by sharp releases of emotion which repattern his sense-impressions and fuse them with the wider sweep of that pre-established musical toughness inherent in his sensibility. This permits us to make a generalization of Debenedetti's observation that a part of his work is a process of lyrical exorcism through self-confession.[20] Even so, it also needs to be stressed that the process does not involve a consistent intellectual effort, only a continuing state of emotional serenity arising from the propitiation of the poet's passions. Whenever the latter are not fully explored and sublimated, his lyricism is deprived of much of its power; and at such moments he loses control over his narration and sacrifices emotional intensity on the altars of factual precision.

Because Saba took a considerable time developing his basic psycho-analytical technique of unifying imagery his lyrical apprenticeship was sufficiently long to allow him to experiment in a number of directions. Sometimes he even tended to abandon his normal open discourse for analogical practices, and in fact a clear cult of analogical forms is already perceptible in the collection *Casa e campagna* (1910). The early lyric, 'A mia moglie', is almost wholly composed of skilfully interwoven analogies and yet it is one of the finest poems he ever wrote. Nevertheless, as is indeed the case in this instance, his analogical approach is not normally strengthened by the underlying metaphysical outlook possessed by the hermetic poets and he tends to rely instead on psychological forces to create his sense of unity. The result is that their imaginative polarization is often less complete, less striking, in their effects. Clearly, however, what also helps to raise 'A mia moglie' above his normal level of analogical writing is a delicate anti-Petrarchism working within Saba's original Petrarchan manner and correcting those excesses of technique and diction which have tended to linger in the Italian sensibility ever since the mannerism of the late Renaissance. Hence what seems at first sight to be a grotesque parody of Petrarchan imagery and syntax is gradually transformed into an authentic lyricism, depicting certain elemental aspects of feminine grace and beauty.

Largely because the poem was written when futurism was still all the rage, Saba was immediately accused of producing a series of gratuitous comparisons. But grotesque and inappropriate as they may seem at first sight, they are not the product of an uncontrolled rhetoric of the kind which the *paroliberisti* were then about to impose upon society. Their incongruity derives rather from the fact that the poet was striving to describe the domestic, maternal and sexual attractions of his young wife as he saw them in reality; and, since he wished to depict a form of beauty based on elemental, instinctive drives, at one stage he even ventured to compare her charms with those of a lanky bitch:

Tu sei come una lunga
cagna, che sempre tanta
dolcezza ha negli occhi
e ferocia nel cuore.

You are a lanky bitch, which always has such sweetness in its eyes and fierceness in its heart.

At another he attributed to her unhesitatingly the buxom gaiety of the pregnant heifer:

Tu sei come la gravida
giovenca;
libera ancora e senza
gravezza, anzi festosa;
che, se la lisci, il collo
volge, ove tinge un rosa
tenero la sua carne.

You are like the pregnant heifer; still free and without heaviness, even festive; who turns her neck, should you stroke it, whence her flesh is tinged with a tender pinkness.

Yet, despite the fact that when taken separately these analogies seem tasteless in the extreme, in combination they are intended by Saba to be so many tender endearments, so many Freudian confessions of his almost visceral love for his wife. Unfortunately their earthy charm did not please the critics, nor for that matter Saba's wife herself; but the poet was particularly incensed by the strictures of the former, because he felt that they had failed miserably to appreciate the psychological appropriateness of his poem's lyrical structure.

In point of fact the judgement of posterity has proved the poet right and the critics wrong; but their short-sightedness may well be excused because this lyric was the very first valid example of the radically new type of poetry which was to emerge out of the wilder experimentation of the futurists. The pre-Freudian unity of the poem is accordingly recognised by everyone nowadays, as is also its subtle intermingling of Petrarchist and anti-Petrarchan features. In combination these contrive to maintain the elemental grace of womanhood while rejecting any semblance of abstract idealism. Their effectiveness depends on Saba's ability to merge narrative with associative elements in a way hitherto unparalleled by his contemporaries; and so this poem, like 'La capra', reveals a judicious blending of an outer temporal world of everyday objects with the inner psychological world of the poet's emotions. The process amounts simultaneously to an intense focussing and an intuitive blending of the senses and the imagination; and it is achieved in such a way that the analogies deployed are neither forcibly involuted like those of the hermetic poets nor wholly dependent upon 'chance' effects like those of Marinetti.

Another significant device subtly modified by Saba is the visual impressionism practised by the decadent poets. Sometimes, it is true, even he indulges in a cult of aestheticism and merges a refined *visività* with a touch of *veggenza*, in lines like

> Sfuma il turchino in un azzurro tutto
> stelle . . .[21]

The blue merges into an azure full of stars . . .

But such a manner is only a passing phase with him and he soon manages to internalize his visual elements and illuminate his normal narrative flow of significant detail by means of highly appropriate memorial flashes of insight. Whenever he strikes a balance between the prosy waywardness of his narrative manner and these deeper but intermittent moments of lyrical perception we again find him capable of producing some remarkably effective verse. Yet, whenever he yields completely to narrative techniques and allows what I.A. Richards would have described as a cumulative wealth of referential data to obscure his poetic emotion, the thread of psychologically based tension toughening his lyricism tends to break and all he succeeds in creating is autobiography in rhyme.[22]

The period of the twenties is notable both for its successes and failures in combining his narrative and imaginative modes of expression. In all, we can distinguish three stages in the process by comparing various lines from the collection *Autobiografia* (1924), the very title of which suggests a coexistence of instantaneous insights and a prosaic form of narration. The first type of text we shall examine contains a fair measure of the poet's narrative charm, precisely because its diaristic manner is underscored by a resilient thread of emotion which raises its lyricism above mere rhymed autobiography:

> Vidi altri luoghi, ebbi novelli amici.
> Strane cose da strani libri appresi.
> Dopo quattro o cinque anni, a poco a poco,
>
> non piú quei giorni estatici e felici
> ebbi, mai piú; ma liberi ed intesi
> della vita e dell'arte ancora al gioco.[23]

I saw other places, I had other friends. I learned strange things from strange books. After four or five years, little by little I no longer had those ecstatic and happy days, ever again; but liberated ones, yet still intent on the game of life and art.

Yet here we immediately sense the constant danger of factual detritus and the equally debilitating presence of a colourless sentimentality. Generally speaking, therefore, the purity of Saba's lyricism is significantly weakened whenever he lingers obsessively over the vicissitudes of his personal life; and, in order to counter this tendency and to authenticate his feelings, he often resorts to atavistic attitudes. A typical instance is to be seen in the following stanza in which he gives us an effective insight into the struggle for survival of a Jewish family, because the imagery contains overtones touching on the age-old oppression of the entire Jewish race:

> Quando nacqui mia madre ne piangeva,
> sola, la notte, nel deserto letto.
> Per me, per lei che il dolore struggeva,
> trafficavano i suoi cari nel ghetto.[24]

When I was born my mother wept alone, at night, in her deserted bed. For me, for her whom pain racked, her dear ones traded in the ghetto.

In a sense this type of veiled perspective runs parallel to that equally generalized mode of evocation to be found in Saba's earlier Leopardian manner. So here, although the narrative strain is now dominant over the descriptive one, the tableau is still dilated memorially by the emotional hinterland which is alluded to in the last line.

A third stage in the same process may be seen in passages where the poet employs colour or at least a series of emotionally charged, colourful details to punctuate his narrative and give it lyrical depth. In the following passage the red shawl worn by his wife and the blue eyes of his daughter offer in combination a strikingly immediate and sensuous introduction into his intimate family life, and so add something indefinable to his poetic texture:

Ed amai nuovamente; e fu di Lina
dal rosso scialle il piú della mia vita.
Quella che cresce accanto a noi, bambina
dagli occhi azzurri, è dal suo grembo uscita.[25]

And I loved once more; and Lina with the red shawl was the better part of my life. She who grows up beside us, a child with blue eyes, has emerged from her womb.

Needless to say, on occasion all three of these neo-narrative modes are used in combination when the poet's inspiration reaches its highest levels. But even if they appear separately their aim is to create the same multi-dimensional impressionism as was previously produced in 'La capra'; and this effect is derived from an interpenetration – not from a mere juxtaposition – of a number of planes of feeling. Within such complex perspectives each image is bound to the others by a powerful psychological relationships, and in this way the factual elements forming the matrix of the poet's narrative style are transcended and acquire profound poetic resonances.

Nevertheless, however sensitive the method proves to be, it also gives rise to certain controversial results. For while all the above-quoted passages possess an undeniable lyrical grace, they can hardly be said to measure up in poetic intensity to poems like 'A mia moglie'. Furthermore, not only *Autobiografia* but also other collections of the twenties like *I prigioni* (1924) and *L'Uomo* (1928) manifestly suffer from a lack of poetic intensity. The result is that Saba's Muse 'dai semplici panni' ('in simple garb') often becomes so engrossed in everyday affairs that she either fails to produce the emotive fire to make her words flesh of the poet's flesh, or else becomes falsely epic in her attitudes and indulges in the following type of rhetoric:

Uscenti dai suoi grandi occhi severi
gli strali
del desiderio andavano, fatali
piú che ad altri a lui stesso, al caro segno . . .[26]

Emerging from his large, severe eyes, the shafts of desire moved, more fateful to himself than others, towards their dear goal . . .

In one way or another almost a decade of Saba's lyrical autobiography suffers from these assorted shortcomings, and during the entire period the poet only reverts to his normal lyrical intensity when, in the interval between his narrative collections, he again experiments with a poetry of discontinuous psychological states. In these moments, of course, associative effects again predominate over the factual patterns of his narrative manner and so authenticate his lyricism. The more satisfactory inspiration of the twenties begins in the collection *L'amorosa spina* (1920), where Saba practises what may already be described as an emblematic symbolism in his attempts to analyse the dominant elements of the feminine personality. Although his method is still anti-hermetic, he now shares with the hermetic poets the orphic mode of suspending his psychological imagery in a timeless poetic sphere. This permits him to turn his eidetic spotlight upon all the complicated emotional characteristics of the female mind, and he seems to possess a particular intuitive grasp on the wayward aspects of passion as it affects the feminine sensibility. The poet's own wife, as Varese stresses,[27] is the main object of his study and she proves by far the most complex of his feminine characters.[28] Since, moreover, she is depicted in her emotive 'essence' rather than in her temporal unfolding, she already appears as a kind of *dea ex machina* guiding the poet's inspiration right from the composition of *Trieste e una donna* (1910-12) onwards. Her shadowy presence continues to make itself felt throughout the twenties, although it is more often to be conjectured than directly experienced by the reader. She broadly represents the stable symbol of the many-sided affections of his married life and we gradually discover that her complex personality highlights the serious feminine duties of motherhood and domesticity. As foils to her, on the other hand, we find figures like Chiaretta, his one-time shop assistant, or Paolina, who together mirror in their fragile grace and coquetry the less serious facets of human relationships.

Probably the penetration Saba shows in analysing the ways in which his feminine characters sublimate their manifestations of desire and repulsion derives from his studies of Freud and other psychologists.[29] Towards the end of the twenties his interest in psycho-analysis increased considerably and, in fact, the collection *Il piccolo Berto* (1929-31) is a lyrical transposition of a course of psychiatric treatment which he himself underwent with Edoardo Weiss and which aimed at a re-exploration of his childhood states and repressions.[30] While maintaining certain reservations on the artistic level, the poet seems to have accepted Freud's central thesis that sexuality is the basis of human behaviour, although he tends to refine the latter's crude concepts about the sex-drive almost beyond recognition by sublimating its manifestations in delicate emotional states. Significantly, too, he permits these forms of sublimated desire to manifest themselves solely within complex social settings, a practice which allows him to introduce into them a strong moral element; and this is no doubt the key factor in his art which is missing in Freud's more scientific treatment of the same phenomena. In short, he uses the very conventions of society to cast light on those fractional changes of mood or shades of consciousness that betray a person's depth of involvement in a given situation. Consequently, in his poetry the psycho-analytical emphasis of his master is largely reversed, and sublimated sexual activity is given greater prominence than the original sexual stimuli from which it springs.

The dynamic balance between convention and personal behaviour normally has to be broken to provide the initial spur for his lyrical dramas. The point may be illustrated in an incident which leads up to Chiaretta's manifestation of outraged modesty in the third lyric of *L'amorosa spina* (1920):

Guarda là quella vezzosa,
Guarda là quella smorfiosa.

Si restringe nelle spalle,
tiene il viso nello scialle.

O qual mai castigo ha avuto?
Nulla. Un bacio ha ricevuto.

Look there at that pretty one, look there at that wheedler. She shrugs her shoulders, keeps her face down in her shawl. O what punishment has she had? Nothing. She has received a kiss.

Equally delicate are her pouting and simple coquetry in an incident related in the ninth lyric, though in this case we can detect a reminiscence from Tasso:[31]

Hai un piccolo scialle, e con quel tutta
ti celi, e i labbrucci spingi in fuori,
quando un bacio ti buschi. Io dico: 'Brutta,

brutta tu veramente'. E invece mai
cosí bella ti godo come allora
che t'adiri, e adirarti, ahimè, non sai.

You have a tiny shawl, and with it you hide everything, and you thrust your lips out, if you obtain a kiss. I say: 'You are truly, truly wicked'. And yet never do I enjoy your beauty so much as when you grow angry, and yet, alas! you cannot rise to anger.

On the other hand, in the collection *Fanciulle* (1925) these simple acts of flirtation give way to a more serious analysis of the effects of passion. It now seems as if the poet intends to essentialize the whole range of sublimated sexuality in the female, and he is especially adept at describing the mingling of desire with a number of residual girlish repressions. So, although in the *Cronistoria* he tells us that young girls tend to be sexual automata and dismisses their feelings as similar to those of statues, the quality of their representation in his poetry still reveals the subtler emotions of timidity and pre-conscious longing behind the indifferent mask of puberty:

Salda fanciulla
cui fascia l'amorosa
zona selvetta ombrosa,
vago pudore di natura. Nulla,

altro ha nulla. Due ancora tondeggianti
poma con grazia unite
pare chiamino il mite
castigo della fanciullezza.[32]

Well-built girl, whose erotic zone a shady woodlet veils, a vague modesty of nature. Nothing, she has nothing else. Two still rounding breasts gracefully united seem to recall the mild chastisement of girlhood.

From this lowest common denominator of sexual ambivalence between childhood and the adult the poet passes on to develop a series of more significant attitudes ranging from the sensuous and dignified poise of the tailoress after her marriage:

Ma chi la vede per la via passare
sul ben calzato piede,
nella vita piú fede
sente, e in se stesso. E si volge a mirare,[33]

But whoever sees her passing in the street on her well-stockinged foot, feels more faith in life and in himself. And turns around to gaze,

to the serene – almost biblical – domesticity of his wife Lina, whose beauty is further enhanced by a suggestive pallor:

Nata da gente antica e disperante,
fiore d'adolescenza,
Lina è Rebecca senza
anfora. E il suo pallore è affascinante.[34]

Born of an ancient, despairing race, a flower of youthfulness, Lina is Rebecca without her pitcher. And her pallor is fascinating.

Moreover, we even obtain a stilnovistic effect in another lyric, though the Cavalcantian echoes are filtered through a more plebeian Campanian optic:

> Questa chi è che par cosí lontana,
> chiusa in se stessa, assente?
> Siede tra la sua gente
> composta ad una maestà popolana.[35]

> Who is this who seems so faraway, closed within herself, absent? She sits among her people composed in a plebeian majesty.

Essentially, then, we can regard Freudian elements as adjuncts to Saba's art rather than as its substance; and oddly enough they lead to a process of perceptual 'inversion' very much like that which we saw previously when comparing Saba and Leopardi. For, unlike Freud, the poet is not primarily interested in tracing behaviour patterns back to the stirrings of sexual instinct; he sets out instead to mask the sexual urge by depicting it as a mere facet of delicate social situations. By such means the process of sublimation is raised to a level of artistic 'veggenza' and instinctive drives are transformed into emblematic symbols of human emotion. Thus we can deduce that, even if Saba might not have been capable of delineating the more subtle aspects of desire without a knowledge of psycho-analytical procedures, it would be equally true to say that without his realization of the necessity to invert Freudian techniques, the Austrian psycho-analyst's methods would hardly have found a place in his art at all.

In addition to the incorporation of psycho-analytical procedures into his poetry we also find during the twenties other innovatory forms which make the period the very crucible of Saba's lyrical evolution. We have already referred to his successful symbolic structures and to his perhaps less than successful narrative or anecdotic manners. As a further way of diminishing his prosaic tendencies he also at times introduced another refinement into his word-music: a device which has the effect of compelling his lyrical cadences to conform more closely to the shape and contours of his intimate emotions. When we compare the musicality of the present period with his earlier poetry, therefore, we sense that it is only now, despite certain isolated moments of insight stretching back to his *Versi militari* (1908), that he emerges from his somewhat patchy apprenticeship. The moment of complete maturity is still perhaps delayed until the publication of *Preludio e fughe* (1928-9), although even in other works preceding it he already achieved a finer nuancing of his imaginative effects by evolving a delicate chiaroscuro scaling of his emotional responses to life.

These tonal transitions are clearly prefigured in *Preludio e canzonette* (1922-3), in which Saba's melodic patterns are already surprisingly mature. The lyrical clarity of 'Canzonetta prima' is a case in point despite its melodramatic note:

> Malinconia,
> la vita mia
> struggi terribilmente;
> e non v'è al mondo, non v'è al mondo niente
> che mi divaghi.

Melancholy, you rend my life terribly; and there is nothing, nothing in the world which amuses me.

But what his fugues contain and his *canzonette* do not is a complete synthesis of his pre-existing lyrical and narrative modes. So only in the latter does he finally transmute narration into the unfolding of subtle emotional states and inflections, in which sensory and musical elements work in double harness to provide graduated – though limpid – images for the expression of his fractionally changing moods.

Moreover, since the structure of these compositions is based on fugue form, they tend to create a musical configuration in which a play of light and shade on the visual, auditory and emotional planes is artfully combined to create a kind of counterpoint. Not only do we come across the normal fugue development and tonal answer, but also at times the device of counter-subject and counter-exposition. In such cases a theme is taken up again and enlarged by the voice which had previously supplied the tonal answer and vice versa. By these means various phonic combinations can replace a corresponding emotional colouring or a colourful emotionally charged image can interact with a dominant auditory pattern in a poem's cadences; and the result is that the entire atmosphere gradually dissolves into half-tints and subtle allusions. Its subtle resonances then eventually prove to be so persuasive that the poet's experiences seem enveloped in shadowy, mysterious forms, as if we were being invited to view his life as a play of images reflected through a photographic negative.

This type of effect is already prominent in 'Prima fuga' where the alternation of two voices expresses a contrast, the first voice symbolizing the darkness of despair and the second the radiance of hope. Since both are modulated within a carefully nuanced pattern of light and shadow, the fluctuating imagery seems to follow the very pangs of the poet's conscience; and, as a result, a subtle dialectic is created in which the poet's moods are alternately either fused or polarized. For instance, in reply to the tender, melancholy strains of the first voice rising pathetically from the gloom of the coalstore:

> La vita, la mia vita ha la tristezza
> del nero magazzino di carbone,
> che vedo ancora in questa strada,

Life, my life is touched with the sadness of the black coalstore, which I still see in this street,

we hear the second voice evoking an allusive gaiety of colour and movement in images which typify Saba's joyful moods:

Io vedo
per oltre alle sue porte aperte, il cielo
azzurro e il mare con le antenne . . .

I see beyond its open doors the blue sky and the sea with its masts . . .

At first the change from melancholy to joy is so dramatic that it almost seems explosive. But once the dominant pattern of tonal contrasts is established, the transitions are more subtly modulated and often blend imperceptibly together. The forms of life are thereby invested with a dynamic plasticity which is wholly regulated by the rise and fall of the poet's emotion. Quite often these fractional changes of mood are skilfully mediated by the use of anaphora, a device which is present in nearly all the fugues. It is especially noticeable in the second tonal answer of the present poem, which links the plastic movement of sea and sky with Saba's innermost feelings:

È bello
il cielo a mezzo la mattina, è bello
il mar che lo riflette, e bello è anch'esso
il mio cuore: uno specchio a tutti i cuori
viventi.

The sky is beautiful at mid-morning, and beautiful is the sea which reflects it, and beautiful too is my heart: a mirror of all living hearts.

By ringing the changes on the dark implacable beauty of the coalstore and the airy configurations of sea and sky, Saba thus not only fuses his two archetypal image-patterns together, but he does so by means of the rich alchemy of his musical effects. As a pre-condition of such a synthesis the gradual removal of all garish colours and harsh contours seems to be required; and it is only when this has been achieved that we breathe the air of total lyrical transfiguration. By then, however, the texture of his verse has reverted to its earlier Leopardian clarity, except that its present maturity and lyrical flexibility stand in marked contrast with the inflexibility and relative superficiality of the poet's earlier efforts in poems like the previously quoted 'La sera'.

What has really happened is that in the whole of *Preludio e fughe* the interfusion of tonal purity and a certain robustness of feeling has led to the complete elimination of all residual crepuscular attitudes and cadences. As a result, Saba's verse no longer seems fraught with sadness and melancholy but is endued with a veiled though pulsating optimism, one which is prompted by his deep, if sometimes diffident, sense of involvement in the wider problems of human existence. The only quality this attitude still shares with the crepuscular poets is an avoidance of crude materialistic effects; yet, while the present poet's artistic detachment, like theirs, results in the last analysis in a process of lyrical refinement, with Saba it is not only detectable by the inward eye but even more by the inner ear. As he develops, the outward features of reality tend to be absorbed by him into a personal pattern of melodic cadences, which nevertheless depict in their rhythmic, phonic and meditative urgency the eternal themes of anguish and elation.

No doubt Frattini was alluding to this particular quality when he described his verse as manifesting a 'doppia tendenza ad accogliere con visiva oggettività il mondo ed insieme ad intimizzarla'[36] ('dual tendency to accept the world with visual objectivity and to intimize it'). The whole process is controlled, as previously suggested, by the poet's melodic fluctuations, in which his images – though robust and significant in themselves – nevertheless play a subordinate role to his word-music. This all-pervading influence of his musicality on his lyrical scenarios is emphasized in the opening of his 'Terza fuga'. In this poem the orphic overtones of the imagery, especially the play of fountains, are again subtly subordinated to the alternating rise and fall of the melody:

Mi levo come in un giardino ameno
un gioco d'acque;
che in un tempo, in un tempo piú sereno,
mi piacque.

Il sole scherza tra le gocce e il vento
ne sparge intorno;
ma fu il diletto, il diletto ora spento
d'un giorno.

I arise as in a pleasant garden a play of fountains; which at one time, in a more serene time, pleased me. *The sun darts among the drops and the wind scatters some of them afar*; but it was the delight, the now dead delight of a day.

Although these images of peaceful gardens and fountains are reminiscent of the crepuscular poets, the fact remains that they are dynamic and plastic in quality, not romantically static and idealized, as they were in the earlier school. In their dynamic flow they remind us of the momentary orphic suspension practised by the hermetic poets, in which case they might aptly be compared, for instance, with the play of fountains described in Campana's 'Canto della tenebra'.

The refined melodiousness of Saba's later work has prompted critics to consider the progressive 'illimpidimento' of his style as the built-in regulator of his art. And, precisely because of the greater fluidity of his poetic line and its retention of popular, realistic touches, Quarantotti Gambini once even went so far as to compare the poetry of this collection, particularly the 'Sesta fuga' for three voices, with the music of Verdi.[37] However unreal such a parallel may seem at first sight, certain Verdian features are undoubtedly present in his manner of writing. Portinari has already alluded to some of them by noting that in Saba's style 'la natura della musica di Verdi, la sua felicità e elementarità semplice della strumentazione, il rischio accettato della banalità' ('the nature of Verdi's music, the joyfulness and simple elementarity of his instrumentation, the accepted danger of the commonplace') are all prominent.[38] Furthermore, both men are well known for the breadth of their emotional range and the variability of their tonal inflections. These qualities allow them to rise unexpectedly to the heights of passion or plumb, equally unexpectedly, the depths of despair, while at the same time suffusing their work with an indefinable elegiac grace normally to be associated with the radiant sadness of the folk-song. With Saba we also perceive that the popular element is offset by a certain classicism of form, a fact which again suggests that his lyricism is a fusion of literary and popular traditions; and perhaps in this too he parallels a trend we see taking place in many of Verdi's operas.

Again, the subtle melodies of the fugues represent only one of the achievements of Saba's maturity. Later, in collections like *Parole* (1933-4), *Ultime cose* (1935-43), or *Mediterranee* (1945), his word-music becomes even more resilient by virtue of his growing ability to use the full range of his stylistic devices with complete lyrical mastery. Nevertheless, a point to be noted once more is that his lyrical progress is by no means strictly chronological, because just as a later poem like 'Bocca' contains a melodic airiness linking it intimately with the fugues:

La bocca
che prima mise
alle mie labbra il rosa dell'aurora,
ancora
in bei pensieri ne sconto il profumo,[39]

The mouth which first placed on my lips the rosiness of dawn, its perfume I still discount in fair thoughts,

so an earlier one like 'Frutti e erbaggi' reveals a new melodic robustness, a much enhanced visual acuity, and a nonchalant colloquial style; and together these elements place it entirely outside their orbit:

Entra un fanciullo colle gambe nude,
imperioso, fugge via.

S'oscura
l'umile botteguccia, invecchia come
una madre.
Di fuori egli nel sole
si allontana, con l'ombra sua, leggero.[40]

A boy imperiously enters with bare legs, runs away. The humble shop darkens, ages like a mother. Outside he moves off in the sun, lightly, with his shadow.

The poet's prosody, in short, largely sheds at this stage its previously evanescent musical qualities and develops by way of compensation a sinuous muscularity.

Some critics have nevertheless doubted the authenticity of such a development and have attempted to attribute Saba's tighter articulation to a skilful imitation of Montale and Penna.[41] But, although certain inflections do indicate a Montalian reminiscence here and there, in the case of Penna the differences in the quality of lyrical texture are at least as important as the similarities. So, if we compare the present lyric with one taken from the latter's *Poesie* (1939), we sense at once that its flavour and poetic articulation are radically different:

Dal portiere non c'era nessuno.
C'era la luce sui poveri letti
disfatti. E sopra un tavolaccio
dormiva un ragazzaccio
bellissimo.
Uscí dalle sue braccia
annuvolate, esitando, un gattino.[42]

In the porter's lodge there was nobody. There was the light above the poor, unmade beds. And on a table slept a handsome boy. A kitten, hesitatingly, slipped from his cloudy arms.

Moreover, we have to remember that the Istrian poet was already using a laconic, colloquial style as early as 'La capra', which indicates that we hardly have to look further than his own lyricism to discover the essential ingredients of the new poetry of 'Frutta e erbaggi'. This is a point that Montale clearly emphasized after the publication of *Preludio e fughe*, and it is one which is no less applicable to Saba's later work.[43] Thus, quite apart from the fact that there is also a certain callow sensuality in Penna's verse which is never detectable in the lyricism of the present poet, other qualities also seem to confirm the view that his influence, if it exists at all, is largely extra-literary.

A further important lyrical feature which tends to justify Saba's growing robust manner is a concealed, though highly personal, form of 'rhetoric' associated with his later style. It has a nonchalant and yet peremptory charm which gives his poetic line a greater virility and vigour than it ever possessed before. It is already observable in poems like 'La brama' in *Cuor morituro* (1925-30), and again its presence at that stage of his career supports a belief in the authentic development of the stylistic features to be found in 'Frutta e erbaggi'. It appears to be the result of a synthesis of Saba's previous allusive word-music and his sporadically attained narrative toughness, and it creates a completely extravert lyrical grace which reaches its climax in *Mediterranee*, especially in lyrics like 'Ulisse':

Nella mia giovanezza ho navigato
lungo le coste dalmate. Isolotti
a fior d'onda emergevano, ove raro
un uccello sostava intento a prede,
coperti d'alghe, scivolosi, al sole
belli come smeraldi. Quando l'alta
marea e la notte li annullava, vele
sottovento sbandavano piú al largo,
per fuggirne l'insidia. Oggi il mio regno
è quella terra di nessuno. Il porto
accende ad altri i suoi lumi; me al largo
sospinge ancora il non domato spirito,
e della vita il doloroso amore.

In my youth I sailed along the Dalmatian coast. Small isles, at wave-level, emerged, where the occasional bird lingered intent on prey, covered with seaweed, slippery, as lovely as emeralds in the sunlight. When high tide and the night blotted them out, sails under the wind flapped further out, to avoid their snares. Today my kingdom is that no-man's land. The port shines its lights for others; my untamed spirit still drives me further seaward, and my painful love of life.

There can be little doubt that this poem strikes as fine a balance as the poet ever achieved between his love of life on the one hand and that deepseated emotional diffidence which bedevilled his sensibility throughout his career on the other. Yet, while the tone is compounded once again from a disturbing clash of feelings, these are now subtly welded together by means of an ebullient, serene, and self-confident rhetoric.

In short, we can regard the manner which has evolved in this lyric to be a felicitous combination of the poet's narrative, imaginative and musical modes. All of them, it must be emphasized, were present in his verse from the very outset, but in his early period they seldom tended to work in harmony with each other. The lyrical synthesis they were later to produce was thus difficult at first to recognize; but, if this seems surprising nowadays because poems with the lyrical resonance of 'Ulisse' are not uncommon even in the Saba of the forties, it has to be borne in mind how great a revelation *Preludio e fughe* proved to be to pre-war critics. It so overwhelmed them that after the somewhat pedestrian nature of the poet's lyrical apprenticeship its tenuous musicality was the only yardstick they thought worthy of applying to his poetry.

By this time, in other words, Saba had shaken off the fetters of traditional prosody altogether and was aiming at maintaining his lyrical tension by means of a sinewy style adhering to the emotional bedrock of the situations he described. From this new attitude of assurance there developed the confident and outward-looking lyricism of his old-age, which, unlike the poetry of many of his contemporaries, is hardly tinged at all with the melancholy of growing old. Instead, the fleeting emotions which he felt previously when confronted with reality are now treated *con brio*; and they throw into relief not only his ambivalent feeling of life's impermanence but also a countervailing sense of lyrical assurance which have all along formed the essential dialectic operating within the *Canzoniere*.

We might even describe the attitude taken up by the ageing Saba as being fundamentally one of disillusioned optimism, a mood which relies simultaneously for its effects upon a deliberate veil of pathos and a sense of commitment. The two collections which contain most of the work of this period are *Uccelli* (1948) and *Quasi un racconto* (1951);[44] but while, strictly speaking, these volumes are extraneous to the *Canzoniere*, they nevertheless tend to provide for it an appropriate epilogue. Naturally with collections written so late in life one can hardly expect to find large-scale innovations of style or technique; yet the poet's sense of drama and pathos is now raised almost to breaking-point, as he reacts to the fact that he feels himself 'morire alle cose'[45] ('dying to things'). The central drama to which they both refer unfolds between Saba and a young poet Federico Almansi[46], although, in fact, the emotional relationship established between them is only finally clarified in the posthumous collection *Epigrafe – ultime prose* (1959). It will therefore be necessary, as a preliminary, for us to touch on one of the compositions in the latter work.

The lyric 'Vecchio e giovane' provides us with the crucial situation, and in it the entire drama is described symbolically, in psychologically orientated language:

Un vecchio amava un ragazzo. Egli, bimbo
– gatto in vista selvatico – temeva
castighi e occulti pensieri. Ora due
cose nel cuore lasciano un'impronta
dolce: la donna che regola il passo
leggero al tuo la prima volta, e il bimbo
che, al fine tu lo salvi, fiducioso
mette la sua manina nella tua.

Giovinetto tiranno, occhi di cielo,
aperti sopra un abisso, pregava
lunga all'amico suo la ninna nanna.
La ninna nanna era una storia, quale
una rara commossa esperienza
filtrava alla sua ingorda adolescenza:
altro bene altro male. 'Adesso basta'
diceva a un tratto; 'Spegniamo, dormiamo'.
E si voltava contro il muro.

An old man loved a boy. As a child – a wild cat to look at – he feared punishments and hidden thoughts. Now two things leave a sweet mark in the heart: the woman who for the first time sets her gentle step to yours, and the child who, in the hope that you will save him, trustingly places his tiny hand in yours. A young tyrant, with eyes like the sky, open on to an abyss, he begged his friend to sing a long-drawn lullaby. The lullaby was a story, which like a rare and moving experience he filtered through his greedy adolescence: other good, other evil. 'That's enough' he said suddenly; 'Let's put out the light and sleep'. And he turned towards the wall.

Our first reaction to these lines is to ask ourselves why the rupture in the two poets' relations should ever have taken place, and Portinari provides the answer by quoting from an unpublished poem of Almansi's. In it the younger poet accuses the older one of attempting to absorb him spiritually into his own hard-won state of serenity, by acting as an all-protecting father-figure:

Se la febbre che divora il mio sangue
non può essere placata, non sorridere.
Il mio peccato è di averti creduto.
. . . .
Non avevi il diritto di recidere
la mia passione per la vita. Forse
perché un giorno ti diedi il cuore in pegno
e tu, come un mercante d'occasione,
l'hai venduto?[47]

If the fever which devours my blood cannot be soothed, do not smile. My sin is having believed in you . . . You had no right to stunt my passion for life. Was it, perhaps, because one day I pledged my heart to you, and you, like a second-hand dealer, sold it?

Having now fully understood the relationships existing between them from this dialogue, we can attempt to bring the underlying mood of 'Uccelli' more clearly into focus. Both it and its companion volume seem to be a delicate form of revenge sought by Saba for Almansi's continual attempts to escape from his influence. There is naturally no malice in the elder poet's verse and to represent it even for a moment as a destructive process would be to give an extremely false impression. But what Saba is prepared to reveal at a few critical points in its unfolding is his scepticism towards the younger poet's outlook of social idealism.

One major theme in these two collections is an allegory dealing with caged birds. They seem to find their imprisonment more pleasant than freedom, and, by way of their grace and charm, offer moments of sheer terrestrial bliss to their doting owner. As a foil to them we are also presented with birds in the wild and the sense of freedom which they possess is similarly emphasized. Moreover, the whole atmosphere is bathed in a type of charm which the very old share with the very young – one which derives from a combination of a deep sense of involvement with an astonishing degree of innocence, or at least with a complete absence of worldly prejudice. Needless to say, Almansi is sometimes compared with birds in the wild and at other times contrasted with caged ones; and, because of his obsessive interest in the younger poet's welfare, Saba may be regarded at this stage as a kind of meditative birdwatcher, as a person who contemplates life analogically through the delicate tracery of an aviary of his own making.[48]

We can illustrate the point by quoting the lyric 'A un giovane comunista'. Although its title may suggest at first that the poet is reverting to his anecdotal style, the poem's main feature is the elaboration of an 'emblematic' mode of storytelling. The emblem subsuming an entire aspect of life is a canary, and it is only in the last line that this wholly allegorico-figurative sphere is forcibly yoked to reality by reference to local political conditions. In an aesthetic sense the intrusive social element has often been considered to break the charm of the lyric, but at the same time it also indicates the deep tension between Saba's and Almansi's relationship, which is not sufficiently stressed without it:

Ho in casa – come vedi – un canarino.
Giallo, screziato di verde. Sua madre
certo, o suo padre, nacque lucherino.

È un ibrido. E mi piace meglio in quanto
nostrano. Mi diverte la sua grazia,
mi diletta il suo canto.
Torno, in sua cara compagnia, bambino.

Ma tu pensi: I poeti sono matti.
Guardi appena; lo trovi stupidino.
Ti piace piú Togliatti.

I have at home – as you see – a canary. Yellow, touched with green. Its mother or its father was certainly born a siskin. It is a hybrid. And I like it all the more since it is our own. Its grace pleases me, its song delights me. I become a child again in its company. But you think: Poets are mad. You hardly look; you find it stupid. You like Togliatti better.

We note in passing that the canary, like Almansi and Saba himself, is of mixed race. Later, when he poses as the ageing Ulysses of *Mediterranee*, the poet refers to the younger man as his spiritual son Telemachus, to whom he wishes to impart the fruits of his long experience. Needless to say, he fails, and the young man's Communism is symbolic of that failure. Yet the poet's reaction is not one of bitterness, it appears more as a complacent scepticism which he entertains in regard to the ethos and the ideals of the younger generation. The lyrical outcome is a greater mellowing of his language and style, which is certainly not indicative of an incipient dotage as some critics have suggested, but of a form of extreme maturity in the artistic and moral spheres.

Such a development explains why De Robertis described Saba's later poetry as a lyricism 'sillabata con l'anima'[49] ('spelt out by the soul'). It reveals in its most intense form the all-embracing humanity present throughout his entire work, which in his old age is more indulgent and perceptive than ever before. The attitude now predominating is one of deep sympathy and respect for the suffering of all creatures; and, as this feeling pervades the reader's mind, he too is able to participate in the drama and experience the crushed emotions of the poet as his spiritual son abandons him. Naturally the act of abandonment takes place before Almansi fully understands the starkness of the implications lying behind human contingency, and the poet's sorrow at having been unable to communicate them to him recalls other similar circumstances in his earlier collections. But, not surprisingly, the lyrical overtones attached to such dramas are now riper, more poignant, than they were previously, and Saba's language is here recompounded afresh to create a pattern of more intricate psychological insights.

In a cultural context his sociological and psychological interests therefore link him closely in spirit – if not in fact – with the Vocians. As we know from Slataper's rejection of his essay on artistic sincerity, he was not really regarded with favour by the group. But he later wreaked his revenge on them by proving to be more Vocian in outlook than they were themselves. So, as the majority of its adherents moved away from life's existential implications and reverted to idealistic attitudes, he continued to emphasize the contingent and delicately sensuous side of the modern poet's inspiration. In this sense a feeling for individual and corporate existence suffuses his entire work and causes his poetry to oscillate between a downright egocentricity on the one hand and a thorough-going altruism on the other. The greatest debt his contemporaries owe to him is that he showed them how to avoid the dangers of solipsism, and he drove the lesson home by endowing his verse with an elusive air of waywardness and human passion while still permitting it to deal below the surface with the recurring problems of destiny. His feigned nonchalance and continual badinage are therefore no more than a beguiling disguise behind which there exists a well-consolidated moral outlook: an approach to life which centres on the humanist doctrine that the fulfilment of the individual produces its own intrinsic set of lyrical values. By reintroducing this factor into art and dealing allusively with the penumbra of social pressures moulding the human personality, he creates a type of lyricism which can virtually be called a psychology of the imagination.

CHAPTER VIII

Vincenzo Cardarelli and the ideal of modern classicism

Of all the poets who have left their mark on Italian literature in the twentieth century Cardarelli is probably the one possessing the most uncompromising artistic temperament. From the beginning of his career his intense feeling for aesthetic propriety led him to conclude that modern society could only be redeemed from within, by means of a process of complete moral and lyrical regeneration. He therefore considered it his duty to analyse all the experiential tensions implicit in his age and to weave them together into a sober and coherent lyrical pattern, reflecting – and yet at the same time modifying – the time-hallowed standards of classical taste. In other words artistic freedom and iconoclasm were in no sense interchangeable terms for him as they had been for the futurists, because, by possessing as he did an unshakeably classical turn of mind, he upheld the principle of self-restraint, even of self-immolation, on the altars of art with remarkable steadfastness throughout his entire career. His view was that the contemporary poet should aim neither at a baroque cult of the marvellous nor at a hermetic involution of imagery, but at the promotion of the maximum amount of lyrical harmony within a strictly defined and Italianate sphere of aesthetic experience. This does not imply that he was narrowly exclusivist at heart; on the contrary, he was fully prepared to acknowledge that attitudes to life had changed dramatically in the present century and that it was no longer possible for the classically-minded poet to exercise a decisive influence on events unless he could come to terms with the more valid of modern artistic principles. But what he could never accept was the replacement of genuine inspiration with a show of virtuosity, and he considered that the main artistic problem facing his generation was to discover at precisely which point in the lyrical spectrum a poet should operate in order to bring about a recrudescence of classical standards.

As we have already seen, such deep-rooted veneration for past tradition runs counter to the principal trends of his day; and, largely because he clung so tenaciously to the classical doctrines that he, Bacchelli and others had formulated in *La Ronda*, he was soon regarded as outmoded and found himself left behind in the race for literary recognition. But the neglect of the public in no way caused him to deviate from his chosen path whose appropriateness to his age seemed to him self-evident. What it did provoke, however, was a sense of bitterness and indignation which he vented against other writers whom he suspected of betraying, or at least adulterating, the pure strain of Italian poetry.[1]

The nature of Cardarelli's peremptory manner is emphasized in De Robertis's portrait appearing in his review of *Il sole a picco* (1930). The critic then wrote: 'Il ricordo primo che ho di Cardarelli, e che non mi si è poi, mai piú, cancellato dalla mente, è il modo come diceva le parole, scandendole, e col dito levato, quasi ad avvertire che a dirle cosí c'entrava un po' la gloria d'averle scoperte, oltre il piacere di pronunciarle, in quel momento, brillanti d'un'aria nuova, e tutte viventi. Una novità dunque accompagnata ogni volta da una dimostrazione perentoria.'[2] ('The earliest memory I have of Cardarelli, and which has never since been erased from my mind, is the way in which he uttered his words, articulating them carefully, and with a finger raised, almost as if to indicate that in saying them in that way he shared a little in the glory of having discovered them, in addition to having the pleasure of pronouncing them, at that moment, resplendent with a new light, and wholly living. A novelty, therefore, accompanied on each occasion by a peremptory demonstration'). But, although his inflexibility seems to be registered here in every gesture, this supposed hardening of his artistic arteries can only be ascribed in part to the excessive aestheticism of his classical temperament: its apparent rigidity is also derived from a much more praiseworthy attempt to absorb, rather than allow himself to become absorbed by, contemporary fashions. So in place of their dispersiveness and fragmentary sensationalism he strove to develop a coherent aesthetic outlook reflected in a style whose maturity he hoped would be matched by a sober renovation of forms. Unfortunately, his call to order was made just at a time when experimentation was at last producing valid results with the major hermetic writers and when even the most die-hard classicists were being won over to the idea that common sense would eventually winnow the wheat from the chaff in the *avanguardia*. His strictures were thus immediately misunderstood or taken as denunciations of the finest modern achievements, and what was also lost in the process was his most valuable lesson: the principle of tonal unity which many earlier poets had utterly disregarded in the popular craze for ever more daring and disruptive experiments.

Again Cardarelli was himself partly to blame for this state of affairs, because his increasing touchiness soon led him to be as wounding in his polemics as he was restrained in his verse. Therefore, as his moral tone became shriller, his criteria for lyrical excellence grew narrower, until the point was reached where the constant note of persiflage underlying his literary judgements produced sufficient irritation to obliterate the solid achievement of his arguments. Likewise he tended to undermine his critical sensitivity by introducing into his writings an arid, ratiocinatory element bordering on sophistry, a feature not only detectable in his views on other poets but one which is even carried over at times into his own verse. So normally it is only in his finest lyrics that his ethical posturing becomes totally transfigured, moving away from a blunt aphoristic assertiveness towards a sinuous and evocative form of imagery. As a general rule he only reached his highest point of inspiration when he drew his lyrical substance from the convergence of his senses and his reflective faculty. At such times, however, a rare fusion of his imaginative and evaluative powers was often achieved, compensating for the excessive cerebration apparent elsewhere in his work.

The principal question we have to ask ourselves when trying to penetrate to the core of Cardarelli's lyrical manner is precisely how he succeeded in producing authentic poetry almost wholly composed of transfigured concepts and lyrical evaluations. To answer it we have to bear in mind that he considered art to consist of a series of meditative reactions by the human conscience to the vagaries of existence. In order to ensure the validity of his own work he felt it was his prime duty to reduce his experiences to their constituent parts by a process of analysis and then to resynthesize them lyrically by means of intense acts of intellection. In the process we can detect three distinct phases in his lyrical manner corresponding approximately to three different temporal states. The first is a descriptive mode reflecting the external world in its temporal flux. In a spiritual sense its unfolding is somewhat opaque and its images are noted more for their extension than their meditative depth. So, largely because this kind of description produces little more than a visual impact, Cardarelli tends to be very parsimonious in its use, and he normally deploys it only to determine the point of departure of his lyrical meditations. But he cannot resist justifying his own restraint by suggesting that 'inferior' writers like Cecchi[3] appear to know of no other manner of composing; and he deplores their over-indulgence in description by asserting that they do not attempt to interpret life in any way, but simply mimic raw sensations at the point at which they first impinge on the artist's sensibility. Hence the process should in his view be restricted to providing a sensuous undertow for the development of otherwise wholly reflective imagery.

The second phase is an associative style which reflects the inner time-flow of living creatures. As was clearly the case with his descriptive style, this phase is again pre-reflective and its cognitions are almost completely intuitive in quality. We can compare it with Bergson's 'temps vécu' ('lived time') inasmuch as it is immediately given and not meditatively structured. For Cardarelli childhood represents unselfconscious physiological time in its true purity, since at that period, as he tells us in 'Tempi immacolati', he always found that

> Tra me e le ore
> vigeva un accordo esatto.

Between myself and the passing hours there reigned a precise harmony.

Artistic representation at this temporal level is in his opinion simply a first hesitant step beyond gratuitous descriptiveness, and reflective thought is still far from being one of its principal constituents.

The third synthetic phase of his art naturally consists of the poet's meditative perspectives and in 'Silenzio della creazione' he tells us perceptively that 'esprimere è restituirsi'[4] ('to utter is to reconstitute oneself'). The poetic vision that such restructuring provides is in his view best illustrated by Petrarch's memorial regressions in the *Canzoniere*. Like Petrarch, Cardarelli regards any kind of temporal experience which is not put into memorial perspective as being wholly pre-literary. Hence to his mind the fullness of life does not lie in external reality, but in the transcendent realms of the reason and sensibility where the contingent elements of existence are first absorbed and then completely transformed by the poet. As he remarks elsewhere, 'il tempo ci rapisce nei nostri oblii. Ogni piú lieve assenza della memoria è uno scatto del suo grande orologio, alla cui sommità meridiana è scritta la nostra fine'[5] ('time steals us away in our moments of forgetfulness. Even a slight absence of memory is a leap of its great clock, at whose high noon our end is written'). From such an observation we deduce that the fundamental distinction he makes between the sphere of art and the world flux is that the former, but not the latter, is capable of reflecting the poet's meditations. One's sense-impressions are accordingly nothing more than the substratum on which one's lyrical evaluations are based, although by a judicious blending of emotion and reflection he also believed that the authentic poet manages to provide his verse with a satisfying touch of sensuous immediacy.

Cardarelli's aesthetic doctrine was symbolically propounded as early as 1912-14 in the poem 'Arabesco' which shows the reflective pattern behind life's flux in its somewhat allusive imagery:

> Se non fossero i ritorni
> che mi assicurano l'eternità!
> I belli orizzonti che ospito

negli occhi con poco amore
e mutano rapidamente,
se non fosse il sagace inganno
che si consuma nella mia memoria
a riserbarmene il senso!
Poi da un barlume, un ricordo,
forse illusorio, ariose nostalgie,
ricuperate realtà distese.
Dalle ignude concezioni
le prospettive ridenti
che si rifanno!
E i suoni, difficile scherzo,
senza dei quali il ritmo non sussiste.

Were it not for the returns which ensure my eternity! The fine horizons which I house in my eyes with little love and which change rapidly, were it not for the subtle deception which is consumed in my memory to retain the sense of them for me! Then from a flash of insight, a memory, perhaps illusory, airy nostalgias, broad realities recollected. From naked concepts what smiling prospects are reconstructed! And sounds, a difficult game, without which rhythm cannot subsist.

But, although this lyric is clearly an *ars poetica*, we shall not dwell at length on its meaning here since this will become evident later. It will suffice to note for the moment that lyrical creation is in Cardarelli's view a series of orphic 'ritorni' within the creative memory, whereby the Leopardian 'inganni' or beguiling deceptions of the contingent world are meditatively reinterpreted to produce the 'belli orizzonti' of an inner perspective. From them arise certain 'ariose nostalgie' in the poet's sensibility and, because of their peculiar property of enduing objects at the very periphery of perception with as much intensity as those present at the centre of attention, such forms of nostalgia finally produce a series of 'ricuperate realtà distese' which actually replace the external world, mass for mass, with an inner artistic reality. Moreover, since this type of artistic representation is neither wholly sensory nor entirely rational in quality, the tendency is for its object-symbols to 'ideate' rather than 'idealize' the poet's lyrical vision.

As we indicated earlier, Cardarelli's descriptive manner marks the lowest level of his artistic activity and it normally makes its appearance at the beginning of a poem in order to set the scene. In the lyric 'Liguria' the poet's allusions to the cyclical background of the seasons are closely connected with the parallel idea of the flux of cosmic time; so that the ponderous and impenetrable beauty of nature's processes fills us with a sense of awe mingled with futility:

È la Liguria una terra leggiadra.
Il sasso ardente, l'argilla pulita,
s'avvivano di pampini al sole.
È gigante l'ulivo.

Liguria is a pleasant land. The burning stone, the clean clay, are alive with vines in the sun. The olive-tree is gigantic.

But usually such hallucinatory descriptions only act as a groundswell of sensations which he subsequently uses as a spring-board for his subtle transformations of reality. At most they represent so many block-dreams whose unpremeditated radiance will later require interpreting and placing in an aesthetic and ethical perspective. The process need not be openly conceptual and in this particular poem the cerebral charge is itself imprisoned in a chain of concrete images. So, just as the initial description deals with the massive works of nature, the final one opens up the resonance-chamber of the human tradition and depicts mankind as it sails eternally towards its spiritual destiny:

O chiese di Liguria, come navi
disposte a esser varate!
O aperti ai venti e all'onde
liguri cimiteri!
Una rosea tristezza vi colora
quando di sera, simile ad un fiore
che marcisce, la grande luce
si va sfacendo e muore.

O Ligurian churches, like ships ready to be launched! O Ligurian cemeteries open to the winds and the waves! A rosy sadness tinges you when at eventide, like a flower fading, the strong light melts away and dies.

In short, all forms are merged figuratively here with the mystical sunset of human life, and the previous opaque description of man's physical habitat thereby acquires an orphic, almost a decadent, dimension.

The physiological rhythm of life is by contrast expressed in more dynamic chains of imagery, and in the lyric 'Scherzo' its careless raptures are rendered meaningful by a studied grouping of events and sensations to bring out the corporate involvement of all creatures in the teeming life of the earth:

Il bosco di primavera
ha un'anima, una voce.
È il canto del cuccú,
pieno d'aria,
che pare soffiato in un flauto.

Dietro il richiamo lieve,
piú che l'eco ingannevole,
noi ce ne andiamo illusi.
Il castagno è verde tenero.
Sono stillanti persino
le antiche ginestre.
Attorno ai tronchi ombrosi,
fra giochi di sole,
danzano le amadriadi.

> The wood in spring has a single soul, one voice. It is the song of the cuckoo, swelling airily, so that it seems blown through a flute. After its gentle call, more deceitful than an echo, we move about bewitched. The chestnut is a tender green. Even the ancient broom is dripping. Around shady trunks, amid a play of sunlight, the hamadryads dance.

Here we find a suspended tableau of the drama of life in which slightly mythicized creatures offer up hymns of praise to nature in order to give vent to those deep feelings of solidarity which the poet believes unite all living forms. Within its magic circle even man can contentedly enjoy his anthropomorphic illusions, and, by attuning himself to the chorus of the lesser creatures around him, insulate himself from the stark indifference of the cosmos. It is almost as if the latter's life-cycles provide a measure by means of which he can regulate his own existence, and through such a symbiosis he too ultimately learns to harmonize his mind with the social myth.

Evidently we are already moving towards a sublimated plane of pure ethical intelligence and at first it may seem as if this procedure is not too far removed from the art of the hermetic poets. But in contrast with their figurative processes Cardarelli tends to dethrone the fancy and subordinates it to a form of conceptual realism. In other words he still regards the hermetic outlook as a neo-romantic one because of its postulation of infolded extra-sensory states towards which the poet's feelings aspire as he seeks to satisfy his deep craving for absolutes. This trend seems nothing more to him than a Promethean revolt against the human condition; and, since mankind can never participate in the absolute life of the gods, the inevitable outcome of such musing is a series of empty gestures combined on the technical level with much sleight-of-hand, especially in the cult of verbal alchemies. The process even fosters the romantic idea of the poet as a 'creator', but again in Cardarelli's view the creative faculty is simply a misnomer for that profoundly unmystical, transfigurative quality whereby the mind interprets its contingent situations by raising sensory experiences on to an evaluative plane. Thus in many ways he considers modern classical art to be a radical revolt against romanticism and also against the residual idealism of his own age. To further its development he proposes a memorial approach in which the intelligence rules the imagination and becomes the directing force behind lyrical composition.

On the other hand, Cardarelli does not wish to deny the imagination a rôle in poetry altogether: he simply stresses the dangers of giving its associative processes absolute free rein. He considers that the cause of many of mankind's aberrations is the complete unruliness of the fancy which idealizes and thereby dehumanizes everything it touches.[6] His remedy for such a tendency is to fall back on ethical transfiguration which, he claims, produces the classical myth; and in one of his short-stories he actually describes the 'idealistic' Plato as the greatest cross the 'ethically' motivated Socrates ever had to bear.[7]

So clear a shift of emphasis from metaphysical to moral preoccupations probably accounts for the difference in the temper of his poetic line from that of the hermetic poets. Consequently, after modern poetry's long excursion into the realms of speculation we find Cardarelli trying to turn back the clock to the halcyon days of humanist culture. He certainly puts aside all hope of extending the human purview in the direction of a mystical 'veggenza' and asserts instead, with the confidence of a Michelangelo, that for the deft hand there is nothing inexpressible in words, stone or clay. As a justification of this attitude he tells us that 'la mia forza è quando mi ripiego. La mia massima musicalità quando mi giustifico'[8] ('my strength is when I reflect. My highest musicality when I justify myself'). Since his art consists of self-evaluation upon an ethical plane, it is only to be expected that he attempts to apply the same evaluative procedures to his stylistic as he does to his meditative practices. In the process he rejects the verbal alchemies compounded by his contemporaries and relies almost exclusively for his effects on discursive techniques.

A tendency to adopt discursive modes itself implies a classically orientated mind, with a special concern for the problems of style and expression. At no point did Cardarelli ever abandon this ideal of craftsmanship and, if anything, his desire for stylistic perfection was the one concession he made to the mystique of form he inherited from the romantic and post-romantic eras. Such a craving is sufficient in itself to account for the penumbral, orphic atmospheres frequently enveloping the otherwise strictly rational unfolding of his image-patterns, although one might also be tempted to ascribe his concept of the super-stylist to a decadent source, to the influence of Nietzsche.[9] Just as the German philosopher considered man to be a metaphysical rebel against nature, so he sees the artist in the same light: 'Chi parla ha da sentire di compiere un'infrazione. È inutile illudersi su questo punto. Niente di quel che noi facciamo può esserci semplificato dalla riposante persuasione che ci sia bisogno di noi, in qualunque modo . . . E non è che l'intuito della sua imperdonabile superfluità che acuisce e rende eccezionali le manifestazioni dell'uomo.'[10] ('Whoever speaks must feel that he is causing an infraction. It is useless to delude ourselves on that point. Nothing of what we do can be simplified by the fond illusion that we are in any way necessary . . . And it is only the understanding of his unforgiveable superfluity which sharpens and makes exceptional the activities of man.') Nevertheless he refuses to take this attitude to extreme solipsist conclusions, but strips it rather of all its speculative elements in order to create purely artistic criteria for the assessment of experience in a human context. The reason for his caution is that he believed man only has control over his destiny within the historical confines of society's gradual evolution; beyond it, on a cosmic level, he always has been and would always remain the plaything of the gods.

Such views ensure that Cardarelli's poetry never abandons tangible everyday objects for romantic dreams of disembodied godhood. In fact, precisely because he was so determined to keep his feet firmly planted on the ground, his lyricism acquires its specific form – an intellectually structured recuperation of experience through a memorial redimensioning of his sense-impressions. The aim of the process is a rational one: to supply evaluative criteria which will put events in their proper historical and aesthetic perspective; and yet, since the poet is aware that such criteria need to be expressed allusively if they are to retain a lyrical charge, he is prepared to yield to representational techniques in all but essentials. Hence, while his manner of image-building is normally cumulative like Gozzano's, his symbols are never as static or as memorially regressive as they are in the earlier poet's work. Instead, in poems like 'Spiragli', they clearly strike an interesting balance between immediacy and meditation:

Che cosa mi colpisce oramai!
Un velo d'ombra di mare
sui monti lontani,
un lembo di nuvola tutelare.
Ma basta levare la testa.
Le cose non stanno che a ricordare.
Piano piano i minuti vissuti,
fedelmente li ritroveremo.

What strikes me now! A shadowy veil of sea on distant hills, a protective patch of cloud. But it is enough to raise one's head. Things only persist in the memory. Slowly we shall faithfully rediscover the moments which we have lived.

Here the imagery at first tends to be impressionistic, but it is soon raised to a cerebral level as the poet lifts his head and re-creates his sense-impressions in a detached memorial sphere. His modes of representation are thereby transformed into a method for the evaluation of his feelings, with the result that he manages to infuse a whole philosophy of life into a few hallucinatory images dealing with the changing shapes of sea and clouds. Although such a procedure is clearly meditative, it is certainly not escapist in any sense of the word. It has little affinity with traditional Platonic transcendence to a conceptual or static world of forms and may more properly be likened to Husserl's gradual transformation of the *Lebenswelt* through *epoché* and disinterested reflection. So, precisely because Cardarelli presupposes a social consciousness as the ultimate reality behind his cultural world, he sees no point in peering beyond existence and trying to catch a glimpse of some inaccessible, metaphysically postulated paradise. In his view the genuine poet should simply aim at producing a figurative transcription of his personal feelings while rejecting the symbolist quest for self-deification through the application of speculative procedures to the concrete products of the sensibility.

Naturally the main danger in an art of this kind is a tendency towards over-cerebration and the very intensity of Cardarelli's meditations, as Bigongiari notes, often leads him 'a uscire dall'esperienza nella saggezza che l'assevera e l'uccide'[11] ('to abandon experience for a sagacity which makes it assertive and kills it'). Whenever this occurs his poetry plunges from the heights of inspiration to a level of utter frigidity and he openly indulges in a cult of sophistry and ratiocination. His main artistic problem is therefore how to establish a balance between intellectual and sensuous elements so as to avoid the danger of a prosaic discursiveness. That he is himself aware of the danger emerges from his own definition of his lyrical methods, for he notes: 'La mia lirica (attenti alle pause e alle distanze) non suppone che sintesi. Luce senza colore, esistenze senza attributo, inni senza interiezione, impassibilità e lontananza, ordini e non figure, ecco quel che vi posso dare.'[12] ('My lyricism (pay attention to its pauses and distances) presupposes only synthesis. Light without colour, presences without attributes, hymns without exclamations, impassibility and perspective, precepts and not images, that is what I can give you.') But unfortunately, despite his being continually on his guard, we find all too frequently that he is haunted by one particularly intransigent demon, a constant desire to wield the categorical imperative. This causes him to prefer concepts or assertions to images, even though by continually striving to express himself in a series of aphorisms he deprives his poetry of many of its sensuous undertones and intuitive insights.

The actual terms which Cardarelli uses in defining his art are well worth further consideration, since they sum up all its essential qualities. Some of them are clearer than others, such as the first term 'sintesi' which simply denotes that act of intellection whereby the various segments of the poet's image-chains are meaningfully welded together. On the other hand, some require further explanations to those which he himself provides, while a few are very obscure indeed. In the first place, it seems that the phrase 'luce senza colore' refers to Cardarelli's tonal radiance which is subdued and reflective because he draws his inspiration from cerebral rather than concrete effects. Similarly his reference to 'esistenze senza attributo' appears to indicate his Leopardian technique of character-sketching and landscaping, which are either consciously generic or spatially dilated, so as not to obscure meaning by over-concreteness. His care over his 'pause' and his desire for 'lontananza' or perspective again show a desire to redimension life and reconstruct it according to pre-conceived intellectual and memorial patterns; while his 'inni senza interiezione' often give us additional insight into his tonal fabric by hinting at the restrained nature of his enthusiasms. By contrast, his concept of 'impassibilità' is less amenable to immediate interpretation, although it seems connected with the symbolists' doctrine of the impersonal nature of all authentic art. Elsewhere he defines the particular term as follows: 'Impassibile è il poeta che, còlto dall'ispirazione, può volgerla indifferentemente su ogni oggetto, come si diffonde la luce.'[13] ('Impassible is the poet who, seized by inspiration, can turn it indiscriminately on all objects, as one diffuses light.') In this sense it no doubt relates to the process of artistic evaluation, but with further implications concerning the tonal unity necessary in all authentic lyricism. What he is suggesting, it seems, is that once a writer has reached a high pitch of emotive intensity he is capable of evaluating any situation he chooses; and indeed nothing could be more calculated than this to throw into relief the fact that his own approach to art is cerebral rather than imaginative. For, whereas the imaginative poet relies mainly on the tactile and visual qualities of precise situations to sharpen his lyrical intelligence, Cardarelli as a typically rational poet deploys his images and situational features as external and largely 'detached' illustrations of his pre-established moods and ideas.

Another of the above-mentioned concepts, the idea of 'lontananza', also deserves closer inspection, since it has an architectonic function as well as an intellectual one. Its perspectives help the poet to develop his objective manner while simultaneously providing him with a cosmically dilated framework for his cerebro-spatial insights.[14] His spatial imagery is indeed nothing less than a meditative re-creation of the universe, though with a mass-distribution depending not on chance but on his aesthetic and intellectual powers of reconstruction. So, when we examine Cardarelli's manner of deploying images, we find that he normally organizes them (as in 'Estiva' or 'Liguria') as if he were creating an ascending series of ever-broadening lyrical perspectives, punctuated by breathtaking moments of languor and rhythmic repose. An apt example is the poem 'Omar Kayyâm' which is especially interesting because it offers a memorial repenetration of the Persian poet's historically defined tastes and feelings. Its inner 'landscape' represents the deeper reaches of Khayyam's personality and each phase in his mind's ascent towards an overall vision of beauty ends on a rhythmic plateau, consisting of a laconic statement of fact accompanied on the prosodic level by a dying fall. Three such falls are apparent in the following passage and they round off various stages of Cardarelli's resonant repenetration of Khayyam's world-outlook:

> Tu hai potuto iridare
> di primordiali curiosità
> l'ombra della vita.
> Dove tutto non era
> che disperata certezza
> tu hai fatto domande,
> proposto accordi e tutto era concluso.
> E quando, non la durezza
> della faccia di Dio,
> pietosamente a te ascosa,
> ma la tua carne stanca
> ti rimbrottava,
> da quell'oscuro e flebile scontento
> nasceva la grazia d'un ritmo.

> You have been able to irradiate with primitive curiosities the shadow of life. Where everything was only a desperate certainty you have asked questions, proposed harmonies, and everything was concluded. And when, not the harshness of the face of God, piteously concealed from you, but your own weary flesh reproached you, from that plaintive and obscure discontent was born the grace of a rhythm.

As is often the case, the poet's lyrical inflections tend here to produce a repetitive or circular movement. Sometimes even the atmosphere of an entire poem is dependent upon such 'ricapitolazioni', as, for instance, in those lyrics in which whole chains of imagery are immersed and re-immersed in the languid warmth of a summer's evening. Poems of this type have a soporific, almost a decadent, flavour about them, and they combine a suppressed Dannunzian sensuality with a gentler Pascolian evanescence. Yet they nevertheless possess an intellectual resilience and a classical appropriateness of tone which prove to be the specific qualities of Cardarelli's genius.

Their full impact is to be seen in poems like 'Largo serale' where a mood of speculative indolence becomes all-pervasive. In one of his letters the poet links heavy summer atmospheres with that essential 'superfluità' he associates with the human spirit, and he notes: 'I riposi dell'estate sono enormi ... perché quasi fuori dell'ordine della natura. La mia poesia è tutta una variazione su questo tema.'[15] ('Summer's moments of repose are enormous ... because almost beyond the natural order of things. My poetry is wholly a variation on this theme.') His habit of aestivating in the balmy warmth of summer evenings is in other words symbolic of his conception of a meditative human maturity, of a period in life to which he attaches overriding importance. Later we shall observe these hothouse atmospheres of maturity changing to autumnal ripeness and decay in old-age, when the poet finally becomes a prey to physical decline and lassitude. It even seems at times as if he intentionally uses the cycle of the seasons as a tonal medium through which to diffuse his thought. Their gradations of warmth and mellowness are intended to bear along his stream of consciousness rather than to possess any specific meaning in their own right. Yet, whenever they are combined with his subtle pauses, his frequent recapitulations, and tremendous efforts at lyrical synthesis, they ensure the validity of his imagery and also its strict adherence to a realist outlook on existence.

When Cardarelli had fully developed his mature figurative manner he thus felt absolute confidence in its potentialities. So, although he was disillusioned even in his early youth by most other forms of human activity, his faith in his art never faltered. He regarded it in all stages of his life as a deep spiritual therapy which led not to mystical insights or to a direct communion with God, but to a satisfying psycho-sensuous equilibrium:

> La speranza è nell'opera.
> Io sono un cinico a cui rimane
> per la sua fede questo al di là.
> Io sono un cinico che ha fede in quel che fa.

> Hope is in the work of art. I am a cynic to whom there remains through his faith this one beyond. I am a cynic who has faith in what he does.

Since at the height of his inspiration his images and ideas fuse instantaneously together to form a subtly modulated lyrical discourse, one could indeed describe his authentic meditations as arising at the very tips of his senses. As a result of the memorial sphere in which they move, their effects are normally elegiac[16] and dwell upon the contingent delights of living, as previously depicted in 'Scherzo' and 'Spiragli'. But, oddly enough, even the irremediable threat of decay is treated in a different fashion by him than by most other modern poets, because it is not only leavened by the consolatory note implicit in his tonal colouring, it also acquires a further resilience from the absoluteness of his acts of intellection and lyrical synthesis.

On the other hand, his cynicism obtrudes whenever his senses and reason fail to move in unison, and the distortion of the psycho-sensuous balance in his imagery often gives rise to what Gargiulo once called 'argomentazioni in concatenazione dimostrativa'[17] ('arguments in chains of assertions'). The main cause of his moments of ratiocinative insensitivity is a relative banishing of tactile and visual elements from his poetry which results in a failure to transfigure. The precise extent of this failure may in fact be measured by the degree of over-conceptuality to which any given composition falls victim. Whenever Cardarelli is under the spell of his rationalizing demon he thus eliminates from his lyrical texture all those chance illuminations and spontaneous psychological asides which enhance the aesthetic beauty of his art. Indeed, their inevitable replacement by schematic structures then inclines his verse towards a form of ratiocination rather than towards the airy grace of the song.

Probably there is a psychological reason for Cardarelli's desire to create *absolute* rational entities – a feeling of precariousness arising from his illegitimate birth and the wounding and ill-natured remarks to which he was constantly subjected in his native town. Hence, although later he could jokingly remark that 'per aver un bel paio di corna non è necessario essere di Corneto'[18] ('to have a fine pair of horns it is not necessary to come from Corneto'), the insecurity of his childhood continued to affect him, as if by reaction, throughout his life. Above all, it instilled into him a heightened sense of the uncertainties of living, in compensation for which he attempted to crystallize his experiences into ever more intractable and quartz-like forms. This explains the solidity and corpulence of his lyrical tableaus and especially their visual acuity. Moreover, it also stresses the main distinction between his work and that of the hermetic poets: for, whereas the latter have been accused of refining away their poetic content to vanishing point, his verse at all times manifests an indisputable lyrical substance. Admittedly, his content largely consists of a small number of obsessively fixed ideas, as Contini has noted;[19] but, far from appearing a serious defect, this recurrence of the same imaginative patterns is part and parcel of his originality. Elsewhere he calls them his 'fulminee ricapitolazioni'[20] ('fulminatory recapitulations') and they form a creative spiral which has implications for his style as well as his thought. At the moment, however, it is with his lyrical substance that we are mainly concerned, so we shall concentrate our attention on his poetic themes. From the very outset these offer a maturity of outlook which permits us to consider them as definitive expressions of his attitude to life; and, in fact, it is their progressive ethico-figurative deepening through constant repetition that represents the true chronology of development in his poetry rather than the slighter conceptual or temporal modifications which they periodically undergo.

★ ★ ★ ★ ★ ★

As a preliminary to an examination of Cardarelli's themes we should, however, emphasize once again the ethical value of his tonal colouring. The suffocating heat of summer and the tepid warmth of autumn create between them a spiritual sensorium within which the poet finds it convenient to depict the various climacterics of human existence. The unfolding of life in his lyricism actually begins with a meditation upon the youthful theme of virginity and it ends with a series of reflections upon the significance of death. Together these two notions mark the limits of the poet's lyrical purview; they are the initial and terminal cut-off points of experience accepted by him without question or prevarication. Between them there lies the intensely self-conscious state of maturity to whose temperate passions he almost entirely devotes his attention.

The theme of virginity marks a point of metamorphosis between immaturity and maturity, between that over-replete sense of Being characteristic of childhood and the self-awareness of one's own contingency that fills the entire outlook of the adult. As we would expect, the poet equates virginity with a state of purity, but it is a purity which is still unconscious of itself and therefore gratuitous. In other words virginity is a phase of life whose very sanctity is expressive of a limit, and this limit in Cardarelli's work finds its symbolic incarnation in the figure of a young girl. In the lyric 'Adolescente' her untouched perfection is inevitably undermined in the course of time by the tensions of living, but as long as she remains a virgin her principal characteristic is an impenetrable, sphinx-like, physical luxuriance: a type of beauty ripe for carnal defilement since its perfection, even at the very moment of its plenitude, is already touched by the promptings of instinct. Being and Existing are thus offset figuratively in her air of artless innocence, mingled as it is with a stifling sensuality; and her very acts of unthinking self-assurance are chilled by tortured doubts as she feels her sexual desires gradually awakening:

Sei l'imporosa e liscia creatura
cui preme nel suo respiro
l'oscuro gaudio della carne che appena
sopporta la sua pienezza.

You are the smooth and impenetrable creature on whom in her very breath there weighs the dark joy of the flesh which can hardly bear its own plenitude.

Most of Cardarelli's virgins are depicted in similar poses and possess the attributes of distant goddesses who, through their very inaccessibility, compel the poet to respond to their presence with a silent act of worship. Unfortunately in the present case the girl's sanctity is quickly undermined by the onset of puberty, and afterwards, instead of treating her as an unattainable ideal, he simply regards her as a banal figure of womanhood and meditates ruefully on her undoing.

One of the first signs of incipient maturity is a certain vacuous laughter which in 'Impressioni' is associated with 'bocche di vergini, d'una ilarità faunesca e misteriosa'[21] ('mouths of virgins, with a mysterious and faun-like hilarity'). It is meant as an outward manifestation of latent imperfection, as a beginning of coquetry. Laughter has indeed had a long history in Italian literature, ranging from Beatrice's gentle smile – traditionally regarded as a specifically human characteristic irradiating the divine – to Laura's culturally 'saturated' smile and its many variants in subsequent Petrarchist poets and the lyricists of today. By contrast, the disruptive laughter Cardarelli depicts appears to be an inversion of this tradition, and far from being charged with spiritual grace, it is symbolic of a certain waywardness or perversity of the senses. As such, it acts as a foil to the absolute air of purity surrounding his young girls and points allusively to a dark anxiety marking their brows and foreshadowing the unruliness of passion. All too soon they break completely free from the cocoon of suspended animation in which they have passed their childhood, yet the poet lingers tenderly over their troubled metamorphosis precisely because of its importance as a climactic event in life. For this reason his *jeunes filles en fleur* continually disturb his sensibility and in the lyric 'Polacca' the girl is described as a contagion and as an expiation of his desires. She symbolizes both an inaccessible ideal and the stark, conflicting appetites of the flesh, and she becomes simultaneously an object of distant adoration and a figure of anguished, sensual yearning. Similarly, in 'Natura', the poet's conception of the eternal feminine is once more swathed in ambiguity:

Tu non conosci l'ampo arco impetuoso del tuo sorriso:
come sfolgori, come si dilati una tua mossa rapida!
Io sono il tuo martire e il tuo testimone;

You do not know the wide impetuous range of your smile: how you corruscate, how any brief gesture of yours is dilated! I am your martyr and your witness;

and here too the lady exudes a certain spiritual radiance combined with an elusive element of coquetry which together make up the Cardarellian ideal of feminine grace. It almost seems as if the poet is attempting to crystallize an aesthetic-ethical archetype out of two of the most powerful forces in human nature, by compelling a vestigial sexual potentiality to coexist with the very sublimation of sex. In so doing he may well be imitating Baudelaire who was the first to fuse together in this way Neoplatonic and sensual elements.

Since Cardarelli's virgins are presented at the traumatic point of their sexual maturation they are not wholly unselfconscious creatures, and the air of provocative grace surrounding them is due partly to their obscure awareness of their own attractions. But he sees the course of their sexual defilement as an inevitable one, even though he is highly perturbed at the easy resignation with which they accept their fates. It prompts him to turn away in disillusionment from the inevitable corruption of the flesh and seek refuge in a purer sphere of meditation. So gradually he inclines his inspiration more towards the side of the 'testimone' and less towards that of the 'martire' of love, although in his view it is the martyr who alone enjoys life to the full, a point which explains why the seducer of his adolescent maiden is not a sage like himself but a callow youth whose own martyrdom immediately follows his carnal knowledge of her. The youth in question is, if anything, even more unselfconscious than the girl himself, and he gratifies his natural urges without attempting to reflect upon them or draw from life anything more durable than its momentary pleasures:

Pur qualcuno ti disfiorerà,
bocca di sorgiva.
Qualcuno che non lo saprà,
un pescatore di spugne,
avrà questa perla rara.
Gli sarà grazia e fortuna
il non averti cercata
e non sapere chi sei
e non poterti godere
con la sottile coscienza
che offende il geloso Iddio.

Yet someone will deflower you, spring-like mouth. Someone who will not know it, a fisherman after sponges will obtain this rare pearl. It will be his grace and good fortune not to have sought you out and not to know who you are and not to be able to enjoy you with that subtle awareness which offends our jealous God.

From such meditations we deduce that the inescapable facts of physiological life present the poet with a major problem: how to depict his ideal of virginity in a satisfying and unchanging form in the face of human corruptibility. How to rise, that is, from a level of passion-torn, physiological time to a reflective state in which true lyricism is alone possible. In his view only a form of virginity owing nothing to the exigencies of the flesh can recapture the state of purity to which he aspires and this requires from the poet almost casuistic acts of lyrical intelligence. Here it may seem as if his thought is already bordering on sophistry, but at present such a charge would be more apparent than real. What he is actually suggesting is a highly original lyrical process which will serve as a counterweight to the inevitable degeneration of objects in the real world. It amounts to a form of ideative 'possession' through the memory. Such 'possession' will, he asserts, leave the objects possessed as undefiled as before, and in fact most of his personal love-affairs are pressed into this wholly reflective mould. Consequently, until a love-situation or a feminine presence has been transformed into a memorial re-creation in his mind, neither will possess for him the qualities of a decisive lyrical experience:

> Sei trapassata nella mia memoria.
> Ora sí, posso dire
> che m'appartieni
> e qualchecosa fra di noi è accaduto
> irrevocabilmente.[22]

You have passed into my memory. Now indeed, now I can say that you belong to me and that something irrevocable has happened between us.

In short, lyrical authenticity is itself a by-product of memorial possession or re-possession and results from the poet's mental reconstruction of his contingent situations. The human values this process of readjustment produces are sufficient unto themselves and contrast starkly with that gratuitous gift of virginity present in normal everyday life. For, whereas their purity is purposefully derived from the recollective faculty of the human spirit, physical virginity is essentially an unearned increment having its origin in the absurdity of the natural world about us. In this sense it does not enter into the previously established criterion of the 'superfluità' of all true human values and is to be classed with those degraded and absurd phenomena which come under the heading of 'necessità'.

A theme closely associated with virginity is the love-theme. Cardarelli's understanding of love turns out once more to be a highly idealized affair, for he cherishes only the ghost of an affection which fades away before it ripens. In his view it is only in a purely platonic, yet psychologically based, form that love can be conserved. As such, it becomes a pure nexus of emotional relations buried in the memory and insulated from the progressive decline inherent in all of our more mundane relationships. Its most satisfactory evocation is to be found in a comparison he makes between its distant promise and a still-born summer storm:

Quale un estivo temporale
s'annuncia e poi s'allontana,
cosí ti sei negata alla mia sete.[23]

As a summer storm threatens and then moves away, so you have denied yourself to my thirst.

Although one would think at first sight that such intangible experiences would not leave the poet much room for manoeuvre in his love-affairs, the opposite proves to be the case; and he soon composes a miniature *Canzoniere* of his fleeting and unrequited passions in which every aspect of the tenuous psychological unfolding of his emotional attachments is irradiated by turn.

Sometimes the anguish of premature abandonment is uppermost in his mind and he expresses it in allusive, antithetical imagery:

Come chi gioia e angoscia provi insieme
gli occhi di lei cosí m'hanno lasciato.[24]

Like one who feels joy and pain at the same time, so her eyes have abandoned me.

At others he investigates the impalpable sensation of repressed desire and shows how it becomes tinged with incipient irony:

Le voglie trattenute
mi stemperano in languide inedie.
E il riso spunta sulle fissità.[25]

Pent-up desires plunge me into languid listlessness. And laughter bursts upon my stagnant moods.

On occasion even his very disillusionment becomes a hallucination of his senses, and then it is the absence, not the presence, of his lady which most stimulates his mind:

Ti porto in me come il mare
un tesoro affondato.
Sei il lievito, il segreto
d'ogni mio male, o amore a cui non credo.[26]

I bear you within me like the sea a sunken treasure. You are the yeast, the secret of all my ills, o love in which I have no faith.

Such refinement explains why we can compare his love-poems with those addressed by Baudelaire to Mme. Sabatier, since both poets wished to worship their ladies from afar and their verse is based on a regression of beauty into the memory where it subsequently produces a consolatory atmosphere of moral purity. With Cardarelli it never amounts to a belief in a form of religious grace such as was engendered when Dante contemplated Beatrice; it creates instead a form of aesthetic harmony symbolized by a lyrically idealized type of womanhood. The poet uses woman, in other words, as Baudelaire did before him, as a pretext to aestheticize the love-theme; and he does so in such a manner that he brings about a displacement of lyrical emphasis away from the lady herself towards the abstract standard of beauty of which she is the emblematic representation. To achieve the effect required he deliberately attenuates her sensory impact or at least channels it into non-sexual avenues. But sometimes the very process of attenuation provokes a feeling of exasperation and this leads to a perversion of both these poets' views towards the opposite sex. Each of them asserts the fundamental incompatibility between man and woman, and indeed, by universalizing the doctrine, Cardarelli further infers a similar unbridgeable communicatory gap between the individual on one hand and modern society on the other.

The distinction between the French and Italian poets' attitudes is largely the one which prevails between the metaphysical and humanistic approaches to experience; and so, while the Italian poet's attitude to sex is clearly neither as complicated nor as perverse as Baudelaire's, the idea of incompatibility still arises from his premisses. We can best explain the position by comparing their respective attitudes to the concept of love. The French poet's views on that subject were wholly founded on the religious doctrine of original sin. Hence the psychological clash between the sexes seemed to him to be the product of a deep-seated theological defect in existence which gives rise to inevitable 'malentendus'.[27] But with Cardarelli such clashes are not founded on religious grounds at all: they are moral problems resulting from the breakdown of social bonds and the subsequent dominance of the laws of chance in human affairs. He thus deplores our modern methods of choosing our sexual partners, yet maintains that authentic relationships can still be developed in a regenerate society. In short, contemporary society has gone awry and only offers us the worst possible choice: 'Noi amiamo la donna che non c'intende e che non ci perdona. L'inferno è sempre da temere incontrandosi con lei, il vuoto e cieco inferno dove l'uomo, che era tanto orgoglioso delle sue conoscenze, torna straniero e solo come al primo giorno, e avanza col respiro sospeso . . . Se è uomo utilitario, vi si acconcia e convive coi metodi e per i fini che tutti sanno. Non si verrà a sostenere che è possibile comporre con lei una situazione piú onesta, piú umana, piú dignitosa.'[28] ('We love the woman who does not understand nor forgive us. Hell is always to be feared when we meet her, an empty and blind hell in which man, who is so proud of his knowledge, becomes as alienated and solitary as on his first day, and moves forward with bated breath . . . If he is a utilitarian man, he adapts himself to it and lives with her by the methods and for the ends which everyone acknowledges. No one will bring himself to the point of arguing that it is possible to maintain with her a more honest, human and dignified arrangement.')

Nevertheless, although the immediate results are the same as with Baudelaire, the explanation advanced to account for them and the possibilities of improvement are very different. For Cardarelli there exists no fundamental flaw in the human condition which leads to an inevitable *échec* in our relations with others: our problems in this regard arise solely from our moral shortcomings. So we are not dealing with unresolvable absolutes in his opinion, only with misguided standards of behaviour, both of which admit of solutions in ethics and in art.

Precisely because of this difference in outlook the two poets also vary in the intensity of their reactions to sexual relations. The French poet expresses horror when confronted with an image of the sexual act and dwells on its grotesqueness with malice aforethought.[29] But Cardarelli postulates perfectly healthy sexual relationships in a regenerate society, because it is not naked desire which horrifies him, only our modern amorous intentions. In his view these aim at replacing the altruism of earlier times with forms of egoism and deceit, with the result that modern man reifies his partner and reduces her to the level of a thing to be enjoyed. This reduction of people to things drives the sensitive being along the road to misanthropy and solitude; and, since Cardarelli was incapable of accepting the hypocrisy accompanying the expression of love in present-day society, he had to satisfy himself with a substitute: those fleeting moments of memorial desire mentioned previously. Because the poet could evoke these attenuated affairs at will, free from all hypocrisy and egoism, he naturally preferred them to reality. Thus we can conclude that, although his attitude to love was superficially linked with Baudelaire's attitude towards that highly angelic figure, Mme. Sabatier, his views on emotional involvement were founded on the existential attitudes of the twentieth century rather than on the theological speculation of the nineteenth, and they are irreproachably humanist in orientation.

We can reinforce the point by comparing the dominant moods of both poets. Whereas Baudelaire's life is clouded with a metaphysically inspired ennui, the Italian poet's radiates a restrained optimism. What he deplores is not original sin but moral drift which creates an anxiety-ridden and shiftless type of personality. Indeed, because of his 'rootlessness' he says that modern cosmopolitan man only associates with his fellows out of an 'istinto di parassita' ('a parasitical instinct') and this process of mutual enslavement is lacking both in human dignity and in aesthetic significance. Human compassion is, in short, replaced nowadays by a form of social cannibalism and it is most apparent in the love-relationship since the latter tends to degenerate into an avid, self-seeking cult of physical enjoyment.

His explanation for this state of affairs, as we have seen, depends on his belief that social bonds are nowadays metaphysically, not ethically motivated. We live, it seems, in an abstract, scientific theocracy in which individuals are reduced to the status of ciphers and are quite unable to create those genuine emotional responses necessary for the formation of authentic characters. Against such a climate he feels it is imperative to revolt, even though his acts of revolt may seem absurd to his contemporaries; and he insists that the offences he gives, however great, are salutory ones, since they are aimed solely at the regeneration of society. No personal attacks are intended at all, only a carefully calculated series of shocks whose object is to undermine the status quo. So, even if Cardarelli's acts of rebellion sometimes seem egotistical in the extreme, they are humanly justified in his view and never aspire to a level of metaphysicality or sentimentality. Like Stendhal, he simply regards egotism as a type of social assertiveness, while romantic sentimentality by contrast implies egocentricity, the kind of solipsist attitude which breaks all social bonds and produces the most gratuitous forms of metaphysical self-aggrandizement. Needless to say, he detects such a cult in the work of the hermetic poets and considers it implicit in their involution of the poetic image. Although his denunciations in this direction may have been taken too far, they were nevertheless not wholly without foundation. For to a certain extent, at least, the hermetic poets still continue, despite their realist orientation, to treat the universe like the symbolists as an epistemological riddle whose lyrical key it is the poet's sacred duty to discover.

It follows that no mere lip-service to religion or to the senses is a satisfactory solution for living in Cardarelli's view. He prefers to exploit all the potentialities, while acknowledging the limits, of the human condition and never indulges in idle speculation about what lies beyond it. Since he considers such speculation as the chief temptation of the hermetic movement, in his opinion it largely accounts for its self-defeating type of introspection; and, because the hermetics become mesmerized by relations in a metaphysical sense, he seems to regard the poets of the school as symbolizing a 'genio sofistico' ('deceptive genius') in contrast with the 'genio morale' ('moral genius') he attributes to the classical cast of mind.[30] His own specific evaluative method in art is consequently somewhat akin to Carducci's classical approach, but with one important difference: his desire to replace the nineteenth-century poet's idealist historicism with a twentieth-century existential outlook. He believes the contemporary classicist's tendency to value human relations for their own sake will rejuvenate traditional classicism and ensure its capacity to represent the social and aesthetic conscience of the modern world.

Such an attitude clearly places Cardarelli in the open or traditional school of contemporary poets, because his lyricism, like Saba's or Gozzano's, aims at being a complex *trobar clar* and not a mystifying *trobar clus*. The principal distinguishing quality between him and Saba, for instance, is simply the way in which the Istrian poet emphasizes feelings instead of ideas and so inclines more whole-heartedly towards the representation of pure unpremeditated experiences. This suggests that Cardarelli's art is founded on a sheer reflective intelligence as opposed to the former poet's canon of psychologically-orientated sentiment; and it also underlines the fact that, while Saba's main artistic pitfall was a tendency towards a maudlin sentimentality, his will always prove to be a propensity towards 'ratio-cynicism', which on occasion leads to a passionless and unfeeling type of verse.

When he becomes a prey to his rationalizing demon, Cardarelli is indeed hardly interested in emotion or sentiment at all: he is exclusively concerned with the transformation of experience into lapidary statements in accordance with the dictates of his extremely cerebral outlook. His inspiration then strays beyond the bounds of lyricism altogether, into the realms of philosophy and sophistry; so that it is only when his ethical intentions run in half-concealed harness with his aesthetic sense that he creates his most suggestive poetic work. In fact, his finest lyrics show him to be a modern myth-maker whose aim is, as he himself puts it, to 'scoprire nell'inconscio atto/ la ferma presenza d'un rito'[31] ('to discover in the unconscious act/ the solid presence of a ritual'). Normally this kind of creation emerges directly from his sense-impressions and its corresponding artistic mode is a form of ethico-lyrical ritualization of moods and events. So only when he completely mythicizes his immediate sense-impressions by first absorbing and then reflecting deeply upon his sensations does Cardarelli ever succeed in reaching the summit of inspiration.

Clearly, the subtle modification of the sensibility which the poet aims at creating is intended to be effected by evolution rather than revolution, and in practice he always tries to strike a balance between innovation and convention, between personal inventiveness and the redeployment of those time-hallowed classical precepts buried deep in the racial memory. He even suggests that originality can only be measured by the amount of innovation one can introduce into lyricism without upsetting its tonal unity; and, while he does not actually name Barrès among his favourite authors, he nevertheless seems to have been influenced like his hermetic counterparts by the French novelist's emphasis on atavistic elements.[32] However, of even greater importance than his atavistic feelings are the artistic doctrines expounded in Leopardi's *Zibaldone*, which he treats deferentially as a type of cultural Gospel. By taking them as guides for his traditionalism, he believed he could combine boldness of innovation with complete tonal propriety, though for good measure he also added, like Leopardi himself, an archaic flavour to his style.

Even so, while fully appreciating the importance of retaining a multiplicity of lyrical resonances from Italy's corporate cultural past in his work, Cardarelli nevertheless mistrusted certain aspects of the national and regional consciousness. Above all he despised the provincialism constantly emerging in literature from the crude pressures exerted on the poet by his immediate environment. We recall once more in this regard the scandal surrounding his birth and the discomfiture he suffered in his youth in Corneto Tarquinia. By universalizing this discomfiture he draws attention to all the dangers implicit in the parish-pump culture of small towns and advises flight before their influence narrows one's horizons permanently:

> Al mio paese non posso dormire.
> Sempre mi leverò coi primi albori
> e fuggirò insalutato.[33]

> In my village I cannot sleep. I shall always rise at first light and flee, without farewells.

Probably the cause of Cardarelli's feelings of unease was a genuine desire to partake in the wider culture of Europe. Even the Italian cultural field was not wide enough to satisfy him completely, and this explains why he turns a deaf ear to appeals to patriotism just in case it should undermine his personal freedom of judgement. So, although he admits in 'Ballata' that visceral, atavistic experiences linger in his mind like 'un tacito agitarsi di memorie e di ombre' ('a silent commotion of memories and shadows'), he never allows their promptings to dominate his reason or his sense of artistic propriety. He prefers instead, while remaining basically immersed in his national cultural ethos, to integrate his experiences into the widest type of lyrical perspective. In his maturity this perspective embraced – as his attitudes in *La Ronda* show – the entire European literary landscape, with perhaps the sole exclusion of its residual romanticism.

Again, his broad purview should not lead us to believe that he was anything other than passionately Italian at heart, for he was quite as aware of the dangers of a feckless cosmopolitanism as he was of a narrow provincial outlook. Perhaps he was even more appalled by those who cut themselves off from 'national' life than by those who lost their way at an 'international' level; and this point is made with special emphasis in 'Incontro notturno', where the inane life of tramps and vagabonds is shown to result from their irresponsible abandonment of the social myth:

Accozzati per pochi dí
su provvisori giacigli,
assieme, nudi, vi coricavate
sotto lo stesso lenzuolo,
vi scambiavate gli oggetti
piú aderenti alla carne,
i vostri idiomi aprivate
forzando spalla con spalla,
ma un'intima parola non ve la dicevate.
Perocché la fatica vi crucciava
e l'un nell'altro odiava la sua pena
e ciascuno mordeva il suo silenzio,
e l'uomo era lungi da voi.

Intermingled for a few days on shiftless beds, together and naked, you slept under the same sheets, exchanged the objects most adherent to your flesh, and extended your vocabulary by rubbing shoulder to shoulder, but an intimate word you could not utter. Therefore stress racked you and you hated in others your own anguish and each one of you gnawed at his silence, and man was remote from you.

In a sense this passage may be taken as a critique of Barrès, since the French writer also tends at times to replace a spiritual with a mere physical type of 'convivenza'. But, more significantly, we can deduce from it Cardarelli's belief that one's moral responsibility to society should override any kind of instinctive urge: a fact which also explains why he denounces nocturnal vagabonds as people whose moral fibre has been completely destroyed. Theirs is the deepest form of degradation he can envisage for mankind because it runs counter to the humanist's function of reconciling individual liberty with social responsibility. By his standards only the free, socially integrated man is a complete human being, and in another poem he proceeds to describe his ideal of the well-adjusted lay personality who takes refuge neither in religion nor in metaphysics but is self-reliant and temperate in all his actions except one, the defence of his freedom of action. The figure symbolizing such an ideal is Ajax, since this ancient hero, while recognizing his essential Greekness of background and character, nevertheless refuses to rely on the divine aid of the Greek gods or on any other kind of mystique to help him build up a society to which he can feel himself attached with the maximum amount of personal freedom:

> Sempre obliasti, Ajace Telamonio,
> ogni prudenza in guerra, ogni preghiera.
> Mai non pensasti ad invocar l'aiuto
> d'una benigna Dea
> che ingigantir potesse le tue forze
> o sottrarti sollecita al nemico . . .
> Nessun Dio ti protesse,
> niun gloria t'arrise incontrastata,
> ti fu solo di scorta il tuo valore,
> o fante antico.[34]

You always forgot all prudence and every appeal in war, Ajax of Telamon. Never did you think of invoking the aid of a benign goddess to giganticize your strength or to rescue you at your bidding from the enemy . . . No God protected you, no glory smiled on you unchallenged, you had only your valour to protect you, o ancient warrior.

Here the word 'valore' has a wider meaning than courage and includes the further concepts of self-reliance and fulfilment. Later the poet reasserts his faith in both by claiming that a rugged self-reliance can save one from the arbitrary paternalism of Communism on the one hand and the equally frustrating strait-jacket of Catholicism on the other.[35] What he hopes to acquire through his cult of temperate wisdom is a renewal of the tastes and moral standards of the ancient classical writers, together with the serenity of their bell-like lyrical tones. For him such tonal clarity is the hallmark of an authentic civilization, because the style in which it manifests itself assimilates traditional values while at the same time projecting the innovations of the individual sensibility on to the cultural ethos of the whole community.

This outlook leads Cardarelli to a buoyant – if reflective – attitude to life, although at times even he becomes infected with a touch of anguish. He then transforms himself into a tortured, speculative thinker who finds it difficult to accept the process of living as an end in itself. Beyond it he postulates mysterious and at first sight meaningless emotional arcana which are the very obverse of his normal mode of perceiving. He once described this extra-sensory perception of life's mysteries as following: 'Tutta la realtà incomunicabile e sacra che ha una sua furtiva azione dietro i sipari della convivenza ha fatto il mio tremore e la mia folle fuga nell'impotenza, per anni'[36] ('All the sacred and incommunicable reality which provokes its own secret activity behind the curtain of society has caused my fear and wild flight into impotence, for years'.) No doubt he is referring here to that area of irrationality lying behind the real world which the ancients called the Fatum and the moderns the Absurd. He too has to acknowledge its impact upon his life and this explains why at times, despite his cult of clear ideas, he felt himself submerged by the very complexity of his sense-impressions. From a lyrical standpoint these complexities are externalized in the orphic resonances of modern imagery, and they are sometimes as effectively evoked by him as by his hermetic contemporaries. In fact, his lyricism frequently depends, like theirs, upon associative processes, and in his best work his image-chains submerge his rational approach to experience and give his verse a delicately sensuous and associative aura. In the latter part of his career this tendency was further marked by a touch of melancholy as he brooded more and more deeply over the transiency of life and allowed his poetry to become tinged with nostalgia and regret. At that stage, indeed, his mental torture proved to be more intense than ever before, because he then struggled to find some rational explanation for life's last great climacteric, death.

As a moralist and sophist the main point at issue for Cardarelli was how to reconcile the death of the body with one's innate sense of the continuity of experience. Needless to say, he never found a satisfactory solution to the problem. So gradually he turned away from the speculative issue and tried to elaborate a psychological theory in which his objection to death would not be its inevitability, but only its possible suddenness. In his view death has only the right to steal upon one and become, as it did for Montaigne, the last of all one's habits. He puts the point succinctly in 'Alla morte', one of the lyrics rounding off his major collection of verse, *Poesie* (1936), where we perceive a distinctive blend of his humanism and the tortured sophistry of his more abstract moments:

Morte, non mi ghermire
ma da lontano annunciati
e da amica mi prendi
come l'estrema delle mie abitudini.

Death, do not seize me but announce yourself from afar and take me as a friend, as the last of all my habits.

At first sight such an attitude may seem reasonably serene, but the whole tenor of Cardarelli's outlook shows that he is even less able to reconcile himself to the inevitability of death than to the mysteries of childhood.

Hence death not only haunts him in his old age but continues to remain the most 'imprevedibile e insoddisfacente delle soluzioni'[37] ('unforeseeable and unsatisfactory of solutions'). The way in which he always felt baulked by its incomprehensible presence may be exemplified by comparing 'Non basta morire' in *Poesie nuove* (1946) with an earlier lyric 'Ultima speme' in *Poesie*, since the later poem develops a belief which the poet first expressed in the earlier one that death is a completely absurd and unknowable state. Thus, whereas the 'cenere superstite' ('surviving ash') of memory in 'Ultima speme' still offers mankind some form of skeletal immortality, in 'Non basta morire' we find an almost Montalian scattering of life's ashen residue, a final dissolution of remembrance itself; and this occurs even though Cardarelli acknowledges that recollection is the only basis of the humanist and elegiac poet's lyrical values. In this poem, in consequence, a dialectical relationship is effectively created between memory and death, as a result of which the individual suffers two kinds of extinction: first physical death, the destruction of the body, and then an even more painful process of disintegration: the loss of one's personality in the memories of the living. When the second stage is completed we become nothing more than the 'comuni abitatori' ('common inhabitants') of our cemeteries and bear all the signs of complete oblivion.

As a traditional Petrarchan poet Cardarelli naturally deplores this state of affairs and tries to counter the erosion of time by providing an equally Petrarchan antidote, a cult of Fame. In his view Fame alone can effectively raise the individual above the level of the transient memories of the living and assure for him a place in the collective memory of the race. The most suggestive modern exposition of this doctrine is perhaps to be found in Ungaretti's 'La morte meditata' where, as we shall see later, the deeper implications of dying are investigated analogically and where death is ultimately transformed into the quickener of life's perspectives. But, although Cardarelli is also aesthetically aware of the shadowy resourcefulness of death, he prefers to lay stress on its absurdity and not on its creative aspects. So, even though he considers the kingdom of death to be the continuum of Fame, for him it still has only a residual power to bring about a spiritual 'convivenza' between the present and the past. Normally in his view the face of death is frozen in an attitude of cosmic indifference, and to meditate upon its implications produces only an increase in our existential anguish. This makes death a thoroughly paralyzing phenomenon for him, the final *nec plus ultra* of human awareness.

It seems then as if Cardarelli's attitude to life is bounded by two opaque states; for, just as the young girl of 'Adolescente' represents the impenetrable face of *pre-conscious* existence, so death symbolizes the equally impenetrable face of *post-conscious* extinction. Both stand as Kantian *noumena* and are completely uninterpretable by the human intelligence. In retrospect, therefore, his world-picture lies between two sharply defined limits: the meaningless perfection of the virgin and the gratuitous perfection of death. It is precisely in the area lying between these two limits that he claims to discover all that is valuable in human life, and so the content of his poetry is almost exclusively concerned with the robust and creative activities of the adult. The proper function of art in his view is the evaluation of the mature human personality and no doubt this explains why from the outset his style seems completely mature. It always appears to have an atemporal aura of serene wisdom about it, a fact which provides ample justification for examining his work thematically in the first instance rather than chronologically, unlike our approach to the other major poets of his age.

★ ★ ★ ★ ★ ★

Once we have fixed in our minds Cardarelli's somewhat singular outlook, we are immediately drawn to an assessment of the means he employs to transform his thought into imagery. What is particularly striking in this regard is the ease and rapidity with which he effects his tonal transitions and their extremely wide range.[38] The three dominant tones in 'Incontro notturno' are a case in point. The poem opens in a nonchalant, journalistic manner and its style is endowed with just the right touch of rhetoric and impressionism to create the desired atmosphere of irresponsibility towards the social contract:

Ah vagabondo, gli esseri come te!
Con le tue scarpe di tela bianche,
i vasti pantaloni di velluto,
e un sigaro spento che pende
fra le tue labbra
come un proposito dimenticato . . .

Ah vagabond, beings like yourself! With your white canvas shoes, enormous velvet trousers, and a burnt-out cigar hanging from your lips like a forgotten proposition . . .

Although the tone is clearly modern here, the poet is nevertheless following the traditional process of providing a thumb-nail sketch of his subject-matter before meditating upon it: he is certainly not opening mysteriously *in medias res* like so many of the hermetic poets. But once he has set the scene he allows his style to become more elevated and in oratorical fashion contrasts the wretchedness of the beggar with the glory and panache of the explorer:

Lo conoscevi tu il mare
prima di percorrerlo?
Sapevi tu l'esistenza
di tante, di tante città?
Su quale atlante hai prescritto,
girando la terra col dito,
gl'itinerari de' tuoi viaggi?
Eppure, di', davanti ai continenti
la tua idiota fermezza
di grande esploratore!

Did you know the sea before crossing it? Did you know of the existence of so many cities? On what atlas have you inscribed, as you move around the earth with your finger, the itineraries of your journeys? Well then, when confronted with the continents, tell of your idiotic stubbornness as a great explorer!

The function of such heavy rhetorical irony is evidently to diminish the stature of the person interrogated and to bring about a tonal clash between the absurdity of his position and the exaggerated exaltation of the poet. But soon this high state of tension gives way in its turn to a desultory – yet still highly appropriate – form of realism, in which the previous undercurrent of irony is replaced by a frightening note of spiritual fecklessness and inertia:

E adesso ambuli terrorizzato
come un fanciullo che non sa che ha fatto.
E biascichi male la tua cicca!
E vai sbirciando per consolazione
la meretrice che porta,
sul marciapiede opposto,
la sua solitudine parallela
con meno rancore di te.

And you now walk in terror like a child who does not know what he has done. And you slobber over your cigarette-end. And you eye for consolation the prostitute who bears on the opposite pavement her parallel loneliness with less rancour than you.

We are consequently presented with a stylistic examination of a state of beggary upon a number of planes of feeling. Yet what is surprising about the actual tonal variations of the diverse linguistic strata employed is that they all tend in the end to fuse together to form a harmonious lyrical structure. In their imaginative sweep they not only cover the entire experiential curve of the individual's life-span, but also frame Cardarelli's lyrical effects within an orphic perspective by way of a curious combination of spiritual, rational and spatial qualities.

We can regard the process as a form of lyrical redimensioning and a further example of its modes of operation is to be found in 'Rimorso'. This poem again opens with a description, then runs the whole gamut of a ratiocinative and psychological analysis, and finally threatens to end on a note of rhetoric. But it is ultimately redimensioned by the allusive cultural resonances of Love's memorial shadow in the closing image, for its smile becomes a spatio-spiritual absolute:

> Voglio dormire all'ombra
> del suo tremendo sorriso.

I want to sleep in the shadow of its tremendous smile.

From a literary standpoint this effect can perhaps be explained as the product of an allusive re-creation of lines taken from Baudelaire's sonnet 'La géante':

> Dormir nonchalamment à l'ombre de tes seins,
> Comme un hameau paisible au pied d'une montagne,

To sleep nonchalantly in the shadow of your breasts like a peaceful hamlet at the foot of a mountain,

to which Cardarelli adds the Dantean image of the beatific smile. Yet the image functions as more than the sum of its sources, creating a tonal unity which lies halfway between the sensual satiety of the French poet and the wholly spiritual atmosphere evoked by Dante. The result is a specifically Cardarellian lyricism combining visual, spatial and cerebral perspectives to denote the hallucinatory powers of his lady's personality.

Another example of spatio-spiritual balance is the poet's airy landscaping achieved in 'Largo serale'. Possibly it derives, as Anceschi suggests, from a combination of D'Annunzio's heavy sensuousness and a gentler Pascolian evanescence:

> È l'ora dei crepuscoli estivi,
> quando il giorno pellegrino
> si ferma e cade estenuato.
> Dolcezza e meraviglia di queste ore!
> Qualunque volto apparisse in questa luce
> sarebbe d'oro.
> I riflessi di raso
> degli abitati sul lago.
> Dolce fermezza di queste chiome
> d'alberi sotto i miei occhi.
> Alberi della montagna italiana.

Di paese in paese
gli orologi si mandano l'ora
percotendosi a lungo nella valle
come tocchi d'organo gravi.
Poi piú tardi, nella quiete notturna,
s'odon solo i rintocchi dolci e lenti.

It is the hour of summer twilights, when the wandering day halts and collapses, exhausted. The sweetness and wonder of these moments! Whatever face might appear in this light would be golden. The satin reflections of the houses on the lake. The sweet firmness of the foliage of these trees beneath my gaze. Trees from Italian mountains. From hamlet to hamlet the clocks ring out the hour, echoing lengthily in the valley like deep organ-notes. Then later, in the nocturnal silence, only hears only a slow and gentle retolling of bells.

Here D'Annunzio's influence is largely an undertone of rich tactile imagery and the plethora of sensations it evokes; while the subtle leavening of Pascoli's impalpable rustic tranquillity comes towards the end, reminding us of the soothing auditory imagery of 'L'ora di Barga'. Moreover, the poem's lyrical effectiveness arises not only from its complex literary background but also from its imaginative transformations and the periodicity of its rhythmic flow. Its almost circular rhythm is mainly the result of the poet's breathtaking recapitulations. By means of these features he manages to build up in the reader's sensibility the impression that he is being treated to a sinuous roundelay movement; and, although the process is not overtly based on anaphora, at times the style adopted closely approximates to that technique, as the repetition of 'dolcezza-dolce-dolci' and 'd'alberi-Alberi' shows. Similarly, the series of dying falls in the prosodic structure again tends to punctuate the ending of each circular phase and announce the beginning of a further parallel one.

Within the characteristic circularity of these modern orphic perspectives, however, we find that Cardarelli's actual imaginative procedures remain highly traditional. He normally prefers the simile to the hermetic lyricists' startling juxtapositions of analogical elements, while at the same time he continues to draw powerful effects from an intense form of visual perception. One example of the almost anatomical concreteness of his descriptive powers appears in 'Adolescente' where he highlights cosmic effects by mirroring them in the young girl's rosy cheeks:

Nel sangue che ha diffusioni
di fiamma sulla tua faccia,
il cosmo fa le sue risa
come nell'occhio nero della rondine.

In the blood which spreads flame-like across your face the cosmos laughs, as in the dark eye of the swallow.

Although such a comparison is highly visual in structure, it contains something far more disturbing than mere *visività*: it also reveals the poet's breathtaking ability to open up in the microcosm of the swallow's eye a tremendous inner perspective of the emotional abyss to be associated with the passions. Their depth is further stressed in this instance by the complexity of the blood-red network of veins in the girl's cheeks which form the matrix for her cosmic laughter; and Anceschi again considers this ability to create the airy grace of infinite resonances within the single concrete image as being a technique akin to Pascoli's cult of distant perspectives.[39] Even so, what the modern poet manages to avoid is Pascoli's 'scacco inconsapevole' ('unconscious échec') which derives from his attempts to replicate his sheer descriptive power on a cosmically sliding scale as a partial substitute for lyrical insight.[40]

Another technique which provides his verse with an underlying lyrical toughness is Cardarelli's use of psychological comparisons. In this field we can contrast his method with Saba's. For, whereas the latter employs psychological features to sharpen the emotional nuances evoked consecutively within his moods, the present poet uses them almost exclusively as illustrations of certain moods or situations in their totality. This implies that they are rarely evaluative in their own right, but tend to underline the evaluative power of a previous lyrical discourse. A case in point is to be found in 'Memento' where the intention is to stress the helplessness of humanity before the ravages of time. The individual's traumatic realization of his contingency in this instance is likened to the psychological disturbances arising in the mind of a neglected child:

Passan l'ore fugaci e malinconiche
come per il fanciullo
che niun vezzeggia ed è vestito a nuovo.

The hours slip by, swift and melancholy, just as for a child whom no one pampers and is dressed in new clothes.

Similarly, a fine psychological comparison also appears in 'Alla morte' where man's expectation of death is likened to the mood of a weary traveller waiting for a train:

Morire sí,
ma non essere aggrediti dalla morte.
Morire persuasi
che un siffatto viaggio sia il migliore.
E in quell'ultimo istante essere allegri
come quando si contano i minuti
dell'orologio della stazione
e ognuno vale un secolo.

> To die indeed, but not to be assailed by death. To be persuaded that such a journey is the best. And at that final moment to be joyful, as when one counts the minutes on a station clock and each one seems a century.

So appropriate indeed are comparisons of this kind that they can virtually be regarded as tonal as well as demonstrative in quality. Thus, in combination with his finely nuanced emotional transitions and his deep sense of spatio-spiritual proportions – especially in the mass-distribution of object-symbols to produce mental as well as physical landscapes – Cardarelli's perceptive psychological insights go far towards authenticating his otherwise elevated and rhetorical manner, and they ultimately convince us of the practicality and authoritativeness of his views on life. In this sense we can affirm that more than with any other contemporary poet his actual style reflects the distinctive quality of his mind. Normally his highly self-conscious way of handling his materials produces a fusion of his inner and outer worlds and causes his imagery to adhere strictly to the configuration of his moods. Because of this strict adherence his work does not arouse the slightest suspicion that a speculative yearning for absolutes – the most dangerous of all contemporary literary temptations – lurks behind his imaginative processes. Yet at the same time he is bedevilled by one specific literary danger of his own, as we have already noted: a tendency towards a ratiocinatory approach to life. This emerges from his lyrical textures whenever he fails to dominate his intellectual faculty and thereby effect an emotional and memorial redimensioning of his themes.

★ ★ ★ ★ ★ ★

Even when we pass from the imaginative to the linguistic level we can see the same procedures at work. He completely rejects the romantic cult of a vacuous, sentimental word-music and never allows his lyricism to acquire functionless incantatory rhythms. In his view every word, every turn of phrase and every inflection must be the product of a significant 'fatto spirituale' ('spiritual factor'), and poetic expression within his melodic line is indeed normally unimpeded by any conscious superfluities or gratuitous adornments of style. If anything, his subtly modulated discourse shows an even greater antagonism towards verbal alchemies than it does towards romantic oratorical flourishes; and, far from accepting the Crocean theory that in the mature lyric thought and form are one, he considers that thought always precedes form and is its necessary precondition. For him, in consequence, conceptual adequacy means *ipso facto* stylistic perfection, but the converse is never true. He observes instead that 'non è la ricchezza dei mezzi verbali che fa lo scrittore. È il modo, è l'accento, è il tono. Arrivare alla grammatica per forza d'ispirazione, questa mi sembra una maniera di scrivere.'[41] ('it is not a richness of verbal means which makes a writer. It is his manner, his emphasis, his tone. To arrive at a grammar through the force of inspiration, that to me seems a way of writing.') Precisely because he holds a deep and unshakeable conviction that the very essence of stylistic and artistic perfection derives from experiential insight, he dismisses out of hand any lyrical approach which regards poetic substance as unimportant or even indirectly dependent for its effects upon structural and phonic procedures.

On the other hand he does not underestimate the importance of poetic form and senses intuitively the infinite resourcefulness of the lyrical echo-chamber of the Italian tradition. Nor is he afraid to allow himself to be influenced by that purity of expression which has its roots in Leopardi's cult of fourteenth-century language. As a result, he studs his work with archaisms from the period and some of these linguistic forms like 'gaudio', 'perocché' and 'niun' have already appeared in previous quotations. Their resemblance to Leopardian linguistic practice suggests that the precepts of the *Zibaldone* are again responsible for their presence; indeed, it is largely from this work that Cardarelli drew his conception of stylistic grace which he defines as a 'felice infrazione all'uso'[42] ('felicitous break with usage'). The formula conforms in every way to the classicist's aim of continually reintroducing an inventive traditionalism into lyricism, and it implies that a poet should not know merely how to express his moods simply and directly but also prove capable of taking well-judged liberties with linguistic norms so as to refashion the language of his age and make it suitable for the representation of contemporary emotional reactions to the pressures of life. Instead of conspiring to shock and dazzle the reader, Cardarelli thus prefers to submit him to the constraining influence of a classical sense of propriety; and the result that he hopes to achieve is one which he claims Dante first produced and which amounts to the discovery of a 'verginità di senso ... sotto la tirannia dell'uso'[43] ('virginity of sense ... under the tyranny of usage'). In short, he considers that it is only when the living poet is willing to acknowledge the restrictions of taste and inventiveness imposed by past tradition that authentic poetry can ever be written in any language.

Such an attitude virtually amounts to an 'ethical' doctrine of stylistic elegance, and in Cardarelli's view a poet's style is only genuine if it succeeds in wresting from the tradition a viable communicative compromise. This, he assures us, is what Leopardi sought to achieve in his philological studies, and he notes that while 'rimanendo in apparenza alla superficie ..., (egli) va molto in fondo alla questione della lingua e ne scopre, se ciò può far piacere a qualcuno, il substrato morale'[44] ('remaining apparently on the surface . . ., he goes deeply into the question of language and discovers, if the expression gives pleasure to anyone, its moral substrate'). Although Cardarelli's own stylistic accomplishments are not quite as far reaching as this, he too was similarly motivated throughout his career. He thereby ranges over the entire spectrum of the Italian language and, by adopting an eclectic approach to art, manages to refurbish the word-music of the traditional lyric so that it becomes capable of representing the whole range of modern thought and emotion. Like Leopardi, however, he was also well aware that such a manner of proceeding was apt to suffer from a surfeit of conventionalism unless the inventive effort involved was really an effective one. Consequently, although he bases his stylistic practice on a perennial ideal of craftsmanship, he insists that in the last analysis the whole problem of representation has more to do with content than with form and that all lyrical solutions finally depend on the deep-seated exigencies of the tradition itself.

We can therefore conclude that his artistic and spiritual impulses are interlocking and that it is precisely because of their harmonious balance that his poetry often possesses a flawless quality of classical grace. As Spagnoletti points out, his lyricism is based on 'una costante di rivelazione angosciosa, ma esatta' ('a constant element of anguished but precise revelation') deriving from 'una dialettica continua e misteriosa dal mito alla passione'[45] ('a continuous and mysterious dialectic from myth to passion'). This ratio-sensuous approach to poetic composition puts him in the forefront of the classical tradition to which the early Vocian writers aspired and which he himself defines in the previously quoted formula: 'esprimere è restituirsi' ('to utter is to reconstitute oneself'). While recognizing the eternal flux of experience he tries to catch the moment of truth at its culminating point of maturity before degeneration sets in to destroy it, and he fixes his artistic goal as an entirely human transfigurative process made up equally from emotive and meditative qualities. In the act of transfiguration he never allows the realities of life to move out of focus or to slip through his fingers, so that in all essentials his art amounts to an ethico-aesthetic re-evaluation of living.

CHAPTER IX

Giuseppe Ungaretti and the hermetic movement

After lending an ear to Cardarelli's disparaging views on hermeticism it is disconcerting to discover that the major poets of the twenties and thirties nevertheless adhered to its lyrical principles. But we have to bear in mind that the latter was something of a die-hard in aesthetics and proposed to ride roughshod over the innovatory aspects of his age while imposing his classical theories willy-nilly on all its artistic manifestations. He was able to pinpoint with devastating accuracy the literary temptations inherent in the doctrines of the movement; and yet, at the same time, he failed to recognise its virtues, even though some of these coincided with his own artistic methods and were often attained by more subtle means than he was prepared to admit – by a careful combination of classical principles with the romantic concept of creativity. So, by misunderstanding the ingenuity and suppleness of their approach, Cardarelli and indeed other hostile critics were eventually led to assert with ever-increasing stridency that the hermetic poets were determined to whittle away matters of lyrical substance for the purpose of concentrating on a pure cult of form.

Although a sharp line of demarcation cannot be drawn between the hermetic poets proper and their immediate predecessors, because we can clearly find stylistic prefigurations of their lyrical manner in poets as varied as Rebora, Onofri and Campana, what is indisputable nowadays is the fact that Ungaretti was its first major representative. The principal reason for his early pre-eminence was that he proved to be the first poet willing to approach the problem of modern lyricism from a critical and an imaginative standpoint simultaneously. In this sense his early collection of verse, *Il porto sepolto* (1916), marks the beginning of a new and fruitful poetic era, in which the fragmentary experimentation of the futurists and the 'crisi di coscienza' ('crisis of conscience') of the Vocians were gradually welded together into a powerful and coherent lyrical perspective. Consequently, with Ungaretti's appearance on the literary scene the hitherto profuseness and lack of direction characterizing modern poetry suddenly and – as it then seemed – almost miraculously acquired a critical focus.

The crucial change in climate which he initiated was not, however, immediately apparent; and, although a small group of critics soon detected the poet's greater perceptiveness and welcomed it, a far larger number regarded his innovations as a sign of spiritual exhaustion or even of further decadent mystification. For the relevant information on these polemics we refer the reader to the two early surveys of Ungarettian criticism made by Anceschi and Mariani.[1] From the documentation which they provide we can deduce that for close on twenty years the poet found himself caught in a critical cross-fire in which the salvoes of invective launched by the more intransigent of his critics were countered by paeans of praise (not all of them relevant to his artistic achievement) produced by his admirers. Fortunately the smoke and dust of the battle has now finally died down and a powerful reaction has set in against the hermetic poets themselves. But, while this was clearly to be expected since each literary movement has its moment of popularity and then becomes a butt of ridicule for its successors, the significant point about present-day reactions is that they have not been directed against Ungaretti himself, who – until his death in 1970 – was regarded as the very embodiment of modern poetry in Italy: they have been aimed almost exclusively against the minor hermetic writers who have been found guilty of putting the involuted humanism of their predecessors into a rigid, formal strait-jacket.[2] The time is ripe at present, therefore, for a reassessment of the whole tangled skein of hermetic aesthetics and for the dominant part which Ungaretti played in it.

Despite the tremendous amount of criticism dedicated to Ungaretti's poetry, it seems as if it has fallen to the lot of his fellow-poet Montale to put his specific contribution to lyricism into historical and aesthetic perspective. On the occasion of his sixtieth birthday Montale remarked that 'egli solo, nel suo tempo, riuscí a profittare della libertà che era già in aria, gli altri non seppero che farsene, e cambiarono mestiere o gemettero "incompresi" '[3] ('he alone, in his time, succeeded in profiting from the liberty which was already in the air, the others did not know what to do with it, and changed their trade or complained of being "misunderstood" '). The truth of this statement was confirmed on a technical level by Bargellini who pointed out that as early as *Allegria di naufragi* (1919) the poet 'ha voluto rendere alle parole il loro potere evocativo, quasi liturgico, di segni e suoni significanti'[4] ('wanted to give back to words their evocative, almost liturgical, power of significant signs and sounds'), a remark which even goes far towards explaining why eventually in the sphere of prosody he undertook the rehabilitation of the *endecasillabo* and adapted it to modern lyrical cadences.

By contrast, Francesco Flora's *La poesia ermetica* (1936) is a powerful attack on Ungaretti's manner in particular and on what he describes disparagingly as 'l'impressionismo atomico' ('atomic impressionism') in general.[5] He regarded its whole ethos as the product of an effete decadentism and the poetry it produced as a form of undigested sensationalism. As he conceived it, hermetic verse was a directionless riot of colours and emotions based on futurist attitudes and seemed completely devoid of that underlying unity so necessary to the genuine work of art. In Ungaretti's particular case he admittedly nuanced this view at times by conceding that a few lyrics like 'L'isola' possess high literary merit, although he again added with disarming insidiousness that 'se la poesia fosse, come del lirismo dice Paul Valéry in *La littérature*, lo sviluppo di una esclamazione, bisogna dire che Ungaretti esclama senza aggiungere sviluppi'[6] (if poetry was, as Paul Valéry said of lyricism in *La littérature*, the development of an exclamation, one has to say that Ungaretti exclaims without adding any development'). In one sense, perhaps, time has not wholly invalidated Flora's thesis, it has simply turned his remarks in another direction – away from the major hermetic poets like Ungaretti or Montale and towards the mannerists. But, while pointing out the dangers inherent in the movement, Flora still failed to throw any positive light on the problems of hermetic aesthetics; and so his earliest views, at least, can hardly be said to have offered a balanced judgement on the achievements of the new trend.

Later, when it became evident from the collections published in the forties and fifties that Ungaretti was by no means emphasizing technique at the expense of poetic substance, his apparently revolutionary modes of expression were welcomed in literary circles and his art was regarded as a highly intelligent revaluation of the lyrical tradition in the cultural atmosphere of the twenties and thirties; while, on the other hand, those dissident voices which still tended to make themselves heard argued over historical or literary principles rather than over the basic propriety of his manner. As a result of the virtual disappearance of a polemical tone a much more fruitful era in the appreciation of his work then began; and from that time on the labours of his critics were often facilitated by Ungaretti's own periodic analyses of his aesthetic outlook. Even so, one major approach to his art still seems to have received scant attention: the problem of the relationship between form and content in his poetic evolution. It is from this standpoint, therefore, that we shall attempt to examine his literary output.

At the outset of his career Ungaretti, like most of the poets of his time, paid his due to the prevailing crepuscular and futurist movements, and at first he even showed a predilection for the kind of virtuosity we normally associate with Palazzeschi. This tendency is particularly noticeable in a small number of poems written during his formative years and later published by De Robertis under the title of *Poesie disperse*.[7] Interesting as these compositions are as literary curiosities, however, they must ultimately be dismissed as belonging to the pre-literary phase in his career, since all the really significant poems he composed during his early period were either included in *Allegria di naufragi* (1919) or in his French collection *La guerre* which appeared in the same year.[8] From these lyrics we note that most of his genuine early poetry derives from his wartime experiences; and, although we have to acknowledge that Ungaretti sometimes reworked his poems to such an extent that their first and final forms are very different, nevertheless the war – despite Serra's categorical assertion to the contrary – had a profound effect not only on him but on the whole of Italian cultural life in the early part of the century.

The poet's virtual mania for reworking his poetry also raises a serious preliminary problem which the critic has continually to bear in mind during any examination he makes of his early work – the importance of his variants. Should he consider the earliest versions of his lyrics to be the only authentic ones or should he reject them in favour of subsequent restructuring? Since Ungaretti always attached great importance to the periodic remodelling of his early poems it is a problem one cannot shirk with an easy conscience, and yet it is one which would require a detailed study in its own right. So, as the necessary space to conduct it is clearly not available at present, we immediately find ourselves on the horns of a dilemma. If, for instance, we take the definitive edition of *Allegria* published in 1942 as our textual standard, we shall seem to be deliberately flouting historical accuracy in order to uphold a kind of aesthetic opportunism; while, on the other hand, if we accept the early versions of the poetry as our principal working basis we shall be doing precisely the opposite and sacrificing aesthetic quality for historical accuracy. There is clearly no adequate solution to this dilemma, but fortunately several critics – notably De Robertis – have already made partial studies of the variants and the consensus of opinion seems to be that, while the definitive edition necessarily falsifies to some extent the historical perspective of the development of Ungaretti's sensibility, it nevertheless represents an 'ideal' version of his work both from the aesthetic and ideological points of view.[9] So, since it is with these aspects that we are mainly concerned, we shall cut the Gordian knot and use the 1942 edition as the basis for our remarks. In so doing, the aim is not to underrate the reservations of a critic of the stature of Montale who sounds a cautionary note;[10] but the fact remains that under our present constraints no lengthy discussion of the problem of the variants can be undertaken.

It is to be hoped, on the other hand, that the very manner of the approach which has been adopted will help to diminish any possible distortions, because the main intention is to stress the relationship between form and content; and, fortunately, content remains surprisingly constant with Ungaretti despite his many variants, since most of his refinements are simply processes of formal purification. Admittedly, there is also a sporadic expansion or contraction of a poem's subject-matter at times, but these changes are not central to his inspiration. In the past, however, so much emphasis has been placed on his lyrical techniques that even the poet himself was at one stage moved to utter a mild protest. He did so in an article in French addressed to a meeting of Unesco, where he insisted that the authenticity of a work of art rests ultimately on the ennobling qualities of the spirit, on its emotional content and tension, rather than on any ingenious display of verbal pyrotechnics: 'Le miracle n'est pas dans le langage, il est dans la tension qui ennoblit le langage, qui le porte à former des objets sublimes et enchanteurs; et si la tension . . . disparaissait du coeur et des pensées de l'homme, l'homme privé de sa dignité deviendrait semblable à la brute.'[11] ('The miracle is not in language, it is in the tension which ennobles language, which causes it to create sublime and enchanting objects; and if tension . . . should disappear from the hearts and thoughts of men, man deprived of his dignity would come to resemble the brute'.) From this we can deduce that he was attempting to open up a new avenue of critical approach to his own poetry and that his main object was to assert that genuine lyricism runs on two levels which are always interlocking: that is, upon meditative and formal planes simultaneously, without either of them being in any way subordinated to the other.

Although it is not our main intention to stress technique at the expense of poetic content, it will perhaps still be advisable to begin our examination with a few stylistic observations in order to put Ungaretti's melodic line into proper historical perspective. When we consider it from this standpoint we at once realize that the fundamental linguistic innovation appearing in *Allegria* is its syntactic essentiality. Superficially the poet's extreme verbal economy will appear to be an attempt to bridge the gap between the completely non-syntactic manner of the *paroliberisti* and the classical, discursive technique exemplified by the traditional Petrarchan lyric. But, while these two poles of literary fashion represent the cultural base within which he works, his true linguistic achievement amounts to a radically new departure, since he evolves a technique which has the effect of raising his poetic manner to a new level of consciousness: one which emerges at the interface between direct emotional experiences and distant lyrical resonances. Apollonio already hints at this process when he observes that despite earlier attempts by the futurists it is Ungaretti who first 'svela . . . la possibilità di respingere il bagaglio della retorica e di risospingere la parola alle origini prime della sua suggestione, alla sua forza primeva, disvelatrice del caos . . . del cosmo'[12] ('revealed . . . the possibility of casting aside the baggage of rhetoric and of pushing back the word to the very source of its suggestiveness, to its primitive power, revelationary of the chaos . . . of the cosmos'). And, since this is the case, we can confidently assume that from the very beginning his style possessed one particularly outstanding quality: an ability to restore words to their pristine, intuitive significance by imposing upon the vacuous freedom of futurist poetry at that period a limited – yet clearly unifying – syntactic structure. In his new hermetic manner we indeed sense for the first time a subtle thread of literary and linguistic intelligence underscoring the immediate responses of the poet's sensibility. His approach involves a flexing of his intellectual muscles to permit him to interpret as well as to stimulate powerful sensations from the present and the past. As a result, Ungaretti had no need to accept the futurists' doctrinaire principles of art in order to channel his moods into coherent and lyrically satisfying imagery. His deeper understanding of the possibilities implicit in the literary climate from the turn of the century onwards allowed him to integrate his own personal feelings in an incisive manner with the historical developments of his age. His aesthetic responses to social and intimate experiences consequently adhere with great fidelity to the subtle contours of his constantly developing and highly allusive moods; and this explains why most of the lyrics in *Allegria* seem to be balanced on the razor's-edge created by the mutual offsetting of sensory, atavistic and purely intellectual tensions.

Normally two quite distinct manners emerge from his early method of writing and the first consists of a laconic, narrative style in which the commonplace events of everyday life are galvanized into an intense form of lyricism through the stark recounting of significant details. A case in point is the following terse analysis of the vicissitudes of a single human destiny in 'In memoria':

Si chiamava
Moammed Sceab

Discendente
di emiri di nomadi
suicida
perché non aveva piú
Patria

He was called Mohammed Sceab. A descendant of the emirs of nomads, a suicide because he no longer had a Fatherland.

The other tends, by contrast, to be a highly associative style tinged with a controlled sensuousness, in which imagery is sharpened, as for instance in

'Levante', by means of the startling interaction of one word upon another:

Picchi di tacchi picchi di mani
e il clarino ghirigori striduli
e il mare è cenerino
trema dolce inquieto
come un piccione.

Tapping of heels clapping of hands and the clarinet strident spirals and the sea is ashen quivers sweet and restless like a pigeon.

In the first of these examples the clipped stylization has an underlying thread of congruous detail summed up in the three words 'emiro – suicida – Patria'; while in the second the intensity of the multiple sensations springs partly from an electrifying juxtaposition of nouns and partly from a gradation of adjectival effects. In both cases, however, it is to be noted that very little use is made of the verb or even of conjunctions and similar link-words. The reason for this is that the secret of Ungaretti's art already lay largely in the involution of his syntax, in his ability to imply an organic structure without making that structure in any way overt.

At first sight it might seem as if the poet was intending to adopt a variant of Marino's doctrine of surprise to startle the reader and fill his mind with a restrained – yet explosive – display of baroque artifices; but this is certainly not the case. What he was really attempting was to 'infold' the highly extravert and superficial baroque techniques of the Italian *seicentisti*. The effect on his lyrical texture was that, instead of startling others by his imaginative use of the element of surprise, it was he who in the first place tended to startle himself. In other words his analogical flashes are not so much effects aimed at creating a feeling of surprise in the reader as a means of showing his own amazement at the unexpected depth and freshness of his own sense-impressions.[13] These moments of self-surprise are, moreover, wholly figurative in quality and, like Baudelaire's lyrical responses, they acquire their baroque intensity from an inner sense of existential disillusionment. Oddly, they also possess an aura of enchantment about them which commits the reader to participate in Ungaretti's transiently regained states of emotional innocence; and, at times, they even make him the poet's accomplice as he explores the arcana of his senses.

The hypnotic state of astonished innocence emerging from the lyrics of *Allegria* is defined in the lyric 'Casa mia', where Ungaretti expresses his surprise at the unexpected intensity of his feelings when he revisits his childhood home:

Sorpresa
dopo tanto
d'un amore

Credevo di averlo sparpagliato
per il mondo.

> Surprise of a love after so long. I thought I had dissipated it throughout the world.

Although this and other similar evocations are normally caught up in a whorl of memory, we do not detect in his verse any breathless pursuit after effect for its own sake such as we often found in Govoni. So, whereas the latter poet's superficial baroque qualities were almost wholly contained within the manner of a Marino, Ungaretti's are more modern and more subtly articulated, emerging authentically from the depths of his own imaginative processes. His baroque outlook might therefore be described as a mental optic or personal mode of perception which only determines his poetic manner indirectly by magnifying or intensifying his pre-lyrical sensory experiences. As such, it can be regarded as virtually a category of his spirit, and yet it is one which is so carefully controlled that it rarely obtrudes openly into his verse. Nevertheless its oblique and open-ended impressions contrast starkly with the closed, symmetrical beauty of classical structures; and so, in spite of his classical propensities, Ungaretti can be regarded as having introduced a genuine baroque vein of dramatic tension into modern Italian verse.

His deep-seated concern with the baroque involution of imagery is also responsible for his ability to use empathy to focus the attention of the reader on his mythology, and his chief technical instrument for guaranteeing an authentic emotional commitment is the analogy. It was undoubtedly his symbolist inheritance which first led him to cultivate this device, an influence which was particularly strong when he studied in Paris just before the First World War.[14] But to the speculative symbolist artifice of the *correspondance* he eventually added the futurist device of *simultaneità*, because he felt intuitively that in order to represent the complex emotions of the modern world it would be necessary to make the image a powerful nexus of dynamic and multi-faceted sensations. This explains why his early work is noted more for its intensity than its duration, and it also accounts for his later theoretical considerations on the subject of analogical representation which involved the raising of the analogy to the level of a poetic principle. On this subject he notes: 'Il poeta d'oggi cercherà . . . di mettere in contatto immagini lontane, senza fili. Dalla memoria all'innocenza, quale lontananza da varcare: ma in un baleno.'[15] ('The poet of today will seek . . . to put distant images into contact, without links. From memory to innocence, what a distance to cross: but in a flash.') We can, of course, still detect an echo of Mallarmean syntax in this definition, but Ungaretti transforms the symbolist *analogie* and the futurist *parola in libertà* into something wholly original – a transfiguration, not a transcendence, of the real; and his revealing analogical flashes often appear in their most intense form in his shorter lyrics. Take, for instance, the compressed – and yet lyrically expansive – imagery of 'Inizio di sera':

La vita si vuota
in diafana ascesa
di nuvole colme
trapunte di sole;

Life unburdens itself in a diaphanous ascent of brimming clouds dappled with sunlight;

or the equally intense sensations of 'Rose in fiamme' in which analogies play simultaneously upon our auditory and visual faculties:

Su un oceano
di scampanellii
repentina
galleggia un'altra mattina.

On an ocean of tinklings suddenly there floats another morning.

Precisely because each of these compositions was written as early as 1917 we can be sure that the poet was attempting to create through his images that multidimensionality of lyrical effects so fashionable among the futurists. But the lyrical tension binding the various parts of his images together is again transfigurative, not purely verbal, like theirs; and it consists, moreover, of a baroque amalgam of richly blended analogies, in which sometimes the first and sometimes the second term of the comparison is deliberately suppressed.

The advantages which Ungaretti drew from the adoption of an analogical unfolding in his imagery were many and varied, but above all the process allowed him to deal *organically* with his moods and situations. Indeed, he was the first poet in contemporary Italy to answer the question of the nature of poetic truth in a meaningful, modern fashion by insisting that it was nothing more than the recording of a state of mind in all its multiple resonances. His refusal to countenance preconceived lyrical structures thus turned him irrevocably away from any cult of Neoplatonic idealism. For, whereas the analogy in symbolist aesthetics ultimately functions as a key to unlock the door to the hidden mysteries of the ideal world, in his art it is employed, as we have suggested, only to provide a realistic assessment or transfiguration rather than a transcendence of his human condition.

The importance of this change in outlook cannot be overstressed, because it not only permitted Ungaretti to elude the clutches of the 'pure poets' but it also cast him into the arms of the humanists. As a result, his verse aims primarily at a delicate exploration of personal experiences and only deals by extension with the metaphysical problems of human destiny.

In practice, the approach Ungaretti adopted to achieve this aim was to project his imagery through what he himself called 'una sua bella biografia' ('a fine biography of his own'). By such means he hoped to provide a temporal account of a single modern life in its manifold complexities, because he always regarded himself as a contemporary 'everyman' with all the tastes, anxieties, and hopes of his time.

From a textural and structural standpoint one other element needs to be emphasized in the composition of *Allegria*, Ungaretti's apparently deep attraction to the *haikai* or normally three-lined impressionist lyric originating from Japan.[16] Chinese and Japanese poetry was extremely popular at the time and a typical translation of the *haikai*, or rather the closely associated *tanke* form, reads as follows:

Son stanco di penare.
Nel profondo del mare
voglio sparir: ma come
potrò dunque portare
con me fino il mio nome?[17]

I am weary of suffering. I wish to disappear into the depths of the sea: but how shall I then carry off with me even my name?

Clearly a connection is detectable between this type of verse and Ungaretti's own early lyrics; but there is also perhaps a more important difference. It derives from the fact that the Italian poet's attitudes permit him to delineate in a still realistic – yet figuratively denser – manner than in the translation of the original Chinese poem the multiple facets of his states of mind. No doubt the same effects were achieved in many similar Japanese and Chinese lyrics in their original languages, although their Italian renderings, as the above instance reveals, fall somewhat short of this ideal. So what really characterizes Ungaretti's verse at the present stage is a kind of magical realism not unlike that associated with Bontempelli; and in the following description of the *dépaysement* of a nomad in 'Dolina notturna', a crisp emotional radiance evokes analogically the actual mood and discomfiture of the person concerned:

Questo nomade
adunco
morbido di neve
si lascia
come una foglia
accartocciata.

This nomad, hook-nosed, soft with snow, abandons himself like a withered leaf.

Consequently, since neither the drama of the situation nor the visual and analogical acuity of the Italian poet's imagery is to be found in the *haikai* model, we must assume that its influence upon him was either entirely structural or else simply confined to the general atmosphere of trepidation associated with the genre's breathless impressionism.

In support of these highly original – if perhaps somewhat eclectic – textural qualities, we also detect in Ungaretti's early verse a finely articulated word-music which intensifies his underlying feelings of grief and nostalgia. Broadly speaking, an attenuated existential anguish is characteristic of his lyrical moods at all stages of his career and in *Allegria* they seem to blend together to form the inner perspectives of a psycho-sensuous dreamland or 'paese innocente' ('land of innocence'). To complete their lyrical impact they normally need to be associated with certain dying falls in his prosody, and whenever these falls emerge a type of emotional serenity tends to emanate from the very inflections of his poetic line, in conformity with the following self-explanatory definition of his lyrical aspirations drawn from 'Girovago':

Godere un solo
minuto di vita
iniziale.

To enjoy a single minute of primal life.

This postulation of a 'paese innocente' is perhaps somewhat romantic in derivation, but with Ungaretti it remains an ideative rather than an idealistic or sentimental concept. It may be characterized as a transfigured world closely associated with his personal life and affections and it often reaches a state of dynamic baroque equilibrium in which no overtly stated ideology or any implication of the pathetic fallacy is allowed to enter. As such, it is fully compatible with Contini's observation concerning the underlying quality of his poetry, that 'nel clima piú rarefatto s'urta in qualcosa di corposo, d'immediatamente reale: come fosse la natura terriera del poeta ineliminabile'[18] (in the most rarefied atmosphere one strikes against something corporeal, immediately real: as if it were the earthy and unquenchable nature of the poet'). In its turn this 'corposità' is itself capable of attenuation and rarefaction; and it often undergoes a kind of ascension through the senses to a state of purified aesthetic contemplation, such as we see in the purely haikai-like form of 'Tramonto':

Il carnato del cielo
sveglia oasi
al nomade d'amore.

The rosy blush of the sky awakens oases in the love-lorn nomad.

Although the imagery here has still not wholly freed itself from symbolist influences, it clearly no longer bears the imprint of the phonic excesses of a René Ghil. Indeed, we rarely encounter in Ungaretti's verse the situation which was all too common in symbolist writing, whereby 'la parola finiva per venire intesa come episodio sonoro d'un ciclo musicale'[19] ('the word ended up by becoming understood as a sonorous episode in a musical cycle'). It seems as if the realist element in his inspiration was responsible for this greater resilience: an element which can again be traced back to a residual decadent strain of sensuality rather than to symbolist speculation and abstraction. So, if anything, Ungaretti's lyrical substance and inflections have a greater affinity with the poetry of Jammes and Verlaine than with the poetry of Mallarmé; because, in spite of his highly self-conscious Mallarmean approach to art, his poetry is far more attuned to the emotional qualities inherent in his human situations than to their metaphysical overtones, although he was naturally aware of both.

On the other hand, Ungaretti also gradually broke away from decadent aesthetics and synthesized his own lyrical manner out of the prevailing crepuscular-futurist chaos. When he had finally achieved his initial aim of essentializing his syntax, he then moved on towards his next lyrical goal: that of reinserting his laconic, analogical modes of expression into the traditional fabric of Italian prosody. Admittedly, this programme was only in its early stages in *Allegria* and the collection's tremulous harmonics and simplified grammatical structures are no more than the pre-condition of the broader and more symphonic lyricism he was later to produce in *Sentimento del tempo*. Yet even at this stage we can already detect the outlook and lyrical responses of a poignant, modern sensibility.

The secret of Ungaretti's early success derives from his unwillingness to dissociate style and lyrical content and to make the cultivation of formal elements a pursuit in its own right. His imagery is notable for its careful reflection of his inner existence and is saved from solipsism by the presence of a curious metaphysical perspective which inverts the concepts of life and death. Such an attitude is another example of his baroque mental optic and it implies that human existence is a prelude to an all-seeing and corporate, orphic state of death. Human contingency is thus described in 'Sono una creatura' as a somnambulist's dream which leads to a process of self-extinction through grief:

La morte
si sconta
vivendo.

One discounts death by living.

Death, by contrast, is not a hollow void for him as it was for Cardarelli, a kind of Kantian noumenon to be ignored because of its inexplicable nature. Instead, it is envisaged as a dynamic process of lyrical recall, as a depository of powerful atavistic emotions, which by operating indirectly on the poet's conscience fills his every wakeful moment with its shadowy perspectives. Its infinite resourcefulness is a constant reminder to the individual of the ever-present shadow of the history and historical tastes of the human race as he moves sluggishly through his own personal life and is lulled by the complacent oblivion of the senses. Indeed, Ungaretti maintains that ever since Petrarch's discovery of the mind's ability to communicate atemporally through the memory,[20] an orphic awareness of human destiny has been the lyricist's principal means of transfiguring experience. So, since memory can be regarded as death's hand-maiden, the means through which the broad expanses of its kingdom may be illuminated and explored, it surrounds past experiences with a halo of nostalgia which gradually, together with the poet's continual existential 'dolore', becomes the main tonal element in modern verse. In combination, these two qualities offset the sensuous pleasure of living and counterbalance the kind of non-perspectual oblivion which the mind creates around itself through its unreflective involvement in the world of the senses.

Not surprisingly, the immediate consequence of this doctrine is that Ungaretti's whole art becomes obsessed with the process of dying. The individual dies a little more each day because dying is really the self-conscious rebirth of experience through the memory. Lyrical contemplation, therefore, is for him a redemptive recollection of the past which, precisely because it is memorial, is filled with the foreknowledge and omnipresence of Death. Paci puts the doctrine in a nutshell when he says 'la vita come vera vita sarà liberazione dall'oblio, un lento continuo svolgersi del Lete sul quale è sedimentata la mia mondanità'[21] ('life as true life will be liberation from oblivion, a slow, continuous flowing backwards of Lethe where my earthliness has been deposited'). By slowly unwinding in his poetry the accumulated memories of past existence, Ungaretti considers it possible to draw back the veil which shuts off the true light of reality from our eyes. When once this new world has been revealed to him in its 'regained' primeval nudity, he hopes that the creative resonances implicit in his orphic dream of death will fill him with its illuminations and endow him with a dazzling lyrical clear-sightedness. He will then become a beacon-light to posterity and whisper the secrets of human destiny down the ages through his lyrical inflections and resonances.

Very early in his career the poet conceived of a dual perspective for recapturing life's lyrical insights. The first of these is connected with his belief that man exists in a state of orphic suspension over an abyss between heaven and hell, a vision which he only makes explicit later in the ending of 'La pietà'; while the second, more technical one is perhaps to be considered in the light of Bergson's theory of 'le néant' or the void. According to Bergson, our conception of the void is not a sense of emptiness but one of substitution.[22] When we pass from one form of reality to another, as for example from the concrete to the figurative, at the very moment of change-over from one sphere to the other there is a momentary hiatus or, at least, a psychological sensation of our having crossed a no-man's land between two very different territories. Ungaretti describes this area as 'l'inesprimibile nulla' ('the inexpressible void') and it marks the point of transition from our everyday language to the transfigured language of art. He expressed the idea as early as 1915, in 'Eterno', where he uses the symbol of the flower as the symbol of artistic creation:

> Tra un fiore colto e l'altro donato
> L'inesprimibile nulla.

Between the flower plucked and the other proffered the inexpressible void.

This brief hiatus between the inner vision he evokes and the outer reality presented to him is in his view the vital condition which allows every genuine poet to transcend the objective situation he is describing and to make his aggregate of object-symbols an eternal interpretation of a mood rather than the passing reproduction of an external scene.

The entire myth of poetic creation implicit in this doctrine is clearly to be regarded in a figurative rather than in a literal sense, but it nevertheless shows that Ungaretti relied mainly upon a process of memorial regression followed by an orphic 'return' to reality to generate his images. As the poems in *Il porto sepolto* (1916) reveal, he made a habit of delving into the racial memory for the purpose of mining from its rich strata of experiences the treasures later to be consolidated in his own culturally saturated lyricism. Although such a ritual of regression from, and then a subsequent reinsertion in, the *real* may seem to border upon a mystique, it has no connection whatsoever with the Neoplatonism of the symbolists, because the lyrical treasures the Italian poet recovers are existential and emotional in quality, not metaphysical abstractions clothed in a veneer of sensuousness. Normally Ungaretti's transfigurations approximate to those of Petrarch[23] and can also be compared with those emerging from Campana's orphic meditations. Although sensuous in quality, they suggest a 'metaphysic' of the senses which permits a concrete image to flash upon the poet's inward eye surrounded by a void of conscious and self-possessed detachment. In short, the process is one of memorial dilation of immediate sensations leading to a distant orphic perspective. Ungaretti himself describes it poetically in an incisive – yet impertinently brief – lyrical poem entitled 'Mattina':

M'illumino
d'immenso.

I illuminate myself with immensity.

Behind this apparently simple statement there lies a whole world of allusion and more than an echo of Leopardi's archetypal 'naufragio' or shipwreck, a concept which for the present poet is nothing more than the previously discussed process of regression to the void for the purpose of changing register and rendering lyrically significant the artist's multitudinous and gratuitously given sense-impressions, frequently against the background of the symbolic light of dawn. Memorial re-ordering of this type is in his view linked with originality and perspective, with the stamping of one's personality on one's art; and it is the one quality he considers absolutely necessary for every modern poet during his struggle to combine his own experiences with the harmonics of the lyric tradition. Hence, by definition, Ungaretti's art is a compromise between his own sensibility and the cumulative cultural ethos of the society in which he lives, and his constant aim is to blend his contingent lyrical 'voice' with the deeper organ-music of the past.

Unfortunately insights of the required intensity are rare, even with the greatest of modern lyricists; and it was an awareness of this fact which prompted the view among the Vocian writers that a modern poem must necessarily take the form of a *frammento*. Nevertheless, despite its disjointed structure, its poetic flash managed in their eyes to encapsulate the cultural responses both of the living and the dead and to merge their very widely diverging modes of feeling into a subtle interplay of sensations and memory. Probably this explains why the present poet's definition of lyrical density is similar to that originally put forward by Leopardi, though transposed into a modern key. For according to Leopardi's aesthetics, as Ungaretti explains, the poet should aim at a type of lyricism in which 'senza niuna, nemmeno minima discontinuità mai, contemporaneamente la memoria s'abolisca nel sogno, e il ricordo dall'oblio si resusciti, dolcemente vago in una infinita malinconia di pensieri'[24] ('without even any minimal discontinuity, simultaneously memory is abolished in the dream and remembrance is resurrected from oblivion, gentle and vague, in an infinite melancholy of thoughts').

Normally the poetry arising from this type of procedure has underlying atavistic elements, and in Ungaretti's case these elements are, as we might expect, partly derived from Barrès. The poet's infinite and melancholy thoughts prove to be so many visceral emanations from the past aiming at bringing about an emotional communion between the living poet and his dead forbears. We can almost regard them as transfusions of blood through time, and their trains of deep instinctive feelings are resolved into sheaves of carefully refined images. The type of communion at which Ungaretti normally aims is summed up in 'Popolo', where the opposition between consolidated atavistic urges and the living poet's passionate hunger results in the ordered song of the tradition:[25]

O Patria ogni tua età
s'è desta nel mio sangue

Sicura avanzi e canti
Sopra un mare famelico.

O my Fatherland, all your ages are awakened in my blood. You move forward and sing securely over a hungry sea.

Some critics – Paci among them – have defined this procedure as one of *smemoratezza*, as a progressive sloughing-off by the poet of his *mondanità* or blind involvement in life as he constantly renews his personal perspectives in the fires of his native culture. It virtually amounts to an aesthetic form of ancestor-worship, or rather to an attempt to intone in the authentic language of a specific ethnic group the ever-present and continuously evolving 'dolore' implicit in the human condition itself.

Ungaretti's main concern when practising this type of art was his fear of a possible lack of authenticity in his poetic utterances, because such a shortcoming would inevitably result in his inability to strike notes which would bring forth the appropriate overtones in the sensitive resonance-chamber of the lyric tradition. Whenever he failed in this regard he felt himself overwhelmed by a sense of paralysing rootlessness such as that which Barrès analysed in *Les déracinés*. So in the long run his fears in this direction caused him to revolt both against the arid and inhibitory bonds of neo-classical convention[26] and against the non-descript cosmopolitanism of his own age. His revolt was projected in his poetry in the form of a living ideal of socially constrained, human freedom, and its embryonic existence may already be recognized in an early French poem entitled 'Calumet'. Here, as Seroni has noted,[27] there first appeared the symbol of the 'agneauloup' ('lamb-wolf') which is already a prefiguration of the later 'uomo di pena' ('man of grief'), especially since it clearly displays a mildly wolfish hunger for experience of a type which persists in Ungaretti's personality throughout his entire lifetime. In *Allegria* the 'agneauloup' undergoes one of a number of metamorphoses and is transformed into the symbol of the bedouin-poet, a figure whose authenticity can hardly be called into question when we recall that Ungaretti himself was born in Alexandria on the edge of the Egyptian desert. Soon the bedouin archetype assumes the emblematic status of a carefree wanderer, eager for new experiences and yet simultaneously the proud preserver of the secrets of his race. By extension, he also proves to be the keeper of the poet's Italianate soul, and he seeks to mirror its qualities in a poetry steeped in the lyrical clarity and dying falls of the Petrarchan tradition.

What we are effectively confronted with in *Allegria* is, therefore, the bedouin-poet's responses to life, and one of Ungaretti's early attempts to repenetrate the racial memory is mirrored in the poem 'Il porto sepolto'. The lyric was originally inspired by the sunken harbour at Alexandria with its wealth of ancient treasures. But the situation is redimensioned in such a way that its imagery contains personal as well as historical overtones:

Vi arriva il poeta
e poi torna alla luce con i suoi canti
e li disperde

Di questa poesia
mi resta
quel nulla
d'inesauribile segreto.

The poet arrives there and then returns to the light with his songs and he scatters them. Of this poetry there remains to me that inexhaustibly secret nothingness.

Here, of course, 'quel nulla/d'inesauribile segreto' is the elusive lyrical harmonic which results from a sudden change of register, from the change-over from realist to figurative language, and it links the contingent voice of the modern poet to the 'absoluteness' of the lyric tradition. At first its orphic and atavistic suggestiveness might seem to imply that the quality and timbre of the song are all that matters. But with Ungaretti timbre and lyrical tone are compounded in some mysterious way from both formal and ideological features. Consequently an amalgamation of form and poetic content is required to give rise to his peculiar sense of lyricism. He himself describes it as a 'miracolo d'equilibrio' ('miracle of equilibrium'), in which the sensitivity of voice and ear frequently succeed in reactivating 'in chiave d'oggi un antico strumento musicale'[28] ('in a modern key an ancient musical instrument'). How, we might ask, is such a miracle performed? How does the poet succeed in striking so subtle a tone that his words are transmuted into the very flesh of the tradition? Ungaretti's approach to this problem was broadly a philological one in the Leopardian sense of the word. It amounts to a type of 'lavoro di scavo' ('work of excavation') in which he plumbs the depth of each word or image's traditionally matured overtones in order to bring forth from his investigations the monolithic radiance of a composite, and yet elemental, flash of immediate emotion. The intensity of the process may be judged from its definition in the following lines from 'Commiato':

Quando trovo
in questo mio silenzio
una parola
scavata è nella mia vita
come un abisso.

When I find a word in this silence of mine, it is dug into my life like an abyss.

Here we can almost feel the poet struggling to create connective links between the present and the past in the tissue of the racial memory. He always regarded the process as a continuous one, as a means of forging in each successive generation new relationships between the already consolidated substance of the past and the as yet unrefined substance of the present. If then we can talk at all about a lyrical mystique with Ungaretti, it is simply a mystique of poetic continuity and distinctiveness, one which he shares with Eliot and many other contemporary European poets.[29]

To some extent, it must be admitted, superstition and ancient orphic ritual also play a part in this kind of lyrical reconditioning of words and images, and one of the most significant ceremonies practised by the early Ungaretti was immersion in water, no doubt to be regarded as an act of purification. A ritual of immersion, for instance, forms the whole substance of 'Universo':

Col mare
mi sono fatto
una bara
di freschezza;

With the sea I have made myself a bier of freshness;

and, furthermore, the phrase 'bara di freschezza' shows us that the poet was already at that time experimenting on his analogical keyboard. The coffin symbol – like a similar image we find in Corazzini – was thus one through which he often hoped to penetrate to the deeper truths behind appearances.[30] It also figures later in association with water as the central image in a more important poem, 'I Fiumi', whose broader perspectives will allow us to examine the symbolic implications of both in a much more adequate manner.

The first thing that strikes us about 'I Fiumi' is its precarious existential setting. Even in its opening lines the contingency of the poet's human condition, as Gutia has explained,[31] is emphasized by his use of demonstratives and tortured imagery:

Mi tengo a quest'albero mutilato
abbandonato in questa dolina
che ha il languore
di un circo
primo o dopo lo spettacolo.

I cling to this mutilated tree abandoned in this gully which has the languor of a circus, before or after the performance.

What then, we might ask, is so compelling about this description? In the first place the obvious point is that it evokes the theatre of war 'sul Carso' ('on the Carso mountains'), but even more significant is the fact that the description of the battlefield is raised to an emblematic level to symbolize modern man's spiritual desolation. In the process the mutilated tree becomes an archetype[32] suggesting the anguish-torn state of the human mind in the aftermath of the decadent age – an era in which art might be considered as having been reduced to the level of a game of ritualistically objective, and therefore solipsist, contemplation. Of this particular state Mallarmé's imperturbable star-gazing is perhaps the perfect illustration, and the only way of escape from so barren a spiritual wilderness is, according to Ungaretti, not through the continuance of pure contemplative inactivity, but through the 'continua invenzione dell'uomo'[33] ('continual invention of man') as he meditates within the tradition. Thus his own tortured landscapes become framed within deeper Leopardian moonlight scenes which stress the importance of the poet's fleeting – yet unique – responses to his situations against the absoluteness of the static, or seemingly static, continuum of a gradually evolving national culture. At present this perceptive Leopardian atmosphere is allusively evoked in the following image:

E guardo
il passaggio quieto
delle nuvole sulla luna.

And I watch the quiet passing of the clouds over the moon.

Now, although such descriptions are clearly impressionistic, they are certainly not sentimental, nor do they attempt to transport us into an escapist, romantic sphere of experience. They seek instead to present a balanced view of life by employing suggestive orphic regressions from reality; and among these rituals is the same kind of mysterious immersion in water as we saw earlier in 'Universo'. Once again the poet attempts here to give the ceremony depth and resonance by means of a train of associated analogies, and their overtones prepare us for flight into a realm of transfigured emotion:

Stamani mi sono disteso
in un'urna d'acqua
e come una reliquia
ho riposato.

This morning I stretched out in a watery bier and like a relic I rested.

Because of our previous encounter with the coffin-symbol we need hardly labour the point that both the *urna* and *reliquia* mentioned here are two of its sub-symbols and represent variations on its dominant modes and inner perspectives, as the poet experiments once more on his analogical keyboard. At the same time such images tend to subvert the human condition and emphasize the fact that Ungaretti has regressed into a suspended state of life-in-death. From this deathlike trance of suspension he is at times brutally reawakened by certain dramatic events, especially by his wartime experiences on the banks of the Isonzo and the harsh discipline which he underwent during his military service. The result is that he undergoes a further metamorphosis, changing from a mere passive relic into a resistant, polished stone, itself shaped by the water:

L'Isonzo scorrendo
mi levigava
come un suo sasso.

The Isonzo as it flowed polished me like one of its stones.

The analogical key here is the word *sasso* which is a typically 'congealed' sensation representing a purified form of 'dolore'; and, in fact, most of the poet's other representations of his anguish are endued with a similar hard and intractable texture. Afterwards we move forward again, possibly to a quasi-religious type of symbol, to an allegorical walking of the waters, which results from the inclusion of a late variant in the poem's imaginative structure after Ungaretti's conversion to Christianity in 1928:

Ho tirato su
le mie quattr'ossa
e me ne sono andato
come un acrobata
sull'acqua.

I gathered up my four spare bones and moved like an acrobat upon the water.

These lines seem to indicate a possible fusion between the poet's religious and artistic impulses and are the beginning of the formation of his ethico-aesthetic ideology. His 'quattr'ossa' adumbrate perhaps a modern Christ on the Cross, while the 'acrobata' links back with the circus scene mentioned above. But clearly the precariousness of his stance again underlines Ungaretti's difficulty in maintaining his sensibility in a state of equilibrium between dreams and reality in the violence of the modern world. Probably the overall traumatic picture of war which acts as a back-cloth to the lyric is intended to indicate the dawning of the poet's belief in his own self-reliance, so that at this point we find the bedouin figure reappearing as the symbolic protagonist of the poem. He is always depicted as a race-proud wanderer and here ritualistically enjoys the light of a symbolic sun as he rests for a moment from the struggle he is waging against the enemies of the tradition he has sworn to maintain:[34]

Mi sono accoccolato
vicino ai miei panni
sudici di guerra
e come un beduino
mi sono chinato a ricevere
il sole.

I squatted near my clothes filthy with war and like a bedouin I bowed to receive the sun.

As a result of his presence all the symbolic elements of the ritual fall neatly into place and the poet feels poised to achieve an orphic communion with his ancestral voices through successive immersions in the rivers of his real and adoptive fatherlands. There are, of course, significant parallels between the rivers he chooses and his own personal life: the Isonzo subsumes his wartime experiences, the Serchio is the river of his Lucchese parents and forbears, the Nile the river of his birth, and the Seine that of his intellectual development. His spiritual ablutions in their waters fill him with a rare feeling of joy which virtually amounts to a visceral – yet highly figurative – unity with the essential spirit of past Italian culture and human destiny:[35]

Ma quelle occulte
mani
che m'intridono
mi regalano
la rara
felicità.

But those hidden hands which soak me through grant me a rare happiness.

We consequently find that Ungaretti has now transported us into a realm of completely transfigured reality whose qualities are suggested multi-dimensionally by an intermingling of present sensations and atavistic imagery. Precisely because he is able to explore the arcana of the racial consciousness in this fashion we note in many of his poems that his inward eye is focussed simultaneously on a whole cone or array of different perspectives. Their density and complexity gradually create that 'infinita melanconia di pensieri' which he lays down as his ideal form of poetic radiance, and its effects are subsumed in the closing image of the poem:

Questa è la mia nostalgia
che in ognuno
mi traspare
ora ch'è notte
che la mia vita mi pare
una corolla
di tenebre.

This is my nostalgia which in each one emerges for me now that it is night, that my life seems to me a corolla of shadows.

After the production of this finely conceived lyric we find that the poet's sensibility is unified by the inner coherence of his symbolism. In the course of time he learns to fuse together into a single perspective all the diverse tensions confronting modern man – tensions ranging from his fluctuating religious hopes to his metaphysical speculations, from his sense of contingent anguish to his artistic hesitancies. By such means he creates a poetry which moves serenely within a sphere of transfigured reality, one which may in a sense be described as a modern counterpart to the romantic paradise, in which, as Ungaretti himself emphasizes, 'l'oggetto s'è alzato dall'inferno all'infinito d'una certezza divina'[36] ('the object has been raised from the infernal region to the infinity of a divine certainty'). The crucial difference, however, between his and the romantic paradise is that it is not idealistically detached from everyday affairs; instead, it is experientially and psychologically wrought from the poet's sense-impressions and attains a state of lyrical serenity through the control of a vigilant intelligence.

At this juncture we should perhaps consider Ungaretti's sense of 'durata', his attitude towards the process of maturation of thought and feeling which takes place over the entire span of an individual poet's lifetime. Again he interprets the process in a Leopardian light, a fact which no doubt explains why the original title of *Allegria* was *Allegria di Naufragi*. A Leopardian 'naufragio', as we have already seen, is considered by him to be a pre-condition for any kind of deepening and enrichment of the sensibility. It involves both a decanting or refining of experience through meditation and a dramatic change of perspective; and it eventually leads to a poetic precipitation, to an imaginative representation in verse of the tensions racking the poet's mind at any given moment. An authentic lyric in this sense can be regarded as a cross-section of the poet's state of maturity at a pre-selected stage in his 'ideal autobiography'; and, by the same token, the quality and intensity of his sense of 'durata' may be assessed by judging a poem's density of implication against the back-cloth of his earlier verse and the ever-broadening human perspectives within which he works.

Even so, the classical sense of balance arbitrating between the poet's lyrical *persona* and tradition is strained in one particular direction by Ungaretti because he normally sees life through a modern baroque optic. Thus the expression of his 'dolore' amounts to an optimistic and dramatic process of nostalgic longing contrasting with Leopardi's classical and consciously restrictive method which adumbrated only the shadowy outlines of life as a condition of hopeful despair. The overall vision that Ungaretti evokes is thereby less cohesive than the earlier poet's, and this is especially the case in the period of syntactic compression found in *Allegria*. Later, however, when he seeks to rehabilitate the *endecasillabo* within a modern context,[37] we no longer suspect that we are being presented with a fragmented series of coloured plates but are returning instead to an organically articulated Leopardian manner. This is the process which takes place in *Sentimento del tempo* (1933), although somewhat paradoxically the collection illustrates a simultaneous heightening of the poet's dislocated baroque perceptiveness and a return to classical forms.

In *Sentimento del tempo* it becomes clear that the poet is once again grappling with the problem of the creative memory, and he adapts to his own purposes the Leopardian method of combining historical perspectives with suspended human dramas in the hope of awakening multiple resonances from within the cumulative features of the racial consciousness. Moreover, as Bigongiari has stressed, there is a 'sentimento dello spazio' ('sense of space') as well as a 'sentimento del tempo' ('sense of time') in this collection, a space-time dilation of the sensibility which was noticeably absent from the instantaneous flashes of *Allegria*.[38]

What it signifies is the introduction of an 'orphic historicism' into the poet's narration of events or moods, and this reveals itself as an unwinding of a continuous sense of 'dolore' behind the discontinuous flashes of insight associated with analogical writing. But there still persists an intermittent baroque tension deep within Ungaretti's otherwise mythically orientated imagery, so that we encounter a curious interaction between the continuously sustained myth and the fragmented impressionistic image, as illustrated in 'Notte di marzo':

> Luna impudica, al tuo improvviso lume
> Torna, quell'ombra dove Apollo dorme,
> A trasparenze incerte.

> Shameless moon, in your unexpected light returns to uncertain transparencies, that shadow where Apollo sleeps.

In this lyric it seems as if emotion coagulates around single object-symbols, although at the same time the analogical flashes are fused together by mythological allusions to provide at least the promise of a continuous narrative. Even so, what is immediately clear is that this type of procedure is at bottom a prolongation rather than a fundamental change in the poet's instantaneous insights into the nature of things. For the principal means Ungaretti adopts in sustaining the poetic flash over a discrete period of time is basically a technical process – a syntactic and rhythmical transformation of his poetic line.

The result is that the breathless memorial involution characteristic of the asyntactic structure of *Allegria* is somewhat diminished in *Sentimento del tempo*: it is indeed subtly replaced by a reawakened sense of traditional lyrical procedures. In this collection Ungaretti not only takes refuge in Leopardi's cultural historicism but also in the melodic and atavistic humanism featured in Foscolo's 'Dei sepolcri'. His atavism, like Foscolo's before him, is ethico-aesthetic in quality and is evoked through that bond of instinctive solidarity, that 'corrispondenza d'amorosi sensi' ('reciprocation of amorous feelings') or 'eredità d'affetti' ('inheritance of affections'), which poets re-create over the ages as they remodulate traditional feeling and the 'mesta armonia che lo governa' ('the sad harmony which governs it'). A case in point is the lyric 'Alla noia' which personifies ennui as a woman and combines the spatial mysticism of Foscolo's sonnet 'Alla sera' with that almost visceral desire to communicate with the dead expressed in 'Dei sepolcri' itself. In consequence, the bell-like clarity of a dominant Leopardian manner is momentarily replaced by a Foscolian perspective, indicative of a generic type of ancestor-worship through the instincts and the memory:

> Memoria, fluido simulacro,
> Malinconico scherno,
> Buio del sangue . . .

Quale fonte timida a un'ombra
Anziana di ulivi,
Ritorni a assopirmi . . .

Di mattina ancora segreta,
Ancora le tue labbra brami . . .

Non le conosca piú!

> Memory, fluid mirage, melancholy sneer, darkness of the blood . . . Like a timid fountain in the age-old shadow of olive-trees, you bring back drowsiness to me . . . In the still secret morning, let me still desire your lips . . . Let me know them no more!

On the other hand, if this inspiration is Foscolian at all, it is certainly a Foscolo steeped in the fluid impressionism of the symbolists and decadents.[39] What is more, this type of poetry tends to move back towards a Leopardian lyrical clarity at the end, as soon as its atavistic feelings have been purified and reorganized in the shape of an auroral myth. So, although Ungaretti's mind at first appears to work at the level of instinct, it always struggles to transcend the appetites of the flesh and to attain to a higher level of mythical insight, through an organic interfusion of present sensations and past perspectives. The memorial resonances which result are deeply coloured by an atmosphere of nostalgia – a form of consolatory melancholy which seems to be the product of a clash between the poet's awareness of the transiency of all things human and his desire for absoluteness of expression.

It was undoubtedly the absoluteness of the past as opposed to the contingency of the present which caused him to use memorial echoes and insights as a back-cloth for his own personal experiences. Indeed, as we read his poetry we always feel that it is modulated on a double string, with individual elements moving in the foreground and the off-stage chorus of the tradition murmuring a mysteriously compelling melody in the wings. The two features are orchestrated by an allusive interplay of sensations, imaginative forms and reminiscences, and their verbal alchemy goes far towards accounting for the depth of implication to be found in key poems like 'L'isola'. From here on, in short, Ungaretti's method of composing differs radically from the absurdly irrational, kaleidoscopic manner of the *paroliberisti*, and the main difference between their art and his lies precisely in his introduction of an integrative process, the dynamic resonance-chamber of memory, together with its technical and lyrical adjuncts.

In future we shall therefore need to distinguish between the active and passive memories in his verse, just as we shall have to separate them even more radically later in Montale's. But Ungaretti's distinction between these two phenomena is rather less startling, since he does not raise them consciously to a metaphysical status nor does he consciously equate the active memory with life and the passive memory with death. He simply regards the former as perceptually orphic in nature and the latter as largely mechanical and factual. He claims, moreover, that the advent of mechanical civilization has prompted an insidious attack on the creative memory and tended to reduce the human personality to the level of an automaton. Since such an attack is wholly inhuman, the only remedy left to the masses has been an adaptation to the futurist aesthetic of speed, definable as a witless form of mechanical repetition.[40] If then the passive memory is ever to regain significance in the modern world, it will have to be reintegrated and brought once more under the control of the creative memory. As it stands at present, however, it is simply a source of endless 'noia'; so he puts the entire problem of the regeneration of society in terms of the reintegration of the two forms of memory inherent in the human mind: 'La civiltà meccanica è dialettica: bene è nata nel secolo di Hegel. Essa è memoria ed è, contrastante, il contrario della memoria. Il male viene dalla difficoltà di rimarginare questa scissura vastissima nell'essere.'[41] ('Mechanical civilization is a dialectic: it was rightly born in the century of Hegel. It is memory and is, by contrast, the contrary of memory. The evil arises from the difficulty of resuturing this vast fissure in Being.')

From the lyrical standpoint the main result of this situation is a continual fluctuation of the mind between active and passive states. One might almost say that the modern spirit has gradually been transformed into a reciprocating engine passing alternately from the one sphere to the other in an endless and largely meaningless cycle. By emphasizing this passive, mechanical element the futurists (in spite of the apparent activity of their aesthetic of speed) soon acquired a taste for accumulating and coagulating meaningless facts and sensations in the imagery of the poem-document; and the aesthetic insignificance of such a process was bound eventually to lead them towards an uncontrolled cult of the *parola in libertà* as they freewheeled in the bombastic void of rhetoric. But Ungaretti, by contrast, emphasizes the pre-eminence of the active memory from the outset, while not perhaps being completely immune to that dissociative activity which characterizes the futurists' vision and which is probably at the root of his own modern baroque outlook. In this field his greater synthesizing power no doubt accounts for his ability to control his imagery yet at the same time bring about a magnification of sensations which is no less intense than that to be found in the work of his contemporaries.

The lack of control evident in the poetry of the futurists perhaps explains why Ungaretti always associated the baroque mentality with a sense of impending disaster. But he also believed a similar feeling to be implicit in all his acknowledged masters – in Racine, Baudelaire and Mallarmé in France, in Shakespeare (especially the Shakespeare of the sonnets) in England, in Góngora in Spain, and in Tasso and Leopardi in Italy itself. So, in contrast with the authentic Petrarchan tradition which tends to 'riparare le rovine minuto per minuto, quasi insensibile alla fuga del tempo, e dando al tempo gradualmente spazio d'infinita profondità storica'[42] ('restore ruins moment by moment, almost insensible to the passing of time, and giving to time gradually the spaciousness of an infinite historical depth'), he claims that the baroque mind stresses the extreme corruptibility of the body and with it the progressive 'affievolimento' ('weakening') of its powers; although at the same time it also inspires the poet with a tremendous desire to drink the wine of life to the lees, in the knowledge that time is constantly passing him by. Its principal lyrical feature is its hallucinatory sense of the void[43] surrounding human life, a foreknowledge of death and destruction which the poet considers to be taken to excruciating lengths in the poetry of Góngora. When analysing the Petrarchism of the *seicento* he thus notes that among its main characteristics is a feeling that 'la memoria ha orrore di sé come d'un vuoto' ('memory has a horror of itself as of a void') and that 'il decoro del secolo precedente è mandato in frantumi e ricostituito in modo che sia armonioso, ma mettendo in risalto una violenza di rovina, senza – sebbene sia stato il Barocco a inventare lo spirito d'evasione insegnando a fare tesoro dell'esotico – lasciare, per potersi uno rivolgere ad altri pensieri, la minima libertà di spazio'[44] ('the propriety of the preceding century is broken up and reconstituted in a manner which is harmonious, but by throwing into relief a destructive violence, without leaving – although it was the Baroque which invented the spirit of escapism by teaching us how to cherish the exotic – the minimum spatial freedom to permit us to turn to other thoughts').

Such an analysis does not mean that Ungaretti's own manner is to be identified with the 'metaphysicals' in England or the Gongorists in Spain, or even with the Marinisti in Italy, but the fact remains that he did experience a similar kind of crisis: one which explains why a 'coscienza del perire' ('consciousness of dying') gradually becomes more and more intense in his work and why, by the time we reach *La terra promessa* (1950), it has taken over his sensibility almost completely. In the interval he had slowly learned to appreciate the significance of the partially unsuccessful attempt made by the earlier baroque writers to dominate the elements of the static memory in the post-Renaissance era.[45] Hence he stresses Góngora's sense of the 'valore ossessivo degli oggetti' ('obsessive value of objects') and illustrates the point in poems like 'Mientras por competir'.[46]

In this lyric memory has been almost totally abolished and the only consolation remaining to the poet is his enjoyment of present sensations which themselves undergo tremendous magnification in order to blot out the hallucinatory spectre of death which lies behind them. For this reason Ungaretti claims that Góngora's work proceeds 'per squilli di tromba' ('by trumpet-blasts') and that 'ciascun elemento ha, per quanto fondendosi, piú che non si fosse mai visto, negli altri, vita avulsa dagli altri, vita crudamente indipendente, vita che vale perché manifesta e sollecita sensazioni di calore, di splendore, di spasimo fisico: ossessive sensazioni visive, tattili'[47] ('each feature has, though merging more than one had ever seen before with all others, a life divorced from others, a crudely independent life, a life which asserts itself because it reveals and incites sensations of warmth, splendour, physical shuddering: obsessive sensations, both visual and tactile').

Even in his own poetry a similar tendency to cling to life and heighten its sensations is often noticeable. It is symbolized, for instance, in the oak-tree of 'Le stagioni' which sternly resists any attempt to sap its strength despite the meagreness of its resources:

Ora anche il sogno tace.

È nuda anche la quercia,
Ma abbarbicata sempre al suo macigno.

Now even the dream is silent. Bare too is the oak, but still deep-rooted in its rock.

Such intense feelings seem at times to be about to break the bonds of the human condition and assume a quartz-like state of Being within the recesses of the passive memory. For Ungaretti, therefore, as for all baroque lyricists, the problem is how to rescue his emotions from these inanimate hypostases, how to make them so dynamic that they become a cone of living impressions whose cutting-edge will make a permanent mark on the reader's sensibility. Only when this is achieved can memory weave a delicate skein of relations between the individual conscience and the continuously evolving tradition. Hence a constantly receding vision of poetic fulfilment haunts his thoughts leaving behind it a gratuitous mood of ennui, as implied in his dreamlike pursuit of the lady in 'Alla noia':

La mano le luceva che mi porse
Che di quanto m'avanzo s'allontana.

Eccomi perso in queste vane corse.

The hand which she offered to me shone, and the more I advanced it receded. Now I am lost in these vain pursuits.

These lines show the fundamental ambivalence of the human condition.

In one sense a poet can protect himself through his art from all such regressive uncertainties, because art offers him both an absolute standard for emulating the past and the guidance deriving from the 'buia veglia' ('dark vigil') of his dead colleagues. But simultaneously he feels himself confronted with the 'beffa infinita' ('infinite mockery') of their selfsame perfection because he is imprisoned, unlike them, in life's contingent state of flux. To counteract the anguish which such a contrast provokes he has to solve the problem of adequate resonance, of adequate communication, through time. Yet, as long as he feels himself condemned to a temporal existence – which he defines in 'Paesaggio' as 'il consumarsi senza fine di tutto' ('the endless disintegration of everything') – he knows it is in the nature of things that he will neither completely assuage his anguish nor attain to a perfect form of communication. There will always persist that residual sense of contingency, that Corazzinian sense of 'sentirsi morire' ('feeling oneself dying'), still implicit even in his own far more robust concept of 'dolore'. Hence Piccioni's acute definition of his art as 'il simbolo del perire, non il dolore della morte'[48] ('the symbol of dying, not the pain of death'). As an ultimate truth he senses that poetry can only fall into final temporal perspective after the poet's demise, when the very society in which he has worked has become fixed in the cultural consciousness, as though enclosed in a self-contained state of historical suspension. This is clearly a paradoxical eidetico-phenomenological way of looking at things; and yet, as we have already indicated, it is one which most hermetic poets tend to adopt.

It also explains why the central problem of *Sentimento del tempo* is the restructuring of time, the modification of the earlier spontaneous poetic flashes of *Allegria* as a result of the poet's desire to regraft his sensibility on to the historical realities about him. In the first section *Prime* (retaining close syntactical links with *Allegria*) time still remains, perhaps, an instantaneous, if not an external, phenomenon. It tends to be symbolized by the changing seasons of the year, although such a device can at best only provide a superficial framework for the study of human maturation and decay. Fortunately its mechanical implications are later intimized as the poet's lyricism becomes more and more dependent on the growth and development of his creative faculty. Similarly, his rising maturity is now associated figuratively with a change in his dominant scenery. We are thus no longer confronted with the youthful wilderness of *Allegria*, depicted in its deserts or war-torn Alpine landscapes; instead, we are encouraged to aestivate, as we were previously with Cardarelli, in the summery stillness of the Latian countryside, whose landscapes are intended to reflect Ungaretti's placid manhood.

In parallel with this more restrained imagery we also note a return to traditional metres in which the Leopardian doctrine of a 'ritmo analogo ai sentimenti' ('rhythm analogous to feeling') is uppermost. Ungaretti now tries by careful auscultation of the lyrical past to re-create the time-hallowed *endecasillabo* in a modern key and to endue it with an impressionistic allusiveness in keeping with the subtle suggestivity of his newly established lyrical manner.

Some examples of a similar process are, admittedly, to be found as far back as *Allegria*, although in that collection they normally tend to be broken up by typographical division. A typical instance is to be seen in 'Chiaroscuro':

nel verde torbido / del primo chiaro,

In the murky green of first light,

and another in 'San Martino del Carso':

È il mio cuore / il paese piú straziato.

My heart is the most shattered country.

Yet neither of these lines has the remarkable elusive qualities of the following ones taken from 'Silenzio in Liguria' in *Sentimento del tempo*:

Scade flessuosa la pianura d'acqua;

Sinuously the watery plain slopes down;

or:

Una carnagione lieve trascorre.

A flesh-soft glow lightly shimmers past.

Each of these shows how much Ungaretti had deepened his sense of artistry in the interval. In the first the imagery is intensified by an undulating rhythm and a delicate interplay of plosives and sibilants which on an auditory level produce the swishing motion of the eddying water; while in the second a momentary flickering of the visual impression is first evoked by the positioning of the adjective and then re-echoed in the fleeting impressionism of the verb. As the collection proceeds similar lines become more frequent and a gradual change-over from Ungaretti's earlier technique of compressed, neo-futurist syntax to a more traditional lyrical discourse is then clearly detectable.

Already in the second section, *La fine di Crono*, the mythology and style gradually become more open and the poet seems aware of the fact that he is undergoing a permanent poetic transformation. He notes it himself in the one-lined poem 'Una colomba':

> D'altri diluvi una colomba ascolto.

I listen to a dove of other floods.

This transformation, moreover, is symbolized by an impending cataclysmic event, the death of Cronus and the end of the ancient world of the Titans.[49] Yet the expressive mode in which it is phrased is still largely the dislocated one of *Allegria*, as may be seen in the eponymous lyric:

> Una fuligine
> Lilla corona i monti,
>
> Fu l'ultimo grido a smarrirsi.
>
> Penelopi innumeri, astri
>
> Vi riabbraccia il Signore!
>
> (Ah, cecità!
> Frana delle notti . . .)
>
> E riporge l'Olimpo,
> Fiore eterno di sonno.

A lilac soot crowns the mountains, it was the last cry to fade. God re-embraces you, numberless Penelopes, stars! (Ah, blindness! Avalanche of nights . . .) And Olympus offers once more the eternal flower of slumber.

Cronus, we recall, was the chief of the Earth-Gods and his name is derived from the Greek word meaning time. This is probably why he is associated with the seasons – especially the harvest – and why this section appears as a sequel to the poem 'Le stagioni' in *Sentimento del tempo*, especially from a syntactic standpoint. The type of cyclical or eternally repetitive time-flow which Cronus represents is similar to the cosmic present of *Allegria*, because the very simultaneity of lyrical effects aimed at by the poet in that collection is itself by definition atemporal. Here, however, the apocalyptic manner of the god's death appears to symbolize the dawning of a new era for Ungaretti – one which involves a change of emphasis from cosmic to human time and from the simple consciousness of youth to a more mature and complex state of self-consciousness with the onset of manhood.

The point is made by allusion to the myth in which the elemental father-figure Cronus is deposed by his more humane and culture-orientated son, Zeus, although the latter's presence is still only hinted at, not openly avowed, in this entire section, either by reference to other Olympians such as Juno and Apollo or by the evocation of Zeus's mortal lover, Leda. With the coming of the new gods, however, a sense of 'durata', of a gently maturing participation in life, begins to predominate; and, because the idea of the lifespan brings with it the terminal concept of death, the whole situation provides an opportunity for a typically Ungarettian inversion of values. In contrast with the all-seeing 'veglia' ('vigil') of death, the individual's lifespan is henceforth apparently to be measured in terms of the slumber of emotional existence and gives rise to the key phrase 'fiore eterno di sonno' ('eternal flower of slumber'). The dream of life in turn leads to a new vision of death, to a fresh orphic cycle, prompted by the new pantheon of gods on Olympus. This will be characterized by an artistic vision of a *human* time-flow rather than by the inanimacy of the previously prevailing *cosmic* time-scale, thereby highlighting contingent, human experiences in place of the eternal cosmic pattern.

By so confining himself to the temporal evolution of humanity Ungaretti senses that he has been transformed into a god in his own right and shows a continuous ability to face up to fresh experiences and assimilate them. The sharpness of his desire to live authentically in the present while still remaining conscious of the whispering of the past around him gives rise to a more mature view of the 'uomo di pena' ('man of grief') who is at this juncture metamorphosed into a nostalgic wolf. In a way the symbol is a partial regression to the 'agneauloup' of 'Calumet',[50] but the difference is that here his character is filtered through the experiences of the bedouin-poet of *Allegria*. He will henceforth be caught up in an ever-deepening whorl of memories; yet, despite his feeling for tradition, the acuity of his senses in 'Con Fuoco' shows that he still retains his intense passion for the here and now:

Con fuoco d'occhi un nostalgico lupo
Scorre la quiete nuda.

Non trova che ombre di cielo sul ghiaccio,

Fondono serpi fatue e brevi viole.

With eyes of fire a nostalgic wolf scours the stark silence. He finds only shadows of the sky on the ice, melting serpents and short-lived violets blend together.

In other words the 'agneauloup', although now more fully conditioned to the anguish of living, is still as capable as ever of drawing intense pleasure from his immediate sensations. The very language of this lyric suggests, therefore, the imminent creation of a new type of figurative realism, the temper of which will be peculiarly baroque in the twentieth-century meaning of the term. In the present section its supreme illustration is the poem 'L'isola'.

The basic theme of the lyric has been described by Leo Spitzer as 'una materializzazione dei temi pastorali della fiamma d'amore e dell'isola d'amore'[51] ('a materialization of the pastoral themes of the flame of love and the island of love'). Its immediate inspiration, as the poet himself once indicated, was a journey he made on foot from Rome to Tivoli and Subiaco. Yet, precisely because he never indulged in futurist gratuitousness, we must reject Friedrich's suggestion that the lyric has no specific meaning, that it is the product of 'die eigenmächtige Sprache' or an automatically generated flow of language.[52] We shall try instead to detect a symbolic message which will link it with Ungaretti's own art and the wider Italian lyric tradition.

On an aesthetic level the composition seems to be concerned with a personal exploration by the poet of the racial memory which he attempts to represent in the emblematic landscapes of art.[53] This explains why we feel ourselves to be in the presence of a recast classical Petrarchism with little more than a touch of decadence in its lyrical texture. A preliminary problem which has to be resolved is the identification of the protagonist in the poem; but, if we assume the normal polyvalency of Ungaretti's images and symbols, the unnamed explorer is probably, in the first place, Zeus, the herald of a new world of feeling, and, in the second, the poet himself as its actualizer. We can consequently regard the landscape of the first stanza as a correlative to the multidimensional exploration of the world of art emerging from the poet-god's meditations as he strolls through the Roman countryside, possibly near some small lake:

A una proda ove sera era perenne
Di anziane selve assorte, scese,
E s'inoltrò
E lo richiamò rumore di penne
Ch'erasi sciolto dallo stridulo
Batticuore dell'acqua torrida,
E una larva (languiva
E rifioriva) vide;
Ritornato a salire vide
Ch'era una ninfa e dormiva
Ritta abbracciata a un olmo.

Down towards a shore where darkness was everlasting through ancient brooding woods he went, and moved on, and a flutter of wings liberated from the throbbing heart-beat of the torrid waters attracted him, and a phantom (it waxed and waned) he saw; on climbing upwards again he saw it was a nymph and she slept with her arms around an elm.

Clearly the ancient meditative woods in this landscape tend to remind us of Baudelaire's 'forêts de symboles' ('forests of symbols'), even though with Ungaretti they have an atavistic rather than a specifically metaphysical aura about them. The sounds of wings – as countless other hermetic images show – are likewise typical orphic features suggesting the transitory beauty of all human experiences; while the nymph whose image waxes and wanes is probably the Italian Muse clinging to the stout elm of her time-hallowed poetic tradition. As we follow the poet into the shadows of his emblematic woods, we therefore appear to penetrate ever more deeply into the mysteries of aestheticized sensation, and we feel ourselves irresistibly caught up in the all-pervasive and nostalgic enchantment of the past which he manages to recapture for us within the immediate context of the present. In short, the very landscape essentializes the corporate sensibility of mankind in a multitemporal orphic continuum, and its subtle resonances invite the poet and his reader to experience the rapture of true love. Its chain of shadowy sensations gradually draws us out of the realm of contingent illusion into a sphere of absolute, aesthetic truth, and then a new kind of realism flashes upon Ungaretti's inward eye: one whose incandescent interiority is moulded into delicate – yet vitreous – Petrarchan imagery:

In sé da simulacro a fiamma vera
Errando, giunse a un prato ove
L'ombra negli occhi s'addensava
Delle vergini come
Sera appiè degli ulivi;
Distillavano i rami
Una pioggia pigra di dardi,
Qua pecore s'erano appisolate
Sotto il liscio tepore,
Altre brucavano
La coltre luminosa;
Le mani del pastore erano un vetro
Levigato da fioca febbre.

Passing waywardly within himself from feigned to true passion, he arrived at a meadow where the shadows grew dense in the eyes of maidens, like evening at the foot of olive-trees; a lazy, pin-like rain dripped from the boughs; here sheep had drowsed in the calm warmth, others were feeding on the glistening sheen; the shepherd's hands were like glass smoothed by a faint fever.

In the first line of this stanza the adoption of a time-hallowed Petrarchan diction at once demonstrates that the poet's responses to his emblematic landscape lie wholly within the tradition; while the movement from a 'simulacro' to a 'vera fiamma' can be interpreted aesthetically not only as a passage from fancy to reality but also from what the Petrarchists call 'imitatio' ('imitation') to a more authentic process of 'aemulatio' ('emulation'). When such a stage is reached the lyrical resonances emerging from the imagery echo the secret melodies of the whole course of Italian lyricism, and the recessive atavistic elements contained in them are symbolized by a continuous darkening of shadows in the eyes of maidens, like evening at the foot of olive trees. Even the choice of olive-tree is emblematic of mediterranean culture, and this culture is suddenly given immediacy as a baroque sphere of pure art by the association of certain reconstituted memories from the past with the poet's immediate sense-impressions. The result is the creation of a psycho-sensuous paradise with disturbing existential overtones, in which a precarious eidetico-existential equilibrium is reflected – almost prismatically – through the contrasting analogical implications of *vetro* and *febbre*.

This explains why almost a greenhouse atmosphere involving the dank arcana of the senses is evoked by a further reference to a 'pioggia pigra' and a 'liscio tepore'. Within such tepid warmth we are presented with modern versions of Petrarch's 'dolci animali' ('gentle animals') described in their peaceful pastoral setting (symbolizing no doubt the unconscious masses who are the unwitting preservers of the tradition.) As they bask like sheep in their atmosphere of cultural saturation, we note that some of them are active and others passive, a fact which reminds us of the previous distinction between the active and passive memories, and also between the articulate and inarticulate members of society. Finally, however, they are all fixed like flies in amber in the glassy imagery stimulated by the shepherd's fever: in a tense, baroque historico-imaginative state which attempts to combine the metaphysical and contingent anxieties inherent in the human condition with the absolute emotions locked in a timeless orphico-cultural state of suspense. When possessed by such a fever the inspired poet usually manages to strike the right harmonics to produce a modern Petrarchan transfiguration of his sense-impressions; and this type of transfiguration, as Paci has explained, tends to acquire a singular *ideative* quality, because it is 'né la ripetizione del dato né una forma puramente ideale: è piuttosto la mediazione tra il dato e l'aprirsi del dato a nuovi sviluppi secondo uno schema'[54] ('neither the repetition of a datum nor a purely ideal form: it is rather the mediation between a datum and the opening of that datum to new developments according to a pattern').

Our conclusion must therefore be that, far from offering an example of automatic writing as Friedrich has suggested, 'L'isola' is intended to evoke the natural configuration of the poet's cultural perspectives within the orphic framework of his analogical keyboard. Intuitively a similar approach was adopted by Petrarch himself in certain lyrics like the well-known Canzone 'Chiare, fresche e dolci acque' where, as we noted earlier, the imagery also seems to have been compounded from a psycho-sensuous alchemy of great purity. As the poet admits, it is from the fourteenth-century poet's art reflected through the aesthetics of Leopardi that he in fact draws his deeper artistic practices and lyrical criteria. For at moments of intense inspiration all three writers put aside extraneous metaphysical and historical considerations and produce a poetry of sheer meditative dimensions, quite undebased by an accumulation of 'fatti prosastici' ('prosaic factors') or by too overt a form of conceptualism.

It is only in this sense that we can consider Ungaretti as a 'pure poet' and not because he tended to adopt a speculative or detached attitude towards lyrical content. Consequently he does not yield to the dangerous temptation indulged in by many other Petrarchists of allowing his inspiration to degenerate into an effete idyllicism. The supreme examples of the latter phenomenon in Italy are, of course, the poets of Arcadia; but, since the present poet has a powerful ethos of his own to express, he never models his art on the funambulatory, pre-Arcadian word-music of a Chiabrera nor on the later superficial practices of the Arcadians themselves. Instead he is content to exploit the ethical realism and meditative approach to art typified by Leopardi; and so, while he avoids all Neoplatonic posturing on the one hand, he equally shuns any suggestion of romantic sentimentality on the other.

The next section of *Sentimento del tempo* entitled *Sogni e accordi* is a technical interlude, in which Ungaretti mainly attempts to extend the range of his analogies and metaphors. Some of his comparisons are rather far-fetched, though on the other hand a play of colours or colourful overtones often enhances the lyrical impact of his intensely complex analogies, as may be seen in the subtle colour alchemy of a description of dawn in 'Sogno':

> Con un volare argenteo
> ad ogni fumo insinua guance in fiamma.

With a silvery flight, in every wisp of smoke she insinuates cheeks of flame.

Although such sequences border on surrealism, it is a surrealism with a peculiarly Italianate ring about it: one which retains throughout a basis of critical intelligence and does not rely simply on external elements and automatic writing for its effects. What the poet is probably trying to achieve in such exercises is to amalgamate as closely and as authentically as possible his previously established symbolism with a vast panoply of linguistic and artistic effects. Such artifices are clearly illustrated in the interplay of alliteration on 'n' and 'm' in the second line of the above quotation.

Again, despite the clear emphasis placed on technique in this section we still detect the poet's intense sense of 'dolore', so that the deeper forms of his lyricism are not even now entirely masked. However, it is often a 'dolore' expressed indirectly through a heightened preoccupation with the transient qualities of life, as indicated in the flickering of day's last embers against a cosmic background in 'Di sera':

Nulla, sospeso il respiro, piú dolce
Che udirti consumarmi
Nel sole moribondo
L'ultimo fiammeggiare d'ombra, terra!

Nothing is sweeter than, with bated breath, to hear you consuming in the dying sunlight my last flaming of shadow, earth!

Here, of course, the poet is clearly employing once more his inversionary technique, because what he is really depicting is 'a *flaming* of earthly shadows'.

The next group of poems, *Leggende*, reverts to the style of a close-knit hermetic discourse and its lyrical texture proves to be dramatic rather than technical in quality. It aims at illustrating through its symbols the convention-innovation dilemma always present in hermetic practices, and the composition entitled 'Il capitano' will serve to exemplify the problems involved.[55] Broadly speaking, the lyric indicates that the human mind possesses a natural disposition towards idealism which can only be overcome by the poet's continual assertion of his 'disponibilità'. In this sense the captain represents one side of the bedouin's character, that of the upholder of tradition, while the poet represents the other, the restless seeker after experience. Behind the captain there also lurks the Baudelairian archetype of 'le vieux capitaine' ('the old captain') of 'Le voyage' who is identifiable with death. But the background presence of death is hardly surprising here, since the equation linking death with past tradition is a frequent one with Ungaretti. Even so, the personality which tends to dominate the entire poem is that of the emerging poet who avoids becoming imprisoned by, even when admiring, the ideal of traditional authority represented by the captain. Hence, while he piously treasures and savours the achievements of the past, he nevertheless emphasizes his complete freedom of action, and he soon feels himself sufficiently emancipated to 'emulate' rather than slavishly 'imitate' its modalities.

The lyric opens with two general statements, the first of which again stresses the receptivity of the bedouin-poet's mind:

Fui pronto a tutte le partenze;

I was ready for all departures;

while the second highlights the orphic arcana which lie behind human activity and which always surround man within his temporally matured tradition:

> Quando hai segreti, notte hai pietà.

> When you have secrets, you have pity, night.

The point need hardly be laboured that here the word 'segreti' leads us back once more to 'quel nulla/d'inesauribile segreto' ('that inexhaustibly secret nothingness') which we previously encountered in *Allegria* and which continues to allude to the subtle harmonics which the poet draws from past tradition by changing register and attuning his lyre to its deeper melodies. Likewise 'notte' signifies – by virtue of Ungaretti's inversionary technique – existence in the raw, just as elsewhere images of light indicate the all-pervasive conditions of Being or Death. 'Pietà' is, by contrast, a relatively new concept and represents something more than pity in the Christian or everyday sense of the word. It approximates more closely to the concept of *pietas* held by the Ancients, though with certain Christian overtones; and it may be defined as a moral and emotional fellow-feeling for all mankind accompanied by an awareness of one's social and religious duties.

Once the poet has laid down his general attitudes to life he proceeds to give us a kind of idealized autobiography. At first he paints an emotively concentrated picture of his childhood in which a dawning consciousness of the continuity of the human tradition, the child's fear of the dark, and the human being's instinctive eagerness to enjoy intense experiences all play a part. Indeed, as he unwinds the temporal thread of his early life, we find that it not only offers an authentic prelude to the attitudes he strikes during his maturity, but it also mirrors through its symbolic ambivalence the dynamic representational principles on which modern aesthetics is based:

> Se bimbo mi svegliavo
> di soprassalto, mi calmavo udendo
> Urlanti nell'assente via,
> Cani randagi. Mi parevano
> Piú del lumino alla Madonna
> che ardeva sempre in quella stanza,
> Mistica compagnia.

> If as a child I awoke with a start, I grew calm on hearing stray dogs howling in the empty street. They seemed to me, more that the light to the Madonna which always glowed in that bedroom, a mystic company.

We equally note in this passage the poet's sense of his existentiality, since the evocation of the terrors of the child waking in a darkened room reminds us of the adult's awareness of the terrifying solitude of existence after he has been overwhelmed by the trauma of a self-conscious awakening to the deeper implications of the human condition. Similarly other symbols now represent a veritable sounding-board of analogical and conceptual resonances. The 'cani randagi' recall for us the earlier symbol of the 'lupo' ('wolf') and suggest the waywardness of the poet's emotional life, particularly through the carefully pointed overtone emphasizing his hunger for sensation. The 'assente via' has a double implication, signifying in the first place the empty street, but also in the second something more – the 'unlived' or 'unplotted' course of the poet's future life. Likewise, the light under the statuette of the Virgin Mary is an indication of Ungaretti's acknowledgement of the religious tradition in Italian culture, even though as a person he only feels himself bound to it at present in the loosest sense.

We can take his understanding of 'religio' here in the etymological sense as a 'binding-together' of the whole of the cultural tradition, because in his early life the poet's faith was founded principally on his sense of communion with his fellow-men. Despite a religious conversion in 1928 he still held no brief for dogmatic forms of worship and his basic credo, as we have stressed, continued even then to be a perennial humanism connected – though by no means wholly identified – with the culture of the past. This accounts for the introduction into the present image-chain of another atavistic perspective paralleling the image of the 'occulte mani' ('hidden hands') we encountered in 'I Fiumi'. But at present the recall of these instinctive, pre-natal urges is largely intended to act as a foil to the true theme of the poem, which focuses on the speed of his growing up and his unpreparedness for the change in his condition which the appearance of a self-conscious adulthood will bring:

E non ad un rincorrere
Echi d'innanzi nascita,
Mi sorpresi con cuore, uomo?

And was it not in chasing pre-natal echoes that I surprised myself at heart, a man?

At this stage a crisis of self-identity looms on the horizon. Consequently, as the instinctive and atavistic echoes of childhood fade away, there arises in their place a soul-chilling despair, provoked precisely by the self-consciousness of adulthood. The poet's first encounter with this new sense of reality proves traumatic, and he feels completely disorientated by life's absurdity as he becomes conscious of his own contingency, a quality which he had hardly noticed earlier:

Ma quando, notte, il tuo viso fu nudo
E buttato sul sasso

Non fui che fibra d'elementi,
Pazza, palese in ogni oggetto,
Era schiacciante l'umiltà.

But when, o night, your face was laid bare and cast upon the rock, I was nothing less than a crazed bundle of filaments manifest in every object, the humility of it was crushing.

Such disorientation is very different from his previous feeling of being 'una docile fibra/ dell'universo'[56] ('a docile filament of the universe') after his ritualistic immersion in the Isonzo. But, clearly, he can now hope to counter his sense of disarray only by reorientating himself decisively within the compass of human culture.

From here on the poem trails off, perhaps, into a somewhat disjointed impressionism, but the basic thread of the argument is still discernible. The captain, for instance, is identified with the serenity and stability of the past tradition or racial memory, and a muted dialogue ensues between him and the poet. It is framed within a dominant Leopardian moonlight scene and the waxing of the moon seems to indicate the dawning of Ungaretti's independent lyrical consciousness. The awakening of a personal lyrical outlook creates a struggle between the demands of his own maturing sensibility and the consolidated tastes of the past represented by the captain's heroic and unyielding pose. After it the tradition is suddenly compelled to yield before his originality as the captain is toppled from his pinnacle:

Nessuno lo vide cadere,
Nessuno l'udí rantolare,
Riapparve adagiato in un solco,
Teneva le mani sul petto.

Gli chiusi gli occhi.

No one saw him fall, no one heard his death-rattle, he reappeared carefully laid out in a furrow, his hands were folded on his chest. I shut his eyes.

Although the literal interpretation of this event is the death of one Captain Cremona in the trenches during the First World War, the symbolic meaning is therefore much more important, for it represents the ultimate assimilation and domination of the past tradition by the poet. The captain's allegorical last rites are performed when the poet piously closes his eyes; and, as he does so, the moonlight which up to that point had not been in evidence in the orphic night of existence, now heralds in Ungaretti's own matured lyrical intelligence. As a veil in a Leopardian sense it also shields both protagonists from the horror of untransfigured reality:

(La luna è un velo).

(The moon is a veil).

At the same time the Captain is transformed into a suspended – though deeply resonant ideal – and his soul floats away, feather-like, into the eternity of the culturally saturated past. Equally curiously, his vicissitudes are described in italics:

Parve di piume;

He seemed feather-like;

and thereafter he symbolizes for Ungaretti those unquenchable potentialities of the racial consciousness from which living poets must derive their lyrical harmonics in order to ensure not only their own success but also the continuity of the cultural tradition itself.

The suspension of reality and the 'epochization' of the human tradition in its legends are probably regarded as two convergent processes by Ungaretti. He even uses different typographical devices to indicate the three levels of his discourse in this composition: roman for the growing confidence and self-assertiveness of the poet; italics, as previously mentioned, for the fading authority of the captain; and parentheses for the 'epochized' condition of the natural world when evoked as artistic representation, since it is no longer a real but a transfigured scene which he is describing.

Evidently this lyric is the key to the entire section. It implies that the poet's 'legends' are to be interpreted as so many latent traditional residues to be revivified by authentic poetic acts and given fresh significance in a modern setting. All of them tend to be composed of personal or communally shared myths, and their stratification in Ungaretti's lyrical memory may be illustrated simply by quoting titles like 'Primo amore', 'La madre', 'Memoria d'Ofelia d'Alba', and 'Dove è la luce'. Although in their pre-lyrical state such myths stand merely as

Cose consumate:
Emblemi eterni, nomi,
Evocazioni pure . . . ,[57]

Worn-out things: eternal emblems, names, pure evocations . . . ,

once they are incorporated into his poetry they are transformed into dynamic symbols of spiritual integration with the previous tradition, becoming authentic images of Ungaretti's own lyrical endeavour and sense of fulfilment. He regards their reabsorption into the present as his highest artistic achievement and he emphasizes the point in 'Epigrafe per un caduto della rivoluzione'. In this poem he links the underlying tradition of his motherland with his own dream of immortality, and he claims that by helping in her secret unfolding

Il mio giovane cuore in sé immortala.

She immortalizes my young heart within herself.

Even so, certain existential doubts and hesitations remain to form the substance of the next section, *Inni*. We might describe these lyrics as so many self-confessions arising out of the poet's attempts to find some underlying purpose in his life. He wonders at first, for instance, in 'Danni con fantasia' what instinctive mystery drives him to participate in such an apparently aimless process:

Quale segreto eterno
Mi farà sempre gola in te?

What eternal secret always tempts me into you?

or why sin is so prominent a feature in the mutability of the human condition:

La vostra, lo so, non è vera luce,

Ma avremmo vita senza il tuo variare,
Felice colpa?

Yours, I know, is not true light, but would we have life without your diversity, joyful sin?

At first it might seem as if he intends the idea of sin to be understood here in the religious sense because the symbolic figure representing its mythicization is Cain. But even Cain is a kind of bedouin whose thirst for living is emphasized in his dynamic actions and raging appetites; and so we must assume that even sin is capable of felicitously extending the mind and personality:

Corre sopra le sabbie favolose
E il suo piede è leggero.

O pastore di lupi,
Hai i denti della luce breve
Che punge i nostri giorni.[58]

He races over fabulous sands and his foot is fleet. O shepherd of wolves, you have the teeth of the brief light which bites our days.

In these lines it is also worth noting that the erstwhile wilderness of *Allegria* again changes subtly: it is no longer a barren desert but a myth-steeped tract of 'sabbie favolose'. Accordingly, instead of a barren waste-land we now encounter the time-hallowed images and experiences accumulated by mankind during its historic journey through time. The only defect which still persists is that residual sense of imperfection or metaphysical sin inherent in the very contingency of human existence. This rather than any

Giuseppe Ungaretti

religious doubt which Cain senses accounts for his overwhelming feelings of anguish and yearning. Its obsessive presence even takes on the form of a brooding, memorial conscience which blots out the vision of the 'paese innocente' evoked earlier:

> Anima, non saprò mai calmarti?
>
> Mai non vedrò nella notte del sangue?
>
> Figlia indiscreta della noia,
> Memoria, memoria incessante,
> Le nuvole della tua polvere,
> Non c'è vento che se le porti via?

> Soul, shall I never learn how to calm you? Shall I never see in the night of blood? Indiscreet daughter of ennui, memory, incessant memory, will no wind ever carry off the clouds of your dust?

All that a human being can do, therefore, is to wait for the eventual expunging of the memory of his sinfulness by death, since only through a return to a state of unambiguous Being can he hope that

> Gli occhi mi tornerebbero innocenti,
> Vedrei la primavera eterna
>
> E, finalmente nuova,
> O memoria, saresti onesta.

> My eyes would become innocent again, I would see the eternal spring, and, finally renewed, o memory, you would be honest.

Such an attitude may again seem like the espousal of a Neoplatonic ideal, but Ungaretti's attenuated Neoplatonism is dynamic, not static, in its approach to reality. Furthermore, this is as far as he will ever go in his acceptance of any type of dogmatic religious values because, as we have seen, his true faith amounts to a 'binding-together' of mankind within a continuous and sustained cultural tradition.

Such an attitude explains why the principal poem of the section is entitled 'La Pietà'[59] and why, while viewing human destiny in a broad metaphysical light, the poet concentrates on the ambivalence of human emotions and the problem of the individual's alienation from the corporate will of society in the modern world:

> Non ho che superbia e bontà.
>
> E mi sento esiliato in mezzo agli uomini,
>
> Ma per essi sto in pena.

> I have only pride and goodness. And I feel myself exiled among men. But for them I am stricken with anguish.

These propositions indeed act as a prelude to a whole range of moral and aesthetic problems with which Ungaretti deals in the poem and which he now finds he has to wrestle with as a man and as an artist. For instance, his fear of lapsing into unwitting lyrical insincerity is expressed in the following self-questioning imagery:

Ho popolato di nomi il silenzio.

Ho fatto a pezzi cuore e mente
Per cadere in servitú di parole?

I have peopled the silence with names. Have I shattered heart and mind to fall into a slavery of words?

And similarly, later on, his metaphysical doctrine of the inversion of the significance of life and death is restated in a rich, baroque form of symbolism:

È nei vivi la strada dei defunti,

Siamo noi la fiumana d'ombre,

Sono esse il grano che ci scoppia in sogno,

Loro è la lontananza che ci resta,

E loro l'ombra che dà peso ai nomi.

In the living runs the road of the dead, we are the torrent of shadows, they are the seed which bursts on us in dreams, theirs is the distant perspective remaining to us, and theirs the shadowiness which gives weight to our names.

Incidentally, the peculiar nature of Ungaretti's orphism is also reaffirmed here without equivocation: it is an outlook which adheres to the subtle melodies and atavistic imagery of the past and which presents the real world as shadows and the shadows of the dead as the only authentic reality.

The frustrations the poet encounters both in his pursuit of distinctive Italian inflections in his lyricism and in his thirst for knowledge of the infinitely responsive keyboard of the kingdom of death actually tend to lead him at times to an emotional échec. But his is ultimately a communicative, not a metaphysical, problem and so differs absolutely from that found in Baudelaire or the symbolists. Here its most explicit ethical formulation reads:

Non ne posso piú di stare murato
Nel desiderio senza amore,

I can no longer bear being walled up in desire without love,

and its appearance is partly due to the poet's obsession with the apparently unbridgeable void separating the consolidated poetic feelings of the past from the seemingly transient lyrical utterances of the present. This attitude is, of course, an aspect of the modern baroque outlook,[60] although again its speculative implications are underplayed and an emotive, almost a Promethean, defiance diminishes the horror of the metaphysical abyss over which each individual now appears to be continually suspended:

Attaccato sul vuoto
Al suo filo di ragno,
Non teme e non seduce
Se non il proprio grido.

Ripara il logorio alzando tombe,
E per pensarti, Eterno,
Non ha che le bestemmie.

Hanging over the void on his spider's thread, he neither fears nor beguiles aught but his own cries. He makes good the wear-and-tear by building tombs, and to think of you, Eternal God, he has only blasphemies.

The process alluded to here is the Foscolian one of tomb-building, and it is positive in that it holds out the prospect of the creation of a strictly human eternity which will resolve man's sense of alienation. By now, indeed, a sense of every human being's continual dying had virtually become a category of Ungaretti's spirit and it provided him with a clear-sighted foreknowledge of death's infinite resources. So, not surprisingly, the next section of *Sentimento del tempo* deals exclusively with a lyrical meditation on the deeper aspects of death while providing us at the same time with an allusive survey of the multiple resonances of death's all-pervading kingdom. Since, moreover, its sphere is largely identified with the Italian cultural tradition transposed on to an aesthetic plane, its treasures offer us both a sense of despair at our imperfection and one of redemption through the perenniality of its traditional values.

We can usefully contrast Ungaretti's treatment of death with Cardarelli's, and in doing so we note that, whereas the latter's approach was metaphysical, or even somewhat casuistic in quality, the present poet's is undoubtedly completely cultural in its implications. Death is not represented by Ungaretti in other words as an inexplicable and soul-searing catastrophe: it is transformed into a heightened state of awareness whose insights and perspectives control the living poet by analogical and allusive means. Consequently we find a confession by the poet in the second canto that his main preoccupation with death is to produce traditional resonances and harmonics as a background to his verse:

Scava le intime vite
Della nostra infelice maschera
(Clausura d'infinito)
Con blandizia fanatica
La buia veglia dei padri.

> The dark vigil of our fathers cuts into the intimate lives behind our unhappy masks (a barrier to the infinite) with a fanatical blandness.

To gauge the full impact of these lines we need to have recourse once more to the notion of Ungaretti's analogical keyboard which evokes feelings and atmospheres rather than a series of direct conceptual statements. In this context the lyrical message is clear: the dark vigil of the poet's forbears delves into the intimate recesses of his mind (a mortal barrier to infinite perceptiveness) through the insistency of an imperious 'blandizia' or 'dolcezza' of almost Petrarchan quality and proportions. It is this cultural pressure which is the true nature and extent of the influence of death – or rather of the literary dead – upon the living, and a few archetypal analogies drawn from 'La morte meditata' will be the best way of illustrating the point.

In 'Canto quinto', for example, death is likened to the impalpable desire created by the fleeting vision of a beautiful woman. The source of the image may well be Baudelaire's 'A une passante' which also influenced Cardarelli, but Ungaretti's image is more ethereal than the French poet's, even though his lady also stirs in his mind a taste for intense sensations mingled with a sharp, spiritual exasperation:

> Sei la donna che passa
> Come la foglia
>
> E lasci agli alberi un fuoco d'autunno.

> You are the woman who passes like a leaf and leave on the trees an autumnal fire.

This feminine presence may well be a perennial Eve representing the two principal aspects of death, sin and redemption. Her presence is also discernible in 'Canto primo', where her responsibility for the Fall may explain why she is described as the 'madre velenosa degli evi' ('poisonous mother of the ages'), and her promise of an innocence regained at the end of time why she also appears as a 'sognatrice fuggente' ('fleeing dreamer'). In this way primeval innocence and that ultimate reborn innocence acquired through mankind's cultural pursuits are linked together in an orphic circle of Being and Becoming, resulting in a form of lyrico-cultural redemption brought about by a cult of aesthetic anamnesis.

In the third canto the same kind of exasperation of the senses as that previously associated with the Eve-Death figure is again detectable and at this point it appears to be more concentrated than ever, because it is closely allied to atavistic and instinctive forces. Moreover, its brooding mystery is conveyed analogically by means of a further irritant, the insistent song of the cicadas in the summer's heat:

Tu, nella luce fonda,
O confuso silenzio,
Insisti come le cicale irose.

You in the deep light, o confused silence, insist like angry cicadas.

Here atavistic perspectives, the inversionary technique whereby light means the darkness of death, and the Petrarchan-like oxymoron of a 'confused silence' awaken sharp resonances within the lyrical texture. In other images, by contrast, the note of irritation is significantly toned down, and then the poetry acquires a more placid attitude towards death, which is, for instance, depicted in 'Canto primo' as an organic symbol of the latent resources of the racial memory:

Da quel momento
Ti odo nel fluire della mente
Approfondire lontananze,
Emula sofferente dell'eterno.

From that instant I hear you in the flowing of the mind probing distances, anguished emulator of the eternal.

Accordingly, it is through an analogical image of distant hope that the poet normally gains his insights into the secrets of death's domain. Even so, at times a touch of despair also arises when he considers himself too deeply immersed in the turbulent stream of life ever to equal the timeless perfection of the consolidated past. When this mood dominates, as in 'Canto terzo', he feels mocked by the bell-like clarity of the pure voice of the lyric tradition and sees no hope of overcoming the scorn which its very perfection casts upon his own puny poetic efforts:

Incide le rughe segrete
Della nostra infelice maschera
La beffa infinita dei padri.

The infinite mockery of our fathers scores out the secret wrinkles of our unhappy mask.

Fortunately these disturbing doubts are counterbalanced at other times by superbly resonant lyrics around which the emotion of the centuries immediately seems to ferment. Occasionally, a bedouin figure also reappears and acts as a further instrument of lyrical consolidation. The bedouin's ingrained historical awareness ensures the full deployment of the poet's hallucinatory analogical techniques and the creation of traditionally saturated transfigurations of his experiences. Thus, when Ungaretti reaches a climax of inspiration, as in 'Canto quarto', he burns both time and space in a momentary communion with death's infinite perspectives, as he meditates on a hill reminiscent of Leopardi's setting for 'L'infinito':

> Mi presero per mani nuvole.
>
> Brucio sul colle spazio e tempo,
> Come un tuo messaggero,
> Come il sogno, divina morte.

Clouds seized me by the hand. On the hill I burn both space and time, like one of your messengers, like the dream, o death divine.

Elsewhere in the section other analogical patterns similarly allude to death's innermost qualities. At one point she becomes 'la rosa abbrunita dei riflessi' ('the darkened rose of reflections'), at another the 'atleta senza sonno della nostra grandezza' ('sleepless athlete of our greatness'); and indeed the whole range of such analogies, when taken cumulatively, provides Ungaretti with a prospect of lyrical redemption cast in an aesthetic key. He feels that within the resonant lyrical eternity of the past he can work out his own poetic destiny with complete confidence, in the sure knowledge that his artistic merits will be measured and assessed by their relevance to, and their transformation of, the tradition's pre-existing aesthetic norms. His art in other words becomes a process of integration, of harmonization, with the development of Italian lyricism as a whole, during which he himself feels constantly stimulated to transmute his contingent bodily and psychic presence into a fully modulated and lyrically historicized symphony. Like Baudelaire in 'Les phares' his view of the poet's duty is that of adding a personal lyrical flavour to the unfolding of the whole course of cultural history and he would certainly have underwritten the French poet's assertion that

> . . . c'est vraiment, Seigneur, le meilleur témoignage
> Que nous puissions donner de notre dignité
> Que cet ardent sanglot qui roule d'âge en âge
> Et vient mourir au bord de votre éternité!

. . . it is truly, Lord, the finest testimony that we can give of our dignity, this burning sob which rolls from age to age and dies away at the edge of your eternity!

The final section of *Sentimento del tempo* is entitled *L'Amore* and again deals on another level with the age-old anguish and perennial aspirations of mankind. Love is now regarded as the handmaiden of death and provides a further perspective on her complex nature. The entire scope of life and the humanistic cohesiveness of the poet's vision of birth, regeneration and death are thus concentrated in the apparent simplicity of the 'Canto beduino' opening the section:

Una donna s'alza e canta
La segue il vento e l'incanta
E sulla terra la stende
E il sogno vero la prende.

Questa terra è nuda
Questa donna è druda
Questo vento è forte
Questo sogno è morte.

A woman rises and sings, the wind pursues and bewitches her, and lays her on the ground, and the true dream seizes her. This ground is bare, this woman is a paramour, this wind is strong, this dream is death.

All the symbols involved here are clearly polyvalent and they can be defined in conceptual terms only in an approximate sense. Essentially, the woman-symbol stands for the instinctive life and the shadowy arcana of death; the wind for atavistic urges and physical passion; the earth for bare existence and regeneration; and the dream for a kind of trance which establishes communication with the past. In this way the poem again acts as a cone of relationships linking together the various perspectives present in Ungaretti's world outlook; and its imagery synthesizes their antinomies in order to present the reader with a lyrical synopsis of a complex, multifaceted view of the world.

The other poems in the section are also brief love-songs expressing in allusive imagery the poet's Petrarchist attitude to this perennial theme. A familiar note, for instance, is struck in 'Canto' where he again considers woman as a modern Eve: that is, as a psycho-sensuous creature guiding him towards a state of contentment and supreme human wisdom:

Quando ogni luce è spenta
E non vedo che i miei pensieri,

Un'Eva mi mette sugli occhi
La tela dei paradisi perduti.

When every light dies away and I see only my own thoughts, an Eve lays on my eyes the canvas of lost paradises.

The allusive humanism and the normal syntax of such a statement, moreover, indicate that a re-created traditionalism has by now partly replaced the dislocation of syntax characteristic of *Allegria*.

★ ★ ★ ★ ★ ★

Il Dolore (1947) was largely written during the war and can be regarded as a personal interlude rather than as a direct continuation of *Sentimento del tempo*. Apart from the first section *Tutto ho perduto*, which appears to retain close links with the themes of the preceding volume, all its compositions deal either with the tragedy of wartime Italy or, more specifically, with a personal, domestic tragedy which at that time almost overwhelmed the poet, the death of his son Antonietto in Brazil in 1939. He indeed expressed his grief at this bereavement with such intensity that his lyricism tends to become narrative rather than hermetic in character, although certain powerful hallucinatory effects are still maintained through the extra dimension now added to his poetic line by his towering emotion and the final maturing of his baroque outlook. Many of these effects derive from Ungaretti's herculean attempts to intimize the savage landscapes of Brazil with their bleak features and evident inhumanity. Yet, once again this expansion of his sorrow against a wider, almost cosmic, background enables him to treat his narrow family tragedy as a typical example of the broader anguish of all men as they are confronted by the twin spectres of old age and death.

The first section of the collection looks forward as well as backwards and provides a universal framework of ageing as a foil to the tragedy of death. Once again in *Tutto ho perduto* the poet mourns the passing of his youth and with it the loss of his deeper lyrical perceptions:

Tutto ho perduto dell'infanzia
e non potrò mai piú
smemorarmi in un grido.

I have lost everything from my childhood and I can never again unburden my memory with a cry.

Here we must bear in mind that 'infanzia' was for Ungaretti a period of unselfconscious 'allegria' ('joyfulness') and that the process of growing up tended in his view to corrode the spontaneity of the senses by submerging them in arid intellectual structures which, eventually, would no longer allow him to unburden his memory of its instinctive feelings through the largely spontaneous and asyntactic 'gridi' ('cries') of his early poetry. At the present stage this effect has finally reached its climax and he finds himself lost in the senseless flux of existence, with only the memory of his childhood dreams to console him:

Di me rammento che esultavo amandoti,
Ed eccomi perduto
In infinito delle notti.

Of myself I remember that I exulted in loving you, and now I am lost in an infinity of nights.

As a result, he is unable to reactivate those processes which formerly provided him with periodic psychological releases of tension and he feels himself reified within the static memory as he is overwhelmed by a mood of black despair. The depth of this despair is conveyed in an intractable image, a 'roccia di gridi' ('rock of cries'), which again evokes distinct Petrarchan overtones within his analogical keyboard:

Disperazione che incessante aumenta
La vita non mi è piú,
Arrestata in fondo alla gola,
Che una roccia di gridi.

A despair which incessantly increases, life is now to me, blocked in the depths of my throat, nothing more than a rock of cries.

To counteract the ossification of his emotions his dominant moods now tend to become steeped in an impotent baroque rage, noted particularly for its emotional violence, giganticized descriptions, and fragmentary – at times even lyrically unresolved – imagery.

The section *Giorno per giorno* introduces these features and it is primarily an intimate diary of the poet's reactions to the various stages of his son's illness. He now magnifies virtually all his experiences as a consequence of his sense of impotence and he channels his sorrow into intense forms of baroque imagery. The following stanza is a case in point, because a play of reflections and a sense of infinite regression to an insubstantial skeletal world – a *mise en abyme* of the entire physical universe – stress the explosive nature of his pent-up feelings:

Agli abbagli che squillano dai vetri
Squadra un riflesso alla tovaglia l'ombra,
Tornano al lustro labile d'un orcio
Gonfie ortensie dall'aiuola, un rondone ebbro,
Il grattacielo in vampe delle nuvole,
Sull'albero, saltelli d'un bimbetto . . . [61]

In the dazzle which screams from the window-panes the shade frames a reflection on the tablecloth, in the faint glittering of a pot reappear swollen hydrangeas from the flowerbed, a drunken swift, the skyscraper in a blaze of clouds, the capering of a child, on a tree. . . .

The sweltering heat and the flashes of reflected light clearly cause the scene to border on an hallucination; and elsewhere we similarly find a swelling emotion almost reaching breaking-point in its intensity as the poet indulges in a new type of 'grido': one which is not analogical but syntactically normal in structure, yet is marked by the same soul-searing – perhaps even excessive – emotionalism:

E t'amo, t'amo, ed è continuo schianto! ...[62]

And I love you, I love you, and it is a continuous shattering! ...

Many critics have considered outbursts of this kind to fall outside the province of art altogether: they no longer seem to form, that is, an aesthetically ordered expression of grief, but become simple ejaculations of pain and distress on a physiological level. Although there is perhaps an element of truth in such criticism, it could also be argued that they provide at the same time a fresh note of authenticity in Ungaretti's poetry, since his previous literary and metaphysical meditations are now momentarily replaced by his unpremeditated emotional responses as a father and as a man. The introduction of so intimate a set of human values at this relatively late date in his career is indeed highly significant and, as we shall see, it gradually helps the poet to reach out towards even broader forms of lyrical consolation.

The immediate outcome of the tragedy recounted minutely in *Giorno per giorno* is a religious crisis, the beginnings of which were detectable as early as *Sentimento del tempo*. Before it finally overwhelms him, the poet develops a full-blown baroque rage in 'Tu ti spezzasti', in which the memory of his son's death and the symbol of the araucaria pine-tree fighting for its life in a stony Brazilian wilderness become the correlatives of his ambivalent state of mind:

E la recline, che s'apriva all'unico
Raccogliersi dell'ombra nella valle,
Araucaria, anelando ingigantita,
Volta nell'ardua selce d'erme fibre
Piú delle altre dannate refrattaria,
Fresca la bocca di farfalle e d'erbe
Dove dalle radici si tagliava,
– Non la rammenti delirante muta
Sopra tre palmi d'un rotondo ciottolo
In un perfetto bilico
Magicamente apparsa?

And the bent monkey-puzzle tree which spreads itself in the only gathering of shade in the valley, breathlessly gigantic, having cast its solitary fibres into the hard flintstone, more refractory than its other damned companions, its mouth cool with grass and butterflies at a point where it tore itself away from its roots, – Don't you remember it, delirious, mute, on three palms' breadth of rounded stone, in perfect equilibrium, a magical apparition?

Here, in short, we see the gigantic, inhuman landscapes of Brazil in all their terror, and they contrast absolutely with the humanely-moulded scenery of Latium forming the background to *Sentimento del tempo*. Despite their apparently classical structure involving hyperbaton, such lines are emotionally symptomatic, through their very linguistic contortions, of the personal and religious crises about to descend upon the poet. Moreover, during this period his private anguish will, in fact, be intensified by the communal despair experienced by all Italians when faced with the devastation inflicted on their country by the Second World War.

Generally speaking, Ungaretti had by this time abandoned his clinically pure, metaphysical imagery, replacing it with an ethically directed, baroque outlook; and he now pursues the trend to its ultimate conclusion. In the section *Roma occupata* the poem 'Mio fiume anche tu' shows that his cult of atavism has been supplemented by a broadly humanist religion which even encompasses the possibility of a personal redeemer, Christ. The figure of Christ might at first seem to be a further metamorphosis of the 'agneauloup', a kind of deified bedouin or 'uomo di pena'. But his presence is simultaneously associated with imagery typical of a more dogmatic and baroque Catholicism than that seen hitherto, since Ungaretti now uses allusions to hell and devilry as a means of objectifying the maceration of his conscience. Even so, his religious creed is probably nothing more than a psychological inclination towards Christianity in the widest sense, a fact which is reinforced by the occasional reappearance of significant traces of his analogical manner. To round off the abovementioned lyric certain hermetic forms are therefore mingled with his now dominant, comminatory imagery, softening its almost Jacoponian tone while also suggesting the reintroduction of an inverted, almost a pagan view of reality:

> Cristo, pensoso palpito,
> Astro incarnato nell'umane tenebre,
> Fratello che t'immoli
> Perennemente per riedificare
> Umanamente l'uomo,
> Santo, Santo che soffri,
> Maestro e fratello e Dio che ci sai deboli,
> Santo, Santo che soffri
> Per liberare dalla morte i morti
> E sorreggere noi infelici vivi,
> D'un pianto solo mio non piango piú,
> Ecco, Ti chiamo, Santo,
> Santo, Santo che soffri.

Christ, thoughtful heart-beat, star incarnate in human darkness, brother who crucify yourself perennially to rebuild mankind humanely, Saint, Saint, who suffer, master and brother and God who know we are weak, Saint, Saint who

> suffer, to free the dead from death and to sustain us the joyless living, with my own tears alone I no longer weep, behold, I call to you, Saint, Saint, Saint who suffer.

The result is a virtual updating of the medieval *Lauda* and a redimensioning of its highly emotional rhythms through the evocation of a series of carefully contrived analogies.

Precisely because aesthetic and humanist elements still play a prominent part in these lines we should perhaps beware of Marvardi's claim that such poems imply Ungaretti's whole-hearted conversion to Catholicism.[63] On the contrary, the poet's occasional religious images appear to emerge more from the peculiar circumstances of his life than from any dramatic change in his outlook, and in no way can they be regarded as incompatible with those broad humanist attitudes which Marvardi has himself appositely defined elsewhere as the natural religion of man. So, in preference to his suggestion of a possible conversion, Piemontese's views seem far more likely to fit the facts. After asking himself whether Ungaretti was a strictly Catholic or merely a religious poet in the broadest sense of the word, the latter observed: 'Certo, se una definizione di tale genere si dovesse adoperare per lui, bisognerebbe accontentarsi della seconda. Ed anche questa apparirebbe, francamente, ancora un po' troppo impegnativo.'[64] ('Certainly, if such a definition were to be adopted for him, we should have to be satisfied with the second. And even that would appear, frankly, a little too committed.') In other words Ungaretti's religious imagery at present reveals another aspect of the complex song of modern anguish, and although it now makes use of specifically Christian symbols, the reason for this is that they happen to be part and parcel of the poet's cultural inheritance and not because he himself has suddenly abandoned his humanist attitude of 'pietas' for an arid, transcendental faith.

Still further proof of Piemontese's contention is to be deduced from the fact that towards the end of the collection some of the poet's most successful lyrics again display that rich atavistic inspiration previously featuring in *Sentimento del tempo*. This is especially the case with 'Non gridate piú' where the poet's social and personal piety – now deepened but not replaced by a sense of religious awe – leads him to plead with his fellowmen for a more reverent and understanding attitude by the living towards the muted voices of the dead. So, since this type of lyricism ultimately tends to draw *Il Dolore* back into the mainstream of Ungaretti's lyricism, the collection can perhaps in the last resort be considered as aiming at something more than a personal interlude in his lyrical development. The point is further emphasized by the reappearance of a narrative style, not wholly unlike the laconic manner we saw in 'In memoria' in *Allegria*. It is a new impressionistic mode of narrative which will later become fully developed in *La terra promessa* (1950); but, although its presence in embryo here already indicates a refocusing of his dominant moods, the tone of the collection proves overwhelmingly to be one of baroque allegory and its lyrical texture is far less hermetically allusive than any of the poet's earlier or subsequent verse.

★ ★ ★ ★ ★ ★

In *La terra promessa* we immediately revert to Ungaretti's verbal alchemies as he tries to re-create the elements of his erstwhile 'paese innocente' upon a more sophisticated level of feeling. Now a Debussy-like melodiousness tends to emerge from his lyrical texture, while the poet's clearer delineation of his mythological framework also gives the collection a richer cultural density than its predecessors. Its starting-point remains that traumatic sense of ageing which already formed the hinterland of *Sentimento del tempo* and which was temporarily phased out in *Il Dolore*. But the continuity of the theme over such a long period is partly to be accounted for by the fact that the key-poem 'Canzone' was first drafted as early as 1935.[65] *La terra promessa* is in this sense the chronological successor of the former volume and is only indirectly affected by the baroque rage of the latter.

As the poet moves towards the threshold of old age he takes up a curiously contemplative attitude to life, one which involves a retrospective examination of all his previous experiences. It almost seems at times as if these are completely detached from his sensibility and placed in a sphere of pure aesthetic suspension. His approach amounts to a virtual metaphysic of the imagination as he considers that he is about to 'rinascere ad altro grado della realtà' ('be reborn at another grade of reality'), to enter a state in which the fires of passion have died away and a feeling of mortality and futility has suddenly become acute. Fortunately, this sense of the approaching void of death does not lead to despair, but provides a heightened form of insight: one which he defines as 'il concoscersi essere dal non essere, essere dal nulla . . . il conoscersi pascalianamente essere dal nulla'[66] ('knowing oneself to be from non-being, being from nothingness . . . knowing oneself to be, Pascalian-like, from nothing'). The problem now to be faced is consequently that of overcoming one's sense of existential emptiness and purposelessness, and the poet gradually adopts a modernized form of Petrarchism as the principal means of reviving his lyricism. In other words, he uses as a palliative to the starkness and arid intellectualism of old age the hallucinatory kingdom of his lifetime's memories, and their lyrical consolidation in the present melancholy circumstances immerses his imagery in an atmosphere of nostalgic consolation. Nevertheless he cannot entirely escape from that 'orrida conoscenza' ('horrible awareness'), the dispassionate self-knowledge, of ageing; and so the secrets he brings back from his lyrical flights into the past are now steeped in a sense of disillusionment. The very obsessiveness with which he deals with the theme of mortality in fact eventually stimulates him to dwell meditatively on this last climacteric in human life, and he stresses its tendency to dissociate the appetite from the reason, especially at moments of physical exhaustion, when each human creature's feeling of insecurity appears to take on a fresh dimension, a sense of mortal foreboding.

Once more the concepts of the active and passive memories provide a basis for a series of lyrical dreams in which the poet highlights his present soul-searing experiences, and this endless dialectic of activity and stasis continues to form the two poles of his world-picture. But in 'Canzone' he tries to orchestrate them in a subtler manner, by creating images which involve an emotive interplay of light and shade at the breaking of dawn. We are fortunate enough to possess Ungaretti's own interpretation of this lyric and his method of approach justifies our earlier remarks on the importance to be attached to the variations he rings on his analogical keyboard.[67] The protagonist is the artist towards the end of his life, at a time when he has at last consolidated his experiential 'secrets' in his poetic memory. These secrets are, as we know, the stuff and substance of his personality and are intended to fill the void which the poet believes haunts every man in old age. As fully matured memories they are symbolized here as beautiful young girls swimming contentedly through the waters of Lethe:

Nude, le braccia di segreti sazie,
a nuoto hanno del Lete svolto il fondo,
Adagio sciolto le veementi grazie
E le stanchezze onde luce fu il mondo.

Naked, their arms with secrets sated, they have swum the bottom of Lethe, slowly liberated the vehement graces and the wearinesses whence the world was light.

The nudity of these young maidens introduces a perceptual sensuousness into the dispassionate state Ungaretti feels he is about to enter after a lifetime's toil; but the scene also stresses that the full light of insight, the clarity of perfect understanding, will only be enjoyed when eventually the poet reaches a point of self-extinction. His state of immortality will indeed then involve the final setting of his entire personality, Petrarchan-like, in the firmament of the racial memory; but in the meantime he has to content himself with an intermediate stage, the recessive void of dying passion:

> Nulla è muto piú della strana strada
> Dove foglia non nasce o cade o sverna,
> Dove nessuna cosa pena o aggrada,
> Dove la veglia mai, mai il sonno alterna.

Nothing is more silent than the strange road where no leaf burgeons, falls or winters, where nothing ever pains or pleases, where waking never, never alternates with slumber.

How can such aridity be overcome? Possibly through a form of poetic death closely followed by a fresh awakening. Then alone will the shades of the prison-house suddenly disappear and a new world of intelligent psycho-sensuous contentment be reached. For this purpose Ungaretti now seems to equate the dramatic crystallization of memory with his previous ideas on changing register, thereby re-creating 'il nulla' in a consolatory Bergsonian sense. This also explains why the process of recollection is symbolized by the coming of dawn, which is an archetypal form of symbolic promise we can read into his lyricism right back to *Allegria*. Here its light is the incarnation of our 'imperfect' human beauty as it is re-evoked at the end of time in the regained 'perfect' beauty of a state of Being. Hence in his view the function of poetry is not to portray an absolute world of Platonic Ideas, it is simply to release echoes of our regained primeval innocence whenever the poet can recapture them in the concrete.[68] The basic aim of *La terra promessa* is accordingly the same as in *Sentimento del tempo*, 'di suscitare una realtà mitica, una realtà che trasfiguri il linguaggio per profondità di memoria, o se volete per profondità di storia'[69] ('to awaken a mythical reality, a reality which transfigures language through memorial profundity, or if you like through historical profundity'). Presumably the new dawn portrayed in the poem is in this sense a glimpse of our 'innocence regained' in the fullness of time, through a gradual aesthetic maturation of thought and language.

The poem's half-light perspectives thus offer the promise of yet another 'paese innocente', which is neither the promised land of death nor that of pre-birth, but the promised land of fulfilled adulthood. To attain this land is the goal of each human soul; and so, although every moment of self-awareness appears to require Ungaretti to break through the crustacean-like growths around his dulled senses before he is intermittently capable of overcoming their fossilization and glimpsing the 'ossessiva mira' ('obsessive goal') of purity associated with the 'prima immagine' ('primal image'), nevertheless the poet is still occasionally able to transform his present negative sense of 'il nulla' and replace its implications of existential emptiness with the 'breve salma' ('brief spoil') of a lyrically matured phenomenological essence, depicted in a pure condition of *epoché*:

> Preda dell'impalpabile propagine
> Di muri, eterni dei minuti eredi,
> Sempre ci esclude piú, la prima immagine,
> Ma, a lampi, rompe il gelo e riconquide.
>
> Piú sfugga vera, l'ossessiva mira,
> E sia bella, piú tocca a nudo calma
> E germe, appena schietta idea, d'ira
> Rifreme, avversa al nulla, in breve salma.

A prey to the tangled skein of barriers, eternal inheritors of time, the primal image excludes us more and more, but in flashes it cracks the ice and reconquers. The truer it is, the more the obsessive goal may flee, and the more beautiful it is, the more it touches nakedly the stillness, and as a seed of wrathful passion, scarcely changed to pure idea, it quivers, opposed to the void, as a brief spoil of flesh.

From such an experience there arises a new kind of human purity, not the purity of death or nothingness but the purity of orphically refined human recollections, evoked as a cone of images against the continually evolving 'voice' of the lyric tradition.

How does one reawaken these resonances and stretch their transient forms over the pure cosmic void? The process of their encapsulation is objectivized in the following hermetically recaptured images of the poet's childhood ranging right back to scenes of the Sahara desert:

> Rivi indovina, suscita la palma:
> dita dedale svela, se sospira.

Streams it divines, uplifts the palm: if it sighs, it reveals daedal fingers.

Fortunately Ungaretti himself explains the underlying meaning of such recalls. The initial stages of the poetic task, it seems, are performed under the aegis of Iris and they involve the combining of the absolute and the contingent. For him this goddess was originally 'la divinità che legava l'eterno all'effimero'[70] ('the divinity which linked the eternal to the ephemeral') and as a result was mythologically well-placed to weave the primal image over the void. But as the task became greater with the growth of civilization it was taken over by Daedalus, with his 'dita capaci di aprire i labirinti'[71] ('fingers capable of opening labyrinths'); and it is under the auspices of this *homo faber* that the modern poet completes his work. From its complexity there emerges imagery capable of evoking a deeper understanding of the multiple facets of modern life, and at this point the bedouin-symbol undergoes yet another transformation: he is now metamorphosed into the archetypal figure of a modern Ulysses. In his old age the poet appropriates the mythological character's obsessive curiosity and wanderlust, even though – like Dante's Ulysses before him – he is all too aware of the fact that the foreknowledge he seeks is that of his own death:

> E se, tuttora fuoco d'avventura,
> Tornati gli attimi da angoscia a brama,
> D'Itaca varco le fuggenti mura,
> So, ultima metamorfosi all'aurora,
> Oramai so che il filo della trama
> Umana, pare rompersi in quell'ora.

And if, still fired by adventure, with time changed back from anguish to desire, I cross the fleeing walls of Ithaca, I know, as a final metamorphosis of dawn, I know henceforth that the thread of the human web seems to break at that moment.

Although we have reached here the ultimate limits of the human lifespan, the spectre of personal death is still not presented in a negative fashion. The poet even sees it as a further adventure: one which will bring him greater clarity and insight and create that ideal state of suspension into which the lyrical personality finally subsides as it becomes consolidated among the timeless poetic hierarchies of the past. Such an accommodation is not of a static Gozzanian order, it takes place in a dynamic sphere of memory and personal fulfilment.[72] The idea is expressed in this lyric by way of a refined artifice, the repetition with totally different implications of those earlier lines which described the aridity of old age:

> Nulla piú nuovo parve della strada
> Dove lo spazio mai non si digrada
> Per la luce o per tenebra, o altro tempo.

Nothing fresher there seemed than the road where space is never degraded through light or shadow, or other time.

The situation is in other words again inversionary and death in its finality is regarded as yet another noviciate.

Because of the subtle articulation of its imagery we gradually realize that despite its apparent fragmentariness *La terra promessa* is the collection in which Ungaretti's art reaches complete maturity. It represents the whole panorama of our human tragedy as seen through the eyes of three separate, but closely connected, mythical figures: Dido, Palinurus and Aeneas. By remaining simply a background figure Aeneas is, admittedly, implicit rather than explicit in the work; yet his attitudes dominate it and he radiates a hidden optimism contrasting with the gloom and despair surrounding the disintegrating personalities of the other two protagonists. Symbolically, therefore, he stands for human constructiveness and poetic liberation as opposed to the manifestations of bodily and spiritual decay evoked in the myths of Dido (the trauma of ageing) and Palinurus (the aridity of blind fidelity).

Dido's drama is the first to be represented and it combines a bodily with a spiritual decline as she first becomes aware of the waning of her beauty and tries to reconcile herself to the approach of old age. This theme runs right through the 'Cori descrittivi di stati d'animo di Didone' which may be considered an intimate diary of damnation. In its poetic texture we find echoes of all Ungaretti's masters ranging from Virgil to Leopardi, while even lines from John Donne transposed in one later chorus reveal his continuing preoccupation with baroque tastes.[73] However, a prolonged examination of sources would be out of place here. What is of greater interest is the tonal maturity which the lyricism now attains, especially after Dido has made the traumatic discovery of the fading of her charms:

Grido e brucia il mio cuore senza pace
Da quando piú non sono
Se non cosa in rovina e abbandonata.[74]

I cry out and my heart burns ceaselessly since I am no longer anything but a ruined and abandoned object.

The depth of this maturity may be measured by the subtleness and allusiveness of the analysis of her decline, in which the still glowing fires of passion are offset by the lengthening shadows of old age.

Before approaching the poem from a textural standpoint we should perhaps note in passing that it unfolds as an essentialized narrative, not unlike that originally found in *Allegria* or in modified form in *Il Dolore*. It is a mode of narration which continues to ignore precise factual detail but nevertheless embraces in its imaginative sweep all the psychological essentials of the protagonist's life, while at the same time casting a cold intellectual light on moments of dramatic stress. In short, what is evoked is neither an account of the vicissitudes of Dido's existence nor of her temporally evolving, emotional transitions, but certain critical psychological foci and the intense lyrical power which they cumulatively acquire. Since this is the case in most of the other poems as well, a deeper insight into the collection as a whole may be obtained by comparing the play of variants from the major lyrics.

The very copiousness of these variants emphasizes once more the painstaking nature of Ungaretti's craftsmanship and indicates the lengths to which he was prepared to go in his efforts to track down the appropriate allusive resonances in the language of his time. Even in 'Canzone' the number of variants is considerable, and the following are just a few drafts of the first line:

Le nude braccia di segreti sazie . . .

Their naked arms with secrets sated . . .

Le care braccia di segreti sazie . . .

Their dear arms with secrets sated . . .

Now, though adequate, neither of the versions actually touches a poetic chord capable of making the whole poem vibrate in unison with the lyricism of the past. Such a harmonic is only found when the poet finally discovers his definitive word-order, as follows:

Nude, le braccia di segreti sazie . . .

Naked, their arms with secrets sated . . .

in which the displacement of the adjective in a typically classical manner gives the line far greater allusiveness and shows how effective the subtle literary exercises performed in the poet's workshop can be. Similar processes take place in the 'Cori' themselves and each produces extremely delicate effects.

Normally in the lyrics addressed to Dido Ungaretti tries to approach as closely as possible to that tremulous aura of fleeting sensations characterizing the inner experience of his protagonist. A typical example is to be found in the second chorus whose definitive form reads:

Lunare allora inavvertita nacque
Eco, e si fuse al brivido dell'acque.

Lunar then and unperceived, Echo was born, and merged with the shimmering of the waters.

These lines refer to memorial stirrings in the mind of the ageing queen as she meditates at the water's edge on the sharpness of her youthful passions, and we can compare their effectiveness with an earlier variant:

Lunare, allora apparve, ma si giacque
Eco, perplessa al tremolio dell'acque.

Lunar then Echo appeared, but lay perplexed by the shimmering of the waters.

From a linguistic standpoint these changes may not seem substantial but they nevertheless account for the final version's greater imaginative resonance. For instance, the verb 'nacque' is far more alert than the colourless 'apparve'; likewise the heaviness of 'si giacque' is replaced by the touch of surprise latent in the sound and sense of 'inavvertita'; while again the imprecision of 'perplessa al tremolio' with its diffuse overtones is transformed into the visio-auditory exactness of 'si fuse al brivido'. Accordingly, these musical modifications bring about convergences between sound and sense which are of crucial importance. So, quite apart from the fact that the enjambement is more dramatic after 'giacque' has been removed, we note in the earlier version a certain lack of fluidity caused by the use of unvoiced plosives or gutturals like 'p' and 't' or 'c' and 'g'. In the final version, by contrast, these are replaced by their voiced counterparts 'b' or 'd' or else are made subservient to an interplay of voiced and unvoiced fricatives and sibilants like 'f', 'v' and 's', which reflect more appropriately the quicksilver motion of the image-stream. From this it follows that in Ungaretti's mature verse it is the combinatorial sensitiveness of the inner ear which finally guides the poet in his lyrical experimentation, through the virtual semanticization as an undertone of appropriate phonemic groups. Despite the still growing complexity of his lyrical situations, however, he does not aim at present at re-creating atmospheres as concretely as he sometimes did earlier: he simply tries to allude to them through subtle and evocative resonances, which tend to integrate his own personal word-music with that of the lyric tradition at all levels of implication. As a result, the authenticity of his lyrical efforts can hardly be called into question, because what he was striving to achieve was an improvement in the receptivity and suggestiveness of his melodic line by making his imagination a more adequate instrument for reflecting the delicacy of his lyrical substance and the rhythmical 'soubresauts' ('quiverings') of his conscience.[75]

Just as Dido is a symbol of waning emotion, so Palinurus is a symbol of the sclerosis of the intellect. The distinction which Ungaretti himself makes between them is that between 'l'esperienza della natura' ('experience of nature') and 'l'esperienza della mente' ('experience of the mind'); and we soon discover that the archetypal analogy depicting this slow calcification of the mind is another 'roccia di gridi' just like the previous one we encountered in 'Tutto ho perduto' in *Il Dolore* (1947). The essentialized drama presented in the 'Recitativo di Palinuro' is an emblematic elaboration of the death struggle of Aeneas's faithful helmsman at the end of his journey from Troy. In classical mythology Palinurus then fell into the sea off the south coast of Italy and was either drowned or murdered by the natives. An analogy is thus drawn by Ungaretti between his unshakeable fidelity and the so-called 'scoglio di Palinuro' ('rock of Palinurus') near Elea, which the poet describes in *Il deserto e dopo*.[76] Like the rock which commemorates him, Palinurus appears to be a symbol of mental fossilization: an attitude to life which can only be overcome by a purposeful and self-fulfilling existence. This explains not only his tragic fate but why Aeneas took over from his helmsman the plotting of the course of Italian destiny after the promised land had been reached. As a further overtone, given Ungaretti's present circumstances, the myth is no doubt intended to express the hope that his own bedouin-like temperament will become regenerated in old age and regain spiritual control over the unfolding of his existence.

The poet provides a short exegesis of certain aspects of the 'Recitativo' in his preface, where he explains that Palinurus is turned into the 'immortalità d'un sasso' ('immortality of a stone') solely because he allows himself to be absorbed by an immutable ideal instead of remaining 'disponibile' or receptive to experience. As his world of fixed emotions disappears with the approach of the promised land, a curious baroque heightening of his senses takes place. It involves the creation of a dialectic between dreams and reality, between purposeful activity and pure contemplation; and eventually he finds himself compelled by some inner demon to opt wholly for the world of dreams, since he is quite unable to make a realist assessment of his new situation by abandoning his obsession of fidelity. The poem is in other words an emblematic act of dying and Palinurus's drama attempts to symbolize his mind's immortal fidelity to a static idealism which inevitably results in a Promethean fury. His mood of frustration derives from an overwhelming desire to eternalize the social habit at the expense of the authentic and uninhibited emotional drive. Yet according to Ungaretti it is that drive's mutable emotional charge which evaluates a situation and causes it to persist in the memory as a meaningful image of life:

Per strenua fedeltà decaddi a emblema
Di disperanza e, preda d'ogni furia,
Riscosso via via a insulti freddi d'onde,
Ingigantivo d'impeto mortale,
Piú folle d'esse, folle sfida al sonno.

Through strenuous fealty I declined to an emblem of despair and, a prey to all furies, battered continuously by the cold insults of waves, I grew gigantic with human impulsiveness, more crazed than them, a wild challenge to slumber.

Such an absolute passion for truth accompanied by a failure to realize that all human truths can only be expressed through the 'breve salma' ('brief spoil') of the image was bound to lead Palinurus to a Leopardian acknowledgement of the 'vanità del tutto' ('vanity of everything'). As his mind discovered the purposelessness of his continued existence, he projected this discovery imaginatively as a philosophy of despair. Such an attitude dissociated him completely from the problems of living, because he was no longer in a position to enjoy the responses of his senses nor appreciate those memorial consolations gained by the hallowing of imagery through time. So essentially Ungaretti reiterates in this poem that redemption is only possible through a psycho-sensuous approach to reality, as implied perhaps in the title of the volume itself.

One other poem is of particular interest in this volume, 'Variazioni su nulla', since it again underlines the difference of approach by the nihilistic philosopher on the one hand and the positive lyricist on the other to the whole problem of time. The distinction established is similar to that which Montanari has drawn between *aevum* and *tempus*[77], the former representing humanized time and the associated idea of 'durata' and the latter the gratuitous flux of 'cosmic' time which does not bear the imprint of human feeling. Although 'Variazioni su nulla' deals mainly with 'cosmic' time, its emphasis on the fleeting presence of a disincarnate human hand suggests an orphic reconditioning of the universe, and time almost becomes humanized as a result, creating and perpetuating a mysterious cosmico-empathic temporality:

La mano in ombra la clessidra volse,
E, di sabbia, il nonnulla che trascorre
Silente, è unica cosa che ormai s'oda
E, essendo udita, in buio non scompaia.

> The hour-glass turned the hand to shadow, and the trifling flow of sand that slips away silently, is the only thing which can now be heard and, being heard, does not vanish in the gloom.

Once he has justified a humanized time-flow, moreover, the poet goes on in 'Segreto del poeta' to justify the artist's representation of the condition of *aevum*; and finally he hopes even to justify in the same way the bedouin outlook, now apparently metamorphosed into that of a modern Aeneas in the 'Cori d'Enea'.[78] Aeneas, the empire-builder, is just the right type of person to rule over Ungaretti's inner empire of memories and he uses the Trojan hero's optimistic attitudes towards life to counterbalance the despair of Dido and Palinurus. Hence we are probably intended to regard the 'promised land' of this collection as a polyvalent symbol of various promised lands which subsume the accumulated experiences of the poet's entire lifespan, not excluding the heightened intelligence of his old age and his shadowy but no less significant premonitions of death. Likewise, throughout the collection's somewhat impressionistic unfolding we find that the two forms of memory, the active and passive forms postulated previously, irradiate and negate by turns the poet's deepest hopes and aspirations.

★ ★ ★ ★ ★ ★

After *La terra promessa* we are hardly surprised to find that Ungaretti seeks from his art some kind of memorial rehabilitation and consolation for the tragedy of living, and the result is a rethreading in the Petrarchan key of his past experiences in *Un grido e paesaggi* (1952). The principal poem contained in the collection is 'Monologhetto' which was first written in prose for Italian radio and broadcast on New Year's Day 1952. Even so, we should not for this reason dismiss the later poetic version as simply a *vers de circonstance*. Instead, it again illustrates the new dramatic and narrative style already formulated by the poet in the experimentation of his previous volume. Yet, precisely because of the pre-existing prose version, the structure of this particular composition is less essentialized, less allusive, and more realistic than most earlier ones. Furthermore, in spite of the fact that the poet's memories are evoked concretely and appear as a series of 'social' masks superimposed on his underlying orphic *persona*, the inner unity of the lyric is again ensured by the imaginative device of 'simultaneità'. This recurrent artifice, we recall, earlier caused all the poet's experiences to converge as a single cone of images, but at present they are projected not through a linear motion in space but by means of a recessive movement in time.

The poet's use of external elements as inverted temporal structures within the confines of his overall myth is reflected in his adoption, as symbols, of the false (because summery) Februaries of the southern hemisphere; while their associated carnival-times are presented as the carnival of the poet's own existence. He starts his story at that time of the year because February was the month of his own birth and also in ancient myth represented an initiation. But behind the whole poem there also lurks the image of the ineluctable flow of the hour-glass as depicted in 'Variazioni su nulla', whose tragic significance is regularly punctuated by the cyclical return of the poet's birthday. As Bigongiari has explained, the aim behind the entire dialectic of the narration is to bring about 'uno scambio tra apparenza e memoria' ('an exchange between appearance and memory'),[79] to create an atmosphere in which Italian experiences can be etched upon Brazilian and Egyptian backgrounds while at the same time Brazilian and oriental feelings and modes of perception are used to redimension the Italian scene. In the process we are provided with a mirror-image of the inner topography of the poet's lifetime and with a cone of memories subsuming his entire human presence. This presence is destined to form, as perhaps the theme of 'Variazioni su nulla' indicated, an integral part of mankind's immortal testimony before the Gods.

The experiences of his life have been so shattering that Ungaretti now finally tempers his poetic faith with a note of deeply felt existential sorrow.

But, even so, a continuing belief in the validity of the life-force is still adumbrated in his elegiac attitudes, and the poem ends on a muted reaffirmation of the importance of human values:

Non c'è, altro non c'è su questa terra
Che un barlume di vero
E il nulla della polvere,
Anche se matto incorreggibile,
Incontro al lampo dei miraggi
Nell'intimo e nei gesti, il vivo
Tendersi sembra sempre.

There is nothing, there is nothing else on this earth but a glimmer of truth and the nothingness of dust, even if, mad and incorrigible, against the flash of its mirages, in gestures and intimate self, the living man always seems to strain.

Such a faith is at bottom the rejection of the metaphysical attitudes advocated by the symbolists and a full acceptance of man's existential condition. It is accompanied by an equally strong reaffirmation of the efficacy of art and its ability to hypostasize momentary experiences. This explains why in 'Monologhetto' the poet continues to aim at a multidimensional synthesis of imaginative and narrative effects, which he achieves by ignoring the negative aspects of external time and by using its cyclical processes as a pattern on which to transform his inner feelings. In so doing, he succeeds in Spagnoletti's words in alchemizing an authentic 'tempo dell'anima'[80] ('time of the spirit') which not only expresses his own self-sincerity, his strict adherence to the rhythm of his intimate development, but which also underlines the general point that modern poets need not resort to a romantic escape from a realistic frame of reference in order to achieve a full and mature form of self-expression.

In this collection in other words we are moving still further into the world of supreme intelligence associated with old age, and now the very attenuation of Ungaretti's senses paradoxically allows him to rekindle the flame of his inspiration in *Il taccuino del vecchio* (1960). Although the choruses to Aeneas still do not appear, the poet again shows that he can be as disturbed as ever by the 'trop-plein' of his momentary feelings. His continuing vigour is particularly emphasized in his desire to reinvolve himself in life, which proves that he had not yet succumbed to the sensory sclerosis which Leopardi had suggested was the inevitable scourge of old age. So in the 'Ultimi cori della terra promessa' he clings to life like the moth to the flame, while at the same time sensing deep within himself the cosmic futility of existence:

È sempre pieno di promesse il nascere
Sebbene sia straziante

E l'esperienza d'ogni giorno insegni
Che nel legarsi, sciogliersi o durare
Non sono i giorni se non vago fumo.[81]

Birth is always full of promise, although it is agonizing and the experience of every day teaches that in fusing together, melting or lasting, one's days are nothing more than wayward smoke.

Clearly this attitude to life is purely Petrarchan, enriched by a hopeful nostalgia arising from a memorial consolidation of experience and an atavistic perspective on death seen as the very sounding-board of man's cultural progress. Here the poet is by no means singing merely to keep his courage up; his intention is to hold a mirror up to life and to meditate deeply upon death as he has always done, thereby proving that it is ultimately a form of absolution, a higher state of consciousness, attainable only after the dissolution of the flesh. The issue is clearly enunciated in *Esercizio di metrica* in 'Un grido e paesaggi' where the process of dying is envisaged as an orphic rebirth:

L'urto patito che scinde,
Sorte ripresati Eterno, se, già
Fetida, l'alvo reclami che
È orrido a ingenui, la spoglia tua,
Giú essa sarà, dal suo mistero esule,
Sparsa nel sonno, non sozza, vera.

Having suffered the cleaving blow, fate having remade you Eternal, if, already mouldering, you seek the tomb which is horrible to the ingenuous, your mortal spoil, exiled from its mystery, down below will be scattered in a sleep, not foul but true.

Because of its steady approach, death is seen here in all its concrete, physical horror; but at the same time it remains the secret orphic activator of the human spirit, the sphere within which the traditional inflections of the Italian race are modulated and its cultural continuity ensured. It is indeed this consistency in his outlook towards art and death which is the touchstone of all Ungaretti's poetry. For in his view, without the two limits of artistic purity and final extinction to measure themselves against, poets would experience no sense of finitude or individuality at all. If then we accept this doctrine as the core of his philosophy, we discover that his hermetic imagery, while being regressive and infolded from a conceptual standpoint, is based fundamentally on an inner logic of ethical and aesthetic resonances. Through a subtle association of concealed conceptual symbols and living sensations he tries to unravel the relationships which bind the modern writer to the past tradition; and, in the process, he exploits the shadowy resourcefulness of death – the ultimate continuum of the racial memory – in the hope of deepening and enriching the fabric of present-day life.

Ungaretti's last collection *Dialogo* (1968) not only contains poems by him but also by Bruna Bianco, a young Brazilian poetess whom he met while on a visit to São Paulo in 1966. He describes his first meeting with her in highly dramatic terms in the poem '12 settembre 1966', where she seems to be the very flame of love in its essence:

Sei comparsa al portone
In un vestito rosso
Per dirmi che sei fuoco
Che consuma e riaccende.

You appeared at the doorway in a red dress to tell me you are fire which consumes and rekindles.

She in turn responded to his love and, when faced with the imminence of his departure from Brazil and his despairing sense of mortality, she raised the clarion-call of youth:

Ma dall'esilio ci libererà
L'ostinato mio amore.

But from exile will liberate us my persistent love.

For a time she does indeed manage to tilt the balance for him away from the stoicism of old age towards a new participation in life. But, although she rekindled the fires of love and Ungaretti himself considered that an eternal – if existential – bond of fidelity had been forged between them, the poetry he addresses to her is always touched with the profundity of his desolation, as may be seen in the second version of 'Conchiglia':

Se tu quella paura,
Se tu la scruti bene,
Mia timorosa amata,
Narreresti soffrendo
D'un amore demente
Ormai solo evocabile
Nell'ora degli spettri.

If you should examine that fear closely, my timorous beloved, anguish-stricken you would tell of a demented love now only to be evoked in the hour of spectres.

So, although she came over to Italy to join in the celebrations for his eightieth birthday and conducted a considerable correspondence with him, surprisingly the poet ultimately transferred his affections elsewhere.

Their object was a Yugoslav girl called Dunja whose name, he tells us, meant 'universe' in Arabic. He again speaks of her with immediate and overwhelming emotion in the second poem he addresses to her:

> Il velluto dello sguardo di Dunja
> Fulmineo torna presente pietà.

The velvet of Dunja's glance becomes present pity in a flash.

He explains that she reminded him of his mother's old servant who was also a Yugoslav; but the most important feature in Dunja's nature is her resemblance to the poet's former Eve archetype, for she symbolizes for him redemption beyond memory:

> D'oltre l'oblio rechi
> D'oltre il ricordo i lampi.

From beyond oblivion you bring flashes, from beyond memory.

When he utters such words it seems as if Ungaretti has finally reached his promised land, which is now no longer a gratuitous and unmemoried state of nature but a remembrance-laden paradise regained, a spiritual kingdom of serenity and fulfilment where he feels that he can commune once more with an equally redeemed figure of womanhood.

★ ★ ★ ★ ★ ★

We can therefore sum up Ungaretti's poetics by referring back to the image of a 'corolla di tenebre' in 'I Fiumi' which the poet subsequently deepened in implication by way of his inversionary techniques. What that early lyric achieved was the creation of a cone of simultaneous sensations in accordance with the aesthetic doctrine advocated by the futurists. Yet at the same time it also provided a lyrical perspective and a mythology of creativity which futurist art did not itself possess. Such acute critical intelligence is closely linked with the growth and development of the hermetic tradition; but, although Ungaretti can be considered both as its guide and master, he was not himself dominated by any preconceived literary doctrines, except in the widest sense of the word. Certainly he had his own metaphysical view of man's perfectibility and he explained his position in the following way: 'Come intendo io, infatti, il mondo, quale è il mio modo particolare d'intendere l'universo? C'era un universo puro, umanamente una – diciamolo – cosa assurda: una materia immateriale. Questa purezza diventa una materia materiale in seguito a un'offesa fatta al Creatore, non so per quale avvenimento. Ma insomma, per un avvenimento straordinario, di ordine cosmico, questa materia è corrotta

– e ha principio il tempo, e principia la storia. Questo è il mio modo di sentire le cose, non è una verità, ma è un modo di sentire le cose: io le sento, le cose, in tale modo.'[82] ('How indeed do I understand the world, what is my particular way of understanding the universe? There was once a pure universe, humanly – let's admit it – an absurdity: a dematerialized materiality. This purity became materialized matter as a result of an injury perpetrated on the Creator, by who knows what event. But anyway, through some extraordinary event, of cosmic dimensions, this matter became corrupted – and time and history began. This is my way of understanding things, it is not truth, but my way of seeing things: I feel things, I feel them in this way.') But, since this whole argument is more of an act of faith than a self-consistent doctrine, it did not have the effect of placing his lyricism in any conceptual or artistic strait-jacket. His aim was not to exemplify a certain theoretical outlook, it was to assert a principle of artistic freedom within the lyrical tradition. As Gaëton Picon remarked, 'ce qui définit l'artiste, c'est la passion qu'il voue à son art: nullement l'illusion d'une vérité absolue.'[83] ('what defines the artist is the passion he devotes to his art: by no means the illusion of an absolute truth'). This is particularly true in Ungaretti's case. So, even though his illuminations seem at first to be 'absolute' bolts from the blue, they are in reality products of a patient inner maturation of thought and a subtle experimentation with language. Together these processes have given rise to a distinctive Italian poetry in the first half of the twentieth century, a fact which is itself remarkable when we consider that all the fashions and aesthetic developments of the age have been clearly weighted towards French – or at least Franco-European – tastes.

The secret behind this success, as we have indicated earlier, was the abandonment by the Italians of the French symbolists' idealist attitude to life in favour of an indigenous realist approach. Hence, whereas the modern French advocates of 'la poésie pure' ('pure poetry') created a lyricism which was preponderantly speculative in tone and inspiration, the hermetic poets in Italy avoided any similar Narcissus-like introspection and attempted to link their basic metaphysical perspectives to the broader emotional, but not crudely political, tensions of the society in which they lived. In the process of lyrical transfiguration Ungaretti may be regarded as the artist of the group and Montale, as we shall see later, its poet. Yet such a definition is again simply a matter of emphasis, because both poets accepted from the outset that a contingent approach to aesthetics was the only way of mediating between the spiritual and material elements of life and of creating a poetry which would ideate – not idealize – the lyrical truths of their age.

Ungaretti's method of accomplishing his poetic task was to encapsulate each of his lyrical insights in an appropriate analogy and to blend together whole series of such flashes into a meditative lyricism. His poetic success is thus linked with the problem of tonal duration, which Silori has defined as 'un fatto d'ordine espressivo in senso latissimo, cioè semantico, psicologico e fors'anche morfologico e fonico, laddove la continuità non sarebbe che un concetto rigidamente temporale'[84] ('a factor of an expressive order in the widest sense, that is, in a semantic, psychological, and perhaps a morphological and phonic sense also, whereas continuity would only be a rigidly temporal conception'). What is, in fact, at its base is the poet's authentically evolving personality, no true example of which can according to Gide 'échapper à sa propre réalisation'[85] ('escape from its own fulfilment'). Ungaretti works out his lyrical destiny, as we have seen, through a dialectical process first noted by the poet himself. For he tells us that his unswerving aim throughout his career was always to perfect 'un linguaggio poetico dove, nella ricerca del vero che è il sacro, la memoria s'abolisca nel sogno e dal sogno rifluisca agli oggetti, e viceversa, incessantemente'[86] ('a poetic language in which, in the search for truth which is sacred, memory abolishes itself in the dream and flows back from the dream to objects and vice versa, incessantly'). Gradually he so refined his aesthetic approach that his poetry became capable of evaluating in a non-prescriptive sense all the nuances of feeling produced by the immersion of his sensibility in the cultural flux of modern society; and for this reason alone he must be regarded as one of the most sensitive and responsive, yet wholly undogmatic, poets of the twentieth century.

CHAPTER X

The poetry of Eugenio Montale

Whereas Ungaretti's verse is a process of self-purification through suffering, Montale's is first and foremost a descent into a realm of existential damnation. Moreover, since we sense that his poetry has been written in the sure knowledge that all has been lost, we find that he normally relegates hopes to the outer limits of perception – to a narrow area of subliminal feelings where the flesh and the spirit uneasily combine. In sharp contrast, therefore, with Ungaretti's analogical perspectives evoking a possible salvation lying concealed within the very fabric of the cultural tradition, he conceives of a shrunken and meaningless universe in which the mind – except for brief periods of illumination – is totally imprisoned within the confines of a metaphysical cell. Yet, while he dismisses the human condition as one of almost completely unrelieved misery, he too searches diffidently at times for inexplicable moments of serenity to assuage the anguish of his metaphysically-based despair; and, to satisfy his sensibility's innate craving for some sort of absolute, he occasionally evokes in passing certain hypostasized states of purely existential grace. On first inspection these moments of liberation seem founded on nothing more substantial than an unexpected balancing of the humours of the body and, as such, they offer the reader little by way of spiritual consolation. But his half-submerged world of memory, instinct and superstition is nevertheless not one of total gloom, despite its sombre hues. He still tries fitfully to draw from its depths some clearer vision of life, and with this object in mind he clings to a single meditative lifeline: his belief in the validity of his artistic procedures. Although he is well aware that art cannot ultimately save his soul from perdition in a *theological* sense, he still thinks it can help him towards some vicarious form of *emotional* redemption, which he hopes to attain through the very act of representing his condition of damnation in as authentic a manner as possible. To this limited and thankless task he consequently devoted his entire literary career, although he also stressed from the outset that he never hoped to reach any universal conclusions or even any enduring form of moral comfort.

Granted his singular outlook on life, it is not surprising that those rare expressions of joy which flash upon Montale's inward eye take on the appearance of so many sudden and unexpected illuminations. Generally speaking, such 'barlumi' or lyrical flashes are breakthrough points, moments of deep memorial perception, in which he glimpses – albeit indistinctly – an ultimate justification for existence. But it cannot be too strongly emphasized that his flashes of insight are wholly 'secular', not 'religious', forms of grace; and, as if to underline the point, they are often inexplicably foreshadowed by the most insignificant objects. A typical illustration is the poet's reference to the freshness of a flower blooming precariously on a volcano's rim, another the remarkable self-possession of the high-flying falcon, and yet another the ecstasy of the eel breeding in parched and barren rocks. Because Montale believed that life smoulders with the greatest intensity in arid and inhospitable places, most of his emblems of hope spring up uncannily within remote spectral landscapes, such as arid wildernesses, dried-up marshes, or rocky coastlines – all situations in which life appears to be at its lowest ebb and is therefore pervaded with a certain breathless anguish of suspension.

A typical Montalian wasteland emerges from the landscape described in 'Vecchi versi', where a ghostly charcoal sketch is given of a nocturnal scene close to the Tino lighthouse on the riviera coast near Monterosso. At times the entire universe seems to dilate and contract in rhythm with the waxing and waning of its slender, probing pencil of light:

> Muoveva tutta l'aria del crepuscolo a un fioco
> occiduo palpebrare della traccia
> che divide acqua e terra; ed il punto atono
> del faro che baluginava sulla
> roccia del Tino, cerula, tre volte
> si dilatò e si spense in un altro oro.

> The whole twilight atmosphere moved with a faint western flickering of the line which divides land and water; and the dead point of the beacon which glimmered on the blue Tino rock grew bright and died away three times in another gold.

At first, perhaps, the poet's evident predilection for ambiguous and precarious situations was prompted by crepuscular and metaphysical considerations, and also by a desire to reproduce in a modern context the atmospheres of Leopardi's meditative moonlight settings. But later his technique acquired further depth and evocativeness in two distinct ways: first, from the halo of personal and literary reminiscences associated with the poet's object-symbols; and, second, from his telescopic use of imagery to enlarge his poetic canvases and provide them with an ever-widening range of memorial resonances.[1]

Montale's normal imaginative patterns accordingly revolve around a few carefully chosen natural states – the shadows of twilight, the intense phantomatic light of high noon, the obscure line of the horizon, or the indeterminate water's edge along the seashore. As time passes these areas are raised to a metaphysical status because of their associations with miraculous events, and cumulatively they impart a peculiar resonance to his lyrical manner. It is almost as if certain psycho-sensuous reactions arise subliminally by osmosis from the dark stirring of his blood, and these reactions cannot be defined as conceptual, instinctive or even emotional in quality, but are an intermingling of all three. In combination, they form the basis of Montale's lyrical intelligence and may be contrasted with the far more rationally orientated attitudes of a Cardarelli. For, whereas in Cardarelli's work we always sense that imagery is striving to be conceptually interpretative, with Montale the aim is almost wholly the reverse: it is to fuse together concepts and sensuous forms in such a way that the resulting poetic symbols will gravitate towards a form of emblematic *veggenza* or lyrical insight endued with an incisive psycho-sensuous charge.

Equally his halftone landscapes recall Gozzano's carefully etched engravings and radiate a similar feeling of irredeemable anguish. But Montale's word-pictures do not amount to a gratuitous cult of fetishes, still less to a series of jaded keepsakes; and the emotion generated between his sensibility and his object-symbols is normally immediate, not mediate, in quality. On the other hand, both poets share the technique of deploying symbolic aggregates within halftone crepuscular backgrounds, since by using ambivalent inscapes of this kind they apparently hope to ensure that their stylistic colouring will be firmly rooted in the cultural realities of their age.

Nevertheless, in spite of his various affinities with the crepuscular poets, one factor always separates Montale's chiaroscuro tonalities from those of his contemporaries and predecessors: their manifestation as a single facet of his poetic inspiration rather than as a complete tonal matrix. To counter the melancholy and despair which he detects in the crepuscular manner, he expresses a firm belief in the significance of resuscitated human experiences; and it is indeed almost exclusively in a sphere involving the memorial revaluation of personal relationships in the present that he considers it appropriate for the modern poet to operate. Gradually, therefore, we see a figurative, moral perspective arising out of the very core of his initial metaphysical conception of existence, and nowhere is this better illustrated than in his concern for the relationships subsisting between the living and the dead. On this subject he proves to be the complete foil for Ungaretti; for, whereas the latter regarded death as the ultimate reality, Montale views both life and death from a relative standpoint, as absolutely equivalent states of anguish.

His implication is that Being has no greater validity than Becoming in a human context, not even a permanent advantage from the standpoint of desirability. So, just as the living are endlessly tortured by a longing for quietus in their perpetual condition of conflict, similarly the dead are often disturbed by a residual desire to participate in life. The specific problem attached to both conditions, as Montale sees it, is one of barrier-breaking, of restoring reciprocal communications; it is certainly not the Ungarettian problem of how to filter the whole of living experience through the particular atmospheres and traditions of the dead. In his view intercommunication results from an ethical position even more than from an aesthetic one. Hence he tends to regard the artist as the complement of the man, whereas with Ungaretti the emphasis was, if anything, reversed.

The first poem dealing with Montale's views on death and communication is 'I morti' in the *Ossi di seppia*. The poem's setting, according to Bonora, is one of the typical cemeteries to be found along the riviera coast like S. Michele di Pagana on the Gulf of Tigullio, where the graveyard lies on a promontory to the seaward side of the town.[2] As the ancestors of the present villagers lie in their tombs the poet imagines that they are occasionally recalled to life by the booming of the sea in their ears, just as elsewhere precisely the opposite process takes place and the living are momentarily transfixed to the spot where they stand by totally unexpected intimations of spectral sights and feelings. When the dead find themselves raised to a state of intercommunication their anguish is naturally increased; and then, unexpectedly wakened as they are to some kind of vestigial existence, they momentarily coexist with the living in a magical sphere of memorial communion. Later, after the mysterious forces responsible for their brief resurrection have waned, they return once more to their normal state of inertia and sink without trace into the sea, the archetypal image of the 'Ocean of Being' for Montale:

Cosí
forse anche ai morti è tolto ogni riposo
nelle zolle: una forza indi li tragge
spietata piú del vivere, ed attorno,
larve rimorse dai ricordi umani,
li volge fino a queste spiagge, fiati
senza materia o voce
traditi dalla tenebra; e i mozzi
loro voli ci sfiorano pur ora
da noi divisi appena e nel crivello
del mare si sommergono . . .

Thus perhaps all repose is taken even from the dead beneath the sod: a power draws them from it more pitiless than life, and drives them around, ghosts gnawed by human memories, even up to these shores, dematerialized and

> voiceless exhalations betrayed by the darkness; and their half-shorn flights graze us even now, hardly divided from us, and they sink in the sieve of the sea . . .

For students of Baudelaire, perhaps, the cohabitation of the living and the dead will not be entirely unfamiliar, because we are immediately reminded of poems like 'La servante au grand cœur' which ends on the following significant line:

> Les morts, les pauvres morts, ont de grandes douleurs.

> The dead, the poor dead, have tremendous sorrows.

But the difference between the homespun Baudelairian theme and Montale's broader, metaphysical conception of death is to be found in the fact that the Italian poet projects the idea of post-mortem existence into a transcendental sphere of intercommunication and makes it one of the principles of his art. The French poet, by contrast, rarely postulates the possibility of the dead rubbing shoulders with the living nor does he ever conceive of the still stranger notion whereby the living momentarily gravitate towards a state of co-presence with the dead in the somnolence of high noon. This, however, does not seem at all strange to Montale, especially in midsummer, when, with the sun overhead, the normal shadows of objects tend to disappear in Italian latitudes and even the living seem dematerialized, as the concrete world around them apparently loses its substantiality. Indeed, for him as for Valéry, midday becomes a moment of complete metamorphosis: a time when the perceptive sensibility of the living sinks into a state of nirvana and the bustle of life reaches its lowest ebb:

> Gloria del disteso mezzogiorno
> quand'ombra non rendono gli alberi,
> e piú e piú si mostrano d'attorno
> per troppa luce, le parvenze, falbe.[3]

> Glory of distended high noon when the trees offer no shade, and all around appearances become more and more tawny, through too much light.

Naturally at such moments his lyricism acquires its deepest resonances, since it operates at a privileged memorial point of intersection between life and death. The two spheres are normally fused together by the use of catalytic emblems and an apt illustration of this is the kingfisher appearing at the end of the above-quoted fragment. Its 'emergence' in the heat of the day almost seems like the introduction of a smouldering living presence into the very kingdom of death:

> L'arsura, in giro; un martin pescatore
> volteggia s'una reliquia di vita.

La buona pioggia è di là dallo squallore,
Ma in attendere è gioia piú compita.

The heat, all around; a kingfisher hovers over a relic of life. True rain is on the other side of wretchedness, but there is more complete joy in expectation.

Here a state of equilibrium has already been achieved by the offsetting of a still-life landscape and a symbol of dynamic existence. Later similar combinations will acquire many diverse implications, through the poet's deliberate cult of telescopically contrived, imaginative and emotional resonances.

Just as momentary states of communication are arrived at by certain chance events, so momentary feelings of happiness also flash fortuitously upon the poet's inward eye. Again these intermittent states arise only when moral, aesthetic and instinctive forces tend to offset each other, and one typically perilous state of lyrical equipoise is to be found in another of the *Ossi*:

Felicità raggiunta, si cammina
per te su fil di lama.
Agli occhi sei barlume che vacilla,
al piede, teso ghiaccio che s'incrina.[4]

Happiness achieved, for you one walks on the razor's edge. To the eyes you seem like a flickering glimmer, to the foot, strained ice which cracks.

In this lyric happiness can be said to lie at the heart of a miraculous cone of circumstances whose instability is stressed in images like the razor's edge, a flickering inner light, and the hair-line crack appearing in ice straining beneath one's feet. So precarious is the situation that one begins to wonder whether Montale ever experienced a true state of happiness at all; and indeed by way of confirmation of this suspicion we find that he is far more adept at evoking a preceding mood of expectancy or a subsequent feeling of disenchantment than at depicting the precise moment of happiness itself. In other words we tend to conclude that such moments of pure unadulterated joy are only vicarious experiences for him, because he knows that to cross 'il varco', the threshold of liberation, one needs to be capable of performing miracles. In his world miracles are, needless to say, the sole prerogative of certain 'elect' souls who have undergone a process of magical involvement in life and have learned, as he puts it allusively, to cast an authentic shadow upon its ceaselessly changing landscapes. All such individuals, it seems, avoid life's pitfalls as if by instinct, and for this purpose they seem to possess some ineffable form of inner awareness.

Unfortunately the poet himself is one of the damned and he has to live his life wholly without miracles. But even he does not lose hope of eventually reaching some inner state of peace characterized by insights derived from the paradox of 'motionless motion'. On achieving this state he feels he may be able to solve in an emotional context Zeno's puzzle of movement-in-repose; while in turn the production of such moments of *epoché* could enable him one day to hypostasize the elements of the world-flux and transmute them into absolute forms of lyrical grace embodying the deepest human values:

Forse un mattino andando in un'aria di vetro,
arida, rivolgendomi vedrò compirsi il miracolo:
il nulla alle mie spalle, il vuoto dietro
di me, con un terrore di ubriaco.

Poi come s'uno schermo, s'accamperanno di gitto
alberi case colli per l'inganno consueto.
Ma sarà troppo tardi; ed io me n'andrò zitto
tra gli uomini che non si voltano, col mio segreto.[5]

Perhaps one morning walking in a glass-like, arid air, on turning round, I shall see a miracle enacted: the void at my back, emptiness behind me, with the terror of a drunkard. Then, as if on a screen, immediately will leap forth trees, houses, hills through the customary illusion. But it will be too late; and I shall go my way silently with my secret, among the men who do not turn round.

Knowledge of the pure orphic void behind us, of the hidden pattern behind the contingency of the human condition, can consequently in some mysterious way give the individual a broader understanding of his future destiny, probably by acting as a fixed and detached standard of values. But the poet's own interpretation of the point is apparently somewhat more abstract even than this, for he notes: 'Qui naturalmente c'è l'idea che la nostra visione delle cose esterne, sensibili, sia puramente illusoria; e se noi ci volgessimo indietro, e questo scenario tarda per un secondo a ripresentarsi, noi ci accorgeremo del vuoto, ecco.'[6] ('Here, naturally, there is the idea that our view of external sensory things is purely illusory; and if we turned round, and this scene delayed for a moment before re-presenting itself, we would notice the void, that is all.') However, it is doubtful whether the situation is quite as arid as he suggests, for the above explanation does not take into account the poet's 'segreto' or orphic perspective which he would acquire as a result of such an experience. So probably what he is proposing is a similar orphic bifocality to the one proposed by Ungaretti, though he places more weight on the expectancy of the damned, on those still caught up in the great 'Wheel of Being', than on the certainty of those who have escaped from it; and, indeed, elsewhere he actually calls the latter's insights a meta-psychology. If then we had to characterize his type of orphism, we could define it as an inversion of ancient orphic values, in that the dynamic expectations of the damned are more cherished than the static memorial insights of the 'elect'.

Such an attitude presupposes a well-developed 'theology' of existence, a fact which is confirmed by Montale's division of life into two parts corresponding to the Nestorian view that the human and divine attributes of Christ are entirely separate and that the latter are completely unknowable. In fact, as time passes the poet becomes more and more resigned to this view of life's inevitable dichotomy; and so, to nurture some ray of hope in what seems a hopeless, dualistic situation, he gradually introduces a ritual of self-sacrifice and altruism into his outlook. His view is that he can only accept his fate as one of nature's damned or 'misfits' if he is able to acquire the power to act as a self-willed victim, as one who, by making a self-conscious sacrifice resulting in his own damnation, can at times effect the psychological redemption of another soul. He wants his lyrical acts in other words to work as a covert stimulus to create positive responses in others, despite their own apparently negative orientation; and he connects this doctrine with his wider conception of the mythical existence of damned and elect souls and the special power of positive or elect souls to cast shadows. Nevertheless, the very shadow-casting ability of the latter may well in the last resort turn out to be a disinterested gift from the insubstantial, shadow-thin personalities of the damned. Indeed, although the Italian language has only one word 'ombra' for 'shadow' and 'shade', the poet makes great play with the two meanings and in the following lines suggests that a 'shadow' represents true character, a 'shade' hardly any personality at all:

Se un'ombra scorgete, non è
un'ombra – ma quella io sono.
Potessi spiccarla da me,
offrirvela in dono.[7]

If you spot a shadow, it is not a shade – but I indeed am one. Would that I could pluck it (a shadow) from me, offer it to you as a gift.

Here the only possible meaning seems to be that the poet regards himself as an unauthentic 'shade' but wishes he were an authentic 'shadow' so that he could detach it from himself and offer it as a gift to another person, thereby performing one of the damned's rituals of sacrificial altruism.

Later, perhaps, the poet begins to doubt the redemptive effectiveness of this particular ritual, but he nevertheless always retains a stoic faith in the powers of the single, decisive and altruistic act to change a person's destiny. Hence, in *Le occasioni* (1939), the poem 'Tempi di Bellosguardo' asserts in its conclusion the possibility that every decisive act may open up the secrets of the universe:

E il gesto rimane: misura
il vuoto, ne sonda il confine:
il gesto ignoto che esprime

sé stesso e non altro: passione
di sempre in un sangue e un cervello
irripetuti; e fors'entra
nel chiuso e lo forza con l'esile
sua punta di grimaldello.

And the gesture remains: it measures the void, sounds out its confines: the unknown gesture which expresses itself and nothing else: an everlasting passion in an irrepeatable blood and brain; and perhaps it enters into the closed sphere and forces it open with the slender point of its jemmy.

From here it is a short step to the supposition that decisive acts are our distinctive personal features and that they form permanent nexuses of relations in the memory of the living to ensure our immortality after death. The point is particularly stressed in the lyric 'A mia madre' written shortly after the poet's mother died in 1942. Her physical absence and memorial presence then became inextricably interwoven and both are recalled by a series of irrepeatable acts and gestures. The background is the empty street symbolizing the void left within the poet's mind by his bereavement; and the web of personal attributes which his mother's recollection evokes both affirms her post-mortem survival in Montale's memory and offers her a kind of residual immortality through his pious act of fidelity towards her:

La strada sgombra
non è una via, solo due mani, un volto,
quelle mani, *quel* volto, il gesto d'una
vita che non è un'altra ma se stessa,
solo questo ti pone nell'eliso
folto d'anime e voci in cui tu vivi;
e la domanda che tu lasci è anch'essa
un gesto tuo, all'ombra delle croci.

The empty street is not a road, only two hands, a face, *those* hands, *that* face, the gesture of one lifetime which is nothing else but itself, this alone places you in the Elysium thick with souls and voices where you live; and the question which you leave behind is also a gesture of yours, in the shadow of the crosses.

It is therefore clear that the whole of Montale's poetry is to be regarded as a dialectic between decisive acts and memory, implying a completely humanist and non-transcendent religion of post-mortem survival. For the poet a dead person can only be envisaged as a nexus of remembered gestures encapsulated in the minds of the living; and the living re-evoke these memories out of the ashen experiential precipitates left by the dead and deposited in their minds, as it were, from the snuffed-out flames of the latter's personalities and characteristic attributes. Such recalls symbolize, in short, skeletal value-judgements by the living on the intrinsic worth of the dead:

ma una storia non dura che nella cenere
e persistenza è solo l'estinzione.[8]

but a life's history only endures in its ashes, and persisting is simply extinction.

Consequently we are again presented here with the hermetic device of *epoché* set in an ethical key, involving the 'eternal' suspension in imagery of dead but still potentially dynamic characters.

One could perhaps argue that such a concept reveals technical similarities with Mallarmé's views on 'ideal absence', but in fact its emotive charge connects it more intimately with Proust's approach to memorial recall.[9] The French novelist emphasizes, for instance, that the involuntary activity of the memory is a form of re-creation, a memorial interlocking of *persona* and *situation*, in which both active and passive forces combine and offset each other. On the subject of the authentic remembrance Proust accordingly speculates: 'Rien qu'un moment du passé? Beaucoup plus, peut-être; quelque chose qui, commun à la fois au passé et au présent, est beaucoup plus essentiel qu'eux deux.'[10] ('Nothing but a moment of the past? Much more, perhaps; something which, common both to past and present, is much more essential than either.') Why, we might ask, is memorial experience intrinsically more valuable to the writer than either the present or the past in its unrecollected state? It is mainly because, as Proust again explains, 'une minute affranchie de l'ordre du temps a recréé en nous pour la sentir l'homme affranchi de l'ordre du temps. Et celui-là on comprend qu'il soit confiant dans sa joie, même si le simple goût d'une madeleine ne semble pas contenir logiquement les raisons de cette joie, on comprend que le mot "mort" n'ait pas de sens pour lui; situé hors du temps, que pourrait-il craindre de l'avenir?'[11] ('a minute liberated from the dominion of time has re-created in us so that we can feel it a man liberated from the dominion of time. And one can understand why such a man has confidence in his joy, for even if the simple tasting of a madeleine-cake does not logically seem to contain the reasons for this joy, one understands that the word "death" has no sense for him; placed outside time, what could he fear from the future?'). As we shall see, insignificant objects like Proust's 'madeleine' prompt equally privileged multidimensional recalls for Montale; but, whereas the French writer's memorial creativity is weighted towards aesthetics, the Italian's is more weighted towards ethics. Hence, although both men postulate the possibility of momentary insights into the nature of things as they sink towards oblivion, Montale's 'temps retrouvé' ('time regained') is basically cherished for its moral efficacy[12] and Proust's for its aesthetic beauty and consolation. In fact, Montale's recalls normally pass from the *involuntary* to the *voluntary* stage before they acquire real significance and value,[13] and yet at the same time both writers operate in a clearly realist, as opposed to an idealist, sphere. In the same way, too, each considers memory to be a region beyond time, even though its elements normally remain concrete ones and do not consist of the abstract relational forms cherished by the symbolists and subsumed so often in their verbal arabesques.

Because of his stronger ethical bias the two poles of Montale's dialectic of memory are connected with his earlier mentioned myth of election and damnation. For convenience we can describe the extremes of the imagination within which these distinctions operate as the active and passive memories; and, in effect, his whole method of lyrical redemption is one which amounts to a series of acts whereby people and things are piously drawn out of the passive memory and momentarily reanimated, for the purpose of restoring them unexpectedly to their pristine reality. In this sense his view of memory has certain affinities with Ungaretti's, but a clear distinction between the attitudes of the two poets still subsists. For, whereas the 'buia veglia dei padri' ('dark vigil of the fathers') causes Ungaretti to draw a series of harmonics from the corporate *racial* consciousness, Montale deals wholly with reminiscences of a *personal* origin. Hence his lyrics are less traditional, less culturally resonant, than his predecessor's, but more highly individuated. Similarly we do not experience in his verse the positiveness of Ungaretti's neo-Christian 'dolore', but only an extreme form of existential anguish and an attenuated memorial hopefulness. We can therefore conclude that the grading of his lyrical values is upon a relativistic rather than the absolute Ungarettian scale, insofar as he disregards the formal standards and continuous myths of the pre-existing tradition; or, at least, if any traditional element is to be found in his lyricism at all, it is once more closely associated with specifically personal processes of recollection.

As a general rule the value of each image Montale deploys depends on how fully it has been liberated from the passive or retentive memory into a sphere of lyrical recall. When fully released it provides a measure of ethical solace; but, when it slips back into the deeper memorial recesses of his mind, it seems to offer little more than a feeling of despair, by virtue of the very starkness and nudity of its dematerialized relationships:[14]

> Memoria
> non è peccato fin che giova. Dopo
> è letargo di talpe, abiezione
>
> che funghisce su sé . . . —[15]

Memory is not a sin as long as it is helpful. Afterwards it is a lethargy of moles, an abjectness which moulders on itself . . . —

This 'utilitarian' doctrine does not, however, imply that fossilized images are wholly eliminated from Montale's work, but simply that they are rarely used without a purpose. In flavour, they are often similar to those produced by Gozzano in his 'vecchie stampe' ('old engravings'); but the present poet has in this regard a distinct advantage over his Turinese counterpart because he believes that life's heritage can be portrayed through a subtle admixture of passive and dynamic elements – always provided, of course, that the lyric concerned is able to 'liberate' experience authentically from the various stratifications of the passive memory.

★ ★ ★ ★ ★ ★

Not surprisingly, Montale's aesthetics runs parallel to his ethics and seems to amount to a corollary of his philosophical outlook. Hence at times of despair we find the poet denouncing lyricism as largely a quietist activity, or even as a psychological substitute for those who wish to opt memorially out of life.[16] Fortunately, he retreats in practice from this somewhat extreme position and makes the paradoxical claim that 'il massimo dell'isolamento e il massimo dell'*engagement* possono coincidere nell'artista e dovrebbero coincidere sempre'[17] ('the maximum of isolation and the maximum of *commitment* can coincide in the artist and should always so coincide'). This type of 'participatory detachment' clearly has its origin in crepuscularism, but where Montale deviates from that particular school is in his dynamic view of imagery. Like the futurists he believes that a hunger for movement, even of movement for its own sake, distinguishes the modern sensibility from its classical counterpart; and, borrowing a well-known dictum from Oscar Wilde, he notes that 'sparito il senso statico della vita, spariti certi universali della cultura classica, è rotto il diaframma fra arte e vita e la vita stessa si presenta come una mostruosa opera d'arte sempre distrutta e sempre rinnovata'[18] ('the static sense of life having disappeared, and certain universal elements of classic culture having vanished, the diaphragm between art and life is shattered and life itself is presented as a monstrous work of art, for ever destroyed and for ever renewed'). However, one should not imagine that he is content with this state of affairs; on the contrary, he always regards the modern lyrical climate as a hysterical, even a pathological, condition, in which the heraclitean spirit of the age 'ha reso l'arte cosí immediata da distruggerla'[19] ('has made art so immediate that it has destroyed it'). To save it from the excesses of sensationalism to which it can so easily fall victim he proposes to raise it completely on to a symbolic plane, to the level of the 'io trascendentale' ('transcendental ego'), where in his view perfect intercommunication through an ethico-realist transfiguration of experience can alone be achieved. The process involves a 'dynamic fixation' of imagery, in which the emblem, such as the kingfisher seen earlier, mediates between the passive and active memories, penetrating and subsuming both in a fulminatory imaginative hypostasis. The poet describes the technique as follows: 'Il tentativo di fermare l'effimero, di rendere non fenomenico il fenomeno, il tentativo di rendere comunicante l'io individuale che non è tale per definizione, la rivolta insomma contro la condizione umana (rivolta dettata da un appassionato amor vitae) è alla base delle ricerche artistiche e filosofiche del nostro tempo.'[20] ('An attempt to absolutize the ephemeral, to make the phenomenon non-phenomenal, an attempt to make the individual ego communicative which it is not by definition, a revolt, in short, against the human condition (a revolt dictated by a passionate amor vitae) is at the root of the artistic and philosophical research of our time.')

Such then are the paradoxical transfigurative means that Montale chooses for bringing about a state of communication between himself and the reader; and, to achieve them, he normally uses emblematic and correlative procedures. Whereas his emblems are capable of subsuming whole aspects of individual character, his emotional correlatives are his underlying lyrical landscapes themselves, and they represent through their symbolic patterns his overall tonal unity. Even so, his symbolic universe is composed of many disparate elements and effectively its range includes the Gozzanian keepsake, the fetish, the talisman, the symbolic aggregate and the emblem in an ascending order of importance. Together they form a scale of ethico-emotional values and depict either the still glowing embers or else the smouldering ash of experience. While they are mostly embedded in the past, they nevertheless often have strong implications for the present, in that their unexpected intrusion into the poet's field of consciousness results – as with Proust – in the momentary creation of epiphanies of the dead or memorially departed. This imaginative rescuing of distantly remembered personalities from the limbo of death has simultaneously a lyrical and a moral function: it asserts the poet's solidarity with his fellow men by creating what he calls a humanist circle of 'cordialità' ('cordiality') and it also weaves in the long run a continuous orphic fabric of experience out of the emotional discontinuities of living. The kind of lyrical texture which results is defined by Anceschi as 'un gioco complicato tra sensibilità e intelligenza, in cui la intelligenza isola certi oggetti che diventano segni di una decisione assoluta'[21] ('a complicated game between sensitivity and intelligence, in which the intelligence isolates certain objects which become signs of an absolute decisiveness'). Although the process takes place to varying degrees in all Montale's lyrics, its complete effectiveness is only realized when his landscapes are deepened in significance by an accumulation of symbolic features acting as variations on his dominant themes. We have thus to interpret his symbols through their contextual repetition like Ungaretti's, and it is only when they are seen in retrospect that their many facets and deeper implications become clear. Cumulatively they create a modern mythology as ambitious as that of a T.S. Eliot, a Pavese or a Calvino, though in a detached and highly individualistic rather than in a culturally or socially orientated sphere.

On the prosodic level Montale's imaginative structures are also underpinned by a rich word-music which draws on a variety of effects. Like most modern poets he aims at being functional, not decorative, in his cadences. He is not content, therefore, merely to represent his thought within the traditional melodic line, he also requires it to have its own articulation and originality, which he calls its distinctive 'qualità di timbro'[22] ('quality of timbre'). Precisely because he believes that distinctiveness of utterance and lyrical authenticity go hand in hand, he gradually enriches his early crepuscular inflections with other elements which make their origin almost unrecognizable. Likewise he indulges far more than the other hermetic poets in the traditional techniques of alliteration, assonance, antithesis, and balance; with the result that we are sometimes reminded of the kind of musical atmosphere created, for instance, by Boito's literary exercises, illustrated earlier. Occasionally his auditory devices even have a tendency to cloy, although in fact his highly contrived musical effects never degenerate into a jingle. His prosodic excesses are not therefore signs of a flagging inspiration, but by-products of his lyrical urgency. Indeed, in the last analysis it is precisely through a subtle interplay of sound and sense that he makes his sensibility incarnate in his rhythmical patterns.

★ ★ ★ ★ ★ ★

Montale's first collection, the *Ossi di seppia*, appeared in 1925 and was republished in slightly enlarged form in 1928. Since then the number of the lyrics included in the collection has remained the same and even the variants to individual poems have been relatively few. This is because, unlike Ungaretti, Montale did not keep his ear constantly attuned to the rapidly evolving poetic tradition and avoided becoming obsessed with its subtleties and lyrical resonances. But his poetry still presents us with many difficulties from a stylistic and symbolic standpoint because his manner is a curious combination of hermetic and discursive techniques. The general structure of the *Ossi di seppia* is nevertheless perfectly clear and the organization of the collection is one of the most logical produced since Baudelaire set the trend for large-scale architectonic design in the fifties of the last century. Even the involution of its imagery is perhaps not quite typical of the hermetic movement, since its so-called obscurity derives more from the suppressed personal associations surrounding his object-symbols than from any conscious attempt on the poet's part to indulge in esoteric lyrical practices. What normally occurs is that we are carried along by trains of allusively articulated feelings concealing deeper conceptual truths; and such a method shows us just how often the poet presses against the limits of expressivity in his attempts to communicate his thought. As for his lyrical flavour, this is undoubtedly a form of inverted baroque which aims at bringing about a diminution rather than the normal baroque magnification of reality. Essentially it is based on Montale's wry self-knowledge, his irony and cult of litotes, which together produce a lilliputian world of stunted growth and intimate damnation against which his elect souls can project their momentary vertiginous flights of insight, self-fulfilment and magnanimity.

Montale's self-depreciation and sophisticated renunciations are largely due to his highly ascetic personality, but his understanding of the existential illusion of life was also fostered by his reading of certain modern poets and philosophers in his youth. Among the philosophers concerned were Bergson and Boutroux, especially the latter, whom the poet regarded as the head of the contingentist school. To them he later added the Russian existentialist Chestov and to a limited extent the indigenous influence of Croce and Gentile. But in him any idealist trend was counterbalanced by more congenial and realist aesthetic pressures, notably those deriving from his fellow-Ligurian poets like Ceccardi, Sbarbaro and the poet-critic Boine. So, despite the fact that he showed an early interest in philosophical trends, he was always keenly aware of the difference between philosophy and poetry and never attempted to write philosophical verse, except perhaps in the most general sense. He even considered such an undertaking to be self-defeating, and stressed that 'il bisogno di un poeta è la ricerca di una verità puntuale, non di una verità generale.'[23] ('The poet's requirement is a search for a precise truth, not a general truth.') We might, moreover, compare this distinction between philosophy and art with another which he makes between art and documentation. From the outset of his career he is perfectly aware of the different demands and functions of the intellect and the sensibility and broadly suggests the same type of distinction between them as I.A. Richards. The latter, we recall, discriminated between scientific or documentary language and poetic or emotive language. By adopting a similar attitude Montale is able to introduce a large number of concrete elements into his poetry while remaining constantly on his guard against the practice of scientific 'reportage'.

The keenness of his appreciation of this danger is underlined by his more recent criticism of the 'avanguardia' poets in Italy whom he felt had fallen headlong into the trap. In his remarks about their work he showed that he was perfectly conscious of the fact that through the use of object-symbols in a highly emblematic fashion he had himself avoided sinking into a lifeless 'mare di oggettività' ('sea of objectivity'), a danger always present in his view in Sanguineti, Sanesi, Pagliarani and others. Perhaps no further illustration of the point is needed than a reference back to the passage previously quoted from 'Vecchi versi', where the poet's mood is reflected concretely in a seascape. Scenes of this kind are very common in his verse and they bring out an important principle in hermetic art: the fact that the poet's aim must always be to absorb as completely as possible his conceptual matter in his imagery. Fortunately, such a procedure does not lead to a cult of 'pure poetry' in Italy, at least not in the sense attributed to the term by French critics, because it does not imply the detachment of the poet from the human realities about him. It ensures instead the dominance of the imagination over the reason, with the result that thought is transfigured and clothed in images possessing a minimum amount of conceptual appurtenances. Admittedly, Montale is not at first as radical as some of his contemporaries in his use of this technique, and in his early verse he does sometimes enunciate metaphysical and aesthetic principles in a conceptual fashion. But in his maturity an appropriate metaphor normally transforms the naked idea into an image, until the point is reached when few insights pass muster unless their conceptual element either remains implicit or appears in a wholly unobtrusive form.[24]

When reading the *Ossi di seppia* we are at once struck by the prominence the poet gives to his dialectic of existence. Already in the first lyric, 'In limine', he emphasizes the fact that the polarities of redemption and damnation will colour his entire outlook on life. He does not, of course, attach any religious connotation to these terms: the so-called Elect in Montale's scheme of things are simply the adjusted members of society and the Damned its misfits. Oddly enough, however, the misfits usually turn out to be the original personalities while the adjusted ones remain rather distant and monochord in their apparent beatitude. This makes us suspect that their sense of 'belonging' and their *gioia di vivere* ('joy of living') are nothing more than illusions in the eye of the beholder, or at most the result of glandular processes working at the instinctive level of the blood. Hence we cannot rule out the possibility that the poet, in projecting their sense of fulfilment, is practising a form of inverted Narcissism. If so, the Elect (of whom Esterina is the stock example) provide nothing more than a foil for his own state of damnation, and each and every one of them may well be evoked solely as a means of dramatizing a largely unreal state of emotional Grace.[25] The metaphysical abyss lying beneath such an attitude hardly needs emphasizing.

On the other hand, his elect souls are not as lifeless as Gozzano's and he manages unerringly to change the latter's fetishes and keepsakes into dynamic emblems of life. Consequently, even when the Elect become virtually disembodied presences in *Le occasioni* (1939), his wraith-like female figures continue to possess a residual sensuousness, and almost a palpable – if memorial – personality. In fact, the 'tumultuous void' they present to the reader's sensibility itself suggests a kind of fulfilment, one which contrasts deeply with the spiritual inertia and memorial palsy of most of Gozzano's alienated characters. Moreover, the anguish of Montale's Damned often has its positive side, since they sometimes realize that their alienation is emotional – not speculative – in nature and that it will not lead them to that mind-chilling metaphysical échec experienced by the symbolists. What they suffer from most is a modern dissociation of the memory resulting from the over-stressing of its passive at the expense of its active qualities.[26] In other words, the swollen state of their cultural awareness prevents them from living a satisfying life in the present, precisely because they have become saturated by the sheer weight of the past. Together with the convolutions and complications of the present this memorial pressure causes them to sink into a state of *noia* which is a fossilized form of life-in-death; and, as living fossils, they are transformed into so many natural repositories of dead or dying imagery. This explains why all Montale's victims yearn after certain obsessive talismans momentarily capable of arousing them from their sunken sleep of death. Through such objects they hope to bring about Boutrouxesque miracles, to stir the dying embers of their senses, and to give their existence a fresh lyrical radiance. Unfortunately, the required miracle often fails to take place; and so both they and the poet find themselves perceiving only glimmers of insight as they live out their lives in a meaningless limbo of despair. Their states of desperation are clearly identified with the sphere of the passive memory, which is symbolized in the collection by cuttlefish bones or other 'spectral' relics of the past.

In fact, such a situation is the point of departure of the first poem, 'In limine', because the poet feels he has been brought to the very threshold of authentic life and yet remains totally unable to enjoy it. He therefore contrasts his condition of unremitting damnation with that of an indefinite female figure who already possesses the deep sense of commitment characteristic of the Elect. And, while acknowledging the 'bifocal' nature of their separate existences, he urges her to abandon herself immediately to the wind of life and leave him alone with his melancholy to fossilize in his reliquary, where he is lulled by a vicariously consoling Gozzanian dream:

> Godi se il vento ch'entra nel pomario
> vi rimena l'ondata della vita:
> qui dove affonda un morto
> viluppo di memorie,
> orto non era, ma reliquiario.

Enjoy it if the wind which enters the garden brings back to it a flood of life: here, where a dead tangle of memories sinks, there was no garden but a reliquary.

In short, the poet's condition of ennui offers paradoxically a possible avenue of salvation for another soul, although the stimulus he provides for her escape is at present simply an instinctive power drawn from the dark stirring of the earth. The implication is that by obeying the life-force one turns the humours stagnating in the barren garden of memory into a seething crucible of life:

> Il frullo che tu senti non è un volo,
> ma il commuoversi dell'eterno grembo;
> vedi che si trasforma questo lembo
> di terra solitario in un crogiuolo.

The fluttering that you hear is not a flight, but the stirring of the eternal womb; see how this lonely patch of ground is transformed into a crucible.

Here the poet chooses his words carefully, because his lady's experience will not be a Mallarmean 'volo' ending in the circularity of a metaphysical échec, but a 'frullo' or energetic fluttering such as we saw earlier with the kingfisher. Henceforth, then, we must bear in mind that a flapping motion will be indicative of redemption, to be contrasted with a corresponding circular movement indicative of life's egocentricity and the vicious circle of damnation.

The most important feature of 'In limine' is its figurative realism. Its emblematic style aims at depicting a realistic myth about modes of life and not an escape into an idealistic sphere. So, although the poet speaks elsewhere of arriving at an absolute, 'il quid definitivo' ('the definitive quiddity'), nevertheless the redemptive sphere he hopes his lady-friend will enter on breaching the wall of existence is not theological in quality but ethico-aesthetic. To enable her to achieve this breakthrough he evokes lucky charms, talismans, even salvatory phantoms, in the hope that they are capable of reawakening the inanimate memorial relics surrounding her to an active emblematic life:

> Un rovello è di qua dall'erto muro.
> Se procedi t'imbatti
> tu forse nel fantasma che ti salva:
> si compongono qui le storie, gli atti
> scancellati pel giuoco del futuro.

> There is a ferment on this side of the high wall. If you proceed you will perhaps encounter a phantom which will save you: here are composed the life-stories, the actions cancelled through the play of the future.

Thus, in the final stanza of the poem he combines Boutroux's philosophy of momentary liberation with his own doctrine of sacrificial altruism, and together they represent a carefully calculated revolt against the limitations of the human condition:

> Cerca una maglia rotta nella rete
> che ci stringe, tu balza fuori, fuggi!
> Va, per te l'ho pregato, – ora la sete
> mi sarà lieve, meno acre le ruggine . . .

> Seek a broken link in the net which tightens about us, you leap out, flee! Go, for you I have beseeched it, – now my thirst will be bearable, less bitter the rust . . .

The consolation he derives from this personal religion of sacrifice is the vicarious one of which we have already spoken, and upon it he tries to build a religion of detached communion with his fellow-men.

Montale's myth of vicarious redemption has a Dantesque ring about it and his salvatory phantom even reminds us of Virgil's function in the *Inferno*. In fact, his lyrical texture never entirely loses its Dantesque resonances, and at the lowest level they manifest themselves in the poet's equating of existence with a sense of ennui amounting to a form of hell on earth. In lighter moments, on the other hand, his mood of expectancy recalls feelings similar to the ones animating the souls in purgatory; while, finally, whenever a fully-fledged miracle obtrudes, we experience that instantaneous sense of 'divine' harmony which is perhaps the secular equivalent of the mood felt by the blessed in paradise. It is accordingly in this sense that we can describe Montale's entire lyrical activity as an investigation into a modern theology of existence, while the one significant difference between his conclusions and Dante's may be explained by the fact that he is not animated by a religious faith and is thereby prevented from regarding redemption as a linear or progressive certainty. Most souls are in his view bedevilled through no fault of their own by long periods of brooding melancholy, in which they rarely experience any moments of 'beatitude' at all. The poet himself is one of their number, although with him the vicious circle of existential despair is often further intensified by an awareness of a higher state of consciousness lying just beyond his grasp.

As we have indicated previously, the *Ossi di seppia* is as highly organized and as carefully divided into sections as *Les fleurs du mal*. Its first section entitled *Movimenti* not unexpectedly reflects the poet's earliest attempts to free himself from his emotional torpor; but his efforts at liberation are still somewhat hesitant and diffident, and the most significant feature of the lyrics in which they are expressed is that they provide the dominant tone which he intends to adopt throughout his poetic career. Almost immediately we are made to realize that his verse will not be based on traditional rhetoric, but deliberately modulated in the minor key and suffused with a tortured realism:

Ascoltami, i poeti laureati
si muovono soltanto fra le piante
dai nomi poco usati: bossi ligustri o acanti.
Io, per me, amo le strade che riescono agli erbosi
fossi dove in pozzanghere
mezzo seccate agguantano i ragazzi
qualche sparuta anguilla;
le viuzze che seguono i ciglioni,
discendono tra i ciuffi delle canne
e mettono negli orti, tra gli alberi dei limoni.[27]

Listen to me, classic poets only move among plants with little-used names: boxwood, privet, acanthus. For myself, I love the roads which lead to grassy ditches where in half dried-up pools children seize a few emaciated eels; the paths which follow the embankments descend among tufts of reeds and emerge in gardens among the lemon-trees.

He also introduces at this stage his symbolic aggregates whose function will be partly tonal and partly conceptual. For example, the emaciated eels and the lemons mentioned above will gradually be transformed into emblems with intense evocative powers in subsequent lyrics. At first the poet possessed only a limited range of these topographical features, although later they became multisuggestive by way of their repetition and telescopic interaction upon each other. So in a sense his train of symbolic implications soon allowed him to construct entire mental landscapes correlative with his moods.

In addition to tonal and symbolic procedures Montale also lays down his main metaphysical principles in this volume. The most important of them is his belief in the possibility of a Boutrouxesque 'liberation' from the laws of cause and effect, which explains why he tries to describe the sensations he experiences when the causal chain of events seems momentarily broken and he feels he is about to penetrate to

> il punto morto del mondo, l'anello che non tiene,
> il filo da disbrogliare che finalmente ci metta
> nel mezzo di una verità.[28]

the dead point of the world, the link which does not hold, the thread to untangle which will finally place us at the heart of a truth.

Solmi has described this state of miraculous expectation as 'un'illusione dell'imminenza dell'al di là'[29] ('an illusion of the imminence of the world beyond'). In the present lyric the illusion is symbolized by a patch of blue sky contrasting with the dismal, rainswept urban scene. Its very brightness works miraculously upon the poet's inward eye reassuring him temporarily despite his almost immediate relapse into a torpid state of ennui:

> Ma l'illusione manca e ci riporta il tempo
> nelle città rumorose dove l'azzurro si mostra
> soltanto a pezzi, in alto, tra le cimase.
> La pioggia stanca la terra, di poi; s'affolta
> il tedio dell'inverno sulle case,
> la luce si fa avara – amara l'anima.

But the illusion fails and time brings us back to the noisy cities where the blue sky appears only in patches, high above the eaves. The rain wearies the earth, then; the tedium of winter intensifies over the houses, the light becomes dim – and the soul bitter.

Here perhaps we detect a touch of despair in the poet's tone, but nevertheless the insignificant phenomena described partially restore his faith in life and set the stage for his future responses. Their immediate effect is to stimulate the production of numerous talismans (magical objects lying halfway between Gozzano's fetishes and his own mature emblems) which acquire intense psycho-sensuous charges and awaken visual or olfactory images deep in his sensibility. A case in point is the image of the lemons in the present poem. When he glimpses the fruit through a half-open door, they recall the glories of the summer sun, melt the ice around his heart, and enrich it with their flood of yellow light:

> Quando un giorno da un malchiuso portone
> tra gli alberi di una corte
> ci si mostrano i gialli dei limoni;
> e il gelo del cuore si sfa,

e in petto si scrosciano
le loro canzoni
le trombe d'oro della solarità.

When one day from a badly-closed portal among the trees in the courtyard, the yellow of the lemons reveals itself to us; and the ice around our hearts melts, and in our breasts sunny trumpets of gold rain down their songs on us.

Clearly this poem marks the emergence of a new type of 'allegory' in the form of an emblematic discourse; and the last scene in particular tends to fall into a Dantesque and Proustian perspective involving, momentarily at least, an unexpected release from damnation. Gradually the dominant aridity of the landscape yields to a promise of regeneration; then the blue sky offers a distant and magical moment of hope; and finally we encounter the flash of the lemons in the courtyard, seen almost as if through the strait gate of salvation which – by being half-ajar – frees the poet for an instant from his condition of memorial insentiency. As we shall see, similar neo-narrative structures repeat themselves continually in Montale's work, and this lyric is only the first of many combining the contingent elements of nature and the absolute world of the emotions. Once the poet had established this specific representational manner he naturally devotes himself to the elaboration of an appropriate emblematic style to exploit it. Hence he concentrates more and more on the task of making his basic symbolic patterns flexible instruments for the expression of his thought and intimate feelings.

At first Montale's techniques for fusing together the external world and his own internal tensions may seem elementary, reproducing the still-lifes typifying Gozzano's manner. 'Quasi una fantasia' is an apt illustration, for it virtually presents a static dream in the form of a tapestry:

Avrò di contro un paese d'intatte nevi
ma lievi come viste in un arazzo.

I shall have before me a landscape of unblemished snow, but feathery as if seen on a tapestry.

Antonielli regards this mode as mirroring Montale's 'superstizione del salvamento'[30] ('superstition of salvation'), but despite its similarity to Gozzano's daguerrotypes it differs from them substantially by operating in the present and future rather than exclusively in the past. His symbolic aggregates accordingly tend to vibrate with a living emotion and do not lie motionless, like dead memories, within his poetic texture. Often they produce embryonic emblems such as the hoopoe, which in *Ossi* XXI symbolizes a momentary state of grace created through the emergence of a dynamic nexus of relationships. Needless to say, this creature announces a mature development in Montale's symbolism: namely, the appearance of those emblematic figures – frequently animals or birds – which represent facets of absolute emotional states or fixed psychic truths lying within the very flux of life.

So far we have only considered modes of momentary transcendence from damnation, but a more permanent product of Montale's ritual of vicarious redemption appears in the lyric 'Falsetto' and is symbolized by a girl named Esterina.[31] She is the very archetype of the Elect and like Cardarelli's 'adolescente' before her she too has just reached maturity. Yet, in contrast with her Cardarellian predecessor, she is not cocooned in a state of passive mystery and breathless suspension. Her purity and contentment spring instead from her ability to participate in life, from her willingness to commit herself single-mindedly to the business of fulfilling herself. Even her apparent chastity is the product of a perfect equilibrium and derives from an innate capacity to practise a serene detachment in her relations with others. As a result, she emerges from the storms of passion more self-assured than ever:

Sommersa ti vedremo
nella fumea che il vento
lacera o addensa, violento.
Poi dal fiotto di cenere uscirai
adusta piú che mai,
proteso a un'avventura piú lontana
l'intento viso che assembra
l'arciera Diana.

We shall see you submerged in the smoky cloud which the wind tears to pieces or thickens, violently. Then you will emerge from its shower of ashes more bronzed than ever, your face, resembling the huntress Diana, alert and inclined to a more distant adventure.

Here the swirling dust and smoke are symbolic of the earlier mentioned ash of experience, and variations on this type of symbolism will reappear countless times with Montale in images describing memorial persistence. Possibly Esterina's salamander-like presence is somewhat overdone, as is the precious comparison which later identifies her beauty in Dannunzian manner with the huntress Diana; but even these images throw into relief the girl's radiant animality, her self-assurance and self-confidence, which reach a crescendo at the end of the poem when she stands poised to dive from a highly symbolic spring-board into the ocean of life.

In fact, the sea has up to this point been a suppressed presence in *Movimenti*, but now it becomes an overt symbol of an all-embracing, plastic existence to be contrasted with the aridity and squalor of the land. Esterina's familiarity with it as one of the Elect is emphasized by her being described as a 'watery creature', and she tends to make the sea her normal habitat and source of her orphic vitality:

> L'acqua è la forza che ti tempra,
> nell'acqua ti ritrovi e ti rinnovi:
> noi ti pensiamo come un'alga, un ciottolo,
> come un'equorea creatura
> che la salsedine non intacca
> ma torna al lito piú pura.

Water is the force that tempers you, in water you rediscover and renew yourself: we think of you as a piece of seaweed, as a pebble, as a watery creature whom the sea's saltiness does not corrode but who returns more pure to the shore.

In short, her human presence – like the bedouin in Ungaretti's work – is ritualistically matured by immersion in its waters; and, as a result, she is able to protect herself from the salty corrosion of living. Her very enjoyment seems to be the climax and embodiment of an act of liberation, and her assurance and unforced laughter – like the smile of a modern Beatrice – symbolize an inner feeling of earthly beatitude:

> T'alzi e t'avanzi sul ponticello
> esiguo, sopra il gorgo che stride:
> il tuo profilo s'incide
> contro uno sfondo di perla.
> Esiti a sommo del tremulo asse,
> poi ridi, e come spiccata da un vento
> t'abbatti fra le braccia
> del tuo divino amico che t'afferra.
>
> Ti guardiamo noi, della razza
> di chi rimane a terra.

You arise and walk forward on the narrow diving-board, above the swirling main: your silhouette is chiselled out against a pearly background. You hesitate on the top of the quivering board, then laugh, and, as if launched by a wind, you cast yourself into the arms of your divine friend who seizes you. We watch you, we of the race of those who remain land-bound.

As the whole scene in 'Falsetto' is raised to a kind of emblematic status, it will be interesting to note in passing that some of the recurring elements of Montale's symbolic landscapes already emerge from it. The narrow spring-board like the 'razor's edge' mentioned earlier represents the difficult path which leads to happiness; the sharpness of Esterina's features mirrored in the pearly depths suggests that she casts a shadow which stresses her decisiveness; while the wind, as previously seen in 'In limine', is a form of experiential stimulus, an 'ondata di vita' ('flood of life'), driving the individual to taste life in all its manifestations. But perhaps the most significant point of all is that we see the land turning here into the specific habitat of the Damned, especially in the last two lines.[32] The riviera coast is therefore already becoming a degraded sphere appropriate only to those who dare not attempt the acrobatics of the Elect in their far less intractable, watery domain. So in this sense we can regard 'Falsetto' as establishing a further important dialectical feature in Montale's early poetry: the polarities of the sea and the land which will later prove to be a key to the overall interpretation of the *Ossi di seppia*.

A short section addressed to his friend Camillo Sbarbaro may be described as an interlude leading up to the next important sub-division, *Sarcofaghi*. It contains another significant Montalian imaginative feature – the typical aggregate of objects he will later associate with the stunted life of the Damned. This form of degenerate symbolism was first deployed by Sbarbaro, and the lilliputian type of imagery it produces is to be seen in Montale's poem 'Caffè a Rapallo', where he describes a children's carnival. Its unruliness and grotesqueness clearly foreshadow the gratuitous world of nature's misfits. In particular, it incorporates in its image-chain the false values, the forced gaiety, and the ceaseless tumult of modern life; and the general impression it gives is that the children's wayward state of *pre-conscious* innocence is merely a prelude to an adult mood of *self-conscious* bewilderment and despair. Their fancy-dress, knick-knacks and shrill music all seem insignificant when set against the thunderclap (compare with Eliot's 'The Waste Land') which threatens to introduce them into a traumatic state of self-consciousness. And after such a state has emerged, the children will, of course, experience the same sense of futility as their elders:

L'orda passò col rumore
d'una zampante greggia
che il tuono recente impaura.
L'accolse la pastura
che per noi piú non verdeggia.

The horde passed with the rumble of a stampeding herd which the recent thunder has frightened. The pastures welcomed them, which for us no longer grow green.

Precisely because the lilliputian world of 'Caffè a Rapallo' seems to be about to capitulate before the blind forces of chance, in the other poem contained in the section, 'Epigramma', Montale provides a guardian-angel for the children, a 'galantuomo' ('gentleman') whose sacred duty it will be to protect their games from disaster and guide their fleet of paper ships – possibly their destinies – safely to port. The very appearance of this male salvatory figure is unusual in Montale's work and is no doubt intended to be a special tribute to Sbarbaro; but the very fact that the symbol is that of a 'galantuomo' again stresses the 'secular' rather than 'religious' nature of the poet's outlook. Like the *deae ex machina* we shall encounter later, he becomes the incarnation of that secret regenerative power implicit in Montale's talismans and lucky charms. Already the world in which he operates is one of incipient damnation, a 'mondo gnomo' ('a gnome world'), whose existence tends to indicate the underlying temptation of escapism to be found in all hermetic art. This fairy-tale world indeed remains the sphere to which his protagonists will turn whenever they wish to avoid facing up to the reality of their circumstances. As such, however, it has only a negative validity and represents no more than a beguiling regurgitation of their passive memories. Probably the next section *Sarcofaghi* is intended to epitomize it, for there the poet is tempted to associate life with statuesque Gozzanian tableaus in many ways similar to those we find on the friezes of Pompeian tombs.[33]

The still-life technique adopted by Montale nevertheless differs considerably from that practised by Gozzano. For his acute self-consciousness causes him to realize that objective poetry can only be authenticated by endowing its fetish-like object-symbols with an emblematic status. He tries paradoxically to achieve this aim while simultaneously maintaining the static atmosphere of the daguerrotype. The first poem typifies the whole series and was probably modelled on Keats' 'Ode on a Grecian urn'. The young girls depicted in its Arcadian landscape are, like Keats' figures, crystallized into eternal poses, and the eerie stillness of the scene suggests a world momentarily resuscitated from the dust of death:

Dove se ne vanno le ricciute donzelle
che recano le colme anfore su le spalle
ed hanno il fermo passo sí leggero;
e in fondo uno sbocco di valle
invano attende le belle
cui adombra una pergola di vigna
e i grappoli ne pendono oscillando.

Where are the curly girls going who bear brimming amphoras on their shoulders and have so firm yet light a step; and in the background a valley's mouth awaits these beauties in vain, whom a pergola of vines shades and from which the grape-clusters hang swaying.

Since these lines are, despite their evocative brilliance, pastiches of classical forms, the poet himself soon begins to wonder whether he should indulge in such pretty exercises. So, when finally he realizes that the charms which they offer are delusive, he warns others not to be led into the same trap:

> Lungi di qui la tua vita ti conduce,
> non c'è asilo per te, sei troppo morto:
> seguita il giro delle tue stelle.

Your life leads you far from here, there is no refuge for you, you are too dead: follow the circle of your own stars.

The admonishment to the reader to pursue his own destiny because he is 'troppo morto' to enjoy such an idyllic life may seem puzzling at first; but it is a parallel to the Ungarettian technique previously described as 'le monde mis à l'envers' ('the world upturned'). Its implication is that the contingent qualities of life are too insubstantial, too prone to dissolution, to permit the living to participate in a world of pure Being, fixed as it is for ever in a statuesque state of immobility.

Precisely because the still-life technique does not offer any emotional satisfaction to the poet, he turns to its nearest artistic neighbour, the photograph; and he experiments to see whether it is worth while exploiting its modalities in his art. To test its effectiveness he used the camera of his inward eye as a means of hypostasizing a situation, and normally, as the shutter clicks, we find that Montale has chosen his angle of vision so carefully that he is able to concentrate the entire emotional tension of a scene upon one or more object-symbols. A central presence in the second lyric is the talisman of a dog which guards a small temple where human footsteps will never again penetrate. Doubtless, this animal is intended to symbolize faithfulness because the same theme is taken up again in the last poem in the section and even develops further into the doctrine of a 'fedeltà immortale' ('immortal fealty') in the poet's later work.[34] Likewise, it is connected with Montale's superstitious belief in the power of Proustian-type imagery to evoke powerful, emotionally charged memories. So, by acting as a kind of amulet, the dog is intended to lift the veil of illusion for a moment and provide an orphically suspended vision of the emotional tensions which have been embalmed in the temple's structure:

> Ora sia il tuo passo
> piú cauto: a un tiro di sasso
> di qui ti si prepara
> una piú rara scena.
> La porta corrosa d'un tempietto
> è rinchiusa per sempre.
> Una grande luce è diffusa
> sull'erbosa soglia.
> E qui dove peste umane

non suoneranno, o fittizia doglia,
vigila steso al suolo un magro cane.
Mai piú si muoverà
in quest'ora che s'indovina afosa.
Sopra il tetto s'affaccia
una nuvola grandiosa.

Now let your step be more cautious: at a stone's throw from here a rarer scene is prepared for you. The corroded gate of a little temple is closed for ever. A strong light spreads over the grassy threshold. And here where human footsteps shall not resound, nor a fictitious anguish, on the ground an emaciated dog lies vigilant. It will never move again in this suspected sultry hour. Over the roof appears a huge cloud.

Other elements afterwards form a symbolic aggregate around the magical, galvanizing emblem of the dog: namely, a corroded door, a few tufts of grass, and a large cloud. According to Beall, the cloud symbolizes the imminent destruction of Pompei by the eruption of Vesuvius; but, despite this possible historical touch, the lyric displays mainly timeless effects, created by the reduction of the background elements to essentials and their immersion in an intensely bright light. In association with the adjectives nuancing it (*corrosa, grande, magro, afosa, grandiosa*), the entire symbolic landscape forms a powerful emotional focus which is further intensified by yet another inversion of life and death expressed in the phrase 'fittizia doglia'. What the poet means by it is the insignificance of the mere anguish of living when compared with the eternal 'doglia' of death. Hence we can assume at this juncture that we have passed into the realm of what Montale elsewhere calls the 'io trascendentale' ('transcendental ego'), where emotion becomes absolute and resolves itself into an aesthetico-ethical transfiguration of experience. When such a type of communication is achieved, the perspective becomes privileged, and then the barren wasteland of the tomb, the mediatory figure of the dog, and the threatening cloud all combine to create a unified picture which is immediately raised to that emblematic status to which all the poet's lyrical evocations aspire.

Montale's main concern in this section is, in fact, how to fix for ever in his art the emotional bond which perpetuates the image of a friend or lover long after time has cast them into the passive memory, itself a kind of tomb:

Ma dove cercare la tomba
dell'amico fedele e dell'amante;
quella del mendicante e del fanciullo;
dove trovare un asilo
per codesti che accolgon la brace

dell'originale fiammata;
oh da un segnale di pace lieve come un trastullo
l'urna ne sia effigiata!

But where to seek for the tomb of the faithful friend and the lover; that of the beggar and the child; where to find a refuge for those who accept the embers of the primal flame; oh, from a sign of peace as trifling as a bauble may the tomb be sculpted!

The solution he suggests is that the urn of memory has to be engraved with the image of a total emblematic presence if the remembrance is to be an authentic and lasting one, since it is only at that stage that it can participate in the eternal flame. How then can a lyrical recall in all its pristine substantiality be actualized? Only, it seems, through the craftsmanship of the artist, for he alone can hint at eternity when evoking insignificant memorial events and he alone is able to endow these events with the strange magical power of leading the mind back along genuine paths of remembrance to the original experience itself:

Lo guarda il triste artiere che al lavoro si reca
e già gli batte ai polsi una volontà cieca.
Tra quelle cerca un fregio primordiale
che sappia pel ricordo che ne avanza
trarre l'anima rude
per vie di dolci esigli:
un nulla, un girasole che si schiude
ed intorno una danza di conigli . . .

The sad artisan on his way to work gazes at it (the sculpture on the tomb), and already a blind desire beats in his heart. Among these (ie the tombs) seek out a primal frieze which may be able, through the memories emerging from it, to draw the uncultivated soul along paths of sweet exiles: a trifle, a sunflower opening, and around it a gambolling of rabbits. . . .

By such means the poet weaves over the 'derelitte lastre' ('derelict slabs') of dead friendships an unbreakable bond of fidelity, and it is by evoking such bonds in powerful talismanic imagery that Montale hopes to achieve a certain measure of vicarious salvation. In the present instance we note that the plants and animals which serve as trigger-mechanisms for the establishment of his emotional relationships possess either idyllic or normal, everyday qualities; but later he considers incongruous, almost unnatural, 'animali buffi' ('comic animals') like porcupines, moles, jackals, storks and okapi to be a more appropriate means of transfiguring his moods.

In the *Sarcofaghi*, therefore, we already see precocious hints at the poet's mature dialectic of memory, outlined earlier. Indeed, there is much more in Montale's memorial technique, as Singh has suggested,[35] than either the fossilized dream or even the emergent emblematic aggregate. In the course of time the act of recollection itself acquires evaluative power and ranges over the whole field of human relationships. Its scale of values is ethico-imaginative in quality, expressing at one instant moments of intense participation and at others moods of almost cosmic indifference. As we might expect from such a doctrine, remembrance often becomes a double-edged sword, attempting and yet normally failing to change long-forgotten incidents into intense foci of lyrical recollection.

Behind the imaginative evaluation implicit in Montale's lyrical recalls there also lies a belief in the irrepeatability of experiences. This is a restatement of his faith in the decisive act which enhances what at first may seem a chance happening so as to make it part and parcel of a human personality. It then becomes the myth and evaluating standard of a single lifespan:

> Ahimé, non mai due volte configura
> il tempo in egual modo i grani! E scampo
> n'è: ché, se accada, insieme alla natura
> la nostra fiaba brucerà in un lampo.[36]

Alas! time never does arrange its grains twice in the same way! And a loophole it is for us: for, should it arise, our life-story together with nature would burn out in a flash.

Without such distinguishing features there would in Montale's view be no possibility of evaluation at all; so that for him the irrepeatable or decisive act is the justification of all artistic practices. It provides us with the means of modifying the sensibility of our age and its inherited tastes, and it produces that endless dialectic we find operating in his work between the passive and active memories. In other words the Montalian image-chain offers us a threefold perspective: the record of an irrepeatable act, its layering in the passive memory, and its subsequent lyrical recall. By using these three elements as our guide we shall find it possible to interpret by far the larger part of his poetic output.

The central section of the *Ossi di seppia* consists of 'frammenti' bearing the title of the collection itself. In them the poet sums up the moral and aesthetic discoveries he has made so far and proceeds to use memorial situations as a means of recalling intensely significant and dramatic situations. The first poem is a general statement of his outlook as one of nature's Damned and, by extension, it gives expression to the damnation of his entire generation:

> Non chiederci la parola che squadri da ogni lato
> l'animo nostro informe, e a lettere di fuoco

lo dichiari e risplenda come un croco
perduto in mezzo a un polveroso prato.
. . . .
Non domandarci la formula che mondi possa aprirti,
sí qualche storta sillaba e secca come un ramo.
Codesto solo oggi possiamo dirti,
ciò che *non* siamo, ciò che *non* vogliamo.

Do not ask us for the word which defines in every sense our unformed minds and in letters of fire announces it and shines like a crocus lost in the depths of a dusty field . . . Do not ask us for the formula which can open up worlds for you, but dead-branch-dry some twisted syllable. This alone we can utter for you today, what we are *not*, what we do *not* want.

In contrast with the damned majority we note in the same lyric the self-assurance of the few, who are, as previously indicated, Montale's Elect. Their imprint is engraved for ever upon the active memory of their age and they are represented here as distant figures boldly casting a shadow upon the wall of life:

Ah l'uomo che se ne va sicuro,
agli altri ed a se stesso amico,
e l'ombra sua non cura che la canicola
stampa sopra uno scalcinato muro!

Ah, the man who goes away confidently, a friend both to himself and others, and who does not care when his shadow is impressed by the dog-days on a crumbling wall!

What then is the reason behind this contrast? Simply that the Damned are caught up in the modern Baudelairian *noia* of metaphysical and existential despair, while the Elect manage to escape from so over-cerebral an attitude and move within an 'absolute' human and emotional sphere. At first the poet's sense of 'il male di vivere' ('evil of living') had nothing to do with social or political conditions; it was, as he himself explained, the result of a flaw perceived in existence;[37] and he gives the idea emblematic status in these 'frammenti' by associating it with certain symbolic aggregates: the withered leaf, the dried-up stream, the broken-winded horse or the human soul itself as it fossilizes into an ancient stoic state of complete indifference in the summer's heat:

Spesso il male di vivere ho incontrato:
era il rivo strozzato che gorgoglia,
era l'incartocciarsi della foglia
riarsa, era il cavallo stramazzato.

Bene non seppi, fuori del prodigio
che schiude la divina Indifferenza:

era la statua nella sonnolenza
del meriggio, e la nuvola, e il falco alto levato.

Often I have encountered the evil of living: it was the gurgling, dried-up stream, the withering of the burnt-up leaf, it was the broken-winded horse. I knew no good except the portent which reveals divine Indifference: it was the statue in the somnolence of noon, and the cloud, and the high-flying falcon.

It is interesting to note that while the poet retains here some of the immobile effects of the *Sarcofaghi*, he is now infusing into his still lifes a few dynamic features like the high-flying falcon. The pattern which emerges is one which plays on the phantomatic qualities of light and shadow, and yet introduces a subtle human element into an otherwise absolute sphere of metaphysical dimensions:

Come quella chiostra di rupi
che sembra sfilaccicarsi
in ragnatele di nubi;
tali i nostri animi arsi

in cui l'illusione brucia
un fuoco pieno di cenere
si perdono nel sereno
di una certezza: la luce. [38]

Like that cloister of cliffs which seem to unthread themselves in webs of clouds; so our burnt minds, in which illusion kindles a fire full of ash, are lost in the serenity of one certainty: light.

This passage reminds us, perhaps, of Baudelaire's 'saharah brumeux' ('misty Sahara') and its associated ennui, but the significant image of fire and ash also provides a positive indication of salvation through experiential suffering. Indeed, the overall effulgence of the scene is symbolic of the muted kind of Bergsonian life-force which Montale believed to be operative throughout life and residually even in death.

From these and other effects we can legitimately conclude that in the *Ossi di seppia* the poet was striving to perfect his imagery and symbolic atmospheres, and he hoped to be able to combine them later with dramatic human situations as an adequate representation of his moods. His approach runs parallel to Eliot's technique of the 'objective correlative', although he insists that it was independently conceived. Both writers, in effect, seem to work on similar planes of empathy in order to attain to higher states of consciousness; but Montale's methods are slightly more elaborate, because they involve an artful intermingling of fetishes, talismans and emblems crystallized into states of momentary poetic equilibrium. A typical illustration of this type of aggregative technique is the lyric 'Meriggiare pallido e assorto' written as early as 1916. But despite its early composition it reveals a maturity of expression which is positively startling for the time:

Meriggiare pallido e assorto
presso un rovente muro d'orto,
ascoltare tra i pruni e gli sterpi
schiocchi di merli, frusci di serpi.

Nelle crepe del suolo o su la veccia
spiar le file di rosse formiche
ch'ora si rompono ed ora s'intrecciano
a sommo di minuscole biche.

Noon-musing, pale and absorbed, near a burning garden wall, to hear among the thorns and brake the caws of blackbirds, the slip of snakes. In the cracks of the ground and on the vetch to espy the columns of red ants which now break formation and now interlace on top of minute hillocks.

Here the atmosphere is wholly instinct-laden and various animal and insect talismans are used to provoke responses deep in the poet's blood. Together they orchestrate those powerful physiological raptures which for Montale pervade the entire flora and fauna of the earth, and their whole emotional charge is related to the symbol of the garden-wall depicting the wall of life, already mentioned in 'In limine' and elsewhere. This wall marks the psychological dividing line between the Elect and the Damned, yet its reappearance highlights the poet's basic dichotomy in another important sense, because it tends to contrast the pre-conscious participation in life of the lower forms of the animal and insect world on the one hand and man's self-conscious alienation from it on the other. The necessity for reintegrating the human sensibility into the sensory world is accordingly emphasized in the last stanza; but it has to take the form of a reintegration through harsh experiential suffering, in which man's meditative and instinctive impulses are unified into a subtler socio-metaphysical harmony. An interpenetration of thought and feeling is no doubt at present the concealed hope behind the poet's melancholy acknowledgement of his alienation, while his realization of the difficulties to be encountered before emotional redemption can be achieved is reflected in the image of the jagged bottle-shards on top of the wall:

E andando nel sole che abbaglia
sentire con triste meraviglia
com'è tutta la vita e il suo travaglio
in questo seguitare una muraglia
che ha in cima cocci aguzzi di bottiglia.

And walking in the dazzling sun to feel with a sad astonishment how the whole of life and its anguish are in following this wall which has sharp bottle-shards on top.

Clearly this poem has its importance auditively as well as imaginatively, since it echoes in its sharp sounds the paradoxical aridity and intensity of Montale's wasteland descriptions. In particular, the alliterative orchestration of sibilants and gutturals in such words as 'schiocchi' and 'frusci' are themselves striking illustrations of the technique, and the same harsh sounds reappear in another lyric where a state of unselfconscious childhood innocence replaces the instinct-driven world of the lower animals:

La farandola dei fanciulli sul greto
era la vita che scoppia dall'arsura.
Cresceva tra rare canne e uno sterpeto
il cespo umano nell'aria pura.

Il passante sentiva come un supplizio
il suo distacco dalle antiche radici.
Nell'età d'oro florida sulle sponde felici
anche un nome, una veste erano un vizio.

The dancing jig of the children on the gravel river-bed was life exploding from the heat. Among scattered reeds and a thorn-brake the human thicket grew in the pure air. The passer-by felt as a torture his detachment from his ancient roots. In the lush age of gold on those happy banks even a name, a garment, was a vice.

In opposition to the closed world of the adult the infinite potentialities of the unselfconscious child are raised here to a level of pure emblematic intelligence, as the entire sensory meaning of existence is unfolded in a few dry and brittle images framed within the promise of a golden age. By offsetting myth and personal experiences in this manner the poet soon proves himself to be a master in the art of casting the salient features of life into imaginative relief, very much as Ungaretti cast them into melodic relief. In the long run, therefore, we can describe both poets as having fundamentally the same aim: the reunification of the chaotic world of the present through the provision of an underlying figurative and melodic pattern for its manifold activities. Significantly they do this by re-creating modern moods within the time-hallowed restraints of traditional forms instead of attempting, as the futurists did, to bring about a complete break with the past.

In contrast with the subtle cacophonies of the *Ossi*, the section *Mediterraneo* attempts to provide a full-throated, almost a rhetorical, representation of the poet's joyful reintegration into life. Its lyricism is a paean of praise to the sea which, by acting as the ultimate repository of pure plastic existence, offers a dynamic background for Montale's own life. Needless to say, the tone of the section is no longer one of cautious indecision; for, as an archetype of Being-in-Becoming, the Mediterranean proves capable of reflecting and absorbing all the Protean forms of human experience. Moreover, since the ocean is projected as a metaphysical infinity towards which all finite minds aspire, it symbolizes the sphere within which a complete form of intercommunication between past and present, the living and the dead, may be capable of actualization.

Montale's choice of the ocean as a sounding-board for his moods no doubt had an orphic and atavistic origin. In this regard we recall that he was born and bred along the riviera coast and lived his whole childhood within the sound of the sea. Very soon it became a category of his spirit and its incorruptible liquidity tends to mirror his own specific paradoxical moods of movement-in-repose. Hence, just as the sea was envisaged earlier as an infinite receptacle welcoming Esterina's absolute experiences,[39] so here it is transformed into an imaginative continuum fusing together the metaphysical sphere and the realm of sensation. It represents, in short, the conjunction of the mind and the body, the individual and the racial consciousness. It is the medium within which the poet's 'io trascendentale' operates, in his attempts to bring about miraculous states of emotional liberation; and, as he communes with the sea's protean spirit and contemplates its 'motionless mobility', he makes its continuous movement-in-repose a fixed principle of his art:

Tu m'hai detto primo
che il piccino fermento
del mio cuore non era che un momento
del tuo; che mi era in fondo
la tua legge rischiosa: esser vasto e diverso
e insieme fisso . . .[40]

You first told me that the puny ferment of my heart was simply a moment of yours; that in the depths of my being was your perilous law: to be vast and diverse and at the same time fixed . . .

After propounding this doctrine it is hardly surprising that Montale should seek to transfigure reality in such a way that its static and dynamic features offset each other and subsume the whole drama of existence. By reflecting the values of human activity in the vast mirror of the sea, he hoped to eternalize these values in their very contingency; and by virtue of their very 'absoluteness' they then tend to acquire a self-justifying element, one which arises at the intersection between the material flux of reality and the constant emotive forces inherent in human nature. The lyrical release that results amounts to a reconciliation of the opposing moods of redemption and damnation, of stasis and motion:

Tu vastità riscattavi
anche il patire dei sassi:

pel tuo tripudio era giusta
l'immobilità dei finiti.[41]

> You, o vastness, redeemed even the suffering of the rocks: the immobility of finite creatures was justified by your exultancy.

Later, as we shall see, the poet even nurtures a desire to 'flow back' into the ocean from his landlocked, and thereby damned, state of mind. He represents the idea by evoking the crumbling away of the rocky landfalls of the riviera coast and by associating the process with the unfolding of his own life.

Experience thus takes on the form of a redemptive erosion of the land only to be completed at the point of death, when each one of us will be orphically restored to a state of Being by ultimate immersion in the briny ancestral deep. When compared with such an absolute goal, our everyday experiences in this life seem petty and insignificant, although each thoroughly decisive act we perform is itself a move in the right direction, when once the process of erosion is under way:

M'affisso nel pietrisco
che verso te digrada
fino alla ripa acclive che ti sovrasta,
franosa, gialla, solcata
da strosce d'acqua piovana.
Mia vita è questo secco pendio,
mezzo non fine, strada aperta a sbocchi
di rigagnoli, lento franamento.[42]

> I fix myself in the shingle which slopes down towards you as far as the ascending bank which hangs over you, slithery, yellow, furrowed by gushes of rainwater. My life is this dry slope, a means not an end, a path open to the mouths of runnels, a slow landslide.

Clearly the very interplay of sea and land in this passage brings into the open the symbolic message of the entire sequence. Their two polarities are consistently maintained and figuratively differentiated throughout Montale's work, a fact which explains why for him the ambiguous line of the tide along the seashore is an area of intense experience. When actually formulating such a symbolism he may well indeed have been thinking in evolutionary terms, since the overstepping of the tide-line proved to be a similar traumatic experience for our aquatic ancestors, one which left instinctive memories at the salty level of the blood.

Not surprisingly, therefore, we constantly find that water and the water's edge are associated by Montale with deep and ungraspable feelings. These feelings similarly emerge from the depths of pools and, although they are themselves formless, they tend to offer infinite perspectives. The lyric 'Vasca' illustrates the point, because by peering into a fountain's bowl the poet describes how he detects a closed world of unformed potentialities in its depths. These potentialities are distorted by the ripples made when a pebble is thrown into the water, and through them there half-emerges a mysterious new world which – like Mallarmé's cosmic kiss in 'Autre éventail' – fades away before it can be given an actual form:

Alcuno di noi tirò un ciottolo
che ruppe la tesa lucente:
le molli parvenze s'infransero.

Ma ecco, c'è altro che striscia
a fior della spera rifatta liscia:
di erompere non ha virtú,
vuol vivere e non sa come;
se lo guardi si stacca, torna in giú:
è nato e morto, e non ha avuto un nome.

One among us threw a pebble which broke the shimmering surface: the gentle mirages shattered. But behold, something else slides on the surface of the resmoothed sphere: to burst forth it does not have the power, it wants to live but does not know how; if you look at it, it slips away, sinks down again: it is born and has died, and has not acquired a name.

In the same way Montale believes all memories are gradually eroded away from the human mind and then become formless shadows revivable only by chance effects or encounters. But at times this play of chance re-creates forgotten circumstances and allows the epiphany of a memory to break through into the poet's consciousness like the magical recapitulation of a paradise lost.

The process is fundamentally a modern form of Petrarchism and involves the same dialectic as we have already seen between the active and passive memories. One favourite theme with Montale, as indeed with all hermetic poets, is the recall of childhood states as perceived through the eyes of the adult. In 'Fine dell'infanzia' the starting-point of this kind of analysis is virtually Cardarellian. In the unselfconscious state of childhood the poet considers that everything is given in an immediate sense, because by definition the child is far closer to the pristine glories and memorial arcana of primitive life than the adult. The result is that the metamorphosis occurring at puberty is a traumatic one, and Montale describes the uncertainties of youth as ones in which the mind first becomes attuned to

la musica dell'anima inquieta
che non si decide.

the music of a restless soul which cannot make up its mind.

Such uncertainties are to be contrasted with the fixed mental horizons of infancy which have clear Campanian associations with a timeless and fabulous dreamworld, where

> ogni umano impulso
> appare seppellito
> in aura millenaria.

every human impulse seems buried in an age-old atmosphere.

So close an association of immediate sensations and myth establishes in childhood a 'consenso' ('harmony') between the individual's inner and outer worlds, providing a centre upon which every other form of activity may be concentrated. Is this sense of unity necessarily lost in the process of growing up? Not inevitably, according to Montale. The adult state of election is, as we have already seen, also a state of self-assuredness, and a male figure of election actually casts his shadow over the landscape of this poem. He is thrown into gigantic relief against the screen of the poet's childhood memories and remains rooted in his mind like a Gozzanian engraving:

> Tra macchie di vigneti e di pinete,
> petraie si scorgevano
> calve e gibbosi dorsi
> di collinette: un uomo
> che là passasse ritto s'un muletto
> nell'azzurro lavato era stampato
> per sempre – e nel ricordo.

Among the scrub of vineyards and pine groves, bald stone-quarries and the humped backs of small hills could be seen: a man passing by over there on a mule was engraved in the washed blue-sky for ever – and in remembrance.

His shadowy profile is, in short, metamorphosed into a talisman, into an intense focus of attention; and it is through these obsessive qualities of remembrance that the child may hope to prolong into adulthood the 'estatico affisare' ('ecstatic fixity') of his 'età verginale' ('callow youth').

Even so, the poet is also aware that most children grow out of their state of preconscious happiness after the stirring of their intellects; and then, just as with Gozzano's characters in 'Paolo e Virginia',[43] the dawning of self-consciousness shatters every illusion:

> Giungeva anche per noi l'ora che indaga.
> La fanciullezza era morta in un giro a tondo.

For us too arrived the moment of analysis. Childhood had died in a circling dance.

Hence for both these writers the immediacy of infancy yields before the mediacy of reflective thought, and it is thereafter the sad fate of most human beings to be cast willy-nilly into that anguished state of *noia* or adulthood regarded by Montale as a state of metaphysical alienation.

Once this deep-seated feeling of frustration is detected by the poet, he explores in the next section, *L'agave su lo scoglio,* various means of mitigating it. The dominant symbols he now deploys are those of the winds, all of which are archetypes of memorial stimulation. Typical Italian winds, in particular, have an instinctive power to arouse his innermost hopes and fears; and, since the 'scirocco' (the name of which originates from the Arabic 'sharq' meaning 'dry') blows from a south-easterly direction over the riviera and brings a sense of deep neurosis with it in local folklore, we find it associated with the obsessive anguish of adult life. In a similar fashion the 'tramontana' or chill north wind is considered to mirror the heraclitean flux of existence and fills the poet's thought with an inescapable sense of dismay, aimlessness and disillusion. It causes him, in fact, to look upon the ceaseless churning of the material world in a detached, almost Olympian, manner:

> Ogni forma si squassa nel subbuglio
> degli elementi; è un urlo solo, un muglio
> di scerpate esistenze: tutto schianta
> l'ora che passa: viaggiano la cupola del cielo
> non sai se foglie o uccelli – e non son piú.

Every form is shaken in the churning of the elements; there is one single howl, a bellowing of shattered existences: the passing hour crushes everything: one knows not whether leaves or birds fly across the cupola of the sky – and are no more.

The 'maestrale' ('north-west wind'), on the other hand, is depicted as a restorer of tranquillity, as a stimulus prompting the discovery of a new harmony. Characteristically, this mysterious harmony is again located at the water's edge where so many of Montale's lyrical metamorphoses tend to take place:

> Una carezza disfiora
> la linea del mare e la scompiglia
> un attimo, soffio lieve che vi s'infrange e ancora
> il cammino ripiglia.

A caress touches the line of the sea and disturbs it for a moment, a light breath which breaks upon it and takes up its journey again.

Probably the real function of the 'maestrale' is to drive away the dust and cobwebs surrounding the passive memory and establish a dynamic state of movement-in-repose. Thus, in association with the sea, these three winds represent a monstrous Hegelian dialectic of destruction, anguish and rebirth, and they produce in combination that miraculous, lyrical balancing-act implied in Baudelaire's line:

> Bercant notre infini sur le fini des mers . . . [44]

> cradling our infinity on the finitude of the seas . . .

Montale's 'Maestrale' indeed recalls Baudelaire's 'Le voyage' and his conclusion, like the French poet's, shows the same disquiet consuming the human soul as it seeks out some absolute truth to slake its thirst.[45]

However, Baudelaire is not the only poet whom Montale draws upon for his ideas and imagery at this stage in his development and it eventually becomes clear that he intends to use the tradition, like Eliot, as a means of enriching his lyrical textures. In his view the artist is engaged in a struggle to awaken progressively deeper resonances in the consciousness of his age; and, as we have already seen, he chooses to evoke these resonances through emblematic procedures. One of his most constant lyrical notes is a mood of hopeful despair which expresses itself in an elemental type of melancholy. It can be illustrated in the following audio-visual image which, by echoing a well-known line from Vigny's 'Le cor', gives us a historical perspective of attenuated human anguish stretching right back to the age of Roland himself:

> Nella sera distesa appena, s'ode
> un ululo di corni, uno sfacelo.[46]

> In the barely unfolded evening, one hears a blasting of horns, a shattering collapse.

Twilight cacophonies indeed often represent for him a modern state of *noia*; they symbolize the lowest common emotional denominator of industrialized life, in which desperation and irritation combine to produce apathy in the sensibility. The only way of escape is through the exercise of a 'volontà di ferro' ('an iron will') because the will alone can erect an effective barrier to protect the mind from the gratuitous changes wrought by society. To avoid his own complete 'déracinement' ('uprooting') the poet formulates certain categorical imperatives which will counter his own spiritual drift and allow his sensibility to take root in the emotional substratum of his age. Hence it is mainly through the power of the will that he now hopes to create the necessary conditions for a series of poetic liberations which will not involve the sacrifice of his nucleus of personal identity.

The poem 'Arsenio' [47] dealing with the 'observed observer' appears to be the result of this desire. It attempts to resolve the finite-infinite paradox inherent in human nature by postulating a state of 'rooted rootlessness' as the ideal condition of the human spirit. Although such a concept may at first seem mystifyingly metaphysical, the poet attempts to convince us of its realizability by using concrete imagery to describe it. The very concreteness of the lyric's stylization thus provides an intimate setting of emblematic eternity, an 'eternità tascabile' ('a pocketable eternity'), for the poem. The precise mental state at which Montale aims seems to be a metapsychological one transposing into emotional terms the paradox of 'motionless mobility'. Its central drama is a metaphorical stroll by Arsenio (to be identified on his own admission with the poet himself) down from the heights above a seaside resort on the riviera coast to the seashore, until he reaches a disturbing point of metamorphosis at the water's edge. As he descends from the hills, each step brings him nearer to the 'Ocean of Being' where individual life and corporate existence intersect. So, when he is finally liberated by contact with its waters, he is able to participate in the corporate emotions of society while preserving intact his sense of personal identity. The feeling which results, one of vicarious beatitude, assumes the form of a universal communicability in which, as Bonfiglioli puts it, 'i fenomeni, liberati da una mera evidenziazione empirica, diventano eventi, figure autonome, termini di un rapporto, destini'[48] ('phenomena, freed from a mere empirical persisting, become events, autonomous figures, terms in a relationship, destinies').

The landscape framing this exceptional experience is a phantomatic one, bathed in the eerie silence heralding the approach of a summer storm. Storms are often used as symbolic archetypes in Montale's work and the suppressed storm in particular represents a point of crisis. In this poem it makes itself felt through a hushed mood of expectancy in the opening scene, when an aggregate of objects drawn telescopically from earlier lyrics gives an emblematic representation of a possible meditative breakthrough:

I turbini sollevano la polvere
sui tetti, a mulinelli, e sugli spiazzi
deserti, ove i cavalli incappucciati
annusano la terra, fermi innanzi
ai vetri luccicanti degli alberghi.
Sul corso, in faccia al mare, tu discendi
in questo giorno
or piovorno ora acceso, in cui par scatti
a sconvolgerne l'ore
uguali, strette in trama, un ritornello
di castagnette.

Whirlwinds raise the dust over the rooftops, in spirals, and over the deserted open spaces, where hooded horses nuzzle the ground, motionless before the

> gleaming windows of the hotels. You walk down the street, facing the sea, on this sometimes rainy and sometimes burningly hot day, during which a clatter of castanets appears to break out to disturb the monotonous hours tightly woven into a pattern.

Orchestral variations on the poet's previous images – spiral forms, flashes of reflected light, rain, and dust-laden whirlwinds – are plainly visible here and are intended to deepen the resonance of the tableau. Afterwards, a clatter of castanets promises entry into another sphere, far removed from the inert atmosphere of *noia* which normally envelops the poet.[49] How then does this scene acquire such a meditative function? Mainly through its multiple reflections and the presence of the powerful talisman of blinkered horses whose attitude, as they nuzzle the ground, is suggestive of an ability to reveal a half-forgotten ontology of existence.

In such a description we have clearly passed well beyond Gozzano's 'decalcomania' and moved into a new symbolic dimension. From this point onwards the picture becomes organic in its unfolding because it does more than reflect the poet's mood, it also offers an orphic perspective of possible salvation by virtue of the referential patterns that lie concealed behind its particular combination of object-symbols. So, although superficially the dominant tone is still a neo-crepuscular one, the underlying emblematic allusiveness of the language provides a far greater sense of life's complexity than does the poetry of the crepuscular poets proper.[50]

The next scene transports us into the metaphysical and imaginative sphere in which Arsenio's emblematic function is to unfold. The experience co-involves the protagonist, the sultry heat of the afternoon, and the impending storm; and the apocalyptic sequence of events which their joint influence creates causes life to retreat to its lowest ebb. Within such a framework the hero's ritualistic journey ends along the water's edge, at the highwater mark. This is the point where the pure plastic motion of the sea and the memorially crystallized immobility of the land intersect, producing in Arsenio's mind a flash of illumination as he crunches along the gravel like a somnambulist. His experience has been described by Solmi as a kind of 'vertigine metafisica' ('metaphysical vertigo'), whose repressed exaltation is concentrated in the awe-inspiring motion of a gigantic waterspout:

> È il segno d'un'altra orbita: tu seguilo.
> Discendi all'orizzonte che sovrasta
> una tromba di piombo, alta sui gorghi,
> piú d'essi vagabonda: salso nembo
> vorticante, soffiato dal ribelle
> elemento alle nubi; fa che il passo
> su la ghiaia ti scricchioli e t'inciampi

il viluppo dell'alghe: quell'istante
è forse, molto atteso, che ti scampi
dal finire il tuo viaggio, anello d'una
catena, immoto andare, oh troppo noto
delirio, Arsenio, d'immobilità . . .

It is the sign of another orbit: you follow it. Go down towards the horizon where there looms a leaden waterspout, high above the deep, more restless than it: a salty twisting billow sucked up from the rebellious element to the clouds; make your footstep grind upon the gravel and let the tangle of the seaweed enlace you: that moment is perhaps the long-awaited one which will save you from finishing your journey, a link in a chain, a motionless motion, oh the too well-known frenzy, Arsenio, of immobility . . .

Probably its spiralling circularity has, at bottom, an orphic implication, to be associated with the 'eternal return' and the ritual of purification through immersion in water already detectable in 'Falsetto'. In the shadow of its brooding emblematic presence Arsenio feels he can walk confidently along the shore in a mood of expectancy, deeply conscious that joy is to be found more in striving than in the completion of one's journey.

Eventually his stroll takes him along the promenade where commercial and other gaudy, materialistic influences make themselves felt. But even the musicians in the waterfront cafés are momentarily silenced by certain mysterious claps of thunder marking Arsenio's arrival, and in this respect we are again reminded of the thunder in the false world of 'Caffè a Rapallo' or of its admonitory function in Eliot's 'The Waste Land'. So at this point the atmosphere almost becomes one of sultry, psycho-ethical incubation, implicit in the humid heat of the suppressed storm and the appearance of the dogstar; and, within it, other symbolic combinations are brought into play to emphasize the protagonist's restless calm. One is a flash of forked lightning like an inverted tree (probably of dawning self-knowledge) which bathes the scene with a pinkish, transitional light, not unlike Campana's orphic sunsets. Eventually, however, all this inward-looking imagery is externalized by an association of the thunderclap with the gypsy-drum of the musicians, and its subdued cacophony implies that the moment of intercommunication is at hand. Indeed, the intersection of the spheres of the active and passive memories, of the present and the past, is imaginatively foreshadowed at this point by the merging of the sea and sky into a single shadow.

On completion of his second stage of initiation Arsenio then encounters the bobbing acetylene lamps on the boats in the harbour and they perhaps suggest flashbacks to the poet's childhood vacations at Monterosso, or even to the stunted childhood state associated with that riviera poet *par excellence*, Camillo Sbarbaro, in an earlier section. A faint mist or rain squall now descends upon the scene and portends a traumatic event, the intensity of which is emphasized by the wind flapping around wet canvas and the hissing of paper lanterns as they fall, rain-sodden, to the ground. The rain then washes out the false world of the musicians with its artificial decorations and at the same time metamorphoses the hero into a vegetative talisman around which there accumulates another 'morto viluppo di memorie' ('dead tangle of memories'). The plant into which he is changed is a reed, described as a mobile yet memorially rooted object, possibly with Dantesque and Barresian associations.[51] Indeed, the vegetative talisman itself suggests a two-stage descent in Dante's hierarchy of Being, from the rational through the sensitive to the vegetative soul with all its instinctive potentialities.

Although caked with mud and trailing its roots it is still a pliant and adaptable life-form, quivering with vicarious joy and irradiating the qualities of a dynamic organism. What then is the nature of the strange power that the rain-drenched and transmogrified Arsenio possesses as he sits on the wet matting of his tent? Probably it is the poet's previously mentioned vicarious power for redeeming others, although it now derives less from chance events than from his newly established sense of personal, if still mutable, identity. In fact, once his redemptive powers have been reaffirmed, his fate is to be re-immersed in the 'onda antica' ('ancient wave') which will reactivate his latent virtues as a talisman. Subsequent to this re-immersion he is once more cast up on the shore among the 'ghiacciata moltitudine' ('frozen multitude') of the Damned, where a mere word or gesture will suffice to enable him to liberate a lost soul; and that soul will in turn find its skeletal memory associated with stardust and transported upwards to an eternal sphere by the wind.

In this sense Arsenio is the 'unmoved mover', the very incarnation of the talismanic spirit animating Montale's personal priesthood. He becomes the initiator and the catalyst of the miracles wrought through the poet's deeply felt religion of sacrificial altruism. By virtue of his passive mutability or active changelessness other souls are revitalized in his presence and are conveyed to the region of the 'io trascendentale' where they glow like jewels of memory among the constellations, very much like Mallarmé's swan:[52]

> e se un gesto ti sfiora, una parola
> ti cade accanto, quello è forse, Arsenio,
> nell'ora che si scioglie, il cenno d'una
> vita strozzata per te sorta, e il vento
> la porta con la cenere degli astri.

and if a gesture brushes past you, a word falls beside you, that is perhaps,

> Arsenio, in the melting hour, the sign of a strangled life rising for you, and the wind carries it off with the ashes of the stars.

The 'via di scampo' ('way of escape') for the Damned is thus to make of themselves a talismanic potency for the redemption of other souls. In this poem Arsenio evolves into a transcendent object-person or talisman through whom a force of aesthetic redemption operates, and his acts provide possible moments of liberation for others. We shall find similar examples of the personification of this force later, particularly in Clizia and the intersubjective voice in 'Voce giunta con le folaghe', where as a memorial power it appears to pervade our everyday experiences and places us all in our 'predestined voids' so that we can fill them emotionally by combining suitable circumstances. The same idea is also apparent in Montale's tendency to envisage the dead soul as an ashen precipitate, as a skeletal nexus of relations, which lingers fitfully in the minds of the living and ultimately 'redeems' itself by finding its proper place in the racial memory.

If then we grant this preoccupation with the afterlife, however wraith-like and insubstantial it may appear,[53] it is not difficult once more to link Montale's cosmology with Dante's; for, as we have already mentioned, he has much in common with Dante's spiritual outlook, if not with the temper of his religious convictions. So, just as Dante postulates a 'spezial amore' ('special love') guiding the human soul to its rightful place in the world of the heavenly intelligences, similarly the modern poet invents a parallel process, except that he makes the stimulus a memorial recall with humanist overtones instead of a divine force with theological implications. All that has changed is the nature of the beatitude offered; because, instead of taking up an anagogical attitude towards the ultimates in human destiny, Montale adopts an aesthetic and ethical one; and his sense of immortality amounts to a lingering memorial deposit left by the deceased's personality in the form of a lyrical *raptus*.

One might be tempted to think that such an impalpable religion of art is itself a mysticism, and to a certain extent we could accuse Montale's pan-psychism of being a disguised Platonism. Yet what distinguishes it from earlier Platonic forms is its uncompromising existentiality, its concrete-ness, especially since the poet never postulates a standard of perfection to be obtained, but only a focus of emotional energy upon which all the faculties of the spirit must be concentrated to create a work of art. Thus art in his view can only function in contingent situations, where it draws its strength from the transiency and interrelevance of an aggregate of images.

Because of its tendency to explore the metaphysical limits of existence, the *Ossi di seppia* deals much less with single human situations than *Le occasioni*; but we do come across prefigurations of Montale's 'occasioni' towards the end of the volume. A case in point is 'Crisalide' which moves away from archetypal attitudes towards at least an embryonic form of a personal relationship. The lyric is addressed to a lady [54] who seems to have become so cocooned in the poet's passive memory that he can only visualize her as a chrysalis: as a disembodied nexus of relations or one of those lost images he earlier attempted to draw out of the murky depths of pools. Because of her remoteness she is naturally much less individuated than Arsenio, although she too is metamorphosed at one stage into a plant and even promises to flower. But in the end she tends to act as a perfect foil to his talismanic presence, because she is transformed into a kind of passive keepsake, whereas he is changed, as we previously saw, into an active redeemer.

What the poet is apparently trying to illustrate through the very spectrality of his fading memory of this lady is the actual process of forgetting which he regards as a kind of dying. His attempt at recollection indeed leads to an échec in her case because time and distance have made her image so obscure in his mind that the bond of intimacy between them has finally been broken. In future they will be mere prisons of regret for each other and will become suspended in a limbo of 'monche esistenze' ('stunted existences') as their respective boats of salvation founder in the shallows of time. Their mutual regression consequently leads Montale to dwell on the underlying futility of life and to doubt the very possibility of moments of communication, of 'liberation', from the closed circle of solipsist experience. Indeed, he now even begins to suspect that his entire doctrine of memorial recall is nothing more than an idle dream and that the will-o'-the-wisp of transcendental communion with another soul must necessarily prove unattainable:

> Ah crisalide, com'era amara questa
> tortura senza nome che ci volve
> e ci porta lontani – e poi non restano
> neppure le nostre orme sulla polvere;
> e noi andremo innanzi senza smuovere
> un sasso solo della gran muraglia;
> e forse tutto è fisso, tutto è scritto,
> e non vedremo sorgere per via
> la libertà, il miracolo,
> il fatto che non era necessario!

Ah chrysalis, how bitter was this nameless torment which rolls us on and carries us far – and then not even our footprints remain in the dust; and we shall plod on without budging a single stone of the great wall; and perhaps everything is fixed, all is written, and we shall not see liberty rising by the wayside, the miracle, the fact which was not necessary!

The elegiac nature of these lines is self-evident, and the failure of communication they suggest can be equated with a sense of Petrarchan 'unrequitedness' on a human and cosmic level. Both protagonists are ineluctably sealed off from one another as they subsist in recessive metaphysical cells of non-communication, with the result that neither is able to act as a self-willed victim for the salvation of the other and the poet suffers intensely from this deprivation:

Il silenzio ci chiude nel suo lembo
e le labbra non s'aprono per dire
il patto ch'io vorrei
stringere col destino: di scontare
la vostra gioia con la mia condanna.

Silence encloses us in its shroud and our lips do not part to affirm the pact which I would like to strike with destiny: to discount your joy through my damnation.

The type of renunciation he now feels is not unlike the universal anguish experienced by Leopardi. For both poets, as Bo suggests in the latter's case, 'il nulla . . . è nello stesso tempo un dato d'arrivo, un risultato e uno stimolo, lo scatto che riporta alla guardia dell'uomo'[55] ('the void . . . is at the same time a point of arrival, a result and a stimulus, the break-through point which brings one back to the defence of man'). Hence we shall not be surprised to find Montale returning time and time again to his grief-stricken religion of vicarious redemption and seeking a state of beatitude at one stage removed as a means of assuaging the anguish implicit in life.

The reason why Montale's pessimism is less intense than Leopardi's is because the modern poet still holds a residual belief in the power of the will to overcome the limits of the human condition. It is the will, in fact, which consolidates for him those 'radici viscide' ('sticky roots') possessed by Arsenio and which allow him to anchor himself within his own particular historical atmosphere. Towards the end of the *Ossi di seppia* his faith in the will of the artist grows, if anything, even more intense than it was at the beginning; so that in the lyric 'Casa sul mare' he attempts to redefine his doctrine of vicarious salvation with the object of making it dependent on conscious, decisive acts, both on the part of saver and saved:

Penso che per i piú non sia salvezza,
ma taluno sovverta ogni disegno,
passi il varco, qual volle si ritrovi.
Vorrei prima di cedere segnarti
codesta via di fuga
labile come nei sommossi campi
del mare spuma o ruga.

> I think that for most people there is no salvation, but that a few upset all designs, pass beyond the threshold, such as have willed it, refind themselves. Before yielding I would like to mark out for you this way of escape as fragile as foam or ripple in the heaving fields of the sea.

Such acts provoke momentary feelings of euphoria which ideally – if not chronologically – tend to change the dominant tone at the end of the *Ossi di seppia* into a hymn of praise. The point is made in 'Riviere'[56] where a serene state of wisdom is acquired through intense suffering:

> Triste anima passata
> e tu volontà nuova che mi chiami,
> tempo è forse d'unirvi
> in un porto sereno di saggezza.
> Ed un giorno sarà ancora l'invito
> di voci d'oro, di lusinghe audaci,
> anima mia non piú divisa. Pensa:
> cangiare in inno l'elegia; rifarsi;
> non mancare piú.

> Sad soul of the past and you renewed will which calls to me, it is perhaps time to link you together in a serene haven of wisdom. And one day there will again be an invitation of golden voices, of bold praise, o my soul no longer divided. Think: to change the elegy into a hymn; to remake oneself; to fail no more.

Admittedly, this imperious tone can hardly be regarded as a prescriptive one, for in his later work it will soon vanish with the loss of the poet's momentary illusions. But the collection as a whole achieves three basic objectives without which Montale's sensibility could not have developed further. First, it propounds a dialectic of the active and passive memories and meditates upon the metaphysical attitudes and moral precepts deriving from this dichotomy; second, it elaborates a vicarious religion of salvation and a magical state of intercommunication between the dead or the absent and the living; and, finally, it familiarizes the reader with the aggregates of object-symbols, emblematic mediators, and emotionally smouldering talismans through which the poet will attempt certain forms of catharsis. In this way it lays a firm foundation for a less generic approach to life in *Le occasioni*, where the poet considerably sharpens his responses to his personal circumstances.

★ ★ ★ ★ ★ ★

In this second collection we soon discover that life is not something to be thought over, but to be lived: lived in the sense that the single situation or agonizing rebuff now replaces the contrived metaphysical limits of experience as the boundary of the poet's insight. Doubtless this is why the overriding personality in *Le occasioni* is no longer an indefinite phantom but a palpitating womanly 'absence' who appears as a distant 'tu' as early as 'Il balcone', the liminary poem of the collection. Despite her ethereality she firmly guides the poet away from his hitherto contemplative existence in the spectator's gallery of life, in the hope of imbuing him with a whole-hearted desire for commitment:

> Pareva facile giuoco
> mutare in nulla lo spazio
> che m'era aperto, in un tedio
> malcerto il certo tuo fuoco.
>
> Ora a quel vuoto ho congiunto
> ogni mio tardo motivo,
> sull'arduo nulla si spunta
> l'ansia di attenderti vivo.

> It seemed an easy game to change into nothing the space which you had opened to me, into an uncertain tedium your certain fire. Now to that void I have linked every tardy motif of mine, on the arduous void there grows a desire to await you alive.

Clearly, her influence is at best intermittent and she herself becomes incarnate only in a series of momentary flashes in the normal Montalian fashion. Most of the time she hardly possesses any substantiality at all and stands as little more than the sum or projection of the experiential lessons learned by the poet during the previous lyrical meditations. In this sense it is perhaps difficult to assert without qualification that *Le occasioni* is a poetry of living, to be contrasted with his previous poetry of speculative observation. But it is nevertheless a representation of the nearest approach the poet was then capable of making to life. Accordingly, an existential element now seems to run in double harness with his distant reflective manner, providing his lady with the attenuated charms and the breathless timidity of a modern Laura.

Often her emotional complexity proves to be the mirror-image of Montale's own personality, as Laura was with Petrarch; although yet another dimension (or lack of dimension) separates her from her early humanist counterpart, her regressive allusiveness. She is in other words a Laura whose character appears to be described in such a way as to conform to the Mallarmean dictum that the poet's approach should be to 'paint not the thing, but the effect it produces'.[57] However, she is to be distinguished from the Mallarmean archetype too, through her ethical function and her possible, if improbable, accessibility. She is, in short, by no means a creature of a different order from the poet, but rather a bridge uniting him *immanently* with the lyrical impulses and social consciousness of his age. In Montale's own words she might be considered the 'occasione-spinta' ('situation-impulse') by means of which the single circumstance is transformed into the 'opera-oggetto'[58] ('objective work of art').

Since her function normally corresponds with that of the emblem, we legitimately begin to doubt her very existence as a person, especially when we discover that her only specific gestures are a few vague acts like the tossing back of her hair. As such, she is reduced to the rôle of a synthesizing intelligence, and by acting solely as the overseer of the poet's aesthetics is slowly transformed into the *dea ex machina* of his lyricism. Even so, her power as a humanizing force gradually increases as the work progresses and prepares us for her somewhat involuted political attitudes appearing in *Finisterre*, a short collection first published in 1943 and later incorporated in *La bufera e altro* (1956). By that stage even the poet had become rather distressed at her evanescent and fragmentary epiphanies and this is perhaps one of the factors which causes him to describe *Le occasioni* as 'un'arancia, o meglio un limone a cui mancava uno spicchio: non proprio quello della poesia pura nel senso che ho indicato prima, ma in quello del *pedale*, della musica profonda e della contemplazione'[59] ('an orange, or better a lemon with a segment missing: not precisely that of pure poetry in the sense that I have indicated earlier, but in the sense of *pedal*, of deep music and contemplation'). Possibly this lack of deeper musicality is to be explained by the lady's failure to develop as a symbol of fulfilment; instead, she remains simply as a mirror-image of his shattered *alter ego* and retains many of his own ambivalent attitudes to living. In the last resort she is only to be distinguished from the disembodied phantom of the *Ossi di seppia* by virtue of her faint aura of humanity: an emotivity which is hardly substantial enough to give rise to specific situations, yet which drives underground, without wholly eliminating it, the poet's earlier, more abstract, approach to life.

Normally the tensions arising in the present volume are the product of a relationship between two people, as was already the case in 'Crisalide'; and, indeed, its lyrics also retain the other principal feature of that poem, a memorial perspective. Hence, although the dialectic dominating them is still that of the active and passive memories, their contradictions seem to be transcended when the lady is totally absorbed as an imaginative figure by the poet's sensibility – when her distinctiveness, that is, emanates solely from the situation in which both are immersed and is filtered vicariously through his particular lyrical perceptions. Such an involution of the lady's character is an essential ingredient in hermetic aesthetics,[60] since any assertion of the self on her part would tend to place her outside the magic circle of emblematic representation of which she is both the archetypal image and the activator. Yet while she remains within its ambit she offers a means whereby Montale's contingent experiences shed their grosser sensory qualities and are transmuted into radiant human values implying a state of ethical and figurative synthesis.

Since she is so completely absorbed by the poet's responses, it is not even of great importance whether this lady remains as one and the same person throughout the work. In fact, her authentic nature is probably represented only in the *Mottetti*, the section corresponding to the *Ossi* in the earlier collection; and, precisely because her individuality is not as significant as her function, her actual identity on the poet's own admission changes in the various sections of the work. What remains constant, on the other hand, is Montale's growing consciousness of her singular powers; and so already in 'Vecchi versi' (1926) she is foreshadowed as the controlling deity of his lyrical situations, even though at this stage she acts merely as the poet's unnamed *confidante* and operates vicariously through another feminine presence, his mother. A similar kind of remote control broods over most of the other lyrics, sometimes becoming more definite and sometimes less so. Structurally speaking, in these poems the poet does not try to plunge us directly *in medias res* ('into the heart of things') like so many other modern poets, but prefers to adopt a modified Parnassian approach to composition; and in the above-mentioned lyric, for instance, he bathes the scene in the mystery of a hallucinatory seascape before describing the curious drama which the situation prompts.

Within the particular atmosphere evoked we note that the sea and the sky merge on the line of the horizon offering a typical Montalian point of departure for the creation of a higher state of consciousness. A talismanic emblem subsumes the exact moment of 'veggenza' or insight and takes the form of a moth which moves in a giddy circling flight around the chandelier of the room where the poet is sitting. A dramatic tension gradually develops between the poet and the insect, since both are seekers after light and both are frustrated in their quest for it by virtue of the limits imposed on them by the vicious circle of their existential condition:

Nel breve
vano della mia stanza, ove la lampada
tremava dentro una ragnata fucsia,
penetrò la farfalla, al paralume
giunse e le conterie che l'avvolgevano
segnando i muri di riflessi ombrati

eguali come fregi si sconvolsero
e sullo scialbo corse alle pareti
un fascio semovente di fili esili.

In the restricted space of my room, where the light quivered inside a cobwebbed fuchsia, the moth entered, reached the lampshade, and the pendants which surrounded it were disturbed, marking the walls with shadowy reflections not unlike friezes, and on the plaster of the walls there ran a self-propelled sheaf of slender threads.

A hidden promise of redemption is no doubt contained here in the imagery associated with the blundering waywardness of the moth. But the complex pattern of relations cast on the walls by the reflections of the glass pendants also serves to illustrate (by analogy) the existence of similar relations surrounding human beings as they blunder about in their particularized situations.

At the next stage the mode of emblematic representation becomes more overt and depicts a scene of emotional shock. The horror evoked is ostensibly that of the poet at the hideousness of the moth; but, in reality, it also implies the horror individuals feel when suddenly confronted with the idea of the precariousness of existence:

Era un insetto orribile dal becco
aguzzo, gli occhi avvolti come d'una
rossastra fotosfera, al dosso il teschio
umano; e attorno dava se una mano
tentava di ghermirlo un acre sibilo
che agghiacciava.

It was a horrible insect with a sharp mouth, with eyes as if surrounded by a reddish photosphere, on its back the human skull; and, all around, if a hand tried to seize it, it gave a sharp hiss which paralysed one.

From this description we can easily identify the death's-head moth and are at once reminded of a similar one appearing in Gozzano's 'Acherontia atropos', quoted earlier. Both poets were undoubtedly aiming at creating a 'frisson nouveau' ('fresh shudder') when evoking it, but Montale's achievement is far more self-conscious than his predecessor's. His description results in the production of a fulminatory image in which the insect's terrifying contingency is perpetuated and given metaphysical significance through a process of *epoché*:

Poi tornò la farfalla dentro il nicchio
che chiudeva la lampada, discese
sui giornali del tavolo, scrollò
pazza aliando le carte –
e fu per sempre
con le cose che chiudono in un giro

sicuro come il giorno, e la memoria
in sé le cresce, sole vive d'una
vita che disparí sotterra . . .

> Then the moth returned again to the niche which enclosed the light, fell on to the newspapers on the table, tossed madly, winging over the sheets – and it persisted for ever like things shut in a closed sphere as safe as day, and memory magnifies them within itself, the sole survivors of a life which has vanished underground . . .

This subterranean realm of subsisting again coincides with the passive memory, the poet's personal hell; and in it lives are crystallized into objects or daguerrotypes in true Gozzanian fashion, until they are momentarily revivified by pious recollection.

What then distinguishes this poem from similar ones in the *Ossi di seppia*? Mainly the stress it lays on the creature rather than on the metaphysical situation in which the latter is involved. Thus a new type of Petrarchism is generated, one which is not abstract and based on still-lifes like the tableaus of *Sarcofaghi*, but rather one in which the emphasis falls on the emblematic reduction of a moment of authentic experience. The same technique is continued throughout the collection, even though the intensity of the emotional release is not always sufficient to ensure an emblematic crystallization of the poet's mood. In fact, by temperament Montale was destined to shy away from dazzling emblematic representations, for he was always highly suspicious of the natural exuberance of poets like D'Annunzio and therefore half-suppressed his more powerful feelings in order to avoid a similar rhetoric. This explains why normally he preferred to convey his outlook through restrained cacophonies like the clashing of metal sheets or the dull thud of cracked jugs rather than through Esterina's more jubilant and carefree peal of bells. Yet, as we have already seen, glimmers of hope still shine through his subtle cacophonies and provide an ethico-aesthetic resilience for his lyricism.

A danger that could easily result from the above type of hypostasis is a cult of verbal 'fixations'. It is indeed a temptation to which Quasimodo frequently succumbs later, but which Montale generally succeeds in avoiding because he is aware that true transfiguration implies empathy as well as a show of imaginative ingenuity.[61] He consequently manages to distinguish clearly between the authentic lyric and the poem- document, although even he is not averse to using the latter occasionally to lay a deliberately false trail. One such trail, it seems, is the kind of mass-hysteria one meets on the sportsfield. An instance of this is recounted in 'Buffalo' whose setting is the Paris velodrome during a bicycle race. In the electrifying atmosphere the poet and crowd apparently 'pass beyond', and the spell sparking off their meaningless exhilaration is the incantatory effect of the word 'Buffalo' itself:

> Mi dissi
> Buffalo! – e il nome agí.

I said to myself Buffalo! – and the word acted.

The final outcome of such gratuitous releases is an empty nominalism illustrated in the next poem 'Keepsake' which simply lists a series of one-dimensional characters drawn from operettas. The most animated is perhaps Robinson Crusoe's Man Friday who has, however, fallen from a state of emblematic grace to the level of a decadent, contemplative talisman:

> Venerdí
> sogna l'isole verdi e non danza piú.

Friday dreams of green islands and dances no longer.

This description is designed to suggest a virtual *reductio ad absurdum* ('reduction to absurdity') of Friday's character, in which the living person is replaced by a decorative fossil lost in 'una piega di memoria' ('a fold of memory'). He represents in other words the point of crisis beyond which character becomes burnt-out and buried in the passive memory, since it moves out of the reach of lyrical recall and then represents a mere *flatus vocis*[62] ('empty sound').

These spectral figures contrast markedly with the other genuine personalities to be found in *Le occasioni*, whose intense individual actions subsume whole areas of existence. While most of them are again women, they are no longer the instinct-driven creatures of the *Ossi di seppia*, but emblems of mature womanhood. A case in point is the Jewess Liuba who carries her own particular state of grace around with her. From the outset we sense the inner tranquillity of her character; and, as if to emphasize further the homeliness and domesticity of her nature, she is closely associated with a talisman or household god, a cat. Such an interlocking of emblem and talisman not only brings out their interrelevance, it also creates a strange atmosphere of equipoise which reappears in 'Dora Markus' despite the lady's suppressed 'irrequietudine' ('restlessness'). Indeed, as this stage Montale is in complete command of his scale of symbolic values from the keepsake to the emblem and he can use figures at one level to offset those at another with remarkable dexterity. The feeling of relatedness that we experience when encountering these various object-symbols actually gives his poetry an aura of close-knit unity, a fact which is reflected in the title of the work and which indicates that generic situations will henceforth yield to precise 'occasioni'. Admittedly, in themselves these 'situations' seem essentially discontinuous, but when closely inspected they have a second order of continuity about them which is connected with the symbolic development of certain themes. Their coherence is also strengthened by the poet's now fully consolidated procedure of producing telescopic flashbacks to the steadily maturing lyrical archetypes of his previous lyricism.

Such mosaics or imaginative cross-references help to throw new light on otherwise perplexing poems like 'Carnevale di Gerti' whose obscurity upon first reading is complete. Even the poet felt obliged to offer a few words of explanation about this lyric and in a footnote he tells us that its central image is based on the fact that fortune-tellers in Italian fairgrounds sometimes cast molten lead into water to divine the future of their clients. They then read their horoscopes from the grotesque incrustations produced on the metal. This information is perhaps itself of rather limited value and sheds little light on the lyric; yet, apart from it and the additional point that Gerti's husband was doing his military service at the time, we are left to our own interpretative devices.[63]

What strikes us first about the poem is that it is constructed upon two temporal planes. It is as if Montale, as Getto has suggested,[64] is indulging in an impossible 'recherche du temps perdu' ('search after lost time'), in which the present is used as a spring-board to initiate false, but kaleidoscopic, flashbacks into a half-remembered past. The real scene is a fairground at carnival-time where the poet has taken Gerti to cheer her up; and the memorial flashback refers to the festivities of the previous New Year's Eve to which Gerti tries to put back the clock so as to be reunited with her husband. In this sense the poem reminds us of a Leopardian 'festa' ('feast' or 'holiday') because the festive occasion is used as a symbolic point of departure for an analysis of human life in the round. Equally, the drama evoked seems to move towards a predestined end, although, as long as it lasts, it is sufficiently hallucinatory to colour the lady's daydream and create an inner sphere of lyrical make-believe.

The opening lines depicting the confusion of the fairground are dominated by a symbolic Wheel of Fate. The atmosphere produced entices the heroine into a fairy-tale world described as a 'tremulous air-bubble', in which she is immediately transported back to the previous New Year and has her fortune told through the plunging of molten lead into water. As she muses, she is herself caught up in a regressive memorial vortex and finds herself cast out of time and space back into a suspended state of childhood innocence, where she encounters a collection of rumbustious toys and dolls, actually the presents offered to the guests at the New Year's party. She soon sinks passively to their inanimate level, thereby becoming in this parenthetic lilliputian limbo an object 'chiusa tra i doni . . . per gli assenti'[65] ('enclosed with the gifts . . . for the absentees'). Consequently we sense here in many respects a similar 'mondo gnomo' to that previously found in 'Caffè a Rapallo' and elsewhere. Its degenerate or damnatory nature is highlighted by the mention of a lottery to distribute the presents (as if by pure chance) and also by Gerti's desire to renounce her present life in order to become identified with the enchanted circle of make-believe she has by now conjured up in her mind. In so doing, she hopes first to re-enact and then eternalize a moment of happiness encrusted in the past; and afterwards the poet evokes another unreal fairyland atmosphere to underline and intensify her sense of escape:

Chiedi
tu di fermare il tempo sul paese
che attorno si dilata? Le grandi ali
screziate ti sfiorano, le logge
sospingono all'aperto esili bambole
bionde, vive, le pale dei mulini
rotano fisse sulle pozze garrule.

Do you ask for time to be stopped in the hamlet which dilates around you? The giant many-coloured sails graze you, the loggias drive out into the open slender fair-headed, living dolls, the waterwheels' paddles whirl, fixed over gurgling pools.

According to Bonora this landscape combines scenarios from two operettas, *Il paese dei campanelli* by Marco Lombardo and *Le campane di Corneville* by R. Planquette.[66] Their artificial tinselled atmospheres offer Gerti a moment of 'false election'; but the feeling soon proves illusory and she is then compelled to reassert her sense of reality and release herself from her self-imposed and regressive, lilliputian existence.

As self-consciousness flows back, all the images of her previous damnation reappear, together with the dominion of time, and her everyday existential condition replaces the sham state of 'Being' which she had created momentarily for herself. Reality's return is represented by the clanking of the 'ruote dei carriaggi' ('wheels of the military trains') which like life not only bump inevitably along, but also remind her of her husband through their military overtones. To lessen the shock of her reversion to the land of the living and her acknowledgement of her husband's continued absence, the poet once again poses at this point as a self-willed victim and tries to offer her some vicarious comfort by stressing the similarity of their fates and the bond of solidarity uniting them. So, since their destinies, as told by the fortune-tellers, are both ones of damnation, the poem ends on a note of melancholy and despair, stressing the fact that there is no way of escape for either of them, for life

> . . . torna alla via dove con te intristisco,
> quella che additò un piombo raggelato
> alle mie, alle tue sere:
> torna alle primavere che non fioriscono.

. . . returns to the street where I grow sad with you, the one which a congealed lump of lead indicated for your and my evenings: returns to the springs which do not flower.

If therefore we had to define what exactly the poem symbolizes, we would say that it underlines the danger of abandoning the grimness of real life for a false sense of well-being, as previously hinted at in 'Buffalo'. Its curve of inspiration rises to a point of artificial exaltation and then gradually sinks back towards a state of complete disillusionment. The poet and the lady, in short, are obliged to accept in the end the pointlessness of their wilful attempts at escapism.

By contrasting Gerti's situation with Liuba's we make the interesting discovery that Montale's emblems can be positive as well as negative, whereas Gozzano's symbols with similar wide-ranging implications were virtually always negative. So, while the neo-crepuscular poet's art marks a half-way stage to the modern sensibility by reducing Pascoli's anthropomorphic imagery to inanimate objects of still-life, Montale's takes the process to its final conclusion by reanimating the nineteenth-century lyricist's symbolism against the dislocated and gloomy background of the modern world. This means that he has a scale of empathy or empathic commitment in his poetry which makes use both of a lifeless Gozzanian symbolism at the one end of the spectrum and of a dynamic, full-blown emblemism at the other. By precise acts of will he rings the changes on the various symbols contained within this hierarchy of object-symbols, and the order of ascension appears to be the keepsake, the fetish, the talisman, the objective correlative, and the emblem, the latter usually evoking a mediatory figure which guarantees a form of complete lyrical communication. These symbolic values naturally work through their subtle combinations, but each is capable of definition in its own right. The keepsake, for instance, is normally a dead relic with, at most, only an obscure sentimental charge; the fetish is an obsessional keepsake to which the poet feels himself intimately linked by past associations; the talisman proves to be a keepsake endued with magical effects which can initiate an emotional 'release'; the objective correlative, as we have already seen, encapsulates a complete mood in a landscape; while the emblem has likewise been illustrated in its cathartic, mediatory function in a number of lyrics. What we have to remember, however, is that the modern lyricist who deploys the symbols holds a very different view of the world from that of the late nineteenth- and early twentieth-century poets. Hence, while with Pascoli lyrical emotion still derives from a pre-conceived mythology, from the supposition that a built-in sympathy exists between the mind and natural objects, Montale rejects the pathetic fallacy altogether, and considers that for imaginative values to be created there must be a one-way flow of emotion only, from the poet to the concrete elements which make up his lyrical texture. Accordingly, no reciprocal mystery subsists in his work of the kind foreshadowed by Baudelaire's 'forêts de symboles' ('forests of symbols'), but only the magic of empathy which imposes the poet's moods upon his lyrical aggregates.

A poem having many affinities with 'Carnevale di Gerti' is 'Dora Markus' which in its second part curiously takes Gerti as its source of inspiration. The combination of these two women into a single character is, as previously hinted, typical of Montale, since it was more the symbolic function of individuals than the distinctiveness of their personalities which ultimately interested him. In the first part of the lyric the heroine is not unexpectedly associated with a talisman or fetish emphasizing her dominant characteristic, her complete trust in life; and it turns out to be a toy white mouse differing in no essential way from the 'morti balocchi' ('dead dolls') found in 'Carnevale di Gerti'. Dora keeps her lucky charm close to her at all times and it is to be found in her handbag next to those other fetishes of her feminine charm, her powder-puff, lipstick and nail-file. But whether or not her determination to make a success of life through the mediation of this amulet is effective is hardly made clear, since the poem was never completed in its original form. The first part dealing with Dora dates from 1926, while the second dealing with Gerti was written in 1939.

One feature which apparently does nevertheless subsist despite the substitution of the one lady for the other is their Jewishness.[67] It shines through the imagery and tonal colouring in which it is embedded and gives the impression of a smouldering, though strictly controlled, passion. As a consequence, the combined figure of Dora and Gerti symbolizes the 'wandering Jew' in a modern sense, and her particular wanderlust is based on a much desired but impossible return to her native land. Dora's self-deluding hope despite her exile and apparent alienation is emphasized by the fact that she is virtually depicted within a landscape resembling a Gozzanian daguerrotype, as she gazes out over Porto Corsini at Ravenna and imagines that she glimpses across the expanse of the Adriatic her distant home of Carinthia. In her mind the prospect at once takes on the appearance of a memorial paradise, and then, by comparison, the Ravennese scene degenerates into a static correlative picture of damnation. Within its sluggish atmosphere Dora's aspirations are offset by Montale's self-conscious and disillusioned melancholy, and both their moods are at once blended together in the image of a brooding and inert spring:

Fu dove il ponte di legno
mette a Porto Corsini sul mare alto
e rari uomini, quasi immoti, affondano
o salpano le reti. Con un segno
dello mano additavi all'altra sponda
invisibile la tua patria vera.
Poi seguimmo il canale fino alla darsena
della città, lucida di fuliggine,
nella bassura dove s'affondava
una primavera inerte, senza memoria.

It was where a wooden jetty ran out to sea at Port Corsini and a few men, almost motionless, lowered or drew in nets. With a wave of your hand you sketched out the other invisible coast, your real native land. Then we followed the canal right down to the docks of the city, which was gleaming with soot in the lowlands where an inert spring was sinking, without memory.

What is significant in this passage is that the bright sootiness of its damnatory atmosphere has the effect of causing Dora's dormant hope to flare up more intensely than ever. It is highlighted prismatically in a single talisman – a dying mullet – which is seen against the ageless pageant of the former exarchate of Ravenna, with its colourful byzantine culture. Such a combination of 'talismano' and 'occasione' almost transforms Dora into a Campanian priestess, and she emerges from the exotic atmosphere like some mysterious oriental figure, the archetypal Jewess endowed with an age-old anguish and gentleness:

E qui dove un'antica vita
si screzia in una dolce
ansietà d'Oriente,
le tue parole iridavano come le scaglie
della triglia moribonda.

And here where an ancient way of life becomes variegated within a gentle oriental anxiety, your words glowed iridescently like the scales of a dying mullet.

Suspended as she is between the contradictory feelings of a deep racial passion and a despairing hope, she is perhaps once again to be compared with Arsenio, especially after he becomes a smouldering presence of

Eugenio Montale

possible salvation for others through his metamorphosis into a reed. Significantly, Dora's equally burning faith is symbolized by a suppressed storm of the same type as that appearing in the earlier poem:

La tua irrequietudine mi fa pensare
agli uccelli di passo che urtano ai fari
nelle sere tempestose;
è una tempesta anche la tua dolcezza,
turbina e non appare,
e i suoi riposi sono anche piú rari.

Your restlessness makes me think of birds of passage which strike lighthouses on stormy evenings; even your sweetness is itself a tempest, it ferments and does not appear, and its moments of calm are even rarer.

Nevertheless, the poet senses deep within himself that her ultimate goal, a return to her native land, is psychologically an impossible one, and he eventually decides that she must, at least to a certain extent, be play-acting in order to keep her courage up. He wonders, therefore, how she manages to stand the strain of constantly nurturing unattainable hopes in her heart; and he concludes, as we might suspect, by suggesting that her faith is based on pure superstition, which is maintained by the amulet of the white mouse which she keeps concealed in her handbag:

Non so come stremata tu resisti
in questo lago
d'indifferenza che'è il tuo cuore; forse
ti salva un amuleto che tu tieni
vicino alla matita delle labbra,
al piumino, alla lima: un topo bianco,
d'avorio; e cosí esisti!

I do not know how, exhausted, you endure in this lake of indifference which is your heart; perhaps a lucky charm saves you which you keep next to your lipstick, powder-puff and nail-file: a white mouse, made of ivory; and thus you exist!

So, in conclusion, we should perhaps consider Dora as a cross between a Gozzanian and a Montalian character who has, through no fault of her own, become alienated from her birthright and yet remains convinced that there is some magical – or at least some emotional – way out of her difficulties.

The second part of the poem shows us a 'redeemed' Dora (or Gerti as the case may be). But we again suspect that her 'redemption' is a false one brought about by her having sunk into the poet's passive memory and become transfixed as a degenerate and frustrated presence in a falsely idyllic setting. The paradise of Carinthia is chosen and re-evoked for the purpose, although its ambivalence is stressed by a play of reflections, especially the flash of pier-awnings and boarding-houses in the water of pools. In fact, Dora now seems at first sight to enjoy an authentic, domestic existence in contrast with the uneasy life as a wanderer which she led in Ravenna; and the incident which recalls her to the poet's mind is a second visit which he makes to the town, this time alone. But, as soon as he tries to focus her idyllic bliss in his mind's eye, the picture tends to be shattered by a series of cacophonous sounds, the throbbing of speed-boat engines and the gaggling of geese; and consequently he is unable fully to recall her earlier presence and can only visualize a blank, orphic screen or skeletal background against which to project her now shadowy personality. Yet this 'interno di nivee maioliche' obscurely reflects in the blackened mirror of his memory the fossilized story or myth of her past life – a myth which has been engraved in the inexpungible recesses of her conscience and of which the metamorphosis of the moth in 'Vecchi versi' is the stock archetype:

. . . e un interno
di nivee maioliche dice
allo specchio annerito che ti vide
diversa una storia di errori
imperturbati e la incide
dove la spugna non giunge.

. . . and an interior of snow-white ceramic tells the blackened mirror which saw you differently a story of coolly-made mistakes and engraves it where the sponge cannot reach.

Can he rescue the lady's image from the sunken fossilized sphere which it now occupies? Even he himself doubts it, because in his mind she is already associated with so much Gozzanian lumber that she merges with the pictures of her equally degenerate and ineffectual ancestors in the attic of his memory:

La tua leggenda, Dora!
Ma è scritta già in quegli sguardi
di uomini che hanno fedine
altere e deboli in grandi
ritratti d'oro e ritorna
ad ogni accordo che esprime
l'armonica guasta nell'ora
che abbuia, sempre piú tardi.

Your legend, Dora! But it is already written in the looks of those men who have weak and haughty side-whiskers in great golden portraits, and comes back with every chord which the broken harmonica utters in the darkening hour, later and later still.

As his memory of her darkens, we again note the reappearance of the cacophonous sounds we detected earlier. They emphasize the disruption of the organic melody of her presence and its replacement by occasional shreds and tatters of memorial harmony emanating from a broken mouth-organ. As such, they seem auditory parallels to the 'barlumi' ('glimmers' or 'flashes') we have already seen on the visual level and lead us in the last stanza to the stark contrast between Dora's artificial sense of bliss and the emotional turmoil of the poet himself. He speaks, in particular, of a 'ferocious faith' which he tells us later is a reference to Nazism,[68] but which also appears to be connected with the 'whorl of immortal fealty' he is soon to offer as a pledge to Clizia in the *Mottetti*. Indeed, the ferocious faith of his will still binds him closely to the lady, although with the passage of time the links in their mutually forged relationship are becoming more and more eroded:

È scritta là. Il sempreverde
alloro per la cucina
resiste, la voce non muta,
Ravenna è lontana, distilla
veleno una fede feroce.
Che vuole da te? Non si cede
voce, leggenda o destino . . .
Ma è tardi, sempre piú tardi.

It is written there. The evergreen laurel endures for the kitchen, your voice does not change, Ravenna is far away, a ferocious faith distils its poison. What does it want from you? One does not yield one's voice, legend or destiny . . . But it is late, later and later still.

As the bond between them becomes more tenuous, despite the freshly created domestic talisman of a 'sempreverde alloro', he and Dora sink into a kind of oblivion for each other and he fears the time will soon arrive when the thread of memory will snap completely. This is precisely what happened in 'Crisalide' and will recur in 'La casa dei doganieri', where the lady manifests herself only as an amorphous, emotional state of *epoché* whose lineaments cannot be restored by an act of remembrance. For Montale such an occurrence is equivalent to death in an intensely *human* sense and is, if anything, more tragic than death in the physical sense. It marks a regression to an area of memory totally beyond recall, where experience feeds cannibalistically on itself and is self-destroying together with the human values it represents.

What the poet describes in 'La casa dei doganieri' is the still-birth of one of his attempts to resuscitate a personal myth. But the lessons that this poem and 'Dora Markus' offer are summed up and further evaluated within a wider mythological framework of possible authentic recall in 'Stanze', where we see the lady actually 'pass beyond' and sense the damnation descending on the poet after her effulgence has moved out of his perceptive range. The pattern of relations she creates is wholly metaphysical, no more than a 'raggera di fili' ('halo of threads') which is then further reduced to an 'ultima corolla di cenere' ('final corolla of ashes'). So, at the point where the lady passes beyond human cognizance, all that is left for the poet to contemplate is the hum of a bowstring, the wake of a ship, or the last bubble rising on the surface of water. Yet even these mnemonic features can be positive, provided that they subsume a human character in the form of a corruscating and stimulating 'absence', because all such authentic 'absences' are capable of operating on the social and personal consciences of the living and of offering us vicarious moments of bliss:

> In te m'appare un'ultima corolla
> di cenere leggera che non dura
> ma sfioccata precipita. Voluta,
> disvoluta è cosí la tua natura.
> Tocchi il segno, travàlichi. Oh il ronzío
> dell'arco che'è scoccato, il solco che ara
> il flutto e si rinchiude! Ed ora sale
> l'ultima bolla in su. La dannazione
> è forse questa vaneggiante amara
> oscurità che scende su chi resta.

> In you there appears to me a final corolla of light ashes which does not endure but, flaking, falls. Willed, unwilled, such is your nature. You reach the goal, surpass it. Oh the hum of the bowstring which has been loosed, the furrow which ploughs the waves and closes again! And now the last bubble rises to the surface. Damnation is perhaps this delirious bitter darkness which descends on those left behind.

This conception of life is clearly the doctrine of modern orphism in a specific Montalian key. It promises a vicarious form of liberation whenever the living conscience of the individual intersects with and reactivates society's mass-memory or group-consciousness, through the re-evoking of the dead or the departed. In this way the lady in the above passage has the effect of momentarily dilating the poet's sphere of perception and allowing him to enlarge his purview of the ultimate bounds of the human condition. Though, naturally, he is forced to return once more to his non-perceptive state of damnation as soon as the moment of illumination she offers has passed away.

In this collection we thus encounter a modern stilnovistic figure, the Woman-Redeemer, even though with Montale she works within an ethico-aesthetic, rather than a religious, sphere. The middle section called the

Mottetti is in fact intended to present the problem of redemption through the virtual reincarnation of a living presence on a memorial plane. The woman whose shadowy figure dominates these 'frammenti' is called Clizia and the poet tells us that during their composition he was obsessed with the problem of 'l'assenza-presenza di una donna lontana' ('the absence-presence of a faraway woman') in reality an American friend.[69] In the poetry she functions as a *dea ex machina* and her various epiphanies, as Glauco Cambon has pointed out,[70] are the result of chance encounters by the poet with certain strange objects which he is able to associate directly with her tastes or personality. So, whereas the emblematic figure normally evoked dependent talismans in his earlier verse, here the reverse takes place and the emblem emerges from the bizarre set of talismanic objects which chance presents to the poet's gaze. A typical example of the process is the poem 'La speranza di pure rivederti' for which we possess the poet's own interpretation. In the lyric there occurs a bizarre, parenthetic description of two jackals which the poet apparently saw being led on a leash in a street in Modena. Their significance is explained as follows: 'Mirco si trovava a Modena e passeggiava sotto i portici. Angosciato com'era e sempre assorto nel suo "pensiero dominante", si stupiva che la vita gli presentasse come dipinte o riflesse su uno schermo tante distrazioni. Era un giorno troppo gaio per un uomo non gaio. Ed ecco apparire a Mirco un vecchio in divisa gallonata che trascinava con una catenella due riluttanti cuccioli color sciampagna, due cagnuoli che a prima occhiata non parevano né bassotti né volpini. Mirco si avvicinò al vecchio e gli chiese: "Che cani sono questi?" E il vecchio secco e orgoglioso: "Non sono cani, sono sciacalli." . . . Clizia amava gli animali buffi. Come si sarebbe divertita a vederli! pensò Mirco. E da quel giorno non lesse il nome di Modena senza associare quella città all'idea di Clizia e dei due sciacalli. Strana, persistente idea. Che le due bestiole fossero inviate da lei, quasi per emanazione. Che fossero un emblema, una citazione occulta, un *senhal*?'[71] ('Mirco was in Modena and walking under the arcades. Anguished as he was and for ever absorbed in his "dominating thought", he was astonished to find life presenting him with so many distractions, as though they were depicted or reflected on a screen. It was too joyful a day for an unjoyful man. And behold there appeared to Mirco an old man in braided livery dragging on a chain two unwilling puppies the colour of champagne, two dogs which at first sight neither seemed to be bassets nor foxhounds. Mirco approached the old man and asked him: "What kind of dog are these?" And the old man replied shortly and proudly: "They are not dogs, but jackals." . . . Clizia loved comic animals. How amused she would have been to see them! thought Mirco. And from that day onwards he never read the name of Modena without associating that city with the idea of Clizia and the two jackals. A strange, persistent idea. That the two animals were sent by her, as though by emanation. That they were an emblem, an occult memento, a *senhal*?')

Now it is only when we are armed with this information that the fragment becomes clear. The unsuspected function of the jackals is to reawaken associations between certain 'animali buffi' and Clizia in the poet's mind and to bring about her momentary epiphany from deep within the recesses of his memory:

La speranza di pure rivederti
m'abbandonava;

e mi chiesi se questo che mi chiude
ogni senso di te, schermo d'immagini,
ha i segni della morte o dal passato
è in esso, ma distorto e fatto labile,
un *tuo* barbaglio:

(A Modena tra i portici
un servo gallonato trascinava
due sciacalli al guinzaglio.)

The hope even of seeing you again was leaving me; and I asked myself whether this which shuts out every sense of you for me, a screen of images, has the marks of death or if something of the past is in it, a flash *from you*, but distorted and fleeting: (in Modena among the arcades a liveried servant dragged two jackals on a leash.)

From this we can deduce that for the poet there is an intervening redemptive stage between absence and total memorial loss, between the deprivation of another person and her ultimate obfuscation in the mirror of remembrance. It lies in a realm of 'ethical release' when the person 'lost' remains suspended as a catalyst in the memory and is still capable of stimulating our deepest feelings. True, the manner of recall at this stage may be highly involuted and idiosyncratic in nature, or at least may seem so to those who do not share with the poet common symbolic referentia. But the exercise itself is a healthy lyrical therapy and provides those intermittent flashes of hope on which Montale feeds in his growing state of melancholy and despair.

Similarly, the other side of the coin of remembrance – the total loss of a relationship – is also described in the *Mottetti*. In the first fragment the poet despairs of ever again being able to re-evoke Clizia in all her pristine beauty; and his sense of loss is intensified by his failure to find talismans in Genoa which are powerful enough to remind him of her former presence, despite the fact that it was in that town that their relationship first developed. Hence for him the emblematic elements of a typical maritime scene now spell out damnation:

Paese di ferrame e alberature
a selva nella polvere del vespro.
Un ronzío lungo viene dall'aperto,
strazia com'unghia ai vetri. Cerco il segno
smarrito, il pegno solo ch'ebbi in grazia da te.
E l'inferno è certo.

Landscape of ironwork and masts thickly wooding the dust of evening. A long droning comes from afar, it grates like a finger-nail on glass. I seek a lost sign, the pledge which I had by your grace. And Hell is certain.

Here he clearly no longer possesses the 'grimaldello' or jemmy to open up the hermetic world concealed in the darkened mirror of remembrance and he depicts his sense of frustration in intractable and nerve-racking imagery, such as the scratching of a finger-nail on a window-pane. This is indeed a precise correlative to the anguish-stricken undercurrents of existence experienced by the Damned and emphasizes the poet's dictum that one must 'vivere la propria condizione senza scappatoie . . . Senza farne merce da salotto'[72] ('live one's own situation in life without boltholes . . . Without making of it drawing-room merchandise'). Only by so doing can one hope to initiate those unexpected recalls which he believes will restore to him Clizia's pristine presence; and likewise, only then does the poet claim that he can complete his circle of 'cordialità' and with her enter 'un gorgo di fedeltà immortale'[73] ('whorl of immortal fealty').

As previously suggested, it is in these moments of memorial apotheosis that life and art coincide for Montale. During them Clizia is not only reincarnated in a series of poetic flashes, but she also acts as the *dea ex machina* of his lyricism, mediating between his sensibility and his human condition and offering a vicarious possibility of emotional redemption. The chanciness of the entire process is often imaginatively underlined. One image describing it is the symbol of the flower blooming on the edge of the precipice. Its tenacity and colourfulness parallel Clizia's mysterious, yet tumultuous, 'absence' and both are fixed for ever in the poet's mind, despite the fact that he and his lady are being continually carried away from each other by the funicular railway of mutual oblivion:

Il fiore che ripete
dall'orlo del burrato
non scordarti di me,
non ha tinte piú liete né piú chiare
dello spazio gettato tra me e te.

Un cigolío si sferra, ci discosta,
l'azzurro pervicace non ricompare.
Nell'afa quasi visibile mi riporta all'opposta
tappa, già buia, la funicolare.

The flower which repeats from the rim of the gorge, forget-me-not, does not have more joyful nor clearer hues than the space cast between you and me. A grinding sound is unleashed, carries us apart, the obstinate blueness does not reappear. In the almost visible sultriness the funicular carries me back to the already dark, opposite station.

What the poet also seems to be illustrating in other similar image-chains in the *Mottetti* is a residual element of memorial mystery which he considers remains latent in the poetic act itself and accounts for the ineffability of its lyrical effects. So, although he certainly does not wish to abandon reason in his creative practices, he insists that 'tra il capir nulla e il capir troppo c'è una via di mezzo, un *juste milieu* che i poeti d'istinto rispettano piú dei loro critici, ma al di qua e al di là di questo margine non c'è salvezza né per la poesia né per la critica'[74] ('between understanding nothing and understanding too much there is a middle way, a just mean which instinctive poets respect more than their critics, but on the one side or the other of this dividing-line there is no salvation either for poetry or for criticism').

The normal way in which he maintains an aura of mystery is by means of emotionally and symbolically allusive statements. Frequently they seem to amount to mere descriptions without any intervening interpretative elements, yet beneath their concrete features close inspection nevertheless reveals a transfiguring symbolism. An example taken from 'Eastbourne' reads as follows:

Freddo un vento m'investe
ma un guizzo accende i vetri
e il candore di mica delle rupi
ne risplende.

A cold wind enshrouds me, but a flash lights up the window-panes and the mica whiteness of the cliffs is resplendent with it.

Here three main elements are discernible: the cold wind, the granite-like appearance of the scene, and the flashing light with its myriad reflections. All of them, however, through their allegorical associations[75] suggest momentary liberation from a damnatory situation because their lyrical resonances are presented to our inward eye as so many flashbacks to previous joyful memories. Incidentally, even the epiphany of Clizia in this poem shows how constant and self-saturated Montale's referential imagery now is, for here again we find the emblem dissolving into an ashen precipitate, a fortuitous wheel of fortune and the flash of light-in-darkness, not to mention a mysterious peal of bells like the one found initially in 'Falsetto':

> Vince il male . . . La ruota s'arresta.
>
> Anche tu lo sapevi, luce-in-tenebra.
>
> Nella plaga che brucia, dove sei
> scomparsa al primo tocco delle campane, solo
> rimane l'acre tizzo che già fu
> *Bank Holiday*.

> Evil conquers . . . The wheel stops. You too knew it, light-in-darkness. In the burning region where you vanished at the first toll of the bells, there remains alone the guttering ember which was once *Bank Holiday*.

The relative intensity of Clizia's incarnations from here on seem to determine her mediatory powers. Sometimes she initiates a transfiguration while at others she loses hope and turns into a tragic figure of Death. Indeed, in this latter rôle she reminds us of one or other of the Fates, spinning, weaving or even cutting the thread of life. Her universal implications, either as an all-seeing goddess of benevolence with magical powers or as the incarnation of the Laws of Chance (a modern Bellona), are first adumbrated in 'Nuove stanze', and the doubt about her function is taken a stage further in 'Notizie dall'Amiata' where she may even symbolize non-communication.

Of the two lyrics the latter has the wider range. By basing our interpretation of it on the dichotomy of memory we have seen running through Montale's entire poetic output, we are led to a somewhat different conclusion in general outline – though not perhaps in detail – from those put forward by Bonora and Tedesco.[76] From a memorial standpoint the poem appears to be a symphony in three parts dealing with life, death and attempted communication, and each of its movements may be interpreted on a literal or a symbolic plane. The opening scene is one which we have come to expect of Montale: an emblematic landscape depicting life's hidden potentialities within a universal or cosmic setting. Moreover, behind its work-a-day miracles, unexpected flarings of passion, and existential anguish there again lurks the image of a rain-squall or impending storm. The poet contemplates this virtually apocalyptic scene or vision from a hut perched high on Mount Amiata in Tuscany, and the rain, mist and lightning flashes deriving from the storm are described in imagery no less allusive in quality than similar phenomena in 'Arsenio', 'Dora Markus' and 'Carnevale di Gerti'. Probably the suppressed storm itself stands as a precarious state of emotional equilibrium within which the poet attains his brief moment of insight. Yet the telescopic allusions implicit in the overall atmosphere are so dense that it seems as if life itself becomes quintessentialized in the opening stanza:

Il fuoco d'artifizio del maltempo
sarà murmure d'arnie a tarda sera.
La stanza ha travature
tarlate ed un sentore di meloni
penetra dall'assito. Le fumate
morbide che risalgono una valle
d'elfi e di funghi fino al cono diafano
della cima m'intorbidano i vetri,
e ti scrivo di qui, da questo tavolo
remoto, dalla cellula di miele
di una sfera lanciata nello spazio –
e le gabbie coperte, il focolare
dove i marroni esplodono, le vene
di salnitro e di muffa sono il quadro
dove tra poco romperai. La vita
che t'affàbula è ancora troppo breve
se ti contiene! Schiude la tua icona
il fonde luminoso. Fuori piove.

The fireworks of foul weather will be the murmur of bee-hives late at night. The room has worm-eaten beams and a smell of melons seeps in through the flooring. The soft swathes of mist, which a valley of elves and toadstools conjures up as far as the diaphanous cone of the summit, blur my windows, and I write to you from here, from this remote table, from the honeycomb of a sphere launched into space – and the covered cages, the hearth where the chestnuts explode, the veins of saltpetre and mould are the picture from which you soon will break. Life which enfables you is still too brief if it contains you! Your icon opens its luminous depths. Outside it is raining.

Hermetic images with this degree of infolding clearly require detailed explanation and they can only be interpreted satisfactorily by constant reference to Montale's previous imaginative textures. In the passage two Montalian polarities seem to complement and offset each other: the violent 'subbuglio degli elementi' ('churning of the elements') of 'Tramontana' and the muted, almost crepuscular, passion for life depicted in the second part of 'Dora Markus'. If we apply telescopic interpretative methods, however, we deduce that the firework display and lightning flashes refer to the inhuman laws of chance associated with a cosmic storm which rages outside the almost Pascolian 'casa-nido' ('house-nest') of the poet's intense domestic scene. As a result, he makes an attempt in the very next line to reduce the cosmos to a human scale by the transformation of its frightening gratuitous thunderclaps and lightning flashes into the more purposeful and intimate activity of droning bees at dusk. To reinforce the visio-auditory cluster of images opening the poem the poet then links them with two olfactory ones, the first alluding to the ravages of time depicted in the worm-eaten beams of the hut and the second to its mellowing effects in the pungent smell of melons, distantly recalling and yet replacing the bitter smell of lemons in the *Ossi di seppia*. Their sweet, mature scent is no doubt intended to contrast with the asperity of the citrus fruit symbolizing the poet's youth, while at the same time emphasizing the fact that fruit still continue to retain a general capacity to trigger off psycho-sensuous miracles in his mind. As for the subsequent scene rising magically out of the mist, this is another deceptive 'mondo gnomo' ('gnome world') which is gradually transformed into a vision of cosmic solitude to stress the communicatory gap between the poet and his lady.

By contrast, the joys of this Earth, as it hurtles through space are compared with a honey-pot which links it back partly with the bee-hive mentioned earlier and partly, perhaps, with Baudelaire's statement that 'La Terre est un gateau plein de douceur'[77] ('The earth is a cake full of sweetness'). So again we see Montale offsetting the senseless mechanical gyrations of the Earth around the sun with images evoking the delights of its intimate environment. Then, within the framework of the rain and the continuing storm, we move away from a cosmic vision of the macrocosm to the microcosm of an archetypal domestic scene. As we have already hinted, the entire process echoes Pascoli's domestic imagery designed to protect the 'inner life' from the destructiveness of the external forces of chance, and so the scene emphasizes the consoling finitude of human feelings as the family sits around the fire roasting chestnuts. Nevertheless there still lingers throughout a certain harshness of tone, a temporal sense of bitterness and decay; and it is from this intimate yet ambiguous setting that Clizia – perhaps an emblem of impending doom – seems about to emerge. A touch of brooding mystery is associated with her epiphany in the image of the 'gabbie coperte' ('covered cages') which already seem to have formed part of a domestic hearth in the reference to a 'gabbia o cappelliera' ('cage or hatbox') in 'A Liuba che parte'. What the poet is probably hinting at is the fact that no finite human mind can now grasp the paradoxical aspects of his lady's cosmicized nature. For she appears to fuse together the separate metaphysical, ethical and aesthetic views already held by a Cardarelli and an Ungaretti by suggesting that certain emotional values hold good over the entire spectrum of human life, even though death itself (or non-communication) is an absurd and irreconcilable condition. In this sense the last image of the stanza is revealing, since it associates Clizia and, by extension, death with an icon whose profundity evokes a mood of rapt, religious awe. Naturally we only catch a momentary glimpse of the icon's intimate secrets, the pit of human values, before we are returned by way of the reappearance of the image of a rainstorm to the *noia* of everyday existence where the laws of chance hold sway. But this momentary flash of insight is enough to encourage the poet to continue his quest for communion with his lady and the secretive world of 'redemption' which she represents.

The introductory landscape, though somewhat artificially constructed, thus aims at depicting life as a symbolic aggregate; and, like Pascoli before him, Montale seems to be attempting to protect the closed and intimate world of human affections from the cosmic storm raging outside mankind's inner spiritual environment. Yet the imagery in which he clothes the message is so concrete that it is virtually transmitted to the reader, as Tedesco has explained, as a series of 'ideas cast into objects'.[78] Afterwards we pass on to a scene which Eliot would describe as 'death's dream kingdom', to a world dominated by ashen precipitates and a sooty radiance, the very features of which once more call to mind the intensely glistening, even though frighteningly inert, landscape described in the first part of 'Dora Markus'.

We can perhaps consider the atmosphere of continual darkness in the second movement as symbolic of the orphic background against which Montale projects the various 'barlumi' of his intense experiences. As their dusty embers are precipitated over the scene, they seem to symbolize the steady accumulative processes of history, although here its elements are evoked and deposited in a lyrical rather than a factual manner:

E tu seguissi le fragili architetture
annerite dal tempo e dal carbone,
i cortili quadrati che hanno nel mezzo
il pozzo profondissimo; tu seguissi
il volo infagottato degli uccelli
notturni e in fondo al borro l'allucciolío
della Galassia, la fascia d'ogni tormento.

And would you followed the fragile architecture blackened by time and soot, the square courtyards which have a very deep well at their centre; would you followed the bundled flight of nocturnal birds, and at the bottom of the ravine the glitter of the Galaxy, the bound of all torment.

In short, the blackened architecture of this perennial city of Dis represents the fragile, orphic remains of that wealth of human experience deposited by past generations. No doubt the courtyards of the city stand for social life and learning, while the well at their centre is the mystery of death itself, already glimpsed in the previous icon-image and persisting in all human societies. Its characteristic talismans and fetishes are immediately apparent in the bundled flight of nocturnal birds in the sky, while on a still wider scale the scene within which this whole vision is contained is the cosmos itself. Hence the Mallarmean image of the galaxy is to be found glittering in the orphic element of water at the bottom of life's ravine.

It also seems probable that a continual orphic 'return' of psycho-metaphysical dimensions ensures the persistence of Montale's skeletal 'City of Death' in the racial consciousness, and this explains why he tries to discover the agents responsible for the constant renewal of the vision. He attributes its avatars, it seems, to the poets whose footfalls alone resound in its mythical streets and who encapsulate experience so successfully that it outlives in the form of aesthetic taste the inexorable collapse and replacement of one tradition by another:

Ma il passo che risuona a lungo nell'oscuro
è di chi va solitario e altro non vede
che questo cadere di archi, di ombre e di pieghe.

But the footsteps which resounds for long in the darkness is of the man who walks in solitude and sees nothing else but this falling of arches, of shadows and folds.

Indeed, such an attitude is already prefigured in the ending of 'Nuove stanze' where Montale also considers the discipline of art and where the 'occhi d'acciaio' ('steely eyes') of his lady help him to overcome the laws of chance. To produce an authentic lyricism the poet has in other words to detach himself from immediate experience and see human aspirations in a privileged aesthetic state of suspension. Through his ability to do so his mode of contemplating existence tends to differ radically from that of his fellow men who are responsible for the inchoate tensions of civilization but are incapable of patterning them and making them lyrically articulate. So, because of his privileged position, the poet establishes a revelationary form of communication which distils out of an ever-changing universe a permanent emblematic representation of the inner truths of his time. Water is again the element used to symbolize such distillations; and, as it drips like quicksilver from the heavily encrusted rooftops of mankind's 'darkened hovels', what Montale is really describing in a hermetically allusive manner is the transmission of aesthetically purified experience through time:

Oh il gocciolío che scende a rilento
dalle casipole buie, il tempo fatto acqua,
il lungo colloquio coi poveri morti, la cenere, il vento,
il vento che tarda, la morte, la morte che vive!

Oh the dripping which slowly falls from the darkened hovels, time made into water, the long dialogue with the poor dead, the ash, the wind, the lingering wind, death, death that lives!

By now, of course, intercommunication across time and space has become a well-worked Montalian theme. But the third part of the poem is not so much concerned with general intercommunication through the rejuvenation of tradition as with a desire to re-establish personal communication with Clizia. With her the poet now appears to suffer from a communicatory block, while she in turn seems to have lost her power to mediate. Therefore he is no longer able to make imaginatively meaningful the opaque, emotional aspects and memorial shreds of their relationship. To mirror his sense of desperation he evokes once more a wasteland correlative to his mood; and his method of delineating it is again simply to evoke the shadowy contours of an apocalyptic scene, after the manner previously used by a Leopardi or a Campana. From this evocation we gather that Clizia has 'passed over' into a static memory as a result of her prolonged absence and is no longer responsive to his appeals for consolation:

Questa rissa cristiana che non ha
se non parole d'ombra e di lamento
che ti porta di me? Meno di quanto
t'ha rapito la gora che s'interra
dolce nella sua chiusa di cemento.
Una ruota di mola, un vecchio tronco,
confini ultimi del mondo.

This Christian struggle which has nothing but shadowy words of lamentation, what does it bear to you of me? Less than the mill-stream has stolen from you as it pours softly down into its cement sluice. A mill-wheel, an old tree-trunk, the last frontiers of the world.

The Christian struggle mentioned here is probably rejected by Montale in favour of his Nestorian broadening-down of experience within a specifically humanist context; but there are also reasons for suspecting that at this point Clizia was already turning away from the poet's mythological beliefs towards a more conventional type of religion. He therefore feels that if he is to bring about any further epiphanies of her presence he will have to resort to a memorial magic; and, significantly, he tries to re-establish their former modes of communication by evoking the powers inherent in certain talismans, particularly in those 'animali buffi' ('comic animals') which, as we know, he had always considered to be intimately associated with her personality. They alone, he thinks, may still prove capable of bridging over the dark void of time and distance separating them spiritually from each other and of reconsolidating in skeletal form the previous conjunction of their minds. We can consequently interpret the slow disintegration of a 'cumulo di strame' ('pile of chaff') in the next lines as a momentary decrystallization of the passive memory[79] which causes the poet's active state of 'veglia' ('vigil') and the lady's passive state of 'sonno' ('slumber') to intersect; and, naturally, at the point of intersection there emerges the mediatory talisman of the hedgehogs or porcupines. Their magic, as is always the case with Montale's talismans, is emotional rather than supernatural, and for this reason they drink in 'un filo di pietà' ('stream of pity'). From its stream of living feeling the poet believes he can draw the strength to revitalize the lady's image and at the same time tentatively reassert his own consolatory belief in his immortal fealty towards her:

Si disfà
un cumulo di strame: e tardi usciti
a unire la mia veglia al tuo profondo
sonno che li riceve, i porcospini
s'abbeverano in un filo di pietà.

A pile of chaff unflakes: and emerging late to unite my vigil to your deep slumber which receives them, the hedgehogs drink in a stream of pity.

This is the note on which the collection ends, and it is clearly one which is far less ambitious and optimistic than the ending of the *Ossi di seppia*. There, we recall, we found a muted cry of triumph in 'Riviere', while here we see at most only the expression of a pious hope as the shadows of memory grow longer and the passions of youth inevitably subside.

This poem is nevertheless a supreme example of how a hermetic poet can destroy almost all the logical links which normally hold his lyrical texture together and yet convey by pure imaginative means a poignant attitude to life. In its imagery we can distinguish two kinds of magical symbol, the fetish and the talisman, and both may conveniently be illustrated by its bird and animal images. The fetish – to which the birds in bundled flight and the enigmatic black asses belong – is intended to be obsessively evocative of a mood and so offers its conceptually opaque, 'atmospheric' side to the reader's gaze; while the talisman – the 'animali buffi' or hedgehogs drinking in a stream of pity – is by contrast basically a meaningful, if allusive, symbol, despite the fact that certain of its deeper personal associations again remain enigmatic. Some critics in the past have condemned both types of image out of hand without distinguishing between them. For instance, with respect to the hedgehogs or porcupines Fusco has noted that 'qualche volta in una stessa lirica ... dalla presentazione in termini precisi, di salda concretezza, si devia bruscamente verso l'immagine metafisica, e si fa il buio'[80] (sometimes in the same lyric ... from a presentation in precise terms, of solid concreteness, one deviates suddenly towards the metaphysical image, and all is darkness'). In one sense Mariani shares the same view, but while stressing the problem of the 'amuleto senza vita'[81] ('lifeless amulet') he at least goes some of the way towards making clearer the distinction between the types of image involved. Both critics nevertheless seem to us to demonstrate an incomplete understanding of Montale's symbolic hierarchy which, as previously indicated, graduates upwards from the keepsake through the fetish and talisman to the emblem. In effect, the poet always attempts to use in each circumstance the kind of symbol which will provide the exact amount of figurative information he feels the situation needs and nothing more; and this explains why some of his so-called examples of involution are negative and others positive in character. Yet, when we study his symbolic range over a period of time, we find in retrospect that it forms an extremely intelligent emotio-cerebral pattern. Indeed, in 'Notizie dall'Amiata' the internal hierarchical appositeness of the symbolism – depending on association rather than on logic – clearly indicates where the originality of the hermetic sensibility lies. It aims fundamentally at achieving through sheer imaginative brilliance a mode of lyrical communication which is, at most, only implicit in the realities of the situations it describes. Nevertheless, such an approach, far from being deliberately obscurantist, is centred on the belief that the hermetic poet is constantly pressing against the bounds of expressivity in language.

From the process of development already traced out it will be clear that in the first stage of his lyrical career Montale was concerned with an investigation of the human condition in the round, while in the second stage of *Le occasioni* he tended to deal with the impact of that investigation on his own personal experiences. His third stage in *La bufera e altro* (1956) is principally concerned with the position of the individual in the world; hence he now discreetly enlarges his canvas to examine the individual's rôle in society as well as the mind's responses to its immediate circumstances. The collection, moreover, incorporates as its opening section a much shorter volume entitled *Finisterre*, first published in 1943. So, partly because it consists of two separate moments of inspiration and partly for other reasons, we find that the volume does not possess quite the organic unity of the two earlier ones. Its development is, in fact, so ambivalent that we can even interpret its title in two different ways: either as alluding to the political upheavals caused by the Second World War or, perhaps more convincingly, in a metaphysical sense as indicating the disruption of the poet's modes of communication with other people. As a result of this ambiguity we note that speculative and political themes are often juxtaposed and intermingled, and at times it is very difficult to decide which forms the true centre of a particular poem. But of the two principal trends probably the metaphysical purview remains dominant, because the poet is rarely prepared to pass beyond the periphery of political life, and so still continues to depict his human situations in a state of suspension or *epoché*.

His metaphysic of communication is again emphasized by the reappearance of Clizia and several other Montalian ladies, all with a clear mediatory function. Nevertheless his feminine figures now compromise more successfully with reality, acting upon a realist as well as a symbolic plane. In other words, while continuing to stand for his metaphysically posited *alter ego*, they also operate partly within a *Lebenswelt* of emotional and cultural values. In this sense their function is considerably expanded and they become the instruments through which the poet hopes to bring about a communicative alchemy between his sensibility and its historical and social settings.

A close adherence to the realities of living in society implies a partial renunciation by the poet of his former search for 'il quid definitivo' ('definitive quiddity'), and his new existential goal is defined in 'Vista a Fadin': 'Essere tra i primi e *sapere*, ecco ciò che conta, anche se il perché della rappresentazione ci sfugge.' ('To be among the foremost and to *know*, that is what counts, even if the reason for the performance eludes us.') Although this seems to be a humanist doctrine *par excellence*, here too Montale still clings to the remnants of his earlier dichotomy of life and continues to describe himself as a 'povero Nestoriano smarrito' ('poor lost Nestorian'). In short, he is striving even in *La bufera e altro* to synthesize his world outlook by combining ethical and metaphysical elements in an imaginative form, although he is now less interested than ever before in final ends, preferring to bring into clearer focus the concept of self-fulfilment, which for him is no doubt a modified form of election.

The result of his change of outlook is that he begins to regard the whole of mankind as an extension of himself and is hesitantly drawn towards participating in human affairs, even if still on a somewhat aristocratic level. So, although Clizia and her circle are gradually transformed into substantial human creatures, in *Finisterre* she still seems somewhat cosmic in nature and acts as his guardian-angel protecting him from the worst excesses of war: 'Ho proiettato la Selvaggia o la Mandetta o la Delia (la chiami come vuole) dei "Mottetti" sullo sfondo di una guerra cosmica e terrestre, senza scopo e senza ragione, e mi sono affidato a lei, donna o nube, angelo o procellaria.'[82] ('I have projected the Selvaggia or Mandetta or Delia (call her what you will) of the "Motets" on to the back-cloth of a cosmic and terrestrial war, without aims and without rationale, and I have entrusted myself to her, woman or cloud, angel or stormy petrel though she be.') When we realize the relative lack of communicativeness implicit in this pose, we begin to wonder how any emotional rapprochement between her and the poet can ever again be realized. But it tends ultimately to be achieved through a reversal of some of Montale's earlier symbols. For instance, one of his most fruitful avenues of approach seems to be through the upgrading of the stunted symbols of his childhood fixations in 'Caffè a Rapallo' and elsewhere. These fetishized objects are now endued with positive meaning and act in poems like 'Nella serra' as trigger-mechanisms stimulating the lady's epiphany:

S'empí d'uno zampettío
di talpe la limonaia,
brillò in un rosario di caute
gocce la falce fienaia.

S'accese sui pomi cotogni,
un punto, una cocciniglia,
si udí inalberarsi alla striglia
il poney – e poi vinse il sogno.

The lemon grove was filled with a pattering of moles' feet, the hay sickle shone with a rosary of cautious dewdrops. A pinpoint burned on the quince-trees, a cochineal, one could hear the pony rearing up at the touch of the comb – and then the dream became overwhelming.

Here the hothouse atmosphere, the intensely visual and lilliputian imagery, and Clizia's normal association with unusual creatures all combine to create a dramatically interrelated pattern of images; and the only thing still missing seems to be a 'decisive act' to encourage the lady herself to 'emerge' from the scene. This act is provided by the rearing of a pony – an identical image to one found previously in 'Carnevale di Gerti' – which now creates a moment of authentic equipoise, a feeling of almost visceral union between the poet and Clizia, rather than a false daydream:

Rapito e leggero ero intriso
di te, la tua forma era il mio
respiro nascosto, il tuo viso
nel mio si fondeva, e l'oscuro

pensiero di Dio discendeva
sui pochi viventi, tra suoni
celesti e infantili tamburi
e globi sospesi di fulmini

su me, su te, sui limoni . . .

> Enraptured and feather-like, I was infused with you, your form was my hidden breath, your face melted into mine, and the obscure thought of God descended on to the few living souls, amid celestial sounds and childlike drums and suspended globes of lightning, on me, on you, on the lemon-trees . . .

Indeed, not only does a Boutrouxesque liberation take place here by the upgrading of former degenerate symbols, but a wholly new Montalian effect is produced, one which might be described as the psycho-sensuous union of two personalities. The concept adds a further dimension to Montale's earlier religion of vicarious redemption by indicating the possibility of the direct participation of the victim in the beatitude of the Elect. However, the process only comes to full fruition later in the collection, since in *Finisterre* the poet still seems to be more concerned with the harmonization of the political and moral tensions in life through the mediation of his ladies.

As the title of the collection shows, the dominant landscape is either that area of northern France bordering the English Channel or of Spain and the Bay of Biscay, beyond which lay the frontiers of freedom during the war. But the word is understood largely in a metaphysical sense by Montale, based no doubt on the overtones of its etymological meaning from the Latin *finis terrae* ('land's end'). So when we bear in mind what the water's edge always signified for him and the tremendous metamorphoses which take place in his lyricism along the tideline, we see how artfully he fuses together at this point his metaphysics and the political stirrings of his conscience. Already the eponymous poem bears an epigraph by Agrippa d'Aubigné clearly alluding to a political theme, yet at the same time he keeps any overt political outlook at arm's length or at least expresses it wholly through the many-faceted character of Clizia residing in far away America. Each memorial loss associated with her absence thus becomes virtually a loss of freedom, while her unexpected recalls take on the form of a veiled salvation which shines in the lightning flashes announcing her mysterious epiphanies. In this way she offers a distant prospect of ethico-political hope, steeped in a metaphysical allusiveness of imagery.

Eventually, however, Clizia regresses almost entirely into the passive memory, as indicated in 'Serenata indiana'. In this lyric her personality disintegrates like those intangible elements which rose momentarily from the depths of pools in poems like 'Vasca'. Earlier, however, it seems as if she still retains her powers of materialization and emerges from one of Montale's typical twilight scenes for the purpose of consoling him. Yet in spite of all his efforts to recapture her pristine wholeness she remains an impalpable mirage, a gratuitous vision sunk in a closed world of memory. What is more, she now seems like an incubus weighing on his mind, and is closely associated with a 'polyp' which in its original Greek form significantly meant 'cuttle-fish'. Accordingly, her degeneration seems to have proceeded so far that she can only find her place henceforth within Montale's lifeless memorial reliquaries. In contrast with her earlier promise of hope, in other words, we are now shown her darker side and, by extension, the negative aspects of Montale's mental hinterland. Within it, Clizia is transformed into an amorphous nightmare and becomes the *reductio ad absurdum* ('reduction to absurdity') of her previous state of grace. This doubtless explains why in the three Shakespearian sonnets that follow, 'Gli orecchini', 'La frangia dei capelli . . .', and 'Il ventaglio' we are reminded of *imprese* ('devices') which aim at restoring by symbolic means her powers to stimulate his conscience. But, since the first- and last-mentioned poems have already been examined by D'Arco Silvio Avalle and Bonora respectively, we shall concentrate our attention here on 'La frangia dei capelli . . .'[83]

As a preliminary, we need nevertheless to quote briefly from 'Il ventaglio' since Montale explains in that lyric his current view of the imaginative use of memory. He suggests that he now sees imagery diminished in size as if viewed through the wrong end of a telescope, but that all imaginative forms thereby acquire a memorial intensity which they do not normally possess. He also draws the parallel between poetry and painting and, by alluding to Horace's phrase 'ut pictura poesis' ('poetry as a picture'), even hints at the possibility that Clizia may be effectively restored to him at present through the aid of the passive memory itself:

> *Ut pictura* . . . Le labbra che confondono,
> gli sguardi, i segni, i giorni ormai caduti
> provo a figgerli là come in un tondo
> di cannocchiale arrovesciato, muti
> e immoti, ma piú vivi.

As a picture . . . Lips which merge together, glances, signs, days now past, I try to fix them there in the circle of an upturned telescope, silent and immutable, but more lively.

But, if this is indeed his intention, he can only hope to achieve it telescopically by causing her to 'emerge' from certain fetishized mementos which bear the emotional stamp of her personality.

An attempt at such an ambitious undertaking is clearly to be seen in 'La frangia dei capelli . . .'. First of all, Montale tries to crystallize Clizia in a characteristic and authentic gesture, in the hope of encapsulating her entire spiritual radiance within a single image. This gesture momentarily releases her from the closed and passive world of memory; and, once released, she again comes to his rescue at a moment of crisis. Her liberation is naturally very attenuated at this juncture, but she nevertheless offers him a veiled form of perceptiveness to guide him through life:

La frangia dei capelli che ti vela
la fronte puerile, tu distrarla
con la mano non devi. Anch'essa parla
di te, sulla mia strada è tutto il cielo,
la sola luce con le giade ch'ài
accerchiate sul polso, nel tumulto
del sonno la cortina che gl'indulti
tuoi distendono, l'ala onde tu vai,
trasmigatrice Artemide ed illesa,
tra le guerre dei nati-morti; e s'ora
d'aeree lanugini s'infiora
quel fondo, a marezzarlo sei tu, scesa
d'un balzo, e irrequieta la tua fronte
si confonde con l'alba, la nasconde.

The fringe of hair which veils your childlike brow, you should not disturb it with your hand. It too speaks of you, in my journeying it is the whole of heaven, my only light together with the jade you have around your wrist, in the tumult of sleep the curtain which your indulgences offer, the wing with which you fly, a transmigrant, immune Artemis, among the wars of the born-dead; and if now those depths are bedecked with airy down, it is you who water their silk, having descended in a swoop, and restlessly your brow merges with the dawn, conceals it.

Here she seems neither a full-blooded human presence nor a mere *dea ex machina*, but rather an 'emergent' creature arising out of an orphic void and intensifying, while at the same time shrouding in redemptive mystery, the poet's experiences. Initially, perhaps, she works on his sensibility as if she were his Muse, making her presence felt through her previously mentioned, decisive gestures; then later she imprints her radiance on his mind through intractable materials like the jade glittering on her wrist;[84] and finally she operates within his soul through a kind of empathy, raising his poetry to that sphere of purity where she herself subsists. All the images surrounding her are, needless to say, highly involuted, but the necessary delimitation of their denotative and connotative fields may again be obtained by a flashback technique – by their association with previous descriptions in similar circumstances.

If we examine the lyric in detail we find that the concentration of Montale's archetypes has now reached saturation point. For instance, the gesture through which the lady apparently identifies herself by tossing aside her fringe of hair is initially prepared in a cosmic setting in the

Mottetti. It begins with a preliminary act by the poet who frees her brow from the icicles of oblivion:

> Ti libero la fronte dai ghiaccioli
> che raccogliesti traversando l'alte
> nebulose . . .[85]

I free your brow from the icicles which you gathered crossing the high cloud-belts.

In the next stage, the image of the lady's brow evolves into a minatory angelic feature, since she develops a winged fringe and a frowning mien:

> Ben altro
> è l'Amore – e fra gli alberi balena col tuo cruccio
> e la tua frangia d'ali, messaggera accigliata![86]

Love is something quite different – and among the trees it gleams with your anguish and your fringe of wings, o frowning messenger!

Then, subsequently, an almost identical image to the one found in the *Mottetti* re-emerges in *La bufera e altro* and characterizes Clizia's salient personal feature as she

> sgombra
> la fronte della nube dei capelli . . .

clears from her brow the cloud of her hair . . .

Even later than in 'La frangia dei capelli . . .' the same gesture reappears once more in 'Voce giunta con le folaghe' where reference is made to her 'biocco infantile ('childlike curl') and the decisive gesture of a 'scarto altero della fronte' ('haughty toss of her brow'). So, all in all, one must assume that it was the poet's intention to categorize the image of brow and hair as a symbolic pointer which introduces Clizia and represents her mysteriously incisive influence upon his sensibility in both a cosmic and personal sense.

A parallel device is the use of intractable materials to provide images with a sharp cutting-edge. Its origin is no doubt in Baudelaire or Mallarmé, but again its association with Jeanne Duval or Hérodiade is of a different quality, because Montale 'pierreries' ('jewellery') tend to have magical or metaphysical, rather than sexual, implications. For instance, the jade bracelet in 'La frangia dei capelli' reappears in different form in 'Il tuo volo' and offers a quartz-like intensification of the poet's emotion. The implication seems to be that such star-like amulets provide the same type of immortality as Mallarmé's constellations:

> (pendono
> sul tuo ciuffo e ti stellano
> gli amuleti).

(amulets hang from your forelock and bestar you).

Moreover, the image of the goddess Artemis is also a telescopic one, deriving from as far back as the 'arciera Diana' ('archeress Diana') in 'Falsetto'. It has the same implication of chastity and purity associated with one of the Elect as the earlier image, while other allusions in the poem to 'il tumulto del sonno' ('tumult of sleep') and 'le guerre dei nati-morti' ('war of the born-dead') are likewise overt references to Montale's dualistic mythology of election and damnation. Even the process of watering silk represents a familiar orphic ritual act, one which permits the poet to transfigure his raw materials through the mediation of Clizia's talismanic presence. As for her descent from on high, this is clearly redemptive in implication and parallels other decisive emblematic bird-images, from the kingfisher and swooping jays in the *Ossi di seppia* onwards. Hence we can conclude that at this stage the poet is no longer an Orpheus in a memorial underworld deploring the loss of Eurydice; on the contrary, the slow fading of his memory of Clizia seems to have been arrested and his lady now keeps close watch over his emotional life by intervening in his personal affairs and endlessly rekindling his hopes. At the same time, as we have already hinted, there may be distant political overtones attached to his present attitude towards her. If so, she may be likened to a transatlantic Statue of Liberty promising eventually a renewed freedom to an enslaved continent, and even the stars frequently associated with her may well be those of the star-spangled banner.

On the other hand, the apotheosis of Woman – whether for aesthetic or political ends – has self-evident dangers, chief among which is the risk of a complacent solipsism. Fortunately Montale is more alert than ever before to this pitfall and he now tries to avoid alienating himself completely from life by regarding Clizia and his other figures as real women. As a result, he associates a certain Petrarchan sensuousness with their lyrical evocations throughout the period. In this collection they are in consequence less Platonic ideals than fleetingly recalled visions of human grace and intelligence, and so the poet lays down as follows in 'Gli orecchini' the limits he will henceforth impose on the pursuit of abstract beauty:

> ... fuggo
> l'iddia che non s'incarna, i desiderî
> porto fin che al tuo lampo non si struggono.

> ... I flee the goddess who does not become incarnate, desires I bear as long as they are not destroyed by your flash.

It therefore seems reasonable to assume that the intention behind this group of Shakespearian sonnets is a twofold one: to stress the redemptive powers of the lady while at the same time restoring her to a concrete plane of existence in order to give her a renewed credibility despite her enforced absence from the period of the war onwards.

Clizia's resuscitated presence paves the way for a further attempt at an empathic identification of souls, as previously practised in 'Nella serra'. But this feeling of empathic unity is now expressed with greater intensity by Montale in respect of another lady, who may even be the original stimulus behind the idea. The process is again complicated by the use of the flash-back technique now so characteristic of the poet's art. Its manifestations take pride of place in *'Flashes' e dediche*, while in the poem 'L'arca' a similar but wider-ranging process of memorial hypostasis is employed to 'perpetuate' in the poet's consciousness his former pets and servants. Many of these reappear in the short stories of *Farfalla di Dinard* (1956),[87] a work which incidentally throws considerable light on the poet's recondite symbolism.

'Flashes' e dediche particularly stresses the importance of unexpected lyrical insights, and the lady presiding over most of the section is not Clizia but another woman whom Montale describes as 'mia volpe' or fox, noting: 'Era una giovane donna e ne è venuto un personaggio diverso da Clizia, un personaggio molto terrestre. Di fronte alla "volpe" mi sono paragonato a Pafnuzio, il frate che va per convertire Thaïs ma ne è conquistato. Vicino a lei mi sono sentito un uomo astratto vicino a una donna concreta: lei viveva con tutti i pori della pelle. Ma anch'io ne ricevevo un senso di freschezza, il senso sopratutto d'essere ancora vivo.'[88] ('She was a young woman, and from her there emerged a different character from Clizia's, a very earthly character. Before my "fox" I compared myself with Pafnuzio, the monk who went to convert Thaïs but was conquered by her. When with her I felt myself to be an abstract man beside a concrete woman: she lived with all the pores of her skin. But even I received a sense of freshness from her, a sense above all of being still alive.') This plurality of Montale's feminine figures does not, as we have said before, detract in any way from the authenticity of his inner development, and the reason is that each of them tends to represent a different aspect of his Muse. However, precisely because of their diverse and highly individuated actions it often seems as if specific existential situations play a larger, and at times a less meta-physicized, part in this collection than in *Le occasioni*.

The one drawback of such a development is that these chance effects or circumstances are no longer controlled by the poet's will; instead they have a fulminatory character arising from fortuitous parenthetic associations and shreds of memory. Thus in the opening poem we feel that Montale has casually opened the Pandora's box of his remembrances and an allusive, but gratuitous, situation has leapt out of it like a jack-in-the-box.

(La fuga dei porcelli sull'Ambretta
notturna al sobbalzare della macchina
che guada, il carillon di San Gusmé
e una luna maggenga, tutta macchie . . .)

La scatola a sorpresa ha fatto scatto
sul punto in cui il mio Dio gittò la maschera
e fulminò il ribelle.

(The flight of the piglets on the Ambretta by night at the shuddering of the car which was crossing the ford, the carillon of St. Gusmé and the May moon, all spots . . .) The jack-in-the-box opened at the moment when my God cast aside his mask and thunderbolted the rebel.

The presence of 'la volpe' ('my fox') in the section is also stressed by reference to certain of her concrete, physical features in contrast with the more evanescent Clizia. Yet even with his fox-lady Montale still remains almost as discreet and generic in his descriptions as Petrarch was with Laura. So, in spite of her sensuousness, she is only materialized indirectly: either through a curl of her hair re-evoked by the flash of trout in the Thames at Reading or by her 'pupille d'acquamarina' ('sea-blue pupils') mediating stilnovistically between the poet and his God in 'Verso Finistère'. In a curious way, however, this type of reticence often makes his ladies seem all the more real to us; and in the fragment 'Di un natale metropolitano' we find that a female presence is first absorbed and then irradiated by the objects lying in her room, even after she has left it and plunged down like some modern Eurydice into the bowels of the earth, symbolized by the London underground:[89]

Un vischio, fin dall'infanzia sospeso grappolo
di fede e di pruina sul tuo lavandino
e sullo specchio ovale ch'ora adombrano
i tuoi ricci bergère fra santini e ritratti
di ragazzi infilati un po' alla svelta
nella cornice, una caraffa vuota,
bicchierini di cenere e di bucce,
le luci di Mayfair, poi a un crocicchio
le anime, le bottiglie che non seppero aprirsi,
non piú guerra né pace, il tardo frullo
di un piccione incapace di seguirti
sui gradini automatici che ti slittano in giú . . .

A piece of mistletoe, a suspended cluster of faith and hoar-frost from childhood on your wash-stand, and on the oval mirror which your *bergère* curls now shelter, among saints and photos of boys slipped somewhat hurriedly in their frames, an empty decanter, small glasses of ash and peel, the lights of Mayfair, then at a crossroads souls, bottles which could not be opened, no longer war nor peace, the late fluttering of a pigeon incapable of following you on the escalator which slides you downwards . . .

We might appropriately contrast this realist and unsentimentalized drama with the one we saw earlier in Corazzini's 'Soliloquio delle cose'. Here the crepuscular poet's decadent 'software' is replaced by more brittle and incisive 'hardware', even though the technique employed to create a living presence by means of objective correlatives is clearly the same. On the other hand, the fact that Montale still returns even now to the writers of the crepuscular movement for techniques and tonalities is further emphasized by the neo-classical, Gozzanian turn of phrase in the opening line and by the use of the word 'bergère' with its 'fin de siècle' overtones. Nevertheless, the crepuscular pitfall which he still studiously avoids is the sentimentalization of situations, and so his underlying message is not an anthropomorphic yearning for immortality but a sense of the certainty of oblivion as the individual descends the escalator of memory. All that the poet can hope to rescue from the ravages of time are the memorial shreds and tatters of his experiences; and he ritualizes them through the pathetic talisman of a pigeon, which is totally unable to follow the lady in her rapid descent into that inferno of shattered remembrances, her life.

Again in the fragment 'Sul Llobregat' a rapid series of events and the distant memory of a particular gesture arc re-sensitivized from within a passive sphere of remembrance. The aim of the poet appears to be to produce a dynamic impression which will allow the reader to penetrate into 'the still point of the turning world' forming the nucleus of a single temperament. From this and other impressionistic recalls of precious experiences it is only a short step to the poet's mystical psycho-sensuous identification with his lady. In the 'Madrigali privati' (also inspired by 'la volpe') another merging of personalities consequently takes place, and it reaches a climax in 'Nubi color magenta':

> Volo con te, resto con te; morire,
> vivere è un punto solo, un groppo tinto
> del tuo colore, caldo del respiro
> della caverna, fondo, appena udibile.

I fly with you, I remain with you; to die, to live is a single point, a squall of wind tinged with your colouring, hot with the breath of caves, deep, hardly audible.

Here the poet describes a state of happiness in a new way: it is the visceral balancing of the humours of *two* individuals in the deeper, instinctive regions of the blood. The process seems to be achieved by a simultaneous weakening of the poet's will and by an intensification of what Pasolini has described as his 'maniac acts of propitiation'.[90] But, even so, Montale still offsets these instinctive feelings with a subtle play of intelligence and the two forces interpenetrate and illuminate each other by turns. The result, as

Giannessi has noted, is that 'nella *Bufera* ogni residuo di petrosità è chiaramente dissolto nel calore incandescente della passione umana.'[91] ('in the *Bufera* all stony residues are clearly dissolved in the incandescent heat of human passion'). Such a development involves a slackening of the metaphysical attitudes adopted by the poet in his earlier verse and a countervailing consolidation of his ethico-historical perspectives, especially in so far as they are concerned with the maturing of his emotions.

A further outcome of his greater reliance on existential circumstances in this collection is that in the section *Silvae* the poet attempts to re-explore all his previous avenues of memorial, imaginative and social communication, and even goes so far as to become openly political in 'La primavera hitleriana'. However, from our present standpoint the most important poem in the section is 'Voce giunta con le folaghe' which is an attempt to re-dimension the myth first appearing in 'I morti' and other compositions in the *Ossi di seppia*, where the spheres of life and death, we recall, were first seen to intersect. The only real difference between the two poems is that here Montale takes a specific instance of memorial recall instead of expounding the doctrine in a somewhat generic fashion. However, because we are dealing with communication between the living and the dead most of the images deployed are again 'inverted' and 'telescopic' in character, referring back to his own work in the first instance and then by extension to the wider imaginative continuity of the Italian tradition as a whole.

The lyrical texture of the poem is again made up of culturally saturated lyrical resonances which are so skilfully orchestrated that they bind together in a virtually mystical communion the poet's dead father, his native Liguria and the absent Clizia. The latter takes up her familiar rôle as an intermediary between the poet and the world outside himself and reflects at one stage removed his inner feelings and perceptions. In the first stanza the pendulum of memory swings towards the shores of the living and the shade of the poet's dead father is momentarily 'recaptured' from the world beyond. He is a soul laid bare rather than a mere wraith and he tends to be mystically identified with the Ligurian landscape with which he was so closely associated during his lifetime:

Poiché la via percorsa, se mi volgo, è piú lunga
del sentiero da capre che mi porta
dove ci scioglieremo come cera,
ed i giunchi fioriti non leniscono il cuore
ma le vermene, il sangue dei cimiteri,
eccoti fuor dal buio
che ti teneva, padre, erto ai barbagli,

senza scialle e berretto, al sordo fremito
che annunciava nell'alba
chiatte di minatori dal gran carico
semisommerse, nere sull'onde alte.

Since the road already covered, if I turn round, is longer than the goat's track which is carrying me to the point where we shall melt like wax, and the flowering reeds cannot soothe the heart but only the shrubs, blood of the cemeteries, here you are, father, emerging from the darkness which held you, upright in the dazzling light, without muffler or beret, in the dull quiver which at dawn used to announce the miners' barges, half-submerged by their great loads, black upon the open sea.

Here cultural reminiscences and distant echoes of Montale's previous imagery form a kind of mosaic. The 'sentiero da capre' symbolic of his life's journey, for instance, reminds us of the 'fil di lama' ('razor's edge') along which he sought out happiness in one of the *Ossi*, while the 'giunchi fioriti' recall either the self-willed sacrificial victim in 'Arsenio' or the 'canneti' ('reed-beds') in another of the *Ossi*. However, these are now metamorphosed into young shrubs or saplings, associated with the blood of cemeteries for two reasons: first, because their sap is intuitively seen as the regenerated blood of the dead, and, second, because of the association perhaps of 'vermena' and 'sangue bruno' in Dante's wood of the suicides. As for the 'chiatte dei minatori' these refer specifically to the barges entering the port of Genova, often seen at dawn by Montale because his father had a small chemical factory in the town; but their foreboding presence reminds us also of the black asses of death in 'Notizie dall'Amiata' and the many burrowing animals like the moles which are prominent in Montale's eschatology and are again probably borrowed from Baudelaire. In the purely literary field we are also immediately led to think of Charon's ferryboat as a possible reference point; and, given the poet's interest in English literature, even Tennyson's 'funeral scarf' in 'Morte d'Arthur'. So what is clear at this juncture is that the poet's lyricism has once more reached a point of cultural saturation.

Quite as important as the imagery in which the poetry is expressed is the doctrine which it expounds. Montale indicates that he himself cannot communicate directly with his dead father, and so Clizia (immediately recognizable by the ritualistic toss of her hair) is introduced as an intermediary to initiate a dialogue in the sphere of the 'io trascendentale'. Because she is one of the Elect, we would expect her to cast a clear-cut shadow; but, since she really represents another type of 'absence' and is nothing more than a memorial projection, her shadow is wholly dematerialized and does not disturb the sensitive plant any more than the shade of the poet's dead father. Their apparently identical status in this sense implies a possibility of communication between them, and the second stanza is designed to lead up to this proposition:

L'ombra che mi accompagna
alla tua tomba, vigile,
e posa sopra un'erma ed ha uno scarto
altero della fronte che le schiara
gli occhi ardenti ed i duri sopraccigli
da un suo biocco infantile,
l'ombra non ha piú peso della tua
da tanto seppellita, i primi raggi
del giorno la trafiggono, farfalle
vivaci l'attraversano, la sfiora
la sensitiva e non si rattrappisce.

The shadow which accompanies me vigilantly to your tomb and rests upon an effigy and has a haughty toss of the brow which clears away a childish curl from her glowing eyes and frowning eyebrows, has no more weight than your own buried for so long, the early rays of the daylight transfix it, dancing butterflies cross it, the sensitive plant grazes it without shrinking back.

The actual dialogue predictably takes place at the point of intersection between the living and the dead, in the sphere we may regard as Montale's memorial purgatory. This may well explain the butterfly image, because Pipa tells us that in the contemporaneously composed stories of *Farfalla di Dinard* this symbol marks 'un moment d'apaisement'[92] ('a moment of tranquillity'). So, although the conversation between Clizia and his father cannot be understood by the poet because his mind does not operate on the right wavelength, he nevertheless makes an intelligent guess at its tenor and believes he detects their reciprocal fears by filtering their anguish through the crying of one of his typical talismans, the coots.

The lady, he assumes, is overcome by religious scruples in her attempted communion with the dead, while he attributes to his deceased father an even stranger fear: that each memorial recall to which he is subject weakens that wisp of memory remaining of his personality in the minds of the living. His son's repeated recollections of him may therefore hasten his regression into the passive memory, the last resting-place of human experience.[93] Fortunately an apparently intersubjective voice – reaching out through the operative talisman of the coots – is able to reassure him. It is a voice of memory which affirms a keeping of faith with everyone and acts as a universal rememberer. Hence at the end of the poem it propounds the previously mentioned 'ethic' of memory as a virtual doctrine of humanist 'redemption' and it is closely linked with that other fundamental principle of Montale's lyricism – his desire to maintain an immortal fealty with his lady:

– Ho pensato per te, ho ricordato
per tutti. Ora ritorni al cielo libero
che ti tramuta. Ancora questa rupe
ti tenta? Sí, la bàttima è la stessa
di sempre, il mare che ti univa ai miei
lidi da prima che io avessi l'ali,
non si dissolve. Io le rammento quelle
mie prode e pur son giunta con le folaghe
a distaccarti dalle tue. Memoria
non è peccato fin che giova. Dopo
è letargo di talpe, abiezione

che funghisce su sé . . . –

– I have thought for you, I have remembered for everybody. Now return to the open sky which transmutes you. Does this rock still tempt you? Yes, the tideline is the same as ever, the sea which united you to my shores since before I had wings, does not fade away. I recall to you those shores of mine and yet I have arrived with the coots to detach you from yours. Memory is not a sin as long as it helps. Afterwards it is the lethargy of moles, an abjectness which moulders upon itself . . . –

Following this brief soliloquy we return to the original scene where Montale was, we recall, paying homage at his father's graveside. There the wind of memory provides a dilated sphere of perception which suggests a strangely impersonal view of life, one approximating to a half-avowed belief in predestination. The poet seems to be suggesting that our characters are moulded by chance happenings similar to those noted in *'Flashes' e dediche* and that in his view memory consists of a series of empty holes into which the individual can, when suitable prompters appear, refit the events of his life. A close fit produces in each individual intense bursts of emotion resulting from a sense of *déjà vu* initially stimulated by the influence of already familiar external objects:

Il vento del giorno
confonde l'ombra viva e l'altra ancora
riluttante in un mezzo che respinge
le mie mani, e il respiro mi si rompe
nel punto dilatato, nella fossa
che circonda lo scatto del ricordo.
Cosí si svela prima di legarsi
a immagini, a parole, oscuro senso
reminiscente, il vuoto inabitato
che occupammo e che attende fin ch'è tempo
di colmarsi di noi, di ritrovarci . . .

The wind of the day merges the living shadow and the other reluctant one in a sphere which thrusts back my hands, and in that dilated spot, the grave surrounding the flash of memory, I catch my breath. Thus there reveals itself to us before it ties itself to images, to words, an obscure reminiscent feeling, the

> uninhabited void that we occupied and which waits until it is time for it to fill itself with us, to rediscover us . . .

But each one of us quickly loses touch with such momentary insights, and then we have to wait for further consolation until the next revelation descends upon us. But the very process indicates that the rôle of Clizia and his other feminine mediators in life is now much less mysterious than it at first appears. They simply prompt recollections and a sense of memorial consolidation.

Probably this form of memorial 'rediscovery' is to be interpreted in an aesthetic as well as ethical sense and, if this is so, it brings Montale's ideas on life and death somewhat closer to Ungaretti's. For here we find him propounding for his father the same kind of orphic immortality as the latter poet propounded for the artists of the past tradition – one which emerges sporadically from the all-embracing shadow of death to obtrude into the socio-cultural consciousness of the living. The same attitude, we recall, was also struck in the poem addressed to his mother in *Finisterre* whose immortality took on positive form through a unique configuration of dynamic features deposited as a memorial precipitate in the minds of her family. Such potentially dynamic, ashen precipitates are clearly to be contrasted with Gozzano's negative sedimentation of 'le buone cose di pessimo gusto' ('the good things of the worst taste'), because with the Turinese poet personal possessions merely become fossilized and non-cathartic through their ultimate lack of human connections. Gozzano's approach to his daguerrotypes can thus be regarded as the negative pole of Montale's dialectic of memory, for it is only at the level of the inert Gozzanian image that we begin to sense in the present poet's work the gratuitous, self-generating emotion of lyrics like 'Buffalo' or 'Keepsake'. To provide a counterweight to the static images which obsess the Damned, Montale sometimes sought to rise above his condition and evoke momentary insights into that dynamic afterlife so dramatically presented, for instance, by Dante in the *Inferno*. This is indeed almost literally true for the story 'Sul limite' in *Farfalla di Dinard* where the entire imaginative framework has a Dantesque ring about it. Yet what the poet produces is a secular, as opposed to a religious, atmosphere for the soul to work out its redemption, and, as we know, this type of redemption is achieved by a sacrificial altruism and an anguished probing of the inner reaches of memory.

In other words, the significant difference between Montale's and Dante's approach is that he works on an existential – not an eternal – plane, and he is more often led to a state of doubt than to theological certainty: a fact which goes far to explain why Clizia turns out to be a far less substantial instrument of salvation than Beatrice. So the residual hope he perceives in almost all situations depends on his unquestioning faith in the validity of his doctrine of 'cordialità' which is perpetually regalvanized and consolidated by the lady's catalytic activity. Through her, a promise of vicarious salvation is even maintained in the lyric 'Il sogno del prigioniero' which rounds off the experience of '*La bufera*'. In this poem a generic political meaning[94] again complements Montale's metaphysical and ethical meditations, and his stoic conclusion is that we should resist all affronts to human dignity imposed by the blind forces of chance, even though we ourselves are likely to be crushed in the process. Politically speaking, in fact, the poet always believed that it was possible to reconcile personal liberty with the legitimate demands of society; and for this reason he would no doubt have accepted the customary liberal definition of freedom, whereby social restraint results from a constant moral fear of encroaching on the equal freedom of others.

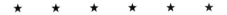

In the first edition of *Satura* (1962) the note of hopeful disillusionment continues to be felt, but the poet now seems to doubt whether he can retain his authenticity within the hermetic ethos. In 'Botta e risposta' he therefore calls into question his entire poetic method and suggests that even his lady, tired of his distant fidelity and adoration, has thrown down the gauntlet and challenged him to redimension his poetry:

> 'Arsenio' (lei mi scrive), 'io qui ''asolante''
> tra i miei tetri cipressi penso che
> sia ora di sospendere la tanto
> da te per me voluta sospensione
> d'ogni inganno mondano; che sia tempo
> di spiegare le vele e di sospendere
> *l'epoché.*'

'Arsenio' (she writes to me), 'I ''given an airing'' here among my gloomy cypresses think it is time to halt the much-by-you-for-me-desired suspension of all earthly illusions; that it is time to spread your sails and suspend the act of *epoché.*'

The way in which he hopes to achieve this aim is by introducing more overt narrative and historical elements into his verse, and yet the mythical survey of his life he now offers still has a touch of orphic suspension about it:

> Uscito appena dall'adolescenza
> per metà della vita fui gettato
> nelle stalle d'Augía.
> Non vi trovai duemila bovi, né

mai vi scorsi animali;
pure nei corridoi, sempre piú folti
di letame, si camminava male
e il respiro mancava; ma vi crescevano
di giorno in giorno i muggiti umani.

Hardly having grown out of adolescence, for half my life I was cast into the Augean stables. I did not find two thousand oxen there, nor did I ever see any animals; even in the corridors, ever more thickly blocked with dung, one walked with difficulty and it took one's breath away; but the bellowing of human beings grew louder there day by day.

Exactly the same thing can be said of his present views on his relations with women, for he still associates their emotional influence upon his sensibility either with relics or with fragmented events:

Poi d'anno in anno – e chi piú contava
le stagioni in quel buio? – qualche mano
che tentava invisibili spiragli
insinuò il suo memento: un ricciolo
di Gerti, un grillo in gabbia, ultima traccia
del transito di Liuba, il microfilm
d'un sonetto eufuista scivolato
dalle dita di Clizia addormentata,
un ticchettío di zoccoli (la serva
zoppa di Monghidoro) . . .

Then from year to year – and who counted the seasons any more in that darkness? – some hands which attempted invisible spirals introduced their mementos: a curl of Gerti's, a cricket in a cage, the last trace of Liuba's transit, the microfilm of a euphuistic sonnet that had slipped from the hands of the drowsing Clizia, a pattering of clogs (the lame servant of Monghidoro) . . .

The cherishing of such fossilized remains is a major feature of Montale's art, and so it will perhaps be interesting to note the high value he still attaches here to certain keepsakes. He hints that they are the basic building-blocks of his imagery, but, as previously indicated, he adds that 'l'importante è che il traslato dal vero al simbolico o viceversa in me avviene sempre inconsapevolmente. Io parto sempre dal vero, non so inventare nulla; ma quando mi metto a scrivere (rapidamente e con poche correzioni) il nucleo poetico ha avuto in me una lunga incubazione: lunga e oscura. *Après coup*, a cose fatte, conosco le mie intenzioni. Il dato realistico, però, è sempre presente, sempre vero.'[95] ('what is important is that transcription from the real to the symbolic and vice versa always takes place within me unconsciously. I always set out from the real, I cannot invent anything; but when I sit down to write (rapidly and with few corrections) the poetic nucleus has had a long incubation inside me: long and obscure. *Après coup*, when the job is completed, I get to know my intentions. The realist datum, however, is always present, always true.')

Where he now makes progress beyond the somewhat opaque involution of his imagery during his hermetic period is in his realization that a cult of object-symbols for their own sake can sometimes lead into blind alleys from which metaphorical liberation is hardly possible. This realization causes him to adopt the stance of an anti-hero who struggles through life despite a foreknowledge of his inevitable failure. Hence he rounds off 'Botta e risposta' parenthetically by telling his lady that she can expect no dramatic positive gestures or sudden bursts of illumination from him. He offers no new lease of life, but remains one of the Damned in modern society who, at best, can only go down fighting:

(Penso
che forse non mi leggi piú. Ma ora
tu sai tutto di me,
della mia prigionia e del mio dopo;
ora sai che non può nascere l'aquila
dal topo.)

(I think that perhaps you no longer read me. But now you know everything about me, about my imprisonment and my afterwards; now you know that the eagle cannot be born from the mouse.)

Although this attitude, as we can see in retrospect, is neither one of satiety nor complete despair, it is nevertheless possible that Montale came to look upon himself in the early sixties as a fly preserved in the amber of his own hermetic techniques. Hence irony, and even the practice of self-parody, tends to be one of his main relaxations at this stage and a rather superior, if precious, 'pièce de circonstance' now sums up through its 'badinage' and contrived elegance his rather ambivalent outlook. It is an epithalamium addressed to Alessandra Fagiuoli, though it is not of the usual laudatory kind: it is filled instead with multiple reminiscences, conceits and internal rhymes emphasizing its origin in a self-conscious, ironic mannerism. Possibly it is also a parody of the multilingual style practised by the *avanguardia* of the period; yet beneath its light-hearted playfulness there subsists an epigrammatic concision reasserting the general drift of the poet's dualistic philosophy of election and damnation:

L'epitalamio non è nelle mie corde,
la felicità non fu mai la mia Musa,
la sposa l'ho vista appena, un attimo tra le sàrtie
di un trealberi giunto dal reo Norte
all'Isola. Il mio augurio è dunque "a scatola chiusa".

Per lei, ma non per me, perché *la boîte à surprise*
è fatta per chi col suo nome decapitò Cassandra.
La gemma che v'è nascosta, frutto di un'inaudita
mainmise del bene sul male, io l'ho chiamata Speranza.

The epithalamium is not one of my strings, happiness was never my Muse, I have hardly seen the bride, just for a moment among the rigging of a three-master coming from the foul North to the Island. My greeting is thus "of the sealed-box type". For her, but not for me, because *the-jack-in-the-box* has been made for one whose name decapitates Cassandra. The pearl which is hidden therein, fruit of an unheard-of *mainmise* of good over evil, I have called Hope.

Such vicarious well-wishing clearly reminds us of the poet's earlier bestowal of Grace on his ladies by acts of self-sacrifice, although the implication is now one of possible 'convivenza' rather than anguished solitude or solipsistic beatitude. The chance element of the jack-in-the-box, it is true, is still present, but probably the surprise awaiting Alessandra is itself a decisive act of choice, giving rise to social good and furthering the corporate will-towards-order in society. In the area of the *Lebenswelt* it leads to the establishment of a social ethic unifying man's aspirations and drawing him towards a distant prospect of Hope. However, Montale's 'Speranza' also reminds us here of Gozzano's 'nonna Speranza' ('Grandmother Speranza') and his 'felicità' ('happiness') of 'La Signorina Felicita' ('Lady Felicity'), both of whom were fossilized creatures inhabiting the passive memory. He thereby dissociates himself from any facile sociological solution while, perhaps, highlighting its advantages as a recipe for happiness in Sandra's case. Moreover, he expresses the idea by means of another evocative literary reminiscence, Baudelaire's three-master in 'Le Voyage'. It is accordingly from a combination of the French poet's idealism and Gozzano's neo-Romantic fetishism that he produces the gem of happiness mentioned in the last lines; and this modern philosopher's stone is at one and the same time a state of emotional serenity for the girl and a symbol of some inaccessible form of ataraxy for the poet.

The views expressed in the early edition of *Satura*, as evidenced by the inclusion of a number of his early unpublished lyrics, tend to mark the end of a phase of Montale's development rather than announce a fresh one. A new outlook only develops when later he turns his back on the muted epic style of 'Botta e risposta' and begins to write poems on a poignant existential level, in memory of his recently deceased wife, Drusilla, in *Xenia*.[96] The differences between the second enlarged edition of *Satura* published in 1971 and the previous one are thus considerable. In particular, the *Xenia* sequence which it now contains is deliberately composed in the minor key, yet despite its domesticity its emotional intensity once again stresses the poet's firmly held belief in the absoluteness of personal relationships. This means that his technique and artistic manner are hardly transformed at all despite his changed mood, and he frequently employs the same trigger-mechanisms for his wife's epiphanies as he did earlier for Clizia's. The vital difference in atmosphere, however, is that here the whole tone is conjugal and domestic rather than metaphysical and apocalyptic:

> Caro piccolo insetto
> che chiamavano mosca, non so perché,
> stasera quasi al buio
> mentre leggevo il Deuteroisaia
> sei ricomparsa accanto a me,
> ma non avevi occhiali,
> non potevi vedermi
> né potevo io senza quel luccichío
> riconoscere te nella foschia.

Dear little insect whom they called fly, I don't know why, last night, almost at the fall of darkness, when I was reading Deutero-Isaiah you reappeared beside me, but you were not wearing glasses, you could not see me, nor could I recognize you in the haze without that glint.

Even so, notwithstanding Drusilla's short-sightedness her insight into the secret world of human relationships was much deeper than was suspected by their friends and acquaintances, and in this respect too she resembles the all-seeing Clizia:

> Non ho mai capito se io fossi
> il tuo cane fedele e incimurrito
> o tu lo fossi per me.
> Per gli altri no, eri un insetto miope
> smarrito nel blabla
> dell'alta società. Erano ingenui
> quei furbi e non sapevano
> di essere loro il tuo zimbello:
> di essere visti anche al buio e smascherati
> da un tuo senso infallibile, dal tuo
> radar di pipistrello.

I have never understood if I was your faithful and distempered dog or you were mine. For others no, you were a short-sighted insect lost in the blabla of high society. Those clever ones were naïve and did not know that they were a laughing-stock to you: to be seen even in the darkness and unmasked by your infallible sensitivity, by your bat-like radar.

A little later we find that she is transformed into his all-comprehending *alter ego*, sharing his outlook on life from a position beyond death (a point, we recall, of true communication) and mitigating through her realistic appraisals of people and situations his own feelings of alienation:

Tu solo sapevi che il moto
non è diverso dalla stasi,
che il vuoto è pieno e il sereno
è la piú diffusa delle nubi.
Cosí meglio intendo il tuo lungo viaggio
imprigionata tra le bende e i gessi.
Eppure non mi dà riposo
sapere che in uno o in due siamo una sola cosa.

You alone knew that motion was no different from immobility, that the void was full and that the blue sky is the most widespread of the clouds. Thus I better understand your long journey, imprisoned in bandages and plaster. Yet my knowing that as one or as two we are a single entity gives me no repose.

Here, of course, it could be argued that the poet's present philosophizing is not radically different from the kind of existential speculation we have seen earlier; but the responses of his sensibility to each and every one of his situations are now far more intimate. So, while his former vicarious humanism required objective, quartz-like imagery to create its impact, his present verse has a suppler texture altogether. It relies more on a direct human *pietas* than on metaphysics for its effects and it enhances Montale's powers of communication so significantly that his images now seem like tangible emanations from an inner elemental self.

The second edition of *Satura* not only contains the early *Satura* and *Xenia* sequences but also a considerable number of other poems written between 1969 and 1970. They tend to show a steady reversion to conceptual thinking and, relatively speaking, we find in them much less imaginative power. Again the revised collection opens with a liminary poem like all the previous major collections, and we now note that the poet considers the human personality and the problem of 'otherness' in an almost Pirandellian fashion:

I critici ripetono
da me depistati,
che il mio *tu* è un istituto.
Senza questa mia colpa avrebbero saputo
che in me i tanti sono uno anche se appaiono
moltiplicati dagli specchi. Il male
è che l'uccello preso nel paretaio
non sa se lui sia lui o uno dei troppi
suoi duplicati.

The critics, misled by me, repeat that my *thou* is an institution. Were it not for this fault of mine they would have known that in me the many are one, even if they seem multiplied by mirrors. The difficulty is that the bird caught in the trap does not know whether he is himself or one of his innumerable duplicates.

The 'one in the many' referred to here is again a speculative concept and may again be associated with the poet's views on the possibility or otherwise of intercommunication. But it is also illustrated at times concretely in his verse, as we have already seen, especially where certain poetic sequences use a number of different ladies to function as lyrical catalysts for a single purpose.

As for the other sections of the collection, they contain few poems which add significantly to Montale's stature, even though they do sharpen some of his philosophical concepts and attitudes. Most of these attitudes we have already considered earlier, but their centrality to his overall outlook on life has perhaps never before been so clearly brought into focus. Montale's belief in the discontinuity of experience, for instance, is expressed in Boutrouxesque terms in 'La storia':

La storia non si snoda
come una catena
di anelli ininterrotta.
In ogni caso
molti anelli non tengono.

History does not unfold like a chain with unbroken links. In any case most links do not hold.

He even goes further in *Dialogo* and observes ironically:

'Se l'uomo è nella storia non è niente:
La storia è *un marché aux puces*, non un sistema.'

'If man is in history he is nothing: history is a *flea-market*, not a system.'

On the other hand, historical discontinuity is ironically contrasted with the unity of religion, despite its innumerable sects:

Tutte le religioni del Dio unico
sono una sola: variano i cuochi e le cotture.[97]

All the religions of the one God are one only: the cooks and cooking vary.

And indeed the poet's anti-clericalism and wry humour are particularly prominent features in this volume.

He nevertheless still clings to his own religion of intercommunication between the living and the dead, the past and the present; and its rituals continue to operate at those points of intersection where communication through the temporal barrier is made possible by way of momentary flashes of emotional insight. Time thus seems to divide itself into a series of parallel tape-recordings, sometimes intercommunicating but mostly not:

> Non c'è un unico tempo: ci sono molti nastri
> che paralleli slittano
> spesso in senso contrario e raramente
> s'intersecano. È quando si palesa
> la sola verità che, disvelata,
> viene subito espunta da chi sorveglia
> i congegni e gli scambi. E si ripiomba
> poi nell'unico tempo. Ma in quell'attimo
> solo i pochi viventi si sono riconosciuti
> per dirsi addio, non arrivederci.[98]

There is no single time: there are many tapes which slide parallel to each other, often in contrary directions and rarely intersect. This is when the single truth becomes manifest which, once unveiled, is immediately expunged by those who control the machinery and interchanges. And then one plummets back into a single time. But in that moment alone a few living people have recognized each other to say farewell, not I'll-be-seeing-you.

Such a doctrine clearly amounts to a thorough-going existentialism interfused with a theory of vicarious salvation through 'veggenza'. Although the poet still continues to regard all religions as of uncertain efficacy, including even his own personal ritualistic mythology, he nevertheless repropounds it as tenaciously as ever in 'Ex voto' and associates it with laric objects:

> Ignoro
> se la mia inesistenza appaga il tuo destino,
> se la tua colma il mio che ne trabocca,
> se l'innocenza è una colpa oppure
> si coglie sulla soglia dei tuoi lari.

I do not know if my non-existence satisfies your destiny, whether yours completes mine which overflows from it, whether innocence is a sin or is gathered on the threshold of your household gods.

Similarly, in the poem 'Divinità in incognito' he again repostulates the existence of *deae ex machina* like Clizia and suggests that even lower grade talisman-mediators like Arsenio have the ability to enact miracles of revelationary communication:

> eppure
> se una divinità, anche d'infimo grado,
> mi ha sfiorato
> quel brivido m'ha detto tutto . . .

and yet, if a divinity, even of the lowest grade, has brushed past me, that shudder has told me everything . . .

What has really happened at this stage is that Montale continues to believe in the effectiveness of his religion of altruism to help others but not himself. He therefore adopts the attitude of a stoic who no longer participates in life (again indirectly symbolized by the sea) yet contemplates it with a certain detached interest from a vantage-point near the shore:

> Nel buio e nella risacca piú non m'immergo, resisto
> ben vivo vicino alla proda, mi basto come mai prima
> m'era accaduto.[99]

> In the darkness and in the slack of the counter-tide I no longer immerse myself, I endure near the shore, fully alive, and feel self-sufficient in a way which has never before happened to me.

One should not, however, regard this attitude as one of complacency, it is simply a resigned acceptance of the human condition; it implies a realization that the individual can only make the most of his destiny emotionally, he can never step outside it in a metaphysical sense and absolutize himself. It is perhaps natural that, once he had embraced this new sort of detachment, all the major themes developed over his long poetic career should have come flooding back to his mind. Yet the lyrically significant part of the collection still seems to be the poems contained in *Xenia* which clearly show that Montale was not indulging in an arid regurgitation of the past but ranging over new and intimate areas of experience and assimilating them to his overall poetic vision.

Montale's next volume *Diario del '71 e del '72* published in 1973 continues the same ironic vein found in *Satura*. In it the poet demonstrated once more his acceptance of – yet subtle self-alienation from – present-day society, since by then he had himself oddly become institutionalized as one of its great poets. He seems on the surface to treat his bourgeois way of life as an empty shell, and this is indeed the impression we obtain from his *pot pourri* of multilingual phrases which ironically mimic the internationalism of the avant-garde writers of the sixties. Most of these are French in origin and for that reason, perhaps, have the flavour of a type of internationalism now in complete decadence. The point is clearly made in human terms in 'Trascolorando' in which a husband takes his wife to the Lebanon after having given her a social 'status', but simply as 'suo nécessaire da viaggio' ('his travelling requisite'). She thereby becomes almost completely reified as a multilingual talking-doll, to be manipulated at his whim:

> Lei lo ricorda in varie lingue, un barbaro
> cocktail di impresti,
> lui la suppone arabizzata, docile
> ai festini e ai dileggi dei Celesti.

> She remembers him in various tongues, a barbarous cocktail of borrowings, he presumes her to be arabized, docile to the feasts and delights of the Celestial Beings.

This supposed shell of decadent bourgeois culture is nevertheless one in which Montale had a fundamental faith, so that his complacent irony hardly attempted to undermine its ideals but rather to strengthen its base through a pious critique of its practical shortcomings. It is for this reason that the present collection resembles a kind of intertext, a self-gloss on the poet's previous work. In a radio programme with Maria Corti and others he pointed out as early as 1971 that 'sarebbe un errore leggere una sola poesia e cercare di anatomizzarla, perché c'è sempre un richiamo da un suono all'altro non solo, ma anche da una poesia all'altra'[100] ('it would be an error to read a single poem and try to anatomize it, for there is not only an echo from one sound to another, but also from one poem to another'). Hence his self-parodies are often more than the mere consolidation of his mythology: they introduce new perspectives, new resonances into his view of the world, and they not only strengthen the coherence of his lyrical outlook, they also widen its range of implication in quite unexpected ways. One good example of a self-gloss which acts in precisely this manner is the poem 'Come Zaccheo'. It appears to hark back to lines in 'Iride' where Montale is dealing in a serious manner with Clizia's religious outlook and where he in fact refers allusively to the same symbolism as he does here – to a sycamore-tree which Zaccheus is later described as climbing to obtain a better view of the Lord:

> Cuore d'altri non è simile al tuo,
> la lince non somiglia al bel soriano
> che apposta l'uccello mosca sull'alloro;
> ma li credi tu eguali se t'avventuri
> fuor dell'ombra del sicomoro
> o è forse quella maschera sul drappo bianco,
> quell'effigie di porpora che t'ha guidata?

> The hearts of others are not like yours, the lynx does not resemble the handsome Syrian who ambushes the humming-bird on the laurel; but you believe them equal if you venture outside the shadow of the sycamore, or is it perhaps that mask on the white linen, that crimson image, which has guided you?

There are many difficulties implicit in this text but for the moment it will suffice to say that the 'bel soriano' has been taken by the critics to mean Christ and the shadow of the sycamore to refer to the Christian religion, as it also does in Nerval's sonnet, 'Delfica'. But in 'Come Zaccheo' an apparently light-hearted approach to the problems of religious belief finally comes to the fore, when in an amusing, yet highly ironic, manner the poet puts his own point of view about God whom he considers either as a 'Deus absconditus' ('hidden God') or even more remotely as 'il sommo Emarginato' ('the Almighty Irrelevance'):

Si tratta di arrampicarsi sul sicomoro
per vedere il Signore se mai passi.
Ahimé, non sono un rampicante ed anche
stando in punta di piedi non l'ho mai visto.

It is a question of climbing up a sycamore-tree to see Christ, if he ever passes by. Alas! I am not a climber and even standing on the tips of my toes I have never seen him.

Even such playfulness, however, is in the last resort an example of Montale's hyper-seriousness. For, in contrast with his dismissal of a metaphysical God, we know that he accepts the existence of human 'gods' and 'goddesses' who act as catalysts in this world and help others to weather the storms of living. The myth goes back at least as far as 'Arsenio', and we have already seen one of its more recent reassertions in 'Divinità in incognito'. Thus poems based on this particular theme may actually be regarded as intertexts of each other, since they both consolidate and at the same time reveal further aspects of a single archetypal myth.

Again, perhaps one of the most significant and all-embracing self-glosses which Montale ultimately wrote was a lyric which appeared in his *Quaderno di quattro anni* (1977), although it was composed as early as 1974. It is once again concerned with the poet's feelings of alienation in his old age and reads as follows:

Senza mia colpa
mi hanno allogato in un hôtel meublé
dove non è servizio di ristorante.
Forse ne troverei uno non lontano
ma l'obliqua
furia dei carri mi spaventa. Resto
sprofondato in non molli piume, attento
a spirali di fumo dal portacenere.
Ma è quasi spento ormai il mozzicone.
Pure i suoni di fuori non si attenuano.
Ho pensato un momento ch'ero l'ultimo
dei viventi e che occulti celebranti
senza forma ma duri piú di un muro
officiavano il rito per i defunti.
Inorridivo di essere il solo risparmiato
per qualche incaglio nel Calcolatore.
Ma non fu che un istante. Un'ombra bianca
mi sfiorò, un cameriere che serviva
l'aperitivo a un non so chi, ma vivo.

> Without any fault of mine they have lodged me in a hôtel meublé where there is no restaurant service. Perhaps I shall find one not far away but the transverse fury of the traffic frightens me. I lie deep in a scarcely soft feather-bed, watching the spirals of smoke from the ash-tray. But the butt-end is now almost extinguished. Yet the sounds outside do not grow fainter. I thought for a moment that I was the last survivor of the living and that formless mysterious celebrants, though harder than a wall, were officiating at the rites for the dead. I was horrified to be the only one spared through some hiccough of the Computer. But it was only an instant. A white shadow brushed past me, a waiter, who was serving an aperitif to someone or other, yet who was alive.

This poem is clearly written in that intimate, yet nonchalant and confidential, style which the poet frequently uses in his later poetry and which distinguishes it so significantly from his earlier writings. But at the same time it contains a veritable mosaic of reminiscences from Italian culture and his own early lyricism, and thereby proves to be a global comment on the meaning of his entire work. What is at once apparent is that he is not fundamentally concerned with social or overt political problems and ideologies; he is instead far more interested in analysing the metaphysical facets of alienation and in commenting on a world slowly turning to dust in his hands. Even so, he still uses his normal artistic and symbolic patterns to describe his feelings, and we note from the phrase 'ma non fu che un istante' that he is dealing with one of his typical flashes of insight. Indeed, the poetic flash could almost be defined at this stage as the momentary recapturing of a personal or literary echo, and this very fact clarifies retrospectively our understanding of Montale's use of the technique throughout his career.

We can, perhaps, interpret the poem not only as a confession of alienation from modern society but also as a mood resulting from a loss of commitment to the world. Already in *Xenia* we hear of the poet's most treasured possessions, his laric objects, being borne away by the Florentine flood as if they were so much detritus of a bygone age:

> L'alluvione ha sommerso il pack dei mobili,
> delle carte, dei quadri che stipavano
> un sotterraneo chiuso a doppio lucchetto.

> The flood has submerged the pile of furniture, papers and paintings which were stuffed in a cellar sealed with a double padlock.

These objects – red morocco-bound volumes, interminable dedications by Du Bos, hair from Ezra Pound's beard, the original of the *Canti orfici*, and so on – had by then clearly sunk into his passive memory and were secured there with a double padlock. They were therefore ready for disintegration into mere keepsakes, eventually to be swept away by the ravages of time. What symbolizes them in this particular poem is a quaintly French 'hôtel meublé', where none of the 'furniture' is the poet's own. The very term gives us the clear impression that we are looking at a decadent period-piece, and the idea of abandonment, of fossilization and alienation is reinforced by the lack of that other vital domestic service, a restaurant. To add to this sense of unease, moreover, the nearest restaurant requires the poet to brave the fast flowing traffic of the modern world: although the phrase 'l'obliqua furia dei carri' is yet another literary reminiscence, a direct borrowing from Parini's 'La caduta'. The mere thought of this danger so discourages him that he flings himself despairingly down on the hard bed of the room – yet another image with literary overtones, this time from Leopardi's 'La sera del dí di festa' – and the allusion hints at the universal anguish of indifference which forms the theme behind the entire poem. As he lies on the bed, the poet contemplates the smoke-rings of his cigar rising idly to the ceiling, and they too recall similar smoke-rings which appear in 'Nuove stanze' where they seem to represent the spiralling of destiny. By now they are merely rising from the stub-end of life, whereas in the earlier lyric the poet still had a future to be lived, even if it were an uncertain and grim one. Again, as in 'Nuove stanze', an ashtray is also in evidence. This might once have symbolized the fortune-teller's crystal-ball in the hands of Clizia, since in it she stubbed out the cigarette of an age of decadence, to replace it eventually with one of renewed hope. At present, however, the cigar of life has almost burnt itself out, and so any residual sense of striving to overcome fate has likewise passed away. The poem thus describes a substitute home, substitute or virtually non-existent services, and the burnt-out ash of a lifetime. Needless to say, we only have to recall the meaning of ashen precipitates in earlier poems to realize that we are now talking of the burnt-out experiences of Montale's own existence. But occasionally the rumbustious present still breaks in on his ear, despite the fact that he imagines himself the last survivor of a lost universe. He feels that he too is about to be buried, and yet the mysterious celebrants at the funeral of his entire generation themselves turn out to be reified, statuesque, ritualized creatures. So in a further Boutrouxesque reminiscence he begins to suspect that mankind's loss is perhaps much greater than he first thought. Despite the noise outside, he may, in fact, be the only fortuitous survivor of human society, through a mechanical quirk in the all-powerful Computer which now symbolizes mankind's degeneration to an automatized and inhuman form of 'convivenza'.

This moment of penetration, as already indicated, comes and goes in a flash, but it is again sufficient to open up fresh vistas by acting as a kind of commentary on his entire work. Such a type of *composition en abyme* ('composition in profundity') naturally can only create a phantomatic universe, and as reality comes flooding back to the poet after his moment of insight, the shadow which announces it is itself skeletal and insubstantial: a waiter who clearly offers a service, but to someone else, to an anonymous client who presumably is as attuned to modern society as Montale himself is unattuned to it. Incidentally, the white shadowy figure appearing here again reminds us of the pawns on the chessboard at the end of 'Nuove stanze'. There the chessmen were desubstantialized by being overwhelmed by the terror of war, while here it is the terror of living which is uppermost in the poet's mind. Indeed, in the *Diario* one of the poems is specifically entitled 'Il terrore di esistere', and in it Montale notes skittishly:

Il terrore di esistere non è cosa
da prendere sottogamba . . .

The terror of existing is not to be taken light-heartedly . . .

It is from this clear-sighted appreciation of the hopelessness of the human condition that there emerges a distinctive note of humane disillusionment, of mellowed ironic *pietas*, in his later work. It is simultaneously a self-commentary on his own life and a wider-ranging commentary on human life in general. It leads to a new kind of closure of the poet's imagery upon itself, again in true hermetic style, as his personal experience is gradually reglossed, made absolute, and cosmicized in its implications through a revitalized poetry of things. For Montale life continues to be a hopeless struggle from the outset, but it nevertheless has its minor compensations, its moments of elation, of insight, of memorial saturation and absolute emotional communication. In his view the poet is unauthentic only when he is not prepared to live the human condition at this humble level without 'scappatoie' or loopholes of any kind; when he tries, that is, to produce a fake rhetoric to conceal the grim realities of his hopeless existential condition from himself. Without doubt the poet's parody of the Dannunzian rhetoric of 'La Pioggia nel pineto' in *Satura* indicates that he regards the latter poet as the supreme self-deceiver in modern Italian literature. As he explains in 'Botta e risposta', no person, not even his lady, can make an eagle out of a mouse, and he seems to imply that in the end all men are mice because of their precarious, existential condition. He puts the point even more succinctly in the *Diario* when he adds in the last poem, 'Per finire':

Vissi al cinque per cento, non aumentate
la dose. Troppo spesso invece piove
sul bagnato.

I lived at five-per-cent, do not increase the dose. Too often it rains on those who are soaking wet.

In contrast with D'Annunzio's posturing, Montale's attitude to life is consequently that of the anti-hero: an anti-hero, however, who paradoxically undertakes the only true heroic action in life – an examination of the absurdity of the human condition without idealistic preconceptions or illusions of any kind. If then we are to look for a positive side to his lyricism, it lies in the fact that he replaces the traditional religious outlook with a wholly lay eschatology, one in which a *religio cordialis* ('a religion of cordiality') or faith in human relationships substitutes for a metaphysical belief in God. Or if God subsists at all in his poetry, it is through the presence of his creatures revivified by the mediation of things.

CHAPTER XI

Salvatore Quasimodo and the collapse of hermeticism

Quasimodo's position in the hermetic movement is rather more complicated to assess than that of the poets considered hitherto, for just as Ungaretti first initiated and then lived the hermetic revolution of the twenties and thirties, so he first stimulated and then largely lived the humanist revolution of the forties and fifties. Moreover, this second revolution, far from being detached and reticent in manner like its predecessor, aimed openly at participating in the real world – at a state of symbiosis between the cultural ethos of society and the single artistic temperament operating within it. Hence, although Quasimodo like Ungaretti before him had his ear closely attuned to the requirements of his age, it was only at the outset of his career that he reacted to his cultural environment specifically as a hermetic poet. Later his manner became so discursive that some critics have maintained that his involvement with the school was the result of a misunderstanding arising out of his collaboration with Montale, Saba and others in the periodical *Solaria*. This thesis too, however, seems somewhat vitiated by the fact that after the appearance of *Oboe sommerso* (1932) he was acknowledged as the hermetic movement's *caposcuola*. In all probability the confusion derives from the spurious critical contention mentioned earlier, which claims that hermeticism is a phenomenon belonging to the thirties alone. Instead, what actually emerged at that time was a revived hermeticism involving a Petrarchist type of mimesis of its earlier forms. Nevertheless one important distinction does seem to exist from the beginning between Quasimodo and his fellow-hermetic poets, namely, his tendency to rely on rational, not associative, imagery for his effects. His addiction to Descartes' geometrical method is clearly detectable in his early imaginative cult of circles, spirals and other mathematical designs, which together tend to reduce his images to a state of Mallarmean abstraction, described by Zagarrio in typically Quasimodean terms as 'un formidabile sforzo di "curvatura" '[1] (' tremendous power of "curvature" '). Such a procedure – often supported by infolded hermetic 'chimismi' – underlines the point that Quasimodo was at that time 'imprigionato nei limiti della propria anima'[2] ('imprisoned within the confines of his own soul'), despite an explicit denial of this tendency made on his behalf by Carlo Bo.

By contrast, the most vital elements in the hermetic ethos which found a response in his sensibility were its atavism and its infolded political overtones, since he soon seems to have realized, as Paparelli has noted, that 'l'ansia dell'uomo contemporaneo – il nostro *mal du siècle* – non è di ordine metafisico o psicologico, ma sociale'[3] ('the anxiety of modern man – our *mal du siècle* – is not of a metaphysical or psychological order, but a social one'). His hermetic posture could therefore only be an uneasy solipsist one, because it tended to distract him from exploring the arcana of authentically felt 'social' relationships and aimed instead at making him the master of a rationally reconstituted, but sensorially degraded, universe of involuted images. So, even though he undertook from the outset an Apollonian pursuit of lyrical clarity, he made the perilous mistake of confining himself within the narrow emotional world of the second-generation hermetics; and their constantly shrinking perspectives eventually provoked in his mind a drama of self-destruction, unfolding in the shattered Inferno of Apollyon rather than in the Elysium of Apollo.

At first sight Quasimodo's poetic development will perhaps seem to consist of two separate phases, but these apparently distinct periods, as Bo has rightly pointed out,[4] have a hidden relationship which removes from them all suspicion of a sudden, gratuitous change of spiritual design. The link between them lies in the poet's belief that every artist should consider himself free to undertake a thorough revaluation of society's moral and aesthetic standards while simultaneously acknowledging its continuing traditions as his guide for living. In his opinion tradition is simply a background force within which the authentic poet operates – normally by reaction. It is at one and the same time a potentially despotic taskmaster and a useful social bond offering him security within a wider scheme of living. Nevertheless this mature attitude is hardly detectable in his first volumes of verse because of his cult of spiritually regressive, memorial abstractions; and so, instead of evoking the social myth and natural landscapes in which to frame it, he makes his early word-pictures function as representations of the flora and fauna of an over-cerebral, private world rationally deducible from his extreme solipsist attitudes. As Stefanile was the first to note, this practice was bound eventually to result in 'un'astratta geometria ... un imponderabile mondo che sfugge a ogni percezione sensibile e solo per simboli si svela al cuore e all'intelligenza'[5] ('an abstract geometry ... an imponderable world which evades all concrete perceptions and reveals itself to the heart and the intelligence only through symbols').

From a symbolic standpoint the gradual widening of Quasimodo's lyrical canvas is punctuated by his acceptance of the sadder, more realistic atmospheres and the darker skies of Lombardy. But in his early career their acceptance still lies some way in the future and the aridity of his hermetic style gives us a clear indication of his dominant moods, most of which alternate between self-negation and escapism. Within such a dialectic his atavism is usually a prominent feature and consists of dynamic, closed emotions literally bursting for expression, but which are often unable to find their appropriate lyrical forms. Since these moods are mostly associated with Sicily, his sense of life's incommunicability tends in the course of time to provoke a psychological fear of alienation from his native land; and this was especially the case after he had left the island in the early twenties to practise as an engineer on the mainland. His exile forced him to cling more closely than ever to his childhood images of Sicilian life and he used their magical effects, very much as Montale used his talismans, as touchstones to guarantee his authenticity as a poet.

Gradually, however, his sense of vocation increased and with it a deep-seated restlessness and dissatisfaction with his chosen career in engineering. Hence, after having based himself for a decade in the south of Italy working in the construction industry, he eventually gravitated towards the literary world of Florence, into which he became fully integrated following his sister's marriage to the novelist Vittorini. From then on he entertained no further doubts whatsoever about his destiny as a poet, although his latent interest in literature had already been stirred as early as 1921, when he undertook a study of Latin and Greek poetry under the supervision of Monsignor Rampolla del Tíndaro. Even so, he only practised the art of lyricism in a somewhat dilettante and intermittent manner until he finally began to collaborate with the writers surrounding *Solaria* in 1930. Later, after having worked as a drama critic with the periodical *Tempo* for a short time, he was finally appointed Professor of Italian Literature at the Giuseppe Verdi Conservatory in Milan 'per chiara fama' ('through clear renown').

During his early years as an itinerant engineer the poet consoled himself, as we have already hinted, by re-evoking the mysterious echoes arising in his sensibility from his intensely Sicilian childhood memories. The attractions of the island's closed and secretive communities and its sun-drenched landscapes even tended occasionally to produce hallucinatory visions – so many manifestations of religion, blood and instinct – in his mind. Thus, as late as 1950, he could still forcefully assert: 'La mia siepe è la Sicilia; una siepe che chiude antichissime civiltà e necropoli e latomie e telamoni spezzati sull'erba e cave di salgemma e zolfare e donne in pianto da secoli per i figli uccisi, e furori contenuti o scatenati, banditi per amore e per giustizia'.[6] ('My hedge is Sicily; a hedge which encloses ancient civilizations and necropoli and latomies and telamones smashed on the grass and saltpetre and sulphur quarries and women in mourning for centuries for their assassinated sons, and furies either unleashed or seething inwardly, and bandits through love or for the sake of justice'.) By that time, in fact, all his Sicilian memories had been concentrated into a single self-perpetuating core of images whose continuing validity may be verified by their appearance in his work in a multitude of moods and circumstances. And they continue to be generated even after he had finally become reconciled with the gloomier landscapes and the less violent colours of the North, a fact which suggests that a slightly sicilianized Lombardy is the point at which he blends his earlier provincial sensibility with the tonal colouring of the wider Italian tradition. Hence within his mature evocations of the unrelieved melancholy of Lombardy with its endless mist and rain we sense a constant desire to recapture multi-dimensionally the intense sensations and richer landscapes of the South.

These archetypal Sicilian features are, moreover, placed in a nostalgic memorial setting in his later work and their sources are the poet's own youthful images appearing in his early collections of verse, where their impact was already heightened by a powerful undercurrent of visual and atavistic sensations. Even at the end of his life they still represented for Quasimodo what Bo calls the 'vert paradis' ('green paradise') of his childhood[7] and they are likely to re-emerge as half-remembered visions of peace and serenity at all critical points in his career. They tend in other words to punctuate the stages of his spiritual development away from solipsism towards a modern form of humanism. Consequently, whereas in his early poetry he evokes many images of failed lyrical redemption like his sleeping or dead angels whom he immerses in an atmosphere of refined but aseptic aestheticism:

> Dorme l'angelo
> su rose d'aria, candido,
> sul fianco,
> a bacio del grembo
> le belle mani in croce,[8]

The angel sleeps, pure, on its side on airy roses, with its beautiful hands crossed over its bosom,

in his later lyrics these static metaphysical ciphers are replaced by more dynamically human figures of Sicilian womanhood bent in an eternal sorrow. Their intensely human postures in other words offer, in place of the statuesque poses of his angelic figures, a far more flexible and emotionally based attitude to life:

> La nostra terra è lontana, nel sud,
> calda di lacrime e di lutti. Donne,

laggiú, nei neri scialli
parlano a mezza voce della morte,
sugli usci delle case.[9]

Our land is far away, in the south, hot with tears and mourning. Women, down there, in black shawls speak in a low voice about death, on the doorsteps of the houses.

Although the main difference between these two word-pictures is the much greater degree of emotional commitment of the second, nevertheless even Quasimodo's early poetry is far from being emotionally threadbare despite its many restraints. The emotion he shows in it, however, is atavistic rather than broadly humanistic in quality, and it springs from his attempts to communicate with his remote Sicilian forbears and to create an emotional bond between their elemental desires and his own sensibility. They stand, so to speak, as the guardians of his secret island civilization, as may be seen in 'Insonnia' or other similar lyrics; and the poet feels himself brought into closer communion with these spirits of the past as he muses over the necropolis of Pantàlica in the Anapo valley. The necropolis in question consists of thousands of chambers cut out of the rock in pre-hellenic times and later used as a cave-town. In the poem Quasimodo feels himself viscerally bound to these early Sicels and tries to counterbalance his own incipient feelings of alienation by evoking an equal and opposite feeling of communion with their brooding telluric souls. In his wakeful dream their primitive passions frequently stir the deepest part of his being:

D'anni e anni, in cubicolo aperto
dormo della mia terra,
gli òmeri d'alghe contro grige acque:

nell'aria immota tuonano meteore.

For years and years, in an open cubicle of my land I sleep, my shoulders laden with seaweed against grey waters: in the motionless air meteors thunder.

But despite the atavistic and even cosmic yearnings implicit in this instinctive mysticism, its final outcome, perhaps, already proves to be a humanism in embryo, one which helps to throw into relief the underlying unity between the poet's two periods of development. Its features are apparent whenever the *intension* of the poet's orthodox hermetic symbolism is counterbalanced by the *extension* of a half-concealed allegory, and a good example of this polyvalency of poetic implication is to be seen in the opening fragment, 'Ed è súbito sera', in *Acque e terre* (1930):

Ognuno sta solo sul cuor della terra
trafitto da un raggio di sole:
ed è súbito sera.

Everyone stands alone on the bosom of the earth transfixed by a ray of sunlight: and it is suddenly evening.

In this poem, as we have shown elsewhere,[10] the three principal object-symbols (*terra, sole* and *sera*) are reductions of real phenomena to orphic archetypes, and in combination they are intended to illustrate the contingency of the entire human condition. They also tend to imply, at a somewhat less esoteric level, the principal stages of the human life-span, and in this sense they are already beginning to break away from the folds of hermetic involution. So, although at one level we can still visualize them as manifestations of a remote orphic iconography, they are simultaneously expanded, at least in part, into an emotional, or even a social, allegory. Their diffuse imagery, as opposed to the centripetal implications of his normal hermetic structures, clearly indicates in what direction Quasimodo's symbolism will eventually move and how it will gradually acquire the power to cope with the wider range of feelings detectable in most of his post-war collections.

Unfortunately, the overall perceptive range of *Acque e terre* does not measure up to that found in its opening composition, and so the poems it contains do little more than alternate in true hermetic style between the active and the passive memories. In all probability we can take the very title as symbolizing the orphic flow of the active memory (*acque*) and the immutability of the passive memory (*terre*) in a clearly Montalian sense. What is more, whereas we associate the purity of running water with the quicksilver of the active memory, we note that the main stress is placed here on a more sluggish memorial state symbolized by *acquamorta* ('dead water'). In the poem of that name Quasimodo consequently creates a minor epic of almost Dantesque intensity, in which he contemplates existence as it declines into an irremediable state of ennui:

Acqua chiusa, sonno delle paludi
che in larghe lamine maceri veleni,
ora bianca ora verde nei baleni,
sei simile al mio cuore.

Il pioppo ingrigia d'intorno ed il leccio;
le foglie e le ghiande si chetano dentro,
e ognuna ha i suoi cerchi d'un unico centro
sfrangiati dal cupo ronzar del libeccio.

Cosí come su acqua allarga
il ricordo i suoi anelli, mio cuore;
si muove da un punto e poi muore:
cosí t'è sorella acquamorta.

> Closed water, sleep of swamps, which in large sheets rets poisons, now white, now green, in the lightning flashes, you are like my heart. The poplar and the holm-oak grow grey all around; leaves and acorns lie still within, and each has its circles from a single centre distorted by the dark drone of the south-wester. Thus, as if on water memory widens its rings, my heart; it moves from a single point and then dies: and so dead water is a sister to you.

For anyone who has read Campana's poetry the orphic elements which abound here will hold few mysteries. But Quasimodo also tends to dichotomize life like Montale, and so symbols of rivers, streams, the sun, stars and life-giving rain denote positive qualities, while stagnant pools and the greenness of vegetable decay express negative ones. In the pool-image and the spectral whiteness of the lightning flash, moreover, we again perceive here the poet's preoccupation with rationalistic geometrical patterns.

In the first stanza a hallucinatory eye-image of the kind previously used by Pascoli and Corazzini is detectable, although with the present poet it is depicted indirectly as a stagnant pool winking intermittently in the lightning flashes of a subdued storm. The somnolence of the scene reinforces the dominant mood of *noia*, which is then further intensified by the overall greyness of the atmosphere and the poisonous corruption of the water. In combination, these elements are evidently intended to objectivize the shattered emotional state of Quasimodo's sensibility; but, when we later move on to the second stanza, the lyrical atmosphere becomes slightly modified and images of trees tend to predominate. Trees, as we shall see later, are almost invariably used by Quasimodo as figures of human anguish[11] and their bareness stresses their virtual inanimacy, as indeed does the fact that they are rooted in a dreary Gidean kind of marshland. So, although they offer some vague promise of rebirth by virtue of their action of storing away a potentiality of leaves and acorns, they too are enclosed in the same vicious circle of negative experience as the stagnant water. Hence they hardly respond at all to the promise of redemption borne by an atavistic wind, which once again has an obvious Montalian connotation. Finally, in the last stanza, we revert in a symmetrical fashion to the indirect eye-image of the first, although the landscape now seems metamorphosed into the inward eye of memory. Yet even memories quickly fade away as they are cast, wavelike, upon the glutinous water, with the result that the poet's heart lapses back into a state of apathy and threatens to abandon the unequal struggle for life.

Is there any way of escape from the poet's present mood of *noia*? Only, it seems, through a constant re-evocation of the rich sensations of his early Sicilian life. So Quasimodo tends from time to time to superimpose the latter upon his otherwise abstract and negative forms of imagery. But at this juncture not even Sicilian images always give rise to the immediate and joyful sensations we would expect, because they too are immersed in a cerebral medium which Macrí has defined as the *parola-mito*[12] ('word-myth'). This type of symbolic structure is both monadic and archetypal in quality and it aims at providing through its meditative abstraction a 'prova di esperienza totale' ('pledge of total experience'). The materials on which it operates are the poet's atavistic urges and his ratiocinatory, Cartesian concepts; and because of their very refractoriness they often produce images surrounded by an air of fragmented orphic mystery.

The outcome of such a technique is Mallarmean in quality, inasmuch as it distinguishes between the 'état essentiel' ('essential state') of the true poetic word and the 'état brut et immédiat' ('immediate crude state') of reality in the raw. The poet does not wish, it seems, to convey his sense-impressions directly through his lyricism but simply uses them as so many concrete pegs on which to hang the secret inner landscapes of his soul. At this stage such landscapes almost seem to be more real to him than reality itself, because they protect the responses of his sensibility from the crudeness of his everyday circumstances as a man imprisoned in a degraded world. Through their agency he tries to yoke together the earth and the heavens in a truly orphic fashion; and an awakening to an orphic state of mind is clearly likened by him in 'Convalescenza' to the regaining of a state of health, although a residual instinctive delirium is still present in the otherwise cosmic texture of the imagery:

Abbandoni d'alga:
mi cerco negli oscuri accordi
di profondi risvegli
su rive dense di cielo.

Languishing of seaweed: I search for myself in the obscure harmonies of deep awakenings, on dense shores of sky.

Such moods tend to border on an orphic romanticism, but fortunately Quasimodo's inspiration is not always of so facile, if disturbing, a quality. Instead a finely distilled realism replaces the orphic dream whenever he succeeds in walking the tightrope between concept and sensation. At such moments, despite the strict geometrical patterns to which he confines himself, he manages to introduce into his verse a refreshing series of visual images, although most still betray a certain generic aura. A good illustration is the poem 'Terra' where the indeterminate geometrical contours of parched hills and rolling plains are ultimately subordinated to the poet's desire to involve himself in the secret cycle of the earth's fertility:

Monti secchi, pianure d'erba prima
che aspetta mandrie e greggi,
m'è dentro il male vostro che mi scava.

> Arid hills, plains of early grass that await herds and flocks, within me is your ache which scourges me.

Such thumb-nail sketches – although isolated – are highly significant, because they are indicative of the struggle taking place in the poet's mind between his incipient realist, and his previous solipsist, approaches to art – a struggle which will gradually be resolved in favour of the realist trend.

Nevertheless, detached, generic images are so prevalent at the present stage in his development that Flora once made an inventory of Quasimodo's pre-war archetypes,[13] leading Antonielli, Romano and others to venture so far as to doubt their authenticity.[14] Yet, despite the fact that their abuse does at times make certain poems highly obscure, their undeniable effectiveness in most cases offers us sufficient guarantees to discount any suspicion or intentional insincerity. What probably gave rise to such misgivings with some critics was the very ambivalence of the poet's *parola-mito*, especially when it operated on the level of the allegory and the emblem simultaneously. Yet even dual functions of this kind are often advantageous, since they allow the poet to construct his landscapes from archetypes which have whole planetary systems of poetic sub-symbols with diverse implications attached to them.[15] For instance, the sub-symbols *mare* ('sea'), *fonte* ('fountain'), *onda* ('wave') are all linked by Quasimodo with the archetype *acqua* ('water'), symbol of life's 'élan vital' and the associated orphic process of purification; similarly *sera* ('evening'), *buio* ('darkness') *ombra* ('shadow') are variants of an archetypal, orphic *notte* ('night') denoting the mysteries connected with pure unformed existence. Other parallel chains derive from *albero* ('tree') symbolizing human anguish, from *cuore* ('heart') indicating the seat of the emotions, *sangue* ('blood') standing for instinct, and even *angelo* ('angel') representing a statuesque and hypostasized type of desire.[16] Normally these sub-symbols can be regarded as examples of *parola-mito* in their own right, despite the fact that they retain powerful allusive overtones linking them back with their respective archetypes. Moreover, such cross-allusions help considerably in maintaining the overall coherence of the poet's early work, even though they can appear somewhat mechanical at times.

The point may be illustrated in a poem with the significant title of 'Albero'. In it a tree puts on new foliage (*fronda*) by accepting the nourishment provided both by the orphic elements of the earth (*terra, acqua*) and the sky (*sole*), whereas the poet, by refusing such nourishment, fossilizes into a virtually insensitive object:

> Non solo d'ombra vivo,
> ché terra e sole e dolce dono d'acqua
> t'ha fatto nuova ogni fronda,

mentr'io mi piego e secco
e sul mio viso tocco la tua scorza.

Alive not only with shadow, for earth and sun and a sweet gift of water have renewed all your leaves, while I bow down and dry out and on my face I touch your bark.

As we can see, he aims in this case at creating a subtle dialectic between interrelated, yet paradoxical, vegetative imagery. The intention behind such networks is to associate delicate chains of meditative responses with dramatic shifts of emphasis arising from unexpected metamorphoses between man and plants.

Similar transformations are characteristic of all levels of his inspiration and remind us at times of the lyricism of minor hermetics like De Libero.[17] The process is, in fact, typical of the later hermetic movement as a whole and was no doubt chosen for its ready adaptability to an intense involution of imagery. With Quasimodo the identification of man and tree is a recurrent theme and in one poem he even describes his melancholy as 'la mia tristezza d'albero malnato'[18] ('my sadness of an ill-starred tree'). Eventually this tendency towards 'lignification' even causes him to descend two grades in an apparently Dantesque hierarchy of intelligence, when his human nature loses its rational and sensitive qualities to degenerate into a pure vegetative state, somewhat like Pier delle Vigne's in the *Inferno*. He describes this state as one of 'verde squallore' ('green squalor') and it is intended once more to highlight his sense of alienation. Thus, although instinctively he continues to feel the uninhibited surging of the green fuse in springtime, his awareness of his loss of humanity provokes a countervailing mood of destructive clearsightedness. His numerous vegetative metamorphoses thereby punctuate his gradual descent to thinghood and simultaneously underline the various stages of his spiritual sclerosis within the hermetic ethos.

The marmoreal beauty of his angel-symbols are also to be associated with this metaphysical, almost ratiocinatory, cult of soul-death. They prove to be so many orphic emblems of dehumanization measuring his steady rejection of living emotions for pure, geometrical figures. By reaction, their insensitivity also indicates that any attempt at wholesale metaphysical possession of the real by the poet will prove a futile and illusory operation. Such an aspiration can never slake man's Promethean thirst for self-knowledge, it can only turn his desires to ice in his hands, as in the following angel-image:

L'angelo è mio;
io lo posseggo: gelido.[19]

The angel is mine; I possess it: ice-cold.

To counteract the frigidity of this emotional wasteland Quasimodo thus often regresses to the experiences of his childhood and associates them with an escape towards distant racial memories. One of the most aesthetically refined examples of atavistic escape in his early verse is 'Vento a Tíndari' where a gradual attenuation of the poet's sense-impressions is counteracted by a rising Sicilian wind of racial passions which allows him to re-establish contact with the pristine realities of his youth.

The poem opens with the evocation of a hallucinatory seascape: a view of the Aeolian isles, home of the God of the winds, seen from the clifftop of Tíndari:

Tíndari, mite ti so
fra larghi colli pensile sull'acque
dell'isole dolci del dio,
oggi m'assali
e ti chini in cuore.

Tindari, gentle I know you are, hanging between wide hills over the waters of the sweet islands of the god, today you assail me and slip into my heart.

Its magic no doubt owes much to the well-known Leopardian technique whereby the poet deliberately limits himself to tracing out the visual outline of a scene so as to produce an infinite or indefinite perspective. But here the subtle contours of Quasimodo's idyll are even further attenuated by a vaporous and varying sense of melody. Indeed, at this stage the poet shows himself particularly adept at producing contrapuntal harmonies to offset subtle changes in his mood, so that at first the rhythm expresses excitement by the introduction of ante-penultimate stresses very much like the medieval *cursus*, while later this excitement subsides and fades away in the dying falls of lines like 'ti chini in cuore'. Of great importance, too, is the vowel pattern beginning with an insistence of the shrill incisiveness of the letter 'i' and then slowly becoming more deeply modulated through the increasing presence of full-throated sounds like 'a' and 'o'. The resulting lyrical alchemy is by no means a forced one: it evokes in our minds a multidimensional picture of a half-forgotten Sicilian strand harking back in its slumber to some long-past civilization. Its atmosphere not only recalls the fabulous mythological infancy of Sicily itself but also the wider cultural perspectives of *Magna Graecia* which are eventually superimposed on it through the 'nitidezza' ('clarity') of Quasimodo's classically orientated, yet often almost Alexandrine, manner.

By the time of the writing of the poem, however, the mysterious call of the poet's island memories had somewhat receded and only continued to stimulate an area at the back of his mind. So, in order to refocus his childhood images in his inward eye, he had to abandon realities – his exile on the mainland – and wind back his thoughts in an atavistic trance, until such time as his early impressions took on flesh again and came flooding back to him in all their pristine freshness:

> Salgo vertici aerei precipizi,
> assorto al vento dei pini,
> e la brigata che lieve m'accompagna
> s'allontana nell'aria,
> onda di suoni e amore,
> e tu mi prendi
> da cui male mi trassi
> e paure d'ombre e di silenzi,
> rifugi di dolcezze un tempo assidue
> e morte d'anima.

I climb up peaks, airy precipices, caught in the wind of the pines, and the happy company which follows me moves off into the air, a welter of sounds and love, and you seize me, from whom I unwillingly drew away and fears of shadows and silences, once assiduous retreats of sweetness and soul-death.

The day-dreaming here is once again activated by a Montalian wind blowing within an otherwise generic Sicilian landscape of peaks and precipices. Yet for all its generic features the scene is strangely reminiscent of the precipitous coastline around Tíndari.

Such a combination of wind and scenery permits the poet to explore the storehouse of his secret Sicilian soul, though many of its haunting reminiscences are now blurred, as if seen through a darkened mirror. The bittersweet of these memories shows that so far he has not been able to insert himself into any tradition which can adequately replace his childhood involvement in the island's provincial mythology, and this accounts for his turning to love as a palliative for his feelings of solitude and isolation. Eventually he hopes that love (and the wife he had then recently married, we note, was a Northerner) will serve as a kind of stepping-stone to reintegrate him into Italian society upon a more satisfying human plane. But at present even love proves ineffective and he is left with a fragmented sensibility as he meditates ruefully on the debilitating effects of exile:

> Aspro è l'esilio,
> e la ricerca che chiudevo in te
> d'armonia oggi si muta
> in ansia precoce di morire;
> e ogni amore è schermo alla tristezza,
> tacito passo nel buio
> dove mi hai posto
> amaro pane a rompere.

Bitter is exile, and the search for harmony I reposed in you now changes to a precocious desire for death; and every love is a screen for sadness, a silent step in the dark where you have placed bitter bread for me to break.

On the other hand the poet's 'tristezza' contrasts markedly with the more despairing 'male di vivere' which dominates Montale's early work. For Quasimodo's sadness is not a product of metaphysical doubt; it does not question the validity of the human condition as such: it is simply a sense of humanistic loss which he experiences as a result of his failure to commit himself to an integrated and fruitful way of life. Eventually it inspires in him a half-suppressed desire to widen his hermetic field of vision, a process which in his post-war career will give rise to a full-blooded cult of humanism: one which will aim at fusing together his atavistic communion with his Sicilian roots and the exigencies of the wider modes of 'convivenza' he later discovers in the North. Even so, at this point there is little more than a slight hint of uneasiness as the poet's immediate audience stands aside in 'Vento a Tíndari' to allow a Sicilian friend[20] to help him regress towards a momentary state of communion with his island's age-old culture:

> Tíndari serena torna;
> soave amico mi desta
> che mi sporga nel cielo da una rupe
> e io fingo timore a chi non sa
> che vento profondo m'ha cercato.

> Tindari returns serene; a kind friend stirs me so that I can thrust myself into the sky from a rock, and I pretend to be afraid to those who do not know what deep wind has sought me out.

Such communion is, of course, atavistically and socially directed and reveals Quasimodo's transitional function as a poet. From it we can assess his relationship with the later hermetic lyricists, which was expressive or technical in nature rather than aesthetic or spiritual. So while their dominant approaches to life were largely metaphysical in orientation, his outlook derives from the involution of the views and attitudes of a fundamentally humanist philosophy.

The point is underlined by an aura of Greek clarity which was already emerging in his verse and which was rapidly to diminish his reliance on stylistic involution. One of his favourite Greek models of the thirties was Sappho whom he greatly admired for her precision and the previously mentioned quality of 'nitidezza'.[21] Quasimodo's Sappho is, however, mediated by Leopardi who in his view provides the link between Greek and Italian art in the modern world. The significance of his turning to a Graeco-Leopardian type of inspiration is that it was instrumental in refining away many of the turbulent sensations of blood and instinct underlying his early poetry. And it is indeed mainly through this twofold influence that he later succeeded in transforming his impetuous youthful emotions into the remarkably purified imagery of his maturity.

Side by side with the strain of 'pure poetry' in *Acque e terre* we also note a neo-crepuscular tonality intermingled with Pascolian effects. The crepuscular influence is more melodic than visual, as the following lines will show by their dying falls:

Mi parve s'aprissero voci,
che labbra cercassero acque,
che mani s'alzassero a cieli;[22]

It seemed as if voices opened up, that lips sought water, that hands were raised to heaven;

while the Pascolian tendency behind it is psychological and tonal. Thus Pascoli's influence is particularly noticeable in those poems which attempt to recapture the poet's childhood experiences, because Quasimodo then virtually allows himself to be absorbed by the elements of the scene he is describing. Such absorption gives rise to anthropomorphic imagery which is often highly effective. A lyric like 'Vicolo' is a case in point, for in it the poet appears to suspend his meditative faculty for a moment and evokes a childhood memory in all its pre-reflective purity. We find, therefore, that the very houses of the hamlet in which he lived whisper to one another in an atmosphere of almost primeval darkness, just as if they were so many secret repositories of Sicilian feelings. In short, we move momentarily into a dilated sphere of atavistic communion, not unlike that close communion with nature we detect in poems like Pascoli's 'Il gelsomino notturno'. The significant lines from 'Vicolo' read:

Vicolo: una croce di case
che si chiamano piano,
e non sanno ch'è paura
di restare sole al buio.

Alleyway: a huddle of houses which softly call out to each other, and do not know that it is fear at being alone in the dark.

Naturally such intense sensations prove more difficult to recapture as time passes; and, when Quasimodo eventually senses the slackening of his grasp on his Sicilian sensations, he dwells on the dissolution of life itself. Experience is thereafter transformed by him into quick-and-dead imagery, and we can almost see a miniature epic of human growth and decay in 'Antico inverno':

Cercavano il miglio gli uccelli
ed erano súbito di neve;
cosí le parole.

Un po' di sole, una raggera d'angelo,
e poi la nebbia; e gli alberi,
e noi fatti d'aria al mattino.

The birds sought millet and were immediately as snow; likewise words. A touch of sun, the halo of an angel, and then the mist; and the trees, and ourselves made airy in the morning.

Possibly the poet is once again transposing here the hermetic distinction between the active and the passive memories on to an ethical plane. The paradox of the individual's limited life-span yet infinite memories is indeed an integral part of Quasimodo's lyrical outlook and we shall soon find him employing it as a spring-board to rise to higher planes of consciousness.

Needless to say, as his world-picture is slowly transformed to allow for a fuller participation in life, the poet's initial sadness gives way to restrained optimism: an optimism which is based on the discovery that atavistic resonances can function not only in the inner suspended world of hermeticism but also in the emotional continuum of a humanist society. He therefore proceeds to subvert the original intention behind modern orphism while at the same time applying its modalities to an exciting new range of social experiences. Eventually the changeover (which incidentally took place during and after the Second World War) had a traumatic effect on Italian literary life; but in Quasimodo's early poetry it still remains nothing more than a latent possibility. Not only is this true of *Acque e terre* but also of *Oboe sommerso* (1932) which, if anything, is marginally more hermetic in orientation than its predecessor. Sanesi, in fact, once described it as a kind of lyricism based on a 'panteismo della memoria'[23] ('pantheism of the memory'), and all that distinguishes it from the preceding collection is its much denser analogical structures and its completely bewildering allusiveness.

The poet's aim appears to be to evoke echoes from his now rapidly receding Sicilian dreamland in the 'drowned' modulations of a 'submerged' oboe, a practice reminding us of the music of Debussy's *La cathédrale engloutie* to which the title probably alludes. As his faraway melodies break through the surface of the water, they seem like reflections shimmering on the surface of pools, and only their vegetative element – which once again indicates a process of decomposition – links them with the real world. But, although a liquid and vegetative balance is achieved by the bitter smell of foliage which permeates the concentrated interiority of the following lines taken from 'L'eucalyptus',

In me un albero oscilla
da assonnata riva,
alata aria
amare fronde esala,

In me a tree quivers from a sleepy bank, wingèd air breathes forth bitter foliage,

the tree-image itself still remains symbolic of unresolved human anguish. Likewise the 'assonnata riva' now stands for some remote strand or 'Saharah brumeux' ('misty Sahara') beyond the bounds of time, in which the poet's Sicilian ancestors mysteriously subsist.

The scene also continues to retain an element of rêverie about it, mainly because of its semi-aquatic atmosphere which is evoked in the same impressionistic fashion as before; while the alchemistic effects of the entire collection are now strengthened by the use of extremely compressed and essentialized syntax. In *Oboe sommerso*, in particular, Quasimodo is always consciously striving to suppress logical links, to practise fulminatory juxtapositions of words and images, and to experiment with prepositions and other particles. Yet at the same time his symbolic archetypes remain surprisingly constant, indicating that despite his many new technical devices they still form the underlying substance of his lyricism.

As we would expect, the hermetic device of metamorphosis is again widespread, and the eponymous lyric indicates that the poet's alienation has already passed beyond the stage of mere vegetative transformation to reach a condition of almost total inanimacy, symbolized by the wilderness of fallow-land:

L'acqua tramonta
sulle mie mani erbose.

Ali oscillano in fioco cielo,
làbili: il cuore trasmigra
ed io sono gerbido,

e i giorni una maceria.

Water darkens on my grassy hands. Wings quiver in a limp sky, transiently: my heart migrates and I am left fallow, and my days are rubble.

Equally startling in the same collection is the orphic insight resulting from the poet's imaginative juxtapositions which cause a dilation of reality. Spatial expansion, for instance, is clearly implied in the following juxtaposition:

Mite letargo d'acque:
la neve cede chiari azzurri.[24]

Gentle lethargy of waters: the snow yields clear azure pools.

Nevertheless, this technique alone is not sufficient to raise the poet out of his state of alienated existence, and so he soon reintroduces into his poetry the muted humanism of his deeper atavistic urges.

The particular route he chooses at this juncture to seek relief from his solipsist position involves him in direct communion with the regenerative humours of the earth. In one lyric even his relations with his mistress become a form of vegetative growth:

Fatto ramo
fiorisce sul tuo fianco
la mia mano.[25]

My hand, changed to a branch, flowers on your flank.

In another he describes the orphic dream in terms which makes its radiance shine through the very dissolution of the flesh in its bier:

Muove nei vetri dell'urna
una luce d'alberi lacustri:
mi devasta oscura mutazione,
santo ignoto: gemono al seme sparso
larve verdi:
il mio volto è loro primavera.[26]

There moves in the glass of the bier a light of lakeside trees: a dark mutation destroys me, an unknown saint: green larvae moan in the scattered seed: my face is their spring.

It follows, therefore, that the attitude implied by the process of decomposition is not as negative as it first seems; for, beyond the physical process, there remains a deeper state of consciousness in which the corpse's mysterious insights are illuminated by dense, if submerged, images like 'una luce d'alberi lacustri'. In the last resort Quasimodo's vegetative decomposition is indeed no more than a means to an end: an attempt to awaken subtle responses in the reader's mind by simultaneous bifocal allusions to realist and orphic planes of existence. In this respect the lyric 'Nell'antica luce delle maree', is a key poem of this collection, just as 'Vento a Tíndari' was a key to the preceding one. In the first place it is another idyll dealing with the poet's desire to re-evoke in its totality the dreamlike atmosphere of his island home. Yet it has another function as well – to foreshadow an orphic rebirth upon a more satisfying lyrical plane by means of a deployment of imagery representative of a ritual descent into the hallowed light of the tides.

To achieve this mystic, watery descent the effect of the flow of the word-music is as important as the images describing it, so that the poet fuses together his image-chains to form a complex, allusive vision of beauty enveloped in a delicate musicality. In the opening stanza there is again an interplay of light and dark vowels carefully graded to diffuse their richness outwards and illuminate the image of the dreaming trees:

Città d'isola
sommersa nel mio cuore,
ecco discendo nell'antica luce
delle maree, presso sepolcri
in riva d'acque
che una letizia scioglie
d'alberi sognati.

Island city submerged in my heart, behold I descend into the ancient light of the tides, near tombs on the banks of waters which liberate a joy of dreamed-of trees.

If then we bear in mind the human anguish already pent up in the Quasimodean tree-symbol, we can interpret the movement from sadness to 'letizia' as a melodic regression towards an infolded orphic humanism. It amounts, in fact, to a further extension of the poet's atavism, symbolized by 'sepolcri in riva d'acque', and provokes a kind of ritualistic descent into the great memorial storehouse of the sea. Together these symbols highlight the composite atmosphere of the poet's island paradise, and we note that its shadowy eternity implies a form of 'convivenza' submerged in his childhood memories. The latter in turn absorb, as if by osmosis, the lingering cultural echoes of *Magna Graecia* and the dramatic tensions of present-day Sicilian life; so that henceforth the poet's technique of 'watering' the silk of his imagery will create a fresh hermetic pattern, one which will permit him to wind back his memories to the point where he can communicate with a central core of ancestral experiences lying deep within his historically attuned sensibility. The transfigurative process involves a vitalistic communion with the grass-roots of sentient life, clearly expressed in visceral analogies of vegetative growth:

E i tuoi morti sento
nei gelosi battiti
di vene vegetali
fatti men fondi:

un respirare assorto di narici.

And I sense your dead in the jealous heartbeats of vegetative veins made less profound: a meditative breathing of nostrils.

Since life and death are now inextricably intertwined and the rising of the green fuse is linked with a slightly carnal, though largely meditative, quivering of the nostrils of the dead, what can we conclude? That the themes of the first two of Quasimodo's collections involve an aestheticized form of orphism in which the spirit is intended to emerge, almost instinctively, through refined sensations. The principal elements of the subject-matter are, first, an atavistic yearning for communion with the poet's forefathers and, second, a kind of Dantesque descent through the hierarchy of Being – from the rational to the sensitive and ultimately to the vegetative soul. Despite its promise of joy through decay, such a theme clearly possesses its own internal tensions which lead to a spiritual crisis in the next volume, *Erato e Apòllion*.

In this collection Quasimodo is faced with the stark choice of opting for a metaphysical or an ethical approach to art. He had either to continue to tread the regressive and ultimately solipsist path of his former hermetic inspiration or else to exploit his still dimly perceived vision of an orphic humanism. A clash of interests is already apparent in the very title of the work, since it juxtaposes the Greek Muse of love-songs and the biblical demiurge Apollyon. However, some ambiguity still persists in the play on words between Apollo and Apollyon, which actually derive from the same root. What finally emerges, however, is that the poet's tendency to blend rational and associative modes of inspiration has not led him to an Apollonian state of serenity: it has simply provoked a desire for self-destruction or self-immolation on the marmoreal altars of a solipsist type of art.

From Quasimodo's analysis of love in the lyric addressed to Erato we can deduce the nature of his échec. In this poem his failure to reach a higher plane of perception has already reduced his Muse to a frigid angel-symbol. So from his own godlike pose of egocentricity and solitude he now regards his relations with her as a supreme example of soul-death:

> Per averti ti perdo,
> e non mi dolgo: sei bella ancora,
> ferma in posa dolce di sonno:
> serenità di morte estrema gioia.[27]

To have you I lose you, and I do not grieve: you are still beautiful, motionless in a gentle pose of sleep: the serenity of death, an extreme joy.

This attitude of lyrical exasperation and of complete detachment represents the *nec plus ultra* of hermetic experience, amounting virtually to a form of gratuitous suspension. Its manifestations range from a feeling of impending catastrophe to a sense of futility; and so in the lyric 'Apòllion' we see a nihilistic resignation completely encompassing the poet's mind:

> L'ora nasce
> della morte piena, Apòllion;
> io sono tardo ancora di membra
> e il cuore grava smemorato.

The moment of complete death is born, Apollyon; I am still weary of limb and my heart lies heavy, steeped in oblivion.

A spiritual wasteland of metaphysical quality and proportions thus proves to be the inevitable outcome of Quasimodo's solipsist lucubrations; yet precisely because of his built-in humanist tendencies a way of escape already seems at hand. He soon realizes that his melancholy is not rooted in any *a priori* defect in the human condition, it derives from his inability to communicate as a man and as a poet. The remedy he proposes is to delve more deeply into an emotional and instinctive way of life in order to re-formulate in social terms a 'convivenza del sangue' ('living together through the blood'), as indicated in 'Nel giusto tempo umano':

> Ci deluse bellezza, e il dileguare
> d'ogni forma e memoria,
> il labile moto svelato agli affetti
> a specchio degli interni fulgori.
>
> Ma dal profondo tuo sangue
> nel giusto tempo umano
> rinasceremo senza dolore.

Beauty deluded us, and the melting away of every form and remembrance, the fleeting motion unveiled to the affections through the mirroring of inward splendours. But from the depths of your blood in a just human time we shall be reborn without anguish.

Here then the poet's metaphysical 'tempo mitico' ('mythical time') is gradually yielding to a 'tempo sociale' ('social time') and the implications of the change become more and more significant as he matures.

The struggle preceding rebirth is foreshadowed in the lyric 'Canto di Apòllion', despite its mythical allusiveness. In it Apollo and Apollyon merge their natures, the former representing the splendour of the humanist tradition and the latter presumably the destructiveness of all neo-symbolist and hermetic aberrations from its canon. The poem opens with a description of one of Apollo's earthly exiles, normally a prelude to amorous adventure:

> Terrena notte, al tuo esiguo fuoco
> mi piacque talvolta,
> e scesi fra i mortali.

Earthly night, sometimes I enjoyed myself in your exiguous fire, and I descended among the mortals.

There follows a coupling of the God with what appears to be an archetypal Earth-Mother, a theme frequently associated with Apollo because tradition has it that he begot many children by mortal women as well as by nymphs. Nevertheless, this particular coupling seems sterile and, when the

God obtains no response from the 'creatura notturna', he feels alienated from all human activities:

> Amavo. Fredde erano le mani
> della creatura notturna . . .

> I loved. Cold were the hands of the creature of night . . .

His rejection of life then transforms him into a God again, under the guise of the New Testament destroyer, Apollyon; and so, what was originally intended as a fertility rite, ends in a meaningless solipsist state of isolation and damnation:

> Mio amore, io qui dolgo
> senza morte, solo.

> My love, I grieve here, deathless and alone.

Consequently the dichotomy of the poet's metaphysical and humanist yearnings have now led to a point of crisis and the Apollo-Apollyon antinomy symbolizes his split personality – the struggle raging in his mind between the convolutions of hermetic art and his burgeoning desire to participate whole-heartedly in the rapidly changing world about him. As might be expected, this titanic struggle is once more waged against a background of apocalyptic desolation.

In the poem 'Sul colle delle ''Terre bianche'' ' with its abstract orphic landscape the poet accordingly imagines himself to be the sole survivor of some dreadful metaphysical calamity. To depict it he has further recourse to the tree-image, because it alone is capable of expressing his anguish:

> Dal giorno superstite
> con gli alberi mi umilio.
>
> Assai arida cosa . . .

> A survivor from day, I humble myself with the trees. An extremely arid object . . .

The outcome of this feeling of barren solitude is that he is forced to adopt at the end of the poem a Mallarmean stance as a star-gazer while at the same time struggling desperately to raise his soul-searing experiences to an immortal geometrical plane, mirrored in the peacefulness of a constellation of stars:

> O la quiete geometrica dell'Orsa.

> O the geometrical silence of the Great Bear.

Similarly, his sense of soul-death is now fetishized in 'Airone morto' through his recourse to an image of this bird stuck in the mud of a marsh, just as Mallarmé's swan was once stuck in the frozen lake of contingency. And again in 'Al tuo lume naufrago' a confused religious probing appears to lead to a Leopardian 'shipwreck', as the poet reaches the very limits of his human purview:

> Sradicato dai vivi,
> cuore provvisorio,
> sono limite vano.

Uprooted from the living, with my makeshift heart, I am a vain limit.

On the other hand, the vegetative imagery previously seen in *Oboe sommerso* now seems paradoxically to offer a means of spiritual escape through the senses. A positive 'naufragio' ('shipwreck'), for instance, takes place along the banks of a Sicilian river in 'L'Anapo', where a drowning is first followed by the normal processes of decomposition and then later by a kind of meditative rebirth. When the dead body finally floats ashore, a new life at once begins, in fact, to stir like a dream within the very putrefaction of the flesh; and during this process life and death appear to be subtly interchanged, suggesting that a secret form of metamorphosis governs the entire image-chain:

> Sale soavemente a riva,
> dopo il gioco coi numi,
> un corpo adolescente:
>
> Mutevole ha il volto,
> su una tibia al moto della luce
> rigonfia un grumo vegetale.
>
> Chino ai profondi lieviti
> ripatisce ogni fase,
> ha in sé la morte in nuziale germe.

There softly rises to the shore, after jousting with the gods, an adolescent body: his face is changing, on his shin a vegetative growth swells in the play of light. Leaning over a profound ferment, he suffers each phase once more, he has death within him as a nuptial seed.

In short, the sterile substance of the dead body gradually becomes a fertile potentiality of orphic, or perhaps even of humanist, life, and in the hero's mysterious dream a woman plays a significant part, prompting his possible resurrection as a new Adam:

> In fresco oblío disceso
> nel buio d'erbe giace:
> l'amata è un'ombra e origlia
> nella sua costola.

Descending into a fresh oblivion, he lies in the darkness of the grasses: his beloved is a shadow, eavesdropping in his rib.

Appropriately, a number of Montalian animal fetishes or stimuli round off the lyric and consolidate its evocation of an airy, wakeful death. These hallowed creatures inhabit a sphere whose liquid translucence raises the poetry to a higher state of lyrical grace:

Mansueti animali,
le pupille d'aria,
bevono in sogno.

Docile animals, their pupils airy, drink in a dream.

It seems, therefore, that the lyric foreshadows a fresh conception of existence on Quasimodo's part. Although still orphic in quality, it points the way towards a silencing of his metaphysical demon and also, in part, to a muting of the 'antiche voci' ('ancient voices') of his Sicilian forebears which had hitherto sapped his sense of immediacy. In their place we find that his spirit is gradually being opened to the possibility of a more balanced, authentic, and socially orientated form of living.

The result of his broader outlook is the collection entitled *Nuove poesie* (1936-42). Its imagery is cast in a clear Leopardian mould while at the same time we find that its prosody is gradually working its way back, as Ungaretti's did earlier, to the traditional hendecasyllable. The major effect which these two changes have on Quasimodo's lyrical texture is that they make it less impressionistic and allusive in its unfolding; so that instead of the fulminatory analogy we are now frequently presented with the closely woven, connective tissue of the classical simile and metaphor. Furthermore, the lyrical tension of the poet's new style tends to inhabit the entire melodic line rather than the isolated word or symbol, and such a change implies that the cult of the *parola-mito* ('word-myth') is definitely on the decline. It does not disappear entirely until much later, but already its stark metaphysicality is gradually being replaced here by something more akin to the emblem or the allegory, both of which will be characteristic of Quasimodo's humanist period.

In the broadest sense the emphasis on content as opposed to form in the present collection indicates the poet's reconciliation with his human condition after his brief excursion among the gods in *Erato e Apòllion*. From this point onwards he will try to integrate and harmonize his verse by responding *immediately* to the emotional pressures of life, and not *mediately* by adopting distant reflective attitudes. Similarly changes are also brought about in his dominant landscapes, and gradually northern scenes become more common than southern ones despite the fact that a residual

Sicilian aura still persists in certain of his image-chains. Typical examples of the poet's coming to terms with northern landscapes are his scenic descriptions in 'Sulle rive del Lambro' or 'Sera nella valle del Màsino'. But behind them, too, there still lingers an orphic perspective, though often representing a spring-like rekindling of hope in spite of the inevitably darker skies evoked and certain residual autumnal or winter settings:

> Gli alberi tornano di là dai vetri
> come navi fiorite.
>   O cara,
> come remota, morte era da terra.[28]

The trees emerge from beyond the window-panes like flowering ships. O my dearest, how remote death was from the earth.

The poet's optimism is largely produced at this stage by his willingness to participate wholly in the realities about him. His closer commitment, moreover, has a further effect on his landscapes, making them less generic and less detached than they were earlier. So, in place of the former geometrical patterns and shadowy hermetic outlines, we now find concrete and variegated scenes filled with hosts of scampering children, leaping animals, birds, plants and flowers, all symbolic of the poet's new-found interest in the active life of the senses. These talismans of living joy are intended to be spiritually positive[29] and are to be contrasted with his earlier metaphysical images which were spiritually negative in their implications. It thus seems as if Quasimodo's world is now becoming rejuvenated from within, and an indication of this rejuvenation is the resurrection of the 'airone morto' ('dead heron') previously depicted in *Erato e Apòllion*. There, we noted, it was a symbol of the poet's despair, but here it deliberately seeks out life again against a background of allegorical and emblematic features:

> . . . già l'airone s'avanza verso l'acqua
> e fiuta lento il fango tra le spine,
> ride la gazza, nera sugli aranci.[30]

. . . already the heron moves towards the water and slowly sniffs the mud among the thorns, the magpie laughs, black against the orange-trees.

Needless to say, the water-symbol is now an allegory of commitment and no longer a *parola-mito* acting only as a speculative or metaphysical representation of the life-flow. While even the chattering of the magpie in the tree is symbolic of human 'convivenza', although the bird retains a touch of orphic mystery by revealing to us nothing more than its dark silhouette. In consequence, Quasimodo can be seen to have purposefully dilated the meaning of his hermetic symbolism in the *Nuove poesie* and to have gone far towards enriching it with a broad emotional charge.

This open and widely based lyricism is maintained even when his landscapes occasionally revert to a Sicilian pattern, so that island-scenes are now normally presented in a concrete and historical, as well as in an orphic, perspective. A case in point is the poem 'Strada di Agrigentum' where historical associations are half-emergent from atavistic resonances and where the classical rhythm of the hendecasyllable further contributes to the toning down of the brittle, abstract nature of the poet's hermetic style. Its landscape is also made emotionally dynamic by the evocation of wild horses, through whose manes an atavistic wind whistles as they gallop slantwise over the Sicilian plains:

Là dura un vento che ricordo acceso
nelle criniere dei cavalli obliqui
in corsa lungo le pianure. . . .

There a wind lingers which I remember burning in the manes of horses galloping obliquely over the plains. . . .

What is significant about this description is its pure existentiality; yet its deep sense of pounding life is still provided with a historical perspective, by an allusive regression to the atmosphere of Ancient Greece. Appropriately the wind stimulates the recall of the historical past as it gnaws at the hearts of the 'telamoni lugubri' ('lugubrious telamones') which lie upturned on the grass and breathe forth the bitterness of their ancient brooding souls. But after this regression we are brought back, equally suddenly, to the present as we hear the recurrent strains of the modern Sicilian peasant's Jew's-harp mingling with the breeze. Under the pure light of the morning star the music echoes and re-echoes within an almost surrealistic landscape, while all around there lingers in the air an aura of secret saracen culture as a carter tramps up a moonlit hill surrounded by the whispering of olive trees. This then is the poet's multidimensionality of evocation at its best, and he uses hermetic and neo-symbolic techniques to reflect Sicily in its many orphico-historical facets:

E piú t'accori s'odi ancora il suono
che s'allontana largo verso il mare
dove Espero già striscia mattutino:
il marranzano tristemente vibra
nella gola al carraio che risale
il colle nitido di luna, lento
tra il murmure d'ulivi saraceni.

And the more you grieve if you hear the sound again as it moves away towards the sea where Hesperus at dawn already slides: the Jew's-harp sadly twangs in the throat of the carter who reclimbs the hill glistening with moonlight, slowly amid the murmur of Saracen olive-trees.

A similar transitional poem which moves away from hermetic techniques towards multiple humanistic tensions is 'Davanti al simulacro d'Ilaria del Carretto'. The opening scene is set on the mainland, in the cathedral of Lucca, where the poet muses over the effigy of Ilaria sculpted by Iacopo della Quercia at the turn of the fifteenth century. Quasimodo feels himself trapped in a dead world like the person buried in the tomb, a fact which is strongly emphasised by an evocation of the indifference of today's young lovers as they stroll along the banks of the Serchio. In fact, the entire situation has an alienated, decadent flavour about it, rendered impressionistically by the description of an autumnal atmosphere which contrasts with the gay colours of the girls' dresses:

Sotto tenera luna già i tuoi colli,
lungo il Serchio fanciulle in vesti rosse
e turchine si muovono leggere.
Cosí al tuo dolce tempo, cara; e Sirio
perde colore, e ogni ora s'allontana,
e il gabbiano s'infuria sulle spiagge
derelitte.

Already under a tender moon your hills, along the Serchio girls in red and blue dresses lightly move. As in your gentle age, my dear; and Sirius grows faint, and each hour more distant, and the seagull rages over the forsaken beaches.

Here the final image of the lonely seagull crystallizes the mood as effectively as does Montale's kingfisher, making the dead woman's solitude and the poet's plight almost coincide. And yet, if anything, his solitude is even more intense than Ilaria's because he is at last beginning to realize the full extent of his hermetic alienation. His solution to his predicament is to try and transcend lyrically the twin states of indifference and death which he senses around him, and he hopes to do so by re-establishing emotional bonds and human values in a world now turned sour by cowardice and bitterness:

Gli amanti vanno lieti
nell'aria di settembre, i loro gesti
accompagnano ombre di parole
che conosci. Non hanno pietà; e tu
tenuta dalla terra, che lamenti?
Sei qui rimasta sola. Il mio sussulto
forse è il tuo, uguale d'ira e di spavento.
Remoti i morti e piú ancora i vivi,
i miei compagni vili e taciturni.

> The lovers go gaily in the September air, their gestures accompany shadows of words which you recognize. They have no piety; and you held by the earth, what do you lament? You have remained here alone. My shuddering is perhaps yours, similar in its anger and fear. Remote the dead, and even more the living, my base and silent companions.

To be successful, such transcendence must clearly be of a 'social' order, although it seems as if Quasimodo's underlying view is that it should also acquire a mythical aura. What he is now attempting to create is perhaps a sense of solidarity between the living and the dead on the one hand and all the individuals living in contemporary society on the other, despite the stultifying political pressures of the fascist era. In this sense the poem's much more tractable imagery and open emotion are refreshing draughts after his previous involution; and these qualities are conveyed by a softening of the angular contours of his imagery and by subtle syntactic and melodic adjustments within his poetic line to ensure a broader range of understanding between the poet and his reader. Indeed, as his integration into the wider Italian tradition proceeds, he gradually adopts a more placid and balanced outlook towards life, after which his corruscating, though still somewhat monolithic, hermetic symbols tend to die away in proportion to his acceptance of his social responsibilities. At length the change becomes so marked that, instead of the almost neurotic, metaphysical tension of his earlier verse, we come across a note of human melancholy in 'Già la pioggia è con noi' and it develops significantly out of a softly-moulded northern landscape:

> Già la pioggia è con noi,
> scuote l'aria silenziosa.
> Le rondini sfiorano le acque spente
> presso i laghetti lombardi,
> volano come gabbiani sui piccoli pesci;
> il fieno odora oltre i recinti degli orti.
>
> Ancora un anno è bruciato,
> senza un lamento, senza un grido
> levato a vincere d'improvviso un giorno.

> The rain is already with us, it shakes the silent air. The swallows skim the dead waters near the Lombard lakes, fly like gulls over small fish; the hay smells beyond the garden fences. Another year is burnt, without a lament, without a cry being raised unexpectedly to win back one day.

From this change we can conclude that, whereas his previous abstract and infolded landscapes were symbolic of his hermetic attitudes, his present gentler and humane ones are stylistic reflections of a gradual social redimensioning of his inspiration.

On the other hand, despite the relative transparency of this type of lyricism we note that the concrete features making up the poet's scenic aggregates, like the rain, stagnant pools, silent air, birds, fish, and other fetishes, all remain the same in both phases of his career. At most the poet is simply making his style and sensibility more supple, he is not radically changing his basic object-symbols nor the topology of the inner landscapes of his mind. Some object-symbols, however, especially his animal fetishes, now seem to be rekindled from within, and the increasing density of their emotive charges punctuates the gradual opening of his lyrical structures. Hence at this stage we encounter a subtle combination of a traditional lyrical discourse with occasional telescopic images harking back to his former hermetic style; and, not surprisingly, this delicate hermetic undertow actually ensures the unity of his inspiration.

The point becomes self-evident in the next collection *Giorno dopo giorno* (1947). This volume was written during the war and sums up Quasimodo's responses to a wide range of wartime sorrows, renunciations and disappointments. By that time he had finally created a tentative narrative style imbued with a steady lyrical charge in place of his earlier pent-up flashes of insight produced by a deliberate dislocation of syntax. Equally the realist content of these poems now lends itself readily to rapid transformations of mood, though from the outset we need perhaps to distinguish between Quasimodo's wartime poetry and the general course of resistance poetry in Italy. As Cherchi has explained,[31] true resistance poetry was developed after the war as a 'ripensamento' ('reappraisal'), in answer to a need to rebuild democratic values; it was not a reaction to the atrocities perpetrated during the war itself nor to the human problems then troubling the consciences of mankind. Yet it was with these latter problems that Quasimodo was almost entirely concerned, and so he offers us no definite solutions, only his personal reactions to man's unremitting inhumanity to man. If he looks ahead at all it is to an impending European crisis, and he employs the horrors of war as emotive pegs on which to hang a wide range of moral reflections. The message which emerges from *Giorno dopo giorno* is consequently a traumatic acknowledgement of the insane brutalities of the period and a distant recognition of hope and possible regeneration – qualities already latent according to Quasimodo in the Italian social fabric at a time when the human spirit still seemed most inadequate before endlessly repeated acts of violence.

Oddly enough, by identifying himself with the then corporate will to survive, the poet suddenly found himself for the first time communicating freely with his fellow men. Like Victor Hugo before him, he momentarily became the 'écho sonore' ('sonorous echo') of the general mood of his day, even though his attitude was predominantly an elegiac one which sorrowfully contemplated the reduction of life to its lowest common denominator of physical survival:

La vita
non è questo tremendo, cupo, battere
del cuore, non è pietà, non è piú
che un gioco del sangue dove la morte
è in fiore.[32]

Life is not this tremendous, dark beating of the heart, it is not pity, it is no longer anything more than a ruse of the blood where death is in flower.

The touchstone of the whole collection is thus a need for faith and steadfastness which will enable the values of civilization to be reasserted as soon as hostilities cease. The point is stressed in 'Alle fronde dei salici' in which, while concealing none of its horrors, the poet hints at the survival during the war of the nobler qualities of self-sacrifice and fortitude. In so doing, he even adopts a biblical tone, one which contrasts present-day barbarity with the age-old Christian compassion inherent in Western society.

This religious note was, in fact, not a new element in Quasimodo's verse, since it can occasionally be detected even in his earliest compositions. But during his hermetic period it posed a major aesthetic and emotional problem, because the juxtaposition of Christian images and overt pagan rituals was, to say the least, disconcerting. But at the present stage any reservations we might harbour about the validity of the poet's religious feelings are less readily entertainable, because he now uses religion simply as a deeply felt, spiritual background to colour his humanist outlook. As such, it becomes a repository of moral and social wisdom, almost a 'binding together' in the original sense of the word. This explains why the 136th psalm rises authentically to his lips in the above-mentioned poem, because its theme deals with a situation of oppression and slavery similar to that which prevailed in Europe during the Nazi occupation. Furthermore, the very texture of the poem emphasizes once again the tremendous changes brought about in the poet's style during the harrowing period of his wartime experiences:

E come potevamo noi cantare
con il piede straniero sopra il cuore,
fra i morti abbandonati nelle piazze
sull'erba dura di ghiaccio, al lamento
d'agnello dei fanciulli, all'urlo nero
della madre che andava incontro al figlio
crocifisso sul palo del telegrafo?
Alle fronde dei salici, per voto,
anche le nostre cetre erano appese,
oscillavano lievi al triste vento.

> And how could we sing with the foreigner's foot upon our hearts, among the dead abandoned in the squares on the grass hardened by ice, amid the lamb-like bleating of the children, amid the black howling of a mother rushing up to her son crucified on the telegraph-pole? As an offering, on the willow boughs our lyres too were hung, quivering slightly in the sad wind.

Such a transformation is proof of Quasimodo's contention (contradicting an equally well-known one made by Serra during the First World War) that, far from changing nothing, 'la guerra muta la vita morale di un popolo,'[33] ('war changes the moral life of a people'). It also suggests that morality and aesthetics will henceforth be closely interrelated in his work, as indeed proves to be the case.

The reintroduction of a sense of social responsibility leads at first to his adoption of a denunciatory tone whose fire-and-brimstone effects again recall the medieval fervour of a Jacopone da Todi. For a time, in fact, Quasimodo took an interest in the form of the medieval *Lauda*, and later, in 1958, he wrote an essay on Jacopone in which he describes him as the first 'legittimo engagé'[34] ('legitimate engagé'). His interest in the medieval poet was naturally more social than religious, and he confessed that at times the latter's religious fervour overstepped the bounds of art. But his committed style nevertheless helped to reawaken Quasimodo's own conscience and inspired his newly-found desire to participate in life. By means of a reimmersion in social affairs he was convinced that he could overcome that sense of alienation he felt had dogged his steps throughout his pre-war career, and at the same time he made it quite clear that the closed delights of his erstwhile hermetic paradise were now gone for ever:

> Giorno dopo giorno: parole maledette e il sangue
> e l'oro. Vi riconosco, miei simili, o mostri
> della terra. Al vostro morso è caduta la pietà,
> e la croce gentile ci ha lasciati.
> E piú non posso tornare nel mio eliso.

> Day after day: accursed words and the blood and the gold. I recognise you, my kin, o monsters of the earth. At your bite pity has collapsed, and the kindly cross has forsaken us. And I can no longer return to my Elysium.

Even so, despite his mildly vituperative attitude he still does not eliminate hermetic features from his verse altogether; he simply feels that he can no longer regard them as the bedrock of his inspiration. The success of *Giorno dopo giorno* depends, therefore, on his ability to strike just the right note between admonition and regret to capture the sympathy of the reader. Such a procedure evokes an atmosphere of mutual understanding between the two, in which the reader feels sure of the poet's solidarity when he is faced with the horrors of bestial crimes and mass-murder.

Possibly this new ethos grew out of Quasimodo's contempt for the bombast of the fascist era and his suspicion that the hermetic movement had by then declined to such a state of decadence that he felt the only way to describe it was as the 'estremo antro fiorentino di fonemi metrici'[35] ('ultimate Florentine lair of metrical phonemes'). His intention was to replace its empty verbiage with the emotive richness of the human heart, and it is on this sense of inner maturity that he hoped to found his post-war cultural outlook:

> Le parole ci stancano,
> risalgono da un'acqua lapidata;
> forse il cuore ci resta, forse il cuore . . .[36]

> Words weary us, rise again from stone-lashed water; perhaps the heart remains, perhaps the heart . . .

In other words the poet had now finally turned his back on the decadent tradition of moral abstention and was well on the way towards a new conception of the function of art, one which – while having many left-wing features – was not to be envisaged in any pedestrian, political sense but as a valid means of reintegrating the artist into society.

An appreciation of the need to retain his own self-coherence during his change of direction accounts for the continuing presence of Quasimodo's hermetic archetypes like 'acqua' or 'cuore' in his verse. But their symbolic quality is rapidly being transformed and his principal modes of communication are now dramatically lowered from a metaphysical to an emotional level. As this reduction takes place the poet replaces the symbolic involution of his youth with the fable or allegory, which he believes will more adequately represent the moral rehabilitation of the post-war world. Accordingly, another virtual pullulation of plant and animal fetishes now tends to dramatize his fresh emotive manner, even though this joyous concourse of living creatures is still offset by the occasional presence of the faintly 'allegorized', hermetic emblem. The device reappears, for instance, with great clarity in 'La muraglia', where the admittedly more relaxed image of a wall nevertheless still reminds us of Montale's stark metaphysical image in the lyric 'Meriggiare pallido e assorto', on which it seems distantly modelled:

> E già sulla muraglia dello stadio,
> tra gli spacchi e i ciuffi d'erba pensile,
> le lucertole guizzano fulminee;
> e la rana ritorna nelle rogge,

canto fermo alle mie notti lontane
dei paesi. Tu ricordi questo luogo
dove la grande stella salutava
il nostro arrivo d'ombre. O cara, quanto
tempo è sceso con le foglie dei pioppi,
quanto sangue nei fiumi della terra.

And already on the wall of the stadium, among the fissures and the clumps of hanging grass, the lizards flash like lightning; and the frog returns to the ditches, a steady song to my distant nights in remote villages. You remember this place where the large star greeted our shadowy arrival. O dearest, how much time has flowed away with the leaves of the poplars, how much blood in the rivers of the earth.

But henceforth the emblematic basis of his poetry will never again militate against the expression of the poet's enthusiasm for life, and this very fact stresses how profoundly his lyrical perspective had been modified as a result of his post-war attempts to convey a greater range of feeling.

The first experimentation with what Anceschi has called 'la distensione della parola' or broadening of poetic style comes in *Giorno dopo giorno*. One particularly noticeable aspect of the process is the emotive use that Quasimodo now makes of the adjectives accompanying his archetypal object-symbols. The aim behind such adjectival shading is twofold: first to emphasize the horror which the poet feels when confronted with human suffering and bondage, and second to retain at least a touch of 'existentialized' hermetic mystery in his lyrical atmospheres. We can often divide these adjectival effects into two broad categories: those conveying an allegoric atmosphere of gloom and corruption through phrases like 'giorni corrosi' ('corroded days'), 'valli fumanti' ('smoking valleys') or, even more apocalyptically, 'i derelitti resti della terra' ('the forsaken remains of the earth'), and those tending to subvert his previous hermetic symbols by giving them negative instead of positive meanings. A typical example of this corrosive trend is the phrase 'sull'erba dura di ghiaccio' ('on the ice-hardened grass'), in which the water-symbol is metamorphosed into ice and its crystallization is employed for the quenching of the vitalistic drive formerly present in the vegetative symbol of the grass. The same thing also occurs in the treatment of the various sub-symbols of the water archetype, and the process accounts for such descriptions as 'fiumi carichi di sangue' ('rivers laden with blood') or the obliteration of whole landscapes by 'fumi maligni' ('malignant smoke'). In short, most of these expressions reiterate the inhuman message seen previously in the intractable symbolism of an 'acqua lapidata', and a similar aura of frigid indifference is also detectable elsewhere. Again, the grass itself at some points becomes an 'erba maligna' ('malevolent grass') and merges diffidently with a 'grigia pianura' ('grey plain') to produce a moral and metaphysical picture of ennui and despair. Likewise, the long-abandoned angel-image is implicitly pressed into service at this point to describe the rising moon as a 'gelida messaggera della notte' ('cold messenger of the night'). But, regretfully, such naïve allegories often have a deleterious effect on the poet's imagination, and they mark too coarse a broadening of his once refined hermetic modes of inspiration to be wholly effective.

On the other hand, certain compensatory and regenerative undercurrents are also to be found in *Giorno dopo giorno* and they may be illustrated by the poet's deployment of further adjectival techniques for the purpose of creating atmospheres of hope. Most of them are again fulminatory or vegetative in nature, as in the phrase 'le lucertole guizzano fulminee' ('the lizards flash like lightning'), which the poet claims is indicative of an 'oscuro sortilegio della terra' ('obscure sorcery of the earth'). Their residual hermeticism undoubtedly marks the effective limits of the changes which have taken place in the poet's sensibility, although even when he is technically most involuted he now no longer tries to be the harsh interpreter of elemental sensations drawn from the very periphery of perception: he aims rather at becoming a purveyor of human sentiment which at times can even degenerate into a cult of sheer sentimentality. He is not so much concerned, in short, with producing 'un grido per tentare il mondo fermo' ('a cry to tempt the closed world') as with his ability to stretch his sensibility in a humanist – just as he once stretched it in a speculative – sense. The image of the 'corvo' ('crow') in 'Una città lontana' later proves to be a case in point. The poet tells us himself that it no longer functions as a hermetic symbol, it is a 'corvo vero' ('true crow') or real-life figure which seeks to integrate itself with its immediate surroundings and seems to perform a fine balancing act between commitment and aloofness. From here on he hopes through similar figures to evoke those inarticulate truths which lie unexpressed in any given society and represent its inner frustrations, yet which, when clearly formulated by the poets of that society, sum up its deeper aspirations and reassert not only the solidarity of its various members but also, by extension, the spiritual compresence of an entire nation in travail.

Such views indicate that Quasimodo was now attuned not merely to the aspirations of post-war society in Italy, but also to the deeper European crisis. As we know, this crisis was destined to lead to a far-reaching reappraisal of social conditions and to equally profound changes in taste. Nevertheless, it was one thing to be aware of the crisis and be able to represent its troubled transitional states and quite another to solve its aesthetic problems, and this Quasimodo ultimately failed to do. So, since

Giorno dopo giorno was, lyrically speaking, an undoubted success, we have to attribute its effectiveness to the fact that Quasimodo was astute enough to choose just the right moment to transform his earlier elegiac poetry into a sustained paean of praise for humanity's post-war struggle to restore its dignity. What, on the other hand he was certainly incapable of bringing about was a solution to the impending lyrical crisis of the period. Hence the volume stands at most as a brilliant exercise in aesthetic opportunism, modulating in a neo-hermetic key the alternating states of euphoria and despair apparent during the immediate aftermath of the war. On the other hand, as soon as this initial mood of anguished hope aspired to something more substantial, the poet's melodic line proved insufficiently resilient to carry the burden, and he never managed to break away effectively from his previous modes of expression. Indeed, when on occasion he sought fresh pastures, his verse often tended to degenerate into a confused and somewhat sentimentalized internationalism.

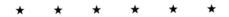

Before we examine the remainder of his post-war verse we must glance briefly at another aspect of his cultural activity which also contributed to the maturing of his style and outlook, because the broadening and purification of his humanist imagery depended in part on his labours as a translator from the Greek, and later even from other languages as well. At first it may be difficult to see how the art of the translator can greatly influence the work of the original poet, but Quasimodo never claimed to be a translator in the usual sense of the word. Instead, in a note appended to his translations from Greek lyrics, he asserted that 'queste mie traduzioni non sono rapportate a probabili schemi metrici d'origine, ma tentano l'approssimazione piú specifica d'un testo: quella poetica'[37] ('these translations of mine are not linked to possible metrical schemes in the original, but attempt a more specific textual approximation: a poetic one'). This statement led Anceschi to stress in his preface that the poet was one of those translators who 'assale con irruenza il testo in un rapido giro dell'anima, e con imperio e quasi con prepotenza lo fa suo,'[38] ('attacks a text with enthusiasm in a rapid whirl of the spirit and with imperiousness and almost with arrogance makes it his own'). His unusual manner of approach, therefore, has deeper implications for the development of his poetic style than if he had confined himself to the humbler work of translation. By concentrating more on catching the spirit rather than the letter of the originals he did, in fact, succeed in enlarging vicariously his own experience, especially during those rare moments when he fully identified himself with the inner feelings of others. Cases of such identification, for instance, are to be found in his translations from Sappho and Alceus, because the poetry of both have left a definite mark on his own work.[39] So in all probability it was through their mediation that he learned, at least partially, to shake off his hermetic strait-jacket and base his themes and melodies on wider lyrical patterns.

A further indication that his early attempts at translation should not be underestimated is given by his subsequent forays into the same field. In one of his later collections of verse he published translations from a number of American writers, notably Pound, Cummings and Aiken. We can only surmise that from Pound he acquired the art of compromising between the rich allusiveness of hermetic poetry and the openness of a restrained narrative tradition. But with Cummings we are on slightly firmer ground, because Quasimodo himself tells us that he was particularly attracted by the latter's 'furiosa ricerca del reale'[40] ('furious search for the real'). Needless to say, such a quality proved to be invaluable when the Italian poet was moving out of hermeticism and attempting to integrate his muse into the social realities about him. So it does seem in the last analysis as if in moments of lyrical crisis he regularly sought communion with kindred spirits in foreign literatures, in the hope of revitalizing his own imaginative procedures.[41]

Precisely because Quasimodo managed only to reflect his inner crisis in *Giorno dopo giorno* and was quite unable to resolve it, his next volume of verse *La vita non è sogno* (1949) is something of a disappointment. One might even be tempted to regard it as a throwback to his earlier hermetic style if it were not for an obtrusive narrative strain which tends to be dispersive of its lyrical effects. His manner of proceeding at this point in his career is to indulge in a certain number of experiments of a propagandist nature, in the hope of discovering an appropriate lyrical resonance for his post-war moods. One such experiment, for instance, is 'Dialogo', and others the lyrics 'Anno domini MCMXLVII' and 'Il mio paese è l'Italia'. In them the poet's diffuse manner can no longer be held in check by the residual hermetic compression of his imagery, and so the balancing trick he successfully performed earlier in *Giorno dopo giorno* between his *parola-mito* ('word-myth') on the one hand and his *poesia-cronaca* ('chronicle poetry') on the other is not repeated. Admittedly, a compromise still does at times emerge between these two incompatible tendencies, but it is only effective when powerful hermetic pressures dominate the existential tensions on which the poems are based.

In the finer lyrics we sense that northern landscapes and attitudes of mind are now more apparent than ever. But, although Quasimodo will henceforth seem fully reconciled to life in his adopted land of Lombardy, sporadic attempts to merge northern scenes with faraway Sicilian memories are still indirectly revived, showing that the vivid topography of his island-home continues to be a force to be reckoned with in his sensibility despite his assertions to the contrary:

La luna rossa, il vento, il tuo colore
di donna del Nord, la distesa di neve . . .
Il mio cuore è ormai su queste praterie,
in queste acque annuvolate dalle nebbie.
Ho dimenticato il mare, la grave
conchiglia soffiata dai pastori siciliani,
le cantilene dei carri lungo le strade
dove il carrubo trema nel fumo delle stoppie,
ho dimenticato il passo degli aironi e delle gru
nell'aria dei verdi altipiani
per le terre e i fiumi della Lombardia.[42]

The red moon, the wind, your colour as a woman of the North, the wilderness of snow . . . My heart is now in these meadows, in these waters clouded by mists. I have forgotten the sea, the heavy shells blown by Sicilian shepherds, the sing-song of the carts along the roads where the carob-tree quivers in the smoke of the stubble, I have forgotten the passing of the herons and the storks in the air of the green uplands for the land and rivers of Lombardy.

So, although we have seen these broad, diffusive trends developing from afar, it would perhaps be true to say that the line of demarcation between his centrifugal humanist inspiration and his former centripetal hermetic strain still continues here to be wafer-thin.

The finest poem in the collection is 'Quasi un madrigale' with its delicate offsetting of allegorical and metaphysical elements. In the first stanza the dominant mood is still hermetic and involves an atavistic descent into a closed world of intimate feelings. However, towards the end there is a clear attempt to establish a balance between esoteric imagery and more extravert emotive forces, between generic and more circumstantial lyrical situations:

Il girasole piega a occidente
e già precipita il giorno nel suo
occhio in rovina e l'aria dell'estate
s'addensa e già curva le foglie e il fumo
dei cantieri. S'allontana con scorrere
secco di nubi e stridere di fulmini
quest'ultimo gioco del cielo. Ancora,

e da anni, cara, ci ferma il mutarsi
degli alberi stretti dentro la cerchia
dei Navigli. Ma è sempre il nostro giorno
e sempre quel sole che se ne va
con il filo del suo raggio affettuoso.

The sunflower inclines towards the west and day already sinks in its ruined eye, and the air of summer thickens and already curves the leaves and the smoke from the boat-yards. This final trick of the sky moves away with a scurrying of clouds and a hissing of lightning. Again, as for years, dearest, the changing of the trees enclosed in the region of the canals has detained us. But the day is still ours, and it is still that sun which departs with the thread of its friendly rays.

The contrast between the cataclysmic world of the sunflower and the realistic picture of the 'Naviglio' area in Milan again reveals here that the poet's hermetic involution is slowly yielding to a more recognizably social pattern of evocation – to an understanding of normal human activities involving a sense of tranquillity and a limited feeling of contentment. But it is to be noted that once more the same archetypes persist as before (especially the tree-image), though they are now no longer metaphysical symbols of anguish but emerge naturally from his new emotional outlook and carry along with them an overt allegorical charge. What they have lost or are about to lose is in other words the last vestige of their metaphysicality, because they are now being redimensioned as a background to a social myth. The humanist implications of this reconstituted pattern are detectable in the closing lines of the poem, where emphasis is placed not on wartime violence but on the dignity and sanctity of life. Thus the symbolism at this stage no longer turns its dark and opaque side towards us but deliberately remains open to inspection. Its lyrical charge, moreover, is hardly ever fulminatory and apocalyptic, but imaginatively controlled and firm. As such, it stresses the poet's anxiety to communicate, both emotionally and conceptually, his desire to put an end to his erstwhile pose of alienation by reintegrating himself into the real life of his age. He therefore hopes at this point to draw directly from his social ethos the values which give intrinsic meaning to his experiences:

Qui sull'argine del canale, i piedi
in altalena, come di fanciulli,
guardiamo l'acqua, i primi rami dentro
il suo colore verde che s'oscura.
E l'uomo che in silenzio s'avvicina
non nasconde un coltello fra le mani,
ma un fiore di geranio.

Here on the canal bank, like children with our feet swinging, we look at the water, the lower branches dipped in its green colour as it darkens. And the man who is approaching silently does not hide a knife in his hands, but a geranium flower.

It will be instructive to examine the symbolism of this passage more closely. Its object-symbols are still largely identical with those expressed in, say, 'Acquamorta' but their lack of involution and obscurity at once show us that the poet had moved far along the road towards a modern humanism in the interval. Accordingly, single objects do not now appear as isolated monolithic images depicting the limits of human aspirations, they act instead as integrated units within a placid but richly textured poetic discourse. For instance, the darkening water is no longer a sealed hermetic symbol of despair but a purely descriptive element, despite its residual link with the greenness of vegetative decomposition. Likewise, the geranium-image contrasts starkly with the violent use of the same symbol as if it were a bloodstain spattered on a wall in 'Lettera' in *Giorno dopo giorno*:

> O mia dolce gazzella,
> io ti ricordo quel geranio acceso
> su un muro crivellato di mitraglia.

> O my sweet gazelle, I recall for you that burning geranium on a wall peppered by machine-gun bullets.

In other words the symbol is now a pliant image of hope for the restoration of human values, not a brittle metaphysical conceit; and so it blends far more successfully than his earlier monolithic images with Quasimodo's new poetic tone. This suggests that he was finally about to abandon the involuted processes of his pre-war verse for a metaphorical manner much more adherent to post-war reconstruction. Indeed, as he becomes more passionately committed to the realities of the post-war era, the elements of his poetic landscaping no longer stand out like so many metaphysical irritants against an inert atmosphere of *noia*, but merge into a series of plastic descriptions suggestive of the tranquil flow of a settled and harmonious way of life. In this sense 'Quasi un madrigale' foreshadows a solution both to the poet's technical and spiritual problems, because it is neither committed to his associative nor to his narrative manners: it represents instead a subtle combination of the two. Its structure is similar to those essentialized chronicles of events we associate with Eliot or Pound, although Quasimodo does not seem fully to have appreciated the nature of his own achievement. He thus allowed other poems in this collection to decline either into a kind of diaristic impressionism or into anecdotal, documentary and *procès-verbal* forms of composition.

Nowadays we associate the poem-document with Marxist poets, since they tend to assume that 'reportage' is the best artistic way of coming to grips with social realities. However, Quasimodo was never obsessed by the crudities of dialectical materialism, he simply shared, as Gide did before him,[43] its active ideal of humanism. In espousing the Marxist cause, his at first unrecognized but clearly long-term aim was simply to introduce a touch of documentary leavening as an undertone into his newly formulated lyricism of universal brotherhood. He was indeed already half-aware of the fact that to identify himself too closely with political facts in his poetry would be aesthetically dangerous, and so he pointed out that authentic humanist poets like Giovanni Della Casa 'non tollerano cronache, ma figure ideali, atteggiamenti: la storia della poesia per loro è una galleria di fantasmi'[44] ('do not tolerate narrative, but ideal figures, attitudes: the history of poetry is for them a gallery of phantasma'). By this he meant that it is the poet's underlying attitude to reality which represents his genuine lyrical substance, not the crude elements of reality themselves, which art should first try to digest and then transcend. As long as the 'social' or 'humanist' poet bears this fact in mind his imagery will continue to possess those tentacular roots capable of plunging down to the innermost reaches of his personality and guaranteeing the authenticity of his vision. Once he allows himself to ape social reality without interpreting it, on the other hand, he stands little chance of ever creating a valid form of art.

This attitude also implies that he was aware of the necessity to combine ethics with aesthetics in modern artistic processes, a fact which explains why he continues to reassert the importance of aesthetic values in his post-war poetry, even though such values seemed to be largely discounted in the practices of the *avanguardia* of the fifties and sixties. He observed, for instance, at the time that moral and social judgements could only be effectively expressed in poetry through 'la sua resa di bellezza' ('its rendering of beauty'), because 'la sua responsabilità è in diretto rapporto alla sua perfezione'[45] ('its responsibility is in direct relation to its perfection'). Accordingly, we are not surprised to find him still using emblems or rather 'fantasmi' in 'La vita non è sogno' as vehicles for his moral indignation. In this respect he replaces his erstwhile ideal of Apollo with that of Orpheus, though an Orpheus who is a singer of human emotion and no longer a mystical priest. The latter's post-war aim was in his view to bring about a regeneration of the human spirit, as Quasimodo himself previously had claimed to do in his slogan of 'rifare l'uomo'[46] ('remake man') as early as 1946:

> E tu sporco di guerra, Orfeo,
> come il tuo cavallo, senza la sferza,
> alza il capo, non trema piú la terra:
> urla d'amore, vinci, se vuoi, il mondo.[47]

And you, Orpheus, filthy with war, like your horse, without the whip, raise your head, the earth no longer shudders: shout with love, conquer, if you will, the world.

Unfortunately, the figure of Orpheus is now too closely modelled on the ideologically motivated propagandist to offer a convincing solution to life's problems, and even the poet's own attitudes oscillate dangerously between ideological and sentimental extremes. At first he confines his attention to the expression of an ineffective, humanitarian horror directed against the bestiality of war, but the lyrical slackness which this style produces normally prevents him from rising above the level of the documentary narrative. Cases in point are those poems in which he sets himself up as the indignant moral chronicler of mankind's misdeeds, as for instance in his descriptions of battlefields or concentration camps:

> . . . Là Buchenwald, la mite selva di faggi,
> i suoi forni maledetti; là Stalingrado
> e Minsk sugli acquitrini e la neve putrefatta . . . [48]

There Buchenwald, the gentle wood of beeches, its accursed ovens; there Stalingrad and Minsk on the water-meadows and the putrefied snow . . .

In the wake of such examples of facile denunciation we begin to detect a regrettable bifurcation in his art, which henceforth will consist of the rich neo-hermetic textures we found in 'Quasi un madrigale' on the one hand and a rather more pedestrian, left-wing expressionism on the other.

The principal defect in Quasimodo's post-war documentary technique is in other words his tendency to emphasize participation at the expense of perspective. As a result, he is often unable to synthesize his moods, since he allows his imagery to adhere too closely to raw facts. His present inability to establish a position of sufficient detachment is thus the very opposite from that which afflicted him in his early verse when his main shortcomings, we recall, were a cult of solipsist detachment and a complete incapacity to participate in life. Hence in the two most significant phases of his literary career he seems to be alternating between the Scylla and Charybdis of over-detachment and over-commitment; and so it was only on relatively rare occasions that he managed to achieve a sufficient spiritual equipoise to produce a balanced lyric which would fully live up to the undoubted richness and subtlety of his poetic vision.

Almost as a reaction against the excesses of emotion in *La vita non è sogno* we find certain orphic overtones reappearing in the next collection, *Il falso e vero verde* (1956), the very title of which is no doubt still to be associated with the vegetative imagery dominant from 'Acquamorta' to 'Quasi un madrigale'. In this collection an example of essentialized narrative with renewed orphic, rather than purely social, implications is 'Le morte chitarre'. Its point of departure is once more a memorially recreated Sicilian scene and its object-symbols are highly personalized and difficult to interpret. The poem may be addressed to either or both of Quasimodo's wives, the first of whom was dead by the time of its composition and the second estranged.[49] Their 'contingent' relations with the poet are, however, offset by his 'idealized' view of the pure and eternal beauty of Sicilian womanhood reflected in the detached world of the brief link-stanza, where young girls comb their hair with nymph-like grace in the mirror of the moon:

Nello specchio della luna
si pettinano fanciulle col petto d'arance.

In the mirror of the moon girls with orange-like breasts comb their hair.

Once again we notice in this lyric the recurrence of all the poet's significant talismans: trees, water, sulphurous flashes, horses and so on, but now they are again recombined with a dreary marshland atmosphere, probably indicative of the *noia* of old age. To these archetypes are also added a few dramatic but largely atavistic symbols like 'coltelli' and 'ferite', which tend to identify the associations of the scene with dark Sicilian passions:

Chi piange? Io no, credimi: sui fiumi
corrono esasperati schiocchi d'una frusta,
i cavalli cupi, i lampi di zolfo.
Io no, la mia razza ha coltelli
che ardono e lune e ferite che bruciano.

Who weeps? Not I, believe me: over the rivers run exasperating cracks of a whip, dark horses, flashes of sulphur. Not I, my race has knives which gleam and moons and wounds which burn.

Essentially, therefore, the poem is a blend of mythicized, memorial elements and occasional vivid images of age-old Sicilian folklore, while its artistry consists of a form of historical allusiveness again standing half-way between an open discourse and the poet's formerly involuted hermetic manner.

Gradually, however, the technique of the lyrical chronicle tends to gain the upper hand over Quasimodo's closed hermetic world, as we would normally expect in a poet determined to reintegrate himself into society. By reaction, he frequently commits himself whole-heartedly to the intricacies of his own personal life in the hope of compensating for the immense sense of solitude resulting from old-age and his growing despair. In another poem of the same collection a third feminine figure, Rossana Sironi, emerges and her death also greatly distresses the poet. Similarly, in the eponymous lyric 'Il falso e vero verde' itself, the uniqueness of a single human life seems to be valued above everything else, and its innate beauty and authenticity are contrasted elegiacally with the meaningless cyclical pattern of nature which represents a false flowering. The poet now draws a Leopardian type of consolation from Rossana's passing, and the anguished meditations she prompts remind us of a similar anguish in Leopardi's 'A Silvia':

> E tu non fiorisci,
> non metti giorni, né sogni che salgano
> dal nostro al di là, non hai piú i tuoi occhi
> infantili, non hai piú mani tenere
> per cercare il mio viso che mi sfugge.

And you do not flower, you do not bring forth days nor dreams which rise from our world beyond, you no longer have your childlike eyes, you no longer have tender hands to seek out my face, which flees from me.

The message in this collection accordingly reasserts the importance of human relationships, first on a personal and then on a social level; and for this reason the poet uses both the absurdity of death and the unfeeling cycle of nature as lyrical foils.

The social element becomes even more evident in the section *Quando caddero gli alberi e le mura*, whose cataclysmic title clearly stresses the poet's sense of the imminent collapse of civilization. The opening composition is a powerful *Laude* written after the manner of Jacopone, in which Quasimodo practises a starker realism than ever before. At the same time the *poesia-cronaca* acquires a new dignity in 'Ai fratelli Cervi, alla loro Italia', which proves to be a restrained and resilient memorial to seven patriots killed in the partisan struggle during the war. Both these compositions intensify their lyrical effects by drawing again on distant cumulative, hermetic features, as indeed did 'Le morte chitarre', although in a more subdued manner. But, by contrast, the poem 'Auschwitz' reveals all too evidently the limitations of the genre, because its dramatic and allusive qualities are diluted either by too close an approximation to the facts of the situation or by an overt indulgence in sentimentality:

> Da quell'inferno aperto da una scritta
> bianca: 'Il lavoro vi renderà liberi'
> uscí continuo il fumo
> di migliaia di donne, spinte fuori
> all'alba dai canili contro il muro
> del tiro a segno o soffocate urlando
> misericordia all'acqua con la bocca
> di scheletro sotto le docce a gas.

From that open Hell hung with a white inscription: 'Work will set you free' there issued forth continually the smoke of thousands of women, driven out at dawn from their hovels and put against the wall as target-practice or suffocated as they cried for pity to the water under the gas-showers with their skeletal mouths.

The collection *La terra impareggiabile* (1958) shares the same merits and demerits as its predecessor, although its imagery is, if anything, less hermetic and its social propaganda more accentuated. The incomparable land to which the title refers is the real, everyday world of the toiling masses, to which the poet now feels himself inexorably bound. Consequently, he asserts that 'un poeta è tale quando non rinuncia alla sua presenza in una data terra, in un tempo esatto, definito politicamente. E poesia è libertà e verità di quel tempo e non modulazioni astratte del sentimento'[50] ('a poet is such when he does not abandon his presence in a given land, in a precise time, defined politically. And poetry is liberty and freedom of that time and not abstract modulations of feeling.') Oddly enough, its first section is yet a further redimensioning of his Sicilian dreamworld, re-evoked within Leopardian moonlight tonalities; and yet at the same time its neo-hermetic symbols are now still further dilated to carry a much smoother flow of emotion. The pessimism and disillusionment of previous years seem therefore to disappear at this point, and in lyrics like 'Visibile, invisibile' we find a reborn enthusiasm for life beneath the serenity of its Leopardian half-tones. In other words Quasimodo's haunting Sicilian memories are now fully integrated into the wider understanding of existence that the poet has gained from his long sojourn on the Italian mainland. This accounts for the almost infinite allusiveness and luminosity of his settings which provide his thoughts with a deep and humane perspective:

Visibile, invisibile
il carrettiere all'orizzonte
nelle braccia della strada chiama
risponde alla voce delle isole.
Anch'io non vado alla deriva,
intorno rulla il mondo, leggo
la mia storia come guardia di notte
le ore delle piogge.

Visible, invisible the carter on the horizon in the folds of the road calls and replies to the voice of the islands. Even I do not drift aimlessly, about me rolls the world, I read my life-story as a nightwatchman reads the rainy hours.

Such a serene and comprehensive outlook is the final outcome of the gradual fusing of orphic and historical elements into a temperate form of wisdom. The poet's manner is no longer as hermetically infolded as it once

Salvatore Quasimodo

was nor does it operate upon a virtual surrealist plane to create alchemistic memorial linkages like those encountered in 'Le morte chitarre'. It works instead in a largely allegorical sphere in which symbolic and realist elements are made to stand in almost perfect reciprocity. This second 'distensione' ('dilation') of Quasimodo's poetic language thus reaches its highest point in this collection, a fact which may be illustrated by comparing the figure of the 'carrettiere' in the present composition with the 'carraio' appearing in 'Strada di Agrigentum'. The latter, despite the already partial opening of the poet's imagery, still tended to possess a certain metaphysical aura about him, indicative of a secret symbolic function, while the proper foil to the present figure is, by contrast, the 'carrettier' ('carter') in Leopardi's 'Il tramonto della luna' where consolatory allegorical implications offset the stark contingency of the human life-span. The last two figures, in short, are symbolic of life's fitful pilgrimage, whereas the former has a narrower involuted, non-historical function. This means that the poet attains to a higher degree of communicativeness whenever his verse no longer proves solipsist and discontinuous in quality but is realistically based and objective, depicting a wealth of social experience as well as his own personal sense of fulfilment. Henceforth he will consider human life to have value in itself and he speaks of the richness of individual memories and their shadowy concreteness rather than of the limitations imposed by death or by hermetic perspectives:

Non mi preparo alla morte,
so il principio delle cose,
la fine è una superficie dove viaggia
l'invasore della mia ombra.
Io non conosco le ombre.[51]

I do not prepare myself for death. I know the principle of things, the end is a surface where the invader of my shadow travels. I do not know the shadows.

Perhaps then the best way of defining the ultimate nature of his humanism would be to claim that it attempts the deepest form of self-possession of which the mind is capable while simultaneously acknowledging the coexistence of a similar self-possession in other minds. To achieve such a degree of humanistic maturity the 'vert paradis' of Quasimodo's youth is at this stage widened dramatically to produce a full-blown social reality with deeply-felt moral overtones. In the process the poet sloughs off the speculative attitudes of hermeticism and replaces them with the connective tissue of a purely emotive discourse – one which continually asserts the poet's readiness to participate fully in everyday life.

From such a humane climate Quasimodo considers that the authentic personality will more readily emerge, and he now uses as his symbol of a fully-developed character the figure of his own father. He had, in fact, long admired his father's rich constructive humanity, his compassion for others, and his unerring ability to adjust to circumstances. So he highlights his positive approach to life by mirroring it in his behaviour during the Messina earthquake, when he offered comfort to his own family and practical help to the bereaved. His father is thereby transformed into an emblem of man's disinterested and hopeful endeavour in the service of others:

Il tuo berretto di sole andava su e giú
nel poco spazio che sempre ti hanno dato.
Anche a me misurarono ogni cosa,
e ho portato il tuo nome
un po' piú in là dell'odio e dell'invidia.[52]

Your beret of sunshine went up and down in the brief space that they always allotted to you. For me too they measured out everything, and I have carried your name a little beyond hate and envy.

In the second section of *La terra impareggiabile*, on the other hand, the poem-chronicle tends to predominate. The section's very title, *Ancora dell'inferno*, gives us the measure of the poet's anguish and sense of commitment, while his mode of lyrical presentation is now clearly allegorico-narrative in quality. For instance, in 'Il muro' the fate of the individual within the social complex is revealed in allusive terms against the background of a wider allegory of unceasing human toil:

Ogni tanto qualcuno precipita
dalle impalcature e subito un altro
corre al suo posto. Non vestono tute
azzurre e parlano un gergo allusivo.

Every so often someone falls from the scaffolding and immediately another runs to take his place. They do not wear blue overalls and speak an allusive jargon.

Similarly in the poem 'Ancora dell'inferno' itself we are presented with a terrifying allegorized scene, the utter devastation following a hydrogen-bomb attack. We have to admit that the poem produces a powerful effect through its fragmentary imagery which accurately reflects the stunned mood of incredulity among the survivors; but it nevertheless remains true to say that, in general, socially based allegories of this type can only have a limited lyrical resonance. Moreover, they tend to lack any resonance at all in poems like 'Notizia di cronaca' where Quasimodo experiments in a journalistic manner with the raw facts of a crime. All that this kind of inspiration can provide is indeed a historical justification for the poet's present social (or socialist) ethos; and in his last collection, *Dare e avere*

(1966), Quasimodo will spend the remainder of his life working out his social Utopia's moral and aesthetic implications.

What is less marked in the collection is the sharp associative-conceptual dichotomy in the poet's earlier lyrical experiences. The climate is mainly reflective and, even though poems like 'Dalle rive del Balaton' are still largely documentary, most of the other lyrics are of a meditative nature, thereby proving to be authentic distillations from the poet's now integrated sensibility. In particular, he offers us a fresh insight into the cultural tradition by adopting the attitude of an interpreter of society's intimate needs and by attempting to define the rôle of the post-war poet. As a consequence, *Dare e avere* is neither wholly symbolic nor allegorical in quality but has the flavour of a reasoned discourse composed of an artful interfusion of both Quasimodo's previous lyrical manners.

Its dominant tone is provided by the poet's sense of mortality, since he had already by this time experienced several severe heart-attacks and the gloomy prognosis for the future had changed him into a kind of despairing optimist. During the entire period he felt as if he was living on borrowed time and this explains the shadowy chiaroscuro effects so noticeable in his imagery. Still, despite the sombre background to his inspiration the main theme of the collection remains a positive one and deals with the process of give-and-take within a regenerated society. Indeed, precisely because of his impending death the poet looks on life as a detached philosopher and warns others that it is only through a love for one's fellow men that one can hope to arrive at a state of happiness:

> . . . ricorda che puoi essere l'essere dell'essere
> solo che amore ti colpisca bene alle viscere.[53]

> . . . remember that you can be the being of being only if love strikes you squarely in the viscera.

Within this overall outlook he examines both human virtue and moral turpitude and, although he equates rectitude with self-sacrifice, he no longer associates nobility of mind exclusively with a slack left-wing emotionalism. All that concerns him now is the full development of the individual within his social context, and he uses the symbol of a Russian nurse, Varvàra Alexandrovna, as an illustration of his ideal merging of one's social and personal consciences. While she looks after him during an illness in Moscow, she consequently becomes transformed into an emblem of human solidarity rising above a national to an international level:

> . . . sei la Russia, non un paesaggio di neve
> riflesso in uno specchio d'ospedale
> sei una moltitudine di mani che cercano altre mani.

. . . you are Russia, not a snowy landscape reflected in a hospital mirror, you are a multitude of hands which seek other hands.

By pinning his faith to this kind of deeply felt humanitarianism Quasimodo is again able to introduce fresh chords into his lyricism, especially a tragic existential note which implies that all human life hangs by a single thread. The point is illustrated in 'Una notte di settembre' in which the elements of the *poesia-cronaca* are remoulded to provide a suggestive work of art.[54] The composition presents us with a new insight into the meaning of life which is now emergent from a whorl of memories, flashbacks and telescopic allusions; and yet its residual hermetic overtones in no way compromise the realities of the situation described.

Consequently, even when he was struck down by a mortal sickness, Quasimodo still strove to catch the inner lyrical resonances of his age, and he later explained that his post-war poetry sought to discover 'un fine etico rapportato alla *comunicazione*'[55] ('an ethical aim linked to *communication*'). Indeed, such a conclusion is already implicit as early as 'Dialogo' in *La vita non è sogno*, where Orpheus's descent into Hell to rescue Eurydice symbolizes a definite act of commitment. In contrast with the outcome of the classical myth, Quasimodo's modern Orpheus expects his lady to be revived and returned to him:

O non eri Euridice? Non eri Euridice!
Euridice è viva. Euridice! Euridice!

O were you not Eurydice? You were not Eurydice! Eurydice is alive. Eurydice! Eurydice!

This revived presence is, of course, an attempted prefiguration of that perfect symbiosis between the individual and society which the poet himself had hoped to realize in the post-war world. He once observed that 'ciò che conta in chi scrive è *la sua presenza umana mentre scrive*'[56] ('what counts in those who write is *their human presence while they write*'); and so at that stage only when social and aesthetic tensions work in harmony did Quasimodo consider the human sensibility vibrant enough to formulate those inarticulate truths which release both the poet and society from their enslavement to the past.

The psychological basis for the poet's post-war development is accordingly his sense of being continually 'disponibile' or receptive in the Gidean meaning of the word. It led him to the conclusion that 'umanesimo non può avere che un significato, oggi: la condizione dell'uomo nelle aperte domande della sua vita'[57] ('humanism can have only one meaning, today: the condition of man in the open demands of his life'). But, as we have previously hinted, he was never wholly successful in producing a lyricism measuring up to his aims, even though his premature death in 1968 cut short his poetic career when it was still full of promise and capable of greater artistic maturity. But in the last analysis whether he achieved his post-war aims or not is beside the point; it is his subsequent influence in the cultural world which is alone significant. This is still considerable, if indirect, because it was essentially his vision in the immediate post-war years which has guided contemporary poets towards a wider understanding of their lyrical potentialities.

Promise as well as achievement have accordingly to be assessed in any consideration of his poetic career and for these very reasons it is difficult to make any clear-cut estimate of his cultural position. In one sense he can be regarded as having achieved – virtually single-handed – the most significant change in literary attitudes since the early decades of the present century. But, by contrast, his post-war accomplishments in the field of humanist poetry are modest when compared with his more lyrically satisfying contribution to hermeticism. This can probably be explained by the paradoxical nature of his aesthetic practice in his later period, because on the one hand he expressed an almost *avant-garde* enthusiasm for innovation, while on the other he also reasserted the necessity for classical restraint in stylistic matters. No doubt it was this paradox which lay behind his and other writers' post-war artistic perplexity, for what in his later years he struggled to achieve was to free himself from the cocoon of solipsist procedures in which he had earlier become enmeshed. In his attempts at liberation he sometimes committed himself too readily to prevailing fashions, a trend which is particularly noticeable whenever he sails too close to the documentary wind. His overriding weakness at that stage was essentially one of failing to provide a coherent perspective, even though his critical intelligence unerringly perceived the general direction in which his inspiration ought to be moving.

At first sight it might seem as if his main problem was not one of prescribing the limits within which post-war poetry should operate but of freeing his aesthetics from its pre-war excrescences. For even his pre-war lyricism reached its highest level of perceptiveness only when in poems like 'Vento a Tíndari' he avoided too intense an involution of his imagery. Yet by means of a curious inversion of rôles we find that his post-war verse also attains a high level of intensity when its coarser narrative strain is interiorized by the raising of its imagery to a form of emblematic limpidity. Accordingly, whenever Quasimodo's inspiration wanes at this period, his poetry tends to display the major defects of both his manners, and it then becomes a gratuitous and perplexing chronicle of events.

During the change-over from the one approach to the other his object-symbols, as we have seen, tend to remain constant, the only difference being that those at the end of his career are no longer symbolically in-voluted but discursive and allegorical in implication. Advantages and dis-advantages accrue from this process. In one sense the more relaxed emotional charge of the allegorical approach gives his poetry a broader spectrum and more humanity than the *parola-mito*, which all too often degenerated to a point of frigidity and provided only an imaginative mausoleum in which to preserve his fossilized emotions. Yet in another sense its distended range of feeling undermined the quartz-like resilience of his hermetic metaphors, and frequently any residual allegorical tension was then insufficient to save his verse from sinking into a morass of social banalities. Because of this slackening of tension we can readily understand why his finest post-war lyrics regress to the point at which his early and later manners intersect and why his authentic art still relies on a merging of hermetic and humanist features at the imaginative level. For it is solely on those occasions that he achieved a harmonious interblending of his two styles and succeeded in writing a poetry which 'si trasforma in *etica*, proprio per la sua resa di bellezza'[58] ('is transformed into an *ethic*, precisely because of its rendering of beauty'). During the major part of his life his 'tempo mitico' ('mythical time') was truly out of joint with his sensibility, because he was unable to run the rhythm of his own highly perceptive conscience in double harness with that of society as a whole. However, despite his somewhat mixed success, we have nevertheless to consider Quasimodo as the chrysalis from which the poetry of present-day Italy ultimately developed. And for this reason his verse marks a new point of crisis and of partial solution to that crisis in the history of the twentieth-century Italian lyric.

Notes

I

1 From 'Le voyage', in *Les Fleurs du mal.*

2 A perceptive survey of the roots of the modern sensibility is to be found in L. Anceschi: *Autonomia e eteronomia dell'arte* (Florence, 1959) (2nd ed.). For the influence of French literature on late nineteenth-century poetry in Italy, see S. Guarnieri: 'Crepuscolari, Futuristi, Vociani', in *Letterature moderne* (1962), 148-66. Guarnieri rightly observes that at this time a new interest in European literature had been aroused, especially in French literature. This interest, he points out, 'spinge a tradurre, a seguire ogni novità straniera' (p.151). Some of the earliest articles on the major French poets of the later nineteenth century appear in the *Gazzetta letteraria* of Turin between 1877 and 1900. (See *La 'Gazzetta letteraria' e la Francia*, memoria di G. Mirandola, Accademia delle scienze, Turin, 1971.)

3 See G. Mounin: 'Une poésie du naturel', in *Cahiers du sud* (1954), 323, 17.

4 See Mario Luzi: *L'idea simbolista* (Milan, 1959), p.10. A similar view was expressed as early as 1908 by G.P. Lucini who wrote: 'Il simbolo considera una realtà, un fenomeno naturale, un fatto storico, un dogma, una leggenda, un atto personale, e ne distingue, un dopo l'altro, non come intenderebbero li esoterici *i tre sensi*, ma le mille leggi, i mille rapporti, le mille significazioni, che formano quella entità e che ne promanano per azione e reazione ... L'Allegoria invece, è un'astrazione della vita; in quella già intervenne, per comporla, un giudizio, una scelta, cioè un'operazione retorica. Non promana dagli enti e dalle loro dirette o indirette relazioni, ma da un modo arbitrario di categoria, quindi da un preconcetto, il quale applica quella astrazione teorica, per cui, anche contro le leggi fisiche, tenta costruire una sua argomentazione.' (In *Ragion poetica e programma del verso libero*, Edizioni di 'Poesia', Milan, 1908, pp.212-3.)

5 For this approach to the Renaissance, see G.T. Wright: *The poet in the poem* (University of California Press, 1960). The writer explains that the classical poet's dependence on the social conscience works through a *persona* or *alter ego*, which may be defined as a projection of his personality acting in full awareness of its limitations and the prescriptions imposed on it by tradition. His conclusion is that in any humanist period 'the conventions of the age largely dictate the areas to which he may apply his song' (p.32).

6 The classic example of the kind of *échec* to which we refer is Baudelaire's, as described in R. Laforgue: *L'échec de Baudelaire* (Paris, 1931), but it reappears in even more exacerbated form in Mallarmé.

7 We can consider the two techniques as forming part of the lyrical pattern which T.S. Eliot defines as the 'objective correlative'. The definition he provides in his essay on *Hamlet* reads as follows: 'The only way of expressing emotion in the form of art is by finding an 'objective correlative': in other words, a set of objects, a situation, a chain of events which shall be the formula of that *particular* emotion; such that when the external facts, which must terminate in sensory experience, are given, the emotion is immediately evoked.'

8 M. Luzi: op. cit., p.15.

9 In *Divagations* (Geneva, 1943), pp.225-6.

10 One of the first critics to distinguish between a 'tendance idéiste' and a 'tendance idéaliste' was A. Aurier in 'Le symbolisme en peinture: Paul Gauguin', in *Le Mercure de France* (March, 1891), 155-65. The idea that all experience is aesthetic and contingent is also one of the tenets of the theory of *Einfühlung*. (For a definition of this type of empathy, see G. Morpurgo-Tagliabue: *L'esthétique contemporaine* Milan, 1960, pp.20-4.)

11 R. Poggioli: 'Simbolismo russo e occidentale', in *Letterature moderne* (1961), 588.

12 Mallarmé's aim was expressed as follows: 'Un désir indéniable à mon temps est de séparer comme en vue d'attributions différentes le double état de la parole, brut et immédiat ici, là essentiel.' ('Crise de vers', in *Divagations*, p.225.)

13 Ibid., p.218. He also believed that this kind of musicality was originally at the root of traditional metres, saying: 'Arcane étrange; et d'intentions pas moindres, a jailli la métrique aux temps incubatoires.' (p.218) The first article written in Italian on Mallarmé was by V. Pica: 'I moderni bizantini. Stéphane Mallarmé' in *La Gazzetta letteraria*, X (1886), 47, 48, 49. For further information, see O. Ragusa: 'V. Pica: First Champion of French Symbolism in Italy', in *Italica* (1958), 255-61; and also by the same author: *Mallarmé in Italy. Literary influence and critical response*, (New York, 1957). E. Paratore, however, describes Pica as 'vox clamantis in deserto' and claims that the real acclimatization of Mallarmé in Italy was at the time of *La Voce* (1908-16). (See 'Naturalismo e decadentismo in Gabriele D'Annunzio', in *Studi dannunziani*, Morano, Naples, 1966.) Pica also wrote on Verlaine in the same periodical in 1885 (Nos. 46, 47, 48).

14 René Ghil, *Traité du verbe* (Paris, 1886).

15 Bachelard investigated the properties of the poet's inner space and concluded that 'chaque objet investi d'espace intime devient . . . centre de tout l'espace. Pour chaque objet le lointain est le présent, l'horizon a autant d'existence que le centre.' (See *La poétique de l'espace*, Paris, 1957, p.184.)

16 Poggioli, op. cit., 588. The expression is originally taken from Kierkegaard.

17 C. Pellizzi was the first Italian critic to see the positive side of decadentism and he wrote as early as 1929: 'La parola *decadente* non deve suonare dispregio o condanna, poiché anzitutto la poesia, che sia tale, non è mai condannabile; e, di piú, questa decadenza significa anch'essa soluzione, sviluppo, progresso, punto di passaggio e di sutura da uno ad altro modo di personalità e di ispirazione.' (In *Le lettere italiane del nostro secolo*, Milan, 1929, p.316.)

18 From 'J'aime dans le temps', in *De l'angélus de l'aube à l'angélus du soir* (Paris, 1898).

19 See W. Binni: *La poetica del decadentismo* (Florence, 1961), p.23 (1st ed. dates from 1936).

20 Letter to Paul Demeny, dated Charleville, 15 May 1871.

21 R. Scrivano: 'Storia critica di un concetto letterario: decadentismo', in *La Rassegna della letteratura italiana* (1961), 452.

22 *Sagesse*, XVI.

23 G. Petrocchi: 'Irrequietudine religiosa del decadentismo italiano', in *Humanitas*, 2, (1946), 1157.

24 Marcazzan's analysis of the difference of degree between romantic and decadent anguish is particularly significant, because he notes that, whereas 'l'angoscia romantica è per la profondità degli spazi e dei cieli, è stupore e sgomento degli abissi nei quali si riflette come capovolta', that of the decadents is to be found 'in direzione della materia e della tenebra terrena, è scandaglio di profondità chiuse, sommovimento d'istinti, esplorazione dell'inconscio, atomismo spirituale e formale di momenti singoli, irrazionalità disarticolata e capillare.' (In 'Dal romanticismo al decadentismo', appearing in *Letteratura italiana: le correnti*, II (Milan), p.746.)

25 From 'Per una signora XXVII', in *In Primavera* (1869).

26 In *Cahiers du Sud*, No. 323, 18.

27 In *Le occasioni* (1939). According to Nascimbeni the scene is the station at Florence where Liuba was fleeing from Fascist persecution. (*Eugenio Montale*, Milan, 1969, p.115.)

28 'La novità del Petrarca era nell'accento che aveva posto sul valore di eredità giacente nella mente umana, valore da considerarsi, per tornare, in possesso, come tenebra da rischiararsi.' (In 'Góngora al lume d'oggi', in *Aut Aut*, 4, (1951), 291.)

29 Sonnet 90. For Montanari's comments on Petrarch's emblematic style, see *Studi sul Canzoniere del Petrarca*, (Rome, 1958). Bigongiari makes a similar point in his review of De Robertis's *Saggio sul Leopardi*, in *Letteratura*, 5, (1938), 156.

30 *Canzone*, 126.

31 From 'La pietà', in *Sentimento del tempo* (1936).

32 See 'La morte meditata' (canto secondo), in *Sentimento del tempo*.

33 In *Orfismo della parola* (San Casciano, 1953), p.459.

34 Preface to *Allegria* (Milan, 1943).

35 Marcel Raymond skilfully illustrates this point by reference to the method of Robert Desnos, about whom he observes: 'Il s'agissait d'essayer une bonne fois de laisser les mots penser pour eux-mêmes; on viendrait voir après ce qui s'ensuivrait. C'est la pêche miraculeuse; mais les miracles sont rares, et la méthode s'est révélée décevante, du moins pour le lecteur.' (*De Baudelaire au surréalisme* Paris, 1933, p.351.)

36 See Tasso's *Discorsi dell'arte poetica e in particolare sopra il poema eroico.*

37 The importance of the racial memory is also taken up by Mallarmé in 'Igitur' and it may well be from him that it passes into modern aesthetics.

38 In the *Zibaldone* (Milan, 1949) (vol. 1), p.1269, para. 2042.

39 See Francesco Petrarca, *Prose* (Milan-Naples, 1955), pp.64-5.

40 See V. Lugli: 'Incontri di Giovanni Pascoli con la poesia francese', in *Pascoli, discorsi nel centenario della nascita* (Bologna, 1958), pp.365-89.

41 Serra, in fact, defines his method as 'una perfezione che suona falso'. (In *Le lettere*, Rome, 1914, p.36.)

42 E. Paci: *Esistenza e immagine* (Milan, 1947), p.144.

43 See J. Sherer: *L'expression littéraire dans l'oeuvre de Mallarmé* (Paris, 1947), p.154.

44 In *Problemi del nostro tempo – La solitudine dell'artista* (Associazione italiana per la libertà della cultura, n.d.), p.3. In 1932 Husserl described his transcendent subjectivity as 'an absolutely independent realm of direct experience'. (See preface to the English edition of *Ideas, pure phenomenology* London, 1931, p.11.)

45 G. Battaglini: 'Fenomenologia, fondazione, estetica', in *Il Verri*, 6, (1961), 23.

46 In *Nuova corrente*, 11-12 (1958), 58.

47 For the origins and interpretation of ancient orphism, see J. Burnet: *Greek Philosophy* (London, 1933); W.K.G. Guthrie: *The Greeks and their Gods* (London, 1950); and E.O. James: *The Ancient Gods* (London, 1960). It is significant that after the rending of the God, even in the degenerate cult of Bacchus, he would revert as a vegetative divinity to the multiple forms of nature: its woods, flowers, streams, lakes, rivers, springs and hills, all images still alive in modern orphic lyricism.

48 For a further consideration of modern orphism, see F. Flora: *Orfismo della parola* (San Casciano, 1953), and more recently M. Perniola: *L'alienazione artistica* (Milan, 1971). An interesting work dealing with more general problems of orphism is E. Eliade: *Le mythe de l'éternel retour* (Paris, 1949), while E. Sewell, *The Orphic Voice* (New Haven, 1960), deals with its cultural resonances throughout history. More specific studies are: E. Kushner: *Le mythe d'Orphée dans la littérature française contemporaine* (Paris, 1961); G. Bays: *The Orphic Vision, Seer Poets from Novalis to Rimbaud* (Lincoln, 1964); W.A. Strauss: *Descent and Return. The Orphic Myth in Modern Literature* (Cambridge, Mass., 1971).

49 No overall study has come to our notice, but an interesting partial one on the myth is P. Cabañas: *El mito de Orfeo en la literatura español* (Madrid, 1948).

50 A. Chastel: *Marsile Ficin et l'art* (Geneva, 1954), p.175.

51 E. Wind writes that the 'hybrid gods of orphic theology follow a logic of their own, which is a logic of concealment . . . By that logic their meaning can be 'unfolded' or made explicit, provided that the rule of 'infolding' has been mastered first, which Cusanus distinguished from *explicatio* by the quaint but fitting name of *complicatio*.' (In *Pagan mysteries of the Renaissance* Penguin Books, 1967, p.204; 1st ed. Faber & Faber, London, 1958.)

52 G. Battaglini, op. cit., in *Il Verri*, 6 (1961), 23.

II

1 The novel in question, *La scapigliatura e il 6 febbraio*, was published in 1861 under the pseudonym of Cletto Arrighi.

2 See A. Romanò: 'La scapigliatura', in *Officina* (1958), 256. Also to be consulted are: E. Gennarini: *La scapigliatura milanese* (Naples, 1961); G. Mariani: *Storia della scapigliatura* (Caltanisetta-Rome, 1967); and A. Romanò: *Il secondo romanticismo lombardo* (Milan, 1958).

3 From this group (founded around 1830) there emerged a whole school of poets, chief among whom were Pétrus Borel and Philothée O'Neddy (Théophile Dondey). The latter wrote the following definition of its aims: 'Tout chez eux puissamment concourt à proclamer/Qu'ils portent dans leurs seins des coeurs prompts à s'armer/De haine virulente et de pitié morose,/Contre la bourgeoisie et le Code et la prose:/Des coeurs ne dépensant leur exaltation/Que pour deux vérités: l'art et la passion . . .' (*Feu et flamme*, Paris, 1926, p.8) Mazzini's 'Giovine Italia' movement was also founded in 1831 but, although it was superficially a parallel movement, it was far more politically orientated than its French counterpart and offered no specific lead in literary affairs.

4 See G. Rovani: *Le tre arti considerate in alcuni illustri italiani* (Milan, 1874) (2 vols.).

5 F. Flora: *Storia della letteratura italiana* (Milan, 1953), vol. V., p.64.

6 See *Tutti gli scritti*, a cura di P. Nardi, (Milan, 1942), p.52.

7 See A. Romanò, op. cit., in *Officina* (1958), 261.

8 See *Prose* (Milan, 1946), vol. 1, 5-56.

9 In *Simboli e strutture della poesia di Pascoli* (Florence-Messina, n.d.), p.9.

10 From 'Il giorno dei morti', in *Myricae* (1891).

11 Umberto Bosco emphasizes Thovez's contribution to the tradition: 'Sta di fatto che il Thovez, poetando tra l'87 e il '95 pone con fermezza dinanzi alla sua propria coscienza d'artista il problema del rinnovamento *ab imis* della forma e della materia poetica . . .' (In 'Leopardi, Thovez e i crepuscolari', in *Convivium, 3 (1936)*. But see also L. Marigo: 'La poetica di Thovez', in *Lettere italiane,* 3 (1970), 351-82, who takes the opposite view.)

12 For a schematic description of the various generations of modern poets in Italy, see O. Macrí: 'Le generazioni nella poesia italiana', in *Paragone*, 42 (1953), 45-53.

13 See *La Stampa*, (10 September, 1910). The article in question, now republished in *La vita e il libro* (Bologna, 1928), pp.120-8, bears the title of *Poesia crepuscolare*. In point of fact, Borgese was by no means favourably disposed towards the crepuscular ethos and describes its basic mood as 'una torpida e limacciosa malinconia' (p.121).

14 The review appeared in three numbers only (15 December 1905, 1 January 1906 and 15 January 1906).

15 Spagnoletti actually considers the futurists as the first twentieth-century poets, saying: 'Ciò che varrebbe la pena di misurare è la distanza che separa, in questa lingua poetica ai primi fermenti, il prodotto futurista meno deteriore ... dal contemporaneo prodotto dei Crepuscolari, assai piú legato alla nostra tradizione formale, proprio per la sua dipendenza da Pascoli e D'Annunzio'. (In *Poesia italiana contemporanea*, Bologna, 1959, p.14). Anceschi, on the other hand, expresses a diametrically opposite view, observing that 'l'inizio del diverso muoversi della parola poetica della prima metà del Novecento fu con i crepuscolari . . .' (In *Lirica del Novecento*, edited with S. Antonielli, Vallecchi, Florence, 1953, p.xvii).

16 See E. Montale: *Stile e tradizione*, in *Il Baretti* (15 January 1925). Like other critics we have slightly changed the text, but not the sense, for our own purposes. The original form reads: 'La verità è un'altra; ed è che, debba o non debba risorgere la nuova arte dal tormento critico, essa non sarà cosa nostra se non risponderà alle piú imperiose esigenze che in noi si sono maturate'. (Reprinted in *Auto da fè*, Milan, 1966, p.19.)

17 In *Lirica del Novecento*, p.xxi.

18 In *Storia della letteratura italiana*, vol. 5, 575.

19 From 'Domenica di Bruggia'.

20 Ibid.

21 Ibid.

22 From *S. Luca*, no. XVIII.

23 See G. Petronio: *Poeti del nostro secolo – I crepuscolari*, in *Leonardo* (November, 1935), 449; now republished in *Poeti del nostro tempo – I crepuscolari* (Florence, 1937).

24 See N. Tedesco: *Quasimodo* (Palermo, 1959); and *La condizione crepuscolare* (Florence, 1970). In the latter work Tedesco puts forward the interesting thesis that a crepuscular tone is a constant feature of modern Italian lyricism.

25 Tedesco: *Quasimodo*, p.52 (note).

26 In Mario Novaro: *Murmuri ed echi* (1912). The present form of the poem is, however, taken from the fifth edition of the work printed in 1941.

27 See F.T. Marinetti: *Discorso futurista ai Veneziani* (1910) later reproduced in M.D. Gambillo & T. Fiori: *Archivi del futurismo* (Rome, 1958), pp.21-2.

28 In *Baionette* (Milan, 1915), p.97.

29 In *Poesia*, 1-2 (1909), 2-4, (French text), 6-8 (Italian text). The Italian texts of the various manifestos appear in *Archivi del futurismo*, from which all quotations will be taken. For an extensive bibliography see P. Bergman: *Modernolatria e simultaneità*, (Uppsala, 1962).

30 See *Archivi del futurismo*, p.17.

31 In *Dal romanticismo al futurismo*, (Piacenza, 1921). Flora was, in fact, one of the first critics to attribute a serious intent to the futurist revolution, which he defined as a 'coscienza della malattia contemporanea e volontà di rinnovazione' (p.61).

32 In *Zang tumb tumb* (Milan, 1914), p.2.

33 Quoted by W. Vaccari: *Vita e tumulti di F.T. Marinetti* (Milan, 1959), p.12.

34 See G. Getto's essay in *Poeti, critici e cose varie del Novecento* (Florence, 1953), pp.56-101.

35 In *Poesie* (Florence, 1949) (6th ed.), pp.22-6.

36 From 'Chi sono', the liminary poem to the collection *Poesie (1904-14)*.

37 See G. Pullini: *Aldo Palazzeschi* (Milan, 1965), (Chapter 1).

38 See E. Falqui: *Il futurismo, il novecentismo* (Turin, 1953). According to him the *verso libero* was first introduced into futurist theory by G.P. Lucini in his *Ragion poetica e programma del verso libero* (Milan, 1908), but in practice it had been widely used earlier. Marinetti later expresses his intention to abandon it in favour of the *parola in libertà* in an article entitled 'Dopo il verso libero le parole in libertà', in *Lacerba* 1 (1913), fascicule 22, 252-4. At the time the main defect he found with the *verso libero* was that it 'canalizza artificialmente la corrente della emozione lirica fra le muraglie della sintassi e le chiuse grammaticali'. On the other hand, he characterizes his new stylistic method as follows: 'Nelle parole in libertà del mio lirismo scatenato si troveranno qua e là tracce di sintassi regolare e anche dei veri periodi logici. Questa disuguaglianza nella concisione e nella libertà è inevitabile e naturale. La poesia, non essendo, in realtà, che una vita superiore, piú raccolta e piú intensa di quella che viviamo ogni giorno, – è come questa composta di elementi ultravivi e di elementi agonizzanti'. The principal outcome of this theory is consequently an a-syntactic, telegraphic style largely devoid of the staid, grammatical practices of the pre-futurist world. On the subject of the *verso libero* see also Marinetti's *Enquête internationale sur le vers libre et manifeste du futurisme* (Milan, 1909).

39 In *I poeti futuristi* (Milan, 1912), p.11.

40 A. Vallone even goes so far as to suggest that Marinetti is a negative foil to D'Annunzio, while adding that 'il fuoco di Marinetti, che piú di ogni altro lo ereditò dal D'Annunzio, diventa motivo di rivolta e distruzione . . .' (In *Aspetti della poesia italiana contemporanea* Pisa, 1960, p.128).

41 The Italian version derives from *Distruzione*, (Milan, 1920), pp.20-1. The first translation of the collection into Italian was published by Edizioni futuriste di 'Poesia' (Milan, 1911).

42 In this respect Frattini speaks of the 'strano associazionismo memoriale-eidetico dei *Cantos* di Pound' and contrasts unfavourably with them the 'associazionismo parolibero teorizzato e realizzato da Marinetti'. He concludes that the shallowness of their approach to associative procedures indicates that the futurists misused a valuable means of poetic regeneration. (In *Da Tommaseo a Ungaretti* (Rocca San Casciano, 1959), p.103.) See also F. Curi, *Perdita d'aureola (Turin, 1977),* in which the futurists' 'materialism' is closely analysed.

43 From 'Battaglia (Peso + odore)'.

44 In 1913 G. Severini noted that '. . . nella nostra epoca di dinamismo e di simultaneità non si può separare una realtà qualunque dai ricordi, affinità o avversioni plastiche che la sua azione *espansiva* evoca *simultaneamente* in noi e che sono altrettante realtà astratte, points de repère, per raggiungere l'azione totale della realtà in questione'. (In 'Le analogie plastiche del dinamismo Manifesto futurista', see *Archivi del futurismo* edited by M.D. Gambillo & T. Fiori, p.77.)

45 This formula appears in a satellite article to the main manifesto of the futurist painters, entitled 'Ricostruzione futurista dell'universo' (see *Archivi del futurismo*, edited by M.D. Gambillo & T. Fiori, p.50). Its very title suggests, however, that it was intended to have universal application to all the arts and not simply to be confined to painting.

46 In 'Il cerchio si chiude', *Lacerba*, 11 (1914), fascicule 4, 49-50.

47 In *I primi principi di un'estetica futurista* (1920); now reprinted in A. Soffici: *Opere* (Vallecchi, 1959), vol. 1, p.690.

48 Soffici: *Opere*, vol. 1, p.662.

49 In *Opere*, vol. 1, 'Guillaume Apollinaire', p.536.

50 In G. Mathieu: *Au-delà du tachisme*, (Paris, 1963), p.224.

51 See 'Simultanisme-Librettisme', in *Soirées de Paris* (15 June 1914), pp.332-5.

52 Soffici's analysis of the 'pure poet' as early as 1909, however, shows us that the whole mood of the time was highly suspicious of this type of art. He wrote: 'Il Poeta ignora e disprezza la vita ... Le avventure spicciole e quotidiane degli uomini non lo riguardano'. (In *Opere 1*, pp.608, 609). He thus preferred the decadent Rimbaud to the purist Mallarmé, because the problems of existence interested the former but not the latter.

53 In *Lirica del Novecento* (edited with S. Antonielli), p.xxxi.

54 See G. Prezzolini: *L'italiano inutile* (Florence, 1964) (2nd ed.).

55 In his address 'Al lettore' in *La Voce* (1909, vol. 1, fascicule 9, p.33) Prezzolini announced the journal's programme as follows: 'Ci si propone qui di trattare tutte le questioni pratiche che hanno riflessi nel mondo intellettuale e religioso e artistico; di reagire alla retorica degli Italiani obbligandoli a veder da vicino la loro realtà sociale; di educarci a risolvere le piccole questioni e i piccoli problemi, per trovarci piú preparati un giorno a quelli grandi ...'

56 As Petrucciani rightly points out, the periodical 'fu nemica dell' imprecisione e dell'astrattezza, puntando ... sulla concretezza dei problemi del momento'. (In *La poetica dell'ermetismo italiano* Turin, 1955, pp.85-6).

57 Quoted by A. Romanò in his introduction to an anthology of the early *Voce: La Voce (1908-14)* (Turin, 1960), p.58.

58 The key article written by De Robertis bears this title and appears in *La Voce*, VII (1915), 488-98. Serra's method may, on the other hand, be summed up by an observation by Luigi Russo, who stresses that for this critic 'una vera critica di poesia dovrebbe essere un commento perpetuo a piè di pagina; di sotto la barbarie arida delle formule, bisogna far zampillare la fresca vena dell'umanità dei poeti'. (In *La critica letteraria contemporanea*, Laterza, Bari, 1942-3, vol. III, p.20.)

59 See G. Scalia: *Lacerba – La Voce (1914-16)* (Turin, 1961), p.93. Of *La Voce letteraria* (sometimes called 'la Voce bianca') Scalia writes: 'In questo ''tavolo riservato'' della letteratura che è stata *La Voce letteraria*, De Robertis si oppone coi suoi strumenti particolaristici, alla comune base ideologica irrazionalistica del tardo ''idealismo militante'' prezzoliniano, del futurismo, del lacerbismo.'

60 In *La Voce*, VII (1915), 498.

61 See A. Soffici: *Arthur Rimbaud* (Florence, 1911).

62 We refer to Bertrand's *Gaspard de la nuit* (Paris, 1842), in which examples of *visività* already abound. See poems such as 'Harlem', 'Le Maçon', 'L'alchimiste', etc.

63 In *Terrestrità del sole* (1927).

64 See A. Onofri: *Orchestrine Arioso*, con una notizia critico-biografica di Giorgio Vigolo, (Venice, 1959), p.13.

65 Prose poem entitled 'Tramonto'.

66 The title of the periodical is a corruption of the title of a fourteenth-century poem by Cecco d'Ascoli, 'L'acerba'. Beneath the title there appeared a line of verse drawn from this poem which reads: 'Qui non si canta al modo delle rane'. It might be more discreet if we allowed this challenge to pass without comment, but Scalia defines Marinetti's function in the periodical as that of a '*colporteur* e polemico amplificatore delle idee altrui' (op. cit., p.31).

67 A letter to T. Cangiullo throws light upon Mussolini's attitude as a politician towards the futurist movement. The implication behind his remarks is that he believed it ineffectual as an activist centre, even though it provided his own movement with a certain cultural panache: 'Noi abbiamo delle simpatie per il futurismo e ne comprendiamo l'intima essenza e la magnifica forza, ma perché dobbiamo trasportare sul nostro giornale una polemica che noi non abbiamo provocato e che non ci può interessare se non in linea accademica? Tutti i nostri sforzi tendono oggi all'azione e a null'altro – non escludiamo che domani si possa anche fare del futurismo e della polemica, su di esso, ma oggi abbiamo piú urgenti cose da fare'. (In *Archivi del futurismo* edited by M.D. Gambillo & T. Fiori, pp.353-4.) Close links were, however,

eventually established between the two movements through the personal friendship of Mussolini and Marinetti.

68 *La Ronda* flourished between 1919-1923. For an assessment of its aims and achievements see V. Cardarelli: 'Passo di Ronda' in *Solitario in Arcadia* (Milan, 1948). This article is now reprinted in *Opere complete*, Milan, 1962, where among other things the former editor explains that the review's aims were to provide 'un accento d'italianità consapevole, con ombre di continuità e di rassomiglianza alla tradizione'. (p.44).

69 Quoted by V. Vettori: *Riviste italiane del Novecento* (Rome, 1958), p.54.

70 In 'Prologo in tre parti', in *La Ronda*, 1 (1919), 5-6.

71 See, for instance, Cardarelli's article on 'Lo Zibaldone' in *Solitario in Arcadia*, where he asserts that 'capire Leopardi significa capire la tradizione e la modernità ad un tempo'. (*Opere complete*, p.518.)

72 In 'Discussione su Pascoli', *La Ronda* (7 November 1919), 15.

73 See Cardarelli: *Opere complete*, p.520.

74 For a survey of the development of the *capitolo*, see E. Falqui: *Capitoli per una storia della nostra prosa d'arte del Novecento* (Milan, 1964).

75 From *Poesie* (Florence, 1942), but first published in *Frontiera* (Milan, 1941).

76 In *Lavorare stanca* (Florence, 1936).

77 This point was first made by Pancrazi who, as early as 1944, wrote: 'Il fascismo urlava, e i poeti del tempo parlavano sottovoce; il fascismo mostrava un'illimitata fiducia nelle piú smaccate iperboliche parole, e i poeti del tempo finirono per non fidarsi piú delle parole oneste, e le smorzavano nel puro suono o le piegavano a significati e allusioni insolite'. (P. Pancrazi: 'Fascismo e letteratura', in *La nuova Europa*, (10 November 1944), 5.)

78 See M. Petrucciani: *La poetica dell'ermetismo italiano* (Turin, 1955); N. Tedesco: *Quasimodo* (Palermo, 1959), pp.23-35, and *La condizione crepuscolare* (Florence, 1970); S. Ramat; *L'ermetismo* (Florence, 1969).

79 See F. Giannessi: *Gli ermetici* (Brescia, 1951); S.F. Romano: *La poetica dell'ermetismo*, (Florence, 1942) (reprinted 1951).

80 Montale writes: 'Non esistono problemi del linguaggio, sperimentalismi, innesti e derivazioni da altre letterature, che abbiano valore normativo. Ogni poeta si crea lo strumento che crede essergli necessario'. (In *Nuovi argomenti*, 55-6 (1942), 43).

81 Ibid., p.100.

82 In *Scrittori del Novecento* (Florence, 1946) (3rd ed.) p.271.

83 Tedesco's conclusion on hermeticism in that 'non vi è stata un'elaborazione letteraria a largo raggio del sostrato linguistico nazionale, ma anzi il tentativo alla fine di sdilinquire la nostra lingua, trasformandola in aristocratico gergo di gruppo'. (op. cit., p. 35). It is for this reason that he can assert that 'Le radici di un antiermetismo di Quasimodo sono molto piú profonde, e sono quelle che ci mostrano la sua sostanziale estraneità alla corrente ermetica: altrimenti non riusciremmo a spiegarci la sua capacità di superamento storico di questo movimento, dopo esserne stato "preso dal fascino esteriore".' (p.23)

84 op. cit., p.101.

85 See H. Brémond: *La poésie pure, avec un débat sur la poésie de R. de Souza* (Paris, 1926).

86 In 'La poetica della parola', now in *Inventario* (1961), 18-41, but originally introducing *Poesie* by S. Quasimodo (Milan 1938), pp.11-61. See also *Esemplari del sentimento poetico contemporaneo* (Florence, 1941).

87 M. Petrucciani: *Poesia pura e poesia esistenziale* (Turin, 1957), p.30.

88 In 'Giorno e notte', in *Aut Aut*, 67 (1962), 44-5; now in *Sulla poesia*, pp.91-92.

89 See G. Pozzi: *La poesia italiana del Novecento* (Turin, 1965), p.203 et seq.

90 In *Pianissimo* (1914), reprinted in *Poesia* (Milan, 1961).

91 From 'Taci, anima stanca di godere', in *Pianissimo* (1914).

92 From *Vidi le muse* (1943).

93 In *Furor mathematicus* (Milan, 1950), p.31.

94 In 'Little Gidding': 'This is the use of memory/For liberation . . .'

95 In *Un Brindisi* (Florence, 1946).

96 Although published after *Nel Magma*, however, it must be pointed out that the poems of *Dal fondo della campagna* were written before it, between 1956-60.

97 Quoted in Spagnoletti, op. cit., p.892.

98 In *Nuovi argomenti*, 55-6 (1962), 44.

99 From 'Laborintus 4', in *Triperuno* (Milan, 1964), p.15.
100 In *Nuovi argomenti*, 55-6 (1962), 38.
101 In 'La libertà stilistica', in *Officina*, 9-10 (1957), 341-6, see 344.
102 Ibid., p.344.
103 The first appearance of the so-called 'Novissimi' was a group surrounding *Il Menabò*, 2 (1960). Among its most important adherents were Pagliarani, Giuliani, Balestrini, Porta and Sanguineti himself. The initial impulse of the new avant-garde, however, goes back to the founding of Anceschi's periodical *Il Verri* in 1956.
104 Published in *Officina* 9-10 (1957).
105 In *Poesia pura e poesia esistenziale*, p.97.
106 See L. Cherchi: *I contrasti della nuova poesia* (Milan, 1961).
107 In *Poesia contemporanea*, now reprinted in *Il Poeta e il politico e altri saggi*, but first appearing in 1946.
108 In *I contrasti della nuova poesia*, p.21.

III

1 In this respect we can contrast the views of Antonielli and De Castris. The former concludes his essay on Gozzano by saying: 'Non vogliamo regalare nulla a Gozzano . . . ma non possiamo fare a meno di accorgerci, ormai, che molti sono gli aspetti dell'opera sua strettamente in rapporto coi caratteri della poesia italiana del Novecento.' (In *Aspetti e figure del Novecento*, p.32.) By contrast, De Castris writes: 'Al suo dramma – e pur assunto nei momenti di sincerità – manca dunque la qualità di dramma storico, cioè una profonda coscienza morale.' (In *Decadentismo e realtà*, p.120.)
2 See 'Poesie sparse' in Guido Gozzano: *Poesie e prose*, a cura di Alberto De Marchi (Garzanti, 1961). This is a reprint with additions and a different preface of an earlier edition of Gozzano's works entitled *Opere*, jointly edited by Calcaterra and De Marchi (Milan, 1953). Recently Mondadori has published a critical edition of his verse: *Tutte le poesie* (Milan, 1980).
3 Bàrberi Squarotti conveniently sums up Carducci's basic manner as follows: '. . . (è) un mondo mitologico in cui tutto si compone in un ordine assoluto, deciso *ab aeterno*, irrelato: il mondo storico e politico del Carducci è sempre un dover essere, mai una realtà.' (In *Astrazione e realtà*, p.23.)
4 See Antonielli, op. cit., p.18. He describes Carducci's influence on Gozzano as 'un esempio di serietà, di disciplina artistica, e un richiamo generico allo studio dei classici.'
5 Despite the affinity of their topographical features, however, Bonfiglioli has emphasized a profound difference in the ideological angles from which the two poets see the world: 'La campagna pascoliana è sempre vista attraverso gli occhi di una piccola borghesia senza terra . . . La campagna gozzaniana invece è sempre vista dalla villa e dal giardino; è la villeggiatura di una decente borghesia proprietaria, o anche, piú gozzanianamente . . . è una villa-rifugio dell'ultimo erede . . .' (In 'Pascoli, Gozzano, Montale e la poesia dell'oggetto', in *Il Verri* 4 (1958), 45, note 7.)
6 He explains the point as follows: 'Il rovello di Pascoli è tutto qui, nella volontà di superare i limiti di una fenomenologia empirica di partenza e nello scacco inconsapevole di chi vede riduplicati gli stessi limiti su scala gigante, nella dimensione degli anni-luce.' (op. cit., p.39.)
7 In *Con Guido Gozzano e altri poeti* (Bologna, 1944), p.73.
8 In *Poesie e prose*, p.235.
9 In *La letteratura della nuova Italia*, vol. VI (Bari), p.377.
10 In *Scrittori d'oggi*, vol. I (Bari, 1953), pp.3-13.
11 In *Guido Gozzano e Amalia Guglielminetti "Lettere d'amore"*, con pref. e note di S. Asciamprener (Garzanti, 1951), p.72. (Letter dated 11 December 1907.)
12 Ibid., pp.94, 95 (dated 30 March 1908).

13 In 'Lo svolgimento della lirica dannunziana', in *La Rassegna della letteratura italiana* 1-2 (1953), 8.

14 See his reference to D'Annunzio's 'superliquefatte parole' in 'Le signore che non mangiano le paste'.

15 In *Le lettere* (Rome, 1914), p.36.

16 Quoted by Moretti in *Il libro dei miei amici* (Milan, 1960), p.158.

17 One blatant witticism borrowed from Musset is the following image in 'La signorina Felicita': 'La luna sopra il campanile antico/ pareva un punto sopra un I gigante.' It derives from 'Ballade à la lune': 'C'était dans la nuit brune, – Sure le clocher jauni,/ La lune,/ comme un point sur un i.' Gozzano's irony resembles Musset's in being both gentle and highly civilized, even complacent.

18 H. Martin: *Guido Gozzano (1883-1916)* (Paris, 1968), p.136.

19 B. Porcelli: 'Gozzano e Maeterlinck, ovvero un caso di parassitismo letterario', in *Belfagor*, 6 (1969), 653-77. This article is now reproduced in *Gozzano, originalità e plagi* (Bologna, 1974), pp.27-64.

20 Antonielli notes in this regard that 'dal preromanticismo di Bernardin de Saint-Pierre fino al Prati, il Gozzano fa una sola sintesi sentimentale dell'età romantica, e tale sintesi la prende a oggetto della sua ironia.' (op. cit., p.14.)

21 One of the strangest characteristics of Gozzano's poetry noted by Montale is its disorganized eclecticism, so that 'spostando i suoi versi potresti proporne una migliore o diversa funzionalità, ma non sopprimerne il carattere.' (See his introduction to *Le poesie di Gozzano* Milan, 1960, p.11.)

22 In 'Solitudine e raccoglimenti dello spirito', from *Memorie e lagrime* (our italics).

23 See 'L'eredità ottocentesca di Gozzano e il suo nuovo linguaggio', in G. Mariani: *Poesia e tecnica nella lirica del Novecento* (Padua, 1958).

24 From 'La basilica'.

25 From 'Lo specchio'.

26 We use the word 'intelligence' here in a meaning akin to that employed by Baudelaire; for in his correspondence the French poet makes the following remark: 'Il y a longtemps que je dis que le poète est *souverainement* intelligent, qu'il est *l'intelligence* par excellence, – et que *l'imagination* est la plus *scientifique* des facultés, parce que seule elle comprend *l'analogie universelle*, ou ce qu'une religion mystique appelle *la correspondance*.' (Letter to Toussaud, 21 January 1856, see *Oeuvres complètes, Correspondance générale (1833-56)*, Conard, Paris, 1947, p.367.)

27 From 'Totò Merúmeni', in *I colloqui* (1911).

28 As Mariani explains, 'Betteloni era stato il primo poeta capace di svuotare dall'interno una situazione romantica pure in tutte le sue sfumature.' (op. cit., p.7.)

29 From the poem 'La via del rifugio', in the collection of that name published in 1907.

30 As a result, certain poems of his mature volumes appear to grow out of earlier ones contained in the *Poesie sparse*. One such instance is 'La via del rifugio' which is patterned on 'Convalescente', while at the more intimate level of poetic texture we can compare the following lines from 'Totò Merúmeni': '. . . In quel silenzio di chiostro e di caserma / vive Totò Merúmeni con la madre inferma,/ una prozia canuta ed uno zio demente!' with others from 'Un'altra risorta': 'Vivo in campagna, con una prozia,/ la madre inferma ed uno zio demente.'

31 From 'La via del rifugio'.

32 L. Mittner: 'L'espressionismo (Bari, 1965), p.31.

33 In fact, many of the objects listed here are still to be seen at Villa Meleto in Agliè which Gozzano also took as his model for Villa Amarena in 'La signorina Felicita'.

34 Gozzano's own view of his lyrical development was given in a letter he addressed to the Director of the periodical *Il Momento* and it is reproduced by Calcaterra and De Marchi in *Opere* (p.1209). In this letter he divided his definitive volume of verse, *I Colloqui* (1911), into three parts: *Il giovenile errore, Alle soglie* and *Il reduce*. Of these three stages he then remarks: 'Il giovenile errore: episodi di vagabondaggio sentimentale; Alle Soglie: adombrante qualche colloquio con la morte; Il Reduce: "reduce dall'Amore e dalla Morte, gli hanno mentito le due cose belle . . ." e rifletterà l'animo di chi superato ogni guaio fisico e morale, si rassegna alla vita sorridendo.'

35 The poem to which we refer is the well-known sonnet which begins:
Chiome d'argento fine, irte e attorte
Senz'arte intorno ad un bel viso d'oro. . .

36 *op. cit.*, p.19.

37 See Marvardi's analysis of this problem in 'Classicità della poesia ungarettiana', in *Letteratura*, 35-6, 94.

38 Quoted by De Castris, *op. cit.*, p.126.

39 See E. Paci: 'Ungaretti e l'esperienza della poesia', in *Letteratura*, 35-6, 90.

IV

1 Even Moretti idealizes Corazzini's lyrical presence and makes him the quintessence of the crepuscular movement by observing that 'nessuno avrebbe potuto contrastare l'idea ch'egli fosse il poeta puro, il poeta vero, che non deve aver passato i vent'anni'. (In *Il libro dei miei amici* Milan, 1960, p.132.)

2 See L. Fontana: 'Évolution poétique de S. Corazzini', in *La revue des études italiennes* (April-September, 1938), 176.

3 An interesting distinction between crepuscular inwardness and futurist materialism has been made by A. Momigliano, who notes that 'sono i crepuscolari i poeti puri, che ritraggono atomicamente se stessi; e i futuristi che ritraggono il mondo esterno, materiale'. (In 'Tendenze della lirica italiana dal Carducci ad oggi', in *La Nuova Italia*, 20 December 1934, pp.381-9.)

4 Fontana, op. cit., p.176.

5 M. Moretti: *Il libro dei miei amici*, p.127.

6 Borgese's denunciation is particularly cutting, for he writes: 'Contro la retorica dell'enfasi vien fuori la retorica ... dell'ingenuità e della semplicità. E, poiché non han nulla da cantare, ma sentono un veritiero bisogno di cantare, s'attaccano alle quisquilie, ai fiori di carta od alle cose buffe e malinconiche ch'erano di moda cinquanta o settant'anni fa. Si sono anche rimessi a idealizzare la tubercolosi, la quale – in quanto tubercolosi poetica – pareva ormai domata dal siero della gaia impostura stecchettiana. La ballata romantica s'intreccia con la delicata e sospirosa elegia di Cosimo Giorgieri-Contri: l'atmosfera sa di incenso e di acido fenico. Poiché il gran campo della nostra poesia fu mietuto con falci d'oro, essi indugiano sui margini della via spigolando i residui del romanticismo e la scorie del classicismo e contentandosi di capire in Pascoli le balbuzie, in D'Annunzio il *Poema paradisiaco*.' (In *La Stampa*, 10 September 1910.)

7 G. Titta Rosa, however, has little faith even in Corazzini's mature work and he characterizes him as follows: 'Corazzini è ... intero nell'alveo della temperie verbale del suo tempo, ed in essa si muove senza polemica; la parola sua è simile a quella altrui, tono e colore, e fare poesia non era dunque per lui cercare una parola diversa dalla comune, ma soltanto mettere in essa un accento proprio, un proprio stato d'animo'. (In *Poesia italiana del Novecento*, Siena, 1953, p.41.)

8 For a brief analysis of this theme in Corazzini's work, see A. Piromalli: 'Poetica e poesia di Sergio Corazzini', in *Saggi critici di storia letteraria* (Florence, 1967), p.154.

9 S. Corazzini: *Poesie edite e inedite*, a cura di Stefano Jacomuzzi, (Turin, 1968).

10 See *Vita e poesia di Sergio Corazzini* (Turin, 1949).

11 First published by E. Veo in the *Messaggero* (8 April 1928).

12 From 'Dolore' in *Le dolcezze* (1904).

13 This poem was written at Nocera in June 1906 during the poet's love-affair with a Danish girl named Sania. (Donini, op. cit., p.145.)

14 This poem entitled 'Partenza' first appeared in the *Rugantino* (14 September 1902).

15 From 'Un bacio', published in *Marforio* (29 November 1902.)

16 L. Baldacci: *I crepuscolari* (Turin, 1961), p.8.

17 From 'J'aime dans le temps', in *De l'angélus de l'aube à l'angélus du soir* (1898). Jammes himself noted an affinity between Corazzini's poetry and his own and encouraged the Italian poet to translate the above-mentioned collection of poems in a letter beginning 'Mon cher confrère et doux poète'. The contents of the letter are summed up in F.M. Martini: *Si sbarca a New York* (Milan, 1930), p.58.

18 The three sonnets entitled 'Amore e morte' appeared in the *Marforio* (1 February 1903). It may well be that the crepuscular poets took the cult of generic adjectives from Baudelaire, who in turn acquired it from Petrarch.

19 We find mention of blood in many of the poet's *juvenilia*, although strangely it dies away somewhat in his later period. See 'Il canto cieco', 'Giovanni delle bande nere', 'La chiesa', 'Il brindisi folle', and even the opening poem of *Dolcezze*, 'Il mio cuore'.

20 From 'Il bacio'.

21 From 'Lettera prima'.

22 Ibid.

23 From 'Dolore'.

24 Even Corazzini's contemporaries note his excessive love of ecclesiastical imagery and Donini (p.67) quotes the following epigram by A. Granelli dealing with the subject:

E Sergio Corazzini che sa tutte le chiès
e che senza quattrini sarà alla fin del mès.

25 From 'Campana'.

26 From 'Acque lombarde'.

27 From 'Giardini'.

28 See L. Anceschi, op. cit., in *Il Verri*, 4 (1958), 25.

29 In the *Piccolo libro inutile* we also find poems by A. Tarchiani. Corazzini's appear on pp.1-36 and number eight in all, three of which had already been published previously in various periodicals.

30 On the different approach of the more significant crepusculars from that of their predecessors Baldacci makes an interesting point when he observes that 'nei crepuscolari l'intento è del tutto diverso: si rischia la prosa magari, ma si vuole che il verso rinunci all'ultima sua ricchezza: quella di una musica precostituita' (op. cit., p.46).

31 In *De Baudelaire au surréalisme* (Paris, 1933), p.59.

32 Pius Servien: *Les rythmes comme introduction physique à l'esthétique*, (Paris, 1930), p.77.

33 When evaluating the lyric 'La morte di Tantalo' which Corazzini composed just before his death, Donini stresses the importance of its musical and symbolic qualities in the following way: 'Con questa poesia Sergio appartiene in pieno alla nuova lirica italiana. La tecnica, il linguaggio, la musica, e quell'ispirazione dove trapela il subconsciente, staccano nella mente *La morte di Tantalo* dai contemporanei crepuscolari e con un salto di vent'anni la pongono accanto *L'Isola* di Ungaretti'. (op. cit., p.202).

34 op. cit., p.179.

35 op. cit., in *La revue des études italiennes* (April-September, 1938), 194.

36 This poem has been attracting a good deal of attention lately, see L. Scorrano; 'Per "La morte di Tantalo" di Sergio Corazzini', in *Studi e problemi di critica testuale,* XI (1975), 188-210; F. Dueros: 'Rhétorique du pathétisme, Lire Corazzini', in *Lingua e stile*, 1 (1978), 59-87; A. Benvento: ' "La morte di Tantalo" di Sergio Corazzini', in *Otto/Novecento*, 4-5 (1977), 159; and F. Livi: 'Saggio sulla poesia di Sergio Corazzini', in *Critica letteraria*, IV (1979), 674-731.

V

1 Titta Rosa states, in fact, that 'fare arte su una realtà morale vissuta, slargandola in valori universali, fu indubbiamente il proposito e l'ambizione dei migliori vociani.' (In *Poesia italiana del Novecento*, Siena, 1953, p.48, note.)

2 Campana does not appear to have contributed at all to *La Voce* while it was under Prezzolini's editorship, even though the latter claims to have received verses from him in 1911. (See *Il tempo della Voce*, Florence-Milan, 1960, p.591.) A poetic fragment by Campana does, however, appear in the *Voce letteraria* (1915, VII, 14, p.902), although it is not listed in the index published by Scalia in *Lacerba-La Voce (1914-16)*, (Turin, 1961), pp.615-27. He also published three poems in *Lacerba* ('L'incontro di Regolo', 'Piazza Sarzano', 'Sogno di prigione'), despite the fact that a somewhat ambiguous

letter addressed to Papini and reported by Falqui (see *Canti orfici*, 4th ed., 1952, pp.342-3) seems to suggest that he had withheld his collaboration. So, while factually nothing could be more tenuous than his links with *La Voce*, aesthetically he tends to represent its avant-garde thought.

3 See Daria Banfi Malaguzzi: *Il primo Rebora, 22 lettere inedite (1905-13)* (Milan, 1964), p.20.

4 Ibid,. p.50.

5 See P. Rebora: 'Clemente Rebora e la sua formazione esistenzialistica', in *Humanitas* 2 (1959), 124. The reference is to Iacopone da Todi (d.1306), a fervent mediaeval writer, who often mingled profane and passionate elements with religious ones in his hymns.

6 In *Clemente Rebora*, iconografia a cura di Vanni Scheiwiller con una nota di E. Montale, (Domodossola, 1959), p.6.

7 In a note prefaced to the *Canti anonimi* in *Poesie* (Florence, 1947). A more complete edition of Rebora's poetry is *Le poesie* (1913-57) (Milan, 1961), although even this is not all-inclusive.

8 From 'L'egual vita diversa urge intorno'. For convenience the titles of Rebora's early poems are taken from the 1947 edition since they are unaccountably omitted from the 1961 edition.

9 Ibid.

10 From 'Città'.

11 Costanzo sums up Rebora's traditionalism as follows: 'L'uomo di Rebora vuole riscattare il mondo dal caos; vuole ristabilirvi, per cosí dire, una prospettiva, un ordine logico e poetico, una gerarchia di valori; ma senza sovvertirlo, rispettando anzi scrupolosamente il suo esserci *dato* . . .' (In *Studi critici*, Rome, 1955, p.9.)

12 The point is emphasized by H. de Bouillane de Lacoste in his critical edition of the *Illuminations* (Paris, 1949), where he notes: 'Nous dirons quelquefois "Les Illuminations" pour la commodité ou la correction grammaticale; mais, en principe, il ne faut pas mettre l'article français devant ce mot anglais . . . Traduisons: Enluminures.' (p.7 note.)

13 From 'Quassú'.

14 See G. Bachelard: *La poétique de l'espace*, p.178.

15 In C. Betocchi: 'Considerazioni di oggi sulla poesia di Clemente Rebora', in *L'Approdo* (April-June, 1952), 82.

16 M. Guglielminetti: *Clemente Rebora* (Milan, 1961), p.100 (note 46).

17 Eight were published by M. Marchione in *La Fiera letteraria* (27 September 1959), and then republished in her book *L'imagine tesa* (Rome, 1960), together with two which had already appeared elsewhere (see pp.245-8). They are now reprinted as (*9 poesie per una lucciola*) in *Le poesie (1913-1957)* (Milan, 1961), since IX and X have been fused together.

18 Quoted by Marchione, op. cit., p.73. See also C. Rebora, *Lettere* (Rome, 1976), vol. 1, p.507.

19 Ibid., p.75. Also in C. Rebora, *Lettere*, 1, p.627.

20 Quoted by Marchione, *op. cit.*, p.64. See also C. Rebora, *Lettere*, 1, p.441.

21 On the transcendent rôle of the city in Rebora, see D. Valli, 'Il dramma esistenziale di Rebora', in *Annali dell'università di Lecce*, Facoltà di lettere e filosofia e di magistero, vol. I, 1963-4, Milelli, Lecce, pp.93-122.

22 In 'Scienza vince natura'.

23 From 'E giunge l'onda ma non giunge il mare'.

24 From 'Al tempo che la vita era inesplosa'.

25 For the categorization of Tesauro's and Gracián's conceits, see L. Bethell: 'Gracián, Tesauro, and the nature of metaphysical wit', in *Northern Miscellany* (1953), 1. The works to which he particularly refers are E. Tesauro: *Il cannocchiale aristotelico* (1654) and B. Gracián: *Agudeza y arte de ingenio* (1642).

26 For the manner and influence of C. Dossi, see E. Gennarini: *La scapigliatura milanese* (Naples, 1961); also A. Romanò: *Il secondo romanticismo lombardo* (Milan, 1958). The most important book produced on Dossi's work, however, is D. Isella: *Lingua e stile di Carlo Dossi* (Milan-Naples, 1958).

27 S. Gamberini: *Poeti metafisici e cavalieri in Inghilterra* (Florence, 1959), p.40.

28 'Tre note su Clemente Rebora', in *Astrazione e realtà (Rusconi & Paolazzi, 1960), p.203.*

29 From 'Curriculum vitae'.

30 Carlo Bo: 'Rievocazione di Rebora', in *Il Verri* 5 (1959), 46.

31 The most extensive study of Rebora's language has been made by F. Bandolini, 'Elementi di espressionismo linguistico in Rebora', in *Ricerche sulla lingua poetica contemporanea*, Quaderni del circolo filologico linguistico padovano, presentazione di G. Folena (Padua, 1966). For two other interesting studies see G. Contini, *Esercizi di lettura* (Florence, 1939), pp.1-17 and M. Marchione, 'Linguaggio reboriano', in *Lingua nostra* XX (1959), 74-8.

32 V. Scheiwiller's *Clemente Rebora*, p.9.

33 See *Esercizi di lettura*, (1947 edition), p.7.

34 From 'O poesia' (our italics).

35 A. Russi: 'L'esperienza lirica di Clemente Rebora', in *Paragone* 30, (1952), 47; now reprinted in *Poesia e realtà* (Florence, 1962), pp.285-305.

36 See U. Marvardi: *La poesia religiosa del Petrarca volgare* (Rome, 1961). Marvardi sums up religious feeling in poetry as follows: 'La poesia religiosa è ... infinita apertura, libera comunicazione con i fratelli, fedeltà alla creazione divina, ordine cosmico e non arbitrario di una invertita personalità, funzione spirituale e non intellettualismo funzionale, e, dal punto di vista etico, non anticipazione di un infinito giudizio provvidenziale sul mondo, ma figurazione della libertà come divina provvidenza.' (p.89.)

37 In C. Pariani: *Vite non romanzate di Dino Campana scrittore e Evaristo Boncinelli scultore* (Florence, 1938), p.47.

38 O. Macrí: *Caratteri e figure della poesia italiana contemporanea* (Florence, 1956), p.30.

39 In *Esercizi di lettura* (Florence, 1939), p.26.

40 Nevertheless, even kaleidoscopic colour-effects often have hidden meanings for Campana, for an analysis of which see F.J. Jones: 'Origine e significato degli schema coloristici di Dino Campana', in *Poesia e critica* 8-9, (1966), 165-95.

41 See *Canti orfici e altri scritti*, a cura di E. Falqui (Vallecchi, 1952) (4th ed.) p.295. All quotations are taken from this edition.

42 'Barche amarrate', in *Canti orfici*, p.95.

43 Pariani, op.cit., p.17.

44 In *La Fiera letteraria*, (26 August 1928).

45 In *Taccuinetto faentino* (Florence, 1960), p.25.

46 In 'Uomo sin dai primevi torbidi', in *Canti orfici*, p.193.

47 In 'Sulle Montagne', *Canti orfici*, p.211.

48 *Canti orfici*, p.28.

49 In *Cahiers du Sud* (1954), No. 323, 16.

50 The usefulness of Carducci's method of image-suspension was always borne in mind by Campana and he once referred to it in the following way: 'Non vi sembra che un cafonismo molto carducciano possa essere una base solida per i miei giuochi di equilibrio?' (*Canti orfici*, p.290.) But at the same time he was well aware of the limits of Carducci's art and wrote the following devastating criticism of his work: 'Tutto è preparazione pittorica ... Già Leopardi vide 'quelle dipinte mura e il sol che nasce da romita campagna ... Quella loggia colà volta agli estremi raggi del dí ...' Ma Carducci, rozzo toscano, non arriva alla purità della vita campestre ...' (Ibid., p.277). With regard to D'Annunzio, on the other hand, he is even more perceptive and he comments on his decadent, sensual classicism as follows: 'Nessuno come lui sa invecchiare una donna o un paesaggio.' (p.284)

51 The influence of Novalis is of a general nature, but that of Nietzsche is more specific and has been examined by E. Falqui in 'Per una storia del rapporto tra Nietzsche e Campana', in *La Fiera letteraria* (14 June 1953). Similarly, for an assessment of Heine's influence, see E. Falqui: *Per una cronistoria dei 'Canti orfici'* (Vallecchi), p.111. A manuscript copy of parts of two of Heine's poems written in Campana's handwriting has been discovered and identified.

52 The problem of Campana's knowledge of foreign languages is considered by Falqui in *Per una cronistoria dei 'Canti orfici'*, pp.109-11. He deduces that his French, though faulty, was adequate for the purposes of literary assessment, and his German, while less adequate, was still sufficiently good for the poet to offer himself to Novaro, then editor of the *Riviera ligure*, as a translator. His English, by contrast, remains a completely unknown quantity. Falqui points out several discrepancies in his citations

of Whitman (p.36), from which we suspect that he had a better oral than written knowledge of the language. This kind of familiarity is perhaps only to be expected from an Italian who had travelled around Europe with a circus and lived for a time in Latin America. One instance of his misquoting – evidently from memory – is his replacement of the world 'glory' with 'flour' in the phrase 'They were the glory of the race of rangers'. Both the misspelling and the substitution again argue for an oral rather than a written knowledge of English, yet amply justify his remark to Novaro that 'conosco abbastanza bene quasi cinque lingue' (p.109). See also a quatrain in English, possibly composed by Campana and quoted by F. Ravagli in *Fascicolo marradese inedito*, Giunti / Bemporad / Marzocco, (Florence, 1972). The quatrain reads:

By what fast heap of snow
Are hid my springtimes (*sic*) roses?
How shall remembrance know
Where buried hope reposes? (pp.17-18)

I have corrected Ravagli's mistaken reading 'hiel' for 'hid' in line 2. If these lines are indeed by Campana, they show an advanced knowledge of English syntax.

53 M. Costanzo: 'Cultura e poesia di Campana', in *Studi critici* (Rome, 1955), p.111.

54 From 'Dualismo' in *Canti orfici*, p.85.

55 In *La Fiera letteraria*, (26 August 1928).

56 We have, however, to draw a distinction between the physical grace of Aphrodite and the 'cultural' grace of Campana's women. In fact, with him mature, experiential beauty is at a premium and physical beauty and mere sexuality for its own sake largely to be discounted. For instance, 'la Ruffiana' in 'La Notte', one of Campana's typically mature and baroque beauties, is described as having a 'testa di sacerdotessa orientale' and, as such, is fully capable of initiating the poet into the orphic mysteries of life; but the 'ancella ingenua e avida' whom he seduces is relegated to the background as 'la sacerdotessa dei piaceri sterili' (See *Canti orfici*, p.15), largely because the former but not the latter bears 'il peso di tutto il sogno umano'.

57 From 'La creazione'.

58 From 'Pampa' in *Canti orfici*, pp.97 & 100.

59 This explains why he notes in 'Storie' that 'L'arte è espressione. Ciò farebbe supporre una realtà. L'Italia è come fu sempre: teologica.' (*Canti orfici*, p.291) In his view Italian art is too rationalistic, too abstractly speculative, to be capable of depicting the type of transfigured, orphic vision to which he aspires.

60 From 'La Notte', in *Canti orfici*, p.21.

61 M. Apollonio: *Letteratura dei contemporanei* (Brescia, 1957), p.207.

62 *Canti orfici*, p.60.

63 R. Lalou: *Vers une alchimie lyrique* (Paris, 1927), p.102.

64 From 'Il ritorno', in *Canti orfici*, p.59.

65 Although the sources making up Campana's orphic background have not yet been thoroughly examined and assessed, Costanzo nevertheless assures us that his adaptation of traditional orphic lore to modern lyrical requirements is highly original. (See 'Ulississimo o orfismo?', in *La Fiera letteraria*, 14 June 1953.) To support this claim the critic compares him with other orphic adepts at the turn of the century and writes: 'Si pensi, infine, al francese Le Cardonnel, i cui *Orphica* (1905-8) nulla hanno a che vedere con gli *Orfici* di Campana; e sono semmai su una linea piú ortodossa e tradizionale di "orfismo" ... Dal francese, ad ogni modo, poté aver notizia dall'amico Binazzi, a proposito del quale sarà bene ricordare un "canto orfico" che è già stato segnalato da Cordiè, 1946, ed è certo anteriore al 1913 ...' (p.6, note). For an analysis of the possible influence of Le Cardonnel and Binazzi on Campana, see my previously mentioned article in *Poesia e critica* 8-9. A line which seems to characterize the modern component in Le Cardonnel's orphism is one which was quoted by G.P. Lucini in *Poesia,* (November, 1908), 8-10. It reads as follows:

'Un grand coq ...
Lancera sa fanfare rauque à l'heure rouge.'

Its orphic overtones may well be reproduced by Campana in 'Giardino autunnale' where redness and a fanfare announce the dying away of the last embers of life. However, Campana's 'heure rouge' is normally sunset, not dawn, as is the case in Le Cardonnel's image.

66 The expression is frequently used in 'La Notte', see *Canti orfici*, pp.16, 17, 26.

67 See G. Gerola: *Dino Campana* (Florence, 1955), p.82.

68 Nearly all Campana's women are examples of baroque beauty and this is why they fit so well into their surroundings. Moreover, they are all daughters of the Mediterranean, as the following evocation will show: '. . . sulla via le perfide fanciulle brune mediterranee, brunite d'ombra e di luce, si bisbigliano all'orecchio al riparo delle ali teatrali e pare fuggano cacciate verso qualche inferno in quell'esplosione di gioia barocca . . .' (See 'Crepuscolo mediterraneo', in *Canti orfici*, p.116.)

69 *Canti orfici*, p.20.

70 In *Aurelia*, 111.

71 In an early version of the poem found among Campana's notebooks her sensuality is perhaps subservient to her priestly function and she is described as 'la regina dei sogni'. (See 'Montagna – La chimera', in *Canti orfici*, pp.250-1.) But, on the other hand, her disembodiment by immersion into her surroundings is not achieved in this fragment and her overall presence is closer to the romantic dream than to Campana's own mature sphere of a 'contingent eternity', peopled by his 'Chimere'.

72 See *Fusées*, X.

73 A. Pellegrini: *Novecento tedesco* (Messina-Milan, 1942), p.123.

74 See W.A. Strauss, *Descent and return. The Orphic Myth in Modern Literature* (Cambridge, Mass., 1971), chapter V, especially p.164.

75 See Pariani, op. cit., p.25.

76 For further details see my article in *Poesia e critica* 8-9. When the alchemists put their materials in the sealed pot of Hermes the sequence of colour changes was as follows: black (putrefaction), yellow (transition), red (salvation). In clear contrast, Campana prefers the reverse sequence: red, yellow, white, with black being reserved to indicate undifferentiated existence, which he calls 'la sopravvivenza nella Morte' (see Pariani, p.65). Thus in his colour-pattern green represents reality; red is transitional, since it represents in Paracelsus's view the colour of the philosopher's stone, the source of mediation between life and death; yellow is a *tabula rasa* stage of 'fertile' aridity; while white definitely marks a first stage of orphic transcendence. To create further elements of his contingent eternity the poet then immerses his orphic vision in powerful olfactory or auditory images. For other variations on alchemistic symbolic practices which may have affected Campana, see F. Portal: *Les couleurs symboliques* (Paris, 1837), and H.J. Sheppard: 'Colour symbolism in the alchemical opus', in *Scientia* XI (1964), 232-6.

77 See Charles Henri: *Le cercle chromatique* (Paris, 1888).

78 See P. Bigongiari, op. cit., pp.15-18. An interesting article written on the implications of orphic colour is H.B. Chipp: 'Orphism and color theory', in *Art Bulletin* (March, 1958), 62-7. Chipp quotes Delaunay as saying: 'I played with colors as one would express oneself in music by a fugue of colored varied phrases.' (Taken from F. Gilles de la Tourette: *Robert Delaunay* Paris, 1950, p.37.) Like Delaunay, Campana seems to have believed in the predominance of colour over form and his colours are far more distinct than his linear features. On the other hand, the futurists claimed that Delaunay's orphism derived from their aesthetics and in an article entitled 'I futuristi plagiati in Francia' U. Boccioni notes: 'L'Orphisme – diciamolo senz'altro – non è che una elegante mascheratura dei principi fondamentali della pittura futurista. Questa nuova tendenza . . . dimostra semplicemente quale profitto abbiano saputo trarre dalla nostra prima esposizione futurista a Parigi i nostri colleghi francesi.' (In *Archivi del futurismo*, p.148)

79 Links with the real are, however, cleverly insinuated into this dematerialized tableau and the sounds of the city and even the trumpet's blast are on the poet's own admission real phenomena. He accounts for the latter, for instance, by noting that 'c'è una caserma vicino', while the Boboli gardens are themselves insufficiently remote from the city for its bustle not to be heard in the distance. (See *Canti orfici*, p.307.)

80 The phrase appears in *Canti orfici*, p.314. A study has been made of two versions of the poem in this sense by G. Bonalumi, who shows that in the final version the lyrical effect is enhanced by 'l'eliminazione di quanto di vago e di astratto pesava nella prima'. (*Cultura e poesia di Campana,* Florence (1955), p.123.)

81 In *Das Buch der Bilder*, (1906), a second and enlarged edition of the original work published in 1902.

82 Pariani, op. cit., p.61.

VI

1 See F. Flora: *Dal romanticismo al futurismo* (Piacenza, 1921), p.204.

2 *La Voce*, (24 April 1913), 1062.

3 Ibid., (May, 1913), 1070.

4 We even find the same claim being made in *Il meridiano di Roma* (14 March 1937), III-IV. Here again he asserts that 'I due primi libri, *Fiale* e *Armonia in grigio et in silenzio*, portano una data che non è priva di importanza storica: anno 1903. Essi segnano dunque non solo una precedenza assoluta sulla poesia crepuscolare del Corazzini e del Gozzano, ma stabiliscono anche inequivocabilmente il preciso punto di distacco della nuova poesia, dalla poesia della triade Carducci, Pascoli, D'Annunzio' (p.III).

5 See Ravegnani's introduction to *Manoscritto nella bottiglia* (Milan, 1954), p.XVI. Even so, opinions differ somewhat on this point and Baldacci, for instance, takes the opposite view: 'La poesia di Govoni, nel quadro di quella crepuscolare, è uno dei fatti piú cospicui.' (In *I crepuscolari*, ed. RAI, 1961, p.66.)

6 From 'Ventagli giapponesi: Paesaggio'.

7 In *Le Fiale* (our italics).

8 From 'Le peonie', in *Gli Aborti* (1907).

9 From 'Città di provincia', in *Gli Aborti*.

10 From 'Cucina di campagna', in *Fuochi d'artifizio* (our italics).

11 From poem XIII, in *Armonia in grigio et in silenzio*.

12 Thus G. Petronio observes: 'Basterebbe confrontare le domeniche del Corazzini con quelle del Govoni a sentire come in questo sull'unità sentimentale prevalgono le singole immagini che sgretolano la poesia e la rendono frammentaria, mentre nel Corazzini prevale un sentimento animatore che fonde in sé le diverse immagini in una sola unitaria impressione.' (In *Poeti del nostro secolo*, 1, in *Leonardo*, rassegna bibliografica (1935), 149.)

13 See C. Varese: 'La poesia di Govoni', in *Nuova antologia*, (May, 1962), 51-60.

14 In *Da Tommaseo a Ungaretti*, p.49.

15 From *Poesie elettriche*.

16 'Paesi', in *Poesie elettriche*.

17 See C. Govoni: 'La caccia all'usignolo', in *Il teatro futurista sintetico* (Biblioteca teatrale dell'Istituto, n.d.), pp.82-3.

18 From Section 11, lines 92-102.

19 G. Boine: *Frantumi, seguiti da Plausi e botte* (Florence, 1918), p.203.

20 From 'La corsa', in *Canzoni a bocca chiusa*.

21 In 'O primavera'.

22 In 'Plastico di Roma'.

23 In 'La cava delle sensazioni: cinquantennio di poesia govoniana', in *Paragone* 40 (1955), 41.

24 Lyric LXV.

25 Lyric XXXIX.

26 A part of this collection was published by Ravegnani in his edition of Govoni's *Poesie* (Milan, 1961). The remainder, however, is still unpublished and this applies also to a part of *I canti del puro folle*, a later collection from which Ravegnani again reproduces a selection. Some additional poems were brought out in *La ronda di notte*, (Milan, 1966) and in *Il vino degli anni* (Rome, 1979), but a vast quantity of unpublished verse still remains.

27 From 'Nuovo lamento su mio figlio'.

28 Lyric III.

29 In *Da Tommaseo a Ungaretti*, p.131.

VII

1 A. Borlenghi: 'Sulla poesia di Umberto Saba', in *Poesia* VII (1947), 92.

2 G. Debenedetti: *Saggi critici* (Milan, 1952). This work contains two important essays on Saba entitled 'La poesia di Saba' and 'Per Saba ancora'.

3 M. Marcazzan: 'La poesia di Umberto Saba', in *Humanitas* 6, (1946), 621.

4 From 'La bugiarda'.

5 From 'Soldato in prigione'.

6 The literary pressures converging on Saba's sensibility were many and heterogeneous, and a number of them will be dealt with later. Among the poets influencing him according to the critics were Petrarch, Metastasio, Parini, Leopardi, Pascoli, D'Annunzio, Ungaretti and Montale. From this list is becomes clear that the dominant impact on his mind was the highroad of the Italian lyric from its virtual inception to modern times. For a detailed analysis of Saba's literary sources, see E. Caccia. *Lettura e storia di Saba* (Milan, 1967), Part 1, Chapter 11.

7 An unpublished letter by Saba to Mr. B.J. Morse emphasizes the poet's predilection for the works of Anatole France in the following way : 'L'anno nuovo mi ha sempre fatto un poco paura, come facevano ad Anatole France i quartieri vuoti che visitava per prenderne uno a pigione. Egli popolava cioè coll'immaginazione dei giorni e delle notti avvenire le stanze che la sorella di Bergeret studiava invece da un punto di vista pratico. Mi è sempre piaciuto Anatole France (che oggi i giovani odiano); e a lei? Forse non è stato un grandissimo scrittore, ma nei suoi libri, in ogni parola dei suoi libri, si condensano 2000 anni di civiltà. Per questo oggi fa malinconia leggerlo.'

8 See R. Lalou: *Histoire de la littérature contemporaine*, Vol. I (Paris, 1947), p.96.

9 *La storia e cronistoria del Canzoniere* (Milan, 1948).

10 See Marcazzan, op. cit., in *Humanitas* (1946), 622.

11 From *L'amorosa spina*, 6.

12 *Quello che resta da fare ai poeti* (Trieste, 1959).

13 Ibid., pp.14-15.

14 This point is confirmed by B. Pento's remark that there is no correlation between Saba's conversational tone and that of the crepusculars, precisely because of their differences of spiritual attitude: 'Della quotidianità diaristica si alimentava in quel primo decennio anche la poesia dei crepuscolari. Ma la realtà morbidamente estenuata di costoro è cosa tanto diversa dalla realtà palpitante e piena, dolorante e gaia, virile sempre, del poeta istriano.' (In 'Galleria degli scrittori italiani: Umberto Saba', in *La Fiera letteraria* (5 November 1950), p.4.)

15 In *Storia e cronistoria del Canzoniere*, p.66.

16 From 'La casa della mia nutrice', in *Poesia dell'adolescenza e giovanile* (our italics).

17 For a study of Saba's style, see G. Bàrberi Squarotti: 'Appunti in margine allo stile di Saba', in *Astrazione e realtà*, ed. cit., pp.123-43.

18 G. Titta Rosa actually defines his style as follows: 'Il suo linguaggio, considerato dal lato tecnico, nei suoi elementi di tradizione, è spiccamente letterario; ma se parole e frasi e costrutti si richiamano a quell'origine, i risultati sono a-letterari, e infine antitradizionali.' (In *Poesia italiana del Novecento*, Siena, 1953, p.86.)

19 For Saba's own views on psycho-analysis in art, see 'Poesia e psicanalisi', in *La Fiera letteraria* (15 September 1946). In this article (in reality a letter in reply to Croce) he rejects philosophy as an element in lyricism and distinguishes between the poet who is 'egocentrico' and the philosopher who is 'egocosmico'. Hence, while the former uses emotive means for the examination of the inner world of the spirit, the latter bases himself on rational and almost wholly self-conscious procedures. Psycho-analysis, therefore, like every other branch of natural philosophy must be limited in art to the rôle of producing a critique of the emotions. See also *Scorciatoie e raccontini* (Milan, 1946), p.136.

20 See preface to *Epigrafe ultime prose* (Milan, 1959), p.11.

21 From 'Meditazione'.

22 See I.A. Richards: *Principles of literary criticism* (Routledge & Kegan Paul, 1961) (reprint). Richards distinguishes two types of language in a way which has a bearing on Saba's style. He notes: 'A statement may be used for the sake of *reference* true or false,

which it causes. This is the *scientific* use of language. But it may also be used for the sake of effects in emotion and attitude produced by the reference it occasions. This is the *emotive* use of language' (pp.267-8). Saba's language normally oscillates between these two extremes, and when it is reduced to a kind of *procès-verbal* it naturally loses much of its emotional impact. When, however, he establishes an emotional or imaginative rather than a factual discourse, he creates a psychological hinterland against which the various tensions of his personal existence are unfolded and set in equilibrium in a thoroughly satisfying lyrical manner.

23 From *Autobiografia*, 9.

24 From *Autobiografia*, 2.

25 From *Autobiografia*, 12.

26 From *L'Uomo*.

27 See C. Varese: *Cultura letteraria contemporanea* (Pisa, 1951), p.304.

28 Saba married Carolina Wölfler who died in November 1956. They had one daughter, Linuccia.

29 In this regard, Saba wrote a letter to Vittorio Sereni which states: 'Tu sai che la mia concezione della poesia è un'altra: niente letteratura (voglio dire il meno possibile; ogni nave ha bisogno, per galleggiare, di un po' di zavorra); molta vita, niente trasposizioni su piani astratti, molto invece di quella "grande immensa rara cosa" che è la sublimazione. . .' (Quoted by Nora Baldi in *Il paradiso di Saba* Milan, 1958, p.50.)

30 See F. Portinari: *Umberto Saba* (Milan, 1963), who emphasizes the influence of the psychologist Otto Weininger in the Trieste of the early nineteen hundreds and mentions the first translation of *Sesso e carattere* (1912). A knowledge of psychological procedures seems to have been widespread in the city at the time, perhaps more than elsewhere in Italy; and these no doubt are accounted for by its close links with Austria. Saba himself acknowledges his debt to Weininger and others in the *Cronistoria* and he pays the following tribute to Dr. Weiss: 'Tutti sanno che il dott. Weiss era un psicanalitico, anzi il "leader" dei pochi, vergognosamente pochi, psicanalisti italiani . . . È chiaro, attraverso la dedica, che il piccolo Berto è rinato durante una cura psicanalitica, il cui procedimento consiste nel rimuovere, o cercare di rimuovere, il velo d'amnesia che copre gli avvenimenti della primissima infanzia' (p.202).

31 See *Poesie* (Milan, 1934), *Rime di vario argomento*, X11, p.763: 'Quel labbro che le rose han colorito/ Molle si sporge e tumidetto in fuore/ Spinto per arte, mi cred'io d'Amore,/ A fare ai baci insidioso invito.'

32 From *Fanciulle*, 1.

33 From *Fanciulle*, 5.

34 From *Fanciulle*, 8.

35 From *Fanciulle*, 6.

36 See A. Frattini: 'Lo svolgimento del Canzoniere di Saba', in *Da Tommaseo a Ungaretti*, ed. cit., p.135.

37 Quarantotti Gambini's article appeared in *L'Italia letteraria* (25 May 1935) under the title of 'Poesia di Umberto Saba'. Saba himself quotes from it in the *Cronistoria*, see p.195.

38 op. cit., p.102.

39 In *Ultime cose*.

40 'Frutta e erbaggi', in *Parole*.

41 Saba acknowledged an extra-literary influence from Penna upon *Parole* in his *Cronistoria* (p.227); but, as Portinari insists, the chronology of the two poets' works shows who was the master and who the pupil.

42 'Interno' in *Poesie* (Florence, 1939). Saba saw the manuscript long before publication, so that an influence is not excluded by the chronological precedence of *Parole*.

43 See 'Ragioni di Umberto Saba', in *Solaria* 5, (1928), 29-34. This article and a previous one appearing in *Il Quindicinale* 10, (1926), 1, are now reprinted in *Sulla poesia* (Milan, 1976).

44 Some of the poems of *Uccelli* also appear posthumously in *Epigrafe ultime prose*.

45 See preface to *Uccelli Quasi un racconto* (Milan, 1951), p.11.

46 For further details of this episode, see Portinari, op. cit., pp.209 et seq.

47 Quoted by Portinari, op. cit., pp.226-7.

48 For Saba's affection for Almansi, see also his preface to Almansi's poems now reproduced in *Prose* (Milan, 1964), pp.676-86.

49 In preface to *Quasi un racconto*, p.35.

VIII

1 In fact, Cardarelli seems to have adopted by turns either a position of incomprehension or one of outright hostility to hermeticism. He notes, for instance, at one stage that 'la letteratura giovane è troppo difficile per me, la poesia pura mi confonde . . . e vorrei perfino dire che dove si adora Ungaretti io non posso esistere . . .' (Op. comp., Milan, 1962, p.678.) Then at another he becomes harsher, more polemical, in tone, and says in regard to the same poet: 'Siamo nemici. Non come uomini, s'intende . . . Come poeta, però, non l'ho mai avuto in considerazione.' (See 'Inchiesta sulla poesia contemporanea', in *Letterature moderne* (1956), 564-6.)

2 See 'Il sole a picco', in *L'Italiano* (1930), but now reproduced in *Scrittori del Novecento* (Le monnier, 1946), p.59.

3 He observes, for instance, that Cecchi's *prosa d'arte* criticism is wholly descriptive and uninterpretative, so when examining his views on Benelli, Chiesa, Panzini and others, he states: 'Che cosa vi ha colpito piú di tutto in questi articoli? Senza dubbio, una insistenza, una progressività addirittura paradossale di rifrazioni fantastiche sopra un punto statico di conoscenza . . . Insolubilità e contraddizione di una conoscenza che non oltrepassa la sua fase descrittiva, *inesplicata*.' (In 'Retorica', in Op. comp., p.993.)

4 Op. comp., p.65.

5 In 'Idea della morte', Op. comp., p.94.

6 See 'Memento', especially the following lines: 'Il mal è nella nostra fantasia/ che perfetto e mirabile si finge/ ogni evento,/ è nell'ansiosa attesa/ del giorno beato,/ del fortunato incontro/ che poi ci disinganna.'

7 See 'Umore di Socrate' in *Solitario in Arcadia* (Milan, 1947), Op. comp., pp.492-3.

8 Op. comp., p.41.

9 Nietzsche, in fact, sums up the Promethean tendency implicit in romanticism in the following words: 'I myself am the *fatum* and, throughout eternity, it is I who condition existence'. (*Werke*, Naumann, Leipzig, 1899-1901, vol. XII, p.399.) Cardarelli, however, in his fable 'Un'uscita di Zarathustra' denounces such solipsist attitudinizing by contrasting the human condition with that of the God Apollo: 'Ogni forma staglia nella tua luce, si avanza verso me in un'aria di solitudine e di estraneità che atterrisce. Il tuo mondo è splendido e inaccessibile. L'uomo troverebbe l'oscurità e la follia se si ostinasse nell'infantile desiderio di descriverlo quale appare. Io credo che l'unico modo di emularti, o Sole, sarebbe, alla nostra maniera, di costruire dei templi.' (Op. comp., p.83.) The construction of temples here is symbolic, it seems, of the propounding of a *religio* or ethical system binding together the whole of mankind. A similar message is to be found in Foscolo's 'Dei sepolcri'.

10 In *Saggezza*, Op. comp., p.64.

11 See P. Bigongiari: 'L'oggetto come occasione in Vincenzo Cardarelli', in *Poesia italiana del Novecento*, p.80.

12 Op. comp., p.41.

13 In a letter addressed to 'Il critico letterario dell'"Osservatore Romano" ' appearing in *Lettere non spedite* (1946). (See Op. comp., p.702.)

14 For the deep love which Cardarelli felt from his early childhood for distance and solitude, see the opening sentence of 'Villa Tarantola in *Il sole a picco* (1929): 'Fin da ragazzo ho amato le distanze e la solitudine.' It is also to be noted that the very title of this collection of reminiscences is a symbolic allusion to the mature state of adulthood represented by high noon in summer.

15 See Op. comp., p.691. In addition, the poet here defines 'enormi' as 'abnormi', an idea which is equally linked with that of man's essential 'superfluità'.

16 B. Romani particularly emphasizes the elegiac nature of his poetry and speaks admiringly of 'quella straordinaria facoltà di Cardarelli di risolvere in elegia le sue descrizioni e le sue fantasie.' (In *Cardarelli,* Padua, 1943, p.54.)

17 A. Gargiulo: *Letteratura italiana del Novecento* (Florence, 1958), p.439; (1st ed. 1940).

18 In 'Il mio paese', Op. comp., p.181.

19 Contini point out that '. . . la poesia di Cardarelli è un repertorio, una storiografia d'idee fisse.' (In *Esercizi di lettura,* Florence, 1947, p.33.).

20 'Non sono vittorioso che in certe fulminee ricapitolazioni.' (Op. comp., p.41.)

21 Op. comp., p.45.

22 From 'Passato'.

23 From 'Attesa'.

24 From 'Amore'.

25 From 'Passaggi'.

26 From 'Rimorso'.

27 See *Mon coeur mis à nu,* XXX.

28 Op. comp., p.79.

29 See, for example, *Fusées*, III.

30 In 'Parole all'orecchio' in *Solitario in Arcadia* he reflects generally on this question and gives a schematized answer:
Relazioni:
genio sofistico – genio musicale
genio morale – stile. (Op. comp., p.467.)

31 From 'Tristezza'.

32 Mme Tison-Braun sums up the position of Barrès by pointing out in the first place that 'un homme sans traditions ne peut être guidé que par ses propres intérêts' and in the second that 'le moi individuel n'existe que comme reflet du moi collectif, puisqu'il n'est que la race incarnée et devenue consciente d'elle-même.' (See M. Tison-Braun: *La crise de l'humanisme Vol. I, Paris, 1955, pp.168-9.)* To this Barrès would himself add an atavistic note, saying: 'Ma pensée ne peut se mouvoir que selon certaines nécessités physiques, discernibles ou non, qui sont en grande partie lorraines.' (In *Mes cahiers* Vol. III, Paris, 1931, p.270.) Cardarelli would no doubt accept the idea of 'l'âme nationale' but would avoid the obtuse kind of provincialism resulting from cultural inbreeding and the narrow tradition of one's native heath.

33 From 'Partenza mattutina'.

34 From 'Ajace'.

35 Cardarelli describes the paternalism of Russian Communism in his *Viaggio d'un poeta in Russia* (1954): '. . . tutto è logico in Russia e arbitrario nello stesso modo. Logico in quanto si può spiegare il comunismo russo storicamente e psicologicamente, come fenomeno nazionale, a dispetto delle ideologie. Arbitrario per le conseguenze che se ne vorrebbero trarre.' (See Op. comp., p.844.)

36 In 'Impressioni', Op. comp., p.46.

37 From 'La morte dell'uomo', Op. comp., p.61.

38 Mario Luzi stresses the breadth of Cardarelli's lyrical range and speaks significantly of 'quella suggestiva alternanza dei toni, dalla gravità allo scherzo, dagli arcaismi alla metafora giornalistica.' (In *L'inferno e il limbo*, Marzocco, 1949, p.91.) On the same point see G. Ferrata's introduction to *Poesia* (Mondadori, 1942).

39 On this subject Anceschi notes: 'È difficile rintracciare un rapporto testuale evidente tra Pascoli e Cardarelli . . . ma suppongo di poter anche dire senz'altro che una cosí fatta leggera e distesa rarefazione degli oggetti come campiti in uno spazio fermo e largo e in un tempo legato non sarebbe possibile se non ci fosse stato il precedente affoltirsi degli oggetti pascoliani . . ., assolvendo gli oggetti da ogni peso, e grave peso di storia.' (In 'Pascoli e il Novecento', in *Il Verri* 4, (1958), 22-3.)

40 See P. Bonfiglioli: 'Pascoli, Gozzano, Montale e la poesia dell'oggetto', in *Il Verri* 4, (1958), 34-54.

41 In *Solitario in Arcadia* (1947), see Op. comp., p.480.

42 Op. comp., p.520.

43 Op. comp., p.530.

44 Op. comp., p.521.

45 G. Spagnoletti: *Antologia della poesia contemporanea* (Florence, 1946,) (Vol. I, p.102).

IX

1 See L. Anceschi, 'Ungaretti e la critica' and G. Mariani: 'Per un storia della critica ungarettiana: i primi giudizi sul poeta', in *Letteratura* 35-6, (1958), 236-45 & 246-63. This entire number is dedicated to Ungaretti.

2 For a balanced attitude towards hermeticism expressed by one of the later anti-hermetic *avanguardia*, see F. Leonetti: 'Esame dei contenuti attuali secondo la serie dei poemetti di Pasolini', in *Nuova corrente* 11-12, (1958), 41-76.

3 See *Letteratura* 35-6, 325.

4 P. Bargellini: *Il Novecento, panorama storico della letteratura italiana*, Vol. XI (Florence, 1950), pp.211-12.

5 F. Flora: *La poesia ermetica* (Laterza, 1936). All quotations are taken from the second edition of 1947.

6 op. cit., p.150.

7 See G. Ungaretti: *Poesie disperse* (Milan, 1945). The work includes an exhaustive list of the variants up till that time and an introductory essay on their significance by De Robertis.

8 See *La guerre. Une poésie de Giuseppe Ungaretti* (Paris, 1919). The collection contains eighteen poems, eleven of which are translations from earlier Italian ones while the rest are original French compositions. Although not wholly without importance, Ungaretti's French lyrics are rather marginal to his development as a poet.

9 Besides De Robertis's crucial study on the variants the following articles have appeared on the same subject: A Seroni: *Ragioni critiche* (Florence, 1944), pp.64-72. L. Piccioni: 'Uno studio' appended to G. Ungaretti: *La Terra promessa* (Milan, 1950); F.J. Jones: 'Sulle varianti di Ungaretti', in *Cenobio* (January-February, 1960), 3-21; P. Bigongiari: 'Sugli autografi del "Monologhetto" ' now in *Tutte le poesie* (Milan, 1969), pp.465-93.

10 For instance, in his 'Testimonianza' on the occasion of Ungaretti's sixtieth birthday Montale writes: 'Ma forse è meglio sorprendere questi segreti della sua fucina nella prima edizione dell'*Allegria di naufragi*, dove la poesia ungarettiana è colta e sorpresa in atto, con quel tanto di piú o di meno, di estraneo o di diverso che la fa sentire in movimento, alla frontiera di due tempi, di due gusti e persino di due lingue diverse.' (See *Letteratura* 35-6, 325.) By contrast, G.A. Peritore in an essay entitled 'Ungaretti 1914-1919', now included in *Alcuni studi* (Imola, 1961), pp.49-70, emphasizes the aesthetic improvements brought about between the works of the early and the later Ungaretti.

11 See G. Ungaretti: 'L'artiste dans la société moderne', appearing in *Témoignages recueillis pour l'Unesco* (Venice, 1952), pp.22-28. The present quotation appears on p.28. (Now reprinted in Italian in *Saggi e interventi*, Milan, 1974, pp.855-66.)

12 See M. Apollonio: *I contemporanei* (Brescia, 1956), p.222.

13 Wölfflin describes the baroque of the seventeenth century as consisting of 'less perception and more atmosphere' when compared with the Renaissance. (See *Renaissance and baroque*, Fontana/Collins, 1971, 3rd impression. p.85.) Probably we could define modern baroque in comparison with that practised by the *seicento* as consisting of *more* perception and *more* atmosphere.

14 During his stay in Paris Ungaretti was in touch with *avant-garde* literary and artistic circles and seems to have become especially interested in the group surrounding Apollinaire. For a detailed account of his cultural life up till 1962, see L. Rebay: *Le origini della poesia di Giuseppe Ungaretti*, Rome, 1962.

15 In 'Ragioni d'una poesia', in *Inventario* 1, (1949), 15. (See also *Saggi e interventi* (Milan, 1974), p.760.)

16 The influence of *haikai* or *tanke* on Ungaretti is somewhat problematical, but probably occurred as a result of the publication by M. Shimoi & G. Marone of their *Poesie giapponesi* (Naples, 1917). These were too late to influence *Il porto sepolto* 1916), although previous publications by Akiko Yosano and S. Maeta in *La Diana,* May, 1916, 99-101 & in November-December, 1917, were undoubtedly known to the poet. In a somewhat heated discussion with E. Palmieri (see *Corriere adriatico* April 13 and

May 21 1933 for the poet's reply) Ungaretti denies any such influence. From a chronological point of view the poet is right, but what Palmieri did not realize was that earlier Japanese poems had already appeared in *Poesia* Nos. 8 and 10-11, (1905-6), translated by Mario Chini. Their form, if not their style and content, may well have determined the structure of some of the shorter poems of *Allegria*.

17 This poems bears the same title 'Annientamento' as one by Ungaretti in *Allegria*. It is one of the series translated by Mario Chini and published in *Poesia* 10-11, (1906), 29.

18 See G. Contini: *Esercizi di lettura* (Florence, 1947), p.48.

19 See S. Antonielli: 'Giuseppe Ungaretti', in *Aspetti e figure del Novecento*, p.51.

20 Of Petrarch's traumatic discovery Ungaretti writes: '. . . il tema poetico principale del Petrarca ... è che dell'universo il centro è la memoria umana e che l'universo si tormenta solo nell'uomo, nella notte dell'essere umano resa bella da alcune luci della memoria.' (In *Il poeta dell'oblio*, in *Primato* 9-10, (1943), 167) Echoes of Ungaretti's atavism, which is, in effect, a type of cultural saturation, are to be found in many poets of the hermetic school. Take, for example the following lines from a poem by Piero Bigongiari entitled 'I vivi e i morti' first published in *L'Orto* (September-October, 1934):

> Chiudono le palpebre ai morti:
> su occhi colmi di acerba ricchezza.

Memory is always an 'acerba ricchezza' or bitter-sweet experience with them, because, although idealized and consolatory, it is nevertheless irrevocably cast into the past and therefore inaccessible.

21 See E. Paci: 'Ungaretti e l'esperienza della poesia', in *Letteratura* 35-6, 83-93.

22 Bergson writes in *Évolution créatrice* (F. Alcan, Paris, 1911, 7th ed.): 'Dans ce va-et-vient de notre esprit entre le dehors et le dedans, il y a un point, situé à égale distance entre les deux, où il nous semble que nous n'apercevons plus l'un et que nous n'apercevons pas encore l'autre: c'est là que se forme l'image du néant . . . (p.303) Elle implique du côté subjectif une préférence, du côté objectif une substitution, et ce n'est point autre chose qu'une combinaison, ou plutôt une interférence, entre ce sentiment de préférence et cette idée de substitution . . . (pp.305-6) . . . La représentation du vide est toujours une représentation pleine, qui se résout à l'analyse en deux éléments positifs: l'idée, distincte ou confuse, d'une substitution, et le sentiment, éprouvé ou imaginé, d'un désir, ou d'un regret' (pp.306-7). Finally, he adds the following telling point which indicates that neither he nor Ungaretti is speaking of a metaphysical void but of a psychological change of register: 'Il suit de cette double analyse que l'idée du néant absolu, entendu au sens d'une abolition de tout, est une idée destructive d'elle-même, une pseudo-idée, un simple mot' (p.307).

23 Ungaretti's view of Petrarch's transfiguring process is summed up in what he describes as 'un verso lapidario, il verso che sembra riassumere tutto il Petrarca:

> *Et m'è rimasa nel pensier la luce.*'

And he goes on to observe: 'L'infinito era dunque per il Petrarca nel pensiero – un pensiero fatto di passato, di memoria; un pensiero tormentato a farsi sempre piú luminoso, a diradare tenebre sempre piú dalla memoria: un pensiero che quantunque fosse luce, non poteva essere se non riflesso di luce.' ('Secondo discorso su Leopardi', in *Paragone* 10, (1950), 3. See also *Saggi e interventi*, pp.451-96.)

24 In G. Ungaretti: 'Secondo discorso su Leopardi', in *Paragone* 10, (1950), 30. See also *Saggi e interventi*, p.488.

25 In a note to 'Popolo' the poet says: 'Il titolo indica il riconoscimento della mia appartenenza a un particolare popolo e al popolo nella sua totalità storica.' (In *Tutte le poesie,* Mondadori, 1969, p.519.)

26 On neo-classicism Ungaretti makes the following significant remarks which immediately distinguish it from his own poetic ideal: 'In realtà la poesia del Neoclassicismo è una poesia che incomincia a lamentarsi della perdita della magia: le parole non hanno piú magia, l'uomo non possiede piú per esprimersi alcuna forza magica: ha l'universalità del due e due fanno quattro.' (In 'Secondo discorso su Leopardi', in *Paragone* 10, (1950), 6. See also *Saggi e interventi*, p.456.)

27 See *Ragioni critiche*, ed. cit., p.48.

28 Ungaretti uses this phrase in respect of certain poems of *Sentimento del tempo* and tells us that at that point in his career he had recognized what his poetic destiny was to be. He wrote: 'Nacquero cosí, dal '19 al '25, *Le Stagioni*, *La fine di Crono*, *Sirene*, *Inno alla Morte*, e altre poesie nelle quali, aiutandomi quanto piú potevo coll'orecchio, e

con l'anima, cercai di accordare in chiave d'oggi un antico strumento musicale che, reso cosí di nuovo a noi familiare, hanno in seguito, bene o male, adottato tutti.' (See 'Ragioni di una poesia', in *Inventario* 1, (1949), 9. The notes on which this article is based, however, appeared in *La Ronda* as early as 1922.) The whole article is now reprinted in *Saggi e interventi*, pp.747-67.

29 Eliot defines the traditional artist's sense of lyrical continuity as follows: 'This historical sense which is a sense of the timeless as well as of the temporal and of the timeless and the temporal together, is what makes a writer acutely conscious of his place in time, of his own contemporaneity.' (In 'Tradition and the Individual Talent'.) Ungaretti expresses the same idea as follows: '. . . nel suo gesto d'uomo, il vero poeta sa che è prefigurato il gesto degli avi ignoti, nel seguito di secoli impossibile a risalire, oltre le origini del suo buio.' (In *Tutte le poesie* Mondadori, 1969, p.505.)

30 Frattini analyses the coffin symbol in Ungaretti's work as follows: '. . . *bara* è lo strumento analogico insostituibile per dar trasparenza e spessore, – su un arco ontologico-musicale – a una vergine rapita invenzione: la morte, l'essenza nuda del dolore e il metafisico distacco della mente che contempla, si accolgono e si fondono in una parola che sembra condensare il terrore del gelo e la dolcezza del riposo sognato.' ('Ontologia del dolore nella lirica di Ungaretti', in *Da Tommaseo a Ungaretti*, p.156.)

31 I. Gutia: *Linguaggio di Ungaretti* (Florence, 1959), pp.7 et seq.

32 On this particular subject we note the following passage in Ungaretti's 'Secondo discorso su Leopardi': 'L'arte della parola esige una metamorfosi radicale. Se dico: albero, tutti hanno nella mente un albero; ma nulla è meno albero di quelle tre sillabe da me pronunciate. È possibile che fosse da principio la parola, voce onomatopeica; ma subito la metafora venne a liberarla d'ogni imitazione della natura, a renderla espressione della natura umana, a ridurla a esprimere stupori, terrori, ebbrezze, necessità, affetti, il sacro, i rapporti prossimi e anche quelli remoti tra oggetti, e la partecipazione animatrice di conoscenza affinché incessantemente potesse convertire la realtà in proprio simbolo.' (See *Paragone* 10, (1950), 18-19; see also *Saggi e interventi*, p.472.)

33 Human invention is, in fact, what offers us a counterweight to cosmic mystery in Ungaretti's view, and so he remarks that 'Il mistero c'è, e col mistero, di pari passo, la misura; ma non la misura del mistero, cosa umanamente insensata; ma qualche cosa che in un certo senso al mistero s'opponga, pure essendone per noi la manifestazione piú alta: questo mondo terreno considerato come continua invenzione dell'uomo.' (In 'Ragioni di una poesia', in *Inventario*, p.7; see also *Saggi e interventi*, p.749.)

34 Ungaretti observes in regard to the bedouin: 'La preghiera islamica è accompagnata da molti inchini come se l'orante accogliesse un ospite.' (*Tutte le poesie* Milan, 1969, p.524.)

35 He notes later in respect of this passage: 'Sono le mani eterne che foggiano assidue il destino di ogni essere vivente.' (Note in *Tutte le poesie*, p.524.)

36 In 'Ragioni di una poesia', in *Inventario* I, (1949), 13; see also *Saggi e interventi*, p.757.

37 Ungaretti counts Leopardi and Tasso as his principal masters in rhythmical matters and observes: 'Il Leopardi, come il Tasso, ha tolto all'endecasillabo ogni rimbombo, ogni lusso, ogni esteriorità, l'ha reso, direi, silenzio. È poesia per sognarci su, e non per declamatori. In essa la mente ascolta l'anima. Il Tasso per l'orecchio è molto vicino al Leopardi. Orecchio virgiliano; il piú fine.' (In *Il Mattino di Napoli* (4-5 March 1927); see *Saggi e interventi*, p.154.) The date of these remarks is highly pertinent because it was at that time that the poet was preparing *Sentimento del tempo*.

38 See P. Bigongiari: 'Per un'analisi della lirica "Sentimento del tempo",' in *Letteratura* 35-6, 168. His contention is that the progression from spacelessness to a sense of space is a feature of the poet's baroque scale of values and is responsible for the type of emblematic discourse which is one of Ungaretti's main contributions to hermetic art.

39 One is reminded here of Verlaine's 'voix anciennes' as depicted in the opening lines of 'L'escarpolette': 'Je devine à travers un murmure,/ Le contour subtil des voix anciennes/ Et dans leurs lueurs musiciennes,/ Amour pâle, une aurore future!' (From *Romances sans paroles*).

40 Certain remarks by Marinetti in 'La nuova religione-morale della velocità' (1916) spring to mind at this point. First he points out that '*La morale futurista* difenderà l'uomo dalla decomposizione determinata dalla lentezza, dal ricordo, dall'analisi, dal riposo e dall'abitudine.' Then, even more significantly, he adds that 'Una grande velocità d'automobile o d'aeroplano consente di abbracciare e di confrontare

rapidamente diversi punti della terra, cioè di fare meccanicamente il lavoro dell'analogia.' (See *Archivi del futurismo*, pp. 52 and 53.)

41 See 'Ragioni di una poesia', in *Inventario* I, (1949), 12, reprinted in *Saggi e interventi*, pp.747-767. Ungaretti's actual solution is, not surprisingly, an ethical one and he notes in this same article that 'se l'uomo d'oggi è costretto a trarre la sua libertà fisica da soggezioni estremamente casuali, è impossibile che il poeta d'oggi non sia portato a tendersi verso una libertà etica decisiva.' (*Inventario*, 13.)

42 See G. Ungaretti: *40 sonetti di Shakespeare* (Milan, 1946), p.13.

43 Ungaretti tells us that he became acquainted with the concept of the 'baroque void' when living at Rome and he associated it with the art of Michelangelo whom he regards as the very quintessence of baroque taste: 'Quell'orrore del vuoto, si può sentirlo a Roma infinitamente di piú, e nemmeno nel deserto, che in qualsiasi altra parte della terra. Lo credo: dall'orrore del vuoto nasce, non la necessità della riempitura dello spazio con non importa quale elemento, ma tutto il dramma dell'arte di Michelangelo.' (*Tutte le poesie*, p.533-4.)

44 In G. Ungaretti: *Fedra di Jean Racine* (Milan, 1950), p.10. Elsewhere, in order to justify the sensationalism of the baroque spirit, he notes: 'L'horreur est donnée au baroque par l'idée insupportable du corps sans âme; un squelette provoque l'horreur du vide.' (*Propos improvisés*, Paris 1972, p.111.)

45 See 'Góngora al lume d'oggi', in *Aut Aut* 4, (1951), 291. Reprinted in *Saggi e interventi*, pp.528-50.

46 The Italian poet's translation of the above sonnet appears in *Da Góngora e da Mallarmé* (Milan, 1948).

47 In 'Góngora al lume d'oggi', in *Aut Aut* 4, (1951), 297. See also *Saggi e interventi*, p.536.

48 L. Piccioni: *Sui contemporanei* (Milan, n.d.), p.283.

49 In a note to this poem Ungaretti writes: 'È una fantasia della fine del mondo. Gli astri, *Penelopi innumeri*, filano la vita finché il loro Signore, il loro Ulisse ritorni ad abbracciarli, ad annullarli in sé.' (*Tutte le poesie*, p.537.) There then reappears the same orphic return of the *status quo*, though perhaps on a higher level of awareness, and the note ends with the following words: 'Tornerà poi l'Olimpo, la quiete assoluta, il non esistere piú.'

50 The significant difference between the present 'lupo' and the 'agneauloup' is that the former is stimulated by a positive 'disponibilità', while the latter was more inclined towards a negative or decadent form of alienation, as may be seen in the following lines: 'Seul ne serait étranger/ au climat/ de la mort/ cet agneauloup/ en exil/ partout.' (*Calumet*)

51 See Leo Spitzer's 'Testimonianza' on the occasion of Ungaretti's seventieth birthday in *Il taccuino del vecchio* (Milan, 1960), pp.120-22. In a note to the poem Ungaretti writes: 'Perché l'*isola*? Perché è il punto dove io mi isolo, dove sono solo: è un punto separato dal resto del mondo, non perché lo sia in realtà, ma perché nel mio stato d'animo posso separarmene.' (*Tutte le poesie*, p.537.)

52 See H. Friedrich: *Die Struktur der modernen Lyrik* (Hamburg, 1956), now translated into Italian under the title *La lirica moderna* (Milan, 1961), pp.206-7.

53 For a detailed analysis of this poem, see my inaugural lecture: *The development of Petrarchism and the modern Italian lyric* (Cardiff, 1969), pp.21-3.

54 E. Paci: *Dall'esistenzialismo al relazionismo* (Messina-Florence, 1957), p.276.

55 Although this poem is based on a particular situation, the death of a friend, Nazzareno Cremona, who was a member of Ungaretti's regiment 'e morí schiantato sul Carso' (see *Tutte le poesie* p.539), nevertheless from even the most poignant human situations we find that Ungaretti draws the universal analogy or 'leggenda', which in this case has to do with authority and individuality or the artist and the tradition.

56 From 'I Fiumi'.

57 From 'Memoria d'Ofelia d'Alba'.

58 From 'Caino'.

59 In this regard Piccioni quotes an interesting observation by Ungaretti concerning the poem 'La pietà romana' which obviously has a general application. It reads as follows: 'La pietà è un antico mito di Roma (vedilo in Virgilio) che converge nel cristiano sentimento.' (In *Vita di un uomo Giuseppe Ungaretti* Milan, 1970, p.124.) This quotation is now to be found in *Tutte le poesie*, p.540.

60 Interesting studies on the baroque poet's sense of the absurdity of human destiny,

the lapse of time, and the inevitable dissolution of the flesh are to be found in J.M. Cohen: *The Baroque Lyric* (London, 1963).

61 'Giorno per giorno', 16.

62 Ibid., 8.

63 See U. Marvardi: 'Carattere della poesia d'oggi e Giuseppe Ungaretti', in *Responsabilità del sapere*, (1947), fasc. 3, 97.

64 F. Piemontese: 'Il sentimento religioso nella poesia di Ungaretti', in *Studium* 5, (1949), 230.

65 Most of the poems in the collection were, in fact, matured over a long period, although one notable exception is 'Il segreto del poeta' added in the second edition.

66 See introduction to *La terra promessa* (Mondadori, 1950), p.12.

67 For an interpretation of 'Canzone' by Ungaretti himself, see *Morte delle stagioni* (Turin, 1967), pp.129-44.

68 The substance of the passage in which Ungaretti describes this idea reads as follows: 'Insommà, come diceva Platone, noi non conosciamo le idee, noi abbiamo reminiscenze, ricordi, *echi* di idee. Cosí, la prima immagine continua ad esistere perché c'è sempre l'aurora . . . C'è dunque un'aurora perfetta, e c'è un'aurora imperfetta che è quella che conosciamo. Noi tendiamo però con tutte le nostre forze a conoscere "la prima immagine" nella sua perfezione, malgrado l'ostacolo dei "muri" che sono gli eredi eterni dei minuti . . . Il nostro intelletto non potrebbe cogliere l'idea pura, ma riesce a coglierla perché in una "breve salma", in una breve immagine, in un breve peso dove ci pare di averla carcerata, noi abbiamo il sentimento che essa contraddica il nulla, la morte: lei è la vita, lei è l'eterno, lei è la verità.' (In *Tutte le poesie*, pp.561 and 562.)

69 Ibid., p.553.

70 In *Tutte le poesie*, p.562.

71 Ibid., p.562-3.

72 In this respect Ungaretti mentions as his two philosophical 'maestri dello spirito' Plato and Bergson. The one provides the eternal world of forms on which he indirectly founds his lyricism and the other the 'élan vital' which gives that world its dynamic qualities and orphic relevance to modern society. (See *Tutte le poesie*, p.561.)

73 We refer in particular to the 'Ultimi cori' appearing in *Taccuino del vecchio* (Mondadori, 1960), where the eighth lyric is evidently based on Donne's 'The Good-morrow'. Likewise an echo of the same poem is detectable in the fifth chorus in this collection.

74 From 'Cori', 111.

75 For a further examination of his allusive musicality, see my previously mentioned study, 'Le varianti di Ungaretti', in *Cenobio* (1960).

76 See *Il deserto e dopo* (Milan, 1961), pp.159-65.

77 For Montanari's distinction, see 'Poesia e durata', in *Studium* 7-8, (1964), 477-83. Of the present poem, 'Variazioni su nulla', the poet observes: 'Il tema è la durata terrena oltre la singolarità delle persone. Null'altro se non un disincarnato orologio che, solo, nel vuoto, prosegua a sgocciolare i minuti.' (In *Tutte le poesie*, p.567) Nevertheless his sense of *aevum* appears to emerge from every line of the composition.

78 These poems have never appeared and Ungaretti speaks of them as follows in his preface: 'Il libro doveva, per apparire un po' meno incompiuto, recare anche i "Cori d'Enea". Sono ancora allo stato d'abbozzo.' (p.14.)

79 In *Poesia italiana del Novecento*, p.162.

80 In *Tre poeti italiani del Novecento* (ed. ERI, 1961), p.60.

81 'Ultimi cori', 3.

82 *Tutte le poesie*, p.560.

83 In *L'écrivain et son ombre* (Paris, 1953), p.87.

84 L. Silori: 'La difficile scoperta di Leopardi', in *Letteratura* 35-6, 225.

85 See *Journal* (1910), August, N.R.F. edition, vol. 1, p.371.

86 In *Fedra di Jean Racine*, p.11.

X

1 For an analysis of Montale's telescopic and memorial techniques, see my article: 'La linea esistenziale dell'arte montaliana', Quaderni del Cenobio, No 30 (Lugano, 1963.)

2 E. Bonora: *La poesia di Montale*, Vol. I, (Turin, 1965), p.133.

3 From 'Ossi', 11 (The poems have been numbered for reference purposes.)

4 From 'Ossi', 12. This lyric has verbal associations with Gozzano's 'Invernale'.

5 From 'Ossi', 14.

6 In 'Cinquant'anni di poesia', in *L'Approdo letterario* 35, (1966), 123.

7 From 'Ossi', 8.

8 From 'Piccolo testamento'.

9 One might indeed consider the following passage from *Du côté de chez Swann* as a definition of the residual immortality which Montale desired for his mother, because it too is one which is capable of being rekindled in the right circumstances: 'Mais quand d'un passé ancien rien ne subsiste, après la mort des êtres, après la destruction des choses, seules, plus frêles mais plus vivaces, plus immatérielles, plus persistantes, plus fidèles, l'odeur et la saveur restent encore longtemps, comme des âmes, à se rappeler, à attendre, à espérer, sur la ruine de tout le reste, à porter sans fléchir, sur leur goutelette presque impalpable, l'édifice immense du souvenir.' (Chapter 1, Gallimard edition, 1919, p.68)

10 *À la recherche du temps perdu, Le temps retrouvé*, vol. XV, (Gallimard), p.14.

11 Ibid., p.15.

12 Critics have varied widely in their interpretation of Montale's 'ethics' and 'theology', often depending upon their own religious and moral outlooks. The orthodox Catholic critic Giovanni Getto, for instance, sees the poet's religious aspirations as 'una religiosità assurda, spoglia di virtú teogali' (In *Poeti, critici e cose varie del Novecento*, Florence, 1953, p.8), whereas L. Malagodi seems, by contrast, to be thinking directly along Montalian lines when he defines living in the following general terms: 'La nostra vita muove da un oggetto reale e si svolge in piena libertà. Noi viviamo sospesi su un vuoto infinito, e ci teniamo abbarbicati alla roccia che sporge; quel vuoto infinito è il mondo della nostra libertà, la roccia è il reale, e procediamo di roccia in roccia, al di sopra di quel vuoto luminoso e limpido.' (In *Poesia come storia, con un'aggiunta sull'attivismo* Florence, 1961, p.89.) Again, Bonora points out the resemblance between Goethe's and Montale's outlooks and quotes the former as saying: 'In me la convinzione della nostra sopravvivenza scaturisce dal concetto dell'attività. Poiché, se io, sino alla fine, non ho mai un momento di riposo, la Natura è in grado di trattenere il mio spirito' (op. cit., p.121). It seems therefore, that Montale's ethics and myth of the active and passive memories have lain dormant in the heart of the humanist tradition for centuries.

13 This voluntary stage of recall may either depend upon the poet or upon the will of the person recalled. Thus in 'Sulla spiaggia' in *Farfalla di Dinard* we find the following significant situation: 'Anactoria o Annabella era stata del tutto soppressa dal mio pensiero per quattro cinque sei anni, ed ora è tornata perché ha *voluto* tornare, è lei che mi fa grazia di sé, non sono io che mi degno di ridestarla andando dilettantisticamente alla ricerca del tempo perduto. È lei l'amorevole, la degna intrusa che rinvangando nel suo passato s'è imbattuta nella mia ombra ed ha voluto ristabilire nel senso migliore della parola una 'corrispondenza'.' (p.233) In short, this 'fenomeno di una scomparsa totale che ad un tratto si rivela presenza' is one which is *willed* by one or both of the personalities involved, and it normally has an ethical and humanist function of 'restoration' as well as a purely aesthetic function of 'representation' in Montale's work.

14 Bigongiari, therefore, seems to be misunderstanding the decisive ethical rôle of Montale's memorial processes when he observes: 'Già nell'azione egli è in atto di memoria, e questa è sorda, non dà la parola precisa: egli non può aprire il mondo con la chiave che la memoria gli offre. Anche *dopo*, essa non è ancora che un triste risveglio, anzi una veglia entro la quale in deflusso tutta la confusione degli occhi aperti passa. Montale non scevera, per la memoria, ma ricade al punto del proprio sangue.'

(In *Poesia italiana del Novecanto*, p.170) The issue at stake, however, is whether the poet *intends* to produce the ethical key to a memory at any given point. Very often he does not, but this does not mean that he rejects the moral effectiveness of memorial recalls.

15 From 'Voce giunta con le folaghe', in *La bufera e altro* (1956).

16 See *Intenzioni (intervista immaginaria)* first published in *La Rassegna d'Italia* 1, (1946), 84-9, but now republished in *Sulla poesia* (Milan, 1976), pp.561-9. The relevant remarks are: '. . . pensai, e ancora penso, che l'arte sia la forma di chi veramente non vive; un compenso o un surrogato' (p.562).

17 In *Problemi del nostro tempo. La solitudine dell'artista*, No. 7, (Associazone italiana per la libertà della cultura, 1952), p.4.

18 Ibid., p.7.

19 Ibid., p.8.

20 Ibid., p.3.

21 In 'Pascoli verso il Novecento', see *Il Verri* 4, (1958), 31.

22 He also warns that a poet 'non deve sciuparsi la voce solfeggiando troppo, non deve perdere quelle qualità di timbro che dopo non ritroverebbe piú.' (In 'Intervista immaginaria', in *Sulla poesia*, p.563.)

23 Ibid., p.564.

24 In actual fact the least metaphorical statements in Montale's early work are connected with moral judgements. For instance, in the following lines, taken from 'Flussi', the metaphor is subordinated to the conceptual element, even though it still makes its presence felt: 'La vita è questo scialo/ di triti fatti, vano/piú che crudele.' Metaphysical problems are also similarly treated at times, as in 'Mediterraneo', 7: "M'abbandonano a prova i miei pensieri./ Sensi non ho; né senso. Non ho limite.' By contrast, broader ideas or moods are already cocooned in metaphor, even in the *Ossi di seppia*, as for example the following: 'Nel futuro che s'apre le mattine/ sono ancorate come barche in rada.' ('Ossi', 22) Later still, even moral and metaphysical concepts undergo similar involution, when Montale is sure that the reader no longer entertains any doubts about their meaning.

25 Montale has never provided an unambiguous explanation of the problem of Grace. But in reply to an inquiry by F. Camon, he once wrote: 'L'ipotesi della Grazia non è recente: era nella *Casa sul mare* e in *Crisalide*, e già qui era solo per altri. In *Crisalide* volevo stringere un patto col destino, per scontare l'altrui gioia con la mia condanna. In *Casa sul mare* penso che per i piú non vi sia salvezza, ma che taluno sovverta ogni disegno e passi il varco. Può essere un motivo cristiano; come può essere un motivo cristiano *Iride*, l'ebrea che io chiamo Cristofora o portatrice di Cristo. Qualche fermento cristiano è senz'altro in me, ma non sono un cristiano praticante: io rispetto *tutte* le Chiese come istituzioni.' (In *Il mestiere di poeta*, Milan, 1965, p.81)

26 One is immediately reminded here of the Baudelairian line: 'J'ai plus de souvenirs que si j'avais mille ans.' ('Spleen') There is a number of traces of Baudelaire in the early Montale, and the idea of the burden of the passive memory may well have been suggested by the French poet.

27 From 'I limoni'.

28 Ibid.

29 See S. Solmi: 'La poesia di Montale', in *Nuovi argomenti* 26, (1957) 13.

30 In S. Antonielli: *Aspetti e figure del Novecento*, p.60.

31 Esterina has been identified with Esterina Rossi, one of Montale's friends. A medallion of her profile by F. Messina appears in *Omaggio a Montale* (Milan, 1966), plate 7. Some aspects of this poem remind us of Aleixandre's Spanish poem, 'Destino trágico', although the heroine of Montale's poem is a complete foil to the Spanish one who was a suicide. Other Spanish poets who may have influenced Montale are Machado, Bécquer and Guillén.

32 On the subject of the dialectic between sea and land in Montale's work, see S. Antonielli, *Aspetti e figure del Novecento*, pp.57-65.

33 The association between *Sarcofaghi* and Pompei is suggested by C.B. Beall in his article 'Eugenio Montale's "Sarcofaghi",' in *Literary and linguistic studies in honor of Helmut Hatzfeld* (Catholic University of America Press, 1964), pp.65-78. Beall does not indicate his source for the information, but it is clear that, if it is correct, the scenes depicted are ones taken from 'idealized' rather than 'actual' Pompeian friezes.

34 The dog symbol here also forms part of what Macrí has termed Montale's "sacertà larica" (See *Realtà del simbolo*, Florence, 1968, pp.139-46). This problem is closely connected with the poet's scale of symbolic values on which the present interpretation of his work largely depends.

35 In G. Singh: 'Eugenio Montale', in *Italian Studies* (1963), pp.128-30. His analysis of memory forms part of a larger article on Montale's development, pp.101-37. See also Getto's remarks in *Poeti, critici e cose varie del Novecento*, pp.111-12, my own article, 'Montale's dialectic of memory', in *Italian Studies* XXVII, (1973), 83-107, and S. Antonielli, 'La memoria di Montale', in *Studi in memoria di Luigi Russo*, (Pisa, 1974), pp.525-32.

36 From 'Vento e bandiera'.

37 'Nel '21 "Il male di vivere" non era certamente il fascismo; era un male di vivere, diciamo cosí, esistenziale, una condizione di vita.' (In 'Cinquant'anni di poesia', in *L'Approdo letterario* 35, (1966), 122.)

38 'Ossi di seppia', 3.

39 One is again reminded here of Baudelaire, especially in 'Le voyage'.

40 'Mediterraneo', 2. (For reference purposes these lyrics have also been numbered.)

41 Ibid., 3.

42 Ibid., 5.

43 Parallel lines in Gozzano's poem read: 'Di tutto ignari: delle/Scienze e dell' Indagine che prostra/ e della Storia, favola mentita,/ abitavamo l'isola romita . . . Ma giunse l'ora che non ha conforto . . .' Although Gozzano's influence on this poem seems very strong, for a different interpretation see A. Seroni: *Esperimenti critici sul Novecento* Milan, 1967, pp.19-29.

44 From 'Le voyage'.

45 Baudelaire expresses the infinite desire of his travellers as follows:

> De leur fatalité jamais ils ne s'écartent,
> Et sans savoir pourquoi, disent toujours: 'Allons!'

The general drift of Montale's ending is of a similar kind:

> . . . sotto l'azzurro fitto
> del cielo qualche uccello di mare se ne va;
> né sosta mai: perché tutte le immagini portano scritto:
> 'piú in là'.

46 From 'Clivo'. Vigny's line reads:

> Dieu! que le son du cor est triste au fond des bois.

47 Several critics have tried to explain the origin of the name Arsenio, especially since it was applied to Montale by his friends during vacations on the riviera coast. G. Kay may possibly have discovered the source in the detective stories of Maurice Leblanc whose well-known 'gentleman-cambrioleur' was called Arsène Lupin (See his introduction to *Eugenio Montale Selected Poems*, Penguin Books, 1969). Montale tells us himself that he learned foreign languages by reading detective stories and there is a slight resemblance between Leblanc's symbol of the sea in *The hollow needle* (trans. by A. Teixeira De Mattos, London, 1960) first published in 1911 and the poet's use of the same symbol throughout his early work. Although Leblanc's book is a 'who-done-it', it nevertheless has a slightly mystical ending, when Arsène is last seen walking towards the sea with his dead wife in his arms, after she has been accidentally killed by Holmlock Shears. We thus conclude that both writers' heroes draw their strength from immersion in the sea and both are highly unconventional figures. However, in a letter to me after the publication of the Italian version of this book, Montale noted as a postscript: 'Non conosco Lupin se non per qualche film' (Letter of 20/5/1975).

48 In *Il Verri* 4, (1958), p.42.

49 A phrase in 'Sulla spiaggia' in *Farfalla di Dinard* links 'castagnette a scoppio ritardato' (p.232) with the sphere of memory. Here, too, it seems to have a recollective action.

50 In this regard A.A. Moles in his 'Analisi delle strutture del linguaggio poetico' (*Il Verri* 14, (1964), 3-21) suggests that the true work of art is above the reader's capacity to assimilate it, and so he feels himself 'conquistato dalla sua ricchezza' while sensing that at bottom 'l'opera d'arte è sommergente' (p.13). This is an idea also suggested by Leopardi (See Chapter I, p.29) and is prevalent among all the hermetic writers. Montale's 'segni' are, in fact, the latest development of a long symbolic tradition examined by E.M. Curtius in *European literature and Latin Middle Ages* (London, 1953), pp.345 et seq. Oddly enough, the historical development he outlines is similar to

that taking place between the neo-crepuscular poetry of Gozzano and Montale's own hermetically inclined inspiration. Curtius claims that the word 'cipher' derives from the Arabic "sifr" meaning an empty emblematic symbol; but the emblem was later used in Renaissance culture, especially in Italy and Spain, as the name for a pictorial device illustrating mottoes. The difference, however, between Montale's and the traditional emblem is that the modern poet's does not carry a rational element, at least in an overt sense. With him the conceit or the concept is largely overlaid by psycho-sensuous elements, although these certainly have unvoiced intellectual and 'cosmic' implications. Hence we can probably regard Montale's manner of emblematic writing as a form of infolded mythmaking and it is this which ranges him alongside the other hermetic poets despite his otherwise imaginative and syntactical orthodoxy. On the subject of the emblem, see Mario Praz: *Studi sul concettismo* (Florence, 1946).

51 One naturally thinks here of the 'giunco schietto' of *Purgatorio*, Canto 1, which for Casini represented 'lo stato dell'animo non perturbato dalla passione, la serenità dello spirito che è fuori del male e però disposto a operare il bene.' (See *La Divina Commedia di Dante Alighieri*, con il commento di T. Casini, vol. II, Florence, p.346.) The Barresian connection would be with his 'déracinés' (See *Les Déracinés*, Paris, 2 vols., 1897).

52 Quite apart from the pun of 'cygne' and 'signe' and the constellation of Cygnus in the last line of 'Le vierge, le vivace et le bel aujourd'hui' which might have prompted Montale's use of 'cenno', the ancient device of immortalizing people among the stars is given a modern gloss in Mallarmé's 'Un coup de dés': 'CONSTELLATION froide d'oubli et de désuetude pas tant qu'elle n'énumere sur quelque surface vacante de supérieure le heurt successif sidéralement d'un compte total en formation.' No doubt it is to similar kinds of 'compte total en formation' that Montale is referring here, as indeed was the case with the poem dedicated to his mother, quoted earlier. A parallel type of immortality to that conceived by Montale also appears in the French poet's 'Ses pures ongles' where a nymph is immortalized by association with the constellation of the Great Bear. The phrase 'la cendre des astres' appears in Mallarmé's *Igitur*, as A. Jacomuzzi has indicated (in *Sulla poesia di Montale* Bologna, 1968, pp.102-3, note 18), and this again points to the Mallarmean implications of the conclusion of 'Arsenio'.

53 Montale's preoccupation with the afterlife is also whimsically treated in the short story 'Sul limite' in *Farfalla di Dinard* (Milan, 1960), pp.222-29. The different regions which he postulates, such as 'Antelimite', 'Limite' and the 'Istituto delle entelechie superiori', can be interpreted as so many regressions into the various stages of the passive memory, especially since in the above-mentioned 'Institute' the personality undergoes 'il processo di smaterializzazione' (p.227).

54 Montale tells us that 'il "tu" di *Casa sul mare* e di *Crisalide* è indirizzato a una donna splendida: era stata attrice e tutti quelli che l'avvicinavano se ne innamoravano. Era sposata con un uomo debole, indifeso: andarono in Sud America. Da allora non ho piú saputo nulla di lei'. (Quoted by G. Nascimbeni: *Eugenio Montale*, Milan, 1969, p.74)

55 In *Eredità di Leopardi* (Florence, 1964), p.25.

56 Although 'Riviere' is placed at the end of the *Ossi di seppia*, it was written in 1920 and must consequently rank as one of Montale's earliest compositions. The real progression in the work as a whole is thus from a mood of optimism to one of pessimism.

57 See letter to Cazalis (1864): 'Peindre non la chose, mais l'effet qu'elle produit'.

58 In *Sulla poesia*, p.567.

59 Ibid., p.567.

60 Montale, in fact, defines his entire manner as one involving 'un totale assorbimento delle intenzioni nei risultati oggettivi' (ibid., p.567).

61 Montale's view of transfiguration as a moment of miraculous emotional equipoise is perhaps defined in 'Intenzioni': 'Il miracolo era per me evidente come la necessità. Immanenza e trascendenza non sono separabili, e farsi uno stato d'animo della perenne mediazione dei due termini, come propone il moderno storicismo, non risolve il problema o lo risolve con un ottimismo di parata' (ibid., p.565).

62 See note to 'Keepsake', in *Le occasioni*, p.105.

63 More recently, however, Montale has provided a little more background material about Gerti, as follows: 'Sempre nell'ambiente di Bobi (Bazlen) avevo conosciuto Gerti: era un'asburgica come Dora e si trovava in Toscana perché il marito era ufficiale di stanza a Lucca. Gerti è la vera protagonista della seconda parte della poesia (i.e.

'Dora Markus'. La vidi una decina di volte. Poi seppi che aveva lasciato il marito. Di lei e di Dora feci un unico fantasma'. (See Nascimbeni, op. cit., p.113)

64 In Montale's regard, Getto notes, perhaps a little unfairly, that 'rimane allora il passato, con la sua vita nella memoria. Però non esiste per Montale, come esiste per Proust, una ricerca e un ritrovamento del tempo perduto. In Montale si dà il tempo che perde e ingoia ogni esistenza' (op. cit., p.111).

65 Bonora associates this kind of imagery with the *flatus vocis* of 'Keepsake' and other similar features appearing elsewhere (See *La poesia di Montale*, Vol. 2, pp.48-50).

66 Ibid., vol. 2, p.48.

67 Liuba, Gerti and possibly Dora were all Jewesses and seem to act as foils to the poet's wife, Drusilla, whom Rebay informs us (despite Montale's denial of the fact to the present author in his letter of 20/5/1975: "Mia moglie NON ERA ebrea, neppure in minima parte") was half-Jewish through her mother. Nascimbeni states that Montale saw Liuba as a pathetic figure on a Florentine station as she was emigrating to London during the persecution of the Jews, in the late thirties; but in the above-quoted letter to me the poet again denies that he had met her at the time, although he did meet her once later on. He also revealed elsewhere that he never met Dora at all: "Sí Liuba, naturalmente era ebrea; e Dora Markus non l'ho mai conosciuta, quella della prima parte della poesia; non so se fosse ebrea anche lei; però nella seconda parte Dora Markus mette in scena Gerti, quella del "Carnevale di Gerti", anche quella un'ebrea austriaca'. (In 'Cinquant'anni di poesia', in *L'Approdo letterario* 35, (1966), 118) The confusion is partly resolved by Rebay who explains that 'L' "occasione" della poesia gli fu suggerita dalla fotografia di due perfette gambe (e nient'altro) che Bobi accluse a una lettera del 25 settembre 1928, nella quale dava a Montale en passant, la seguente notizia: 'Gerti e Carlo: Bene. A Trieste, loro ospite, un'amica di Gerti, con delle *gambe meravigliose. Falle una poesia*. Si chiama Dora Markus'. (In 'I diaspori di Montale', in *Italica* 1, (1969), 48) Evidently there is something wrong with the date of the letter or with Montale's date of composition of the poem if Rebay's hypothesis is correct.

68 See 'Cinquant'anni di poesia', in *L'Approdo letterario* 35, 118. However, if we accept this stanza as dealing mainly with political unease at the time, it tenor would seem to run counter to the overall, metaphysical implications of the poem. As Montale says himself, 'l'arte vive e sopravvive anche attraverso gli equivoci' (ibid., p.118), so that it seems reasonable to assume that social and personal themes are always closely intermingled in the poetry of *Le occasioni*.

69 The poet took Clizia's name from an unauthenticated sonnet by Dante addressed to Giovanni Quirini. Mythologically speaking, Clizia was a nymph who loved and whose love was not reciprocated by Apollo; and so she was transformed by him into a sunflower, a plant which was already a favourite with Montale in the *Ossi di seppia*. Clizia's real name, Irma Brandeis, has recently been revealed by L. Rebay in 'Montale, Clizia e l'America', in *Forum Italicum,* vol. 16, No 6 (Winter 1982), 171-202. Rebay illustrates his point by commenting on the puns which Montale makes on her name in his poetry, including one which splits up her name into two German components 'Brand' and 'Eis' and which accounts for her association with 'fuoco' and 'ghiaccio'.

70 See G. Cambon, 'Motets': The occasion of Epiphany,' in *PMLA* 7, (1967), 471-84.

71 See 'Due sciacalli al guinzaglio', in *Corriere della sera* (16 February 1950) but now reprinted in *Sulla poesia*, pp.84-7. See pp.85-6.

72 In 'Intenzioni', see *Sulla poesia*, p.565.

73 From 'Mottetti', 11 (Again numbered for reference purposes).

74 *Sulla poesia*, p.87.

75 For Montale's allegorical element, see A. Pipa: *Montale and Dante* (University of Minnesota Press, 1968). The difference between Montale's emblemism and Dante's however, is that the earlier poet's allegorizing is rational and didactic in scope, while his is emotionally adherent to his moods and forms part of their multidimensionality.

76 See Bonora, op. cit., vol. 2, pp.135-50, and N. Tedesco: 'Di Montale e del crepuscolarismo (leggendo Notizie dall'Amiata', G. Mori & Figli (Palermo, 1960). See also Tedesco's *La condizione crepuscolare* (Florence, 1970), where his views are somewhat modified.

77 From 'La Voix'.

78 op. cit., p.17: 'idee calate nelle cose'.

79 This interpretation seems confirmed by lines to be found in 'Ezekiel saw the wheel', where Clizia is referred to as 'una mano straniera' and we find that her hand 'frugava

tenace la traccia/in me seppellita da un cumulo,/ da un monte di sabbia che avevo/in cuore ammassato per giungere/ a soffocare la tua voce . . .'

80 See E.M. Fusco: *La lirica*, Vol. 2 (Vallardi, 1950), p.520.

81 op. cit., p.168, note.

82 In 'Intenzioni', in *Sulla poesia*, p.568.

83 See D'Arco Silvio Avalle: *'Gli orecchini' di Montale,* (Il Saggiatore, 1965), and E. Bonora, op. cit., vol. 2, pp.101-10.

84 According to Macrí, however, R. Bilenchi was of the opinion that the objects enumerated in 'Gli orecchini' were 'ciò che di prezioso fu strappato alle salme dopo i massacri e i forni' (*Realtà del simbolo*, p.85). Granted Montale's preoccupation with the Jewish race and the wartime atmosphere of the poems in this section, such an interpretation is quite possible. It would also account for the residual 'giade' glittering on the lady's wrist in 'La frangia dei capelli . . .'

85 From 'Mottetti', 12. Again, perhaps, the icicles are a play on the syllable 'Eis' in the lady's name, Brandeis.

86 From 'Elegia di Pico Farnese'.

87 *Farfalla di Dinard* (Venice, 1956); second edition (Milan, 1960). All quotations are taken from the second edition.

88 See Nascimbeni, op. cit., p.156.

89 This lady, however, is not 'la volpe', see Nascimbeni, p.154. We actually know that 'la volpe' is Maria Luisa Spaziani, since her name is spelled out acrostically in the first letters of the lines of the poem 'Da un lago svizzero'.

90 In *Passione e ideologia*, p.297: 'atti maniacamente propiziatori'.

91 See Giannessi's review of *La bufera e altro*, in *Il Ponte* 8-9, (1956), 1576.

92 See A. Pipa: 'Le mythe d'un papillon, Montale et Anouilh', in *La revue de littérature comparée*, vol. XXXVI 11, 3, pp.400-13.

93 Again in the short story 'Sulla spiaggia' in *Farfalla di Dinard* Montale clarifies this idea, saying: 'Penso agli scherzi della memoria, al pozzo di San Patrizio del ricordo . . . Ero consapevole di custodire nello scrigno della memoria una folla di fantasmi possibili, virtuali . . . Reminiscenze cosi fatte, spore inesplose, castagnette a scoppio ritardato . . . Io credevo insomma dimenticanze relative e quasi volontarie, a un processo, come chiamarlo?, tayloristico della mente che mette in pensione quanto non può giovarle' (pp.232-3). This is perhaps the first stage of memorial loss.

94 Montale's clearest statements on political matters are contained in his articles in *La Nazione* after he had joined the 'Partito d'azione' in 1945. For further details see U. Carpi: 'Montale dopo il fascismo: i primi anni di collaborazione al "Corriere della sera" ', in *Belfagor* 2, (1968), 197-230. This is now reprinted in *Montale dopo il fascismo dalla "Bufera" a "Satura",* Padua, 1971.

95 See Montale's letter in *Aut Aut* 67, 44-5. For a detailed examination of 'Botte e risposta', see also F. Croce 'Due nuove poesie di Montale', in *La Rassegna della letteratura italiana* 3, (1963) 493-506.

96 Montale's wife (née Drusilla Tanzi) was affectionately called 'Mosca', probably on account of her shortsightedness which compelled her to drone waywardly around the house. She died on 12 October 1963 and 'Xenia' was published privately in her memory in 1967. In addition to the original 14 fragments another 14 were published in *Strumenti critici*, 2 and 5, and were later reproduced in *L'approdo letterario*, 42. They now form part of the enlarged edition of *Satura* (1971). Xenium meant in Greek an offering made by one guest to another at dinner and conventionally these gifts were miniatures or still-lifes. Their connection with Montale's and, by extension, with Gozzano's art is self-evident. The word was also used by Goethe who is probably the poet's immediate source for it, since there is a reference in *Faust* (I) to mischievous 'Xenien' appearing as insects. (For further information see M.M. Grimshaw: 'Vertical and horizontal sightings in Montale's Satura', in *Italian Studies* XXIX, (1974), 74-87).

97 From 'La morte di Dio'.

98 From 'Tempo e tempi'.

99 From 'Botta e risposta', 2, part 2.

100 See ' "Satura" di Eugenio Montale', in *L'Approdo letterario* 53, (1971), 107-16. The above-quoted intervention by Montale appears on p.115.

XI

1 G. Zagarrio: *Quasimodo*, Il Castoro 33, Florence, 1969, p.33.
2 In *Otto studi*, p.210.
3 G. Paparelli: 'Humanitas e poesia di Quasimodo', in *Letterature moderne* (1961), 734.
4 See introduction to *Giorno dopo giorno* (Milan, 1947).
5 In *Quasimodo* (Cedam, 1943), p.33.
6 From 'Una poetica', in *Il poeta e il politico e altri saggi* (Milan, 1960), p.23.
7 From *Otto studi*, p.216.
8 From 'L'angelo'.
9 From 'A me pellegrino'.
10 See F.J. Jones 'Osservazioni sulla simbologia di Quasimodo', in *Cenobio* (May-June, 1961), 254-74.
11 In this respect we have to bear in mind Quasimodo's interest in Greek mythology and the fact that the central figure of orphic myth was the god Dionysus, who was originally a tree-god and often depicted as half-man and half-tree. We also recall the archetypal image of a tree in Rilke's *Sonette an Orpheus*, especially in sonnet 17 of the first part, where the tree has clear atavistic implications.
12 See O. Macrí: 'La poetica della parola', saggio introduttivo a *Poesie* di Salvatore Quasimodo, (Milan, 1938), pp.11-61. This essay is now reprinted in *Inventario* (1961), numero unico, 18-41, from which all quotations are taken. Macrí sees a dichotomy in Quasimodo's work between a 'poesia naturale' and a 'poesia geometrica', but nevertheless claims that his figurative intention is to provide 'una prova di esperienza totale' (p.25). Each word struggles to liberate a 'fantasma' which, like the angel-figure previously mentioned, becomes 'una puntuale percezione di marmo' (p.27).
13 See F. Flora: 'Salvatore Quasimodo: preludio sul lessico della poesia d'oggi', in *Letterature moderne* (1951), 2. Reprinted in *Scrittori italiani contemporanei* (Pisa, 1952).
14 Antonielli notes, for instance, that '. . . si potrebbe stendere un elenco di parole da lui amate, che tornano e ritornano in vari componimenti e frasi . . . che sembrano a volte costituire pretesto d'avvio, una sorta di commozione su cui un'intera poesia tenti poi d'accentrarsi' (op. cit., p.71). Likewise Romano stresses the point in a general way by saying that 'questo concepire il mondo come *parola* è in Quasimodo sovente un sentimento troppo insistito, che si irrigidisce in meccanismo'. (*La poetica dell'ermetismo*, Sansoni, 1942, p.88.) Finally Tedesco states openly that 'Spazio' is an example of the poet's 'immaginismo incomprensibile' (op. cit., p.41). When condemning the poet's archetypes in this way, however, we must always be careful to distinguish between mere repetition and a carefully conceived orphic 'return' of similar images which the poet uses to build up an appropriate atmosphere in his verse. It is presumably to his weaving of meaningless lyrical arabesques and their repetition that critics have applied the term Alexandrinism.
15 The splitting of landscapes into their constituent elements reminds us of the rending of the god in ancient orphism. The purpose was, of course, to illustrate the presence of the one in the many, and Quasimodo makes use of the anthropomorphized elements of nature as a means of mythicizing modern life, a practice he no doubt drew from ancient cultures.
16 For a detailed analysis of Quasimodo's image-chains, see my article in *Cenobio* mentioned earlier.
17 See, for instance, O. Macrí, 'De Libero e la crisi del naturalismo poetico', in *Caratteri e figure della poesia italiana contemporanea* (Florence, 1956), pp.235-52.
18 From 'A me discesa per nuova innocenza', in *Oboe sommerso* (1932).
19 From 'L'angelo', in *Oboe sommerso*.
20 The 'soave amico' mentioned in the poem is Salvatore Pugliatti who reawakened Quasimodo's interest in poetry in 1929 and later encouraged him to publish *Acque e terre*. During this period the poet regularly crossed over from Reggio Calabria to meet him in Messina and they made several trips to Tíndari together, during one of which the poem was drafted. For Pugliatti's own account of these events, see 'Preistoria di un colloquio amicale', in *Fiera letteraria*, (17 July 1955). The article is republished in the above-mentioned number of *Inventario*.

21 Of Sappho's poetry Quasimodo wrote: 'Pura è infatti la poesia di Saffo, espressa, cioè, con un linguaggio concreto e lineare – ignoto ai suoi contemporanei – la cui architettura rivela immagini forti, chiuse in una sfera, dove né un aggettivo, né un verbo possono penetrare.' (In *Il poeta e il politico e altri saggi*, pp.99-100.)
22 From 'I morti'.
23 'Ma è un panteismo della memoria. Il passaggio da *Acque e terre* a *Oboe sommerso* è unicamente di densità: il moto prosegue, anzi si rinfranca.' (In 'La poesia di Quasimodo', now reprinted in *Inventario* (1961), p.112.)
24 From 'Anellide ermafrodito'.
25 From 'Senza memoria di morte'.
26 From 'Metamorfosi nell'urna del santo'.
27 From 'Sillabe a Erato'.
28 From 'Sulle rive del Lambro'.
29 Quasimodo himself later refers to his 'cari animali' as 'talismani d'un mondo appena nato' in 'Dalla rocca di Bergamo alta', in *Giorno dopo giorno* (1947).
30 From 'Ride la gazza, nera sugli aranci'.
31 Cherchi's point is put as follows: 'Da noi non c'è stata una poesia della Resistenza, se mai è sorta dopo, come ripensamento; ma si può parlare di una poesia *sulla* Resistenza . . .' (In *Nuove dimensioni* 20-21, (1964), p.13.)
32 From 'Lettera'.
33 In *Il poeta e il politico e altri saggi*, p.27.
34 Ibid., pp.119-26.
35 Ibid., p.27.
36 From 'Forse il cuore'.
37 In *Lirici greci* (Milan, 1944), p.227.
38 Ibid., p.18.
39 For instance, we can trace back his cult of animal fetishes so common in *Giorno dopo giorno* to lines of the following kind which he translated from Sappho:

Leggiadri veloci uccelli
sulla nera terra ti portarono
densa agitando le ali per l'aria celeste.

40 See his essay on the 'Poesia di E.E. Cummings', in *Il poeta e il politico e altri saggi*, p.141.
41 We also note in this regard his translations from East European poets in the fifties like Mickiewicz, Sándor Petöfi and Tudo Arghezi.
42 From 'Lamento per il sud'.
43 Quasimodo, for instance, would undoubtedly have accepted Gide's remark at the time of his conversion to Communism, to the effect that '. . . je prétends rester parfaitement individualiste en plein assentiment communiste et à l'aide même du communisme. Car ma thèse a toujours été celle-ci: c'est en étant le plus particulier que chaque être sert le mieux la société.' (In *Littérature engagée*, N.F.R. ed., p.85.) It seems then that G. Grana goes too far when he asserts that l'imperativo della 'realtà' spesso è materialmente inteso da Quasimodo come in genere dai Marxisti. Realtà sono i fatti esterni, realismo per lui vuol dire passaggio dal 'mondo intimo' al 'mondo esterno' . . .' (In *Profili e letture di contemporanei*, Milan, 1962, p.230.) Probably the poet would not have gone further than G. Lukacs in his so-called worship of the material world, and would have acknowledged that 'la novità decisiva e feconda è sempre un contenuto nuovo che proviene dal mutamento della realtà storico-sociale.' (In *Il Marxismo e la critica letteraria* Turin, 1953, p.11) On this subject, however, see also Quasimodo's essay entitled 'Il poeta e il politico'.
44 From *Il poeta e il politico e altri saggi*, p.48.
45 Ibid., p.36.
46 Ibid., p.17.
47 From 'Dialogo'.
48 From 'Il mio paese è l'Italia'.
49 The poet's two wives were Bice Donetti and Maria Cumani. He married Bice in 1927 and she was somewhat older than Quasimodo himself. She is described as the 'donna emiliana' in his poetry and was born at Cremona. She died in 1947 and her death is commemorated in 'Epitaffio per Bice Donetti' in *La vita non è sogno*. In 1949 he married Maria Cumani who had already borne him a child, Alessandro, some time earlier. Their marriage was not a happy one and the couple soon parted. It is for this

reason that we read both of death and estrangement into this poem. I am indebted for the above information to Signora R. Quasimodo Samarelli and to Dr. D.E.E. Vittorini.

50 See *Il poeta e il politico e altri saggi*, p.36.

51 From 'Visibile, invisibile'.

52 From 'Al padre'.

53 From 'Solo che l'amore ti colpisca'.

54 For a full analysis of this poem, see my article: 'Il nuovo periodo della poesia quasimodea', in *Nuove dimensioni* 7, 3-11.

55 In 'Domande a Quasimodo', intervista di G. Finzi, in *L'Europa letteraria* 30-2, 24.

56 Ibid., p.24.

57 *Il poeta e il politico e altri saggi*, p.85.

58 Ibid., p.36.

Bibliography

A) POETIC WORKS OF THE PRINCIPAL POETS TREATED

Dino Campana (1885-1932)
Canti orfici (Ravagli, Marradi, 1914).
Canti orfici, a cura di Bino Binazzi (Vallecchi, Florence, 1928).
Canti orfici e altri scritti, a cura di E. Falqui (Vallecchi, 1952) (4th ed.).
Il piú lungo giorno (Archivi-Vallecchi, Milan, 1973) (2 vols.).
Opere e contributi, a cura di E. Falqui (Vallecchi, 1973) (2 vols.).
Orphic Songs (trans. by I.L. Salomon), October House Inc., New York, 1968.

Vincenzo Cardarelli (pseudonym of Nazareno Caldarelli) (1887-1959)
Poesie (Novissima, Rome, 1936).
Poesie (Mondadori, Milan, 1942) (con prefazione di G. Ferrata).
Poesie nuove (Neri Pozza, Venice, 1946).
Poesie (Fiumara, Milan, 1949).
Opere complete, a cura di R. Raimondi (Mondadori, Milan, 1962); 2nd ed. (Mondadori, 1981).
Invettiva e altre poesie disperse, a cura di B. Blasi e V. Scheiwiller (All'Insegna del pesce d'oro, Milan, 1964).

Sergio Corazzini (1886-1907)
Le dolcezze (Rome, 1904).
L'amaro calice (Tip. operaia romana cooperativa, Rome, 1905).
Le aureole (Tip. operaia romana cooperativa, Rome, 1905).
Poemetti in prosa (Rome, 1906).
Piccolo libro inutile (Tip operaia romana cooperativa, Rome, 1906). (Also contains poems by A. Tarchiani)
Elegia (Tip. operaia romana cooperativa, Rome, 1906).
Libro per la sera della domenica (Rome, 1906).
Liriche (Ricciardi, Naples, 1908).
Liriche (raccolta definitiva con pref. di Fausto M. Martini) (Ricciardi, Naples, 1922).
Poesie edite e inedite, a cura di Stefano Jacomuzzi (Einaudi, Turin, 1968).

Corrado Govoni (1884-1965)

Le Fiale (Lumachi, Florence, 1903); 2nd ed. (Garzanti, Milan, 1948).

Armonia in grigio et in silenzio (Lumachi, Florence, 1903).

Fuochi d'artifizio (Ganguzza-Lajosa, Palermo, 1905).

Gli aborti (Taddei, Ferrara, 1907).

Poesie elettriche (Edizioni futuriste di 'Poesia', Milan, 1911); 2nd ed. (Taddei, Ferrara, 1919).

L'inaugurazione della primavera ('La Voce', Florence, 1915); 2nd ed. (Taddei, Ferrara, 1919).

Rarefazioni (Edizioni futuriste di 'Poesia', Milan, 1915).

Poesie scelte (1903-1918) (Taddei, Ferrara, 1918); 2nd ed. (1920).

Tre grani da seminare (Palmer, Milan, 1920).

Il quaderno dei sogni e delle stelle (Mondadori, Milan, 1924).

Brindisi alla notte (Bottega di Poesia, Milan, 1924).

Il flauto magico ('Al tempo della fortuna', Rome, 1932).

Poema a Mussolini (Tip. Cuggiani, Rome, 1937).

Canzoni a bocca chiusa (Vallecchi, Florence, 1938).

Pellegrino d'amore (Mondadori, Milan, 1941).

Govonigiotto (S.T.E.L.I., Milan, 1943).

La fossa carnaia ardeatina (Movimento comunista d'Italia, Rome, 1944).

Aladino (Mondadori, Milan, 1946).

L'Italia odia i poeti ('Pagine nuove', Rome, 1950).

Antologia poetica (1903-1953), a cura di G. Spagnoletti (Sansoni, Florence, 1953).

Patria d'alto volo (Maia, Siena, 1953).

Preghiera al trifoglio (Casini, Rome, 1953).

Manoscritto nella bottiglia (Mondadori, Milan, 1954).

Stradario della primavera (Neri Pozza, Venice, 1958).

Poesie (1903-1959), a cura di G. Ravegnani (Mondadori, Milan, 1961).

La ronda di notte (Ceschina, Milan, 1966).

Il vino degli anni (L'Officina libri, Rome, 1979).

(For a selection from the unpublished volumes, *Conchiglia sul quaderno* (1948) and *I canti del puro folle* (1959), see *Poesie (1903-1959)*, a cura di G. Ravegnani.)

Guido Gozzano (1883-1916)

La via del rifugio (Streglio, Turin, 1907).

I colloqui (Treves, Milan, 1911).

Opere, a cura di Carlo Calcaterra e Alberto De Marchi (Garzanti, Milan, 1953).

La moneta seminata, intro. e note di F. Antonicelli (All'Insegna del pesce d'oro, Milan, 1968).

utte le poesie, Testo critico e note a cura di A. Rocca, intro. di M. Guglielminetti (Mondadori, Milan, 1980).

he man I pretend to be: the Colloquies and selected poems, translated by M. Palma (Princeton University Press, 1981).

ugenio Montale (1896-1981)

ssi di seppia (Gobetti, Turin, 1925); 2nd augmented edition (Ribet, Turin, 1928).

a casa dei doganieri e altre poesie (Edizioni dell'antico Fattore, Florence, 1932).

e occasioni (Einaudi, Turin, 1939).

nisterre (Edizioni Quaderni di Lugano, Lugano, 1943); 2nd ed. (Barbera, Florence, 1945).

a bufera e altro (Neri Pozza, Venice, 1956).

ccordi e pastelli, a cura di Vanni Scheiwiller (Tip.U. Allegretti di Campi, Milan, 1962).

atura (Officina Bodoni, Verona, 1962).

enia, (Tip. C. Bella barba, Sanseverino, Marche, 1967).

atura (Mondadori, Milan, 1971) (2nd enlarged edition).

iario del '71 e del '72 (Mondadori, Milan, 1973).

utte le poesie (Mondadori, 1977).

uaderno di quattro stagioni (Mondadori, Milan, 1977).

'opera in versi (Einaudi, Turin, 1980).

ltri versi e poesie disperse, a cura di G. Zampa (Mondadori, 1981).

elected poems, introduction by G. Cambon (New Directions, New York, 1965).

elected Poems translated by G. Kay (Penguin Books, Harmondsworth, 1969).

ew Poems, translated by G. Singh (Chatto & Windus, London, 1976).

alvatore Quasimodo (1901-1963)

cque e terre (Solaria, Florence, 1930).

boe sommerso (Circoli, Genoa, 1932).

dore di eucalyptus e altri versi (Edizioni del antico Fattore, Florence, 1933).

rato e Apòllion (Scheiwiller, Milan, 1936).

oesie (Primi Piani, Milan, 1938).

Ed è subito sera (Mondadori, Milan, 1942).

Con il piede straniero sopra il cuore (Edizioni 'Costume', Milan, 1946).

Giorno dopo giorno (Mondadori, Milan, 1947).

La vita non è sogno (Mondadori, Milan, 1949).

Il falso e vero verde (Schwarz, Milan, 1953); 2nd ed. (Mondadori, 1956).

La terra impareggiabile (Mondadori, Milan, 1958).
Poesie scelte di Quasimodo, a cura di Roberto Sanesi (Guanda, Parm 1959).
Tutte le poesie (Mondadori, Milan, 1960).
Dare e avere (Mondadori, Milan, 1966).
Selected Poems, translated by J. Bevan (Penguin Books, Harmondswort 1965).

Clemente Rebora (1885-1957)

Frammenti lirici (Libreria della 'Voce', Florence, 1913).
Canti anonimi (Il Convegno Editoriale, Milan, 1922).
Le poesie (1913-1947) (Vallecchi, Florence, 1947).
Canti dell'infermità (All'Insegna del pesce d'oro, Milan, 1956); 2 enlarged edition (1957).
Le poesie (1913-1957) (All'Insegna del pesce d'oro, Milan, 1961).
Aspirazioni e preghiere, raccolte da V. Scheiwiller (All'Insegna del pes d'oro, Milan, 1963).

Umberto Saba (pseudonym of Umberto Poli) (1883-1957)

Il mio primo libro di poesie (Trieste, 1903).
Poesie, con pref. di S. Benco (Casa editrice Italiana, Florence, 1911).
Coi miei occhi (La Voce, Florence, 1912).
La serena disperazione – Cose leggere e vaganti (Libreria antica moderna, Trieste, 1920).
L'amorosa spina (Libreria antica e moderna, Trieste, 1921).
Canzoniere (Libreria antica e moderna, Trieste, 1921).
Preludio e canzonette (Primo Tempo, Turin, 1923).
Autobiografia (Primo Tempo, Turin, 1924).
I prigioni (Primo Tempo, Turin, 1924).
Figure e canti (Treves, Milan, 1926).
L'Uomo (Trieste, 1928).
Preludio e fughe (Solaria, Florence, 1928).
Tre poesie per la mia balia (Presso l'Autore, Trieste, 1929).
Ammonizione e altre poesie (Presso l'Autore, Trieste, 1932).
Tre composizioni (Treves-Tumminelli-Treccani, Milan, 1933).
Parole (Carabba, Lanciano, 1934).
Ultime cose (Edizioni della collana di Lugano, Lugano, 1944).
Il Canzoniere (1900-1945) (Einaudi, Turin, 1945).
Mediterranee (Mondadori, Milan, 1946).
Il Canzoniere (1900-1947) (Einaudi, Turin, 1948).
Trieste e una donna (1910-1912) (Mondadori, Milan, 1950).

:celli (Edizioni dello Zibaldone, Trieste, 1950).
:celli – Quasi un racconto (Mondadori, Milan, 1951).
ɔigrafe – Ultime prose (Il saggiatore, Milan, 1959).
Canzoniere (Einaudi, Turin, 1961).
ntologia del Canzoniere (Einaudi, Turin, 1963).
ɔesie e prose scelte (Mondadori, Milan, 1976) (Oscar).
Canzoniere 1921, ed. crit. di G. Castellani (Fondazione Arnaldo e Alberto Mondadori, Milan, 1981).

iuseppe Ungaretti (1888-1970)

porto sepolto (Stab. tip. Friulano, Udine, 1916).
ı guerre. Une poésie de Giuseppe Ungaretti (Établissements Lux, Paris, 1919).
'llegria di Naufragi (Vallecchi, Florence, 1919).
porto sepolto (Stamperia Apuana, La Spezia, 1923).
'Allegria (Preda, Milan, 1931).
ntimento del tempo (Novissima, Rome, 1933).
'Allegria (Novissima, Rome, 1936).
ntimento del tempo (Novissima, Rome, 1936).
ita d'un uomo: L'Allegria (Mondadori, Milan, 1942).
ita d'un uomo: Sentimento del tempo (Mondadori, Milan, 1943).
·ammenti per la Terra Promessa (Concilium Lithographicum, Rome, 1945).
ita d'un uomo: Poesie disperse (Mondadori, Milan, 1945).
erniers jours 1919 (Garzanti, Milan, 1947).
ita d'un uomo: Il dolore (Mondadori, Milan, 1947).
ı terra promessa (Mondadori, Milan, 1950).
ridasti: Soffoco . . . (Fiumara, Milan, 1951).
n grido e paesaggi (Schwarz, Milan, 1952).
ita d'un uomo: La terra promessa (Mondadori, Milan, 1954).
ita d'un uomo: Un grido e paesaggi (Mondadori, Milan, 1954).
taccuino del vecchio (Mondadori, Milan, 1960).
ita d'un uomo: Il taccuino del vecchio (Mondadori, Milan, 1961).
5° compleanno: Il taccuino del vecchio, Apocalissi (Le Noci, Milan, 1963).
ngaretti: Poesie, a cura di Elio Filippo Accrocca (Nuova Accademia, Milan, 1964).
pocalissi e sedici traduzioni (Bucciarelli, Ancona, 1965).
Carso non è piú un inferno (Scheiwiller, Milan, 1966).
lorte delle stagioni (Fógola, Turin, 1967).
ialogo (Bruna Bianco – Giuseppe Ungaretti) (Fógola, Turin, 1968).

Croazia segreta (Grafico Romero, Rome, 1969).
Tutte le poesie (Mondadori, Milan, 1969).
Selected Poems, translated by P. Creagh (Penguin Book Harmondsworth, 1969).
L'impietrito e il velluto (Grafico Romero, Rome, 1970).
Selected Poems of Giuseppe Ungaretti, translated by A. Mandelbau (Cornell University Press, 1975). (First appearing as *Life of a ma* Hamilton, London; New Directions New York; Scheiwiller, Mila 1958).
Vita d'un uomo. 106 poesie (1914-1960), a cura di G. Raboni (Mondado Milan, 1982).

B) GENERAL BIBLIOGRAPHY

(The poetic works of the principal poets treated are excluded from th bibliography since they have been dealt with in Bibliography A. Pro works by the same authors, however, have been listed if reference has bee made to them in the text.)

E.F. Accrocca, *Ritorno a Portonaccio* (Mondadori, Milan, 1959).
S. Agosti, *Il testo poetico* (Rizzoli, Milan, 1972).
A. d'Alba, *Baionette* (Ed. fut. di 'Poesia', Milan, 1915).
V. Aleixandre, *Poesias completas* (Aguilar, Madrid, 1960).
G. Almansi, 'Earth and water in Montale's poetry', in *Forum for mode language studies*, 2 (1966), 377-85.
Eugenio Montale (Edinburgh University Press, Edinburgh, 1977), c author with B. Merry.
'Ipotesi e documenti per il primo Montale', in *Paragone*, No. 3((1975), 86-104.
L. Anceschi, *Autonomia e eteronomia dell'arte* (Sansoni, Florence, 1936 reprinted (Vallecchi, Florence, 1959).
Saggi di poetica e di poesia (Parenti, Florence, 1942).
Lirici nuovi (Anthology) (Hoepli, Milan, 1942); reprinted (All'Insegr del pesce d'oro, Milan, 1958), and by Mursia (Milan, 1964).
'Pascoli verso il Novecento', in *Il Verri* 4 (1958), 9-33.
'Ungaretti e la critica', in *Letteratura* 35-36 (1958), 236-45.
Le poetiche del Novecento in Italia (Paravia, Turin, 1972) (4th ed.).
Da Ungaretti a D'Annunzio (Il Saggiatore, Milan, 1976).

L. Anceschi & S. Antonielli, *Lirica del Novecento* (Anthology) (Vallecchi, Florence, 1953); reprinted in 1961.

C. Angelini, 'Discussione su Pascoli', in *La Ronda* (7 November 1919), 13-15.

A. Angioletti, *E fu subito sera* (Marotta, Naples, 1969).

L. Angioletti, *Invito alla lettura di Guido Gozzano* (Mursia, Milan, 1975).

S. Antonielli, *Aspetti e figure del Novecento* (Guando, Parma, 1955).

'La memoria di Montale', in *Studi in memoria di Luigi Russo* (Nistri-Lischi, Pisa, 1974), pp. 525-32.

G. Apollinaire, *Oeuvres complètes* (Bibl. de la Pléiade, Gallimard, Paris, 1956).

Oeuvres complètes, sous la direction de M. Décaudin (Ballard & Lecat, Paris, 1966) (3 vols.).

M. Apollonio, *Ermetismo* (Cedam, Padua, 1945).

Letteratura dei contemporanei (La Scuola, Brescia, 1956); reprinted in 1957.

U. Apollonio (ed.), *Futurist Manifestos* (Thames and Hudson, London, 1973).

C. Arrighi, *La Scapigliatura e il 6 febbraio* (Sonzogno, Milan, 1861).

A. Aurier, 'Le symbolisme en peinture: Paul Gauguin', in *Le Mercure de France* (March, 1891), 155-65.

D'Arco S. Avalle, *''Gli orecchini'' di Montale* (Il Saggiatore, Milan, 1965).

Tre saggi su Montale (Einaudi, Turin, 1970).

La poesia nell'attuale universo semiologico (Giappichelli, Turin, 1974).

R. Aymone, *Saba e la psicoanalisi* (Il Sagittario, Guida, Naples, 1971).

G. Bachelard, *La poétique de l'espace* (Presses universitaires de France, Paris, 1957).

L. Baldacci, *I crepuscolari* (ed. ERI, Turin, 1961).

A. Baldazzi, A. Briganti, L. delli Colli, G. Mariani, *Contributo a una bibliografia del futurismo* (Cooperativa Scrittori, Rome, 1977).

N. Baldi, *Il paradiso di Saba* (Mondadori, Milan, 1958).

G. Baldissone, *Il male di scrivere – L'inconscio e Montale* (Einaudi, Turin, 1979).

A. Balduino, ' ''Verso Vienna''. Lettura di una lirica montaliana', in *Studi Novecenteschi,* (June-September, 1977), 173-204.

D. Banfi Malaguzzi, *Il primo Rebora, 22 lettere inedite (1905-13)* (All'Insegna del pesce d'oro, Milan, 1964).

G. Bàrberi Squarotti, *Astrazione e realtà* (Rusconi e Paolazzi, Milan, 1960).

'Mito e realtà di Campana', in *La situazione* (1960), 13-14.

'Montale, la metrica e altro', in *Letteratura*, 51 (1961), 53-66.

Poesia e narrativa del secondo Novecento (Mursia, Milan, 1961); reprinted in 1967.

Simboli e struttura della poesia del Pascoli (D'Anna, Messina-Florence, 1966).

La cultura e la poesia italiana nel dopoguerra (Cappelli, Bologna, 1968).

Il codice di Babele (Rizzoli, Milan, 1972).

Gli inferi e il labirinto (Cappelli, Bologna, 1974).

Barbuto, A., *Le parole di Montale – glossario del lessico poetico* (Bulzoni, Rome, 1973).

P. Bargellini, *Il Novecento*, Panorama storico della letteratura italiana, vol. XI (Vallecchi, Florence, 1950).

L. Barile, *Bibliografia montaliana* (Mondadori, Milan, 1977).

M. Barrès, *Les Déracinés* (Plon, Paris, 1897) (2 vols.).

Mes cahiers, Vol. III (Plon, Paris, 1931).

Scènes et doctrines du nationalisme, Vol. I (Plon, Paris, 1945).

R. Barthes, *S/Z* (Editions du Seuil, Paris, 1970).

L. Bartolini, *Pianete* (Vallecchi, Florence, 1953).

'Memorie di Dino Campana', in *Scritti d'eccezione* (Il Càmpano, Pisa, 1942).

L. Basso & L. Anderlini, *Le riviste di Piero Gobetti* (Feltrinelli, Milan, 1961).

M. Bataillon, *L'essence de l'Espagne* (trans. of M. Unamuno, *En torno al casticismo*) (Plon-Nourrit, Paris, 1923).

P. Battaglini, 'Fenomenologia, fondazione, estetica', in *Il Verri*, 6 (1961), 18-31.

C. Baudelaire, *Oeuvres complètes*, ed. J. Crépet (Conard-Lambert) (19 vols.) (Paris, 1922-53).

C. Baumgarth, *Geschichte des Futurismus* (Rowohlt Verlag, Reinbek Verlag, Reinbek bei Hamburg, 1966).

G. Bays, *The Orphic Vision, Seer Poets from Novalis to Rimbaud* (University of Nebraska Press, Lincoln, 1964).

C.B. Beall, see A. Crisafulli.

A. Béguin, *L'âme romantique et le rêve* (Corti, Paris, 1946).

A. Benvento, ' "La morte di Tantalo" di Sergio Corazzini', in *Otto/Novecento*, 4-5 (1977), 159.

P. Bergman, *Modernolatria e simultaneità* (Studia litterarum Uppsaliensia, Uppsala, 1962).

H. Bergson, *Essai sur les données immédiates de la conscience* (Alcan, Paris, 1906) (5th ed.); first published 1889.

Matter and memory (Allen & Unwin, London, 1950); first published 1896.

Évolution créatrice (Alcan, Paris, 1911) (7th ed.); first published 1907.

La pensée et le mouvant (Presses universitaires de France, Paris, 1946) (22nd ed.); first published in 1934.

A. Bertrand, *Gaspard de la nuit* (À l'enseigne du pot cassé, Paris, 1946); first published in 1842.

L. Bethell, 'Gracián, Tesauro and the nature of metaphysical wit', in *Northern Miscellany,* 1 (1953), 19-40.

C. Betocchi, 'Considerazioni di oggi sulla poesia di Clemente Rebora', in *L'Approdo letterario* (April-June, 1952), 79-83.

V. Betteloni, *In primavera* (Treves, Milan, 1869).

P. Bigongiari, Review of De Robertis's *Saggio sul Leopardi,* in *Letteratura,* 5 (1938), 156.

Il senso della lirica italiana (Sansoni, Florence, 1951).

'Per un'analisi della lirica "Sentimento del tempo" ' in *Letteratura*, 35-6 (1958), 168-73.

Poesia italiana del Novecento (Fabbri, Milan, 1960).

Poesia come funzione simbolica del linguaggio (Rizzoli, Milan, 1972).

'Struttura dell' "Allegria" di Ungaretti', in *L'Albero*, 52 (1974), 3-35.

'Nel cuore del Sentimento del tempo: da "simulacro a fiamma vera" ', in *Paradigma 1* (La Nuova Italia, Florence, 1977), 151-233.

W. Binni, *La poetica del decadentismo* (Sansoni, Florence, 1961) (3rd ed.).

Poetica, critica e storia letteraria (Laterza, Bari, 1964).

M. Blanchot, *L'espace littéraire* (Gallimard, Paris, 1955).

M. Blasi, 'Gozzano, sua umanità e sua poesia', in *Città di vita*, 5 (1960), 665-76.

C. Bo, 'Nozione di poesia', in *Corrente* (15 June 1939).

Otti studi (Vallecchi, Florence, 1939).

Nuovi studi (Vallecchi, Florence, 1946).

'Riflessioni critiche sul futurismo', in *Paragone* 36, 21-35.

'Rievocazione di Rebora', in *Il Verri*, 5 (1959), 37-53.

Eredità di Leopardi e altri saggi (Vallecchi, Florence, 1964).

C. Bo & G. Mounin, 'La nouvelle poésie italienne', in *Cahiers du sud*, 323 (1954), 3-22.

N. Bobbio, *La filosofia del decadentismo* (Chiantore, Turin, 1944).

U. Boccioni (and others), 'La pittura futurista manifesto tecnico', in *Archivi del futurismo*, a cura di M.D. Gambillo and T. Fiori (De Luca, Rome, 1958).

G. Boine, *Frantumi, seguiti da Plausi e Botte* (La Voce, Florence, 1918).

A. Boito, *Re Orso* (Brigola, Milan, 1865).

Tutti gli scritti (Mondadori, Milan, 1942).
G. Bonalumi, *Cultura e poesia di Campana* (Vallecchi, Florence, 1955).
P. Bonfiglioli, 'Pascoli, Gozzano, Montale e la poesia dell'oggetto', in *Il Verri, 4* (1958), 34-54.
N. Bonifazi, *Dino Campana* (Ed. dell'Ateneo, Rome, 1964).
G.D. Bonino, 'Il taccuino del vecchio e il 'terzo tempo' della poesia ungarettiana', in *Letteratura*, 51 (1961), 47-52.
E. Bonora, *La poesia di Montale,* (Tirrenia, Turin, 1965) (2 vols.).
Le metafore del vero, Saggi sulle "Occasioni" di Eugenio Montale (Bonacci, Rome, 1981).
G.A. Borgese, 'Poesia crepuscolare – Moretti, Martini, Chiaves', in *La Stampa* (10 September 1910); reprinted in *La vita e il libro* (Zanichelli, Bologna, 1928) (2nd ed.), pp.120-28.
A. Borlenghi, 'Sulla poesia di Umberto Saba', in *Poesia* VII (1947), 88-97.
Fra Ottocento e Novecento, note e saggi (Nistri-Lischi, Pisa, 1955).
U. Bosco, 'Leopardi, Thovez e i crepuscolari', in *Convivium,* 3 (1936) 263-72.
H. de Bouillane de Lacoste, *Illuminations* (Mercure de France, Paris, 1949) (see Rimbaud).
V. Bradshaw, *From pure silence to impure dialogue* (Anthology) (Las Americas Publishing Co., New York, 1971).
H. Brémond, *La poésie pure, avec un débat sur la poésie de R. de Souza* (Grasset, Paris, 1926).
S. Briosi, *Marinetti* (Il Castoro, La nuova Italia, Florence, 1969).
R. Broggini, 'Briciole montaliane', in *Strumenti critici*, 25 (1975), 383-90.
F. Bruni, ' "Verso Vienna" ': ipotesi per l'occasione', in *Sigma* 1 (1980), 21-36.
J. Burnet, *Greek philosophy* (Macmillan, London, 1933).
P. Cabañas, *El mito de Orfeo en la literatura española* (Consejo superior de investigaciones cientificas, Madrid, 1948).
E. Caccia, *Lettura e storia di Saba* (Bietti, Milan, 1967).
C. Calcaterra, *Con Guido Gozzano e altri poeti* (Zanichelli, Bologna, 1944).
'Modi petrarcheschi nell'arte del Gozzano', in *Studi petrarcheschi*, Vol. 1. (1948) Minerva, 213-23.
G. Cambon, *La lotta con Proteo* (Bompiani, Florence, 1963).
' "Motets": The occasion of Epiphany', in *PMLA*, 7 (1967), 471-84.
Giuseppe Ungaretti (Columbia University Press, New York/London, 1967).
Eugenio Montale (Columbia University Press, New York/London, 1972).

La poesia di Ungaretti (Einaudi, Turin, 1976).

Eugenio Montale's Poetry. A dream in Reason's Presence (Princeton University Press, 1982).

D. Campana, 'Sogno di prigione, L'incontro di Regolo, Piazza Sarzano', in *Lacerba* (15 November 1914), 315-16.

Dino Campana – Sibilla Aleramo: Lettere (Vallecchi, Florence, 1958).

Taccuinetto faentino (Vallecchi, Florence, 1960).

Fascicolo marradese inedito, a cura di F. Ravagli (Giunti/Bemporad/Marzocco, Florence, 1972).

Dino Campana oggi, Atti del convegno Firenze 18-19 marzo 1973 (Vallecchi, Florence, 1973).

Le mie lettere sono fatte per esser bruciate, a cura di Gabriel Cacho Millet, (All'Insegna del pesce d'oro, Milan, 1978).

V. Cardarelli, 'Omaggio a Cardarelli', in *La Fiera letteraria* (22 May 1950).

'Inchiesta sulla poesia contemporanea', in *Letterature moderne* (1956), 564-5.

Opere complete, a cura di G. Raimondi (Mondadori, Milan, 1962)

Lettere a un vecchio amico ed altri scritta (Edizioni italiane moderne, Bologna, 1970).

Epistolario, ordinato da Bruno Biasi (Centro Studi Cardarelliani del Lions Club di Tarquinia, Tarquinia, 1981).

F. Carnasciali, 'Didascalismo e poesia nel poemetto gozzaniano sulle farfalle', in *La revue des études italiennes,* 1 (1977), 49-61.

U. Carpi, 'Montale dopo il Fascismo: i primi anni di collaborazione al "Corriere della sera" ', in *Belfagor,* 2 (1968), 197-230.

Montale dopo il Fascismo, dalla "Bufera" a "Satura" (Liviana, Padua, 1971).

'La Voce'. Letteratura e primato degli intellettuali (De Donato, Bari, 1975).

J. Cary, *Three modern Italian poets* (New York University Press, 1969).

G. Cassieri, *La Ronda (1919-23)* (ERI, Turin, 1969).

B. Cattafi, *Nel centro della mano* (La Meridiana, Milan, 1951).

G. Cattanei, *La Liguria nella poesia italiana del Novecento* (Silva, Milan, 1966).

G. Cattaneo, 'Montale e la lirica italiana', in *Palatina,* 2 (1957), 20-30.

G. Cavalli, *Ungaretti* (Fabbri, Milan, 1958).

O. Cecchi, *L'aspro vino. Ricordo di Saba a Firenze '43-'44*, con due inediti del poeta (All'Insegna del pesce d'oro, Milan, 1967).

Cecco d'Ascoli, *L'Acerba* (Carabba, Lanciano, 1916).

L. Cellier, *Fabre d'Olivet* (Nizet, Paris, 1953).

A. Chastel, *Marsile Ficin et l'art* (Droz, Geneva, 1954).
L. Cherchi, *I contrasti della nuova poesia* (Maestri, Milan, 1961).
'Poesia della resistenza', in *Nuove dimensioni*, 20-21 (1964), 11-30.
'Ipotesi sul futurismo' in *Poesia e critica* 8-9 (1966), 46-64.
F. Chiappelli, *Langage traditionnel et langage personnel dans la poésie italienne contemporaine* (L'Université de Neuchâtel, 1951).
'Glossa ungarettiana: una corolla di tenebre', in *Letteratura,* 35, 271.
H. B. Chipp, 'Orphism and color theory', in *Art Bulletin* (March, 1958), 62-7.
R. Christoflour, *Le Cardonnel, pelérin de l'invisible* (Plon, Paris, 1938).
A. Cima & C. Segre, (editors), *Eugenio Montale* (Rizzoli, Milan, 1977).
J. Cohen, *Structure du langage poétique* (Flammarion, Paris, 1966).
J.M. Cohen, *The baroque lyric* (Hutchinson University Library, London, 1963).
G.B. Conte, *Memoria dei poeti e sistema letterario* (Einaudi, Turin, 1974).
G. Contini, *Esercizi di lettura* (Parenti, Florence, 1939); reprinted by Le Monnier in 1947.
Un anno di letteratura (Le Monnier, Florence, 1942).
Pour présenter E. Montale, (Introduction to *Choix de poèmes*, ed. du Continent, Geneva, 1946); also in *Paragone*, 48 (1953), 3-13.
Letteratura dell'Italia unita (Sansoni, Florence, 1968).
Altri esercizi (Einaudi, Turin, 1972).
Esercizi di lettura (Einaudi, Turin, 1974).
F. Contorbia, 'Aggiunte per Montale critico', in *La Rassegna della letteratura italiana*, 2-3 (1970), 417-38.
C. Cordiè, 'Louis Le Cardonnel e Bino Binazzi' (con un appendice di lettere inedite), in *La Rassegna d'Italia* (July, 1946), 53-67.
M. Corti, *Principi della comunicazione letteraria* (Bompiani, Milan, 1976). (See also under Montale, E., interview with poet in L'*Approdo letterario* (1971).)
M. Constanzo, 'Ulissimo o orfismo . . .?', in *La Fiera letteraria,* (14 June 1953), and in *Studi critici* (Bardi, Rome, 1955).
B. Crémieux, *Panorama de la littérature italienne contemporaine* (Kra, Paris, 1928).
A. Crisafulli, *Linguistic and literary studies in honor of H.A. Hatzfield* (Catholic University of America Press, Washington, 1963) (Contains C.B. Beall, 'Eugenio Montale's "Sarcofaghi" ', pp.65-78).
B. Croce, *Estetica* (Laterza, Bari, 1950) (9th ed.).
La poesia (Laterza, Bari, 1953) (5th ed.).
La letteratura della nuova Italia, Vol. VI (Laterza, Bari, 1957) (4th ed.).

F. Croce, 'Due nuove poesie di Montale', in *La Rassegna della letteratura italiana*, 3 (1963), 493-506.

F. Curi, *Corrado Govoni* (Mursia, Milan, 1964).

Perdita d'aureola (Einaudi, Turin, 1977).

E.M. Curtius, *European literature and the Latin Middle Ages* (Routledge & Kegan Paul, London, 1953).

L. Dall'Albero, ' "Petrarchismo" e memoria poetica in Leopardi', in *La Rassegna della letteratura italiana,* 1-2 (1983), 88-101.

G.D'Annunzio, *Il trionfo della morte* (Treves, Milan, 1924).

Poema paradisiaco: Odi navali (Treves, Milan, 1925).

Le laudi: Alcyone (Zanichelli, Bologna, 1949).

G. Debenedetti, *Saggi critici* (Mondadori, Milan, 1952); first ed. (Solaria, 1929).

'Ultime cose per Saba', in *Nuovi argomenti*, 30 (1958), 1-19.

Introduction to U. Saba, *Epigrafe ultime prose* (Il Saggiatore, Milan, 1959).

Poesia italiana del Novecento (Garzanti, Milan, 1974).

L. de Castris, *Decadentismo e realismo* (Adriatica, Bari, 1960).

L. De Libero, *Solstizio* (Novissima, Rome, 1934); reprinted in 1936.

Testa (Ed. della Cometa, Rome, 1937).

L. De Maria, *Marinetti e il Futurismo* (Mondadori, Milan, 1973).

G. De Matteis, *Cultura e poesia di V. Cardarelli* (Lucera, 1971).

G. de Rienzo, *Guido Gozzano* (Rizzoli, Milan, 1983).

G. De Robertis, 'Saper leggere', in *La Voce*, VII (1915), 488-98.

Scrittori del Novecento (Le Monnier, Florence, 1946) (3rd ed.).

'Sulla poesia di Campana' in *Poesia,* VI (1947), 80-94.

'Sulla formazione della poesia di Ungaretti', in G. Ungaretti, *Poesie disperse* (Mondadori, Milan, 1954) (2nd ed.).

Altro Novecento (Le Monnier, Florence, 1962).

Scritti vociani (Le Monnier, Florence, 1967).

C. Di Biase, *Invito alla lettura di Cardarelli* (Mursia, Milan, 1975).

A. Dolfi, *A. Onofri,* (Il Castoro, La Nuova Italia, Florence, 1976).

F. Donini, 'Poesie disperse di S. Corazzini', in *Nuova antologia* (August-September, 1942).

Vita e poesia di Sergio Corazzini (De Silva, Turin, 1949).

J. Donne, *Complete poetry and selected prose* (Nonesuch Press, London, 1929).

F. Dueros, 'Rhétorique du pathétisme. Lire Corazzini', in *Lingua e stile* 1 (1978), 59-87.

M. Eliade, *Le mythe de l'éternel retour* (Gallimard, Paris, 1949).

T.S. Eliot, 'Tradition and the Individual Talent' (1919) in *Selected Essays* (Faber & Faber, London, 1982).

Collected Poems (1909-62) (Faber & Faber, London, 1963).

R. Esposito, *Ideologie della neo-avanguardia* (Liguori, Naples, 1976).

L. Fallacara, *"Il Frontespizio"* (S. Giovanni Valdarno, Rome, 1961).

E. Falqui, *Il futurismo, il Novecentismo* (ERI, Turin, 1952).

'Per una storia del rapporto tra Nietzsche e Campana', in *La Fiera letteraria,* (14 June 1953).

'Dino Campana in bacheca con Nietzsche' in *Novecento letterario*, serie quarta (Vallecchi, Florence, 1954), pp.88-97.

Novecento letterario, serie seconda (Vallecchi, Florence, 1960).

Campana, *Opere e contributi* (Vallecchi, Florence, 1973) (2 vols).

Per una cronistoria dei 'Canti orfici' (Vallecchi, Florence, 1960).

Capitoli per una storia della nostra prosa d'arte del Novecento (Panorama, Milan, 1938); reprinted Mursia (Milan, 1964).

M. Farber, *The foundation of phenomenology* (Harvard University Press, Cambridge Mass., 1943).

G. Faso, *La critica e Ungaretti* (Cappelli, Bologna, 1977).

G. Ferrata (and others), *Avanguardia e neo-avanguardia* (Sugar, Milan, 1966).

G. Finzi, *Invito alla lettura di Salvatore Quasimodo* (Mursia, Milan, 1973).

Poesia in Italia (1959-78) (Mursia, Milan, 1979).

F. Flora, *Dal romanticismo al futurismo* (Porta, Piacenza, 1921).

La poesia ermetica (Laterza, Bari, 1936); reprinted in 1947.

Saggi di poetica moderna (D'Anna, Messina-Florence, 1949).

'Salvatore Quasimodo: preludio sul lessico della poesia d'oggi', in *Letterature moderne,* 2 (1951), (Reprinted in *Scrittori italiani contemporanei,* Nistri-Lischi, Pisa, 1952).

Orfismo della parola (Cappelli, Rocca San Casciano, 1953).

Storia della letteratura italiana, Vol. V (Mondadori, Milan, 1953), (7th ed.).

La poesia e la prosa di G. Carducci (Nistri-Lischi, Pisa, 1959).

La poesia di Giovanni Pascoli (Zanichelli, Bologna, 1959).

G. Folena (and others), *Ricerche sulla lingua poetica contemporanea*, Quaderni del circolo filologico padovano presentazione di G. Folena, (Liviana, Padua, 1966) (Essays on Rebora, Saba, Ungaretti, Montale, Pavese).

L. Folgore, *Il canto dei motori* (Ed. fut. di 'Poesia', Milan, 1912).

A. Folli, 'Il laboratorio poetico di Govoni: 1902-1908', in *La Rassegna della lett. it..* (1974), 437-455.

L. Fontana, 'Évolution poétique de S. Corazzini', in *La revue des études italiennes* (April-September, 1938), 176-202.
P. Fontana, 'Nota sullo stile di Rebora', in *Letteratura,* 53-4 (1961), 36-43.
M. Forti, *Le proposte della poesia* (Marsia, Milan, 1963).
Eugenio Montale (Mursia, Milan, 1973).
F. Fortini, *I poeti del Novecento* (Laterza, Bari, 1977).
U. Foscolo, *I sepolcri* (Piazza, Palermo, 1890).
A. & R. Fouque, 'I novissimi' in *Cahiers du sud,* 382 (1965), 163-93.
A. Frattini, *Poeti italiani del Novecento* (Accademia di studi 'Cielo d'Alcamo', Alcamo, 1952).
Da Tommaseo a Ungaretti (Cappelli, Rocca San Casciano, 1959).
Poeti italiani tra primo e secondo Novecento (I.P.L., Milan, 1967).
Poesia nuova in Italia tra ermetismo e neoavanguardia (I.P.L., Milan, 1967).
Dai crepuscolari ai 'Novissimi' (Marzorati, Milan, 1969).
H. Friedrich, *La lirica moderna* (Garzanti, Milan, 1961) (translation of: *Die Struktur der modernen Lyrik,* Rowoholts Deutsche Enzyklopädie, Hamburg, 1956.).
E.M. Fusco, *La lirica* (Vallardi, Milan, 1950) (2 vols).
R. Fuselli, *Vincenzo Cardarelli* (Edizioni italiane moderne, Bologna, 1977).
C. Galimberti, *Dino Campana* (Mursia, Milan, 1967).
A. Galletti, *Storia della letteratura italiana: il Novecento* (Vallardi, Milan, 1935).
S. Gamberini, *La poesia di T.S. Eliot* (Istituto universitario di Magistero, Genoa, 1954).
Poeti metafisici e cavalieri in Inghilterra (Olschki, Florence, 1959).
M.D. Gambillo & T. Fiori, *Archivi del futurismo* (De Luca, Rome, 1958).
A. Gargiulo, *Scritti di estetica* (Le Monnier, Florence, 1952).
Letteratura del Novecento (Le Monnier, Florence, 1958) (3rd ed.).
E. Garin, *La cultura italiana fra Ottocento e Novecento* (Laterza, Bari, 1962).
Storia della filosofia italiana (Einaudi, Turin, 1966) (3 vols.).
P.M. Gathercole, 'Two kindred spirits: Eugenio Montale and T.S. Eliot', in *Italica*, 3 (1955), 170-9.
A. Gatto, *Poesia* (Vallecchi, Florence, 1943).
Nuove poesie (Mondadori, Milan, 1950).
J. Geninasca, ' ''Evento'' di Mario Luzi', in *Revue romane* (1970), 17-38.
E. Gennarini, *La Scapigliatura milanese* (Scalabruni, Naples, 1961).
G. Gerola, 'Cronologia del Quaderno', in *La Fiera letteraria* (14 September 1952).

Dino Campana (Sansoni, Florence, 1955).
G. Getto, *Poeti, critici e cose varie del Novecento* (Sansoni, Florence, 1953).
Carducci e Pascoli (Zanichelli, Bologna, 1957).
'Guido Gozzano e la letteratura del Novecento', in *Lettere italiane*, 4 (1966), 403-26.
R. Ghil, *Traité du verbe* (Giraud, Paris, 1886).
F. Giannessi, *Gli ermetici* (La Scuola, Brescia, 1951).
'La bufera e altro', in *Il ponte,* 8-9 (1956), 157-77 (review).
A. Gide, *Journal*, Vol. 1 (N.R.F., Paris, 1940).
Littérature engagée (N.R.F., Paris, 1950).
M. Gigante, *L'ultimo Quasimodo e la poesia greca* (Guida, Naples, 1970).
F. Gilles de la Tourette, *Robert Delaunay* (Massin, Paris, 1950).
E.M. Girardi, 'Problematica e poesia di Saba', in *Vita e pensiero* (1957), 731-38.
E. Giunta, *E. Montale. Ovvero il linguaggio come sintesi* (Centro Pitrè, Palermo, 1976).
D. Gnoli, *Poesie edite e inedite* (Società tip. ed. nazionale, Turin-Rome, 1907).
P. Gobetti, *Opere complete* (Einaudi, Turin, 1969) (3 vols.).
C. F. Goffis, *La lirica italiana del Novecento* (Tilgher, Genoa, 1975) (2 vols.).
G. Govoni, 'La caccia all'usignolo', in *Il teatro futurista sinetetico* (Bibl. teatrale dell'Istituto, Milan, n.d.).
'Revisione della poesia futurista', in *Il Meridiano di Roma*, 14 (March, 1937), 3-4.
G. Gozzano, *Lettere d'amore di Guido Gozzano e Amalia Guglielminetti*, a cura di S. Asciamprener (Garzanti, Milan, 1951).
B. Gracián, 'Agudeza y arte de ingenio', in *Obras completas* (Aguilar, Madrid, 1944).
A. Graf, *Poesie (1893-1906)* (Loescher, Turin, 1915).
A. Gramsci, *Letteratura e vita nazionale* (Einaudi, Turin, 1950).
G. Grana, *Profili e letture di contemporanei* (Marzorati, Milan, 1962).
A. Grande, *La Strada al mare* (Vallecchi, Florence, 1943).
E. Graziosi, *Il tempo in Montale – Storia di un tema* (La Nuova Italia, Florence, 1978).
G. Grazzini, 'Lettere inedite di Clemente Rebora' (to Countess Bice Jahn Rusconi (1926-31)), in *L'osservatore politico letterario,* 11 (1961), 47-68.
L. Greco, *Montale commenta Montale* (Pratiche editrice, Parma, 1980).

A.J. Greimas (editor), *Essais de sémiotique poétique* (Larousse, Paris, 1972).

M.M. Grimshaw, 'Vertical and horizontal sightings in Montale's Satura', in *Italian Studies,* XXIX (1974), 74-87.

L. Guaita, *La scienza dei colori e la pittura* (Hoepli, Milan, 1893).

S. Guarnieri, 'Crepuscolari, Futuristi, Vociani', in *Letterature moderne* (1962), 148-66.

G. Guglielmi & E. Pagliarani, *Manuale di poesia sperimentale* (Mondadori, Milan, 1966).

M. Guglielminetti, *Clemente Rebora* (Mursia, Milan, 1961).

La "scuola dell'ironia" Gozzano e i viciniori (Florence, 1984).

S. Guglielmino, *Guido al Novecento* (principato, Milan, 1978).

M. Guidacci, *La sabbia e l'angelo* (Vallecchi, Florence, 1946).

W.K.G. Guthrie, *The Greeks and their Gods* (Methuen, London, 1950).

I. Gutia, 'Il tempo mitico di Quasimodo', in *Letterature moderne* (1951), 331-41.

Il linguaggio di Ungaretti (Le Monnier, Florence, 1959).

P.R.J. Hainsworth, 'The poetry of Andrea Zanzotto', in *Italian Studies,* XXXVII (1982), 101-21.

M. Hamburger, *The truth of poetry* (Penguin Books, 1972); 1st ed. (Weidenfeld & Nicolson, London, 1969).

M. Hanne, 'Ungaretti's La terra promessa and the Aeneid', in *Italica,* 1 (1973), 3-25.

E. Heller, *The disinherited mind* (Penguin Books, 1961); 1st ed. (Bowes & Bowes, Cambridge, 1952).

C. Henri, *Le cercle chromatique* (Verdin, Paris, 1888).

C. de C.L. Huffman, *Montale and the Occasions of Poetry* (Princeton University Press, 1983).

E. Husserl, *Ideas, pure phenomenology* (Allen & Unwin, London, 1931).

D. Isella, *Lingua e stile di Carlo Dossi* (Ricciardi, Milan-Naples, 1958).

Eugenio Montale, Mottetti, (Il Saggiatore, Piacenza, 1980).

R. Jacobbi, *Invito alla lettura di Campana*, Mursia, Milan, 1976.

A. Jacomuzzi, *Sulla poesia di Montale* (Cappelli, Bologna, 1968).

S. Jacomuzzi, *S. Corazzini* (Mursia, Milan, 1963).

Poesie edite e inedite di Sergio Corazzini, a cura di S. Jacomuzzi (Einaudi, Milan, 1968).

R. Jakobson, *Questions de poétique* (Ed. du Seuil, Paris, 1973).

E.O. James, *The Ancient Gods* (Weidenfeld & Nicolson, London, 1960).

F. Jammes, *De l'angélus de l'aube à angélus du soir* (Mercure de France, Paris, 1898).

F.J. Jones, 'Sulle varianti di Ungaretti', in *Cenobio,* 1 (1960), 3-21.

'Osservazioni sulla simbologia di Quasimodo', in *Cenobio,* 3 (1961), 254-74.
'The poetry of Salvatore Quasimodo', in *Italian Studies,* XVI (1961), 60-77.
'Gozzano e la poesia moderna', in *Nuove dimensioni,* 3-4 & 5 (1961), 3-9, 3-13.
'Il nuovo periodo della poesia quasimodea', in *Nuove dimensioni,* 7 (1962), 3-11.
'La linea esistenziale dell'arte montaliana', in Quaderno del Cenobio, 30, (Lugano, 1963).
'Origine e significato degli schemi coloristici di Dino Campana', in *Poesia e critica*, 8-9 (1966), 165-94.
'The Petrarchism of Mario Luzi', in *Gallica,* essays presented to J. Heywood Thomas (University of Wales Press, Cardiff, 1969), pp.219-40.
The development of Petrarchism and the modern Italian lyric (University of Wales Press, Cardiff, 1969).
'Montale's dialectic of memory', in *Italian Studies* XXVIII (1973), 83-107.
La poesia italiana contemporanea (da Gozzano a Quasimodo), (D'Anna, Messina-Florence, 1975).
Giuseppe Ungaretti (Edinburgh University Press, Edinburgh, 1977).
'The mythological status of Arsenio in Montale's ideology', *A.T.I. Journal* No. 38 (1983), 73-7.

E. Kushner, *Le mythe d'Orphée dans la littérature française contemporaine* (Nizet, Paris, 1961).

J. Lacan, *Écrits* (Seuil, Paris, 1966).

R. Laforgue, *L'échec de Baudelaire* (Editions Denoel et Steele, Paris, 1931).

G. Lagorio, *Sbarbaro, un modo spoglio di esistere* (Garzanti, Milan, 1981).

R. Lalou, *Vers une alchimie lyrique* (Les arts e le livre, Paris, 1927).
Histoire de la littérature française contemporaine (Presses universitaires de France, Paris, 1947) (2 vols.).

F. Lanza, *A. Onofri* (Mursia, Milan, 1974).

E. Lazzara, *Introduzione alla lettura di Quasimodo* (D'Anna, Messina-Florence, n.d.).

F.R. Leavis, 'L'impersonalità creativa di Montale', in *Nuova Antologia*, (July, 1971), 324-30.
'Xenia', in G. Singh, *Eugenio Montale, New Poems* (Chatto & Windus, London, 1976), pp.xxiii-xxxiii.

M. Leblanc, *The hollow needle* (Bodley Head, London, 1960); original French edition: *L'aiguille creuse* (Lafitte, Paris, 1909).
F. Leonetti, 'Esame dei contenuti attuali secondo la serie dei poemetti di Pasolini', in *Nuova corrente*, 11-12 (1958), 41-76.
M. Bernardi Leoni, *Informale e terza generazione* (La Nuova Italia, Florence, 1975).
G. Leopardi, *Opere* (Mondadori, Milan, 1949) (5 vols.).
F. Livi, *Dai simbolisti ai crepuscolari* (I.P.L., Milan, 1974).
'Saggio sulla poesia di Sergio Corazzini', in *Critica letteraria,* IV (1979), 674-731.
Ida Li Vigni, *Orfismo e poesia in Dino Campana* (Il Melangolo/Università 9, Genoa, 1983).
G. Lonardi, *Il vecchio e il giovane e altri studi su Montale* (Zanichelli, Bologna, 1980).
V. Lotman, *Analysis of the poetic text*, (Ardis, Ann Arbor, 1976).
G.P. Lucini, *Ragion poetica e programma del verso libero* (Edizioni di 'Poesia', Milan, 1908).
'Louis Le Cardonnel', in *Poesia* (November, 1908), 8-10.
Various authors, 'Lucini e il futurismo', in *Il Verri* (1970), 33-4.
V. Lugli, 'Incontri di Giovanni Pascoli con la poesia francese', in *Pascoli discorsi nel centenario della nascita* (Zanichelli, Bologna, 1958).
L. Lugnani, *G. Gozzano* (Il Castoro, La Nuova Italia, Florence, 1975.).
G. Lukacs, *Il Marxismo e la critica letteraria* (Einaudi, Turin, 1953).
R. Luperini, *Il Novecento* (Loescher, Turin, 1981) (2 vols.).
G. Luti, *Invito alla lettura di Ungaretti* (Mursia, Milan, 1974).
M. Luzi, *Opium chrétien* (Guanda, Modena, 1938).
Un'illusione platonica e altri saggi (Ed. di rivoluzione, Florence, 1941); reprinted by Boni (Bologna, 1972).
Biografia a Ebe (Vallecchi, Florence, 1942).
Un Brindisi (Sansoni, Florence, 1946).
L'inferno e il limbo (Marzocco, Florence, 1949).
Studio su Mallarmé (Sansoni, Florence, 1952).
Onore del vero (Neri Pozza, Venice, 1957).
L'idea simbolista (Garzanti, Milan, 1959); 2nd ed., 1976.
Il giusto della vita (Garzanti, Milan, 1960).
Nel magma (All'Insegna del pesce d'oro, Milan, 1963).
Dal fondo delle campagne (Einaudi, Turin, 1965).
Tutto in questione (Vallecchi, Florence, 1965).
Su fondamenti invisibili (Rizzoli, Milan, 1971).
Vicissitudine e forma (Rizzoli, Milan, 1974).
Discorso naturale (Quaderni di Messapo, Siena, 1980).

Trame (Rizzoli, Milan, 1982).

A. Machado, *Poesias completas* (Colleccion Austral, Espesa-Calpe, 1959).

O, Macrí, 'La poetica della parola', introductory essay to Salvatore Quasimodo, *Poesie* (Primi Piani, Milan, 1938).

Esemplari del sentimento poetico contemporaneo (Vallecchi, Florence, 1941).

'Le generazioni nella poesia italiana', in *Paragone,* 42 (1953), 45-53.

Caratteri e figure della poesia italiana contemporanea (Vallecchi, Florence, 1956).

'Le origini di Luzi', in *Palatina,* 19 (1966), 3-27.

Realtà del simbolo (Vallecchi, Florence, 1968).

M. Maeterlinck, *Le double jardin* (Fasquelle, Paris, 1904).

L'intelligence des fleurs (Fasquelle, Paris, 1910).

La vie des abeilles (Fasquelle, Paris, 1911).

L. Malagodi, *Poesia come storia, con un'aggiunta sull'attivismo* (La Nuova Italia, Florence, 1961).

L'Anti-Ottocento (La Nuova Italia, Florence, 1972).

S. Mallarmé, *Divagations* (Skira, Geneva, 1943).

Oeuvres complètes (Editions de la Pléiade, Gallimard, Paris, 1945).

G. Manacorda, *Storia della letteratura italiana contemporanea (1940-65)* (Editori riuniti, Rome, 1967).

Montale (La Nuova Italia, Florence, 1969).

A. Mandelbaum, *G. Ungaretti – Life of a man* (Hamish Hamilton, London), (New Directions, New York), (Scheiwiller, Milan, 1958); reprinted as *Selected poems of Giuseppe Ungaretti* (Cornell University Press, 1975) (with additional poems).

M. Marcazzan, 'La poesia di Umberto Saba, in *Humanitas*, 6 (1946), 617-27.

'Dal romanticismo al decadentismo', in *Letteratura italiana: le correnti*, II (Marzorati, Milan, 1956) pp.663-896.

G. P. Marchi, *Incunaboli quasimodiani* (Verona, 1973).

A. Marchese, *Visiting angel* (S.E.I., Turin, 1977).

M. Marchione, 'Linguaggio reboriano', in *Lingua nostra,* XX (September, 1959), 74-8.

L'immagine tesa, La vita e l'opera di Clemente Rebora, ed. di Storia e di Letteratura, Rome, 1960).

'Carteggio inedito di C. Rebora e G. Prezzolini (1909-23)', in *Stagione* (1961), 21.

G. Mariani, 'Per una storia della critica ungarettiana', in *Letteratura,* 35-6 (1958), 246-63.

Poesia e tecnica nella lirica del Novecento (Liviana, Padua, 1958).
Storia della Scapigliatura (Sciascia, Caltanissetta-Rome, 1967).
L. Marigo, 'La poetica di Thovez' in *Lettere italiane,* 3 (1970), 351-82.
F.T. Marinetti, *La ville charnelle* (Sansot, Paris, 1908).
'Manifesto del futurismo', in *Poesia,* 1-2 (1909), 2-4 (French), 6-8 (Italian). Previously published in French in *Le Figaro* 10 February 1909; now reprinted in *Archivi del futurismo* (De Luca, Rome, 1958).
Enquête internationale sur le vers libre et manifeste du futurisme (Ed. fut. di 'Poesia', Milan, 1909).
Uccidiamo il chiaro di luna (Ed. fut. di 'Poesia', Milan, 1911).
I poeti futuristi (Ed. fut. di 'Poesia', Milan, 1912).
'Dopo il verso libero le parole in libertà', in *Lacerba,* 1 (1913), fascicule 22, 252-4.
Zang tumb tumb (Ed. fut. di 'Poesia', Milan, 1914).
'La nuova religione – morale della Velocità', in *'L'italia Futurista* (11 May 1916). Now in *Marinetti e il futurismo,* a cura di L. De Maria (Mondadori, Milan, 1973), pp.182-189.
Les mots en liberté futuristes, (Ed. fut. di 'Poesia', Milan, 1919).
Distruzione (Sonzogno, Milan, 1920); 1st ed. (in French) (Vanier, Paris, 1904); 1st Italian translation (Ed. fut. di 'Poesia', Milan, 1911).
(See also *Teoria e invenzione futurista*, Mondadori, Milan, 1968).
G.B. Marino, *Opere scelte di Marino e i marinisti* (Utet, Turin, 1949 & 1954) (2 vols.).
M. Martelli, *Il rovescio della poesia, interpretazioni montaliane* (Longanesi, Milan, 1977).
H. Martin, *Guido Gozzano (1883-1916)* (Presses universitaires de France, Paris, 1968).
H.W. Martin, *Futurist art and Theory* (Clarendon Press, Oxford, 1969).
C. Martini, *La Voce* (Nistri-Lischi, Pisa, 1956).
F.M. Martini, *Tutte le poesie* (ed. IPL, Milan, 1969).
Si sbarca a New York (ed. IPL, Milan, 1975); 1st ed. (Mondadori, Milan, 1930).
U. Marvardi, 'Carattere della poesia d'oggi e Giuseppe Ungaretti', in *Responsabilità del sapere* (1947), fasc. 3, 77-97.
'Classicità della poesia ungarettiana', in *Letteratura*, 35-36, (1958), 94-103.
La poesia religiosa del Petrarca volgare (Ed. Studium, Rome, 1961).
'Ungaretti poeta del mistero', in *Studium*, 9 (1970), 1-10.
'Il simbolismo francese e la poesia di Ungaretti', in *La letteratura italiana e la cultura straniera del Novecento* (Rome, 1971), pp.153-99.

G. Marzot, *D'Annunzio e Gozzano* (Edizioni Italiane Moderne, Bologna, 1979).

G. Mathieu, *Au-delà du tachisme* (Juillard, Paris, 1963).

M.S. Mazza, *The story of the Frontespizio* (Columbia University Press, New York, 1948).

C.A. Mazzacappa, *Noia e inquietudine nella vita di un uomo di G. Ungaretti* (Rebellato, Padua, 1970).

A. Merini, *La presenza di Orfeo* (Schwarz, Milan, 1953).

M. Merleau-Ponty, *Phénoménologie de la perception* (Gallimard, Paris, 1945).

B. Merry, 'The anti-oracle in Mario Luzi's recent poetry', in *Modern Language Review,* 68, 2 (1973), 333-43.

(See also under Almansi)

C. Michelstaedter, *Opere* (Vallecchi, Florence, 1958).

B. Migliorini, *Saggi sulla lingua del Novecento* (Sansoni, Florence, 1941).

G. Minafò, *Quasimodo, poeta del nostro tempo* (Le Monnier, Florence, 1973).

G. Mirandola, *La 'Gazzetta letteraria' e la Francia*, (Accademia delle Scienze, Turin, 1971).

L. Mittner, *Espressionismo* (Laterza, Bari, 1965).

A.A. Moles, 'Analisi delle strutture del linguaggio poetico', in *Il Verri,* 14 (1964), 3-21.

A. Momigliano, 'Le tendenze della lirica dal Carducci ad oggi', in *La Nuova Italia* (December, 1934), 381-9.

'Lo svolgimento della lirica dannunziana', in *La Rassegna della lett. it,* 1-2 (1953), 5-19.

Ultimi studi (La nuova Italia, Florence, 1954).

L. Mondo, *Natura e storia in Guido Gozzano* (Silva, Rome, 1969).

E. Montale, 'Stile e tradizione', in *Il Baretti* (15 January 1925), 7; reprinted in *Auto da fè* (Il Saggiatore, Milan, 1966), pp.15-19.

'Ragioni di Umberto Saba, in *Solaria*, 5 (1928), 29-34; reprinted in *Sulla poesia* (Mondadori, Milan, 1976), pp.218-22.

'Sulla poesia di Campana', in *L'Italia che scrive,* 9-10 (1942), 152-4; reprinted in *Sulla poesia*, pp.248-59.

'Due sciacalli al guinzaglio', in *Corriere della sera* (16 February 1950); reprinted in *Sulla poesia*, pp.84-7.

Problemi del nostro tempo – La solitudine dell'artista (Associazione italiana per la libertà della cultura, Rome, n.d.).

La poesia di Gozzano (Garzanti, Milan, 1960).

Clemente Rebora, a cura di V. Scheiwiller, con una nota di E. Montale (All'Insegna del pesce d'oro, Domodossola, 1956).

Farfalla di Dinard (Neri Pozza, Venice, 1956); 2nd ed. (Mondadori, Milan, 1960).
T.S. Eliot, tradotto da E.M. (All'Insegna del pesce d'oro, Milan, 1958).
'Testimonianza a Ungaretti', in *Letteratura*, 35-6 (1958), 325.
Reply to '*Sette domande sulla poesia*', in *Nuovi argomenti*, 55-6 (1962), 42-6; reprinted in *Sulla poesia*, pp.587-92.
'Giorno e notte' (letter) in *Aut Aut*, 67 (1962), 44-5; reprinted in *Sulla poesia*, pp.91-2.
'Variazioni', in *Il Mondo*, 2 (1945), 6; reprinted in *Sulla poesia*, pp.104-6.
Auto da fè, Saggi di arte e di letteratura (Il Saggiatore, Milan, 1966).
'Cinquant'anni di poesia' (interview), in *L'Approdo letterario*, 35 (1966), 107-26. (See also L. Piccioni)
Fuori di casa (Ricciardi, Milan-Naples, 1968).
' ''Satura'' di Eugenio Montale', in *L'Approdo letterario*, 53 (1971), 107-16 (interview with Maria Corti).
Nel nostro tempo (Rizzoli, Milan, 1972).
La poesia non esiste (All'Insegna del pesce d'oro, Milan, 1973).
Sulla poesia (Mondadori, Milan, 1976); *Sulla prosa* (Mondadori, Milan, 1981).
Autografi di Montale. Fondo dell'Università di Pavia, a cura di M. Corti e Maria Antonietta Grignani (Einaudi, Turin, 1976).
Selected Essays (Carcanet, Manchester, 1978) (translated by G. Singh).
Prima alla scala (Mondadori, Milan, 1981).
Quaderno genovese (Mondadori, Milan, 1983).

F. Montanari, *Studi sul Canzoniere del Petrarca* (Studium, Rome, 1958).
'Poesia e durata', in *Studium, 7-8 (1964), 447-83.*

R. Montano, 'Interrogativo montaliano. Miss Brandeis o Clizia', in *Segni* (October, 1978), 15-17; also 'La Clizia di Montale e altre precisazioni', in *Segni* (April-June, 1981), 22-23.

M. Moretti, *Poesie scritte col lapis* (Ricciardi, Naples, 1910).
Il libro dei miei amici (Mondadori, Milan, 1960).
Tutte le poesie (Mondadori, Milan, 1966).

G. Morpurgo-Tagliabue, *L'esthétique contemporaine* (Marzorati, Milan, 1960).

G. Mounin, 'Une poésie du naturel', in *Cahiers du sud* 323 (1954), 13-22.

G. Nascimbeni, *Eugenio Montale* (Longanesi, Milan, 1969).

R. Negri, *Leopardi nella poesia italiana* (Le Monnier, Florence, 1970).

G. de Nerval, *Sylvie suivie de Léo Burckart et de Aurélie* (Ed. du Rocher, Monaco, 1946).
Oeuvres (Gallimard, Paris, 1952-6) (2 vols.).

A. Noferi, 'Le poetiche critiche novecentesche "sub specie Petrarchae" ', in *L'Approdo letterario*, 46 (1969), 61-88.

Le poetiche critiche novecentesche (Le Monnier, Florence, 1970).

(See also introduction to M. Bernardi Leoni, *Informale e terza generazione,* La Nuova Italia, Florence, 1975.)

N. Noto, *La spazialità poetica in Ungaretti* (Celebes, Palermo, 1976).

M. Novaro, *Murmuri ed echi* (Ricciardi, Naples, 1912).

P. O'Neddy, *Feu et flamme* (Editions des Presses Françaises et 'Les Belles Lettres', Paris, 1926).

T. O'Neill, 'Ungaretti and Foscolo: a question of taste', in *Italian Quarterly,* XIII (1968), 73-89.

'The problem of formalism in Ungaretti's poetry', in *Italian Quarterly,* XIV (1970), 59-73.

'Ungaretti tra Leopardi e Góngora: appunti per una lettura di "Tu ti spezzasti", in *Rivista di Letterature moderne e comparate*, 1 (1974), 56-64.

'Pier Paolo Pasolini's dialect poetry', in *Forum italicum,* IX (1975), 343-67.

A. Onofri, *Terrestrità del sole* (Vallecchi, Florence, 1927).

Simili a melodie rapprese in mondo (Al tempo della Fortuna, Rome, 1929).

Orchestrine Arioso (Neri Pozza, Venice, 1959); first published in Naples, 1917.

Poesie edite e inedite (1900-1914) (Longo, Ravenna, 1982).

C. Ossola, *Giuseppe Ungaretti* (Mursia, Milan, 1975); new enlarged edition, 1982.

E. Paci, *Esistenza e immagine* (Tarrantola, Milan, 1947).

Dall'esistenzialismo al relazionismo (D'Anna, Messina-Florence, 1957).

'Ungaretti e l'esperienza della poesia', in *Letteratura*, 35-6 (1958), 83-93.

'Sulla stile della fenomenologia', in *Aut Aut*, 57 (1960), 133-42.

La filosofia contemporanea (Garzanti, Milan, 1961) (3rd ed.).

S. Pacifici, *A guide to contemporary Italian literature* (Meridian Books, Cleveland & New York, 1962).

E. Pagliarani, *Cronache e altre poesie* (Schwarz, Milan, 1954).

'Per una definizione dell'avanguardia' in *Nuova corrente*, 31 (1966), 86-92.

A. Palazzeschi, *Poesie* (Vallecchi, Florence, 1949) (6th ed.).

P. Pancrazi, 'Fascismo e letteratura', in *La nuova Europa*, (10 December 1944), p.5.

Scrittori d'oggi (Laterza, Bari, 1953) (2 vols.).
E. Panofsky, *Meaning in the visual arts* (Penguin Books, 1970).
G. Paparelli, 'Humanitas e poesia di Quasimodo', in *Letterature moderne* (1961), 719-48.
'Poesia e poetica di Quasimodo', in *Il Baretti*, 9-10 (1961), 134-9.
G. Paparelli & C. Scibilia, *Letteratura italiana del Novecento* (Conte, Naples, 1978).
G. Papini, 'Il cerchio si chiude', in *Lacerba*, 11 (1914), fascicule 4, 49-50.
L'esperienza futurista (Vallecchi, Florence, 1919).
Stroncature (Vallecchi, Florence, 1927) (7th ed.); 1st ed. ('La Voce', 1916).
Ritratti italiani (Vallecchi, Florence, 1932).
Poesie in versi (Vallecchi, Florence, 1947); 1st ed. (1932).
Tutte le opere (Mondadori, Milan, 1958-66) (10 vols).
M.C. Papini, *Corazzini* (Il Castoro, La Nuova Italia, Florence, 1977).
E. Paratore, *Studi dannunziani* (Morano, Naples, 1966).
M. Parent, *Francis Jammes* (Les Belles Lettres, Paris, 1957).
C. Pariani, *Vite non romanzate di Dino Campana scrittore e Evaristo Boncinelli scultore* (Vallecchi, Florence, 1938).
G. Parini, *Poesie e prose* (Ricciardi, Milan-Naples, 1951).
A. Parronchi, 'Ipotesi su Monologhetto', in *Paragone*, 40 (1953), 24-9.
'Genova e il "senso dei colori" nella poesia di Campana', in *Paragone,* 48 (1953), 13-34.
G. Pascoli, *Myricae* (Giusti, Livorno, 1891).
Canti di Castelvecchio (Mondadori, Milan, 1959); 1st ed. (1903).
Prose (Mondadori, Milan, 1946), (3 vols.).
(See also criticism by various authors in *Discorsi nel centenario della nascita*, Zanichelli, Bologna, 1958.)
P.P. Pasolini 'Il neosperimentalismo' in *Officina*, 5 (1956), 169-82.
'La libertà stilistica', in *Officina,* 9-10 (1957), 341-6.
Passione e ideologia (Garzanti, Milan, 1960).
Le poesie (Garzanti, Milan, 1975).
Poems (*Random*, London, 1982).
V. Passeri Pignoni, 'Umberto Saba, poeta contro corrente', in *Città di vita* (1960), 506-22.
W. Pater, *The Renaissance* (Fontana Library, Collins, Glasgow-London, 1961).
J. Paulhan, 'Testimonianza', in G. Ungaretti, *Il taccuino del vecchio* (Mondadori, Milan, 1960), pp.47-9.
C. Pavese, *Lavorare stanca* (Solaria, Florence, 1936).
Verrà la morte e avrà i tuoi occhi (Einaudi, Turin, 1951).

C. Pavolini, *Cubismo, futurismo, espressionismo* (Zanichelli, Bologna, 1927).
A. Pellegrini, *Novecento tedesco* (Principato, Messina-Milan, 1942).
C. Pellizzi, *Le lettere italiane del nostro secolo* (Libreria d'Italia, Milan, 1929).
S. Penna, *Poesie* (Parenti, Florence, 1939).
Tutte le poesie (Garzanti, Milan, 1970).
B. Pento, 'Galleria degli scrittori italiani: Umberto Saba', in *La Fiera letteraria,* (5 November 1950), 4.
Poesia contemporanea (Marzorati, Milan, 1964).
Lettura di Quasimodo (Marzorati, Milan, 1966).
G.A. Peritore, 'Ungaretti (1914-19)', in *Letterature moderne* (1956), 181-96.
Alcuni studi (Galeati, Imola, 1961).
M. Perniola, *L'alienazione artistica* (Mursia, Milan, 1971).
F. Petrarca, *Il mio segreto,* translated by L. Asioli (Hoepli, Milan, 1924).
Rime, trionfi e poesie latine (Ricciardi, Milan-Naples, 1951).
Prose (Ricciardi, Milan-Naples, 1955).
G. Petrocchi, 'Irrequietudine religiosa del decadentismo italiano', in *Humanitas*, 2 (1946), 1156-63.
'Mario Luzi e venti anni di poesia', in *Humanitas*, 2 (1958), 122-30.
Poesia e tecnica narrativa (Mursia, Milan, 1962).
G. Petronio, *Poeti del nostro tempo: I crepuscolari* (Sansoni, Florence, 1937); first published in *Leonardo*, XIII-XIV (1935), 145-51; 294-303; 449-55.
M. Petrucciani, *La poetica dell'ermetismo* (Loescher, Turin, 1955).
Poesia pura e poesia esistenziale (Loescher, Turin, 1957).
'Ungaretti e Campana', in *Lettere italiane,* Anno XXXIV, 1 (1982), 33-54.
R. Pettinelli & A.Q. Giovanni, 'Bibliografia montaliana', in *La Rassegna della lett. it.* 2 (1966).
V. Pica, 'I moderni bizantini, Paul Verlaine', in *La Gazzetta letteraria* (1885), 46, 47, 48.
'I moderni bizantini, Stéphane Mallarmé', in *La Gazzetta letteraria*, (1886), 47, 48, 49.
L. Piccioni, *Sui contemporanei* (Fabbri, Milan, n.d.).
'Cinquant'anni di poesia', L. Piccioni a colloquio con Eugenio Montale, in *L'Approdo letterario*, 35 (1966), 107-26.
Vita di un poeta Giuseppe Ungaretti (Rizzoli, Milan, 1970).
Ungarettiana (Vallecchi, Florence, 1980).
G. Picon, *L'écrivain et son ombre* (Gallimard, Paris, 1953).

F. Piemontese, 'Il sentimento religioso nella poesia di Ungretti', in *Studium*, 5 (1949), 217-31.
M. Pieri, *Biografia della poesia: sul paesaggio mentale della poesia italiana del Novecento* (La Pilotta, Parma, 1979).
A. Pinchera, 'Figure e stile di Umberto Saba', in *Letteratura*, 53-4 (1961), 44-58.
U. Saba, (Il Castoro, La Nuova Italia, Florence, 1974).
A. Pipa, 'Le mythe d'un papillon, Montale e Anouilh', in *La revue de littérature comparée*, XXXVIII, 3, 400-13.
Montale and Dante (The University of Minnesota Press, Minneapolis, 1968).
A. Piromalli, *Saggi critici di storia letteraria* (Olschki, Florence, 1967).
Ideologia e arte in Guido Gozzano (La Nuova Italia, Florence, 1972).
R. Poggioli, 'Simbolismo russo e occidentale', in *Letterature moderne* (1961), 586-602.
B. Porcelli, 'Gozzano e Maeterlinck, ovvero un caso di parassitismo letterario', in *Belfagor*, 6 (1969), 653-77.
Gozzano, originalità e plagi (Pàtron, Bologna, 1974).
Momenti dell'antinaturalismo, Fogazzaro, Svevo, Corazzini (Longo, Ravenna, 1975).
F. Portal, *Les couleurs symboliques* (Treutell & Würtz, Paris, 1837).
F. Portinari, *Umberto Saba* (Mursia, Milan, 1963).
Giuseppe Ungaretti (Borla, Turin, 1967).
A. Pozzi, *Parole* (Mondadori, Milan, 1939).
G. Pozzi, *La poesia italiana del Novecento* (Einaudi, Turin, 1965).
E. Praga, *Tavolozza* (Brigola, Milan, 1862).
Penombre (tip. degli autori-editori, Milan, 1864).
Poesie (Treves, Milan, 1922).
G. Prati, *Poesie* (Salani, Florence, 1936) (2 vols.).
M. Praz, *Studi sul concettismo* (Sansoni, Florence, 1946).
G. Prezzolini, *Repertorio bibliografico della storia e della critica della letteratura italiana dal 1902-1932* (Edizioni Roma, Rome, 1937-9).
Repertorio bibliografico della storia e della critica della letteratura italiana dal 1933-1942 (Vanni, New York, 1946-8).
Il tempo della Voce (Longanesi-Vallecchi, Florence-Milan, 1960).
L'italiano inutile (Vallecchi, Florence, 1964) (2nd ed.).
M. Proust, *A la recherche du temps perdu* (Gallimard, Paris, n.d.) (15 vols.).
G. Pullini, *Aldo Palazzeschi* (Mursia, Milan, 1965).
S. Quasimodo, *Lirici greci* (Mondadori, Milan, 1944); 1st ed. (Edizioni di Corrente, Milan, 1940).

Poesia italiana del dopoguerra (anthology) (Schwarz, Milan, 1958).
'Domande a Quasimodo', interview with G. Finzi, in *L'Europa letteraria*, 30-2 (1964), 21-6.
Il poeta e il politico e altri saggi (Schwarz, Milan, 1960).
Lettere d'amore a Maria Cumani (Mondadori, Milan, 1973).
Quasimodo Salvatore – La Pira Giorgio, *Carteggio* (All'Insegna del pesce d'oro, Milan, 1980).

G. Quiriconi, *Il fuoco e la metamorfosi: La scommessa totale di Mario Luzi* (Cappelli, Bologna, 1980).

O. Ragusa, *Mallarmé in Italy. Literary influence and critical response* (Vanni, New York, 1957).
'V. Pica: First Champion of French Symbolism in Italy', in *Italica* (1958), 255-61.

G. Raimondi, 'Ritratto di Vincenzo Cardarelli', in *L'Approdo letterario* (April-June, 1952), 59-64.

P. Raimondi, *Invito alla lettura di Saba* (Marsia, Milan, 1974).

S. Ramat, *Montale* (Vallecchi, Florence, 1965).
L'ermetismo (La Nuova Italia, Florence, 1969).
Storia della poesia italiana del Novecento (Mursia, Milan, 1976).

F. Ravagli, *Dino Campana e i goliardi del suo tempo* (Marzocco, Florence, 1941).
(See also Dino Campana, *Fascicolo marradese inedito*, a cura di F. Ravagli, Florence, 1972).

G. Ravegnani, *I contemporanei* (Ceschina, Milan, 1960) (2 vols.); 1st ed. (Bocca, Turin, 1930).
Poeti futuristi (La Nuova Accademia, Milan, 1963).

M. Raymond, *De Baudelaire au surréalisme* (Correa, Paris, 1933).

L. Rebay, *Le origini della poesia di Giuseppe Ungaretti* (Ed. di Storia e Letteratura, Rome, 1962).
'I diàspori di Montale', in *Italica* 1 (1969), 33-53.
'Sull' "autobiografismo" di Montale', in *Innovazioni tematiche espressive e linguistiche della letteratura italiana del Novecento* (Atti dell'VIII Congresso dell'Associazone Internazionale per gli studi di lingua e letteratura italiana, New York, 25-28 April 1973), (Olschki, Florence, 1976, pp.73-83).
'Montale, Clizia e l'America', in *Forum Italicum*, 3 (1982), 171-202.

C. Rebora, *Mania dell'eterno* (All'Insegna del pesce d'oro, Milan, 1960).
Lettere famigliari (All'Insegna del pesce d'oro, Milan, 1962).
Il primo Rebora, 22 lettere inedite (1905-13), a cura di M.D. Banfi Malaguzzi (All'Insegna del pesce d'oro, Milan, 1964).

Lettere (1893-1930) (Storia e Letteratura, Rome, 1976); *Lettere (1931-1957)* (Storia e Letteratura, Rome, 1982).
(See also *Omaggio a Clemente Rebora*, Boni, Bologna, 1971.)
P. Rebora, 'Clemente Rebora e la sua formazione esistenzialistica' in *Humanitas*, 2 (1959), 114-25.
M. Remâcle, *L'élément poétique dans 'A la recherche du temps perdu'* (Académie royale, Brussels, 1954).
I.A. Richards, *Principles of literary criticism* (Routledge & Kegan Paul, London 1961).
M. Richter, *La formazione francese di Ardengo Soffici* (Vita e Pensiero, Milan, 1969).
L. Righi, *Dino Campana, poeta della notte* (Collana 'Gli inediti', Tip. Sbolci, Fiesole, 1971).
R.M. Rilke, *Sonnets to Orpheus*, translated by J.B. Leishman (Hogarth Press, London, 1936).
Das Buch der Bilder (1902), now in R.M. Rilke, *Sämtliche Werke*, vol. 1 (Insel Verlag, Frankfurt am Main, 1955), pp.367-477.
A. Rimbaud, *Illuminations,* édité par H. De Bouillane de Lacoste (Mercure de France, Paris, 1949).
Oeuvres complètes (Bibl. de la Pléiade, Paris, 1951).
R. Risi, *V. Cardarelli, prosatore e poeta* (Francke, Berne, 1951).
B. Romani, *Cardarelli* (Cedam, Padua, 1942).
A. Romano, 'Osservazioni sulla letteratura del Novecento', in *Officina*, 2 (1957), 417-44.
'La Scapigliatura', in *Officina* (1958), 255-63.
Il secondo romanticismo lombardo (Fabbri, Milan, 1958).
La Voce (1908-14) (Einaudi, Turin, 1960).
S.F. Romano, *La poetica dell'ermetismo* (Sansoni, Florence, 1942); reprinted 1951.
Various authors, *La Ronda (1919-23)* (tip. Bondani di G. Bolognesi, Rome) (8 vols.)
L. Rosiello, *Struttura, uso e funzioni delle lingue* (Vallecchi, Florence, 1965).
L. Rossi, *Situazione dell'estetica in Italia* (Paravia, Turin, 1976).
G. Rovani, *Le tre arti considerate in alcuni illustri italiani* (Treves, Milan, 1874) (2 vols.).
R. Ruberto, 'A conversation with Eugenio Montale', in *Italian Quarterly* 68 (1974), 35-56.
A. Russi, 'L'esperienza lirica di Clemente Rebora', in *Paragone*, 30 (1952), 45-56.
Poesia e realtà (La Nuova Italia, Florence, 1962).

Gli anni dell'antialienazione (Mursia, Milan, 1967).

L. Russo, *La critica letteraria contemporanea* (Laterza, Bari, 1954) (3 vols.); first published by Bari (1942-3).

'La lirica pura', in *Belfagor*, 2 (1965), 125-9.

'Poesia e psicanalisi', in *La Fiera letteraria* (5 September 1946).

U. Saba, *La storia e cronistoria del Canzoniere* (Mondadori, Milan, 1948).

Quello che resta da fare ai poeti (Ed. dello Zibaldone, Trieste, 1959).

Epigrafe ultime prose (Il Saggiatore, Milan, 1959).

Prose (Mondadori, Milan, 1964).

Ricordi-Racconti (1910-1947) (Mondadori, Milan, 1964).

Ernesto (Einaudi, Turin, 1975).

L'adolescenza del 'Canzoniere' e undici lettere (Fogola, Turin, 1975).

Amicizia, a cura di C. Levi (Mondadori, Milan, 1976).

C. Salinari, *Miti e coscienza del decadentismo italiano* (Feltrinelli, Milan, 1965).

R. Sanesi 'La poesia di Quasimodo', in *Inventario* (1961) numero unico, 107-24.

E. Sanguineti, 'Da Gozzano a Montale', in *Lettere italiane*, 2 (1955), 188-207.

'Documenti su Montale', in *Il Verri*, 2 (1962), 68-80.

Triperuno (Feltrinelli, Milan, 1964).

Ideologia e linguaggio (Feltrinelli, Milan, 1965).

Poeti e poetiche del primo Novecento (Giappichelli, Turin, 1966).

Guido Gozzano, indagini e letture (Einaudi, Turin, 1966).

Poesia italiana del Novecento (anthology) (Einaudi, Turin, 1969) (2 vols.).

G. Savoca, *Quaderno per 'Le occasioni' di Montale* (Liberia ed. Bonaccorso, Catania, 1973).

C. Sbarbaro, *Pianissimo* (La Voce, Florence, 1914).

Trucioli (Vallecchi, Florence, 1920).

Scampoli (Vallecchi, Florence, 1960).

Poesie (All'Insegna del pesce d'oro, Milan, 1961).

G. Scalia, *Lacerba-La Voce* (1914-16) (Einaudi, Turin, 1961).

'I crepuscolari', in *Officina*, 8 (1957), 301-11.

'Per uno studio sulla cultura di sinistra nel dopoguerra', in *Officina*, 12 (1958), 511-34.

C. Scarpati, *Mario Luzi* (Mursia, Milan, 1970).

Invito alla lettura di Montale (Mursia, Milan, 1973).

V. Scheiwiller, *Clemente Rebora* (All'Insegna del pesce d'oro, Domodossola, 1959).

L. Scorrano, 'Per "La morte di Tantalo" di Sergio Corazzini'; *Studi e problemi di critica testuale,* XI (1975), 188-210.

'Marginalia per Guido Gozzano e Sergio Corazzini', in *Studi e problemi di critica testuale* (April, 1982), 188-210.

R. Scrivano, 'Storia della critica di un concetto letterario: decadentismo', in *La Rassegna della letteratura italiana,* 3 (1961), 418-52.

Riviste, scrittori e critici del Novecento (Sansoni, Florence, 1965).

L. Scrivo, *Sintesi del futurismo* (Bulzoni, Rome, 1968).

A. Seppilli, *Poesia e magia* (Einaudi, Turin, 1962).

V. Sereni, *Frontiera* (Ed. di 'Corrente', Milan, 1941).

Poesie (Vallecchi, Florence, 1942).

Diario d'Algeria (Vallecchi, Florence, 1947).

Gli strumenti umani (Einaudi, Turin, 1965).

A. Seroni, *Ragioni critiche*, (Vallecchi, Florence, 1944).

Nuove ragioni critiche (Vallecchi, Florence, 1954).

Esperimenti critici sul Novecento letterario (Mursia, Milan, 1967).

Maura del Serra, *Mostra bio-bibliografica su Dino Campana*, (Gabinetto scientifico letterario G.P. Vieusseux, Florence, 1973).

L'immagine aperta (La Nuova Italia, Florence, 1973).

Clemente Rebora (Vita e Pensiero, Milan, 1976).

R. Serra, *Le lettere* (Bontempelli, Rome, 1914).

Scritti (Le Monnier, Florence, 1938) (2 vols.).

P. Servien, *Les rythmes comme introduction physique à l'esthétique* (Boivin, Paris, 1930).

E. Sewell, *The Orphic Voice* (Yale University Press, New Haven, 1960).

P.B. Shelley, *Poetical Works* (Oxford University Press, London, 1947).

H.J. Sheppard, 'Colour symbolism in the alchemical opus', in *Scientia*, XI (1964), 232-6.

J. Sherer, *L'expression littéraire dans l'oeuvre de Mallarmé* (Droz, Paris, 1947).

M. Shimoi & G. Marone, 'Poesie giapponesi', in *La Diana* (May, 1916).

Poesie giapponesi (Ricciardi, Naples, 1917); reprinted as *Lirici giapponesi* (Carabba, Lanciano, 1927).

L. Silori, 'La difficile scoperta di Leopardi', in *Letteratura*, 35-6 (1958), 224-9.

G. Singh, 'Eugenio Montale', in *Italian Studies,* XVIII (1963), 101-37.

Leopardi and the theory of poetry (University of Kentucky Press, 1964).

'Eugenio Montale e la critica', in *Le parole e le idee*, 3-4 (1965), 163-86.

'The poetry of Umberto Saba', in *Italian Studies*, XXIII (1968), 114-37.

Eugenio Montale, a critical study of his poetry, prose and criticism (Yale University Press, New Haven & London, 1973).

C. Sini, *La fenomenologia* (Garzanti, Milan, 1965).

L. Sinisgalli, *18 poesie* (All'Insegna del pesce d'oro, Milan, 1936).
Vidi le Muse (Mondadori, Milan, 1943); 2nd ed. (1945).
I nuovi campi Elisi (Mondadori, Milan, 1947).
Furor mathematicus (Mondadori, Milan-Verona, 1950); 1st ed. (Urbinati, Rome, 1944).
Cineraccio (Neri Pozza, Venice, 1961).
The Ellipse, Selected Poems (Edizioni Moderne, Bologna, 1979).

A. Soffici, *Arthur Rimbaud* (Casa editrice italiana, Florence, 1911).
Giornale di bordo (La Voce, Florence, 1918).
Kobilek: giornale di battaglia (La Voce, Florence, 1918).
I primi principi di un'estetica futurista (Vallecchi, Florence, 1920).
Marsia e Apollo (Vallecchi, Florence, 1938).
Opere (Vallecchi, Florence, 1959-65) (8 vols.).

S. Solmi, 'Ossi di seppia', in *Il Quindicinale*, 3 (1926), 9.
'I canti orfici', in *La Fiera letteraria* (26 August 1928).
Scrittori negli anni (Il Saggiatore, Milan, 1963).

G. Spagnoletti, *Sbarbaro* (Cedam, Padua, 1943).
Antologia della poesia italiana contemporanea (Vallecchi, Florence, 1946) (2 vols).
Antologia della poesia italiana (1909-49) (Guanda, Parma, 1950).
'La cava delle sensazioni', in *Paragone*, 40 (1953), 30-42.
Tre poeti italiani del Novecento (Ed. ERI, Turin, 1956).
Poesia italiana contemporanea (1909-1959) (Guanda, Bologna, 1959).
Il verso è tutto (Carabba, Lanciano, 1979).

L. Spitzer, 'Testimonianza', in G. Ungaretti, *Il taccuino del vecchio* (Mondadori, Milan, 1960), pp.120-22.

A. Staübe, 'Un manoscritto di Gozzano e l'elaborazione di "Convito" ', in *Lettere italiane*, 2 (1970), 247-52.

M. Stefanile, *Quasimodo* (Cedam, Padua, 1943).

W.A. Strauss, *Descent and Return. The Orphic Myth in Modern Literature* (Harvard University Press, Cambridge Mass., 1971).

T. Tasso, *Opere* (UTET, Milan, 1955) (2 vols.); also *Poesie* (Rizzoli, Milan, 1934).

N. Tedesco, *Quasimodo* (Flaccovio, Palermo, 1959).
'Di Montale e del crepuscolarismo (leggendo Notizie dall'Amiata)' (G. Mori & Figli, Palermo, 1960).
La condizione crepuscolare (La Nuova Italia, Florence, 1970).
L'isola impareggiabile (La Nuova Italia, Florence, 1977).
La coscienza letteraria del Novecento (Flaccovio, Palermo, 1979).

E. Tesauro, *Il cannocchiale aristotelico* (St. di Fabio de Falco, Rome, 1664); 1st ed. (1654).

M. Tison-Braun, *La crise de l'humanisme* (Nizet, Paris, 1955) (2 vols.).

G. Titta Rosa, *Poesia italiana del Novecento* (Maia, Siena, 1953).

T. Todorov, *Littérature et signification* (Larousse, Paris, 1967).

P. Tortorelli, 'Motivi e tradizioni letterarie nella poesia di Guido Gozzano', in *Il giornale italiana di filologia,* 3 (1958), 220-32.

C. Toscani, *Moretti* (La Nuova Italia, Florence, 1975).

L. Traverso, 'Profilo della poesia di Mario Luzi', in *L'Approdo letterario*, 17-18 (1962), 34-44.

G. Trombatore, *Scrittori del nostro tempo* (Manfredi, Palermo, 1959).

M. de Unamuno, *Cancionero, diario poetico* (Losada, Buenos Ayres, 1953).

Essenza di Spagna, a cura di Carlo Bo (Ed. Antonioli di C. Pastore, 1945). (Translation of *En torno al Casticismo*; see also M. Bataillon).

G. Ungaretti, 'Del piú e del meno', in *Il Mattino* (4-5 March 1927). (Now in *Saggi e interventi*, pp.154-69).

Difesa dell'endescasillabo', in *Il Mattino* 31 March-1 April (1927). (Now in *Saggi e interventi*, pp.154-69).

Metrica o estetica', in Il Mattino 19-20 April (1927). (Now in *Saggi e interventi*, pp.154-69).

'Haikaismo', in *L'Italia letteraria* (21 May 1933).

'Immagini del Leopardi e nostre', in *Nuova antologia* (16 February 1943), 221-32. (Now in *Saggi e interventi*, pp.430-450).

'Il poeta dell'oblio', in *Primato*, 9-10 (1943), 165-78. (Now in *Saggi e interventi*, pp.398-422).

40 sonetti di Shakespeare (Mondadori, Milan, 1946).

Da Góngora e da Mallarmé (Mondadori, Milan, 1947).

'Ragioni di una poesia', in *Inventario*, 1 (1949), 6-19. (Jottings from *La Ronda* (1922), *Gazzetta del popolo* (1930), and *Cantachiaro* (1948). (Now in *Saggi e interventi*, pp.747-767).

'Secondo discorso su Leopardi', in *Paragone*, 10 (1951), 3-35. (Now in *Saggi e interventi*, pp.451-496).

Fedra di Jean Racine (Mondadori, Milan, 1950).

'Góngora al lume d'oggi', in *Aut Aut*, 4 (1951). (Now in *Saggi e interventi*, pp.528-50).

'Difficoltà della poesia', in *L'Approdo letterario*, 1 (1952). (Now in *Saggi e interventi*, pp.792-814).

L'artiste dans la societé moderne, Conférence internationale des artistes, Venice, 22-28 Sept., 1952; reprinted in *Témoignages recueillis pour (UNESCO, Paris);* (*H. Vaillant Carmanne, Liège,* 1952), pp.23-30.

'L'artista nella società moderna', in *Aut Aut*, 11 (1952), 381-90. (The Italian version of the above item now in *Saggi e interventi*, pp.855-66).

Responsabilità del poeta, Preghiera e Poesia. Atti dell'11 Convegno internazionale per la pace e la civiltà cristiana (Tip. L'impronta, Florence, 1954).

Il deserto e dopo (Mondadori, Milan, 1961).

Visioni di William Blake (Mondadori, Milan, 1965).

Lettere a un fenomenologo (All'Insegna del Pesce d'oro, Milan, 1972).

Saggi e interventi (Mondadori, Milan, 1974). (Contains many of the above items).

Lettere dal fronte a Gherardo Marone (Mondadori, Milan, 1978).

Invenzione della poesia moderna. Lezioni brasiliane di letteratura (1937-1942) (Edd. Scient. italiane, Naples, 1984).

(See also the special numbers of the following periodicals: *La Fiera letteraria* (1 November 1953), 3-6; *Letteratura* (1958), 35-36; *Books abroad* (Autumn, 1970); *L'Approdo letterario* (1972), 57; *Forum italicum* (1972), 2).

G. Ungaretti & J. Amrouche, *Propos improvisés* (Gallimard, Paris, 1972).

Various authors, *Giuseppe Ungaretti, Atti del Convegno internazionale di Studi*, Urbino 3-6 Ott., 1979, (Stibu Ed. Urbino, Urbino, 1981) (2 vols.).

W. Vaccari, *Vita e tumulti di F.T. Marinetti* (Omnia, Milan, 1959).

A. Valentini, *Semantica dei poeti* (Ungaretti and Montale) (Bulzoni, Rome, 1970).

Lettura di Montale: "Ossi di seppia" (Bulzoni, Rome, 1971).

Lettura di Montale: "Le occasioni" (Bulzoni, Rome, 1975).

Lettura di Montale: "La bufera e altro" (Bulzoni, Rome, 1977).

P. Valéry, *Oeuvres* (Gallimard, Paris, 1960) (2 vols.).

M. Valgimigli, *Pascoli* (Sansoni, Florence, 1956).

V.D. Valli, 'Il dramma esistenziale di Rebora tra forma e idea', in *Annali dell'Università di Lecce*, 1 (1963-4) (Milelli, Lecce, 1965), 93-122.

Saggi sul Novecento poetico italiano (Milelli, Lecce, 1967).

A. Vallone, *Aspetti della poesia italiana contemporanea* (Nistri-Lischi, Pisa, 1960).

I crepuscolari (Palumbo, Palermo, 1960).

T.A. Van Dijk, *Some aspects of text grammars. A study in Theoretical Linguistics and Poetics* (Mouton, The Hague-Paris, 1972).

C. Varese, *Cultura letteraria contemporanea* (Nistri-Lischi, Pisa, 1951).

Pascoli decadente (Sansoni, Florence, 1964).
'La poesia di Corrado Govoni', in *Nuova antologia* (May, 1962), 51-64.

E. Veo, 'Sergio Corazzini e le amiche speranze', in *Messaggero* (8 April, 1928).

M. Verdone, *Cinema e letteratura del futurismo* (Ed. di bianco e nero, Rome, 1968).

P. Verlaine, *Oeuvres poétiques complètes* (Gallimard, Paris, 1941) (3 vols.).

V. Vettori, *Riviste italiane del Novecento* (Gismondi, Rome, 1958).
La Voce (1908-1916) (Stab. tip. Aldino, Florence). (See also Romanò and Scalia).

C. Vivaldi, *Poesia satirica nell'Italia d'oggi* (Guanda, Parma, 1964).

V. Volpini, *Antologia della poesia religiosa italiana e contemporanea* (Vallecchi, Florence, 1952).

K. Wais, 'Tre tipi di atteggiamento stilistico nella lirica italiana contemporanea', in *Convivium* (May-June, 1962).

O. Weininger, *Intorno alle cose supreme* (Einaudi, Turin, 1923) (2nd ed.).
Sesso e carattere (Fratelli Bocca, Milan, 1943); 1st Italian edition (1912); see also: *Sex and Character* (Heinemann, London, 1906).

R. West, *Eugenio Montale: Poet on the Edge* (Yale University Press, 1981).

E. Wind, *Pagan mysteries in the Renaissance* (Penguin Books, 1967); 1st ed. (Faber & Faber, London, 1958).

H. Wölfflin, *Renaissance and baroque* (Fontana/Collins, London, 1964); 3rd impression (1971).

G.T. Wright, *The poet in the poem* (University of California Press, 1960); reprinted by Gordian Press (New York, 1974).

F.A. Yates, *The art of memory* (Routledge & Kegan Paul, London, 1966).

G. Zagarrio, *Luzi* (Il Castoro, La Nuova Italia, Florence, 1968).
Quasimodo (Il Castoro, La Nuova Italia, Florence, 1969).

A. Zanzotto, *Vocativo* (Mondadori, Milan, 1957).
Poesie (1938-1972) (Mondadori, Milan, 1973); reprinted (1980).
Pasque (Mondadori, Milan, 1973).
Prefazione, Selected Poetry of Andrea Zanzotto (Princeton University Press, 1975).
Filò (Edizioni del Ruzante, Venice, 1976).
Il Galateo in Bosco (Mondadori, Milan, 1978).

Index